CHILDREN AND THEIR ART, *Fourth Edition*

CHARLES D. GAITSKELL

AL HURWITZ
Maryland Institute College of Art

MICHAEL DAY
University of Minnesota

cHildREN

HARCOURT BRACE JOVANOVICH, INC.

New York   San Diego   Chicago   San Francisco   Atlanta
London   Sydney   Toronto

FOURTH EDITION

AND THEIR ART

METHODS FOR THE ELEMENTARY SCHOOL

CHILDREN AND THEIR ART, *Fourth Edition*

Gaitskell, Hurwitz, and Day

ISBN: 0-15-507299-4

Library of Congress Catalog Card Number: 82-80129

Printed in the United States of America

Cover photo by Marion Bernstein. Part opening photo on p. 2 by Ken Karp; part opening photo on p. 180 by Jim Cron/Monkmeyer Press. Drawings on pp. 81, 84, 85 by Howard Fussiner. Drawings on pp. 219, 256, 257, 270, 295, 298, 317, 318, 321, 332, 356, 359, 365 by Charles Gottlieb.

Passage by Burt Silverman, pp. 389–90, copyright © 1977 by Burt Silverman. Reprinted by permission of Watson-Guptill Publications from *Painting People*.

PREFACE

Every new edition of *Children and Their Art* represents a commitment to convey the best of current thinking in elementary art education, and the addition of a team member is one way to provide readers with the most significant recent developments. Therefore, the authors of the earlier editions are happy to have Professor Michael Day join them in the fourth edition. Professor Day has a distinguished record as writer, teacher, researcher, and head of a major department of art education.

The fourth edition of *Children and Their Art* continues to offer a comprehensive introduction to the teaching of art in the elementary schools. As in previous editions, the book covers both the theoretical basis of art education and the practical methods of teaching. In an effort to make a range of complex ideas accessible to classroom teachers, art specialists, and teachers in training, we have presented a broad creative program as a continuum of issues—including the nature of art, problems of pedagogy, and art's unique function in the lives of children. Difficulties that arise in the day-to-day tasks of teaching are given close attention, as are the preparation of an artroom, the handling of displays, the correlation of art with the overall school curriculum, and the evaluation of children's progress. These are matters that concern all teachers at one time or another, and, as space permitted, we have considered all of them.

Increased interest in certain areas of art education—such as the tendency toward greater integration of art into other areas of learning and the use of art in teaching retarded and handicapped children—has resulted in more extensive treatment of these topics in this edition. Chapters on the teaching of art appreciation, and on the challenge of working with the gifted child, have also been enlarged, while the section on curriculum planning has been simplified to make it more useful to the classroom teacher as well as to the art specialist. The third edition devoted more time to an examination of behavioral goals and competency of performance; these subjects have been abridged in this edition not only because there has been a shift in practice among art educators but because we have revised our own philosophy.

In this edition, chapter aids too have been improved. New activities have been added for all chapters; as before, the activities suggested for classroom use have all been tested in the classroom. Many of the picture captions have been expanded to provide more information, and the bibliographies now appear at the end of each chapter, where, it is hoped, they will be easier to use. Lists of film and art-reproduction distributors are still in the back of the book.

Many of the illustrations come from three highly regarded school systems: the Dade County schools in Florida, the Newton schools in Massachusetts, and the Metropolitan Separate School Board of Toronto. In Dade County, Jacqueline Hinchey contributed student work which reflected her own talents and skill as a teacher; in Newton, the students of Maida Abrams, Lori Schill, Carolyn W. Shapiro, Arlene D. Bandes, Susan Jenkinson, Susan Varga, and Lily Ann and Ben Rosenberg were equally creative. Special thanks are also due Yvonne Andersen, Jim Robison, George Olson, and Margaret DiBlasio for their helpful comments on specific areas.

We also wish to express our thanks to the Metropolitan Separate School Board of Toronto for submitting a large collection of slides illustrating various aspects of the art production of children and for permitting us to use some of these slides. In particular, we thank Albert St. R. Mallon, Assistant Superintendent of Curriculum (Visual Arts), and the following art consultants and resource teachers: Margaret Adamson, Gabrielle Tutak, Eleanor Copeman-Harris, Susan Ashour, and Taida Supronas. Together, these six collected student work from some 230 schools.

The writers are all active members of the International Society for Education Through Art (INSEA), the only world organization for art teachers, and two of us have served as presidents. It is therefore fitting that the illustrations in this edition, gathered from our travels and personal contacts, continue to reflect our view of visual expression as a universal phenomenon.

We are most grateful to the following INSEA members who gave or lent us the work of children in their countries: Mahmoud El-Bassiouny, Qatar University; Mitsui Nagamachi, Japan; Jan Meyer, South Africa; and Jan de Grauw, the Netherlands. Others who not only contributed art work but served as generous and enthusiastic hosts during Al Hurwitz's travels must be especially noted: Izzika and Jaffa Goan and Ayila Gordon, Israel Museum; Moshe Tamir, Ministry of Education, Israel; Jawad Hakim, Paley Art Centre, Jerusalem; Ahmad Al Fayyumi, Al-Aásam School, Béersheva, Israel; Valentina Hudoshina, Hermitage Museum; Eleana Lazarus, De Cordova Museum, Lincoln, Massachusetts; Jack Condous, President, INSEA, Adelaide, Australia; Andrea Karpati, University of Budapest;

Magda Koltai, Komlo, Hungary; Jane Winney, Auckland, New Zealand; Ray Thorburn, Department of Education, New Zealand; Ray Sampson, Head Inspector of Art, Western Australia; Chong-hiok Yoon, Hong-Ik University, Seoul, Korea; Choi Duk Hyu, University of Seoul, Korea.

Some Americans who made specific contributions in reviewing material are Brent and Marjorie Wilson, Pennsylvania State University; David W. Baker, Louisiana State University; Donald Brigham, Attleboro schools, Massachusetts; Phyllis Gold Gluck, Brooklyn College; and Judith Grunbaum, Newton, Massachusetts. Edmund B. Feldman, University of Georgia, kindly permitted us to use transcripts of his classroom teaching.

Neil Jacobs, Doncaster, England; Coby van Herk, Rotterdam; Christopher Small, Newton; and the staff of the De Cordova Museum provided many of the photographs. Michael and Helen Hurwitz and Maria Hester gave us invaluable secretarial assistance in preparing the manuscript.

The many members of the editorial and production staff of Harcourt Brace Jovanovich served as a model for an author-publisher relationship. Their concern for detail and their seemingly infinite patience in dealing with three authors, rather than just one, should provide a standard which other publishers might emulate.

Charles D. Gaitskell
Al Hurwitz
Michael Day

CONTENTS

Contents   ix

CHILDREN AND THEIR ART, *Fourth Edition*

PART ONE

PREPARING

TO TEACH ART

foundations

of CONTEMPORARY

ART EducATION

If art could do nothing better than reproduce the things of nature, either directly or by analogy, or to delight the senses, there would be little justification for the honorable place reserved to it in every known society. Art's reputation must be due to the fact that it helps people to understand the world and themselves, and presents to their eyes what they have understood and believe to be true.*

ONE

The foundations of art education have been built over the years on increased knowledge and changing beliefs about the nature of the visual arts, conceptions of children and adults as learners, and the values of society as conveyed through educational goals and practices. During this century, the visual arts have gone through rapid shifts in emphasis, far-reaching innovations, and technological advances similar to those in science, social institutions, communications, and transportation. Those who study world culture understand that changes in the various aspects of human endeavor are often interrelated and interdependent and that art often reveals, truthfully and sensitively, aspects of existence common to

*From Rudolf Arnheim, *Art and Visual Perception,* p. 374. Copyright © 1954 the University of California Press, and used with permission.

different societies and eras. Changes in art, which is the content for art education, naturally affect what is taught in educational programs and how it is taught.

Because teaching is an activity that emerges from some conception about how learning occurs, changing views of the learner and of the teaching-learning process affect educational programs probably as much as changes in the content of education. Advances in psychology, as they are applied by educators, have made major contributions to the foundations of art education. Knowledge of the psychological characteristics of learners and their implications for education are essential factors of enlightened art programs.

A third major element in any educational program is the impact of society's values and beliefs. Political, economic, and social changes result in changes in educational institutions and practices. This chapter provides a brief survey of contemporary art education as we review changes in art, in conceptions of the learner, and in the types of education valued by society.

Nature of the Visual Arts

To obtain a basic understanding of art, we must project ourselves back into history, before the advent of personal adornment, even before the age of cave paintings. If we can push ourselves back far enough into the dim recesses of time, we may recognize the importance of one early achievement: the invention of containers. The seemingly simple realization that a hollow space would allow someone to store water or grain must have been one of the wonders of primitive technology. How long people were satisfied with this breakthrough we do not know, but at some point someone must have noticed that if greater attention were given to such considerations as the *shape* of the space as well as the consistency of the thickness of its walls, the container would somehow be more satisfactory. In perfecting the form in order to improve the function, that anonymous fabricator was working on the level of enlightened craftsmanship.

At a later stage the person making the container, or pot, felt an impulse to make adjustments on the *surface* of the vessel. This phase was highly significant simply because what appears on the *skin* of the pot has nothing at all to do with its *function*—that is, with how much the pot can carry or how much wear it can survive. Decoration can only make the handling and the seeing of the object a more *pleasurable* experience. There was yet another difference in this stage: whereas technical considerations (the relation of size to thickness and to function) somewhat circumscribed the pot-maker's choice of size and style, the decorative stage released unlimited options for technique and design. Once the object was formed, shapes could be inscribed or painted in patterns that might include swirls, loops, straight lines, or combinations of any of these.

The next stage, which followed decoration, placed primitive people directly in the line of their more sophisticated descendants, for they soon discovered that decoration could have *meaning*, that signs could stand for ideas. They found that symbols not only clarified their fears, dreams, and fantasies but communicated their state of mind to other people. Cave paintings reflect this function, for in these the animals depicted are more than recognizable shapes taken from the experience of the group—they represent a magical ritual whereby hunters could record concern for survival.[1] Decoration now moved into the more profound sphere of the image as metaphor, and not every member of the tribe was capable of making such a transference. Those who could we now call *artists*.

To produce art, however, artists must master tools, materials, and processes. They usually achieve such mastery only through rigorous self-discipline, which keeps them striving for excellence of production. All artists worthy of the name engage in this search for excellence, never ceasing in the attempt to surpass in quality their earlier output.

As a result of this struggle for mastery, an artist may produce an organization or assembly of materials to which others respond favorably. This assembly is usually given such names as *composition*, or *design*. "The musical composition is arresting," we say, or "The design of the bridge is excellent." Clive Bell called an arresting artistic assembly a "significant form." "In each [work of art]," he said, "lines and colors combined in a peculiar way, certain forms and relations of forms, stir our aesthetic emotions . . . these aesthetically moving forms I call 'significant form' and 'significant form' is the one quality common to all works of art."[2] Although Bell's statement is an important one, he failed to make entirely clear the meaning of *significant*. To do so, we must recognize that art possesses qualities beyond fine form or design. Bell did not, however, equate significance with beauty. Art can be controversial, stimulating, abrasive, and, at times, shocking. The important consideration is that it engage us through its uniqueness.

Common to all art is individuality of expression. All great art bears the imprint of the personality of its creator. "Even the art that allows the least play to individual variations," says Dewey, "like, say, the religious painting and sculpture of the twelfth century, is not mechanical and hence bears the stamp of personality."[3]

The personal nature of art is related to two factors: the source of the subject matter and the manner in which the design is developed. All great

Art may begin anywhere— even, as for this first grader, on the school parking lot.

[1] Albert Elsen, *Purposes of Art*, 2nd ed. (New York: Holt, Rinehart & Winston, 1968).
[2] Clive Bell, *Art* (New York: Stokes, 1914), p. 8.
[3] John Dewey, *Art as Experience* (New York: Putnam, 1958), p. 251.

A wall of prints by fifth and sixth graders displays a range of individual expression. (Photo by Roger Graves.)

art represents the personal reaction of its creator to personal experiences. The genius of El Greco, Picasso, Goya, Cézanne, Matisse, and other great artists is reflected in the thought and emotion generated by contact with their environment. The greatest artists are those who have discovered a personal mode of expression that suits the reaction to experience they wish to convey. Thus, we can glance at a work of art and say immediately, "That is a piece of sculpture by Henry Moore," "That is a painting by Jasper Johns," or "That is an etching by Rembrandt." In the individuality of the work rests its timeless and universal appeal.

We see, therefore, that art results from an act of self-expression involving emotions and intellect. Thus we may say that *art is an expression of a person's reactions to experiences in his or her life, given form through the use of design and materials.* It is this concept of art—a traditional one—that governs to a great extent the art programs in our schools today.

The history of art contains many periods in which views on the nature of art have changed, leading to changes in modes of expression. The educator's understanding of what art is and how it changes with time in an evolving environment is a crucial factor that influences what is taught and how it is taught. The boundaries of acceptable art are constantly exposed to pressure by the *avant-garde* (leading innovators in the visual arts). A painting by Jackson Pollock, for example, would not have been accepted as art in Rembrandt's time, and, until the invention of mobiles by Alexander Calder, sculpture was considered to be by definition immobile. Of

Foundations of Contemporary Art Education

course these developments in art are often valuable because they reveal new potentialities for expression. Although they may upset the standard of production for a little while, they tend ultimately to enrich the mainstream of art. Each mode sinks into this stream, leaving some influence or disappearing entirely according to its merits. A brief survey of change and innovation in Western art will demonstrate the dynamic nature of art.

The view that art must be identified with concepts of beauty has a limited extent in the history of world art. As Sir Herbert Read points out, it probably arose in Greece as the offspring of a humanistic philosophy of life, survived Rome, and reappeared during the Renaissance.[4]

THE CONCEPT OF BEAUTY

The chief aim of Greek art was the portrayal of an *ideal* of humanity, one that gave great emphasis to physical beauty. But this, continues Read, is only one of several artistic ideals. The Byzantine ideal was the representation of the divine rather than the human; the primitive ideal was the control of awesome forces through powerful images; the Oriental ideal was the expression of abstract, metaphysical concepts. It would be difficult to bring beauty into service of all the artistic expressions of these several ideals.

Despite the fact that many artists have relied on beauty as a basis for expression, it is merely one of many possible approaches. Goya, for example, found inspiration in the horrors of war as well as in the beauty of the human body; Daumier found themes for expression in political revolution; Toulouse-Lautrec, in the degradation of the body and soul. Art, in fact, embraces all of life, not only that small segment of it that may be considered ideally beautiful.

Beauty, to the uninitiated in art, is most often identified with execution as well as with subject matter. Thus, in salon painting, nobility and virtue are associated with technical virtuosity; high-blown sentiment with "realistic" rendering.

So powerful is the Greek-Roman-Renaissance influence on Western civilization that even today the concept of ideal beauty as a primary concern of art still exerts a major influence on professional art and, hence, on art education in the schools. Nevertheless, to impose such a limiting concept on children, as some teachers have done, is to deny them the opportunity of exploring the rich variety of themes that artistic expression traditionally includes.

Many innovations or movements in the modern era of art history began in revolutions against accepted artistic tradition or, in many instances, academic dogma. So it was that a group of French painters, including Manet,

IMPRESSIONISM

[4] Herbert Read, *The Meaning of Art,* 3rd ed. (New York: Pitman, 1951).

Monet, Renoir,[5] and others, rejected the narrow aesthetic views of the state academy of artists and developed new purposes and images in painting. These artists, dubbed *impressionists* as the result of a remark by a sarcastic critic, responded to the invention of the camera as a recording device that surpassed the painter in accuracy and to the new scientific knowledge of optics. They began to concentrate on the creation of images that the camera could not achieve as they emphasized mood and visual impression.[6]

The traditional hierarchical organization of subject matter was abandoned in favor of a relatively modern preoccupation with light and color. Flat tones and clear edges were avoided in favor of small strokes of color and indefinite contours, both of which tended to convey a sense of diffuse and often sparkling light. Artists moved their studios outdoors, and painters such as Monet found themselves doing multiple studies of a particular subject as they focused on the light of early morning, high noon, and twilight in relation to a cathedral, a bridge, or a haystack. One might say the Impressionists were primarily interested in the effects of light on objects in contrast to their successors, the *Post-Impressionists,* who were interested primarily in problems of theme, technique, and personal expression.

POST-IMPRESSIONISM

The more immediate forebears of twentieth-century art were a group of painters known as the Post-Impressionists because of their close relationship to the earlier Impressionist movement. The most significant of these artists were Vincent van Gogh,[7] Paul Cézanne, Paul Gauguin, and Georges Seurat.[8] These four men, all highly individualistic, contributed their own distinctive perception of art to those who were to follow. The vivid, emotionally charged works of Van Gogh left their mark on the Expressionists; the broad, flat tones of Gauguin were to find their echoes in the work of Henri Matisse; and the construction of forms in terms of planes undertaken by Paul Cézanne opened the door to Cubism, perhaps the most revolutionary of twentieth-century styles. Cézanne refused to limit his vision to the forms given by the tradition of painting and thus examined the structure beneath the outward aspects of objects. He invited the viewer to study his pictorial subjects from multiple points of view, and he made the space between objects as meaningful as the objects themselves. Cézanne

[5] See Keith Roberts, *Painters of Light: The World of Impressionism* (New York: Dutton, 1978).

[6] Especially revealing of the Impressionists' technique is Robert Herbert's lavishly illustrated article, "Method and Meaning in Monet," *Art in America*, September 1979, pp. 90–108.

[7] See Griselda Pollock and Fred Orton, *Vincent Van Gogh: Artist of His Time* (New York: Dutton, 1978).

[8] See John Rewald, *Post-Impressionism from Van Gogh to Gauguin*, 3rd ed. (New York: Museum of Modern Art, 1978).

Foundations of Contemporary Art Education

rejected the hazy softness of Impressionism and applied his paint in clearly articulated flat strokes of color, which appeared literally to build his paintings as one small passage led to larger areas. This method of organizing the structure of a painting served to unify the entire work into a "fused, crystallized unit, within which the shapes and colors work together."[9]

Fauvism and Expressionism can be considered together, since they are closely related to one another and, in the early years of this century, were linked together under the rubric *Expressionismus*. Expressionism, although difficult to define because it took numerous forms, was clearly the outgrowth of certain features in Post-Impressionism, most notably those found in Van Gogh's work but also to some degree those found in Gauguin's as well. Some scholars have claimed that the main feature of this movement was the expression of the artists' feelings rather than their ideas. Others have stated that the movement relied chiefly on design used very abstractly to achieve an order and a rhythm that had greater significance than could be found in art that relied on nature as a basis for expression. Still others assert that Expressionism was mainly decorative.[10] In general, Expressionism celebrates the artist's individual expressive statement and allows for nearly unbounded abstraction and experimentation.

The Fauves may be represented by Henri Matisse, Georges Rouault, and André Derain. Matisse was the leader of this group of painters in France who extended the new use of color created by Gauguin and Van Gogh, carrying it to the point where the group earned the critically derisive term *Fauves,* or wild beasts. The art-viewing public at the turn of the century, having just begun to accept the radical innovations of the Post-Impressionists, could not cope with the Fauves' strident use of pure color, their free-flowing arabesques, purely decorative line, and total disregard of local color (the specific color of a natural object). The Fauves were trying to paint according to Derain's clarion call of 1906: "We must, at all costs, break out of the fold in which the realists have imprisoned us."[11] The Fauves were creating their own reality, and they conceived of painting as a vehicle for expression that was totally autonomous, wholly independent of the viewer's perception of the world.

Expressionism, generally speaking, may be said to place emphasis on emotions, sensations, or ideas rather than on the appearance of objects.

[9]Burton Wasserman, *Modern Painting* (Worcester, Ma.: Davis, 1970), p. 36.
[10]Concerning the nature of Expressionism, see Sheldon Cheney, *The Story of Modern Art* (New York: Viking, 1941) and *Expressionism in Art* (New York: Liveright, 1941), and Herbert Read, *Art Now,* 2nd ed. (New York: Pitman, 1960).
[11]Quoted in Werner Haftmann, *Painting in the Twentieth Century* (New York: Praeger, 1965), p. 36.

The history of modern art reflects a varied approach to the problems of design and expressiveness. An example of Fauvism: *Red Room (Harmony in Red)*, 1908–09, by Henri Matisse. Oil on canvas, approx. 71″ x 97″. (Hermitage, Leningrad.) An example of Expressionism, Georges Rouault's *The Old King*, 1916–38, also carries forward the traditions of medieval stained glass windows. Oil on canvas, approx. 30¼″ x 21¼″. (Collection, Museum of Art, Carnegie Institute. Patrons Art Fund. © 1974 by SPADEM PARIS.)

Expressionist artists present their reactions in a form that is almost invariably a pronounced distortion of the camera view of the environment. These qualities did not originate in France; Expressionism, in its narrower sense, was a development of early twentieth-century German art in response to the aesthetic furor taking place in France at the same time. We can think of the Expressionist artists of Germany, Scandinavia, and Austria as merging the color and design theories of the Post-Impressionists of France with attitudes toward subject matter that were uniquely Germanic in origin.[12] This merger gave German Expressionism its distinguishing characteristics: a heightened use of color, an extreme simplification of form and distortion of representational conventions for emotive reasons, a preoccupation with hallucinatory religious experience, and the investment of conventional or "public" subjects, such as landscapes and human figures, with private visionary or mythic meanings. Considerably influenced by the Fauves, the German Expressionists in turn affected French painters

[12]The works of Edvard Munch, Arnold Böcklin, and the artists of the Jugendstil such as Gustav Klimt had great influence on the formative years of German Expressionism.

Foundations of Contemporary Art Education

such as Rouault, especially in terms of the ideological substructure of art. Eventually, the artistic manners and attitudes of the German Expressionists were to have a wide influence and to assume the more generalized characteristics described previously. As time went on, Expressionism took the form of extreme abstraction, and had liberating effects on painting and on art education.

It was in 1907, when he painted *Les Demoiselles d'Avignon*, that Pablo Picasso took Cézanne's ideas one step further toward what is now known as Cubism.[13] *Les Demoiselles* combined the simultaneous perspective of Cézanne with the simple, monumental shapes and sharply faceted surfaces of African and primitive Iberian art. As Picasso developed his ideas along with Georges Braque, the forms of Cubism became more complex. By 1911, Cubist compositions grew in complexity as planes overlapped, interpenetrated, and moved into areas of total abstraction. Space and form were now handled with a minimum of color, in contrast to the rich hues of Fauvism and Expressionism. Their spontaneity and painterly qualities, born of their own emotionalism, were superseded by a more intellectual concern for order. As Werner Haftmann describes it:

CUBISM

[13]Robert Rosenblum, *Cubism and Twentieth Century Art* (New York: Abrams, 1960).

The Cubists, reflecting a new consciousness of the relativity of time and space, offered the viewer a flexible visual experience by presenting, simultaneously, different views of objects. Juan Gris, *Breakfast*, 1914. Pasted paper, crayon, and oil on canvas, $31\frac{7}{8}'' \times 23\frac{1}{2}''$. (Collection, The Museum of Modern Art, New York. Acquired through the Lillie P. Bliss Bequest. © ADAGP 1975.)

Cubism embraces all the aspects of the object simultaneously and is more complete than the optical view. From the information and signs conveyed on the rhythmically moving surface, the imagination can reassemble the object in its entirety . . . . Cubism corresponds to that new modern conception of reality which it has been the aim of the whole pictorial effort of the 20th Century to express in visual terms.[14]

Within Cubism can be found many of the central concepts of modern art: manipulation and rejection of Renaissance perspective, abstraction to the point of nonobjectivity, emphasis on the integrity of the picture plane, introduction of manufactured elements in collage, and experimentation with different conceptions of reality.

SURREALISM

The precursors of Surrealism were artists such as Paul Klee, Giorgio di Chirico, and Marc Chagall, all of whom dealt with fantasy, dreams, and other states of mind. We may add to these influences the Dada movement, whose anti-art theatrics and demonstrations challenged the most basic assumptions about art.[15] André Breton, a poet, first used the term *surrealist* in his own publication, thus reflecting the close connection between an art movement and a literary one, a common situation in the history of art. The artists who were ultimately to be identified with the movement—Max Ernst, Hans Arp, Salvador Dalí, Joan Miro, Yves Tanguy—all shared Breton's interest in Sigmund Freud's ideas regarding dreams, psychoanalysis, and the relation of conscious and subconscious experience as the subject matter for art. They strove to divorce themselves from rational and logical approaches to art. In searching for a definition of Surrealism that would apply equally to literature and art, Breton wrote, "Surrealism: the dictation of thought free from any control of reason, independent of any aesthetic or moral preoccupation . . . rests upon a belief in the superior reality of certain forms of association hitherto neglected, in the omnipotence of the dream, in the disinterested play of thought."[16]

NONREPRESENTATIONAL ART

One of the most revolutionary developments in the art of the early twentieth century was the shift toward what was at first called *nonobjective* art. Wassily Kandinsky, a Russian who lived in Germany and France, is considered the father of nonobjective painting.[17] The concepts subsumed under this term are now usually referred to as nonrepresentational and cover a much wider range of styles than originally. Nonrepresentational art now

[14] Haftmann, *Painting in the Twentieth Century*, p. 80.
[15] Hans Richter, *Dada, Art, and Anti-Art* (New York: McGraw-Hill, 1965).
[16] Herbert Read, *A Concise History of Modern Painting* (New York: Praeger, 1959), p. 132.
[17] Wassily Kandinsky, *Concerning the Spiritual in Art and Painting in Particular* (New York: Wittenborn, 1964).

An example of Post-Impressionism: *Boy in a Red Waistcoat*, 1893–95, by Paul Cézanne. Oil on canvas, 35¼″ x 28¼″. (Collection Mr. and Mrs. Paul Mellon.) An example of Dadaism: *To Be Looked at (from the Other Side of the Glass) with One Eye, Close To, for Almost an Hour*, 1918, by Marcel Duchamp. Framed double glass panel with oil paint, collage, lens, 20⅛″ x 16¼″. (Collection, Museum of Modern Art, New York. Katherine S. Dreier Bequest.) Surrealism: *The Eye of Silence*, 1943–44, by Max Ernst. Oil on canvas, 42½″ x 55½″. (Collection, Washington University, St. Louis. © 1974 by SPADEM PARIS.)

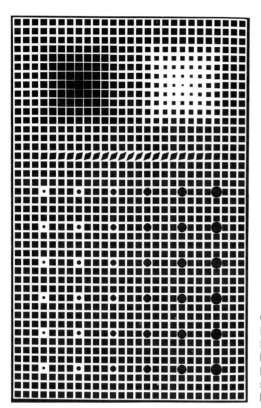

Clockwise from left: An example of Op Art: *Supernovae*, 1959–61, by Victor Vasarely. Oil, 59¾″ x 95½″. (Tate Gallery, London. © 1975 by SPADEM PARIS.) Abstract Expressionism: *Painting 1952*, 1955–56, by Franz Kline. Oil on canvas, approx. 77″ x 100″. (Present location unknown.) Pop Art: *Marilyn Monroe Diptych*, 1962, by Andy Warhol. Silk screen on canvas, 82″ x 114″. (Leo Castelli Gallery. Collection Mr. and Mrs. Burton Tremaine, Meriden, Ct.)

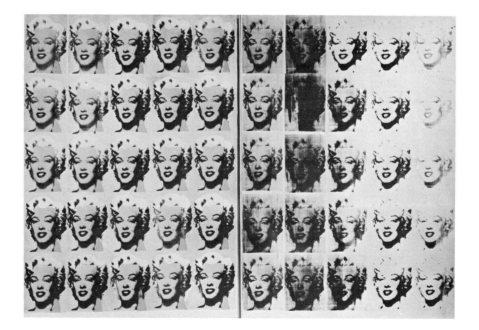

16

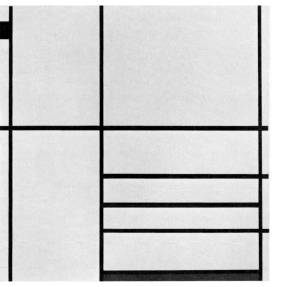

In the early part of this century, certain artists turned completely away from representational functions of art and became solely concerned with the creation of pure relations among the design elements. One of the major figures in this movement was Piet Mondrian, whose *Composition in White, Black and Red*, 1936, is a prime example of what has come to be called pure abstraction. Oil on canvas, 40¼″ x 41″. (Collection, The Museum of Modern Art, New York. Gift of the Advisory Committee.)

includes the works of such diverse artists as Kandinsky, Piet Mondrian, Hans Arp, Constantin Brancusi, Jackson Pollock, Mark Rothko, Louise Nevelson, and the artists associated with the Op,[18] Minimal, and Hard Edge schools of art, such as Bridget Riley, Victor Vasarely, Donald Judd, Kenneth Noland, and Frank Stella. Before the arrival of nonrepresentational art, the subject matter of painting and sculpture derived almost universally from the natural world, although the degree of correspondence ranged widely from photographic likeness to highly abstract statement. The nonrepresentational artist, however, asserts that expression is based on the manipulation of the elements of design—line, mass and space, light and shade, texture, and color—without reference to the visible world. Subject matter is, in a sense, eliminated. Although nonrepresentational painting has perhaps declined in popularity recently, art education has profited greatly from the nonrepresentational artists' experiments with media, techniques, and pictorial composition.

When Picasso included fragments of newspaper clippings in his cubistic paintings, he was attacking much the same problem as the Futurist artist Umberto Boccioni did at an earlier time, when he integrated a real windowframe into a piece of sculpture. Both were struggling with a traditional concern of the artist—that of stating the nature of reality in terms of one's

FRAGMENTATION AND RECONSTRUCTION

[18] See *Understanding Op Art*, sound filmstrip (Stamford, Ct.: Educational Dimensions Group, 1973).

own time. The *fixed* point of view, which began with the Renaissance painters' discovery of perspective, was seriously questioned by Cézanne and the Cubists and was followed by further movements that were not only to redefine traditional ideas of space and subject matter, but also to question the role of the very surface of the canvas itself. The collage approach, which combined diverse and unrelated "found" textures, eventually led to the addition, some thirty years later, of real objects such as Rauschenberg's stuffed birds and pillows. Artists such as Louise Nevelson and George Segal have either employed the real object as an adjunct to painting and sculpture or have used it to create a new kind of symbol derived from both arts. The idea of creating situations wherein found objects are set in fresh perspective by the creation of radically different frames of reference seems to be a part of the current thinking of artists, who have been freed from the limitations imposed by fixed media classifications.[19] Thus, sculpture is not merely painted, it moves; and paintings wired for sound may speak to us literally as well as symbolically, thereby steadily weaning the viewer away from an attitude of passivity and contemplation toward greater participation.

CONTEMPORARY TRENDS

How is the art teacher to respond to contemporary ideas that may seem shocking, frivolous, or even vulgar? The aesthetics of Minimal, Abstract, and Conceptual art[20] are admittedly difficult and perhaps cannot be introduced in every elementary classroom—yet there was a time when a problem in collage was considered very advanced.

The current scene in art is not dominated by a single style or movement, but exemplifies a pluralism that includes contemporary manifestations of nearly all that has gone before. Technical facility through modern technology is displayed by the Photo-Realists such as Chuck Close and Richard Estes, while at the same time conceptual artists such as Walter De Maria and Christo emphasize art as an aesthetic experience rather than as an object. Time will tell which of the art movements currently in vogue are merely fads and which have significance for learning in art. It is pointless to be avant-garde when students have no idea of the meaning behind the activities assigned them, yet there is much of contemporary art from which students can derive value and enjoyment. Scrap sculpture, for example, is closely allied to the mysterious monochromatic assemblages of Louise Nevelson, and working with raw film, box cameras, and photograms (see Chapter 10) allows children to relate designs to the technology of their time. Teachers can ask students to create collages out of paper—

[19] Marcel Duchamp, "Apropos of 'Readymades,'" in *Esthetics Contemporary*, ed. Richard Kostelanetz (Buffalo: Prometheus, 1977).

[20] Gregory Battcock, ed., *Idea Art* (New York: Dutton, 1973). See also Sol LeWitt, "Paragraphs on Conceptual Art," in Kostelanetz, *Esthetics Contemporary*, p. 414.

why not create three-dimensional forms out of found objects? The art of our time, if presented through judicious use of slides and reproductions, field trips, and visiting artists, may provide a greater depth of understanding and excitement for both student and teacher. Students curious about color could learn much from the Hard Edge or Op Art painters; teachers preparing for an annual PTA poster project could stimulate students by showing them the calligraphy and silkscreen prints of Corita Kent.

The burden of presenting activities that relate not only to the art of today but also to that of the past falls on the art specialist, but it is the responsibility of the classroom teacher to express to the art consultant an interest in such ideas. Conversely, the art specialist should recognize that the recent history of art has extended our perceptions, so that the general public can now accept a ballet setting that uses surrealist images, for example, or illustrations and paintings that do not conform to the rules of photographic realism. The art teacher can and should look to the history of art as a rich source of ideas. There is a time for children to focus their attention on the external world and there is a time to honor their own dreams and inner desires; there should be opportunities to experiment with form; and there should be situations wherein the modes of one medium can borrow from another. The history of art provides ample evidence to support all such activities.[21]

Conceptions of the Learner

Is the mind of a child a blank tablet waiting to receive the imprint of the teacher? Are learners passive receivers, active seekers, or some combination of both? Does learning take place most efficiently through the use of all the senses? Are drill and repetition necessary? Does learning transfer from one task or problem to another? Is learning self-determined or is it the result of influences from the environment? Obviously the views a teacher holds on these and other issues in learning theory will influence educational practice. Whether the various conceptions of learning are developed by individual educators or are implied by psychological investigation, their practical influence cannot be overlooked.

Contemporary education, like modern art, is not entirely a product of the last three or four decades. Many of the basic ideas to be found both in aesthetics and in teaching theory today may be traced to ideas held by philosophers and teachers who lived long ago, as well as to the psychologists of recent years.

[21] For a fascinating view of recent art history from primary sources, see the *ArtNews* seventy-fifth-year anthology, *The Art World*, ed. Barbaralee Diamondstein (New York: Artnews Books, 1977).

Contemporary art education, then, is a field that is fed by the history of art and of general education. The development of current practice in art education is also supported by the investigation of psychologists into the learning process as a whole.

EARLY EDUCATORS

What a modern ring some of the ancient writings have. In the *Republic* of Plato (427–347 B.C.), for example, we find the germ of the concept called *the search for excellence*. Montaigne (1533–92) and Francis Bacon (1561–1626) emphasized the need to base teaching on first-hand experience rather than on "logic chopping." Comenius (1592–1670) developed this idea in his *Didactica magna* and later made it practical when he asserted that children should not memorize what they do not understand. Rousseau (1712–88) believed that teaching should be related to childhood interests and that education should be concerned with the everyday life of the child. He emphasized these ideas in his *Émile* (1762):

> What must we think of the barbarous education, which sacrifices the present to the uncertain future, which loads a child with chains of every sort, and begins by making him miserable, in order to prepare him, long in advance, for some pretended happiness which it is probable he will never enjoy?

Let children be children, Rousseau advocated, and let them learn through self-initiated activities. On the matter of competition—a question still being debated in education—Rousseau declared that self-competition is preferable to rivalry with other children. It must be admitted that Rousseau was a theorist and a dreamer and that some of his ideas about teaching were quite impractical. It remained for future teachers to make pedagogical order out of Rousseau's theories. Three teachers—Johann Pestalozzi (1746–1827), Johann Friedrich Herbart (1776–1841), and Friedrich Froebel (1782–1852)—contributed to this process.

Unlike most of his predecessors, the gentle Swiss, Pestalozzi,[22] gave particular emphasis to the idea that education is more than the process of recording sense impressions on a passive mind. Learners must be active participants and must reorganize the experiences that they encounter. As a pioneer and experimenter, Pestalozzi made many mistakes, and he lacked the ability to systematize his thoughts into a teaching methodology. The task of developing a systematic pedagogy was left to Johann Friedrich Herbart, a learned German (see pp. 21–22). Herbart gained inspiration to perform this task from Pestalozzi's school.[23] Although Herbart's method-

---

[22] See Pestalozzi's novel *Leonard and Gertrude* (1781) and his book on education *How Gertrude Teaches Her Children* (1801).

[23] Herbart wrote *ABC of Sense Perception* to explain Pestalozzi's views.

ology seems cold and formal to teachers today, his teachings nevertheless recognized in the learning process the natural capacities, interests, and activities of children.

Froebel, also a German and something of a mystic, established his first kindergarten in 1837 after visiting Pestalozzi's school. His teaching methods were founded on the naturalism preached by Rousseau and practiced by Pestalozzi. His mystical ideas prompted him to use in the kindergarten objects that have a basic geometric shape—cubes, spheres, prisms, and so on—on the theory that a child would gain an awareness of unity, and indeed deity, by being in contact with some of these "perfect" forms. Froebel's strong beliefs that children should be taught from the concrete to the abstract and that a school should be a miniature society are still considered sound.

In this respect at least, Froebel predated the theories of children's concept development of Jean Piaget (see p. 26), for both saw sensory experience as providing the natural basis for distinguishing between material and social realities. (For example, if *working together* is one of the teacher's goals for the class, role-playing or painting a class mural will be of greater educational significance to a first grader than will a discussion of the subject.)

Although the educational theories and practices just described have had their effects on art teaching, an even stronger influence is to be found in the development of psychological thought. Because a complete and detailed study of the effects of psychology on methodology is not possible here, we shall consider only a few of the most important influences on teaching methods in art. These influences include (1) the two branches known as *faculty* and *Herbartian* psychology; (2) the *functional* school of psychology, from which developed E. L. Thorndike's stimulus-response theory of learning and much of John Dewey's philosophy; (3) the *Gestalt* school of psychology; (4) *behavioral psychology* and the work of B. F. Skinner; (5) *humanistic psychology* as developed by Carl Rogers and others; (6) the developmental psychology of Jean Piaget; and finally (7) the so-called *split-brain* research on hemispheric functions.

Examples of the use of Froebel's "basic shapes."

The *faculty* psychologists believed that the mind was composed of a series of separate compartments, each of which housed a *faculty* such as memory, will, or reason. In order to train the mind, a person must perform a series of intellectual exercises. Those whose faculties had not been trained by suitable exercises, or who were deemed lacking in faculties, had to be content with lowly social positions. Because the faculty psychologists taught that the mental powers developed through exercise could be applied to all areas of human endeavor, including artistic effort, influence on early art education was great.

HERBART AND FACULTY PSYCHOLOGY

Herbart, in addition to extending the work of Pestalozzi, is known as the father of scientific pedagogy based on psychology. Herbart thought that the mind acted as a unit, and that it had the power of what he called *apperception*—the capacity to assimilate new ideas through ideas already acquired. Herbart developed teaching methods that he believed assisted the mind in making use of the power of apperception. His methods "elevated the importance of the teacher and made the pupil a listener, whose mind was to be molded according to a preconceived plan of studies and by formal steps of method."[24] By the middle of the nineteenth century, the Herbartian steps of teaching had become common practice—indeed, slogans—in almost every North American normal school. The methods used in drawing lessons were determined by these steps.[25]

FUNCTIONAL PSYCHOLOGY

In the United States, interest later developed in a psychological concept related to Darwinian biology. According to this concept, the mind was thought to be the chief factor in adapting to the environment. Hence the mind was said to consist of functions rather than of the static structures suggested by earlier psychologies; this concept led to the so-called *functional* school of psychology.

John Dewey (1859–1952) is considered one of the founders of the functional school of psychology and was, in his early years, closely associated with it. As a philosopher, of course, Dewey later ranged far in his ideas, but they were unmistakably colored by functionalism. He was greatly concerned with the relationship of learners to their environment and to the society in which they live. He regarded education as the "continuing re-creation of experience." According to Dewey, experience and education are not synonymous: education involves the direction and control of experience, and a meaningful experience implies some measure of control for future experience. Knowledge is not static, Dewey said, nor is it gained in a static environment to be used in a static society. Learning must lead to more learning—the process is never ending. Dewey's ideas readily lend themselves to the teaching of art. Indeed, he was a philosopher of aesthetics as well as of education and produced an admirable book on the subject, *Art as Experience*.

John Dewey's ideas were supplemented by the work of G. Stanley Hall in the Child Study Movement during the early part of this century. Both Dewey and Hall saw school-centered situations giving way to the child-centered curriculum. Hall thought that the selection of all learning activity should proceed from the study of child development and that a

[24] James Mulhern, *A History of Education* (New York: Ronald, 1946), p. 389.

[25] The Herbartian steps of teaching are as follows: preparation, association, generalization, and application. See Herbart's *Text Book of Psychology* (1816) and *Outlines of Educational Doctrine* (1835).

Foundations of Contemporary Art Education

teacher's primary obligation was to study the child rather than the subject. As early as 1901 Hall states, "The guardians of the young should strive first of all to keep out of nature's way and to prevent harm, and should merit the proud title of defenders of the happiness and rights of children."[26] Statements such as that provided the groundwork for the laissez-faire methods of art instruction of the Progressive era. Attention was focused on the learner more than on subject content or on society's goals. Teachers were encouraged to say, "I don't teach art (or math or science), I teach children."

Another psychologist associated with the functional school of thought was E. L. Thorndike (1874–1949). Thorndike joined the staff of Teachers College, Columbia University, in 1901 and remained there until his retirement in 1940. Among his achievements were the development of a systematic animal psychology, the production of the first standardized tests in education, and the investigation of many learning problems.[27]

Thorndike based his educational theories on what is called a *stimulus-response* or *S-R* theory. According to this theory, learning consists in the establishment of a series of connections, or pathways, in the brain, resulting from a specific response to a stimulus. Between each nerve ending is a gap, or synapse, which tends to resist the impulse of the stimulus but which can be bridged by repeated stimuli. These physiological data led Thorndike to believe that learning was a matter of repetitive drill. The most efficient teaching would result from breaking a school subject into minute parts. Drill based on these minute details would then allow the learner to develop "a wonderfully elaborate and intricate system of connections."[28] Although psychological studies have progressed beyond Thorndike's initial thought, it is not difficult to discover curricula based on his notions in today's schools, especially in the areas of reading and mathematics. Thorndike's notions were not particularly compatible with the teaching of art.

The system of psychology called *Gestalt* has had a strong influence on contemporary art education. In *The Growth of the Mind*, Kurt Koffka (1886–1941) produced evidence to show that, in learning, an organism acts as a total entity and does not exercise only certain parts.[29] During World War I, Wolfgang Köhler, a German psychologist, performed experiments with primates that supported the Gestaltist theories. In his experiments,

GESTALT PSYCHOLOGY

[26]G. Stanley Hall, *The Forum*, 32 (1901–02), pp. 24–25.

[27]In 1913 and 1914 Thorndike published his three-volume *Educational Psychology*, comprising Vol. I, *The Original Nature of Man;* Vol. II, *The Psychology of Learning;* Vol. III, *Work, Fatigue, and Individual Differences.*

[28]E. L. Thorndike, *Educational Psychology: Briefer Course* (New York: Teacher's College, 1914), p. 173.

[29]Kurt Koffka, *The Growth of the Mind* (Totowa, N.J.: Littlefield, Adams, 1959).

primates showed "insight" in solving problems. On the basis of such evidence, the Gestaltists maintained that wholes are primary; parts derive their properties and their behavior from them. The learner, in other words, acquires knowledge not by building bit by bit a system of neurological connections, but by achieving "insight," that is, understanding the relationships among the various aspects of the learning situation.

Rudolf Arnheim, in his book *Art and Visual Perception*,[30] has provided art teachers with the clearest and most completely stated view of Gestalt psychology. His book includes material ranging from an analysis of Picasso's *Guernica* to a discussion of the development of children's perception. Gestalt psychology has proved to be useful to many art educators because of the *gestalt* nature of the visual arts. A painting, for example, can be analyzed part by part, but for it to be perceived aesthetically the entire painting must be viewed. Within works of art, each part affects all the other parts simultaneously so that if one aspect is altered, such as the area or brightness of a color, the entire work is changed. In art and in Gestalt psychology, the whole is more than the sum of its parts.

B. F. SKINNER AND BEHAVIORISM

Current educational literature reflects aspects of these earlier developments as well as the strong influences of two divergent philosophical and psychological viewpoints known as *behaviorism* and *humanism*. The behaviorist orientation, most notably represented in the works of psychologist B. F. Skinner,[31] considers the learner to be a passive organism governed by stimuli supplied by the external environment. Through proper control of environmental stimuli the learner's behavior can be controlled. According to this view, human behavior is governed by the same universal laws that govern all natural phenomena and the scientific method is appropriate for the study of the human organism.

Skinner is widely regarded as the most influential figure in modern psychology, as well as one of the most controversial. His study of behavior as an objective science has resulted in developments such as programmed instruction and teaching machines, which have made computer instruction a common reality in many schools. Terms such as *operant conditioning* and *positive and negative reinforcement* and apparatus for research such as the *Skinner box* are associated with his work. The essential and controversial aspect of the behaviorist view has to do with control of behavior:

> Science is steadily increasing our power to influence, change, mold—in a word, control—human behavior. It has extended our understanding . . . so

[30] Rudolf Arnheim, *Art and Visual Perception*, 4th ed. (Berkeley: University of California Press, 1964).
[31] Examples of B. F. Skinner's writings include: *Walden Two* (New York: Macmillan, 1948), *Science and Human Behavior* (New York: Macmillan, 1953), and *Beyond Freedom and Dignity* (New York: Knopf, 1971).

Foundations of Contemporary Art Education

that we deal more successfully with people in nonscientific ways, but it has also identified conditions or variables which can be used to predict and control behavior in a new, and increasingly rigorous, technology.[32]

The influence of behavioral psychology on education is immense. In addition to programmed instruction, teaching machines, and computer-assisted instruction, educators have gone through phases of emphasis on the writing of behavioral objectives for all aspects of the curriculum. Educational evaluation, measurement, and testing have gained emphasis under this orientation. The so-called accountability movement in education has relied largely on the assessment of observable behaviors.[33] Although these trends have resulted in more precision in some areas of educational endeavor, the behaviorist movement is not without its severe critics—especially educators who recognize the unique contributions of the arts to a balanced education.

The contemporary antithesis to Skinnerian behaviorism is conveyed by humanistic psychology in the writings of Rollo May, Abraham Maslow,[34] and especially Carl R. Rogers (1902–).[35] Humanists consider the learner, not the environment, to be the source of all acts. The learner is free to make choices, and behavior is only the observable expression of an essentially private, inner world of being. The individual exists uniquely within a subjective world of feelings, emotions, and perceptions, many of which are not acted out in behavior.

HUMANISTIC PSYCHOLOGY

Research in humanistic psychology has followed the direction of clinical work with human subjects, as opposed to the behaviorists' controlled scientific methodology in the laboratory with animals as subjects. Rogers has devoted most of his professional life to clinical work with individual subjects in an endeavor to provide therapy and gain understanding.[36] He believes that only a tremendous change in the basic direction of education can meet the needs of contemporary culture. Education must respond to the dynamic, changing nature of society. An educational climate must be developed "in which innovation is not at all frightening, in which creative capacities of all concerned are nourished and expressed rather than stifled."[37] The goal of education, according to Rogers, must be

[32] Frank Milhollan and Bill Forisha, *From Skinner to Rogers: Contrasting Approaches to Education* (Lincoln, Neb.: Professional Educators, 1972), p. 46.

[33] See B. F. Skinner, *The Technology of Teaching* (New York: Appleton-Century-Crofts, 1968); Benjamin Bloom, ed., *Taxonomy of Educational Objectives: Cognitive Domain* (New York: David McKay, 1956), and *Affective Domain* (1964); and Robert Mager, *Preparing Instructional Objectives* (Palo Alto: Fearon, 1962).

[34] Abraham H. Maslow, "Existential Psychology—What's In It for Us?" in *Existential Psychology*, ed. Rollo May (New York: Random House, 1961).

[35] Carl R. Rogers, *Freedom to Learn* (Columbus, Ohio: Merrill, 1969).

[36] Carl R. Rogers, "A Theory of Therapy, Personality, and Inter-Personal Relationships, as Developed in the Client-Centered Framework," in *Psychology: A Study of Science*, Vol. III, ed. S. Koch (New York: McGraw-Hill, 1959), pp. 200–01.

[37] Milhollan and Forisha, p. 116.

the facilitation of learning, for only the person who has learned how to learn, to adapt, and to change is an educated person. The humanistic view of education coincides with the beliefs of many art educators who would emphasize the creative and expressive facets of the human personality.

PIAGET AND DEVELOPMENTAL PSYCHOLOGY

Through his work over fifty years, Swiss psychologist Jean Piaget (1896–1980) became the major influence in developmental psychology. His work had an extensive impact on education. It represents one of the most systematic and comprehensive theories of cognitive development. Often in collaboration with Barbel Inhelder,[38] Piaget examined such topics as the evolution of language and thought in children; the child's conceptions of the world, of number, time, and space; and other aspects of a child's intellectual development.

Piaget outlined three major stages or *periods* in the child's cognitive development: the sensorimotor period, the period of concrete operations, and the period of formal operations.[39] Piaget believed that the child develops through interaction with the environment rather than exclusively through either heredity or environment. He saw sensorimotor activity as a basis for higher intellectual development and stressed the active use of the senses in learning. According to Piaget, the child neither "flowers," as described by Rousseau, nor is "programmed" in the manner of Skinner. Rather, the child develops sequentially through Piaget's three stages. An essential notion of Piaget, and of developmental psychology in general, is that intellectually a child is qualitatively different from an adult, and this difference varies according to age and to progress within the three stages. For educators, this implies that knowledge of the learner's characteristics is essential to curricular and instructional decision-making.

SPLIT-BRAIN RESEARCH

A discussion of changing conceptions of the learner would not be complete without some mention of recent research[40] into the functions of the two hemispheres of the human brain and of the effects of this research on education.[41] For many years, scientists have known that the human brain

[38] See, for example, Barbel Inhelder and Jean Piaget, *The Growth of Logical Thinking from Childhood to Adolescence* (New York: Basic Books, 1958) and *The Early Growth of Logic in the Child* (New York: Norton, 1964), and Jean Piaget, *Science of Education and the Psychology of the Child* (New York: Viking, 1971).

[39] Kenneth Lansing, "The Research of Jean Piaget and Its Implications for Art Education in the Elementary School," *Studies in Art Education*, Vol. 7, No. 2 (Spring 1966).

[40] For example, see R. W. Sperry, "Hemisphere Disconnection and Unity in Conscious Awareness," *American Psychologist* 23 (1968), pp. 723–33; J. Levy, "Psychobiological Implications of Bilateral Asymmetry," in *Hemisphere Function in the Human Brain*, ed. S. J. Dimond and J. G. Beaumont (New York: Wiley, 1974); and J. Paredes and M. Hepburn, "The Split-Brain and the Culture-Cognition Paradox," *Current Anthropology*, Vol. 17 (March 1976), p. 1.

[41] A sample of articles includes: Madeline Hunter, "Right-Brained Kids in Left-Brained Schools," *Today's Education*, November-December 1976; Elliot Eisner, "The Impoverished Mind," *Educational Leadership*, Vol. 35, No. 8 (May 1978); and Evelyn Virsheys, *Right Brain People in a Left Brain World* (Los Angeles: Guild of Tutors, 1978).

is composed of two physically equivalent hemispheres and that each half controls movement in the opposite half of the body. Knowledge of brain function has increased through careful study of individuals with brain damage caused by strokes, accidents, or tumors. Recently, brain researchers have devised indirect methods for studying hemisphere functions by presenting competing sounds simultaneously in right and left ears, by presenting visual information to one eye or the other, and by measuring eye movements of subjects after posing different types of questions. The most dramatic advance in this area of research occurred when physicians developed a surgical technique, which involved severing the nerve fibers joining the two brain hemispheres, to control violent epileptic seizures. The relatively small number of patients who have agreed to submit to this last resort for their debilitating seizures have been the subjects of careful study of right and left hemisphere functions.

Results of these split-brain studies have supported the notion that the right and left brain hemispheres are somewhat specialized in their functions. In a summary of these findings, Howard Gardner explains that

> the left hemisphere has manifested a clear advantage in dealing with language, particularly with consonant sounds and rules of grammar. Processing of vowel sounds and access to the meaning of words seem to reside in both hemispheres. The left hemisphere also assumes a more dominant role than the right in classifying objects into standard, linguistically defined categories; it can ferret out from a set of objects all the large red cones or all the pieces of furniture.
>
> The right hemisphere has no cognitive preferences equivalent in strength to the left hemisphere's for languages. Nonetheless, the right hemisphere does seem relatively more important in spatial tasks. We may tend to rely on it in finding our way around an unfamiliar site or in mentally manipulating the image of a two- or three-dimensional form. The right hemisphere also seems crucial in making fine sensory discriminations; these range from the recognition of faces to the detection of unfamiliar tactile patterns.[42]

Less cautious researchers label the left hemisphere as verbal and analytic in function and the right brain nonverbal and global. Taken further in theory, the left brain becomes analytic, rational, logical, and linear, and the right brain is viewed as nonrational, analogic, intuitive, and holistic.[43] The implication for education is that both sides of the brain should be recognized and developed in a balanced educational program. Most schools are likely to attend to the verbal, symbolic, logical, and analytical aspects of brain function, but critics say the intuitive, holistic, and analogic aspects are usually ignored. Schools, it would seem, are effective in educating only half of the human brain.

[42] Howard Gardner, "What We Know (and Don't Know) About the Two Halves of the Brain," *Harvard Magazine*, March-April 1978.
[43] Betty Edwards, *Drawing on the Right Side of the Brain* (Los Angeles: Tarcher, 1979), p. 40.

Whether or not the left and right brain hemispheres in normal people function as separately and independently as the above view indicates, split-brain research has focused attention on many of the human capacities that have been largely ignored in school programs. These capacities are often emphasized in the arts, where intuition, holistic viewing, nonrational and nonverbal thought and expression are valued and developed.

It is not necessary for educators to take sides about learning theory, but it is a good idea for all educators to be aware of the major positions and their implications for teaching practice. Knowledge of major orientations will assist the individual in sorting out and evaluating the profusion of ideas, assertions, and programs.

The Values of Society

The society in which the learner matures and develops shapes that learner's system of values and beliefs as well as the educational systems available to the learner. It is not our purpose here to review comprehensively the influences of social, political, economic, and technological events in history, but rather to discuss briefly a few of the social issues that have had an impact on contemporary art education.

FREEDOM AND ART

Since art is very personal, creative people must control the activities that engage them. To be in control of their work, artists must have freedom to choose both their subject matter and their manner of expression.

At certain periods in history, political and aesthetic restrictions have been placed on artists. Sometimes these restrictions have resulted not from the normal discipline of artistic production but from the repressive actions of dictatorships, such as the Nazi regime in Germany. Nazi repression was promulgated for political reasons, as are similar restrictions on artists in the Soviet Union today. In other historical periods, various groups of artists, salons, and academies have attempted to restrict artistic activities, often for the purpose of maintaining a status quo in which their members strongly believed. In England and France, individuals or groups of influential artists have from time to time set forth canons for art and discouraged any deviation. Sometimes one person of remarkable ability and persuasive power has been able to influence artistic thought until it became derivative rather than creative. Under all such conditions, the art of the times has suffered.

Sheldon Cheney offers a number of examples to demonstrate the disastrous effects that unnecessary restriction has on artists' output.[44] He

[44] Sheldon Cheney, *A New World History of Art* (New York: Holt, Rinehart and Winston, 1956).

mentions the Chinese, who, with their passion for regulating design, did not escape the cramping effects attendant on the codification of rules of composition. Cheney also cites the codification of the rules of architecture by the Roman architect Vitruvius. Originally written in the first century A.D., these rules or *orders* were rediscovered and enthusiastically adopted by the architects of the Renaissance. The ascendancy of Vitruvius' orders has touched the environment of us all. Cheney maintains that until the second decade of this century, submission to the classical mode of architectural design seriously impeded the development of a creative art of building based on human need.

The freedom necessary for the success of an aesthetic act cannot be separated from the freedom of thought and action that is the prerogative of the individual living in a democracy. A fact generally overlooked is that art educators have been among the pioneers in developing a pedagogy compatible with democratic practices. What assisted them as much as anything else was their understanding that art could not be taught successfully unless it was presented in an atmosphere designed to develop individual and, in a sense, nonconformist expression.

Freedom in the art program, however, does not mean unlimited license. Teachers, in attempting to move children beyond a plateau of development, must constantly make certain decisions regarding their instructions. In so doing, they are always guided by the need for options—choices to be made by the individual child during the course of the art activity. It is this recognition of the value of personal decision-making that separates the art class from most other classes.

Many art programs emphasize the development of the individual as a person as well as a producer and consumer of art forms. Thus the individual's behavior in relation to associates takes on considerable significance. Contemporary art education has been affected by the idea that the school is the place where pupils live as well as learn.[45] This suggests that one aspect of education is to foster growth in the child's social skills and awareness, and the art class may include certain group activities designed to bring about this end. By using field trips, by introducing art history, and, in some cases, by coordinating art with other subject areas, the teacher is able to direct the child's attention to the arts as they exist beyond the museum, beyond even personal creative efforts.

Individuals operate on two levels: the interpersonal relationships just mentioned, and social or political behavior. First we learn to respect and live with our neighbors; then we attempt to improve the quality of everyone's life by taking the appropriate political action to affect the broad social and environmental issues confronting the community. These broad

PERSONAL DEVELOPMENT

[45] Phillip Jackson, *Life in Classrooms* (New York: Holt, Rinehart and Winston, 1968).

social concerns are relevant to art education if we are genuinely concerned about ultimate life goals. We must extend our view beyond the individual to society at large. A trip to a new housing project may be as important and as enlightening as a trip to a museum; a visit from a landscape designer as significant and engaging as one from a potter.

ENVIRONMENTAL AWARENESS

Encouraging sensitivity to environment in children is a difficult task for many teachers to accept because of its distance from what they conceive as the creative process. Social awareness through art asks that the students who have contact with an art program become so concerned with issues relating to the world in which they move that, as adults, they seek ways in which they may exercise control over that world.[46] Once they are committed to some program of action that they feel will better the community, they take on the role of worthy or enlightened citizens. In particular, children must be made aware of the rule that art can play in refining the quality of living. Such topics as pollution, conservation, and urban planning are now seen as aspects of design.[47] The ordering of visual elements extends from a painting to a poster, from a building to a housing development, even to a city.

Beginning in the 1920s, critics began to express serious concern about the general level of aesthetic taste. Roger Fry stated that in aesthetic matters people were "satisfied . . . with a grossness, a sheer barbarity and squalor which would have shocked the thirteenth century profoundly."[48] As early as 1934, Dewey asked, "Why is the architecture of our cities so unworthy of a fine civilization? It is not from lack of materials nor lack of technical capacity . . . yet it is not merely slums but the apartments of the well-to-do that are aesthetically repellent."[49]

Statements like these offered a challenge to education, for such condemnation referred indirectly to the masses of people educated in public schools. The inference was that the art education program was not effective in developing the ability to recognize good design from bad. As a result, art educators have only recently begun to seriously consider methods of developing a critical sense in children.

Today it has never been more apparent that aesthetic conditioning of one sort or another is constantly at work on the populace. The impact of the mass media, the changing faces of cities, the birth of new towns, and the despoliation of natural resources must somehow be brought to the attention of children—and in the most dramatic terms. How effective art

---

[46] June McFee, *Preparation for Art* (Belmont, Ca.: Wadsworth, 1966).

[47] June McFee and Rogena Degge, *Art, Culture, and Environment* (Dubuque, Ia.: Kendall-Hunt, 1980).

[48] Roger Fry, *Vision and Design* (New York: Meridian, 1956), p. 23.

[49] Dewey, *Art as Experience*, p. 344.

teachers can be in their attempts to create a visual sensitivity is still a matter of speculation. Our world abounds in vulgarities of every sort—on television, in magazines, in our littered streets, and in our polluted waterways. The future designers and planners in our society share the task of creating environments that will humanize and enhance our lives.

The place of art in the curriculum of the public and private schools of the United States and Canada has always been directly and drastically affected by the values, events, and trends of the society as a whole. The influences of democracy and freedom already discussed are fundamental and have been in operation since the founding of this country. Other values and attitudes toward art perpetuated from early times have not all been beneficial to art education. Unlike Europeans, American pioneers did not grow up in the midst of an artistic and architectural tradition. Aesthetic and artistic concerns often were low in priority, since the tasks of survival and practical living required much time and energy.[50] In place of an aristocracy, the traditional patron of the arts, our thriving democracy produced business leaders and politicians. Since business and politics are often based in practicality, only when the arts could be viewed as making a profitable contribution were they placed higher in priority. The attitude that art is a frill to be turned to only after the "real work" is done[51] is still quite evident and is largely the reason that art has never achieved a place in the school curriculum comparable to the three Rs, science, and social studies. Nevertheless, art education has progressed in theory and in professional practice to the point where the most enlightened educators view it as an essential rather than as a peripheral aspect of a balanced curriculum.[52] A 1980 Harris poll indicated that 59 percent of Americans rejected the idea that the arts are only for a privileged few; 93 percent felt that children should be exposed to a variety of arts activities in the schools; and 56 percent believed that children do not have enough opportunities for exposure to the arts.[53] These positive attitudes toward art education might

[50] Harry Green, "Walter Smith: The Forgotten Man," *Art Education*, Vol. 19, No. 1 (January 1966).

[51] Bernard Forman, "Early Antecedents of American Art Education: A Critical Evaluation of Pioneer Influences," *Studies in Art Education*, Vol. 9, No. 2 (Winter 1968).

[52] In a statement entitled "The Essentials of Education," released in 1978 by a group of professional organizations, the study of art and the aesthetic growth of youth were cited as essentials. The organizations were: American Alliance for Health, Physical Education, Recreation and Dance; American Council on the Teaching of Foreign Languages; Association for Supervision and Curriculum Development; International Reading Association; Music Educators National Conference; National Art Education Association; National Association of Elementary School Principals; National Council for the Social Studies; National Council of Teachers of English; National Council of Teachers of Mathematics; National Science Teachers Association; Speech Communication Association.

[53] *Americans and the Arts, III*, 1980 Louis Harris survey of 1,500 American adults. Quoted in the Minnesota Citizens for the Arts *Newsletter*, Vol. 4, No. 1 (February 1, 1981).

be the result of the dedicated service of thousands of art teachers in many countries during the past fifty years. At least the positive change in attitude toward the arts—as verified by attendance records for art museums, theaters, concerts, and so on—directly correlates with the increased attention paid to the teaching of art in the schools.

If art education is making progress with the general public, it seems to be faced continuously with challenges that affect society as a whole. When the Russians launched the Sputnik satellite in 1957, the reaction of educators and politicians put a tremendous emphasis on teaching mathematics, science, and foreign languages in the schools. Federal money was made available for curriculum development and implementation and for advanced education of teachers in these subjects. Similar funding was not available for other subject areas, causing inequities for teachers and for the curriculum.

SOCIETY AND ART EDUCATION

The post-Sputnik era signaled the growth of public spending and public influence in general education. Local school leaders' vocabulary expanded to include grant proposals, government guidelines, and accountability. The complexity of schooling increased during the civil rights movement of the 1960s and 1970s. School superintendents were made responsible for racial integration, equal opportunity, and affirmative action. Busing was used to achieve racial balance within school districts. In the late 1970s and early 1980s schools were made, by law, increasingly responsible for providing equal educational opportunity for handicapped and special learners. Each of these changes required schools to provide more services at increased expense.

High inflation rates and leapfrogging energy costs together with society's increased expectations for services have resulted in severe financial problems for many school districts. Tight budgets often mean teacher layoffs and cuts in programs—and art programs are often the first to be affected. Along with all of these factors, art education programs in the schools also have had to contend with the "back to basics" movement in education[54] and the additional severe financial stresses caused by the population decline of school-aged children, economic lags, and taxpayer revolts. The degree of emphasis and the quality of art programs varies widely from state to state and from school district to school district according to the values of legislators, school leaders, and communities and according to varying degrees of financial stability. One effect of this seemingly perpetual adversity is the development of art programs based on well-thought-out rationales.[55] Probably no other group of educators has

[54] Stephen Dobbs, ed., *Arts Education and Back to Basics* (Reston, Va.: National Art Education Association, 1979).
[55] Michael Day, "Rationales for Art Education: Thinking Through and Telling Why," *Art Education*, Vol. 25, No. 2 (February 1972).

had to work as diligently as art educators to provide sound educational justifications for their programs.

History of Change in Art Education

The history of art education is a fascinating, ongoing tapestry of interwoven threads that form a complex design. Three of the most prominent threads—the nature of art, conceptions of the learner, and the values of society—we have already discussed. Others represent the works of individual artists, writers, and teachers, and the advances in technology, curriculum projects, and even legislation. It is difficult to gain a view of the emerging pattern while the design is still being developed. Fortunately we can gain some perspective from the few historical accounts written on the subject. The following brief discussion is an attempt to identify some of the more prominent threads in the historical development of art education.

ART EDUCATION FOR INDUSTRY

In the United States, for example, the origins of art in the schools are related to the requirements of business and industry. American business leaders witnessed how the English had raised their standards of industrial design in order to compete favorably with European business in taste, style, and beauty. England's Schools of Design were revitalized in the 1850s, and they produced a corps of skilled designers for industry. In the United States, a few shrewd businessmen noted cause and effect and urged skeptical merchants and manufacturers to see the practical necessity of education in art for competition in world trade markets. Following the British example, the Americans recruited Walter Smith,[56] a graduate of England's South Kensington School, and appointed him concurrently director of drawing in the public schools of Boston and state director of art education for Massachusetts. Smith began his monumental task in 1871, just a few months after the Massachusetts legislature passed the first law in the United States making drawing a required subject in the public schools.

Walter Smith approached his work with great vision and vitality and began the development of a sequential curriculum for industrial drawing. Within nine years, he had founded and directed the Massachusetts Normal Art School, the first in the country, and had implemented his curriculum in all Massachusetts primary grades up to high school. In addition, Smith's writings and the teachers trained at the Normal School extended Smith's influence across the country. Smith's publications included a vol-

---

[56]Green, "Walter Smith."

ume entitled *Art Education, Scholastic and Industrial* and many series of drawing books for instructional purposes. In format, the series of drawing books was very similar. Usually the purpose of the series was "the laying of a good foundation for more advanced art training." The following statements about the particular aims of the books are typical:

1. To train the eye in the accurate perception of form, size, and proportion and to exactness in the measurement of distances and angles.
2. To train the hand to freedom and rapidity of execution.
3. To train the memory to accurate recollection of the forms and arrangements of objects.
4. To cultivate and refine the taste by the study, delineation, and recollection of beautiful forms.

This beginning of art education was quite different from what we experience today. Smith's instruction led teachers and children through a rather rigid sequence of freehand, model, memory, and geometric and perspective drawing. Rote learning, copying, and repetition were common aspects of the sequential curriculum.

> Smith's method of presenting the content depended upon class instruction and relied heavily upon the use of the blackboard, from which the students copied the problem the teacher drew. Prints and drawings were also copied by the students. Smith justified copy work in two ways: that it was the only rational way to learn, since drawing was essentially copying; and that it was the only practical way to teach, since classes were large and only a very limited amount of time was allotted in the school week to drawing.[57]

Although we would reject this type of art program today, Smith's accomplishments were well ahead of his time. His program broke new ground and gave art education in the United States a firm foundation upon which to build, a status the subject had never before had, and a precedent that could never be ignored.

CIZEK AND CHILDREN'S ARTISTIC EXPRESSION

Until the advent of Expressionism, art education remained remarkably aloof from artistic tradition. Expressionism first had its effect on art education largely through the work of one outstanding teacher, Franz Cizek. Cizek, an Austrian, went to Vienna in 1865 to study art. At the close of his formal period of study, he turned to art education. In 1904, after achieving success in several teaching posts, he accepted the position of chief of the Department of Experimentation and Research at the Vienna School of Applied Arts. His now-famous art classes for children were developed in this department.

[57]Green, "Walter Smith," p. 5.

A picture produced in Cizek's school in Vienna.

Cizek eliminated certain activities from these classes, such as making color charts and photographic drawing of natural objects. Rather, he encouraged children to present, in visual form, their personal reactions to happenings in their lives. In the output produced under his guidance—much of which has been preserved—the children depicted themselves at play and doing the things that naturally engage the attention and interest of the young. Cizek always maintained that it was not his aim to develop artists. Instead, he held as his one goal the development of the creative power that he found in all children and that he felt could blossom in accordance with "natural laws."[58]

Much of the work produced in Cizek's classrooms reveals the charm of expression of which children, under sympathetic teachers, are capable. There are indications, however, that Cizek and his staff discouraged the children from venturing much beyond the concept of beauty as a theme for artistic expression. Some of the output seems oversweet and discloses pretty mannerisms, such as a profusion of stars in the sky areas of compositions or a stylized expression of childish innocence in the faces. These mannerisms imply that some of the classes may have been overly super-

[58]W. Viola, *Child Art and Franz Cizek* (New York: Reynal and Hitchcock, 1936).

vised, and that the artistic development of the children was brought about as much by some of Cizek's teachers as by "natural laws." Nevertheless, Cizek is an important figure in art education, and his work deserves the widespread admiration it has received. The contemporary belief that children, under certain conditions, are capable of expressing themselves in a personal, creative, and acceptable manner derives largely from his demonstrations in Vienna.

Although several observers of Cizek's methods found merit in the idea of "creative expression," they were unable to develop an adequate pedagogy to make his ideas practicable. Such teachers were convinced that the child could grow naturally, untrammeled by adult interference. Freedom to grow "according to natural laws" meant to them that children should have license to do more or less as they liked without the teacher's intervention. This belief resulted in art programs that lacked direction or discipline and that too often became chaotic. When children are left to their own devices in the school setting, without stimulus and guidance from a teacher, the educational outcomes are often minimal. Optimal learning can be fostered in a setting where individual expression and creativity are balanced with meaningful structure and guidance by a sensitive teacher.

THE TEACHERS: DOW AND SARGENT

Other threads appear in the warp and weft of the history of art education. Great teachers emerged, such as Arthur Wesley Dow of Columbia University, Walter Sargent of the University of Chicago, and Royal B. Farnum of the Rhode Island School of Design.[59] Dow was concerned with analyzing the structure of art and sought to develop a systematic way in which it could be taught. He developed and taught what we know today as the *elements and principles of design*. The artist works with line, value, and color, composing these elements to create symmetry, repetition, opposition, transition, and subordination, which can be controlled to achieve harmonious relationships. Many contemporary art curricula are organized on the basis of a list of design elements and principles.

Walter Sargent's contribution to art education came from his focus on the process by which children learn to draw. He described in acceptable psychological terms the three factors that he believed influence children's ability to draw. First, the child must want to say something, must have some idea or image to express through drawing. Second, the child needs to work from devices such as three-dimensional models or pictures in making his drawings. Finally, children often learn to draw one thing

---

[59] Stephen Dobbs, "The Paradox of Art Education in the Public Schools: A Brief History of Influences," ERIC Publication ED 049 196 (1971), 48 pp.

Foundations of Contemporary Art Education

well but not others, so that skill in drawing is specific; a person could be good at drawing houses or boats and not good at drawing horses or cows.[60]

It is a tribute to Sargent that these three points are echoed in the current literature of art education, such as the work of Brent and Marjorie Wilson:

> Tony's drawings, like the spontaneous drawings of most chidren, are produced to tell a story, to relate an event or to tell what some subject is like.[61]

> The process of losing innocence in art involves the acquisition of artistic conventions—this imitative process which has for too long remained hidden . . . this borrowing and working from pre-existing images sometimes began before the age of six.[62]

> Our third major observation is that individuals employ a separate program for each object which they depict . . . . In the case of those objects that are well drawn, they have repeatedly played essentially the same program, sharpening their ability to recall the desired configuration easily from memory. . . .
>
> On the other hand, programs that are poorly run are characterized by vague memories of graphic configurations, halting movements and transitions, few established sequences with which to flow through. . . .[63]

Royal B. Farnum was one of many art educators who were involved in the *picture study* movement during the 1920s, 1930s, and onward. When it became possible through advances in printing technology to produce inexpensive color reproductions of paintings, many art educators of that era took the opportunity to present children with lessons in art appreciation. It was characteristic that the pictures chosen for study were not contemporary with the time, represented a narrow standard of "beauty," and often carried a religious or moral message. In his book *Education Through Pictures: The Practical Picture Study Course*,[64] published in 1931, Farnum lists no works of art by Picasso, Dalí, Matisse, Cézanne, Van Gogh, or even Monet or Renoir. Instead the works are chosen from earlier times, with at least fourteen of the total of eighty being pictures on religious themes (*The Holy Night, Saying Grace, Madonna and Angels*), others especially for children (*Goldie Locks and the Three Bears, With Grandma*), and a number with animal subjects (*The Sheepfold, Boy with Rabbit, Feeding Her Birds*). The following passage represents the flavor of the book:

FARNUM AND PICTURE STUDY

[60] Elliot Eisner and David Ecker, eds., *Readings in Art Education* (Waltham, Ma.: Blaisdell, 1966).

[61] Brent Wilson and Marjorie Wilson, "Children's Story Drawings: Reinventing Worlds," *School Arts*, Vol. 78, No. 8 (April 1979).

[62] Brent Wilson and Marjorie Wilson, "An Iconoclastic View of the Imagery Sources in the Drawings of Young People," *Art Education*, January 1977, p. 5.

[63] Wilson and Wilson, "An Iconoclastic View," p. 9.

[64] Royal B. Farnum, *Education Through Pictures* (Westport, Ct.: Art Extension Press, 1931).

Pasturage
Louvre, Paris

Troyon, Constant 1810–1865
French School

In *Pasturage* we find a splendid example of the artist's ability to make a harmonious effect in color and atmosphere by the massive forms of cattle against the sky and verdure. Before Troyon, no animal painter had painted with such a combination of strength and reality the long, heavy gait, the quiet resignation of cattle, and the poetic feeling of autumn light—or the morning mists lightly rising from the earth.

The deeply furrowed road gives an undulating effect; we seem to be looking over the broad limitless surface of the earth. A young girl, one hand on upraised skirt and the other grasping a short branch, is driving her charges homeward. The two cows, the flock of geese, the helpful dog and the sheep, all seem to be quietly browsing along with perhaps an occasional excursion off to the side for a last choice nibble. We wonder if the dense thunder clouds swiftly rolling up have not caused their protectress to urge them home earlier than usual.

Suggestive Questions: 1–Name the different animals in this picture. 2–Do you think the girl is looking after them all? 3–Where is the strongest color? 4–Have you seen clouds like these? 5–Have you ever tended animals? 6–Where do you think this scene is laid? 7–Do girls tend geese in our country? 8–What are geese used for besides food?[65]

Although it is easy to be critical of these early attempts at art appreciation, we must recognize the pioneering nature of this type of art education. Nevertheless, as Elliot Eisner has pointed out, "until very recently art education as a field has been quite unresponsive to contemporary developments in the world of art. Art education until as late as the middle of the twentieth century was more a reflection of lay artistic tastes than it was a leader in shaping those tastes and in enabling students to experience the work on the artistic frontiers of their day."[66]

THE OWATONNA PROJECT

The Owatonna Art Project in Minnesota was the most successful of several community art projects funded by the federal government in the 1930s. The objective of the Owatonna Project was to create art activities based on the aesthetic interests of community members. Rather than importing exhibits of avant-garde art from the city, this project promoted "home decoration, school and public park plantings, visually interesting window displays in commercial areas."[67] The idea was to apply principles of art in everyday life for a richer experience. The Owatonna project was a successful cooperative effort that involved many sectors of the community, the

[65] Farnum, *Education Through Pictures*, p. 50.
[66] Eisner and Ecker, *Readings in Art Education*, p. 6.
[67] Dobbs, "The Paradox of Art Education," p. 24.

local schools, and the University of Minnesota. Unfortunately it was interrupted by the outbreak of World War II and never achieved the impact it might have had under different circumstances.

Another influence in the late 1930s was the Bauhaus, a German school committed to integrating the technology of its day into the artist's work. As a result of its influence, modern art materials, photography, and visual investigation involving sensory awareness found their way into the secondary-school art program. Interest in the technology of art—notably in the communications media—concern for the elements of design, and an adventurous attitude toward new materials are all consistent with the Bauhaus attitude. The Bauhaus stimulated a growing interest in a multisensory approach to art as well as a tendency to incorporate aesthetic concerns into environmental and industrial design, especially in secondary schools.

THE BAUHAUS

Art educators' interest in the development of creativity is well documented by the titles of prominent books published in the field, especially during the 1940s and 1950s. Victor D'Amico's *Creative Teaching in Art* (1942)[68] and Viktor Lowenfeld's *Creative and Mental Growth* (1947)[69] were two of the most influential. Creativity interested not only art educators but also psychologists. The progressive education movement laid the groundwork by relating the free and expressive aspects of art creativity to a theory of personality development. When the movement expired in the late 1950s, members of the American Psychological Association, acting on the suggestion of their president, J. P. Guilford,[70] assumed leadership in applying more rigorous techniques to problems such as the analysis of creative behavior and the identification of characteristic behavior of professionals in both the arts and the sciences. Within a decade, what had formerly existed on the level of a philosophical mystique had been replaced by a science.

CREATIVITY AND ART EDUCATION

The research tools of the psychologist—tests, measurements, computers—were brought to bear on the delicate, mercurial process whereby people of all ages and in all areas of learning arrive at fresh solutions to problems. In considering the creative process, psychologists went beyond the visual arts and established commonalities of experience among all types of people involved in solutions to creative problems. Creativity was no longer the private preserve of the art room. For example, as a result of discovering how the creative process served the teacher of mathemat-

[68]Victor D'Amico, *Creative Teaching in Art* (Scranton, Pa.: International Textbook, 1942).
[69]Viktor Lowenfeld, *Creative and Mental Growth* (New York: Macmillan, 1947).
[70]J. P. Guilford, "The Nature of Creative Thinking," *American Psychologist*, September 1950.

ics, ideas emerged that would permit art teachers to view their profession with new understanding. Art teachers have always suspected that art, taught under proper conditions, can promote values that transcend the boundaries of the art lesson. So many art educators' beliefs have been verified in significant psychological studies that it is impossible for nonart educators to ignore them. Indeed, the movement to examine creative behavior has been a key factor in educational reform of learning theory to the present day.

One effect of the new research has been to question the validity of the I.Q. test. Scholars were concerned about the limitations of a test that relied so heavily on cognitive learning, and they felt that whole areas of a child's intellectual makeup were ignored by objective, machine-scored tests. It is precisely the nonverbal capabilities neglected by the I.Q. test that much research in creativity has concentrated on. Belated attention has been given, for example, to the speculative and intuitive factors in problem-solving.

One way to characterize creative behavior is to project a composite picture of the kind of adults we might want our children to be. In this manner we can identify as creative those children who are flexible in coping with new problems, who are not intimidated by the unknown, and who, in later years, can maintain the spontaneity of childhood. The teacher's task, then, is to teach for such characteristics. But this is difficult if the teachers themselves do not value creative behavior as defined by psychologists or if, as teachers, they are highly structured persons, wedded to a subject rather than a process. As Asahel Woodruff views the situation:

> The creativity problem transcends the field of art, and it seems to me its significance can be enhanced by looking at it as part of the broader concept. I am not sure how best to approach it, so I will just start listing some of the elements of the problem. . . . [C]reativity is often associated with rebellion, delinquency and social disruption. Studies of creative people tend to support this notion by showing that creativity is associated with preference for change rather than stability; tendency to delay closure rather than to structure ideas; tendency to challenge old structure; tendency to let incoming perceptions dictate their own patterns, rather than to force preconceived patterns on them, and so on. Opposed to these tendencies are the overwhelmingly dominant tendencies of most people to maintain structure, and to find security in the maintenance of an unchanging environment. This tendency is deep-seated in the facts of human adjustment. It is perfectly natural, then, for most people to resent those who are unstructured and who are responsive to freshness and differences because they are threats to security.[71]

[71]Quoted in R. C. Burkhart and H. M. McNeil, *Identity and Teacher Learning* (Scranton, Pa.: International Textbook, 1968), p. xvii.

Foundations of Contemporary Art Education

It is difficult to separate concern for creativity from philosophical belief, and so it comes as no surprise that the leading figures in the study of creativity range from empirical researchers such as Jacob Getzels and Philip Jackson[72] to innovative investigators E. Paul Torrance and Frank Barron. The teacher might use research findings and theories to make the art room a laboratory wherein theory and statistics provide the basis for more sophisticated instruction.

The creativity rationale for art education and the interest in personality development so strongly advocated by Lowenfeld and others dominated the field well into the 1960s, when a new generation of scholars and educators began to question that direction and to suggest, for the first time, that the study of art was worthwhile *per se*. Attention was focused on art considered as a body of knowledge that could be learned by children, as well as a series of developmental activities. Jusifications for art in the schools had followed a long tradition of contextual rationales: the study of art is warranted because of its contribution to some other valued goal, such as development of competent industrial designers, development of creativity, achievement of general educational goals, or personality integration. Writers such as Edmund Feldman,[73] Elliot Eisner,[74] Ralph Smith,[75] and June McFee[76] have justified the study of art on the basis of what functions art performs and why those functions are important to understand. This position, as Eisner points out, is that of an essentialist, and it "emphasizes the kinds of contributions to human experience and understanding that only art can provide; it emphasizes what is indigenous and unique to art."[77]

Contemporary art programs often explicitly recognize the body of art knowledge and offer art-learning activities that foster understanding and response to art as well as activities that result primarily in art production. Students are exposed to the visual arts of the ancient and modern eras through films, slides, and reproductions as well as actual art objects in galleries, studios, and museums, when possible. Awareness of the world of art and of the concepts, language, and approaches useful in responding to art can help students understand and appreciate the art of others and become increasingly sensitive in their own art production.[78]

Looking back at the changing history of art education, the conscien-

ART AS A BODY OF KNOWLEDGE

[72] Jacob Getzels and Phillip Jackson, *Creativity and Intelligence* (New York: Wiley, 1962).
[73] Edmund Feldman, *Art as Image and Idea* (Englewood Cliffs, N.J.: Prentice-Hall, 1967).
[74] Elliot Eisner, *Educating Artistic Vision* (New York: Macmillan, 1972).
[75] Ralph Smith, ed., *Aesthetics and Criticism in Art Education* (Chicago: Rand McNally, 1966).
[76] McFee, *Preparation for Art.*
[77] Eisner, *Educating Artistic Vision*, p. 2.
[78] Michael Day, "Child Art, School Art, and the Real World of Art," in Dobbs, *Arts Education and Back to Basics.*

tious teacher realizes that although personal conviction and experience can occasionally be a valid basis for curriculum planning, it can just as easily limit the program. It is imperative, therefore, that competent art teachers see beyond their own experiences to the expertise of others. This is why graduate programs, professional literature, and conventions exist.

Some Basic Beliefs in Contemporary Art Education

Art education today is still very much a composite of what has gone before. It is not difficult to identify the many threads in the pattern that we have discussed. The development of strong professional associations such as the National Art Education Association in the United States, the CSEA in Canada, the SEA in the United Kingdom, and the INSEA in Europe; the publication of an impressive body of literature in the field, including a burgeoning research literature; and the emergence of well-founded teacher-education programs in colleges and universities have resulted in an enlightened group of art educators. This increased level of professional communication has not resulted in a narrow unanimity of thought about the goals of art education in contemporary society, although some points are agreed on by most art educators. The following statements might be regarded as some of the basic beliefs on which many current art education programs are founded.

1. Both through the production of works of art and through our contemplation of them, we use the arts to help us understand ourselves and the world around us. One of the traditional and unique functions of the arts has been to emphasize individual interpretation and expression. The visual arts today continue to be a means whereby we attempt to give form to our ideas and feelings and to gain personal satisfaction through individual accomplishment. The growing complexity of our contemporary culture, including its visual aspects, also requires of every individual a capacity for visual discrimination and judgment.

2. Through the ages we have used the arts to build and enrich our personal and shared environment. Art experiences should help us understand the visual qualities of these environments and should lead to the desire and the ability to improve them. An art education program which consistently emphasizes the ability to make qualitative visual judgments can help citizens to assume their share of responsibility for the improvement of the aesthetic dimension of personal and community living. Acceptance of this responsibility is particularly important during periods of rapid technological development and social change.

3. The visual arts contain a record of the achievement of humanity since the values and beliefs of a people are uniquely manifested in the art forms they produce. A critical examination of these forms can lead to a better understanding of both past and present cultures.

Foundations of Contemporary Art Education

"A Shepherd Near My Village," tempera by a nine-year-old girl from Cyprus. The placement of the sun in the corner is universal, but the extended concentration that this painting demonstrates appears to be a trait developed in particular cultures. The ability to develop an idea beyond its first stage through sustained concentration is an attribute of the visually gifted child. It may also result from the availability of more art time in American schools or from a more structured sequential approach to picture-making.

"Tree," tempera. This painting reflects the lack of self-consciousness and the sensual enjoyment of painting that we associate with children in the primary grades. The painting is an extension of a symbolic image that is usually first realized as a drawing.

4. Art has four aspects: *seeing* and *feeling* visual relationships, *producing* works of art, *knowing* and *understanding* about art objects, and *evaluating* art products. A meaningful school art program will include experiences in all of these areas. A planned program in art should be provided at all educational levels from kindergarten through high school. At each grade level, art experiences should be selected and organized with different emphases and different degrees of intensity and complexity so as to result in a broadened understanding in all four aspects of the art subject: perceiving, performing, appreciating, and criticizing.[79]

In addition to these general statements about the nature of art and its place in culture and society, many art educators share beliefs about the learner vis-à-vis art education. The belief that all children can benefit from art education is related to the notion that all children possess innate creative abilities that can be nurtured through art. Art expression in its purest form is an expression of the individual's interaction with life. In order to create this personal statement, an artist requires significant freedom of

[79] These statements were published by NAEA in *The Essentials of a Quality School Art Program* (1965).

thought, feeling, and mode of expression. Although many aspects of life allow for creative behavior, the arts are especially appropriate for creative development because of the value placed on divergency, uniqueness, and individuality. Although technical facility is essential for artistic expression, creative behaviors can be engaged in by beginners in the arts at even the initial levels. Artistic activities require the utilization of perceptual abilities, whether for production or response. Through a program of art education these perceptual capacities can be developed.

There are, of course, many other beliefs held by people engaged in art education that are not widely shared. It is likely, also, that some of these statements are subjects of controversy. Nevertheless, a review of literature in the field will verify that the beliefs and assumptions stated above are quite pervasive. Awareness of them will assist teachers in accepting or rejecting them as experience suggests or developing and testing new ideas about art education.

Activities for the Reader

1. Study a group of children enrolled in (a) a kindergarten or first grade and (b) a fifth or sixth grade. As you observe the children at work and at play, make a note of what you consider to be their creative acts.
2. Study an art session under the supervision of an expert teacher. Make observations of: (a) the ways in which the children develop artistic skills; (b) the ways in which freedom of thought is encouraged; (c) some of the experiences the children use as bases for expression.
3. Compare the methods of G. Stanley Hall and Walter Smith as they might be applied to a drawing lesson for sixth graders.
4. Select a reproduction of a well-known painting or some other professional artwork and discuss the nature of the artist's reaction to experience that the work exhibits.
5. Select reproductions of two art objects that are limited to being expressions of beauty and compare them with two that are not.
6. Observe an art lesson and describe it, making particular note of any Post-Impressionistic or Expressionistic influences on the teaching methods.
7. Describe any attempts at dictatorial control in any area of the arts that you may have experienced personally, and explain their ill effects.
8. Outline an art lesson according to the "five Herbartian steps." Appraise it for its strong and weak points.
9. Devise an art lesson based on the S-R theory of learning. Explain how it might fail.
10. Thinking of your own pupils, would you make any additions or corrections to the beliefs and objectives listed in this chapter? Explain what you would add, or which of the beliefs discussed are most important to you.
11. Teachers should realize that creativity can be developed in all areas of the curriculum. The following signs of creative behavior have been taken from Paul Torrance's observations of his own classes at the University of Minnesota.[80] Indicate the ways in which Torrance's observations might apply to the teaching of art.

[80] From "Nurture of Creative Talents," in Ross L. Mooney and Taher A. Razek, eds., *Explorations in Creativity* (New York: Harper & Row, 1967), p. 190.

Intense absorption in listening, observing, doing

Intense animation and physical involvement

Challenging ideas of authorities

Checking many sources of information

Taking a close look at things

Eagerly telling others about one's discoveries

Continuing a creative activity after the scheduled time for quitting

Showing relationships among apparently unrelated ideas

Following through on ideas set in motion

Manifesting curiosity, wanting to know, digging deeper

Guessing or predicting outcomes and then testing them

Honestly and intensely searching for the truth

Resisting distractions

Losing awareness of time

Penetrating observations and questions

Seeking alternatives and exploring possibilities

Suggested Readings

Arnheim, Rudolf. *Art and Visual Perception*, 4th ed. Berkeley: University of California Press, 1964. Gestalt psychological view of art, perception, and artistic development.

Chapman, Laura. *Approaches to Art Education*. New York: Harcourt Brace Jovanovich, 1978. Chapters 1, 2, 3, and 6 invite comparison with this text.

Dewey, John. *Art as Experience*. New York: Putnam, 1958. The classic text by the great philosopher of education. Essential for art educators.

Diamondstein, Barbaralee, ed. *The Art World*. New York: Artnews Books, 1977. A fascinating illustrated compilation of highlight articles from seventy-five years of the publication, *ARTNews*.

Dobbs, Stephen, ed. *Arts Education and Back to Basics*. Reston, Va.: National Art Education Association, 1979. An anthology of articles by prominent educators on the "back to basics" movement in education.

Eisner, Elliot. *Educating Artistic Vision*. New York: Macmillan, 1972. The views of a prominent art educator on art education.

_____, and David Ecker, eds. *Readings in Art Education*. Waltham, Ma.: Blaisdell, 1966. For a general overview of the field of art education, see Chapter 1, "What is Art Education?"

Feldman, Edmund. *Varieties of Visual Experience: Art as Image and Idea*, 2nd ed. Englewood Cliffs: Prentice-Hall, 1972. A well-illustrated and articulate discussion of art.

Gardner, Helen. *Art Through the Ages*, 7th ed. Rev. by Horst de la Croix and Richard G. Tansey. New York: Harcourt Brace Jovanovich, 1980. A classic general textbook on the history of art.

Kaufman, Irving. *Art Education in Contemporary Culture*. New York: Macmillan, 1966. See Chapter 13, "Popular Culture and Taste," and Chapter 9, "The Visual World Today," for the relationship of art education to society at large.

Logan, Fred M. *Growth of Art in American Schools*. New York: Harper & Row, 1955. The essential book on the history of art education in the United States.

McFee, June, and Rogena Degge. *Art, Culture, and Environment*. Dubuque, Ia.: Kendall-Hunt, 1980. Sociological and anthropological perspectives on art education.

Smith, Ralph, ed. *Aesthetics and Criticism in Art Education*. Chicago: Rand McNally, 1966. An anthology of writings that helped shape the modern era of art education.

TEACHING METHODS IN ART EDUCATION

[A] description of my teaching seems to me poor compared with what actually happened. The tone, the rhythm, the sequence of words, place and time, the mood of the students, and all the other circumstances which make for a vital atmosphere cannot be reproduced; yet it is the ineffable which helps form a climate of creativity. My teaching was intuitive finding. My own emotion gave me the power which produced the student's readiness to learn. To teach out of inner enthusiasm is the opposite of a mere preplanned method of instruction.*

TWO

The term *methods* is not often used in the literature of art education, perhaps because it carries with it outmoded connotations. Whatever term or phrase is used, the problems that occur in day-to-day instruction still exist. Methodology as dealt with in this chapter is not a rigidly prescriptive series of step-by-step directions on the "how" of teaching. Certainly there are a multitude of methods that can be used by any one teacher. If curriculum deals with the content of instruction, methodology concerns itself with the most effective means of moving students toward the realization of the curriculum. A program can be well planned and supplies plentiful, but if a teacher is unaware of the processes of getting chidren to move in a pro-

*From *Design and Form* by Johannes Itten, Copyright © 1964, by Reinhold Publishing Corporation, p. 7.

ductive way, then the art program that the teacher (and students) envision will probably never materialize.

There are some factors, such as intelligence and personality of students, over which the teacher has little control, but methodology does bring to mind certain principles and techniques of motivation and control that can be studied, observed, and reflected upon. If we concede that methods are determined by the varying nature of the children and of the task, then methodology invites an eclectic approach. Here are three major styles of instruction:

1. The *directive* method is appropriate for transmitting skills, techniques, or processes.
2. The *Socratic* or questioning method, employed with groups or individuals, is used to *guide* students in finding answers. This method requires certain skills of the teacher and takes more time, but it is particularly appropriate for art appreciation or any realm of instruction that deals with ideas, theories, interpretation, and analysis.
3. *Discovery*, formerly known as the "free expression" method, is the method in which the teacher must set the stage for lessons that are open ended, speculative, and problem-solving.

Not all students are ready for all styles of learning; moreover, the teacher may use several modes simultaneously. All these methods—directive, Socratic, and discovery—suggest different problems and therefore different methods of presentation, degrees of motivation, and styles of pupil-teacher relationship. For example, the directive approach might involve demonstrating the use of a file and saw; the Socratic method might call for a comparison of styles of sculpture, the discovery mode might involve a student's planning and carving an imaginary totem out of soft wood.

All three of these methods could be used in the course of one sequence of three-dimensional activities. The approach recommended is flexibility: a teaching style that draws on a number of strategies or methods of instruction suitable for a particular child, material, or idea.

The three approaches discussed thus far are general. Another level of methodology deals with the specific aspects of instruction. When a teacher suggests a particular way of developing a painting ("Begin large, then work small and choose your brushes to match the problem," or "Before you mix a color, think of the amount of paint you will need to cover the space"), he is working at the most immediate level of methodology. When two teachers discuss the most effective way of teaching lettering, or when a teacher plans to introduce a new tool in such a way as to minimize waste or accidents, this is methodology operating at both an immediate and

Teaching Methods in Art Education

practical level. How does a teacher get students to become aware of the forms and colors they have missed? What does he or she say or do to open students' eyes, to heighten their perceptions, to get in touch with their latent ideas or feelings? What kinds of questions do most teachers feel are at the heart of their profession? Before dealing with such questions, we must turn our attention to the larger issues that provide the setting for the level of instruction just described.

Curricula should be based on well-grounded convictions about the nature and worth of art experiences. If teachers have these convictions, methodological issues from broad to specific will follow with logical consistency. Planning involves the relation of parts to wholes; the wholes are the larger basic decisions which in turn determine the components. In drawing a portrait, for example, we do not begin with an eye or a nostril; we start by sketching the rough dimensions into which secondary areas must fit. So too in building an art curriculum.

Implications of Poor Teaching

Art as a field of study in the elementary school can be harmful as well as beneficial to learners. What determines in no small measure the value of art instruction is the teaching method employed. Faulty teaching can create in children a thorough dislike for art that may remain with them for the rest of their lives. A feeling that any artistic activity is wasted effort, a resentment against original thought in all forms of artistic endeavor from architecture to literature, a sense of insecurity when called on to make choices involving aesthetic judgment or taste—these are but a few of the possible effects of faulty teaching. Added to these may be a thorough disrespect for the school that forces on learners a subject in which they can see no value and find no personal challenge, and from which they derive no knowledge of lasting worth. Likewise, as a result of inappropriate teaching methods, more than one teacher in the past has experienced "discipline problems" during art sessions because of an insensitivity to children's preferences in material and subject matter.

On the other hand, children may be enthusiastic about art as a school activity. When such is the case, art can influence the whole atmosphere of a school, and other fields of study seem to benefit by its good effects. Thinking becomes livelier, and children take a greater interest and pride both in their school and in themselves. School halls, classrooms, and the principal's office are changed from drab areas into places of real visual interest. Children proudly bring their parents to school to see exhibitions of work. Principals report a greater degree of cooperation not only among the children themselves, but also among members of the teaching staff and between the public and the school. As well as discussing recommended teaching practices, this chapter will describe some methods that appear to be either ineffective or actively harmful to the artistic development of children. First, however, it will be well to consider just what type of teacher can teach art.

Trained *versus* Nontrained Art Instructors

Most countries in the world do not have trained art specialists in the elementary grades. (Israel, Canada, and the United States are a few exceptions.) In most countries it is assumed that art will be taught by the classroom teacher. (Great Britain, Korea, Australia, New Zealand, and Japan have very active art programs conducted by non–art-specialists.)

The teacher who has sufficient ability, tact, and liking for children to teach, say, language, arithmetic, or social studies can probably teach art as well. Like any other subject, art requires of the teacher some specific knowledge and skills—such as a knowledge of pictorial composition and other forms of design, an acquaintance with professional artwork, and some ability to use materials such as paint, wood, and clay. With relatively little effort, however, a competent teacher may gain the knowledge and master the skills associated with art education. The problems in teaching art, including classroom management and control, discipline, presentation of lessons, assistance of pupils, and appraisal of the success of the program are, broadly speaking, not different from the general school program. One may assert, therefore, that it is possible for a proficient teacher in an elementary school to be a capable teacher of art.[1]

Indeed, one of art's unique characteristics is that it allows for much learning to be attained if the teacher simply assigns the right task. In mathematics, the teacher cannot assign a problem in fractions without first knowing the mathematical processes used with them. Yet a fourth grade teacher without art training can talk about the functions of machines and ask children to design a machine for a particular task, be it fanciful or realistic. Obviously, an art teacher, dealing with the same topic, is in a

[1] See Luella Cole's summary of the characteristics of a good teacher in H. J. Klausmeier and K. Dresden, *Teaching in the Elementary School*, 2nd ed. (New York: Harper & Row, 1962). The trouble, of course, with many such summaries is that most frail humans cannot measure up to the list of excellent traits suggested by the authors. In real life, however, these same frail humans often make good teachers.

Marion Richardson unconsciously reveals in her book *Art and the Child* (Peoria, Ill.: Bennett, 1952) the qualities of a great teacher, among them tact, sympathy, knowledge of subject, sensitivity to art and children, and a number of intangibles. Natalie Cole, whose books *The Arts in the Classroom* (New York: John Day, 1940) and *Children's Arts from Deep Down Inside* (New York: John Day, 1966) are read by art teachers eager to approach children, teaching, and art on an intuitive basis.

better position to develop the idea in terms of design or more effective use of materials, but a non-art teacher can still be very effective. A non-art teacher can also master a few basic processes such as papier-mâché, clay, or printmaking, and can certainly learn how to distribute paints to the class. In other words, teachers do not have to be artists in order to know how to begin art activities. If they can handle basic materials with some degree of enthusiasm, and if they have some idea of what tasks, subjects, or topics are appropriate for the grade level, then teachers can provide children with an art program of value.

There are basically three types of teachers who can offer some degree of art instruction:

1. The classroom teacher with little or no preparation who encourages children to use art by assigning problems and avoiding unschooled criticism.
2. The classroom teacher who has taken the time for an inservice course, to study on his or her own, and who is able to begin art activities that go beyond crayon and pencil.
3. The professional art teacher who has the knowledge to advance the child's work through a trained, critical mind.

One of the purposes of this book is to serve all three of these types of teachers.

The taped discussions of classroom teachers at work in Manuel Barkan's *Through Art to Creativity*[2] clearly demonstrate that a teacher's ability to communicate with children can compensate for a lack of professional art training, at least in the lower elementary grades. In a policy statement for the Commission on Art Education, Barkan wrote as follows:

> At the kindergarten and early elementary grade levels almost any truly good classroom teacher who accepts the commitments of the basic components of general education for young children can learn to teach art well. At the middle and upper elementary grade levels, however, special background and knowledge about the nature of art is essential.[3]

The National Art Education Association's publication seems to have greater confidence in the role of the classroom teacher, because it states:

> . . . Many people consider that it is the classroom teacher who knows the child and can best relate art experiences to the other areas of learning that the child is encountering in his daily program. They feel strongly that through such relationships and understanding, art becomes a means for

[2] Boston: Allyn and Bacon, 1960.
[3] In Jerome J. Hausman, ed., *Report of the Commission on Art Education* (Washington, D.C.: National Art Education Association, 1965), p. 84.

expression and communication which is needed for every other learning experience in the daily class program.[4]

Pauline Johnson feels that "Every elementary school should have at least one person trained in the visual arts who can give leadership and assistance to the program. This person will be in a position to contribute a great deal to the effectiveness of the school in general and to become a unifying force."[5] Even if every elementary school were suddenly to be allotted its own art teacher, however, there would still be the problem of finding hours in the week for each child to be reached by a single specialist. The realities of the situation are such that, at best, the classroom teacher should serve as a partner to trained art personnel in planning and should take on a significant share of the program.

Most elementary schools in the United States do not have the arts personnel Johnson described. We therefore must assume that the average classroom teacher with the will to conduct an art program is capable of providing art activities of value.

Some Sound Teaching Practices in Art

The following discussion of teaching methods contains nothing novel.[6] Almost anyone who has taken a course in methods of teaching will be familiar with the ideas presented below. They are outlined merely as a reminder of certain facts about pedagogy that any teacher, whether in service or in training, would do well to keep in mind.

One important lesson learned from past experiences is that a *teacher* is needed while elementary-school children are engaged in art activities. Teachers who conducted a laissez-faire type of program did not play a sufficiently strong role in the classroom. As a result, their art programs, although largely founded on commendable ideas, failed through lack of suitable teaching methods. The contemporary program, on the other hand, rests on the foundation of a strong belief in the need for both positive guidance and a methodology that is consistent yet flexible.

A good teacher begins where the child's natural creativity ends. During the Progressive era of the early 1930s, teachers were apt to accept everything children did as evidence of their optimal potential. We now

[4] Mary M. Packwood, ed., *Art Education in the Elementary School* (Washington, D.C.: National Art Education Association, 1967), p. 28.

[5] In W. Reid Hastie, ed., *Art Education*, Sixty-fourth Yearbook of the National Society for the Study of Education (Chicago: University of Chicago Press, 1965), p. 84.

[6] Earl C. Kelley and Marie I. Rasey, *Education and the Nature of Man* (New York: Harper & Row, 1952), is a book that makes excellent generalizations about teaching and learning and is highly recommended for reading in conjunction with this chapter.

recognize the fact that much of what children do on their own without guidance, motivation, or special material is repetitive and not a clear indication of the children's true capabilities. The teacher, weary of seeing the same array of rainbows, cartoon characters, and other stereotypes, obviously must teach for the capability of the child. A good teacher realizes that one does not take away without giving something in return; that it is possible, even advisable, to build on stereotypes, so that even second-hand images can provide a basis for original thinking.

Methodology begins before the students enter the art room. Classroom teachers send out cues by preparing a section of the room for visual activities. They should avoid commercial give-aways from product manufacturers and instead display reproductions of artworks or natural objects such as flowers, driftwood, or plants. Art teachers with their own rooms can create an environment rich in visual stimulation, well organized, and reasonably clean and orderly. When students first enter either teacher's room, they immediately receive cues about the possible delight that the room can hold. The teacher who stands at the door and greets the children, who does not begin the class until order is established, who has a pleasant expression, is teaching. The questions that all teachers must ask themselves are quite simple: "If I were a child, what set of circumstances in this room would direct my thinking and my attitudes? What will a child feel like in this space?"

SETTING THE STAGE

Children can be motivated by their experiences to produce art. As children live from day to day, they have many experiences that arise from life at home, at play, at school, and in the community in general. They bring to each new experience the insight they have acquired from previous experiences. If, on the one hand, the new experience arouses their interest, and if it is sufficiently reminiscent of former experiences, learning should occur. If, on the other hand, children are not interested in the new experience, they will probably not profit from it. The majority of experiences that children enjoy, however, do arouse their intellect and stimulate their feelings, and so may be considered suitable subject matter for artistic expression. Indeed, no other kind of subject matter is worthy of a place in art education.[7]

MOTIVATING CHILDREN IN ART

[7] Paul R. Mort and William S. Vincent, *Modern Educational Practice* (New York: McGraw-Hill, 1950), has good sections on motivation and "motivational devices" in general. See, for example, the section called "Stimulating Situations and Problems." Also included in the book are excellent summaries under the title "Reasons Why . . ." in which the authors give succinct statements derived from psychology and sociology to justify their suggestions about method. Every statement of this type might profitably be read by art teachers.

Two examples of taking a close look at things in the young child's environment—a sign of creative behavior and a source of motivation. Above: "Pipes under the sink," kindergarten. Below: "Tables and chairs," first grade.

A major source of motivation, then, is the children themselves. The teacher who can regard students as thinking, feeling organisms who function intimately with both the world of the senses and that of fantasy, imagination, and dreams, will have greater insight into the possibilities of motivation. Because the *total* makeup of the child provides sources for motivation, the teacher must go beyond sensory experience and probe to a

Teaching Methods in Art Education

certain extent what might be called the children's "inner landscape"—that is, their dream world, their fears, their desires and reveries, even their nightmares. A very real function of the art program is to provide visual objectification for the internal as well as external experiences.

In general, the teacher makes a distinction between *extrinsic* motivation, which consists of outside forces (such as contests and grades) that influence the child's level of motivation, and *intrinsic* motivation, which capitalizes on internal standards and goals that the child recognizes as having value (such as the desire to perform well). The teacher should avoid striving for the short-term gain of the former, and work to bring out the latter kind of motivation, which is far more valuable in the long run to the child's development.

The teacher, having decided on the source of motivation, must consider this question: "What are the most effective means of getting the children to use their experiences with the materials I have provided?" At this point the teacher must be sensitive to the variables of the situation, linking subject to materials with techniques capable of capturing the attention of the class. The teacher may decide to focus on the excitement of untried materials, introduce the lesson with a new film, or set up a bulletin board using materials from outside the classroom. The teacher may engage the class in a lively discussion or bring in an animal or unusual still life, plan a field trip, invite a guest speaker, or demonstrate how a particu-

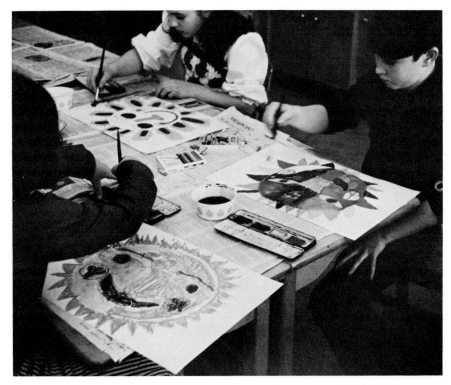

An example of a method of motivation. Fourth graders create their own sun faces after a slide show on the sun image in the history of art.

lar skill might be used. In some instances several such ideas may be combined.

When a discussion is to provide the basis of motivation, the teacher should master the techniques of dialog, involving more children than the usual number of bright extroverts and letting the class members do most of the talking until *they* have come up with the points to be emphasized.[8] The teacher may find it wise to promote intimacy in the classroom by seating the children close together. In this kind of instruction the teacher's personality, enthusiasm for the task, acceptance of unusual ideas, and flair for communciation all play an important role. When energy level is low and the class has to be "brought up" to a productive level, the motivational phase can be enhanced by a touch of showmanship.

It is important to remember that children do not normally connect their experiences with artistic acts. If a teacher tells children to paint a picture of any item of experience that appeals to them, or, in other words, "to do whatever they like," the results are usually disappointing. Under such circumstances the children are often at a loss as to what to paint or make. A well-known cartoon of children looking up at a teacher and asking with rueful expressions, "Do we have to do anything we want to?" illustrates the point.[9] It was not that the children in the cartoon lack experiences suitable for expression, but rather that they have not connected them with expressive artistic acts.

WHEN AND HOW MUCH TO TEACH

Teaching in art is the technique of helping children to say what they want to say in the terms in which they want to say it. Teaching is concerned, therefore, with the development of an idea (once the main theme or subject has been selected), through the use of tools and materials. Since the child must remain in control of the ideas being expressed and of the tools, media, and composition used to express them, the teacher should be sensitive to how he or she critiques the work in progress. (We will show later the disastrous results if a child is subjected to dictatorial pressures.) Two important problems facing a teacher are the timing of teaching and the amount of teaching to be done.

Timing. Teaching must be timed so that it occurs neither too soon nor too late. Once each child has accepted an idea for expression and has selected the tools and medium, there comes a period of hesitation or doubt that any creating person, whether child or professional artist, experi-

[8] For some good examples of dialog, see Barkan, *Through Art to Creativity.*

[9] "No competent and responsible educational leader has ever said anywhere at any time that the pupil is to do what he wants to do." William H. Burton, *The Guidance of Learning Activities,* 3rd ed. (New York: Appleton-Century-Crofts, 1952), p. 65.

ences.[10] The teacher should assist the child in selecting a topic and setting up as a goal a particular act of expression. But even when this is done, the child's thoughts about both the theme and the goal tend to be nebulous. It would be a most extraordinary child who knew instantly what the subject matter, composition, and handling of media were to be. Should children have stereotyped answers to all these aspects of their work, their efforts would no longer be creative. Once children have settled on a theme, therefore, they should be allowed to think about it and to explore it, both mentally and physically, with the medium they have selected.

The experimentation that occurs at this time should not consist of random activity; it should be determined by the problems and goals previously established. Although some of the child's ideas may lead to blind alleys, false moves resulting from controlled experimentation are not a waste of educational time and materials, since they narrow the number of choices the learner has as to the best means of arriving at a satisfactory solution to problems and the achievement of goals. The testing and retesting of ideas, the sifting, discarding, and coordinating that go on, are all traditional functions of a creative act and, at the same time, are highly educative. An activity undertaken without a period of personal struggle does not fall within the definition of art. It is safe to say, in fact, that no real art has ever been produced without it.

Artists accept the necessity of this period of exploration, for they must rely on their own initiative to arrive at a satisfactory solution to their problems. Children, on the other hand, are immature and cannot be expected always to solve their problems and to reach their goals to their own satisfaction. Sometimes they must rely on the teacher for help. The most important question, therefore, arises: when should a child receive help? The answer must be dictated largely by common sense and the teacher's intuition. When the child, because of limited experience, has exhausted the possiblities of experimenting and can proceed no further without help, the teacher must offer assistance. Because each child is different, each requires individual treatment. One child may need assistance soon after work has begun; another may not need help until well into the project.

In deciding when to offer assistance, therefore, the teacher must constantly study every child engaged in art work, making note of such problems as: John is not wiping his brush free of excess paint and hence is spoiling his page with superfluous drops of paint; Mary is making her main figures too small; Elizabeth is unable to draw a house; the background in Peter's picture interferes with the center of interest he has established. When children have reached the end of their resources, when

[10]Described in detail by John Dewey in *How We Think* (Boston: Heath, 1933). In his *Democracy and Education* (New York: Macmillan, 1916), p. 182, he says: "The most significant question . . . which can be asked . . . about any situation or experience proposed to induce learning is what quality of problems it involves."

they have struggled to the full extent of their capacity with the problem at hand, they must receive help. There is no formula or rule of thumb the teacher can follow. Only a personal knowledge of every member of the class, together with good judgment, can indicate when help must be forthcoming. Assistance given too soon will take away the child's initiative; given too late it will leave the child frustrated.

Amount of Teaching. The teacher has noted John's difficulty with the brush, Mary's trouble with small figures, Elizabeth's dilemma with the house, and Peter's problem with the background. The children need help, but how much assistance should they have? If too much help is given, the teacher will be thinking for the children; if too little is offered, the children will still be unable to proceed. The amount of guidance offered must be such that the child is helped to overcome the immediate difficulty and at the same time is left free to face further problems as they may occur. Moreover, whenever practical and possible, the help provided should ideally lead the child to the position of solving the problem independently.

Obviously, the amount of help must be governed by the stage of development of the child. Because John is only six years old, he must be shown precisely how to dip a brush in paint and how to wipe it free of

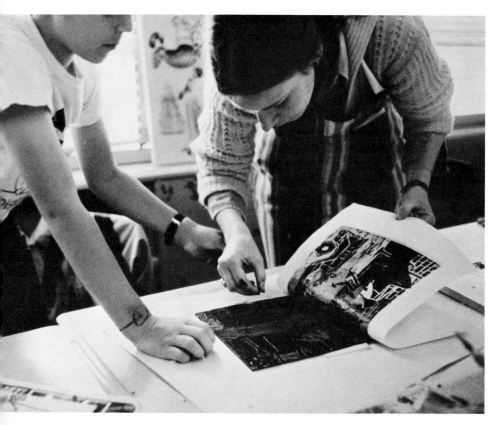

Pulling the first print provides a special excitement that is never quite achieved in other stages of the print process. When the print is completed, the student must decide on the size of the edition, the choice of. paper, the ground or support—shall it be white or colored, collage or montage?—and the color of the ink itself. In each of these stages, the teacher should try to lead the child toward solving the problem independently.

excess drops. He may require several demonstrations of this process before he can use the brush successfully. Mary is seven, and the teacher can ask her to observe her work from a distance and tell why it is difficult to see the figures. Then Mary can be asked how she would change the picture so that everyone in the class will enjoy seeing her figures. Some of her classmates may help her arrive at a satisfactory solution. Elizabeth is ten, and she can be asked to observe houses closely, and perhaps make some sketches of them. Peter, who is twelve, can have his attention drawn to the work of others so that he can study how they overcome difficulties in painting backgrounds. Later, he may be taught how to mix tints and shades of color for use in the background. Occasionally, the teacher will observe that many members of the class share a common difficulty and that a short general lesson to the group is needed. Unless the majority of the class will profit from a group lesson, however, help should be offered on an individual basis.

Media are the materials that a pupil employs in art activities. Their proper use in class depends on the teacher's knowledge of how children will use them.

SELECTING THE MEDIA AND TOOLS

Different types of media suit various stages of physical development of the pupils. At certain stages of development, for example, children have difficulty using soft chalk and require instead a harder substance such as wax crayon. Too hard a medium, however, makes it difficult for children to cover paper readily and will interfere with their expression.[11] Very young children, who have not learned to use their smaller muscles with dexterity, require large surfaces for painting or assembling large objects. Yet children of all ages periodically have a desire to render detail, and there should be occasions when pencils are permitted for small-scale work, in which case the lead should be soft and the paper not too large.[12] As children mature and gain greater muscular control, they can work with smaller surfaces and objects. Some children, however, may wish to work on a large scale no matter what stage of muscular development they have reached.

Children often show marked preferences for a particular medium. One child may find greater satisfaction in using clay than in using card-

[11] See Chapter 6, "Drawing and Painting," for further discussion of suitable media.

[12] Rudolf Arnheim, in *Art and Visual Perception*, 4th ed. (Berkeley: University of California Press, 1964), and Dale Harris, in *Children's Drawings as Measures of Intellectual Maturity* (New York: Harcourt Brace Jovanovich, 1963), both state the case for encouragement of detail as a means of clarification of concepts. On p. 168, Arnheim states: "Unquestionably the modern methods have given an outlet to aspects of the child's mind that were crippled by the traditional procedure of copying models with a sharpened pencil. But there is equal danger for *clarifying line observations* of reality and for learning to concentrate and create order." (italics added)

board; another may prefer colored inks to tempera paint. Unless these children are given reasonable, although of course not exclusive, opportunities to employ the media of their choice, their art output may be inadequate.

Children may also have preferences as to tools. A certain size and type of brush may suit one child but not another. A fine penpoint may appeal to some, while coarser nibs may be right for others. Teachers should be sensitive to the relationship between tools and paper size, bearing in mind that small tools (pencils and crayons) inhibit design on paper larger than 12 by 18 inches, and that large brushes limit detail and observation on smaller sizes of paper.

The teacher who makes an effort to provide a variety of materials and tools is following an accepted practice in art. Nearly every artist develops preferences among the many media and tools available, but this does not prevent exploration of further choices of favorite materials or testing of new materials.

TEACHER TALK

One of the most important factors in instruction is student-teacher dialog, or, to put it more simply, "teacher talk." Attending any exhibition of children's work, we are struck by either shared characteristics or the lack of common attributes within groups of children's art works of different teachers. These group differences are caused not only by materials and

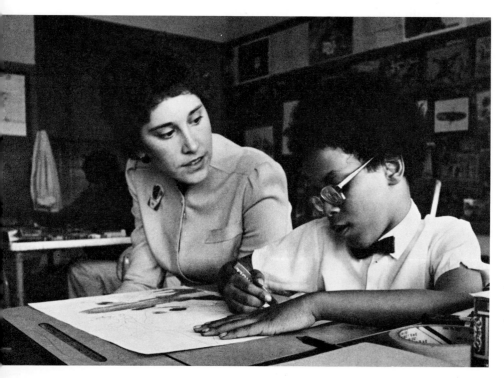

Teachers can communicate their preferences to students through their way of dress, attitudes, personalities, and language. At the same time, teachers should know each child in the class in order to judge when to offer assistance.

subject matter (one teacher prefers clay to other materials, while another may stress observational drawing) but also by the kind of language each teacher uses. *And it is through language that teachers convey much of their philosophy about art.* While teachers communicate much to their students through their way of dressing, their attitudes, and their personalities (little is missed by even the youngest child), their language probably has the most direct influence on how the work of their students develops.

The authors of this book observing teachers in a school system noted instances of student-teacher exchanges over a four-week period. The following dialogs are typical of teachers who attempted to tread a fine line between direct and indirect teaching.

First Grade: *Flower problem in tempera*

TEACHER: I like your shapes, they move all over in so many ways. Tell me about this—it isn't a flower, is it?
STUDENT: It's a bug, yes, a bug.
TEACHER: Does it have a name?
STUDENT: A grasshopper.
TEACHER: Grasshoppers are long and skinny, aren't they? How about a different-shaped bug? Can you think of one?
STUDENT: I can paint a snake—
TEACHER: Well, a snake isn't a bug, but a snake is very nice.

Second Grade: *"My Pet," drawing in felt-tip pen*

TEACHER: That's a good rabbit, but he looks awfully small.
STUDENT: It's a girl rabbit.
TEACHER: Yes, well, it looks kind of lonely by itself. What can we add to keep it company—you know, to make the picture bigger?
STUDENT: It has a cage.
TEACHER: Cages are good; where do you keep your cage?
STUDENT: Outside, on the porch.
TEACHER: Well, if it's outside, there are other things to draw, aren't there? You put them in and let me see if I can tell you what they are.

Third Grade: *Clay animal*

STUDENT: It doesn't look like a dog, it's all lumpy.
TEACHER: I think you are going to have to decide what kind of a dog—
STUDENT: A German shepherd. I like German shepherds. My uncle has one.
TEACHER: What makes a German shepherd different from, say, a beagle?
STUDENT: The ears stick up.

TEACHER: Okay. Then let's begin there. Pull its ears up and I think you can smooth out some of those lumps.

Fourth Grade: Box sculpture

TEACHER: Having trouble, Chuck? You don't seem very happy.
STUDENT: I hate it, it's not turning out.
TEACHER: What seems to be wrong?
STUDENT: I don't know, it's a mess. Nothing seems to go together; I wanted this neat truck—
TEACHER: Well, I think you've been a little careless in joining the sections together (demonstrates joining process with tape). See what I mean?
STUDENT: Yeah, I don't know. It still won't look like a truck.
TEACHER: Look, Chuck, try to think ahead. You have a cereal box and a medicine carton and they both have pieces of letters and different colors showing. Why don't you join it, then paint it, I think you'll like it better.

Fifth Grade: Linoleum print

STUDENT: It won't work.
TEACHER: What won't work?
STUDENT: The tool, it keeps sliding and slipping.
TEACHER: Let me try. No, the blade's okay. Here, try standing and let your weight press the blade, and for goodness' sake, keep your left hand out of the way of the blade or your mother will be calling me tonight about an accident, okay?
STUDENT: Okay.
TEACHER: Say, I haven't checked your drawing, can I see it before you continue?

Sixth Grade: Landscape painting

TEACHER: Very nice, John, very nice.
STUDENT: It all looks the same.
TEACHER: What do you mean?
STUDENT: Well, there was more color—
TEACHER: You mean more kinds of green in the trees—?
STUDENT: Yeah, that's right.
TEACHER: Look, you keep using the same color green. Come on, you know how to change a color.
STUDENT: It will be messier.
TEACHER: You've got your palette set up; try out some mixtures, add yellow, try a touch of black—

STUDENT: Black?
TEACHER: Why not, Try it, it won't bite you. You can always paint over it.

Each teacher in these dialogs had to be sensitive to the range of vocabulary, the nature of the assistance needed, and the tone of address. The role of language is complex and plays a vital role in art education. The best way to learn how to use language more effectively is to observe good teachers in action, either in an art or general classroom situation.

Some Questionable Teaching Practices in Art

Now let us examine some hypothetical cases of teachers whose teaching practices are questionable. A study of these examples may serve not only to clarify the principles of good teaching practice but also to assist the student in avoiding some of the pitfalls of negative teaching methods.

Every year when spring approaches, Miss L, a conscientious second grade teacher, provides the class with yellow and green construction paper. She has designed a pretty pattern of a daffodil in which the leaves are green and the flower yellow. She demonstrates first how to cut the petals and then shows how to make the leaves. "The children," says Miss L, "love to make a daffodil. It provides a most effective art lesson."

THE TEACHER WHO ADVOCATES COPYING

Miss L is correct in saying that the children love to make a daffodil. Spring is in the air and the bright new paper is fascinating. Motivation of the children is not difficult for Miss L, a friendly, likable, sympathetic person, who has timed her activity well. Miss L is incorrect, however, in saying that her assignment constitutes an effective art lesson. The activity is not art: it is "busy work." In producing the flower, no one but Miss L has done any planning. She has not only solved all the problems, but any expression of feelings about the flower is hers alone. The children may have developed some skill, but they have done so without thought and feeling. The children have been subjected to a mechanistic form of teaching.

The children's liking for a particular activity does not necessarily mean that the work is art or even an educationally sound pursuit. With very little motivation, children may be led to break windows or to chop down trees in public parks. Given sufficient approval, they will like these activities even more than they do making daffodils according to Miss L's directions. Actually Miss L has wasted precious educational time and materials in this work. Miss L has taught dictatorially, and not according to the children's needs.

THE TEACHER WHO UNDULY EMPHASIZES NEATNESS

Mr. W is a tidy person; he presents a neat appearance and his classroom is a model of order. "I like things to look right," says Mr. W, as he goes about his duties in a fourth grade classroom. "I have no use for sloppy work," he asserts, "in drawing, painting, or any other subject, for that matter." Mr. W encourages neatness so vigorously that his pupils have grown afraid to experiment. Those who first tried to experiment with ideas and media ran into difficulties with both the media and Mr. W. Now they hold fast to thoroughly familiar materials and well-tried clichés in artistic thought, which pleases their teacher.

Sometimes even under these conditions Mr. W is not altogether satisfied with the neatness of the children's work. In these cases, with bold application of chalk or paint he "touches up" the youngsters' work. He is so clever at this that the output of his class occasionally wins prizes. Only an expert in children's art could tell where the work had been doctored, and very few such experts judge children's art work on a competitive basis, because well-informed art educators are skeptical about competition of this kind.

The children's mural work must also be neat. Sometimes in this activity, too, the children do not meet Mr. W's standards of neatness, and this embarrasses him, particularly when the principal visits the classroom. However, he has developed what he considers a "good" system or mural-making. Now the children draw and paint only the backgrounds, in which work they cannot be too untidy if properly supervised. They then cut out figures from magazines and glue them into place. The new system is much easier because no real effort is required and total control is maintained.

Although no one would advocate untidiness for its own sake in a classroom, children must be allowed to experiment freely with ideas and media. Children's lack of skill in organizing both subject matter and materials makes it inevitable that their art production is often untidy. Tidiness in executing artistic activities will occur only after the children master the skills associated with the activities. To demand extreme neatness at all times is to handicap children in producing creative work. Among the basic principles of teaching neglected by Mr. W are that the products of expression must be the children's own and that teaching must be built on the children's interests. Exploration, even if it leads to blind alleys of thought, can be valuable.

THE TEACHER WHO MISTAKES LACK OF GUIDANCE FOR FREEDOM

Down the hall from Mr. W's classroom is Mrs. deP. She is tall and dark and looks "artistic" because she wears extraordinarily large pieces of jewelry. Mrs. deP spends each summer studying with painters and is a supporter of all forms of avant-garde art.

Mrs. deP says she is a lover of freedom to the extent that she is reluctant to interfere with any form of childlike expression in art. "Art is the

Teaching Methods in Art Education

free expression of an untrammeled spirit," she says. The output of her pupils seems to be lusterless. The principal claims that the pupils are noisy and inattentive and inclined to be rude to Mrs. DeP. Quite often, when not obstreperous, the pupils are listless. They say that they often do not know what to do. The situation is unfortunate, for Mrs. deP has much to offer. Her feeling for art is apparently deep, but she has failed to understand the meaning of teaching. She would have more success as a teacher if she recognized the following basic teaching principles: the pupils must be assisted in establishing personal themes for expression; teaching is most effective when the situation deals with some need; the teaching of art should not be used as a vehicle for frustrated artists to satisfy their own egos.

Miss Z, the teacher of a third-grade class, is clever at mathematics. One of her favorite art lessons consists of having the children resolve objects into triangles, squares, oblongs, and circles. She admires the precision resulting from this activity. "The children are learning to handle basic forms," she explains. Thus the children are taught to draw houses by means of a triangle supported by a rectangular oblong; a chicken by using two circles; a young girl, strangely enough, by resorting to triangles and squares.

THE TEACHER WHO RELIES ON A FORMULA

Miss Z is another example of a teacher who prevents children from expressing themselves in their art activities. Moreover, the designs she insists on are inaccurate in relation to the objects depicted. The forms of houses, chickens, and girls cannot be successfully arrived at through mathematical shapes supplied by the teacher. They can be depicted adequately only by means of personal experience and experiment on the part of the children. Miss Z's system is, in reality, a false and rather ugly one using someone else's pictogram shorthand; it is certainly anything but art. Miss Z should recall at least two basic principles of teaching: personal experience is the basis of learning, and skill (precision in the use of tools and materials) is best gained when closely connected with expressive acts engaging the thoughts and feelings of the learner.

Two Studies of Inappropriate Teaching Methods

The teaching methods described in the preceding section are based on practices inappropriate to artistic development. Study of both art and children reveals that these methods are either ineffective or harmful. But exactly how ineffective or harmful are they? There have been numerous experiments attempting to find an answer to that question. Two extreme cases are described below.[13] The first of these is concerned with dictatorial teaching practices, the second with laissez-faire practices.

THE EFFECTS OF DICTATORIAL TEACHING PRACTICES

The first experiment was performed with 250 children between six and eight years of age, all of whom had enjoyed a creative program of art up until the time of the experiment. They were in what is known as the "symbol" stage of expression and were able to relate symbols to their environment.[14] In brief, they were capable of creatively producing pictures about their experiences. The children were paired according to their mental ages into two groups called Group A and Group B.

For Group A, consisting of 125 children, the creative program in picture-making was brought to an abrupt halt. In its place the teachers substituted ten activities of a restrictive or dictatorial nature: cutting a triangle and a square from colored paper, to be pasted on paper to form a house; drawing an apple in the form of a circle, which the teacher had previously drawn on the blackboard; copying the outline of a tree that had been drawn on the blackboard; coloring a flower that had been drawn by a teacher and mimeographed; copying a drawing of a bird from a mimeographed outline; drawing a snowman according to the teacher's verbal directions; tracing the outline of a car prepared by a teacher; copying a drawing of a girl from the blackboard; drawing a tulip according to visual demonstrations on the blackboard; and following verbal directions in the use of circles to draw a cat.

While Group A was engaged in this work for ten days, Group B, consisting of the remaining 125 children, continued to make pictures creatively. On the eleventh schoolday, both groups were taken to a firehouse where the firemen had consented to act as hosts. After the children had explored parts of the building and the equipment, they were given light refreshments by the firemen. The excursion was an obvious success and a stimulating experience.

The next day all the pupils were subjected to the similar styles of motivation. Then they were asked to develop a picture from their experiences. All the children in Group B were, in varying degrees, successful in this work. Their drawings and paintings illustrated personal reactions to their observations and were produced in a variety of media and with different techniques. In Group A, however, 44 percent (fifty-five of the children), instead of presenting their reactions to the outing, resorted to drawing houses, birds, and the like, as they had been taught during the previous ten schooldays. Others reverted to manipulation of the media, a stage of development that precedes production of symbols.

[13] These were part of a research program directed by C. D. Gaitskell and sponsored by the Ontario Department of Education.
[14] The symbol stage and other stages of development are discussed in detail in Chapter 5.

66

"Animal Tower," line drawings, grade 5. When children feel that art cannot be taught, a teacher may want to change their views on the nature of teaching. Here, the teacher gave the class a problem involving memory and imagination. Children were asked to "draw a tower of animals." No motivation, assistance, or criticism was offered. In the following session, the same topic was assigned, but only after a lively discussion was held on the problems that might attend a group of animals attempting to form a tower. (The story of "The Musicians of Bremen" was referred to.) Ideas then were developed from the first pencil sketch, which was enlarged and transferred to 12-by-18-inch paper with colored felt pens. In the third session, watercolor was added. The combination of exciting art media, motivational dialog, and assistance when needed convinced the children that art could indeed be "taught," and in the process, the art of teaching was redefined.

The children in Group A were studied intermittently thereafter for a period of two years. At the end of this time, no fewer than 8 percent (ten children) were still inclined to produce the stereotyped work they had been taught during the ten days. If only ten days of dictatorial work in art[15] interfere to this extent with their artistic expression, one may well wonder how inhibiting, say, a whole year of this kind of teaching may be on the minds of children, and how durable may be its effects.

A related study is Heilman's investigation of the influence of workbook exercises on the art productivity of second grade children.[16] His evidence shows clearly the retrogressive effects of copying and points out how severely limiting such activity can be on the wider range of symbolization among primary-school children. But it is well to bear in mind that children can be just as inhibited by working from a teacher's model as they can be by using coloring books.

THE EFFECTS OF LAISSEZ-FAIRE TEACHING PRACTICES

The second experiment was designed to discover the extent to which children can get along without art instruction. Two hundred children were selected for observation and divided into two groups. One hundred of them, whose ages ranged from five years to six years, three months, with an average chronological age of five years, eight months, were in the first group studied. Sixty-two of these children were still in the manipulative stage; the remainder were making symbols to represent some objects in their environment.

For five days their teachers provided a variety of materials already familiar to the children, including tempera paint, clay, plasticine, and construction paper and glue. No aid in motivation and no teaching assistance were offered. During the first day and largely during the second, the children got along well. They kept themselves busy either manipulating materials or forming symbols. On the second day sixteen children showed a lagging interest in the work, and on the third, fifty-nine indicated this tendency. On the fourth and fifth days nearly every child indicated lack of interest in the activities, and all the work produced lacked vitality.

It is interesting to note that the older children in the group seemed to miss the attention of the teacher to a greater extent than did the younger. Perhaps this was because they had grown more used to motivation and guidance than had the younger pupils, and because the symbolic stage of expression requires more help from the teacher than does the manipulative stage. Of further interest is the fact that about 22 percent of the chil-

---

[15] We must not forget to take into account also the effects of variable interval reinforcement that usually accompanies such a program.

[16] Horace F. Heilman, "An Experimental Study of the Effect of Workbooks on the Creative Drawing of Second Grade Children," unpublished doctoral dissertation, Pennsylvania State University, 1954.

dren who originally had reached the symbol stage reverted to the manipulation of materials and failed to produce any symbols.

The same procedures were repeated with the second group of 100 children, ranging in age from seven years, two months to nine years, one month, with an average chronological age of eight years, three months. The results of this study were similar to those obtained with the first group, except that from the first day there was a noticeable lack of interest in the work. This attitude was almost universal on the second and subsequent days.

It was concluded that the youngest children, particularly those in the manipulative stage, apparently benefit from an occasional art period in which the teacher does not attempt to provide motivation or assistance. Too many such sessions in sequence, however, rapidly have adverse effects on the art activities of all children, but particularly on the work of those children who have advanced beyond the manipulative stage of development.

Teaching in Action: Planning for the First Session

All teachers must plan for the first meeting with their pupils. The taped dialogs transcribed here represent two approaches to this first meeting. The first conversation depicts a teacher's attempt to get a grass-roots definition of art from disadvantaged children in the third grade; the second demonstrates how a first planning session with middle-class children sounds.

TEACHER: My name is Mrs. D. Do any of you know who I am? (*pause*)

FIRST DIALOG

TOMMY: You an art teacher?

TEACHER: That's right. I am your art teacher. Now, can anyone tell me what an artist does?

SARAH: He paints you pictures.

TEACHER: Very good. What other kinds of artists are there? (*longer pause*)

FLORENCE: Are you going to let us paint pictures?

TEACHER: Certainly, we'll paint pictures, but we'll do things that other kinds of artists do too. Can you think of other things we can do that other artists do? (*pause*) Well, think of going shopping with your mother. Can you think of the work of artists in a shopping center?

TOMMY: (*suddenly*) I know! He can paint you a sign. . . .

TEACHER: (*enthusiastically*) Yes, yes, sign painters are artists, too--what else?

TOMMY: (*picking up the enthusiasm*) And if you had a butcher shop and you had a good—I mean a *good* artist, he could paint you a pork chop on the window. . . .

The above conversation is a fragment of a discussion held by Mrs. D during the first meeting with a group of third graders in an inner-city school. The purposes of the teacher's discussion were to (1) learn the children's concept of art; (2) establish the kind of rapport that comes only through a relaxed exchange of ideas; and (3) prepare the children for the program she had planned for the year. As a result of her discussion, Mrs. D set aside quite a few activities she had planned because she realized they were inappropriate for the children. A skilled and experienced teacher like Mrs. D would be sensitive to the range of differences among children and would understand that they all come to the art class with their own ideas of what constitutes an art program. To some, art represents part of social studies; to others it means carrying out school services. For one child it is the high point of the week, while to another it is a traumatic period during which the student is constantly cautioned against making a mess.

SECOND DIALOG

Let us examine another discussion taking place at a meeting of an art consultant and some pupils. These pupils are fifth graders in a middle-class neighborhood. A content analysis of the pupils' comments is provided in the outer column.

Analysis of Pupil Comments

This remark may be interpreted as a sign of disappointment that Mr. H will not be their regular art teacher.

Mark is ready to go to work. In his eyes the art period (there are so few of them) is not a place to talk, but to make things.

If the art teacher is thinking of giving appreciation lessons that involve close looking in relation to a new vocabulary, he will find that Mark's attitude may provide a clue to the general class readiness for discussion as opposed to actual art work. The teacher has to find ways of making exciting activities of observation and discussion.

Teacher-Pupil Dialog

MR. H: Good morning. My name is Mr. H. I'm an art teacher as well as your art supervisor, and I'd like to talk with you about some of the things you're going to be doing this year with Miss G, your regular art teacher.

SUSAN: You mean you're not going to be our art teacher?

MR. H: No, but I hope I'll be coming in now and then to see what Miss G is doing, and perhaps later on I'll take a few classes myself.

MARK: What are we going to do today?

MR. H: Well, as I said earlier, I'd like to take this time to talk about what you'd like to do this year.

Teaching Methods in Art Education

SUSAN: Will Mr. S be back?

MR. H: I don't know. Who is Mr. S? (*great commotion*) One at a time—could we please use our hands? Deirdre? (*The children had prepared name tags.*)

DEIRDRE: Mr. S illustrated books and he showed us how he did his pictures.

OTHERS: Yeah—he was cool. Boy, could he draw!

MR. H: (*going to the blackboard*) Well, we have our first request. You'd like to meet a real artist. (*Writes this on board.*) Anything else?

MARCIA: The raccoon—the raccoon?

MR. H: The raccoon?

OTHERS: Yes—Miss G brought in this raccoon. We petted him. It climbed up the bookcase.

MR. H: All right—let me see—how shall I put it? How about "Drawing from Live Subjects"—that way we can use live fifth graders as well as other kinds of animals. (*laughter*) Very good. I think drawing from nature is a great idea—it would be even better if we could get a baby elephant in here—(*laughter—other animals are suggested that are equally unrealistic*)—All right, now, keep going—yes, Barbara?

BARBARA: I liked the field trip to the Museum of Fine Arts.

MR. H: Oh, what did you see?

BARBARA: It was Rembrandt.

PAUL: No it wasn't. (*others join in quick argument*)

MR. H: Does anyone remember the exact title of the show?

PAUL: I know! "The Age of Rembrandt," that's what it was.

MR. H: O.K. Let's put in "Field Trips." I'll write it under "Visiting Artists," rather than "Drawing." What else?

SUSAN: Are we going to paint?

MR. H: Certainly—what's an art class without painting?

DAVID: I don't like to paint.

MR. H: Why not?

DAVID: I don't know. I like making jewelry.

MR. H: Well—we can't like everything, can we? You must feel about painting the way I feel about lettering. Let me put down "Crafts," David. That'll hold the door open to other materials. Who'd like to name some?

POLLY: Clay.

PAUL: Clay is sculpture.

POLLY: Bowls are clay and . . .

PAUL: Clay is more sculpture.

"Mr. S" was a participant in the Creative Arts Council's program designed to bring performing artists of all kinds into the schools. The children's interest in observing professionals at work thus opens the door for potters, printmakers, painters, and the like to step into the art curriculum.

Marcia's mention of the raccoon allows the teacher to emphasize as much drawing from observation as he feels is appropriate. Should he decide to have the children do contour-line drawings from a posed figure or brush drawings of animals, or use any of these as a basis for subject matter or point-making, he has Marcia's suggestion to which he may refer.

Paul and Barbara's suggestion has given the teacher the opportunity to plan additional field trips—or a first lesson in art appreciation based on the Dutch School.

In setting up categories the teacher hopes to get the children to begin making distinctions within the arts. This is a technique that will be developed further in the informational part of the art program.

The teacher did not skirt David's dislike of painting. By acknowledging it publicly he hopes to create a threat-free environment in which differences of opinion are discussed openly.

The discussion of the function of clay results in adding sculpture to the list of activities.

MR. H: Actually, clay can be either. If it is something we use, we generally refer to it as "craft"; if it's something we admire in the way that we admire a painting, we usually call it "fine arts." In any case we can put down "Sculpture" as long as you mentioned it. Can you name some other crafts?

EMMA: Batiks. We did batiks once.

PAUL: Weaving. That's crafts.

SUSAN: Are we going to do all these?

MR. H: I'm afraid not—but let's get them down anyway so we'll see what we've done. Say—I've got one for you. How about movies? We can make a movie.

OTHERS: Movies? How?

PAUL: I took pictures with my father's camera. It's an 8mm.

MR. H: Well, I had in mind another kind, something we could all do together. We can scratch designs right on the raw film, put all the pieces together, and put it to music. How does that sound?

Now that the teacher has rapport with the class he can contribute his own ideas. Others that eventually followed were activities in architecture (redesigning the school playground) and design ("making a picture"). Sculpture was also broken down into several media, and printmaking was added.

The important thing to note in the above dialog is that the teacher knew in advance what the rough content of the year's work would be. In communicating with the pupils he could have:

1. Doled out the projects on a piecemeal basis as the year progressed without attempting to communicate the overall structure. This would be an *improvised*, teacher-directed approach.
2. Described the entire year's activities to the class, providing a *planned*, directed program.

Instead the teacher chose a third approach, in that he:

3. Involved the class in the planning. In so doing, many of the teacher's own ideas were made to seem to originate in the class. By engaging the students' participation, he ensured a climate of acceptance for new ideas that normally might not be well received.

ANALYZING THE TEACHER: FIVE PHASES OF INSTRUCTION

Teaching art can be far more complex than most new teachers realize. The following list is composed of significant factors that could bear on the success of a teacher. It is an evaluation instrument with which teachers can get a "profile" of their own style. Note that this form is not descriptive; it merely asks whether any of the factors listed were present, not present,

72

or present in some exemplary way. Description of any one item could be elaborated if desired. The lesson is divided into five segments: preparation, presentation, the class in action, evaluation, and teaching style. Obviously no one lesson could possibly encompass all the items listed. The list also provides some indication of the possible variables in teaching.

Preparation for Instruction and Classroom Management
1. Display areas:
   a. Display pupils' work
   b. Relate materials to studio activity
   c. Relate materials to current events in art, school, community
   d. Show design awareness in the arrangement of pupils' work
2. Supplies and materials:
   a. Organized so that the room is orderly and functional
   b. Organized so that the room is orderly but inhibiting
   c. Organized so that the room is disorderly but functional
   d. Organized so that the room is disorderly and nonfunctional
   e. Distributed systematically
3. Resource materials (aids, art books, art magazines, file materials, live art, film loops and other audio-visual support):
   a. Provided by school system and school
   b. Not provided by school system and school
   c. Derived from teacher's reference file
   d. Not provided by teacher
4. Nonobservable data:
   a. (Pupil's work) Kept in portfolio for reference
   b. (Reference file) Made available for student use

Presentation of Lesson
1. Objectives clearly stated
2. Objectives arrived at through dialog
3. Discussion related to topic or objective
4. Discussion related to levels within group
5. Interaction between pupils and teacher:
   a. Teacher interrupts pupils
   b. Teacher welcomes disagreement
6. Demonstrations oriented toward multiple solutions
7. Demonstrations convergent on single solution
8. Class is flexible:
   a. Chairs easily reorganized for viewing demonstrations
   b. Children can come to teacher freely for additional material
   c. Several projects in operation at same time
   d. Children can move freely from project to project

The Class in Action
　　1. Teacher:
　　　　a.　Listens to pupils
　　　　b.　Asks open questions
　　　　c.　Asks closed questions
　　　　d.　Praises work of pupils in general terms
　　　　e.　Praises work in specific terms that are relevant to the problem
　　　　f.　Uses other forms of verbal reinforcement
　　　　g.　Is able to reach pupils who request consultation
　　　　h.　Talks at length to some pupils
　　　　i.　Relates comments not only to objectives but to pupils' frame of reference
　　　　j.　Motivates those who have become discouraged
　　　　k.　Remotivates those with short attention spans
　　　　l.　Is flexible in permitting deviation from assignments
　　　　m.　Uses art vocabulary
　　　　n.　Is competent in handling discipline problems
　　2. Pupils:
　　　　a.　Are self-directive in organizing for work
　　　　b.　Are self-directive in organizing for cleanup
　　　　c.　Use art vocabulary

Evaluation Period (For final group evaluation)
　　1. Evaluation relates to goals of lesson
　　2. Pupils encouraged to participate
　　3. Pupils do participate as a group
　　4. Only one work evaluated
　　5. Several works evaluated
　　6. There is no final evaluation
　　7. Pupils do not feel embarrassed or threatened by public evaluation
　　8. Pupils generally negative to evaluation process

Teaching Style (Personality)
　　1. Teacher takes positive attitude toward instruction
　　2. Teacher shows rapport with pupils' age group
　　3. Teacher demonstrates sense of humor
　　4. Teacher has sense of pace: controls flow of lesson
　　5. Teacher is innovative in following respects:
　　　　a.　　　　　　　　　　c.
　　　　b.　　　　　　　　　　d.
　　6. Teacher is aware of language (vivid phrasing, imagistic speech, clarity of expression)

1. Describe any situation you have experienced in which children disliked art. Explain how the dislike arose and indicate the means you might use to alter the children's attitude.
2. Describe the traits of a personal acquaintance whom you consider to be an effective teacher of art.
3. Observe some art lessons given by expert teachers and note especially (a) the motivational devices employed; (b) the manner in which themes are defined; (c) the way in which goals are established; (d) the problems that arise and the means by which a solution to them is found. Can you add any items to the analysis instrument at the end of this chapter?
4. Describe how you would motivate a class for a lesson in increased sensitivity to color based on fall colors in nature.
5. Take a close look at your personality and try to project your teaching "style" from it. Apply your style to a specific teaching situation—demonstration, evaluation, or selection of topic.
6. Describe the steps you might take to improve the following situations: (a) a third grade art class whose members are outrageously untidy and wasteful of materials; (b) a class of fifth graders who have always been taught to copy during their art sessions and feel they are unable to create; (c) a group of sixth grade boys who think art is "sissy"; (d) a group of kindergarten children whose parents or older brothers and sisters have given them formulas for the drawing of objects.

Suggested Readings

Eisner, Elliot, and David Ecker, eds. *Readings in Art Education*. Waltham, Ma.: Blaisdell, 1966. Chapter 4, "Can Art Be Taught?"

Lansing, Kenneth. *Art, Artists and Art Education*. Dubuque: Kendall-Hunt, 1976. Chapter 8, "The Teaching of Art."

design: a basis

for art activity

To perceive a visual image implies the beholder's participation in a process of organization. The experience of an image is thus a creative act of integration. Its essential characteristic is that by plastic power an experience is formed into an organic whole. Here is a basic discipline of forming, that is, thinking in terms of structure, a discipline of utmost importance in the chaos of our formless world.*

THREE

Design is not a separate and distinct area of art; it is an integral part of any art form. The message a creating person wishes to convey is made apparent by the formal organization produced. In any work of art, whether by a child or an adult, design is automatically included in the production. A piece of clay sculpture by a child in the first grade, a Chinese stoneware vase, a painting by Cézanne, a symphony by Beethoven, or a play by Arthur Miller all involve design, structure, and the relation of component elements to a unified whole. Design, therefore, is presented in all art forms and may be intuitively achieved or consciously dealt with. One function of art education is the development of a child's awareness of design.

*From Gyorgy Kepes, *Language of Vision* (Chicago: Theobald, 1945), p. 13.

In this chapter we will discuss design as it applies to visual forms of expression. This discussion will include an analysis of the parts, or elements, that make up design, and an outline of the methods employed by artists to coherently use these elements. The teacher without a knowledge of design is handicapped. The information in this chapter is presented as professional background knowledge. Chapter 7 will deal more directly with the application of design knowledge in the classroom.

The Elements of Design

Design is the organization of parts into a coherent whole. "In visual terms, design is the organization of *materials* and *forms* in such a way as to fulfill a specific *purpose*."[1] The designs of accomplished artists should convey the feeling that nothing in the designs could be changed without violating their structure. All the elements of design in use should make a complete and, as far as can be judged, harmonious whole.

The act of designing is common to all human beings. Primitive tribes bring some order and coherence to the jungle while constructing their village; homemakers follow the desire for order in rearranging furniture in their living rooms. Lawmakers bring order to a legislative session and gardeners bring order to their gardens. Because the desire for order is universal, artistic acts, which demand that a form, composition, or design be achieved, have potential significance for us all.

Design, if we are to follow the Gestalt psychologists, may be related to the factor of closure—that is, "behavior that signifies pattern completion, goal realization, the resolution of tension, or the process of effecting a balance."[2] Our psyches are probed even deeper when our response to design is homeostatic in nature, that is, arising from the organism's need for stability and order. John Dewey likens design to an essential seeking for order, for reason and structure out of chaos.[3]

Philosophers have long been fascinated by the faultless organization of good design and have attempted to analyze it. Repeatedly they have asked: What are the parts or elements that make up these splendid organizations? These philosophers, however, know full well that any intellectual dissection of a particular work can never adequately account for the significance of the entire design. From observations of life in general, people have sensed for a long time what the Gestalt psychologists stated a rela-

[1] Marjorie Elliott Bevlin, *Design Through Discovery*, 3rd ed. (New York: Holt, Rinehart, and Winston, 1977), p. 10.
[2] Carter V. Good, ed., *Dictionary of Education*, 2nd ed. (New York: McGraw-Hill, 1959), p. 102.
[3] John Dewey, *Art as Experience* (New York: Putnam, 1958).

Design: A Basis for Art Activity

tively short time ago—that the whole is greater than the sum of its parts, and that to separate the whole into parts can destroy the object we attempt to analyze. Thus any form of intellectual analysis applied to design can destroy the organization we are trying to study.

Even with this realization, we are nevertheless justified in searching for a design's *elements*. Although the original object can be fully understood only in terms of itself and not its parts, the partial knowledge acquired may be helpful later when considering the object in its entirety.

Those who have attempted to isolate the elements of design have reached only partial agreement. Nevertheless, nearly all agree that the elements of design include *line*, *shape* (or *mass*), *space*, *light and shade*, *texture*, and *color*. Design in three dimensions includes the element of *mass*, which is analogous to two-dimensional shape. The term *form* has several connotations in art and design. Form is:

1. The underlying structure or *composition* in a work of art.
2. The shape or outline of something.
3. The essence of a work of art—its medium or mode of expression.[4]
   For example, pencil drawing is a form of creative expression.

These elements are, in effect, the building blocks of all visual art; they are all that the artist has to work with. The elements will be discussed individually so that teachers may not only acquire some insight into design as it appears in the work of children, but also develop a vocabulary for this segment of art education. Even a rudimentary knowledge of the vocabulary of design can provide the teacher with a basis for discussing works of art.

Contemporary artists, particularly the Abstract Expressionists, have worked against what they feel are static effects such as symmetry, balance, and classic proportion. Instead, they have placed a premium on accident, stridency, and deliberate avoidance of a "closed" image. Despite this change in the concept of design, the elements exist in all styles, and for purposes of elementary instruction we can still use design vocabulary in referring to both the child's work and the work of professionals. The language of design provides a basis for discussing the work of students, which can begin as soon as a child understands—through use and recognition—the meaning of the vocabulary.

Design also has another meaning that does not bear as directly on this chapter but which nevertheless is worth noting. Design as a verb can also refer to the planning of useful or decorative objects, such as fabrics, appliances, automobiles, or interiors. We can therefore design a container or create a painting wherein elements and principles of design operate

[4]Bevlin, p. 391.

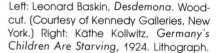
Left: Leonard Baskin, *Desdemona*. Woodcut. (Courtesy of Kennedy Galleries, New York.) Right: Käthe Kollwitz, *Germany's Children Are Starving*, 1924. Lithograph.

effectively. The *principles* of design differ from the *elements* in that the term *principles* refers to precepts or generalizations regarding the structure of forms, be they from fine arts or commercial design. The elements of design interact to make up the *principles of design*. Feldman[5] lists *unity, balance, rhythm,* and *proportion* as the major design principles. Since it is important to convey to young children the meaning of the elements (line, shape [or mass] and space, light and shade, texture, and color) as well as the principles, this chapter will discuss both sets of terms. The danger in planning activities related to the design elements is that too often teachers neglect a second, vital stage—that of making connections between the elements. The ultimate goal of design education is to become aware of the interaction of the elements and principles, in both the children's work and that of professional artists the children study. Teacher and pupil must share some common language, and the terminology of design constitutes the beginning of a mode of discourse that can be referred to during the entire span of the elementary art program.

LINE   *Line*, the path traced by a moving point, is perhaps the most flexible and revealing element of design. If we are angry and doodle a line, our anger is clearly revealed in the marks we make. If we are placid, calm, or pleased, our scribbling takes on a different character. Artists readily express their

[5] Edmund B. Feldman, *Art as Image and Idea* (Englewood Cliffs: Prentice-Hall, 1967), Chapter 9.

Design: A Basis for Art Activity

Paul Cézanne's *Card Players*—a significant organization of the elements of design. (The Metropolitan Museum of Art, New York. Bequest of Stephen C. Clark, 1960.) Above: A diagrammatic indication of the movement of the lines in the *Card Players.*

feelings by means of line. In communicating hatred of war and brutality in general, an artist may use slashing, angular, abrupt lines; presenting feelings about the beauty of a summer landscape, the artist's lines might be gently undulating and flowing.

Line may be used strongly and directly. Käthe Kollwitz uses line as a primary means to achieve her end; the strong, powerful line supports her anger at society and her compassion for its victims (see page 80). Leonard Baskin creates form and integrates figure and background through massed lines. Artists may also imply line—that is, convey it indirectly—by forming edges of contrasting tones that move from one part of a painting to another. Notice the implied line used by Cézanne in his painting of the *Card Players* (above). In the line diagram, we can see how the linear movement begins over the back of the cardplayer on the right, then swings down over his arm, only to be caught up by the line across the back of the center player. Swirling around this center cardplayer's hat, it moves up over the arm and around the back of the standing man and, falling across the shoulders of the player on the left, ends in the sweep of the chair. Folds in the draperies and shadows in the background augment the sweep of Cézanne's expressive line.

Just as most people eventually develop a personal style of handwriting, so artists develop a line peculiar to themselves. By skillfully commanding line, artists can make that element speak of their experiences. Study of line in art works therefore, is a worthwhile pursuit, for line lets us know something of what its creators think and feel and helps us respond to

The Elements of Design

81

whatever they have in mind. In fact, line has sometimes been called the "nervous system" of a work of art. For most of us, linear experience is our first contact with art—if only because of the availability of pencil, pen, or crayon.

The study of line is particularly effective with elementary-school children because they have a linear rather than a shape or volume orientation to picture-making, which derives from their earliest preschool drawings. The children will find their own words to distinguish between the "scratchy" lines of Ben Shahn, the "funny" lines of Paul Klee, or the "squiggly" character of Oriental calligraphy. That sort of exercise provides a basis on which to build the vocabulary of art. But the study of line need not be limited to drawing or painting, for line can be observed and enjoyed in architecture and sculpture and, in many instances, in nature.

SHAPE

The term *shape* refers to the general outline of something. Shapes can be drawn with lines, painted, or cut out of paper or other two-dimensional materials. Shapes can be categorized as geometric or natural. Geometric shapes include squares, rectangles, circles, triangles, and so on. Natural shapes are those that are found in nature, such as rocks, trees, clouds, and the organic shapes of animal and plant life. Geometric shapes are sometimes found in nature also, as in the honeycomb, some seashells, and cellular structures. In addition to the geometric and natural shapes found in the environment, adult and child artists can create new shapes at will.

Mass, as discussed earlier, is the three-dimensional equivalent of shape, although it may be found in artworks that give an illusion of mass, such as Michelangelo's paintings in, say, the Sistine Chapel. The cube, pyramid, and sphere are the three-dimensional equivalents of the geometric square, triangle, and circle. Mass refers to the volume or bulk of objects in a work of art, and *space* refers to the areas that surround mass. The aesthetic effect of mass is perhaps most readily grasped in architecture and sculpture. The great mass of an office building and the delicate mass of a church spire have the power to move us. In sculpture, we are equally affected by the weight, shape, and balance of the masses created by the sculptor.

SPACE

In art there are two types of space: actual space and pictorial space. Actual space is two-dimensional, as in drawings, paintings, or prints produced on flat surfaces; or it is three-dimensional as in sculpture, architecture, or crafts such as weaving or ceramics. Artists have learned to be as sensitive to the organization of space as they are to line and shape. As soon as a line or a shape is placed on paper or canvas it relates to the surrounding space. Placement might be high on the paper, low, near the edge, or in the center.

82

When a second line or shape is added to the composition more spatial relationships are created. Two shapes can be close together or far apart, above and below, side by side, or crowded in a corner. The possibilities multiply as each new shape or line is added to the composition.

Sculpture is three-dimensional and exists in actual space—taking up space and relating to surrounding space. The sculptor is aware of these spatial relationships and makes purposeful decisions to pierce space with sculptural forms and to cause forms to move in space—as with mobiles or kinetic sculpture.

Pictorial space is the flat surface of the paper, canvas, or other material, and is known also as *the picture plane*. On this surface artists often create the illusion of three-dimensional space. For example, a landscape picture often has a foreground of objects that appear near to the viewer, a middle ground farther away, and a background such as the sky or distant hills that is behind most of the objects in the picture. To achieve this illusion, the artist can overlap objects or place them lower or higher on the picture plane, or can make objects in the background smaller than similar objects in the foreground.

Linear perspective is a system developed by artists of the Renaissance that approximates the visual phenomenon of apparently diminishing size of objects as their distance from the viewer increases. This system, which utilizes a horizon line and one or more vanishing points, is rarely learned spontaneously and usually requires instruction and practice for mastery.

Whatever line or shape is placed on the picture plane immediately creates a *figure-ground relationship* in which the mark or shape is the "figure" and the surrounding area is the "ground." With three-dimensional works of art, the object is the figure and the space behind or around it is the background, or just the ground. The placement of any figure in a pictorial space shapes the ground according to its position. Every shape and mass is surrounded by the element of space. As an example of the use of space in architecture, consider the courtyards separating the buildings in a modern housing development. Here the architect has carefully planned the amount of space that should be provided between one building and another. If the space had been planned smaller, the buildings might appear to be huddled together; wider, the buildings might not appear to belong to a coherent plan.

The artist working in two dimensions must also regulate the spaces between shapes. In an Andrew Wyeth painting, for example, the intervals between the shapes have their own qualities, ranging from confined to open areas. Children can learn to appreciate these qualities when they create designs by pasting pieces of dark paper on a white background.

Children should be made aware of the action that takes place among all elements of a picture, and one way to call their attention to it is by showing them how artists deal with the problem of shape and space. The

A diagrammatic indication of the distribution of shapes and spaces in the *Card Players*.

illustration here is a diagram of the shapes and spaces in Cézanne's *Card Players*. The masses formed by the players, the table, and the draperies are presented in a sculptural unity relieved by variations in light and shade, texture, and color. The simplicity of the spaces offers a significant contrast to the detail of the shapes.

LIGHT AND SHADE The creating person may make use of the elements of *light* and *shade* in art work. When drawing with chalk, the pressure applied to the drawing tool regulates the degree of lightness or darkness of the marks produced. By adding black or white to a standard hue of paint, the degree of lightness and darkness is regulated. Architects and sculptors control these elements by a variety of devices. A building may be designed with deep recesses to produce shadows in contrast to a facade that catches the light. Sculptors

This cut-paper collage shows how a sixth grader differentiated the light and dark areas in the accompanying photograph. (Photo by Margaret Bourke-White.)

A diagrammatic indication of the distribution of the chief areas of light and shade in the *Card Players*.

take great pains in controlling the "hollows" (negative areas) and "bumps" (positive areas) they make so that light and shade are used to their best advantage.

The illustration here diagrams the arrangements of light and shade in Cézanne's *Card Players*. Every dark area seems to have a corresponding light area that gives it significance. Notice, for example, the contrast of the white face of the player at left against the dark clothes of the standing figure, or the dark hat and profile of the player at right against the light space of the background.

Chiaroscuro is another word for light-dark contrasts. In Rembrandt's work, the light appears to glow from within the subject. Monet bathes his haystacks in light, and Orozco and Caravaggio use dark-light contrasts for powerful emotional effects. Children enjoy the dramatic interaction that only opposites can provide. Children are capable not only of identifying light-dark effects but also of applying chiaroscuro in their own work.

The dramatic effects that light and shade are capable of producing have been well demonstrated in black-and-white films, where, if the elements are used effectively, we as the audience may be quite content that color is absent. Modern artists also use electric light in the forms of neon tubes and laser beams to create sculptures of actual light.

Motion, although not listed as an element of design, is often an important factor in sculptures that utilize electric light as well as in kinetic sculptures, which are moved by motors, water, or wind.

TEXTURE

Texture is the degree of roughness or smoothness of any surface. Every surface has a texture; a pebble on the seashore, a veined leaf, the wrinkled face of an old man, a brick wall, a sheet of glass, all display varying kinds and degrees of texture. We derive a sensuous enjoyment from texture. We

"My Father," a collage by a ten-year-old Arab girl, was cut directly from a variety of papers. The sections were moved about until the placement satisfied the artist.

COLOR

like to run our hands lightly over the surface of a tweed jacket or a fur coat; we enjoy holding a smooth stone lightly in our hands or gently stroking a baby's hair. When we go to bed we may take delight in the smoothness of the sheets or, on the other hand, in what the poet Rupert Brooke called "the rough male kiss of blankets."

Texture appeals to people for aesthetic as well as sensuous reasons, although it is doubtful if the two can be entirely separated. The texture that artists use may be actual or simulated. Paper for watercolor paintings is carefully chosen for its textural qualities. Some painters stipple a surface with gesso before painting on it with tempera or oils. The paint itself may be applied with careful regard for its textural effects. Paint applied thickly has a degree of roughness, but it can also be put on with silky smoothness. Cutting tools allow children to create texture on such surfaces as linoleum. Sometimes artists devise textural effects that are not actually rough or smooth, but only appear so. In some parts of a drawing, for example, lines may be crisscrossed or a pattern of dots may be devised so that the area has a rough appearance. Other areas may be left untouched or washed with smooth or flat color to create a textural contrast.

The delight children take in surface quality provides the basis for activities involving collage. Again, teachers can develop tactile sensitivity by discussing the treatment of texture and surface in the work of such artists as Kurt Schwitters, Corrado Marca-Relli, Picasso, and William Harnett, whose "trompe l'oeil" effects simulate rather than use real textures.

Because of the complexity of *color*, both artists and scientists have for years tried to arrive at a theoretical basis for its use. Feldman has noted:

These two paintings by second graders illustrate the moving and powerful quality of color and convey the children's delight with its possibilities.

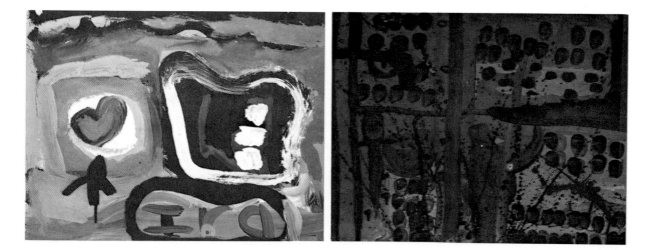

Color theory provides speculative answers to questions which are not often asked in the course of examining works of art. Some color systems seem related to the physiology of perception more than to the aesthetics or psychology of perception. Others may have evolved from industrial needs for the classification and description of dyes, pigments and colored objects. At any rate, artists work with color—pigment, to be exact—more on an intuitive than a scientific basis.[6]

In teaching children about the nature of color, the teacher may vary the methods, using intuitive approaches in the primary grades and gradually moving toward teaching color terminology and its application in the middle and upper grades. (Chapter 6, "Drawing and Painting," discusses the properties and definitions of color that provide the basis for more effective color activities and picture-making.)

Color is a powerful element, and it serves to emphasize the extent to which all the elements are interdependent. Although the elements have been discussed here separately, in reality they cannot be dissociated. The moment we make a mark on paper with a black crayon, light and shade (see p. 84) are involved. If paint has been applied, color is present. As soon as a shape is drawn, it interacts with the space around it. Only for the sake of convenience have we treated these elements as separate entities. Color functions on two levels. On the cognitive level, color conveys information in purely descriptive terms, as when leaves change color in the fall, and in symbolic terms, as in flags or traffic signals. On the affective level, color evokes psychological associations and thereby creates moods and feelings. As any industrial-design consultant is aware, color affects us physiologically as well as psychologically and can be discussed in terms of the wavelengths of light as legitimately as in terms of the interaction of pigments. Indeed, so pervasive are color's effects that the vocabulary of color theory can be used metaphorically in a wide variety of contexts—such as music, when we refer to tone color, or in writing, when we speak of "purple prose."[7]

The Language of Color. Scientists may define color as an effect of physical forces on our nervous system through impact on the retina. To painters, however, color is far more complex: it is a vital element that is closely related to all the other design elements at their disposal. The sensitivity with which painters use color can convey a personal style and the

[6] Feldman, p. 248.
[7] The relationship between color and music has intrigued musicians and artists for a long time. Color and sound "organs" were developed as early as 1730. Using Newton's optical theories as a basis, these "organs" related seven colors to the seven tones of the diatonic scale. Charles Parkhurst discusses the terminology of art and music in his pamphlet "Light and Color," included in Bernard S. Meyers and Trewin Copplestone, eds., *Art Treasures of the World* (New York: Harry N. Abrams, 1955), p. 6.

meaning of a particular work. Ultimately it can influence the varied responses of viewers to a work of art.

The painter's color terminology also differs from the physicist's, whose primary reference is light rather than pigment. In art, a consistent terminology has come to be accepted as a means of discussing and using color, both in looking at works of art and in producing them. The following definitions provide some guidelines for instruction in painting, design, and the appreciation of art.

Hue is another word for color, as in the phrase "the varied hues of the spectrum." Scientifically, a hue is determined by the wavelength of light reflected from an object. As the wavelengths change we note those distinct qualities that we call hues. Hues, therefore, are identifiable segments of light waves.

To the scientist working with light, the primary colors are green, yellow, and red, since these are the irreducible hues from which all other colors can be derived. To the painter working with pigment, on the other hand, the primaries are red, yellow, and blue. Most children can recognize and work with the painter's primaries as well as violet, green, and orange, known as secondary colors because they can be created by mixing the primaries. The tertiary colors result from mixing primary and secondary colors and may be more difficult for children to achieve, since they require a greater control of paint. The tertiaries are also called *grays* and provide richer hues than the simple mixing of black and white will yield.

Value, or *tone*, refers to the degree of darkness or lightness of a hue. The lighter a color, the higher its value; the darker a color, the lower its value. Hence, if white is added, the value is heightened, if black is added, the value is lowered. Hues also may be changed by the use of a *glaze*, or a veil of thin transparent color, which is brushed over the hue. This method of changing a color was much favored during the Renaissance but is rarely used today.

Intensity indicates the freedom from admixture with another color—in other words, the ultimate purity of a color. Any hue that has not been mixed with another color is considered to be at its maximum intensity, although the purity of color can be enhanced or neutralized by adjacent colors in a painting. Although a color can be made more intense by the addition of another color (as in the addition of some oranges to some reds), the original color may lose its distinctive identity if mixing is carried beyond a certain point.

Complementary is a term that refers to the relationship between primary and secondary colors on a color wheel. On the wheel, these colors are in opposition to one another, as red to green, blue to orange, and yellow to violet. The complementaries are antagonistic in the sense that neither color in a pair possesses any property in common with the other.

88

Mixing such colors, therefore, will neutralize them and create a wide range of grays, which, as noted earlier, are potentially more interesting than grays composed of black and white.

Analogous colors are intermediate hues on the color wheel and may be explained to children in terms of families of color. All colors are conceptually on a continuous spectrum, thus allowing analogous colors to be likened to a family in which, for example, a red man and a blue woman produce a violet child. Analogous colors always get along; it is the complementary colors that often disagree.

Warm and *cool* refer to the psychological properties of certain colors. We normally call reds, yellows, and oranges warm colors, which we generally perceive as coming forward, or "advancing," in a field of color. Blues and greens are usually identified as cool and "receding" colors. The movement forward or backward of any color, however, depends entirely on its relationship to the surrounding hues. A red with a touch of blue can appear even cooler than it would by itself when placed next to an intense orange, and may well recede behind it, while yellow with a touch of green, normally warm, will seem very cool when placed next to red-orange, which will advance. Experimentation with recession and advancement of color, in Hans Hoffman's terms "push and pull," is of special interest to the Hard Edge and Color Field painters.

Color wheels, referred to in the preceding definitions, are chiefly useful as guides to understanding color relationships. No teacher should ever restrict pupils to the schematized set of relationships shown on the wheel. If color wheels have any virtue at all, it is to enlarge the options available to pupils rather than narrow them.

Many art forms are produced in which color is lacking—black-and-white films, most forms of sculpture, many of the etching processes, drawings in which black-and-white media are used. Any design, moreover, to which color is applied before due consideration is given to the arrangement of the other elements would probably be unsuccessful. Color, then, is a complex element—at once dependent, powerful, and very moving in its sensual appeal. As for the interests of children, teachers will discover that color has an appeal far in excess of the other elements of design.

The Principles of Design

It would be convenient to offer a formula for the production of satisfactory designs, but of course, if designs were subject to rules and regulations, art would cease to exist. Every good design is different from every other good design, and all artists have unique ways of producing designs. We may ask, however, whether there are any common denominators in all satisfactory designs. We can examine some general principles broad enough to allow for the variations to be found between one good design and another. We will now discuss individually those principles mentioned earlier: *unity, rhythm, proportion,* and *balance.*

UNITY

We have already mentioned the highly integrated nature of design. We described design in terms of order and coherence, and we considered it analogous to a world of stability. These are the most obvious characteristics that result from a successful art form, whether musical, dramatic, literary, or graphic. Each element is so arranged that it contributes to a desirable oneness or wholeness. In a drawing, a line ripples across a certain area to be caught up elsewhere; shapes and spaces set up beats and measures in a kind of visual music. Colors, textures, areas of light and shade, all contribute to the orchestration of the visual pattern. This oneness or wholeness we call *unity,* and unity of design is the first characteristic of all successful art.

Without oversimplifying or intellectualizing a process that is largely one of feeling, we may analyze to some extent how unity is achieved in a visual design. Three aspects of design that contribute to the unity of a work of art are the rhythms, the balances (or proper proportions), and the centers of interest established.

RHYTHM

The controlled movements that are to be found in all good designs are called *rhythms.* They may be established through the use of any of the elements of design—lines, areas of light and shade, spots of color, repetitions of shapes and spaces, or textured surfaces. For example, in a particular work of art a line may ripple in one direction, then undulate in another. This movement may be momentarily halted by an obstructive, brightly colored shape before it darts away elsewhere along a pathway formed by areas of light and shade. Rhythm is used by artists to give orderly move-

Three examples of "exploding" design created by sectioning paper and pasting the pieces on a contrasting background. These are by fourth and fifth graders.

In these flexible design activities, the adjustable components and the duplications of geometrical shapes permit an unlimited number of arrangements. (Education Development Center.)

ment to the manner in which our eyes move over a work of art and to control the pace at which our gaze travels.

There appear to be at least two main types of rhythm in works of art. The first has the character of a flow, and is usually achieved either by lines or the elongation of forms. (The work of El Greco is an outstanding example.) The second type has the character of a beat. An element may be used in one area of a work and repeated elsewhere, either as an exact duplication of the original theme or motif or only as an echo of it. In traditional paintings we are more likely to find reminiscences of an original motif than duplications. The stripe paintings of Gene Davis are examples of visual rhythm and visual beat.

The size relationships within a composition refer to its *proportion*.[8] Proportion often involves an ideal relationship that the artist strives for. Things that are "out of proportion" are often awkward or disturbing, such as an oversized sofa in a small room, a tiny painting hung alone on a broad expanse of wall, or a part of a figure or other object that is too large or small for the other parts. The ancient Greeks developed an elaborate system of proportion by which they built temples and other edifices.

PROPORTION

> The proportions of a classical Greek temple, for example, were rigidly prescribed in a formula that can be stated mathematically as $a:b = b:(a + b)$. Thus, if a is the width of a temple and b the length, the relationship between

[8]Bevlin, p. 128.

the two sides becomes apparent. Similar rules governed the height of the temple, the distance between columns, and so forth. When we look at a Greek temple today, even without being aware of the formula, we sense that its proportions are somehow supremely "right," totally satisfying. The same mean rectangle that determined the floor plan of the temple has been found to circumscribe Greek vases and sculpture as well.[9]

Some artists adhere to systems of proportion to achieve their expressive aims. Others convey ideas and feelings by distorting proportion or controlling it in other ways.

BALANCE

Closely related to the aspect of proportion in design is *balance.* When the eye is attracted equally to the various imaginary axes of a composition, the design is considered to be in balance.

Many writers, particularly those associated with the Post-Impressionist movement, attempted to explain balance in terms of physics, usually referring to the figure of a seesaw. Unfortunately, the concept is not quite accurate, since physical balance and aesthetic balance, while possibly related, are not synonymous. Balance in aesthetics should be considered as attraction to the eye rather than as simple gravitational pull. Aesthetic balance refers to all parts of a picture—the top and bottom—and not only to the sides, as the seesaw analogy suggests. Size of the shapes, moreover, while having some influence on aesthetic balance, may easily be compensated, and indeed outweighed, by a strong contrast of elements. A small, bright spot of color, for example, has great visual weight in a field of gray, as does an area of deep shade next to a highlight.

In many books on art there is still some discussion about "formal" versus "informal" balance. The arrangement of a composition with one well-defined figure placed centrally and with balancing elements placed on either side of this center, as in Duccio's *Maestà* or Fra Angelico's *Coronation of the Virgin,* is called *formal* or *symmetrical* balance. All other arrangements, such as in Miró's *Painting* or Orozco's *Barricade,* are called *informal* or *asymmetrical.*

Attraction to one kind of balance or another seems to be dictated by the ebb and flow of artistic fashion. The history of art shows us that most civilizations (including the Hindu, Aztec, and Japanese) have gone through a symmetrical-design phase. The High Renaissance prized symmetry and was followed by the Mannerists, who rejected the limitations of two-point perspective. The Dadaists of the 1920s and the Abstract Expressionists of the 1950s discarded all semblance of conventional visual order; yet, during the 1960s, many Hard Edge painters and Pop artists revived it for the simplicity and directness of its impact on the viewer.

[9]Bevlin, p. 130.

Design: A Basis for Art Activity

Many works of art—perhaps the majority—are arranged so that one center of interest has paramount importance. Just as any of the elements may be used in the development of rhythms, so also may they be used in the establishment of centers of interest. A large shape centrally placed, a bright color area, a sharp contrast between light and shade, an area more heavily textured than its surroundings, a series of lines leading to a certain place—these are some of the means at the disposal of the artist to attract and hold the observer's attention.

CENTERS OF INTEREST

The elements of design, then, must be unified if the resulting work is to be successful. It is possible, however, to produce a design that has all the attributes of unity but is neither interesting nor distinguished. A checkerboard, for example, has a rhythmic beat, a series of centers of interest, and a balance, but as a design it is unsatisfactory because it is monotonous and lacks tension. Likewise, a picket fence, a line of identical telephone poles, and a railway track are as uninteresting as the ticking of a clock. A stone wall, however, might have great design interest because of the lack of similarity among its units. Even in a brick wall, in which shapes are similar, people generally prefer the variety of color, tone, and texture found at random in old, used brick.

VARIETY OF DESIGN

Painters like Edward Hopper and Stuart Davis have used house gables, telephone poles, and railway tracks as subject matter for their work. But while maintaining an overall unity, they have introduced variations into the delineation of these objects. Mondrian has even gone so far as to use a single basic shape, the rectangle, as the foundation for his post-Cubist compositions. He has, however, varied the size, color, and relationships of this shape sufficiently to generate considerable visual interest.

An example of variety of design: subtle variations on the same basic shape. Edward Hopper, *Early Sunday Morning,* 1930. 35″ x 60″. (Collection Whitney Museum of American Art.)

While the perceptual process, as we have noted, seeks closure, or completeness, educated vision demands that in art, at least, a degree of complexity be attained if our attention is to be held. Every element, therefore, must be employed to bring about a desirable variety within unity.

This variety within unity is, in fact, an expression of life. Philosophers have postulated that design, or form, is a manifestation of people's deepest and most moving experiences. In the designs they produce, people are said to express their relationship to the universe. In *Art as Experience*, Dewey mentioned the mighty rhythms of nature—the course of the seasons and the cycle of lunar changes—together with those movements and phases of the human body, including the pulsing of the blood, appetite and satiety, birth and death, as basic human experiences from which design may arise.

Sir Herbert Read, commenting on Platonic doctrine, tells us that

> the universality of the aesthetic principle is Plato's philosophy: the fact that it pervades not only man-made things in so far as these are beautiful, but also living bodies and all plants, nature and the universe itself. It is because the harmony is all pervading, the very principle of coherence in the universe, that this principle should be the basis of education.[10]

Dewey, Plato, and Read would, then, seem to assert that the search for order, which the design impulse seeks to fulfill, is important not only for an individual's art work, but also as a reflection of that person's larger integrative relationship with life itself and can indeed be viewed as a metaphor for life.

The Attitudes and Mental Processes of the Artist

What do artists think and feel when they produce a design? How do they know when their work is "right?" There are divergent views on this subject. Some artists feel that the act of designing is a feat of intellect; some hold that it is an emotional adventure. The Gestalt psychologists point out, however, that the human organism acts in totality: when people are occupied with an act of artistic expression, both their feelings (impulses) and intellect (ideas) are involved.

It is true that creative people in different art careers tend to have a particular orientation: architects and industrial designers lean toward an intellectual approach to design, whereas painters and poets generally favor feelings and an intuitive approach. Nevertheless, both intellectually

---

[10] Herbert Read, *Education Through Art*, rev. ed. (New York: Pantheon, 1958), p. 64.

Design: A Basis for Art Activity

and intuitively inclined artists apparently alternate between feeling and thinking. "I feel that this should be done" is followed by "I think that this is right," or vice versa. Thus, emotion enlivens an artistic statement and intellect tempers it. Exactly when intellect is the dominant force in artistic acts, or precisely when feeling replaces intellect, is difficult to detect. Often creative people themselves are unable to analyze their approach.

In producing a design for functional purposes such as a design for a building, a piece of pottery, or an item of furniture, some consideration for practical requirements is needed. In such a case, designers' decisions are governed by an honest respect not only for the materials used but also for the purpose to which they are put.[11] Efficiency cannot, of course, always be identical with aesthetic quality, since extreme functionalism, as required in, say, airplanes, must eliminate the personal choices that are necessary to artistic acts.

Thus one important difference between "fine" artists and industrial or commercial designers is the amount of autonomy enjoyed by the former. Unless their work is commissioned, fine artists answer only to themselves; they are members of no team, responsible to no board of directors, and subject to no limitations of time or budget imposed by others. The blessings of freedom, needless to say, place other burdens on them, but it is only through this state of freedom that artists periodically produce works that are unique, authentic, and innovative.

Using the Elements and Principles of Design

Art does not lend itself readily to rules and regulations, and any statement concerning principles must be outlined with caution. Should learners come to rely on the principles they have developed from their experiences to such an extent that they cease to look for new, deeper truths in art, their thinking will become stale. Whatever universal beliefs we may hold about art must, it seems, be subject to continued revision and further inquiry. General truths about art, in short, must always be regarded in a pragmatic light. A principle may not be adequate when we have enjoyed new experiences and gained new insights into design.

The current attitude toward honesty in the use of materials reflects this idea. If we are still to hold to the idea that artists must respect the integrity of their materials and work from the accepted definitions of painting and sculpture, what are we to say of George Sugarman, who paints his sculp-

IMPLICATIONS FOR TEACHING

[11] See Robert C. Niece, *Art: An Approach* (Dubuque: Ia.: Brown, 1963).

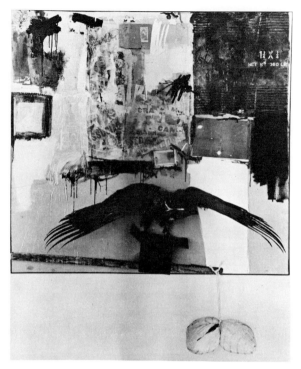

In this combine painting Rauschenberg has mixed three-dimensional objects with two-dimensional forms. Children respond enthusiastically to mixed-media approaches. *Canyon*, 1959. 86½" x 70" x 23". (Courtesy of Leo Castelli Gallery. Collection Mr. and Mrs. Michael Sonnabend, New York/ Paris.)

ture, or of Marisol, who adds drawing to the same combination? Should we adhere to the "rules" and reject their work, or should we keep ourselves open to the element of surprise and amusement when confronted with such combinations? Obviously, today's children should be prepared for the art of their time, and there is no reason why there cannot be room in their life for both the "integrity" of a fresco by Michelangelo and the multimedia combines of Robert Rauschenberg. (We must bear in mind that in the opinion of many of his contemporaries, Michelangelo violated the integrity of the human figure by distorting human proportions.

Each learner arrives at a personal statement of principles that reflects personal experience and its resulting insights. If the pupil has worked thoughtfully with all the elements of design and has mastered, with some degree of success, problems related to unity and variety of composition, two principles of design somewhat like the following may be arrived at:

Every successful design exhibits unity of composition.

Within its unity, every successful design exhibits variety in the use of its elements.

Design: A Basis for Art Activity

The learner who has studied and worked with many materials will probably enunciate a third principle:

In a successful design the character of the materials must be utilized for ends that are consistent with the nature or function of the final product.

The learner who has studied and produced some functional objects might state:

The successful design of a utilitarian object is largely governed by the function for which it is produced.

In considering experiences with all types of design activities, the learner will probably advance a principle as follows:

All successful design in art bears the stamp of the personality of its creator.

To these principles, some readers will wish to add others that have emerged from their own thinking. No matter what principles one may formulate, however, they should be employed only as temporary working hypotheses.

Exploring space through simple materials and using the entire body. Activities of this sort are similar to dance and sculpture and suggest new possibilities for design education. (Photo by Karen Gilborn.)

Activities for the Reader

The preceding discussion about design consists of a verbal and intellectual analysis of a process that is visual and, in considerable measure, intuitive. At best, such a discussion can afford the reader only a partial insight into the nature of design concerns. It would be well, therefore, for the reader to attempt the production of some works to experience directly what designing actually involves. Accordingly, several activities that the reader may try are described below.

Activities Emphasizing Line

1. Select black chalk and a sheet of inexpensive paper, such as newsprint, measuring about 18 by 24 inches and having a natural color. Play some stimulating music and begin to draw a line, not to depict an object but rather to develop a nonobjective arrangement. Draw the line freely, without attempting to produce a particular effect. Repeat the operation, but in this second case consider the variety of the line. See that it swoops and glides, ripples and pauses. Repeat again, this time thinking of the unity of the composition produced. Play music of a completely different mood and produce some further compositions in line.

2. Cover your hand with cloth or paper. With a short pencil draw an object under observation, such as a park bench, a person, or a flower. "Blind" contour drawing of this type tends to place more emphasis on line than on any other element. Analyze your handling of edges and do not worry about the relationship of parts. After doing several such drawings, select the most successful and draw it again, referring this time to your paper to "connect" parts to wholes. Continue this exercise, progressing to more complex forms—fruit to houses, boxes to people, stools to bicycles.

3. Study the paintings and sculpture of such recognized masters as Picasso, Rembrandt, and Henry Moore. Make a line analysis of one of the works. Such an analysis should emphasize the main flows of line in the composition without copying the objects themselves. Pen and ink, soft lead pencil, and crayon are suitable media.

4. Take a subject that is small, such as a bit of crumpled paper or some nuts and bolts. Using a brush, try to blow the detail up on a sheet of mural paper that measures at least 3 by 4 feet. Consider the space between the lines and how the figure (the object) relates to the ground (the surrounding space).

Activities Emphasizing Shape, Mass, and Space

1. Cut some rectangular shapes from paper of various tones but generally neutral in color. Move these shapes on a piece of white cardboard until a satisfactory arrangement of the shapes and spaces has been found, then glue them in place. Take similar shapes and drop them from above the cardboard so that they fall in an accidental pattern. Continue this procedure until you come upon an arrangement that pleases you. Compare the "found" design with the planned one. Which do you prefer and why? Does the accident offer an element of surprise that the planned design seems to need?

2. Take toothpicks or balsa strips and glue them together to form a nonobjective three-dimensional construction having interesting internal space relationships.

3. Using pieces of cardboard or wood scraps, make the same type of construction described in Activity 2. Concentrate on the way flat planes work with internal space relationships—confirming them, allowing one space to flow into another, and so on. If this sculptural approach to mass and space has caught your interest, try combining the lines of the balsa strips with the planes of the cardboard. You can further articulate your space by connecting one area to another with string and by cutting the cardboard for a colored glass or cellophane insert.

4. Study the drawings and sculpture of such artists as David Smith, Louise Nevelson, and Alexander Calder for the manner in which they have arranged masses and spaces. Make a drawing that emphasizes these elements.

5. Work a mass of clay (of about 8 lbs.) into a good-sized block. With simple tools, scoop out sections of the clay and then note how light and shade can be manipulated. When you have established a relationship between shallow and deep areas and the surface of the clay, take a flashlight and study how the character of your work changes with the light

Design: A Basis for Art Activity

source. Think of this in relation to architecture as well as to sculpture. Notice how this problem overlaps with the category below, light and shade.

6. To investigate line and space, try the exploding design (see p. 90). Divide a sheet of dark paper into sections and place the sections on a white background. Observe how pulling the sections apart creates everything from a thin white line to a dominant segment of white. Do this also with curving lines that bisect the paper.

Activities Emphasizing Light and Shade

1. Paint six or seven containers found around the house (cereal boxes, tea tins, cigar boxes, soupcans) a single unifying tone of white. Group these before you on a table, and draw them with black chalk on gray paper, using white chalk for highlights. Let the color of the paper play through for middle tones and reserve the white and black for the extreme values. Try one view with the flat side of your chalk and another with the point, carefully building your tones by massing strokes and lines.

2. Place the three pieces of sculpture produced to illustrate problems of mass and space in the path of a strong light. Manipulate them until the shadows and highlights on the objects themselves, together with the shadows cast from one object to another, form an acceptable unity. Observe the pattern of the shadows behind the sculpture.

3. Analyze the work of several well-known artists, such as Jasper Johns, Helen Frankenthaler, and Andrew Wyeth, for their arrangements of light and shade. Make an analytical drawing of one of the paintings to emphasize the use of these elements.

4. Project a slide of a group of buildings on a sheet of light paper. Forget that you are dealing with buildings and fill in the image with dark and light patterns. As a follow-up, take your sketch outdoors and see if this exercise in concentration on pattern and mass and light and shade has aided you in seeing (and drawing) an actual building.

Activities Emphasizing Texture

1. Cut pieces from printed pages that utilize various kinds and arrangements of type. Paste the pieces on cardboard or paper so that an interesting textural arrangement is developed.

2. With pen and ink, draw a continuous line in such a way that enclosed spaces are formed. By using dots, crossed lines, small circles, and the like, create a design having an interesting textural quality.

3. Repeat 2 using a sheet of aluminum foil, but this time merely press the foil with a pen.

4. Roll out a slab of clay and cut it into various shapes—square, round, rectangular, triangular. Create textural patterns on the surface by pressing found objects (coins, scissors, nuts, wood scraps) into the clay. With softer materials such as sponge, burlap, combs, and string, make patterns even closer to the surface. Use your imagination to think of items other than the ones suggested above.

5. Crumple a piece of paper and spray it with black paint from one angle only. Let the paper dry and press it flat. Notice the startling dimensional quality of the texture.

6. Create a collage that changes texturally in one direction from glassy smoothness to extreme roughness. Feel it with your eyes closed and compare it with those of your classmates. Vary the feel by adjusting the size and location of your textural samples.

Activities Emphasizing Color

1. Paint freely with a large brush, noting the apparent changes in hues as one color is placed next to another. How do the adjacent colors affect each other? Cut out various-sized windows in black paper and move them about your painting, noticing the variety of compositions and color interactions that are possible.

2. Dampen a sheet of heavy white drawing paper and drip tempera paint or watercolors so that different hues run and blend. Note the new colors so formed.

3. Study the work of such great colorists as Rembrandt, Van Gogh, Seurat, and Matisse. Study the color effects obtained by Hard Edge and Op Art painters.

4. Join the class in bringing in a swatch of color you think is red. When placed next to one another, the swatches of paper, paint, and cloth will produce a surprising range of tone and value in a subtly modulated monochromatic collage. Try other colors as well, including black and white. Notice in each case how the surface texture contributes to the effect of the color.

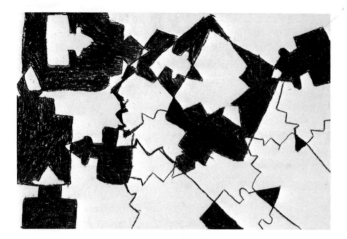

The overlapping shapes of an ink bottle treated in black and white show a balance of positive and negative areas. Fourth grade.

5. Cut out six squares of any single color and paste on them circles of six different colors. Notice how each of the circular background colors changes the nature of the constant foreground color. Is color a fixed entity or does it have relative characteristics?

Activities Emphasizing Function
and Adequate Use of Materials

1. Collect your study pictures of "families" of similar objects such as automobiles, chairs, yachts, and kitchen equipment. Compare one brand with another from the point of view of function. How does a Porsche, for example, compare with a Cadillac or a Datsun in this respect? What concessions have the manufacturers made to style at the expense of function? Why have they done so? To what extent are they justified in doing so? Start a scrapbook of "horrors" that concentrates on the most poorly designed products.
2. Find a number of objects in which a certain material has been processed to resemble another, such as cardboard to resemble leather, or plastic to look like woven cloth. Why has the manufacturer resorted to such practices? What are the opinions of designers and critics about them?

Other Activities

1. Emphasizing analogies: Take a photo or an actual familiar object, and draw another object that the first one appears to resemble. For instance, a fence may remind you of teeth, a fireplug of a robot, and a rock of a loaf of bread.
2. Emphasizing positive and negative patterns of dark and light: Draw an overall pattern using the shape of a common object like scissors, tableware, or an ink bottle. Where the forms overlap, switch back and forth from black to white, so that the objects are fragmented and the viewer becomes engaged in reestablishing the form of the object.
3. Emphasizing variety within a single form: Select any geometric shape as a working module. Using any medium you like, create an arrangement based on your shape, obtaining variety in the design by adjustment of the size or color of the shape, by overlapping, and other effects.
4. Emphasizing change in a single pattern: Design, cut, and paste on paper a simple pattern of dark and light geometric shapes. Make a "window" by cutting out a piece of paper curved vertical shapes, no two alike. Move the cutout over the design from right to left and notice how the patterns change as the shapes seen through the openings grow and shrink.

Design: A Basis for Art Activity

Bevlin, Marjorie Elliott. *Design Through Discovery*, 3rd ed. New York: Holt, Rinehart & Winston, 1977. A contemporary, nicely illustrated book on the elements and principles of design and their application.

Collier, Graham. *Form, Space and Vision*, 3rd ed. Englewood Cliffs: Prentice-Hall, 1972. A fine drawing textbook, beautifully illustrated in black and white, that emphasizes the use of design principles.

Feldman, Edmund. *Varieties of Visual Experience: Art as Image and Idea*, 2nd ed. Englewood Cliffs: Prentice-Hall, 1972. Part III, "The Structures of Art."

Fry, Roger. *Vision and Design*. New York: Meridian, 1956. Reprint. New York: New American Library. A landmark book that established the principles and elements of design in the vocabulary of art.

Garrett, Lillian. *Visual Design: A Problem Solving Approach*. New York: Reinhold, 1966. Reprint. New York: Krieger, 1975. Presents a particular approach to design using problem-solving as a method.

Hurwitz, Elizabeth Adams. *Design: A Search for Essentials*. Scranton: International Textbook, 1964. The principles of design in nature and in objects fabricated by humans.

Itten, Johannes. *The Art of Color*, new ed. New York: Van Nostrand Reinhold, 1973. A carefully written and illustrated book on the fundamentals of color.

Knobler, Nathan. *The Visual Dialogue*, 3rd ed. New York: Holt, Rinehart & Winston, 1980. An introduction to the appreciation of art. This text emphasizes the language of design and uses this language to discuss works of art.

McFee, June King, and Degge, Rogena M. *Art, Culture and Environment*, Belmont, Ca.: Wadsworth, 1977. Part II, "Organizing and Designing," Section IV, "A Search for Meaning and Structure." Although not always in complete agreement with Feldman, above, McFee provides sound foundation statements.

Pye, David. *The Nature of Design*. New York: Reinhold, 1964. A basic text on the elements and principles of design.

Tritten, Gottfried. *Teaching Color and Form*. New York: Van Nostrand Reinhold, 1974.

Films

The *Discovering Art* series: *Color; Composition; Creative Pattern; Dark and Light; Line; Texture*. Bailey-Film Associates.

CURRICULUM

PLANNING: DEVELOPING

A PROGRAM OF STUDIES

The central task of curriculum development is to (a) anticipate what levels of learning groups of children may be capable of achieving in relation to the common goals for the teaching of art and (b) select curriculum components to provide the experiences that can bring forth the intended learnings. Whether the curriculum components are in the form of studio activities, reading or observation, discussion or analysis, the teacher's attention must be fixed on the teaching goals. The activities selected are valuable only to the degree that they provide experiences through which the intended goals are realized*

four

Procedures vary from one educational system to another as to the delegation of responsibility for developing the art program. In some systems curriculum-makers and general administrators at the highest levels of administration are concerned with art education. These officials may even supervise the creation of courses of study and ensure that the courses, once designed, are effective. In the past, some city and state educational authorities set down exact statements of what to do from fall to spring, or during January, or for Easter, or in preparation for summer. The teacher who attempted to follow directions closely usually discovered, however, that much of the work prescribed was unsuitable for a particular class. It

*From Manuel Barkan, "Art in the Elementary Schools," in Jerome J. Hausman, ed., *Report of the Commission on Art Education* (Washington, D.C.: National Art Education Association, 1965), p. 81.

103

is difficult, if not impossible, for anyone who is remote from the classroom situation to prescribe an adequately detailed art program.

Who Designs the Art Program?

The tendency for central offices to set down a detailed art program has changed in the past two decades. Pamphlets about art are still published by large administrative bodies, and these publications, at least in the United States, range from those that deal with broad aspects of programming (as in the State of Ohio guide) to those that set out highly detailed behavioral goals or competency descriptions, like those of Palm Beach and Dade County, Forida. Most guides deal with philosophy, goals, objectives, tasks, and evaluation, but almost never with the methodology of instruction, since this is the most personal dimension of the curriculum. In other words, administrators are now saying to teachers, "You should be going from here to there, but how you do it is your decision."

In Canada, provincial departments of education have tended to provide not one but a series of publications for the schools of a province. In some respects these bulletins are more detailed than those from the United States, but they still do not prescribe a program to be followed rigorously.

In most educational systems today, only those directly engaged in art instruction—the local teaching and supervisory staff—attempt to determine in any detail the nature of the program to be followed. If the local art supervisors, or consultants, and the school principals are up to date, they will allow the art program to develop according to a number of educational circumstances peculiar to the classroom in which art is taught. To ensure that this idea prevails locally, some state departments of education are issuing attractive pamphlets urging that superintendents of education rely on the local art specialists and teachers to devise art programs to suit local conditions.

Classroom and art teachers are the key figures in the development of an effective art program, for only they know the needs and capabilities of the students who will benefit from the program. The teachers' concerns are both philosophical and psychological in determining what values to seek and in deciding what can reasonably be expected of the pupils. On these values and expectations they build an art program, working in concert with local art consultants.

THE TEACHER-CONSULTANT RELATIONSHIP

A large part of the success of any art program depends on the type of working relationship established between the art teacher and the art consultant. One school system* attempted to determine the nature of this

*Newton Public Schools, Newton, Ma.

important relationship by varying not only the *structure* of the relationship (art teaching as opposed to art consulting) but also the *ratio* of teachers and schools to art specialists. In some situations the art personnel did all the teaching on a scheduled basis; in some they served as advisors rather than teachers; and in still other cases they maintained a balance between scheduled teaching and nonscheduled "open," or flexible, use of time. The strengths and weaknesses of these combinations are described below.

Scheduled Teaching. This approach lends itself to a systematic and structured curriculum. The art specialist who can count on coming in for a planned number of art sessions per year can teach sequences of activities, assured that certain minimal programming will be carried out and that the activities will have continuity. The disadvantage in scheduled teaching lies in the tendency of the classroom teacher to abandon the role of art teacher, leaving the burden of the entire program on the art specialist. If the classroom teacher is prepared to offer follow-up activities between the art teacher's classes, the possibilities of the program are greatly expanded.

Open, Flexible Consulting. A system of flexible consulting assumes that the classroom teacher accepts the primary responsibility of conducting the art program and calls on the art specialist to solve problems that require special help. While this is a good concept in theory, it does not always work in practice. Those teachers who do not place a value on art activity may never call on the art teacher, while others who do not need help may call on the art teacher's services either to bolster an already strong program or to supply themselves with a "free" period.

The dilemma posed by these two situations suggests that no relationship will work unless the classroom teacher assumes some planning role in working with the art specialist-consultant. The fact remains that the majority of art instruction in the United States and Canada is still carried out by the classroom teacher. The principal and the art specialist must find ways to impress classroom teachers with the importance of the art program in the school curriculum and must offer them opportunities to improve their skills, and hence, their attitudes. Until the public schools have reached the enlightened stage of having one art teacher for each elementary school, the art specialist and classroom teacher must work together to provide the children with the range of art activity to which they are entitled.

Key Decisions in Planning an Art Program

The development of the program of studies must, like other aspects of art education, be considered a creative endeavor. It requires the planner to take into account such factors as (1) the learning situations related to the goals; (2) media, tools, and techniques; (3) the social setting of the class; and (4) standards of accomplishment as they relate to growth expectations. As the art program unfolds in the classroom, the successful teacher learns to anticipate difficulties in carrying out the program and is prepared to employ alternate procedures. No plan should be so rigid that it does not allow for change at any point.

FREEDOM OF CHOICE

Chapter 1 pointed out that although a mature artist may select, from a whole range of experience, particular themes suitable for expressive acts, such is not usually the case with children. Children who are told to do "anything they like" in art often are reluctant to express themselves artistically, simply because no specific stimulus prompts this expression. The teacher should provide a limited number of specific stimuli strong enough to motivate expression, but the pupils must have the freedom to select those aspects of the ideas that interest them. The problems and themes chosen by the teacher must always allow the children to select their own subject matter.

"Musical Lesson," tempera by a six-year-old boy, South Africa. The human figure involved with a musical instrument is an excellent subject because of its positive associations with creating music and because it transforms the figure from symbol to active element.

A balance between teacher and pupils should be developed; a partnership in which the teacher makes certain basic decisions and encourages students to reach their own solutions. The relationship between student and teacher is then quite similar to that which exists between teacher and supervisor. For example, if a teacher wants his fifth grade students to make a painting based on a trip to the aquarium, he should let them know in advance that they will be expected to rely on either memory or on-the-spot sketches; spend some time reviewing their impressions after the trip; and discuss the options for media open in the final painting phase (tempera? watercolor? mixed media?). In any case, the final selection and interpretation of the topic is left to the children.

Just as controlled freedom is desirable in the children's selection of a subject for expression, so it is often recommended in choosing media and tools. Most themes can be given expression in a number of different media and with a variety of tools. The trip to the aquarium could be depicted in a painting by means of watercolor, tempera, chalk, or wax crayon; it could be shown in sculpture employing paper or clay; it could be developed in a textile design, carved in linoleum, or even woven in colored yarns. Obviously, the simultaneous use of all these media and their attendant tools would create an impossible teaching and administrative burden in the classroom. But because each of these materials provides valuable educative experience for most children, the art program should be developed so that a wide range of media and tools can eventually be selected for classroom use.

SELECTION OF MEDIA, TOOLS, AND TECHNIQUES

Another area of decision-making is technique. In working with each medium the children can use more than one method of manipulation. They can stipple with a paintbrush as well as use it to stroke on color. They may use thin paint over a "resist" area (an area where wax has been applied). They may "add to" a basic body of clay or "draw out" from it. They may work with or without an inner support for the clay mass.

Generally the children will have time to use only one technique in a single art session, but in the evaluation period the teacher may describe other techniques for handling materials. For instance, children who have worked with wood in printmaking should know that they can also print with vegetables, cardboard, and linoleum as well; that a print can be treated as a single image, as a repeat pattern, or as a dominant pattern printed over a picture clipped from a magazine, a collage, or a painted surface; that one effect can be achieved when two plates are made for color separation, and an entirely different effect will result when a single plate is moved around for an overlapping image. Multiple solutions apply also to activities in sculpture, drawing, and painting.

THE SOCIAL SETTING

In preparing the art program, the teacher must look closely at the social requirements of the class. Should the art work be performed by a group, providing valuable social learning, or by an individual, providing valuable experience in independent work? Sometimes work like mural-making, a light show, or puppetry demands that the children pool their efforts to ensure the project's success. Other art activities such as painting, drawing, or clay modeling demand solitary efforts, in which a group of people cannot profitably work together.

The teacher's awareness of the classroom social setting also affects seating arrangements, the chemistry among the students, and the social makeup of the students. Disadvantaged children may not feel as comfortable in a class discussion as upper-middle-class children. Emigré children may have language problems. Mainstreaming adds to the classroom children with special needs who may require more time and more patience from the teacher.

STANDARDS OF ACCOMPLISHMENT

Finally, the teacher must make decisions about standards, based on expectations according to age. How "excellent" must the children's work be? Children are experimenters, and sometimes as a result of experiments the artistic quality of their work deteriorates. How much should one encourage experimentation at the expense of an artistic standard? Although unnecessary untidiness, incomplete work, and similar shortcomings in artistic production are detrimental to the finished expressive product, too great an emphasis on neatness not only inhibits experimentation but also has a negative influence on the product. Criteria will vary with the task. Obviously there will be greater agreement on the success in lettering skills than in the more subjective areas of picture-making. The problem of success or merit in a work should be discussed in advance with students. If children understand the goal of a lesson and concentrate on achieving it, teachers should not say that the children have failed. Children can "fail" in attitudes; they can be inattentive, sloppy, destructive, have short attention spans, or keep others from working. If such is the case, however, teachers must examine their own behavior to determine if they, not the children, are the problem.

THE CHILD'S ROLE IN DECISION-MAKING

Teachers with carefully developed strategies help students to make wise choices in their art activities. Some years ago, an experiment that is now a classic in the field was conducted in which children were allowed to participate in the development of an art program.[1] At that time, many teach-

[1] In the Powell River and District Schools, British Columbia, Canada, 1940–43, during which time one of the authors was the Supervisor of Art for this area. About 150 pupils in grades 1 through 6 participated. No kindergartens operated at that time in the publicly supported educational system of British Columbia.

Curriculum Planning: Developing a Program of Studies

ers were expected to follow a fairly rigid art program, often designed by a central committee. However, in this four-year experiment, every child in a representative experimental group of pupils from the first to the sixth grade was allowed a certain freedom to select an art activity. The choices that the pupils could make were necessarily restricted so that the teachers could offer adequate stimulation and assistance.

At the beginning of the experiment only two choices each of theme, tools, media, and technique were open to the children. Thus a child in the first grade could, for example, either work at picture-making in paint or construct objects out of boxes. Soon, however, four choices were allowed, and this range of choice was maintained in all classes for the remainder of the four-year study. The teachers were careful in arranging the choices that the children could make at any one time. The four available activities always included at least one involving two-dimensional work, while the other three might require work in three dimensions. Occasionally, activities involving historical or theoretical work, such as a study of local architecture or a survey of the output of local painters, were included, particularly in the higher grades. Also in the higher grades, group activities were frequently introduced.

The results of the four-year testing period showed that the children had selected for themselves a broad and comprehensive art program. Every child had included both two- and three-dimensional work and, when offered, activities involving both individual and group effort. From time to time the children had even selected work of a theoretical or historical nature. A comparison of the art output of the children in the experimental group with that of the pupils who were more restricted revealed that the freedom of the experimental program appeared to have beneficial effects. The experimental group's work exhibited a greater variety of techniques, a wider range of subject matter, and surprisingly, superior qualities of design.

It was concluded, therefore, that children should be given considerable freedom to select their art activities. Under conditions of freedom, modified only by a necessary pedagogical strategy, they appeared to select a reasonably broad program of art and to improve the artistic standard of their output.

Influences on Decision-Making

As the development of the art program progresses, a variety of choices in many different situations will be apparent to both pupils and teacher. The best choice of medium or of learning problem in any given case is more likely to be taken if the following influences are given adequate attention.

THE TRADITION OF ART

Every major area of learning has developed traditional attitudes and subject matter as well as activities and a historical background peculiar to itself. The traditional attitudes of art—that is, freedom of expression with respect to subject matter and design, willingness to work to capacity—were discussed previously. In Chapter 1 it was suggested that the sources of art have remained constant throughout the centuries, in the sense that the subject matter has always reflected the reactions of the artist to the environment.

The activities that have engaged people in artistic expression are similarly traditional. The educational background of many artists includes experience in both two- and three-dimensional art forms, although most artists tend to reach eminence working in just one form. Expression in drawing and painting is often more powerful if the artist has enjoyed some experience in three-dimensional output; sculpture and ceramics also have tended to be more successful if the artist has worked in two-dimensional fields. Every child should thus be given an opportunity to produce pictures as well as various types of sculpture and modeling. Any media require that we deal with a subject through the particularities and limitations of the material. Clay, for example, makes us regard the figure in one way, and

Traditional education for artists includes experience in both two- and three-dimensional work. Henry Moore's drawing *Two Seated Figures in a Shelter* and his sculpture *Family Group* illustrate the value to the artist of such experience. (Drawing: City Art Gallery, Leeds, England.) Sculpture: bronze, cast 1950. 59¼" x 46½", at base 45" x 29⅞". (Collection, The Museum of Modern Art, New York. A. Conger Goodyear Fund, 1948–49.)

drawing another. Using both media can facilitate a reciprocity of understanding.

Study of the historical background of art cannot begin too early in the elementary school. Even kindergarten children have much to gain merely by being exposed to carefully chosen works. Naturally, children's limited understanding will restrict their insight into the nature of the works they are shown. If, however, examples are related to the children's current expressive work, a beginning may be made in acquainting them with their vast cultural heritage in art.

Advocates of art education base their many different justifications for it on their own definitions of art, and, although many of these justifications share the same purposes (personal fulfillment, development of visual acuity, increased sensitivity to the environment), even these purposes may acquire different shades of meaning when translated into class activities. Nor is such diversity a peculiarly American problem. Maurice Barrett, a British art educator, reviews six existing rationales for art education on all levels as follows:

1. The *conceptual or art-based* rationale employs the student's ideas, impulses, and feelings, and uses art as a basis for connections with other art forms—drama, movement, language, and music.
2. The *design* rationale stresses the interrelationship between art and industry and other practical functions. It draws social and economic issues together into the area of aesthetic awareness.
3. The *visual education* rationale concentrates on the study of design elements, visual analysis, problem-solving, and on establishing a foundation for analytical research in as objective a manner as possible.
4. The *fine art* rationale arrives at a personally enriching process that can make leisure time more productive through personal expression or appreciation of the work of others. It is nonfunctional in the practical sense and sees the artist as a model.
5. The *art and craft* rationale uses crafts rather than fine art as a center of activity and sees the development of taste through concern for the decorative as well as the practical aspects of textiles, clay, wood, and fiber.
6. *"Graphicacy"*: Barrett's term for a rationale that stresses communication, especially through the use of current or neglected media—from computer graphics, town plans, maps and diagrams to films, photography, models, posters, signs, symbols, photogrammetry, pattern recognition, linear and angle measurement—indeed anything that helps to illustrate space-time relationships through visual data.[2]

[2] Maurice Barrett, *Art Education, A Strategy for Course Design* (London: Heinemann Educational Books, 1979), pp. 61–73.

Obviously there is much overlapping among the six categories, such as between design and visual education or fine arts and arts and crafts. In the United States, Vincent Lanier recommends abandoning studio activity in favor of a "dialog curriculum" based on the study of the popular arts (comics, video, films, posters), a philosophy that has many echoes in the British theories listed above.

Whatever the philosophy, a teacher must begin curriculum planning on some basic level, because philosophy helps one state a rationale, which, in turn, suggests goals that can then be translated into objectives.

If this book stands for a studio–activity-based approach, it does not mean that other approaches are questioned. Because time for art instruction is limited in the elementary-school curriculum and because children possess a natural desire and need to form, shape, and give vent to their ideas, a studio–art-based program is recommended. Indeed, the most effective way to touch on issues other than personal art-making is to rely on the power of direct experience as a means of linking activity to ideas. The problem is not so much to draw, paint, or sculpt, but rather to determine the best ways of dealing with traditional fine arts practice. Matrix C (pp. 124–25) suggests that the sources of art are perennial and that they have honorable historical precedents. It also suggests that they are not so numerous as to be impossible to deal with, and that both traditional and contemporary modes and media of expression can be dealt with imaginatively and with variety within the normal constraints of time and budget.

READINESS OF THE LEARNERS

So broad is the subject matter of art that it can accommodate a learner of practically any age, personality type, or experience. Competent teachers realize that just as no two children are alike, so also classes or groups of children differ. A program of art suitable for the class of a year ago may not be suitable this year.

The previous educational background of children has an important bearing on the art program. Sometimes a group of children may have enjoyed little creative work in art, but instead may have been taught according to dictatorial methods. Then the teacher's task is to help the pupils think for themselves and not place too much reliance on their teacher. Other children may have had an exceptionally rich background of experience, in which case the teacher must offer a more challenging program. In former classes, children may not have been given sufficient group work in art, with the result that they are at a loss as to how to proceed in an activity involving a number of individuals. Other children may not have mastered sufficiently the technique of working individually. Some children may have suffered from an overemphasis on certain types of art work at the expense of other types. A previous teacher, for example, may have laid undue emphasis on "craft," or three-dimensional, projects at the cost of

Curriculum Planning: Developing a Program of Studies

providing opportunities in picture-making. The teacher must be prepared to modify continually the nature of the program so that a balance of art experiences is offered to the children.

The capacities of the children to learn will obviously influence the art program. Variations in intelligence, contrary to popular opinion in some quarters, may affect art output as well as general learning about art. Slow learners in academic fields of study are often also slow to profit from art activities—especially when they have an insensitive teacher—and because of this their program must be arranged so that the right things are expected from them. Intelligent children, on the other hand, will usually profit from art work that continually challenges their creative energies. Children who vary in temperament also require different and carefully arranged degrees of stimulation.

One strategy the teacher may employ is diagnostic, that is, assigning a problem or series of problems at the beginning of the year to assess certain levels of student achievement. For example, if a class is asked at the first class meeting to draw their most memorable summer experience, such simple pictorial abilities as handling of space, the figure in action, use of memory, and diversity of color can be noted. The teacher can also get some idea of older children's attitudes about art by designing simple true-false or multiple-choice tests. Such tests also instill a sense of seriousness about the art program and establish a certain attitude from the first encounter.

The teacher may test attitudes regarding the purposes of art, the nature of art, and the reason for studying art in school. Children may build up distorted views about all of these, sometimes through misinformation. A simple questionnaire can do three things: it can tell the teacher how much information children have on these basic issues; it can open the door to discussion and suggest activities and goals to the teacher; and it can, like the tests mentioned above, instill a sense of seriousness in the children by reminding them of these issues.

The needs, capacities, and dispositions of the children demand diversification of the basic ingredients of every art program—materials to be used, problems to be solved, concepts to be dealt with. Just as we all enjoy different kinds of food, so also do we all exhibit different preferences in art. There is a minimum aesthetic standard, however, by which each of us determines whether or not what we observe or produce is art. Those who recognize this standard will not countenance that which is shoddy, insincere, or trite. The development of artistic taste is said to begin in childhood and to continue throughout one's life. Some people seem to improve their taste more readily than others, but all can do so to a considerable degree.

If the teacher's taste is reasonably sensitive and aesthetic standards sufficiently high, every art activity in the classroom will tend to be acceptable, and praise or some other manner of emphasis should be given to

If few materials are available for the teacher to use as a stimulus for subject matter, then perhaps the teacher and pupils can bring in objects from the home and the environment. Here a child studies an object on a still-life table composed of various toys, antiques, junk, billboard segments, and the like. (Photo by Roger Graves.)

aspects of the students' work worth noting. The teacher's taste, influenced by personality and cultural background, will also be reflected in his or her critical comments on the works of art selected for study. Such decisions set the aesthetic tone of teaching and have ensuing effects on the pupils.

THE SCHOOL SETTING

Manifestly the art program is greatly affected by the school setting. The climate of opinion in the school with respect to art education, the classroom accommodation, the supplies and equipment available, will all have a bearing on what the teacher can hope to accomplish. A wide variation exists in these respects from one locality to another. Sometimes, but fortunately not often, the school authorities may be of the "old school" type and resent spending money on anything but the most "basic" subjects. In some schools, virtually no special provision is made in classrooms for art, and little money is allocated for the purchase of supplies and equipment. Occasionally the teacher is in a school where the schedule is inflexible, and art has to be taught at certain periods and deal with specific themes. By integrating art with other subjects the teacher may offer even more art than by adhering to the hourly period once a week.

No matter how discouraging the situation may be, with determination and ingenuity, the teacher can always find a way to develop a reasonably acceptable art program. If themes are specified, then the children must become sufficiently conversant with them and excited about them to express themselves in a creative manner. If sufficient supplies cannot be purchased, then they must make use of scrap materials. Various conveniences may be built in the classroom at little or no cost. Although an initial lack of supplies and accommodations may limit an art program, these conditions need not prevent the teaching of art.

THE COMMUNITY SETTING

As has been pointed out previously, the substance of art is to be found in the immediate environment. Artists have invariably discovered subject matter in those experiences peculiar to the part of the world they know. In this sense, art is always local. The art of children, of course, will always be greatly affected by their community, and this is fitting. Only thus will their art activities rest on the sole reliable foundation for aesthetic expression.

In the past, some teachers have felt that art should arise from an event romantically remote from the humdrum local scene. Children living in an eastern seaboard city might draw pictures of the Rocky Mountains, and those in a rural community might depict the skyscrapers of some mythical metropolis. But the strength and vitality of children's expression do not, in the long run, arise from objects and events remote from their lives. Such attributes are more likely to come from their own immediate environment. It is the teacher's responsibility to encourage artistic expres-

Children's immediate environment may include an outdoor setting. Direct painting from nature is difficult and can be a frustrating experience if it has not been preceded by preparatory activities. It also demands a well-organized teacher who can bring all the materials to the desired location and set them up in working order. Yet landscape painting is also complex and challenging, and can be a fitting climax to the study of color, a group of artists, or painting itself.

Here, a class of combined fifth and sixth grades has an outdoor painting session. This particular class spent some time studying the Impressionists (see Chapter 1) prior to going outdoors. As a final motivational phase, the teacher reviews problems of technique and vocabulary through a brief demonstration.

Children do not mind working on the ground if they can use drawing boards. They particularly enjoy the additional space and the opportunity to move about before choosing the view they wish to paint. (Two choices are the example here and the one on the opening page of this chapter.) The session's work can be informally exhibited for review. Since these pictures were painted in acrylic, they dried quickly.

sion derived from personal experience and to make children aware of the visual possibilities all around them.

The community served by the school not only can provide much of the subject matter for an art program but also can perhaps supply materials for expression. In the most populous cities any original local materials have largely ceased to exist, and supplies must be purchased or gathered from scrap. Business and industry can provide various kinds of surplus scrap material such as cartons, wood trimmings, and cardboard tubing. In rural areas, suitable woods for sculpture, clays for modeling and ceramics, grasses for weaving, and so on may be found locally. These materials, of course, should be exploited fully, and their use will have bearing on the development of the art program.

Sometimes the general character of the community will influence the art program. In Oregon, the authors observed a far greater use of wood in the art program than in Miami, where sand casting was popular. Communities in which there is a well-defined interest in local history might again influence some of the activities in the art program. In many communities, ethnic groups still maintain a few traditional arts and crafts of which they are proud.

The teacher and students will do well also to study physical aspects of the community, noting distinguishing characteristics of trees, buildings, public plazas, and places of recreation. Perhaps the class can go on a field trip to observe the community. Is the area hilly or flat, old or contemporary, cluttered or open? Answers to such questions can provide rich teaching material for the art program.

Perhaps the greatest resource of a community is its people. Some teachers have inventoried the careers of their students' parents and sent out form letters requesting volunteers to serve as aids on field trips, to give demonstrations in class, or to speak about their art work or their careers. Other teachers have made arrangements with local institutions such as libraries or banks for exhibition space. Others have worked closely with their Parent-Teacher Associations and received financial support for the art program. The art program can reflect the nature of the community and at the same time use it as a valuable resource.

Curriculum Formation

GOALS AND OBJECTIVES

The shaping of any curriculum must begin by establishing a direction. Although teachers may bring to this problem some knowledge of art, of children, and of sound educational practice, the content of the curriculum begins to take form when teachers use all their knowledge and experience as a basis for setting down what they hope to accomplish in terms of art goals and objectives.

Ralph Tyler, in his brief but classic essay on curriculum planning, cites four questions that are generally accepted as a reasonable if not inevitable place to begin. These are as follows:[3]

1. What educational purposes should the school seek to attain?
2. What educational experiences can be provided that are likely to attain these purposes?
3. How can these educational experiences be effectively organized?
4. How can we determine whether these purposes are being attained?

The "purposes" that Tyler alludes to may also be viewed as goals, and his "experiences," the vehicles by which goals or purposes are attained.

Students and teachers may differ in their goals and may strive consciously or unconsciously to achieve them. Decisions regarding goals are perhaps the teacher's most complex task because they represent the articulation of the teacher's philosophy as it relates to his or her knowledge of the children's capacities and desires. Thus goal formulation is a key area of decision-making in the curriculum-planning process.

Kenneth Lansing refers to the problem of goal definition when he states:

> Another thing that makes the formulation of goals difficult is the fact that some of them must be cognitive, while others must be affective and psychomotor. In other words, youngsters must know and understand certain things about art; they must have relevant attitudes and values; and they must possess certain skills. Their knowledge must cover life in general, artistic procedures, composition, art history, and aesthetics. Their attitudes must include an interest in the making and appreciating of art, confidence in their own ability to make and appraise art, tolerance of the various forms that art might take, and a willingness to work hard. And their skill must center around the efficient manipulation of art tools and materials.[4]

If we accept Lansing's statement, we can see that goals may exist in both broad and limited categories. An art program may be conceived of as having a design—that is, as being composed of a series of learning units, the components of which all contribute to the sense of wholeness. The

---

[3] Ralph Tyler, *Basic Principles of Curriculum and Instruction* (Chicago: University of Chicago Press, 1950).

[4] Quoted in Mary M. Packwood, ed., *Art Education in the Elementary School* (Washington, D.C.: National Art Education Association, 1967), p. 72.

teacher must discriminate between the broad goal and the subgoal or objective—and distinguishing between the two can be difficult. A lesson in color mixing, to cite one instance, does not fulfill the goal of "establishing color sensitivity"—an objective so inclusive that color mixing is obviously just one step in a sequence that might also include color matching from magazines, color identification in paintings, using color to express a mood, and finding color parallels to music and other sounds.

Objectives for a particular lesson will, of course, vary with the nature of the task. If the class is drawing pictures to send to a school in Europe or another part of the country, one objective might be to present as much specific information as possible, so that the recipients can determine from the drawings how Americans in Idaho, for example, dress and live. If the community has just experienced a hurricane, snowstorm, or torrential downpour, the objective could be to "create colors to show what it was like." Or, if sixth graders are having their first lesson in contour-line drawing, the objective could relate to the amounts of variance in the line as evidence of clearly observed edges. Objectives should thus be presented in "manageable segments" and in clear, meaningful terms for the child.

Unless some sort of objective, however general, has been discussed in the early phase of the lesson, evaluation cannot be effective at the conclusion of the art period. The more specific the statement of the goal, however, the more effective the evaluation. The teacher who tells students, "Today we will concentrate on bright colors" does not help the students during the critique period as much as one who says, "Today let's see how much variety we can get out of a single color by changing it through the use of black, white, or its complement."

Goals are broad general aims, whereas objectives are more immediate ways of achieving a goal. Some statements of goals, however, are so vague as to have little meaning for student or teacher. The following examples of useful and nonuseful goals may help clarify these differences.

> *Art Appreciation:* Stated in lofty terms, a goal for this area might be: "To learn to appreciate art." This is a virtually meaningless statement, because no critic or aesthetician would claim that this achievement is totally possible for college students, much less for ten- or twelve-year-old children. It also gives no indication of the kinds of learning activities expected to take place. A more useful goal for the same topic would be: "To increase the enjoyment of artworks through discussion and studio experiences based on the work of professional artists."

Other useful objectives that might come under such a goal could provide the basis of lessons to follow. These could be:

"To apply mental operations such as comparing, interpreting, describing, and arguing in response to artworks."

"To demonstrate some connection between a studio exercise and the study of a style, a personality, or a period in art."

"To employ newly acquired art vocabulary when discussing either professional or student artwork."

Objectives are intended to develop behaviors that students were not able to perform prior to some phase of instruction. It is hoped that if the children could not demonstrate the stated behavior in September, they should be able to do so in January. If they cannot, then either the teaching objective is unrealistic or the teacher lacks the skill to teach for the desired change.

Another approach to setting goals for the curriculum is *competency planning*. The following definitions are central to the competency approach to education. Since school systems often require such specificity in describing what the children will be able to do, it is well to note the meanings of these terms for possible future reference.

A *performance objective* is a positive goal, stated as a declarative sentence. Example: "The student will be able to select, discuss, draw, center, and so on." In the case of a single activity, such as centering clay, the goal is specific; in the case of a sequence of activities, such as making a one-minute animated film, the goal is broad. It is also possible to set a goal for a group. Example: "The class will be able to conduct the cleanup period without teacher intervention."

A *set* is a cluster of performance objectives that the student will have to accomplish in order to complete the *carrier project*, or task that leads to an end-product.

A *concept* precedes the choice of the carrier project and is a statement about art, such as, "Styles in painting vary with time." Concepts may ultimately be transformed into "overt" perceptual acts, such as asking the student to sort chronologically the work of a cave painter, Giotto, Manet, and Rauschenberg.[5]

Behaviorists in art education also recommend that the three major domains of learning be maintained. These domains, or classifications of

[5]These terms originated in several conferences organized by the National Art Education Association with the assistance of Professor Asahel Woodruff of the University of Utah. Since the first conference proceedings in 1968, most art teachers have used Woodruff's vocabulary; these are the most widely accepted interpretation of the terminology.

learning, distinguish between cognitive (knowledge, facts, intellectual abilities), affective (feelings and attitudes), and psychomotor (ability to handle specific processes involving physical coordination) skills.

A teacher, instead of suddenly deciding on Friday that drawing would be a good way to begin the week on Monday, will go through a considerable sequence of antecedent steps:

Think about the philosophy of art education.

Decide on the goals for the year for a particular age level. (This means considering what the art program can do to convert the philosophy into a realistic life process.)

Select both broad and specific strategies based on areas of art learnings to be covered.

Determine the sets for each carrier project.

State the performance objectives within sets.

State how the product will be evaluated.

Essential Elements. In developing performance objectives, program planners should also consider these elements.

1. *Identification of the individual or group* that will perform the desired behavior.
2. *Identification of the behavior* to be demonstrated through the product to be developed. The behavior should be described, as precisely as possible, in terms of an *action* that can be followed; or, similarly, the product should be described precisely as an *object* that can be observed.
3. The *primary conditions* under which the performance is expected to be measured: these might include restrictions placed on the project during the performance of specified tasks.
4. *Establishment of the minimum level of acceptable performance.* This step is the critical phase and the one that poses the most problems. What is the criterion for success?
5. *Establishment of the means of assessment,* which will be used to measure the expected performance or behavior. What form will the assessment take: checklist, informal observation, anecdotal record?

Determining objectives within the behaviorist or competency approach is much easier in the psychomotor domain than in the emotional or affective domain, since the personal side of expression resists precise evaluation. Centering clay or sharpening a tool, on the other hand, is quite easy to note. There is also the problem of separating short-term from long-term objectives.

Many teachers have serious reservations about the competency approach because it defines results prior to process and does not deal adequately with experimentation or with learning through certain kinds of failure. Another argument some teachers have against this system is that it is not the way artists operate, since artists do not always know exactly how their work will turn out. Artists might even ask what the point is of creating art while already knowing exactly how it will turn out.

The art teacher today has a great number of options in approaching curriculum planning. One basic decision to be made is whether to take a planned approach or an improvised approach; to avoid completely a plan in the hope that spontaneity and improvisation among the students will determine the course of the year's work, or to take the initiative in deciding what the priorities must be, establishing certain plans as "organizing centers" intended to bring about specific art learning.

THE PROCESS OF PLANNING

Since the class time allocated to art is generally limited, all teachers must be selective as to the activities used, setting their own priorities according to their long-range goals. For example, one teacher may decide that blowing paint through straws is fun and the results are occasionally exciting to look at, while another may decide that an extra session on contour drawing would move the children closer to a goal of increasing their ability to observe analytically. This book provides ample material for various kinds of planned programs. An example of a planning approach, recommended as an "organizing center" for the unit on color, is given in Table 4.1. This plan considers the character of the children and what can be expected of them in art before the content and activities of the program are decided on.

The unit outlined in Table 4.1 should take eight class sessions, so that if a class meets once a week, there would be two months of class contact. This may seem like an excessive amount of time to spend on color, but many kinds of learning are called into play: judgment, intuition, use of information, historical contexts, at least five kinds of media, and observation. The unit concept allows for an in-depth approach and permits sequencing of activities within a broader context. Needless to say, the classroom teacher's support in offering additional art activities can greatly enrich the value of this or any unit.

One way for teachers to get their thoughts on paper is to use a matrix as a graphic guide for sorting ideas. The matrix is simply a grid that indicates where key issues intersect. Matrix A (Table 4.2) demonstrates how basic concerns can be related: What will be studied (art content)? To whom will

MATRIX SYSTEMS FOR CURRICULUM PLANNING

TABLE 4.1

Unit on Color for Upper Grades*

A *unit* is a cluster of activities on one major theme. This is the simplest way to begin, and it can easily be extended into the vocabulary of competency planning by adding concepts, evaluation, and the division of activities (carrier projects) into *sets* or secondary groupings of objectives.

Expectancies in art: The student will be able to master art processes involving physical manipulation; sharply increase color perception; relate art vocabulary to art problems; recognize formal elements of design; and be able to organize a painting.

Content	Activities	Materials	Art References
1. *Color:* The distinction between primary and secondary colors	Creation of a design, based on a still life, that utilizes primary and secondary colors	Tempera	Expressionist paintings
2. The meaning of tints and shades	Creation of a design based on natural forms, using one color as a base and shades or tints of that color on top	Tempera	Cubist paintings
3. The emotive power of color	Creation of a nonobjective painting that reflects a mood or state of mind	Watercolor	Kandinsky, German Expressionists Film: *Fiddle-dee-dee* (National Film Board of Canada)
4. How color neighbors affect each other	Formation of a collage from samples of an assigned color chosen by each child	Colored paper, clippings from advertisements, fabrics, wallpaper	Josef Albers Victor Vasarely
5. Difference in function between mixing colors and selecting colors	Matching of colors in a painting, first with paint, then by pasting colors from magazine advertisements	Magazine advertisements, tempera, and construction paper	
6. Difference in effect between broken color,† mixed color, and flat, pure color	Painting of one tree in a painterly manner and another in a Hard Edge manner	Tempera	Impressionists such as Monet and Pissarro, and Hard Edge painters such as Stuart Davis, George Ortman, and Frank Stella
7. How color behaves in relation to light	Experimentation on acetate or old slides	Tempera, hole punchers, nail polish, acetate, and slide projector	

*"Color" is one of several units planned for the semester. Other areas of focus for art learning might be "Forms in Space" and "Printmaking." See also example of "Environment" unit.

†Broken color refers to the Impressionistic manner of painting an area in short, flickering strokes of different hues.

TABLE 4.2

Matrix A—The First Stage

	Art Content Areas			
	Art History	*Art Appreciation*	*Design Awareness*	*Drawing*
Upper Grades	X	X	X	X
Middle Grades		X	X	X
Primary Grades			X	X

it be taught (kinds of students)? In what order (sequence)? Before these questions are answered, the teacher should have given some thought to the two principal concerns that must precede the issues mentioned above: the philosophy of the teacher (What do I believe?) and its attendant goals (What do I hope to accomplish?).

This matrix is but one instance of a wide variety of possibilities. It would also be possible to organize a program around one particular content area. For example, one could subdivide design awareness so that the study of color would be a major area of activity for all grades. Sawyer and de Francesco plan their matrix around five basic "needs": communication, industry, personal living, society, and commerce.[6] Just as good a case, of course, can be made for the awareness of design as for communication, and obviously the latter cannot succeed without the former. The difference is one of emphasis, and in articulating goals the teacher justifies the content and emphasis selected.

Matrix A is the first stage of planning. The subdivisions of each content area must now be indicated so that more specific information can be accommodated.

The second stage shown in Table 4.3, Matrix B, moves to the heart of instruction and should also deal with concepts (statements about art, which Eisner describes as "principles or generalizations to be used by the teacher as a focus for subsequent work with students"[7]). The " Objectives" column translates the concept into a performance objective. The "Activities" column lists the major tasks that are designed to engage the child in learning the concept. The next column deals with materials, support, or resources that may be needed to fulfill the performance objectives that serve to realize the concept. The final column contains suggestions for evaluation, although this information could be reserved for the third, or lesson plan, stage.

[6]John R. Sawyer and Italo de Francesco, *Elementary School Art for Classroom Teachers* (New York, Evanston, and London: Harper & Row, 1971), p. 143.
[7]Elliot Eisner, *Educating Artistic Vision* (New York: Macmillan, 1972), p. 174.

TABLE 4.3

Matrix B—The Second Stage

		Art Appreciation		
Concept Statements	*Objectives*	*Activities*	*Media and Resources*	*Evaluation*
"Styles vary with time and artist."	"The student will be able to recognize and distinguish between the works of Surrealists, Expressionists, and Cubists."	Sorting postcard reproductions of works of artists	Slides Films Filmstrips Games Packages File material Postcard reproductions	After examining Cubist paintings of Braque and Picasso with the aid of the teacher, pupils can assign a painting by Juan Gris to the Cubist School on their own.

TABLE 4.4

Matrix C—Semester Planning

Grade _____
No. of
class sessions _____

Basic Modes of Expression/Media

Sources of Art	*Drawing* Pencil Ink Crayon, craypas	*Painting* Watercolor Tempera Acrylic	*Printmaking* Monoprints: linoleum calligraphy vegetable	*Sculpture* Assemblage Clay Cardboard Wood scraps	*Crafts* Wood scraps Papier-mâché Clay	*Mixed Media* Collage-ink Crayon resist Craypas Crayon etching
Observation						
Problem-Solving						
Hidden Landscape (dreams, imagination, fantasy)						
Narrative Art (storytelling, illustration)						
Language of Art (design, line, form, color)						
Art History						
Art Appreciation						
The Environment						

Matrix C (Table 4.4) suggests another format; organizing thoughts for an entire semester. "Sources of Art" are listed in the first column. The other columns offer choices of how they can be given form—that is, through a choice of "Basic Modes of Expression" and "Media." The matrix assumes that the source of art is where to begin, and that media and modes are means to ends, rather than ends in themselves. As an example, students can exercise observation through drawing (pencil, ink), sculpture (clay), or painting (tempera). The source categories often overlap: a lesson on environmental awareness can involve drawing landscapes or discussing slides of local architectural styles (art history and art appreciation). When examining the concept of utopia through environmental improvement, the student is working from Source 2, Imagination and Fantasy. The Source category provides a focus of attention, a central core around which succeeding sessions may be planned. Most teachers, particularly those teaching on the secondary level, begin with the basic modes and then search for subject matter; but Matrix C is arranged to *begin* with subject matter, since this lies closer to the goals of art education.

Using Matrix C, teachers should try to achieve some balance between the sources and the different media used to deal with them, and to plan for some coverage of basic experiences that can be accommodated in the time allotted. For example, if there are fifteen class meetings in one semester, the teacher could accommodate three basic modes of expression that deal with four sources of art, or could deal with fewer sources and develop them through a wider range of media or modes. One plan for the first semester of a fifth grade environmental unit involved the following activities:

1. Viewing films of landscapes, including aerial views.
2. Studying painters who painted landscapes, from Constable (realistic) to Hundertwasser (abstract).
3. Making student self-portraits as skydivers, with views of the earth below.
4. Making a relief collage of an imaginary landscape viewed from above.
5. Direct painting from landscape, preceded by a study of broken color.

This is another example of a unit approach—a way of organizing a sequence of art experiences that enables children to concentrate on a single artistic problem through a group of related tasks and materials.

Table 4.5 presents another plan for the fifth and sixth grades, in this case for an entire year—thirty-four class sessions. The number under each activity refers to the list of sources, some of which are brought into play when the students perform each of the sequences of activities.

TABLE 4.5

A Program—5th and 6th Grades

Sources from which activities are drawn:
1. Confronting the Exterior World
2. The Hidden Landscape: Fantasy, Imagination, Speculation, Dreams
3. Design: The Language and Structure of Art
4. Cultural Content: History, Criticism, and Ethnic Settings
5. Memory and Experience: Sports, Family, Vacations, Weekends, Personal History
6. Artist and Society: Practical Purposes, Commercial Art, Environmental Art, Industrial Design
7. Integrated Art: Art activity in relation to language arts, social studies, mathematics.
8. Public Rituals: Celebrations, Exhibits, Parties, Holidays, Events

Activity	Session	Sequences of Activities	Objectives
Drawing (may be used as a diagnostic instrument)	1	Memory drawing	
	2	Observational drawing: mechanical objects (bicycles, insides of watches, movie projectors, vehicles, toys, tools)	Ability to handle detail, to relate whole to parts, and to work with new visual structures
Mapping 2, 3, 4, 7	3	Introduction, planning, sketching of decorative maps	To develop imagination through maps. To create symbols and situations and to use design for embellishment. To relate all this to historical context of Portuguese cartography
	4	Development and drawing	
	5	Finishing	
Painting and Color 3, 6	6	Warm/Cool, Approach I: number/letter design	To see new possibilities of color. To deal with compositional problems in relating form and color to total space
	7	Warm/Cool, Approach II: still life selected for unusual shape	
	8	Complete still life	
Collage 1, 3	9	People collage, drawing, design	To develop design awareness through the collage technique (texture applied to surface). To use one activity (drawing) as a basis for subsequent activities
	10	Development	
	11	Complete collage	
Fish Mobile 1, 3, 6, 7	12	Developing drawing, working in tissue	To master a new craft process. To exploit the possibilities of transparency as a means of dealing with color
	13	Decorating and stuffing	
Clay: Dinosaurs, Mythological, etc. 1, 2, 3, 4, 5, 6, 7	14	Presentation, working	To deal with modeling and shaping techniques. To study and use mythological forms as a basis of art. To relate details (surfaces, anatomical structures) to large shapes
	15	Working, finishing	
Drawing: Crayon Engraving 1, 2, 3	16	Line drawing, animals	To learn how processes and stages of development can enrich and extend the possibilities of image development. To learn the values of extended concentration on a project. To learn a mixed-media technique
	17	Color phase	
	18	Paint phase	
	19	Engraving phase	

TABLE 4.5
A Program—5th and 6th Grades (Continued)

Activity	Session	Sequences of Activities	Objectives
Linoleum Print 1, 2, 3, 5	20	Introduction, free choice of subject: animal, design, personal experiences	To learn how stages of processes can extend imagery. To acquire skill in using new tools. To use accident and pure design to achieve unexpected effects in printmaking. To use sources of design to generate ideas. To deal in balances of dark and light areas
	21	Introduction to tools; work on block	
	22	Work on block	
	23	Work on block	
	24	Work on block, start printing	
	25	Straight printing	
	26	Explorative printing	
Critical/Historical Study 4, 7		Selecting an artist whose work suggests some formal or conceptual problem (Klee, Matisse, Picasso); discussing meaning and intent as they relate to style and technique.	To learn about a new artist or painting. To discuss art: description and interpretation, analysis. To create a connection between art history and students' own creative decisions
Celebration: Masks, Headdresses, and Face-Painting 1, 2, 3, 4, 6, 8	27	Begin by modeling the form of the mask in clay	To see art as a social process that can enhance public rituals. To relate design to the human form. To discover imaginative solutions to paper sculpture used as body ornament. To establish relationships between costume and face-painting
	28	Begin covering with papier-mâché	
	29	Continuing papier-mâché	
	30	Finishing and planning surface treatment	
	31	Painting and decorating	
	32	Creating headdresses and decorating faces	
Evaluation of Program	33	Objective written examination to assess information retained. Celebration-eat, parade	To assess attitudes and knowledge as a basis for decision-making
	34		

The creation of a lesson plan is the culminating exercise for student and beginning art teachers. Although most teachers stop using lesson plans after a few years of experience, it is a good exercise to analyze the final stage of curriculum planning—the point at which a new area of the curriculum is introduced. Lesson plans can cover a day or a longer period of

THE LESSON PLAN

time. A good lesson plan anticipates what can and should happen; it is a scenario for achieving an objective. Just because the actual events do not always go according to the plan, the value gained from writing lesson plans should not be dismissed.

The sample plan that follows is the final stage of column 4, "Drawing," on Matrix A.

Art content area: Drawing.

Concept statement: Contour or edge drawing is one way to become aware of the variety of edges of shapes and the overall structure of a form.

Time: Two lessons.

Objectives: The students will be able to make a continuous contour drawing of a group of simple objects selected from around the room or from their own pockets. (Several arrangements will be set up for those who prefer groups of large objects.) The students will demonstrate their handling of detail and edges of the subject, both characteristics of contour drawing.

Concepts and processes to be stressed at the introduction of the lesson: Drawing will be defined as "a record in line of forms in space." Contour drawing will be defined as "a record of the edges of shapes," as opposed to drawing that uses lines and tones to suggest volume or mass.

Materials to be used: Soft pencil or crayon on white paper.

Perceptual processes to be emphasized: The ability to focus on the edges of shapes and to see the shapes that are constituent parts of an object. The students may accomplish this by covering their hands with a sheet of paper so that they will not be tempted to compare object and drawing.

Group evaluation: The drawings of students and professional artists will be pinned up so that successful parts may be noted.
Questions for consideration in a group evaluation:
"How does contour drawing differ from other kinds we have done?"
"What did you notice in your subject that you had not seen before?"
"Let's take a look at some contour drawings by professional artists. How have they handled the edges of things?"

Art history: Picasso, Matisse, Ben Shahn.

"A Day at the Beach," by a nine-year-old girl from South Africa, combines drawing and painting, observation and memory, all handled within the content of the symbolic stage. If there is such a thing as a classic problem, this is one.

The plan that covers the stages discussed above is an exercise in relating wholes to parts. If the teacher begins with a broad conceptual frame, then the art lesson has a clearly stated context. The novice teacher, however, too ofen begins at the other end of the scale, and as a result the students receive a potpourri of scattered experiences without any underlying logic.

Obviously, planning a program can be arduous and time-consuming if teachers feel they must do the entire job themselves rather than consult existing models. Most teachers, in any case, will not be expected to plan entire programs on their own. The planning system described above is intended as a brief introduction for readers who suddenly find themselves on a team that is required to produce a total art program in depth and detail.

The idea of approaching art instruction in a disciplined manner may seem rather extreme to the teacher who feels that art lies beyond careful planning. But every teacher, regardless of philosophy or field, must face the results of classroom work, and planning for art simply requires that the instructor consider the end results before beginning to teach.

Planning, however, should never be so tight that attention cannot be given to any child who is unable to begin work. One difficulty may be that the child has not found the assigned task sufficiently interesting to become involved. A teacher may find it necessary in this case to help the child work on another task that is compatible with the goal. For example, the teacher might eventually suggest variations of the assignment, or if need be, depart from the original plan in order to motivate the child. The solution may lie in a change of medium or subject matter. Vicarious experiences, such as stories from literature, films, radio, or television, may capture the reluctant child's interest and provide sufficient motivation to begin work. In any event, new bases for expression, from either actual or vicarious sources, must be explored until the child is prompted to action.

Case Histories of Art Program Development

By now it must be obvious that the development of an art program demands much strategic thinking on the part of the teacher. Although local factors affect the character of the program, the teacher must keep in mind the traditional nature of artistic effort, so that whatever work is produced in the name of art will have the attributes of art.

Many teachers have been eminently successful in developing a program of art in keeping with these concepts. It is instructive to study the efforts of some of them, to observe how they have coped with the various factors affecting the program. Accordingly four case histories are presented to illustrate the manner in which these teachers solved, to the general satisfaction of all concerned, the problems associated with the development of an art program.*

A SCHOOL IN A DEPRESSED URBAN AREA

Mr. G is an art teacher in a school situated in an old and deteriorated section of an American east coast metropolis. The buildings of the district are rundown and monotonous, living conditions are poor. There is neither a playground nor a public park within convenient reach of the school.

Mr. G enjoys his work because he senses a great need for it. His own classroom is a model of neatness, order, and attractiveness. He has sponsored the formation of a pupils' committee that is responsible for hanging attractive displays of art work in the halls of the school. Because the school board has had the halls and classrooms painted in attractive colors, entering the building after leaving the drab street is a happy experi-

*Should the reader consider some of the settings extreme, it must be pointed out that often an extreme example more clearly demonstrates an educational strategy.

ence. In the hallways, the students have painted murals of neighborhood scenes.

The program followed by Mr. G is similar to that found in many other teaching situations. The pupils make pictures related to their lives and intersperse this activity with some three-dimensional projects. If some of the pupils' output displays negative interests resulting from a depressed environment, their expressions at least have the saving graces of honesty, clarity, and a sharp perceptual response. Indeed Mr. G is quite aware of the special perceptual problems of his pupils. He devotes much of his time to discussions and activities that deal with sharpened visual awareness, size and color discrimination, relation of parts to wholes, filtering out of irrelevant details, and study of symbols in the environment.

Since many of his children are black or Hispanic, Mr. G makes certain that many examples of the work of black and Hispanic artists are used either for general display or in conjunction with instruction. He discusses posters, record album covers, cartoons, comic books, television, and music as readily as more formal art; he knows that it is more important what a student discovers than where the discovery begins. He even uses grafitti as a subject for discussion, and he knows that the inner lives of his children have special validity when choosing subject matter. He would like to give his students cameras and teach them simple film animation. He is trying to find out where and how he can get the needed equipment.

Mr. G has also paid a good deal of attention to home and community planning. The members of his class work at problems related to this theme—such as designing a park, an apartment, or a recreation center. On one occasion, the pupils reconstructed the entire neighborhood in miniature. Some of the boys and girls have planned a "dream house" and others have designed the bedroom or kitchen they would like to occupy. As frequently as possible Mr. G takes his students on expeditions to see the layout of the city parks, new housing developments, or other building projects worthy of note. At times he feels he is more of a social studies teacher than an art teacher.

Mr. G was faced with grave problems arising from the choice of theme and the social setting. Should the pupils continue to express sordid things, or turn to subject matter remote from their present world? Fortunately Mr. G had sufficient insight into art to realize that expression must arise from what the pupils knew, even though what they knew was often far from socially desirable. He realized that reliance on artificial subject matter would probably only adversely affect the pupils' artistic taste. Therefore, he made sure that the pupils had some socially commendable experiences that they could employ as themes. The discipline of art was still operative, expression was still within the artistic tradition, but now it embraced the real world. This was the objective of his strategy, which he felt succeeded as far as was artistically expedient.

Mr. Y accepted his first teaching position in an isolated community in the Tennessee mountains. Only seven families supplied the twenty-six children enrolled in his school. Mr. Y noticed that many of the parents had little good to say for their neighbors and that their conversation about them contained many unkind references. No social gatherings in the community had occurred for some years; instead, the people were in the habit of seeking their entertainment in the small town some fifteen miles away. In summer, the people were able to drive to this town, but in winter traveling became almost impossible because of snow or mud.

Mr. Y was young and liked people and he determined to begin his program by defining art in its social function. He organized a dance to take place in the schoolhouse. Two men—one who played a fiddle and the other a guitar—consented to make the music, and each family was asked to bring something to eat.

The children were excited about the forthcoming dance. The drab appearance of the classroom, however, had escaped their notice. Indeed, in that area no one seemed to be concerned with interior decoration, at home or elsewhere. Mr. Y brought the matter before the class. "What could we do to make the classroom pretty for the dance?" he asked, producing a few art supplies. After much discussion a theme for decoration was agreed on: Summer in the Mountains. The children drew or sculpted in paper the flowers, birds, and trees of the surrounding country. They painted a mural depicting a trip to the neighboring town. They wove paper mats to place under the food, and they constructed paper hats for the guests. Since the area had a particularly rich heritage of folk music, some children also illustrated the themes and stories of this music.

When the parents and a few visitors arrived at the schoolhouse on the night of the dance, not many people commented on the cheerful appearance of the schoolroom. But the decorations were nevertheless noticed. "That teacher's a smart artist," a parent commented. When they learned that the work was entirely that of the children, the parents could scarcely believe it. Later, after they realized that the children had been responsible, some small bickering developed as to whose children were the "smartest" artists.

Let us examine how the influences discussed on page 120 affected Mr. Y's decisions. The tradition of art exerted itself largely from the standpoint of the "function" of the project. Since the community was primitive artistically and otherwise, nothing but a "practical" or functional form of art, such as the project clearly proved to be, would probably have been acceptable to the parents. The problem was well within the understanding of the children, and they were ready for the activity; the art activities being of a simple nature largely because of the lack of supplies, the young teacher needed no special training to be able to assist the pupils. Finally, the community setting provided a theme for decoration. Local themes were the logical choice to appeal to the parents and to evoke real artistic responses from the children. Mr. Y was perceptive enough to use a social occasion as a means of getting a number of new ideas going. Later, he was to capitalize on the success of the event by developing other activities from what had been accomplished on the night of the dance.

Mr. Y, as well as doing the community a social service, had cleverly launched an art program in a region where art, if it had ever been considered at all, had been relegated to outsiders and "highbrows." He had demonstrated to the people that school art was practical and acceptable.

On the seaboard of the northwestern part of the state of Washington was a thriving settlement of some 20,000 people. Here lumber and other wood products were produced in a number of large sawmills. The district was wealthy, and no reasonable expense for the school system was refused. Art rooms were models of efficiency; supplies were abundant.

A SCHOOL IN A WELL-TO-DO, SCENIC AREA

Miss A accepted a position in one of the large elementary schools in this town and was assigned to teach art in the fourth, fifth, and sixth grades. In studying the children's art output under the guidance of her predecessor, she was disappointed to discover that the program had been extremely rigid. Its nature was evidenced by still-life drawings of flower arrangements and exercises in perspective and color theory.

Miss A was a competent painter whose work was sensitive rather than powerful. She was, furthermore, an experienced art teacher and thoroughly familiar with contemporary ideas in art education. Her former home in North Dakota was a complete contrast to northwest Washington. As she looked about her, Miss A was deeply impressed by her new environment. At her back rose the great mountains, before her was the sea, and in the distance the peaks of an island mountain range showed their caps of snow. At night she could hear the rumble of the mills and watch the moving lights of the ships as they came and went with their cargoes. She became familiar with the art of the local native tribes. Moved by all she saw, Miss A recognized that here was all manner of inspiration for art.

The people of the settlement went busily about their affairs, apparently giving little aesthetic attention to their environment. The children also seemed unaware of their surroundings. Miss A, however, was enthused. Somehow, she decided, she must make the pupils really see and feel this place.

She began her program simply. The pupils were asked to produce pictures based on the usual happenings in their lives. Their first work was neither more nor less inspired than one would find in many other schools. Gradually, however, she introduced them to the folklore of the coastal native tribes. She showed them the artifacts of the native Americans, pointing out their strength and originality, and after some investigation discovered that a number of local artists, both Caucasian and native American, were available to meet with children and talk about their work. Whenever possible, she placed exhibit catalogs of their work on display.

She played music of the sea, powerful compositions such as the "Sea Interludes" from Britten's *Peter Grimes* and Mendelssohn's *Fingal's Cave*. Occasionally she read them excerpts from the stories of Joseph Conrad and the poems of John Masefield. After the children had produced some pictures on sea themes she showed them reproductions of works by John Marin, Henry Mattson, and Albert Pinkham Ryder, and *The Great Wave* by Hokusai.

Following the motivation related to the sea she introduced the subjects of the mountains and valleys, and later the forests and the lakes. In each case she made use of related literary and musical interpretations of these subjects. Then she told her classes stories of the explorers of the West Coast. Finally she turned to the mills and to the drama of heavy industry.

As time passed the art program expanded in many directions. Miss A discovered, for example, a local wood that was suitable for carving. Later she introduced various kinds of textile printing and encouraged the children to use motifs inspired by the local environment. She helped the children organize fist-puppet shows, for which they wrote scripts about life, either past or present, on the West Coast.

As an artist, Miss A knew intimately the nature of art as a discipline. She possessed many artistic skills and her taste was impeccable. Her pupils also possessed some skills and a reasonably developed taste. Her strategy, then, was first to make the local scene acceptable to the pupils as a basis for expression; second, to get the pupils to use the abundance of two- and three-dimensional materials wisely in expressing their reactions to the locality; and third, to make use of important historical facts having artistic significance.

She carried out her strategy by exhibiting the work of artists and artisans who had lived in, and had been moved by, similar surroundings and by inspiring the pupils through her own deep and commendable enthusiasm. Perhaps the most important change Miss A brought about was to reveal the environment to the children.

ART IN A BRITISH OPEN CLASSROOM

Someday a situation may arise in which the art program will be rethought in terms of a national philosophy. For some years, the primary schools of Great Britain moved toward the "open classroom" or the "integrated day," as the new approach to teaching was called. This approach affected the

Curriculum Planning: Developing a Program of Studies

TABLE 4.6

Comparison of Educational Approaches

Structured Education	Open Education
Graded Organizational Pattern	Nongraded Organizational Pattern
One Teacher	Team Teaching
Group-Paced Learning Experiences	Self-Paced Learning Experiences
Group Instruction	Individualized Instruction
Restricted Space	Flexible Use of Open Space
Systematic/Logical Learning	Discovery Learning
Subject-Centered Education	Life-Centered Education
Direct Teaching	Indirect Teaching

methodology as well as the content of teaching and, in general, improved art instruction. Art under the new practices changed from a separate subject to an integrated part of the curriculum. A comparison of educational practices between the traditional structured and the newer open is listed in Table 4.6.

The case study that follows describes the way in which a classroom teacher might handle art activities in the context of an open classroom.

Mrs. H taught a primary-school class in an industrial town in Yorkshire. Unlike her typical American counterpart, she had only three years of professional preparation rather than four, and like her American colleague, she had little or no training in art to prepare her to conduct an art program competently. Mrs. H did not have an art specialist to consult, but she did have two advantages over an American teacher: she was working within a movement that strongly endorses not only the role of visual art but of all of the arts, and she had a strong inservice program to assist her in filling the gaps in her art background. She looked on professional development as an ongoing process rather than as one that ended with the completion of her schooling. If strong inservice training had not been offered, she and her colleagues most likely would have demanded it.

Despite the disadvantages of a limited budget and a large class (well over thirty children), Mrs. H managed to carry on an art program on two levels. One might be called "art for art's sake," where the children had a set time of the day or week to work in a medium or subject of their choice; and the other was an integrated program where art was used in conjunction with other subject areas—illustrating stories, making scale models, creating decorative maps and charts, and the like. Mrs. H could not be a master of every material her students worked with, but other staff members helped: one day she might send someone to a teacher who knew fabric printing, while the following week she in turn would help students from another class with linocuts, a special interest of hers. The "head," or principal, was particularly strong in ceramics and had a weekly class on an informal basis for those students who were interested.

Mrs. H's school was quieter than an American one; there was a seriousness about the way work was carried on, and this showed in the care and extended concentration the students brought to their art. One girl worked on a large painting of the school playground for several weeks, while a team of boys took considerably longer to create a life-sized diorama of underwater life. Some students enjoyed doing outdoor sketches of the school grounds. If ideas ran out, there were the everpresent but always-changing still lifes that both Mrs. H and the class were arranging. These could be based on a particular idea, such as a color; a specific geometric shape; objects used by local workers, such as coal miners' tools; or interesting bits of junk or castoff pieces of machinery collected along the way to school. The children were thus urged to use their environment in as many ways as possible as a source of ideas for art. Whatever the children drew or painted was mounted with care, exhibited in an organized way, and carefully labeled. It was obvious from visiting Mrs. H's school that art was considered very much a part of general education and that, far from being a special case, her class reflected the philosophy of the school, which in turn was part of a national trend in education.[8]

The programs of the four teachers just described, although varying in detail, have several characteristics in common. Each teacher, while stimulating and helping the pupils, allowed them sufficient freedom of expression and choice of activity within the framework of a theme. All the programs were successful because the teachers were sufficiently competent in both pedagogical and artistic matters to make each program effective and all were sensitive to the local character of the children and the community setting.

[8] This description is a composite of impressions taken during the author's visit to four "open" schools in Yorkshire. For greater insight into the subject, read the articles on art in *The Open Classroom Reader*, Charles E. Silberman, ed. (New York: Vintage Books, 1973).

Activities for the Reader

1. Describe in some detail the significant planning decisions that must be made in an art program developed in the following situations: (a) a sixth grade classroom in a new, wealthy suburb of a large city; (b) a third grade classroom in a temporary school for the children of construction workers in an isolated part of North Carolina; (c) a mixed-grade classroom (first through fourth grades) in a mission school for Indians located in New Mexico.

2. Describe how you would constructively handle a situation in which your principal was more interested in having an art program based on a rigid program of outdated concepts than on a contemporary, creative approach. Choose a classmate and do some improvised role-playing on this subject.

3. If a fellow teacher who gave evidence of atrociously bad taste in art asked you for an honest appraisal of his or her artistic efforts, what would you say or do?

Curriculum Planning: Developing a Program of Studies

4. You are elected chairman of an eight-person *ad hoc* committee in a city school system to submit ideas to a central authority for the improvement of the art program. You are expected, furthermore, to select the eight members of the committee. State the kinds of people you would choose. Describe the agenda you would draw up for the first hour-long meeting.

5. Because of negative associations with a previous art program, your fifth grade pupils do not seem interested in helping you develop an art program. Describe how you might improve matters.

6. A former teacher had for two years taught nothing to fourth, fifth, and sixth grade pupils except the copying of either comic strips or picture postcards. How would you proceed in developing an art program in your new teaching position?

7. Improvise the conversation you might have with a parent who thinks teaching art is a waste of taxpayers' money, which should be used for "more important fundamentals." Try this conversation with various types of parents: professionals, lower-middle-class factory workers, local shopkeepers.

8. Compare the features of structured and open education; list specific instances involving art under the items shown in both columns in Table 4.6.

9. Plan a sequence of six art activities for the middle grades, all based on the theme "Above and Below the Earth." Try one sequence for a limited budget and one for a generous budget.

10. Divide the painting experience into "tight" (performance) objectives and "loose" objectives (more personal interpretations).

Suggested Readings

Barrett, Maurice. *Art Education, A Strategy for Course Design.* London: Heinemann Educational Books, 1979. A concise guide to curriculum planning stated in an operational, practical way.

Chapman, Laura. *Approaches to Art Education.* New York: Harcourt Brace Jovanovich, 1978. Chapter 18, "Planning the Art Program." This is one of the best books for art curriculum development.

Hurwitz, Al. *Programs of Promise: Art in the Schools.* New York: Harcourt Brace Jovanovich, 1972. See sections by Elliot Eisner, Ronald Silverman, Guy Hubbard, and Mary Rouse for structured approaches to art programming.

the development
of children's art

The child begins to express itself from birth. It begins with certain instinctive desires which it must make known to the external world, a world which is first represented almost exclusively by the mother. Its first cries and gestures are, therefore, a primitive language by means of which the child tries to communicate with others.[*]

five

Expression in art relies on both its creator's unique personal qualities and experiences in life. Since children neither possess identical personalities nor react in wholly similar fashion to experiences, their output in art must of necessity vary. Nevertheless, at certain periods of their development, children pass through various stages of artistic production and adopt recognizable modes of artistic expression. It is highly desirable that a teacher be familiar with the developmental stages of artistic production and with the accompanying conventions of artistic expression. Often the stage of expression that children have reached will give clues not only to the type of subject matter that may interest them, but also to the tools, materials, and activities with which they may cope successfully.

[*] From Herbert Read, *Education Through Art*, rev. ed. (New York: Pantheon, 1958), p. 108.

Ignorance of children's artistic development can result in inappropriate intervention by adults who respond to children's art products and who attempt to guide them in their learning about art. Even a general understanding of the stages of artistic development can assist the teacher in being more confident and competent as an art educator. Familiarity with a child's stage of expression will also help the teacher to determine what kind of stimulation, assistance, and general educational treatment the child requires.

This chapter will first discuss the relation between art and children's personality. Then it will describe the several stages of children's artistic development, and investigate the relationships between children's art products and the works of adult artists.

Art and Personality

An important value of the art process is the way art activity reflects or expresses the personalities of children. Although teachers should not try to be amateur psychologists, they can be aware of some of the connections between art and personality as background for effective teaching.

Personality is usually considered to be a complex of behaviors dealing with temperament, character, and intellect. Most people think of those elements in just that order—am I warm, open, or furtive; introverted or extroverted (temperament); rather than honest or dishonest (character), bright or stupid (intellect). Casson reminds us that "Personality has much the same popular usage as character, perhaps without the moral tone of the latter term. In psychology, it refers to the combinations of emotional tendencies, habits, opinions, attitudes, mental and physical factors that determine an individual's behavior and make him the person he is."[1]

In terms of art, Irving Kaufman notes, "there is little doubt that all art work, whether in the classroom or artist's studio, captures some individual quality of the creator, that the form has locked in its essence some residue of the psychological nature that shaped it." Kaufman also cautions, however, that psychological interpretation of every action or idea that goes into a work of art "may well divert the course of art education into undesirable directions, demanding of both teacher and students an esoteric understanding that requires both very strenuous and specialized training."[2]

Most art teachers, of course, do not make psychological interpreta-

[1] F.R.C. Casson, *Introduction to Psychology* (New York: Arco, 1965).
[2] Irving Kaufman, *Art and Education in Contemporary Culture* (New York: Macmillan, 1966).

tions except in the most general terms, and are content to concern themselves with criticism of the art work of the child, discussing the development of design, drawing skill, and the like. How then should teachers regard the qualitative aspects of the work—that is, the child's personalized manner of handling pictorial elements, the personal style, the individual handling of media, and so on? This kind of judgment, while statistically unrealizable is quite familiar to the teacher. The psychologist Dale Harris comments on the problem: "Such evaluations are not based on accumulations of points, as in a scale; rather they are based on impressions of 'Gestalt' effects produced by the arrangements and interrelationships (often vaguely and very subjectively appraised)."[3] This is how most teachers must operate when they feel the need for appraisal of personality characteristics.

Until complete scientific verification of this kind of interpretation is achieved, several assumptions, representing a body of research, are held by many art educators. The most significant of these are as follows:

1. Interpretation of children's art is most valid when based on a series of a subject's drawings rather than when based on one drawing. A single drawing can be deceptive.
2. Drawings are most useful for psychological analysis when teamed with other available information about the child. Drawings should not be viewed as isolated phenomena.
3. Free drawings are more meaningful psychologically than drawings of directed or assigned topics. "Overteaching" can destroy the spontaneity required of a direct visual statement even though it may advance them in aesthetic terms. Each child adopts a schema or style of drawing which is peculiar to that child and which becomes highly significant psychologically. The teacher should make the extra effort of interpretation.
4. Drawings should be interpreted as wholes rather than in segments. The *gestalt* of a work usually tells us more than any single detail.
5. The use of color in drawings can be significant for studying personality—but only if choice of color has been part of the process. The more children know about color, the greater the possibility for colors in their art work to reflect some inner state of mind.

Research up to now has dealt primarily with drawing and painting, and of these, drawing has received the most attention. For drawing, a secondary set of generalizations may be made; for example, that early scribbles are not necessarily random; that there are analogous patterns

[3] Dale B. Harris, *Children's Drawings as Measures of Intellectual Maturity* (New York: Harcourt Brace Jovanovich, 1963).

between both writing and drawing; that as children develop the patterns change from simple to complex, from generalizations to specifics or formal detail, and so on.

PROBLEMS OF INTERPRETATION

One way to study the problem of personality and art is to match recurring visual factors against an array of personality characteristics. Alschuler and Hattwick used such an approach with 150 schoolchildren ages 4 to 7.[4] In a study of the children's paintings over several weeks, they concentrated not only on color choice but also on shapes, linear patterns, and other evidence of formal structure. In most cases, during the psychological investigation the children worked freely and spontaneously without any teacher intervention. They also collected related data on the behavior of the children from the children's homes and schools. The researchers saw clear relationships between behavior and the colors used and concluded that warm colors (yellow, orange, and red) connoted open, affectionate, outgoing personalities, while children who preferred cool colors (blue, green) tended to be quieter, more controlled, and less emotional. An excessive use of black, brown, and dark purple also indicated some form of emotional stress.

Alschuler and Hattwick's conclusions reflect the general psychological effects of color so familiar to such artists as theatrical designers—who, in a sense, manipulate the emotions of an audience. The question that arises from the study is: Do children take on, at an early stage, some of the psychological and, to some degree, culturally conditioned associations of color and form held by adults? Psychologists have been content to let Alschuler and Hattwick's study stand without verification at later stages of growth. There are, as yet, no comparable studies of the relation of painting and personality in preadolescent, adolescent, or adult behavior.

What are the clues for interpretation when studying the work of anyone—child or teenager? A partial list would be the following:

1. *Persistency:* the incidence and degree of repetition.
2. *Omission:* What the child does not include may be as important as what is present in a picture.
3. *Exaggeration:* the distortion of form, subject matter or content of the picture.
4. *Use of color.*
5. *Personal handling:* of line, rhythm, and movement.

The art of children is therefore a significant source of information for a fuller understanding of the child. Whether or not we can "read" the

[4] Rose Alschuler and La Berta Weiss Hattwick, *Painting and Personality* (Chicago: University of Chicago Press, 1947), Vols. I & II.

work, we are aware that frustrations, conflicts, and dreams are buried somewhere in the end results. We "read" an artwork by utilizing the specific visual information listed above. For example, aggression might be manifested in scribbled, chaotic forms. Depression might be reflected in the child's selection of paper (usually a small size).[5] Some states of mind are, of course, more difficult to define than others. It has not yet been determined, for example, whether excessive use of empty spaces indicates a feeling of inferiority, isolation from a group, or other forms of anxiety.

Regardless of how theorists may disagree with each other, many art educators share the belief that art reflects personality and can be a desirable path for the psychological development of children. Art is productive in that it can also play a fulfilling role in enriching the personality.

The teacher must believe in the unique role of art, in its potential for growth. The new teacher should begin the year with a few diagnostic problems so that some idea can be gained of the range of students' art work. A suggested sequence of problems assigned to the whole class is as follows:

THE TEACHER'S ROLE

> *Exterior:* A picture based on close observation of the environment or of natural forms.
> *Interior:* A picture based on the "hidden landscape" of dreams, fantasies, reveries.
> *Memory:* A picture based on the recollection of a personal experience.
> *Design:* A picture based on a problem of pure design, that is, the organization of line, light and shade, shape, mass and space, color and texture.

Dealing with four problems rather than one is important, because most children will not respond with equal enthusiasm to all situations. Some may resist the observational exercises while others may be fascinated by them. Drawing from observation can provide information about personality as well as can drawing from dreams, if to a lesser degree. (Twenty children all painting from the same still life will still produce twenty different paintings.)

The element of freedom of choice is vital to the kind of unforced effort that allows the child to be an individual. The teacher who develops a standard way of working, one that becomes immediately identifiable as coming from a particular class, is overteaching, imposing his or her goals on the students. This obviously leaves little knowledge to be gained about the individual personalities of the children.

[5] Viktor Lowenfeld, *Creative and Mental Growth*, 3rd ed. (New York: Macmillan, 1957).

Developmental Stages

Scholars have long been interested in the art of children. Read indicates that this interest probably began with John Ruskin's book *The Elements of Drawing*, which appeared in 1857.[6] As Read notes, the "first documents in a long and increasingly complicated process of research" were published in 1885 and 1886. These were articles written by an English schoolteacher, Ebenezer Cooke, for the *Journal of Education*, London.[7] Read then lists at least a dozen writers, from James Sully[8] in the 1890s, who defined some of the stages of development in terms similar to those we use today, to Helga Eng,[9] who in the 1930s made a searching analysis of the modes of expression found in children's drawings.

Psychologists' interest in the nature of children's artistic production and their desire to classify it has grown in the last century. The methods of researchers, however, vary considerably. Kellogg[10] developed her ideas from the study of approximately one million drawings, while Eng and Piaget studied only a few children. It is difficult, therefore, to arrive at a scientifically validated, comprehensive theory regarding the psychology of early drawing—although one can infer general concepts from a consensus of the major theorists. Today there are numerous classifications of children's artistic development, but basically they all agree on at least three main stages that occur before adolescence.

The first stage is one at which children manipulate materials, initially in an exploratory, random fashion. Later in this stage the manipulation becomes increasingly organized until the children give a title to the marks they make. During the next stage, the children develop a series of distinct symbols that stand for objects in their experience. These symbols are eventually related to an environment within the drawing. Finally comes a preadolescent stage, at which the children become critical of their work and express themselves in a more self-conscious manner. The fact that these stages appear in the work of most children in no way detracts from the unique qualities of each child's work. Indeed, within the framework of the recognized stages of expression, the individuality of children stands out more clearly. Stages of artistic development are useful norms that can enlighten the teacher, but should not be considered as the goals for art education. The effects of a positive, supportive educational environment

[6] Herbert Read, *Education Through Art*, rev. ed. (New York: Pantheon, 1958), p. 108.

[7] Read says, "These articles . . . are . . . remarkable as an anticipation of subsequent theories." *Education Through Art*, pp. 169–70. Extracts of the articles may be found in the appendix.

[8] James Sully, *Studies of Childhood*, rev. ed. (New York: Appleton-Century-Crofts, 1903).

[9] Helga Eng, *The Psychology of Children's Drawings*, trans. H. Stafford Hatfield (New York: Harcourt Brace Jovanovich, 1931).

[10] Rhoda Kellogg, *Analyzing Children's Art* (Palo Alto, Ca.: National Press Books, 1969).

can be seen in the children's art work, and their progress can be enriched and accelerated by the efforts of well-prepared and sensitive teachers.

It is difficult to indicate precisely at which grade level or age each stage of artistic development occurs. Lowenfeld attempted to do this, but urged flexibility in relating activities to adults' expectancies. Some writers, probably trying to steer away from too rigid a classification of developmental stages, present so general a list of expectancies that their statements become meaningless. Although this chapter attempts to be as definite as possible in describing the developmental stages and modes of expression, teachers should understand that human behavior, especially in art, is more often unique than it is uniform.

Drawing is a natural and virtually universal activity for children all around the world. From infancy onward, children mark, scribble, and draw with whatever materials are available. As soon as they can grasp a marking instrument of some sort—a crayon, a pencil, or even a lipstick or a piece of charcoal—children make marks and scribbles. Many adults discourage this behavior in their offspring, especially when it occurs on walls, floors, and other surfaces not intended for graphic purposes, and they are relieved when their children outgrow the tendency to engage in scribbling.

These parents, and often teachers, too, do not realize that scribbling can be a worthwhile learning activity for very young children. By scribbling, an infant literally "makes a mark on the world," in one of the earliest examples of personal causation: children come to realize in physical and visual terms that they can affect their environment—that they can make things occur. The infant is fascinated by its ability to make oral noises, babblings, cries, gurgles, and laughs. All of these sounds cease instantly upon completion and leave the child no residue for observation. Graphic marks that the infant makes remain, however, and provide evidence of the marking behavior. The child marks and sees the marks with the dawning awareness that it can alter them and add to them. This is a significant realization for such a tiny person and, as Eisner explains, is also a source of pleasure:

> The rhythmic movement of the arm and wrist, the stimulation of watching lines appear where none existed before are themselves satisfying and self-justifying. They are intrinsic sources of satisfaction.[11]

Through their scribbles, children aged 1 through 3 or 4 develop a repertoire or vocabulary of graphic marks, which they create primarily for the

[11] Elliot Eisner, "What Do Children Learn When They Paint?" *Art Education*, Vol. 31, No. 3 (March 1978), p. 6.

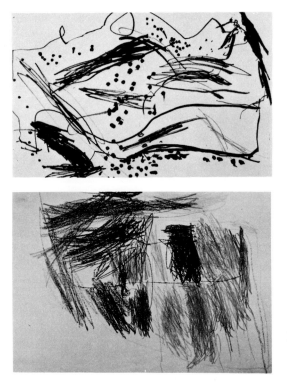

Children who engage in scribbling develop a repertoire of lines and marks that they will use later in more advanced drawings.

An example of organized, controlled scribbles. The child is exploring concepts of color and visual organization.

kinesthetic rewards inherent in the manipulation of lines, colors, and textures.

Scribbled marks are precursors to the visual symbol system of drawing that each child develops independently and uses idiosyncratically. Children who have the necessary opportunities to scribble develop the ability to produce a wide variety of lines, marks, dots, and shapes during the first two or three years of life. This repertoire of graphic marks is utilized later by the child for the invention of visual symbols in the form of drawings. The child who develops a variety of graphic marks during the scribbling years will manifest this visual vocabulary to produce symbolic drawings that increase in richness and sophistication as the child matures. Children who engage minimally in early graphic activities usually exhibit a narrower vocabulary in their drawings and sometimes require considerable encouragement to continue to develop their drawing abilities.

This initial stage of artistic production is referred to here as the manipulative stage and usually lasts through ages four or five in many children. Older children and even adults engage in manipulative behavior such as scribbling, but the older groups produce symbols and possess other advanced graphic skills. The manipulative stage is also known as the

The Development of Children's Art

scribble stage, but whereas the word *scribble* implies a distinct early phase of image development, *manipulative* implies a general stage of initial exploration and experimentation with any new materials or ideas. Scribbling is the beginning of the manipulative stage and, indeed, of all artistic expression, and usually lasts until the children are in kindergarten or first grade.

Periods of producing scribbles last several days, weeks, or months, depending on the child's muscular development, intelligence, general health, and the time devoted to practice. As time goes on, the scribbles are increasingly controlled; they become more purposeful and rhythmic. Eventually many children tend to resolve their marks into large circular patterns, and they learn to vary their lines so that they are sweeping, rippling, delicate, or bold.

The great variety of circular patterns, or "mandalas," according to Rhoda Kellogg's analysis of thousands of children's drawings, appears as a final stage between scribbling and representation. The term *mandala* is usually used to describe a circle divided into quarters by two crossed lines. Carl Jung and Rudolf Arnheim both view the mandala as a universal, culture-free symbol that evolves out of a physical condition (that is, as a basic property of the nervous system) as well as a psychological need (the quest for order on its simplest level). It is interesting that the mandala, like other manifestations of children's early drawing, can appear as readily among Nigerian children as among children in an American nursery school.

As they experiment with making marks and as they gain experience, normal children progress through the manipulative stage. They develop a greater variety of marks, and different marks and scribbles are combined in many ways. Random manipulation becomes more controlled as children invent and repeat patterns and combinations of marks. Lines of all types are used by children in their marking, including vertical, horizontal, diagonal, curved, wavy, zigzag, and looping lines. Some children will attend to drawing intently for periods of thirty minutes or more and will produce a series of a dozen or more drawings within a brief time.

Children aged 2 to 5 begin to learn about qualities of materials. They are fascinated by the materials around them, the multitude of textures, colors, smells, tastes, weights, and other properties. They are interested in art materials because of the intrinsic visual and tactile properties. They can manipulate art materials and can even transform their characteristics. With a brush they can make paint into a line or a shape or various textures. How thrilling for the child to learn that colors change when mixed together—and that the child is the agent of change. Similarly, the child can make a piece of clay into a coil or pinch it into small flat shapes or scratch it with an object to create an interesting texture. Children experience the same exploratory process with other media such as scraps of wood, cardboard boxes, and so on. After perhaps five or six weeks of work with several art media, most children gain sufficient skill to repeat line or shape with paint, clay, boxes, or scraps of materials.

Picture-making in general comes naturally to children at a surprisingly early age. Some children will grasp a crayon and make marks with it before they are fifteen months old. Children's bodily movements are overall movements and result in a broad rhythmic action. When very young children paint, they do so from their fingertips to the ends of their toes. Not until they grow older and gain control of the smaller muscles do their muscular actions in art become localized to the arm and hand.

As well as exhibiting an ability to design in two dimensions, the preschool child often learns to produce three-dimensional designs. By the time some children have reached the age of 3, they have experimented with sand and—sometimes to their parents' horror—mud. They are capable of joining together scraps of wood and cardboard boxes or using building blocks to bring about the semblance of an organized three-dimensional form.

On entering kindergarten at the age of 4 or 5, even those children who have had practice at home with art materials and who have produced pleasing designs tend to lose the ability to design in a natural and charming manner. Sometimes their work loses the qualities of balance and rhythm. Often children at this level show little feeling for space as an element of composition. Variety in the use of line, shape, and color may produce only a state of confusion.

The causes of these conditions are not hard to find. In the first place, the children are passing through a period of adjustment to a strange social setting. Many of them are away from the protection of their parents and their homes for the first time. Unfamiliar faces and situations surround them, and a new and powerful adult in the form of a teacher must sometimes be placated. The confused state of their art is simply a reflection of a slightly upset personality. A second reason for the deterioration of their design at this period is that many are passing through a new phase of artistic development. From the scribble or manipulative stage they are progressing into the stage of symbols. As we mentioned earlier, in the symbolic stage marks can no longer be placed at random on a sheet of paper but rather must be set down with greatly increased precision. In their attempt to achieve greater command of symbols, children tend to lose their natural sense of freedom. Not until they feel more at home in their new environment will qualities of spontaneity and directness return. Regressions in ability occur with each child from time to time and may be observed at any level of development. Absence from school, illness, or temporary emotional upsets are clearly reflected in the design output of any child in the elementary school.

Judith Burton describes three types of conceptual learning accomplished by children in the manipulative stage. When children are able to grasp the outstanding features of lines, shapes, and textures, and when they learn what materials can be organized in many different ways, they have formed *visual concepts. Relational concepts* are formed when children can construct relationships of order and comparison and when they can apply these relationships knowledgeably.

> For example, when organizing a painting, children make careful decisions about the placement of their lines and shapes, whether they are to be close together or far apart, positioned in the middle, top or bottom of the page, or enclosed within each other."[12]

Expressive concepts are formed when children recognize the connections between their actions with art materials, the visual outcomes, and the sensations these actions cause. Children begin to describe lines as "fast" or "wiggly" and shapes as "fat" or "pointy." The fact that children can control and select the qualities of the elements of design and can organize them in ways that express happiness, bounciness, or tiredness represents significant artistic development. It means that children have developed a graphic language with which they can begin to express and communicate their ideas and feelings.

Up to this point children have neither established a theme of expression nor given a title to their work. Eventually, however, children will lift their eyes from their work and say, "It's me," or "It's a window," or even "That's Daddy driving his car." The manipulative process has at last reached the stage at which the product may be given a title. We may assume that, in general, children up to this stage share these characteristics:

1. The work of art is primarily instrumental in nature; in other words, it is an adjunct of another thought process rather than an end in itself. This does not preclude, however, drawing as a self-rewarding act.
2. Early drawings are general rather than specific; that is, they deal with dominant impressions as opposed to differentiation. (Noses may be more significant than the roundness of the head.)
3. Each stage of development is usually accompanied by a period of retrenchment, often regression, during which the schemas are repeated in a seemingly mechanistic way. Eng calls this "automatism."[13]

[12] Judith M. Burton, "Beginnings of Artistic Language," *School Arts*, September 1980, p. 9.
[13] Helga Eng, *The Psychology of Children's Drawings.*

A child two years and nine months old drew the circular shapes among other scribbled lines and marks. He pointed to one of the shapes and said, "This is me. I made me. I made a happy boy."

We cannot overemphasize the importance of this "naming of a scribble" in the life and development of a child. Many parents watch with great anticipation and record the exact age when their child takes the first step; the child's first word is another memorable occasion; but neither is as intellectually significant as the child's invention of a graphic symbol. This ability places the child far ahead of all other mammals and reveals the tremendous mental potential of human beings.

We have no precise knowledge as to how children arrive at this pictorial verbal statement. On the one hand, it has been suggested that the shapes they produce in their controlled manipulations remind them of objects in their environment. On the other hand, the dawning realization that marks or shapes can convey meaning, together with a newly acquired skill to produce them at will, may prompt them to plan symbols. Perhaps the symbol appears as a result of both mental processes, varying in degree according to the personality of its author. Whatever the process may be, the ability to produce symbols constitutes an enormous advance in the child's educational career. The kindergarten child has now developed a new means of expression and communication with associates that is definitive, personal, flexible, and artistically effective.

The first named scribble is usually a circular or generally round shape. The child sees the shape as it appears among random scribbles and marks and learns to repeat the shape at will. The production of symbols demands a relatively high degree of precision because a symbol, unlike

The Development of Children's Art

most of the results of manipulation, is a precise statement of a fact or event in experience.

As we have seen, the manipulative period in artistic expression includes three overlapping but recognizable phases: (1) scribbling, random manipulation, (2) controlled manipulation, and (3) named manipulation. Although it is impossible to assign any stage of expression to any age group, or to predict how long each learner will take to pass from one stage to the next, certain generalizations can be made about rates of development. Much depends on the children's preschool or nursery-school experience with art media and on their muscular development. If the children are provided with materials and encouragement, they may begin random manipulation during their second year and reach the stage of relating symbols to an environment before they enter kindergarten. Other children, who have been given no practice in using art media, may be capable only of random manipulation when they enter kindergarten.

The teacher of the early elementary grades must be prepared, then, to find pupils at many stages of development and to see pupils progress at different rates. In the case of most normal children, however, the teacher might expect satisfactory progress through the three phases of the manipulative period to take about six weeks to two months. At the end of this period most children will be entering, or ready to enter, the symbol stage.

Actually, no one leaves the manipulative stage entirely. Confronted with an unfamiliar substance or a new tool, we are likely to perform some manipulation before we begin to work in earnest. After buying a new pen, for example, we generally scribble a few marks with it before settling down to write a letter. Artists who purchase a new kind of paint will in all likelihood experiment with it before they paint seriously. Indeed, the manipulation of paint has been one criterion of art since the Venetian painters of the Renaissance, and more recently was one of the chief characteristics of Abstract Expressionist painting. Moreover, the painterly surface is one of the hallmarks of all Romantic art, much as the repression of painterly effects is a distinguishing characteristic of classicism. Surface manipulation plays the same role in sculpture. The teacher should realize that manipulation is not a waste of educational time and materials; it is a highly educative process. The control of tools and materials that the children gain through manipulation allows them to enter the symbol phase of expression.

Eventually the normal child makes a mental connection and assigns meaning to a drawn shape, and the shape becomes a primitive symbol. Initially, this shape is used to stand for whatever the child chooses. A shape designated as "Mommy" might appear very similar to another shape that the child calls "house." The early symbol is, in the terms of psycholo-

THE SYMBOL-MAKING STAGE (AGES 6–9, GRADES 1–4)

Once they discover the concept of symbol, children elaborate on the basic circular shape. Above: a three-year-old girl drew "People with eyelashes and a fish." Left: diagrams showing some symbols that represent person, tree, and house. These diagrams, proceeding from simple to complex, were all taken from the work of kindergarten children.

gist Rudolf Arnheim, *undifferentiated*.[14] It serves the child by standing for many objects. A parallel use in the verbal symbol system is demonstrated when a young child who has learned to say "doggie" in relation to the family pet points to a sheep, cow, or other furry four-legged animal and says "doggie." Adults correct the child and introduce the appropriate term. The child then has a more differentiated symbol to apply: "doggie" for one kind of animal, "sheep" for another, and so on.

A similar process develops with children's drawings. The initial primitive symbol can stand for whatever the child chooses it to represent. As the child's symbol-making ability progresses, the child produces more sophisticated graphic symbols. This can be seen especially in children's early representations of the human figure. The primitive circular shape stands for "Mommy." Later, a line and two marks inside the shape are "Mommy" with eyes and mouth. The primitive shape is differentiated further by the addition of two lines that represent legs, two lines for arms, and a scribble that stands for hair.

It is at this point that a fundamental misunderstanding of children's graphic representation occurs. Most adults, including some experts in chil-

[14] Rudolf Arnheim, *Art and Visual Perception* (Berkeley: University of California Press, 1967). See especially the chapter entitled "Growth."

dren's artistic development, view these early drawings of people as heads with arms and legs protruding. They have been termed "head-persons" or "tadpole" figures because the head apparently dominates. The question is asked, "Why do children draw figures this way?" Those who are experienced with children at this level realize that the children understand human anatomy much differently than their drawings would suggest. They know the parts of the body and they know that arms do not protrude from the head. They are aware of shoulders, chest, and stomach. Why, then, do these early drawings appear to represent heads with arms and legs and no torso? Arnheim's explanation is eminently logical and useful:

> Representation never produces a replica of the object but its structural equivalent in a given medium. . . . The young child spontaneously discovers and accepts the fact that a visual object on paper can stand for an enormously different one in nature.[15]

This means that the child's primitive symbol, the circular shape, stands for the entire person, not just the head. This is a person with eyes and a mouth, a person with arms and legs, a person with hair. It does not represent only the head of a person with inappropriately placed appendages. This interpretation eliminates the apparent discrepancy between what children draw and paint and their understanding of the world around them, especially the human figure. We must recognize that children's symbols are not replicas of the world and that the materials used by children will influence their symbol-making.[16]

As children grow and develop from this early symbolic behavior into the symbol-making stage, they produce increasingly differentiated representations. The human figure appears with more details, such as feet, hands, fingers, noses, teeth, and perhaps clothing. It is interesting to note again how children create structural equivalents rather than replicas of their subjects. Hair might be represented by a few lines or by an active scribble. Fingers are often shown as a series of lines protruding from the hands with a "fingerness" quality, but with little regard for exact number.

Eventually a body is drawn with the head attached and with arms and legs in appropriate locations. This more true-to-life figure drawing is usually achieved through a process of experimentation with the medium. Sometimes the space between two long legs becomes the body. Some children add another larger circular shape for the body and draw the head on top. Once the child's representation of the human figure has reached the point where all of the body parts are explicitly included, the symbol can be used in many ways and can be elaborated upon in significant ways. The

---

[15] Arnheim, p. 162.
[16] For a careful verification of this principle, see Claire Golomb, *Young Children's Sculpture and Drawing* (Cambridge, Ma.: Harvard University Press, 1974).

A four-year-old boy's drawing of his family. Note the figure sitting on a chair. Some family members are drawn more than once.

child can draw men and women, boys and girls, and people with different costumes and occupations. Most children also develop symbols for other objects in the world, including animals and birds, houses and other buildings, cars, trucks, and other vehicles, and in general anything that interests the child.

Children do not usually concentrate on fully developing any one category of symbols. Many diverse objects receive their attention simultaneously and are developed in symbolic form at a rate governed by their knowledge of and interest in the objects depicted, together with their skills in portraying these objects. Between kindergarten and second grade, two or more symbols delineating different categories of objects might appear in their output. This development may sometimes occur almost simultaneously with the appearance of the first symbols, although it may occur some days, or even weeks, later. When the development occurs, however, the children have made an advance into a second phase of symbolic expression.

Relating Symbols to an Environment. Whenever pupils produce two or more symbols related in thought within the same composition, they have demonstrated an advance in visual communication, for they have realized that a relationship of objects and events exists in the world. The problems that confront them at this point revolve around a search for a personal means of expressing satisfactory relationships between symbols and their environment. In striving for such a means of expression, normally by the age of 7, they are engaged in the main task of all artists.

The Development of Children's Art

This development can occur only if educational conditions are right. Unfortunately, during these delicate developmental stages problems may develop if adults view children's art as a crude version of adult work rather than an entity unto itself. Children's work up to this point sometimes appears to the eye of the uninitiated as untidy, disorderly, and often unintelligible. To make children's work neater or clearer, adults sometimes use certain "devices" such as outlining objects for them to color, giving them the work of others to copy and trace, and providing kits of circles, squares, and triangles from which they can shape the forms of people, birds, and houses. All these activities, often designed by well-meaning people, can interfere with the developmental processes mentioned earlier.[17] In performing such prepared activities, children begin to rely on the activities and cease to search for adequate modes of personal expression.

Children may begin relating a symbol to its environment by simple means. They may render in paint, clay, or some other suitable medium two similar symbols for human beings, to which they give the title "Me and My Mother." Soon they begin to put together symbols for diverse objects that have a relationship in their thought. Their work may be given such titles as the following:

Our House Has Windows
My Dog Fetching a Stick

[17] For further discussion, see C.D. Gaitskell and M.R. Gaitskell, *Art Education in the Kindergarten* (Peoria, Il.: Bennett, 1952).

Parents and teachers can learn about children's conceptual development through their drawings. This drawing by a five-year-old boy indicates his understanding of birds—how they fly, make nests, and lay eggs.

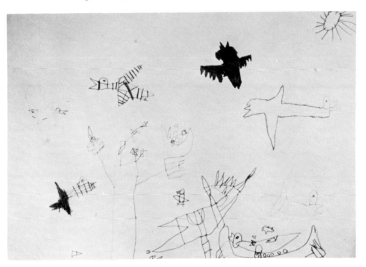

I Am Watching Television
Riding to School with Daddy
Kicking the Ball to Maria
Mommy and I Are Cooking

Frequently children weave into one composition events that occur at different times. In a sense, they may treat the subject of a painting as they do that of a written composition. For example, in a painting entitled *Shopping with Mother*, they may show themselves and their mother driving to a shopping center, making various purchases, and finally unpacking the parcels at home. Here we have, as it were, a story in three paragraphs with all the items placed on one painting surface. Some of these compositions may be arranged aesthetically, while others may contain items that tend to be pictorially unrelated. If not always related aesthetically, however, the items are at least related in thought.

Expression based on vicarious experiences—stories told or read to them, events they have seen on the television or in the movies—may appear in children's art. Brent and Marjorie Wilson have studied the themes of children's drawings and describe the surprisingly broad range of thought and feeling depicted by them. In order to encourage children to draw stories, the Wilsons provided paper divided into frames and made the following request:

> Have you ever drawn pictures to tell stories? Have you ever drawn adventures that you, or heroes, or animals might have? Have you ever drawn adventures that could not happen? Have you ever drawn stories about strange creatures in strange worlds? Have you ever drawn stories of battles or machines, even of plants and insects? Have you drawn stories about sports or vacations or holiday celebrations? Have you drawn stories about everyday things that happen to people? Please draw a story using boxes to show what first happens in your story, what happens next, and how things finally turn out.[18]

In analyzing many children's graphic narratives (story drawings), the Wilsons found about twenty different themes.

> Children continually draw *quests* ranging from space odysseys to mountain climbing; *trials* depicting tests of strength, courage and perseverance; and they show *contests* and *conflicts* in which individuals and groups engage in battles, sports contests, and fights. The process of *survival* is a persistent theme, where children depict evasive actions, but here the characters make little effort to fight back. Little fish are eaten by big fish, and people eat the big fish. Children show *bonding*, love or affection between individuals, animals, plants (and even shoes) in any combination. The process of *creation* is

[18] Brent Wilson and Marjorie Wilson, "Drawing Realities: The Themes of Children's Story Drawings," *School Arts*, May 1979, p. 16.

The Development of Children's Art

shown through all kinds of depictions of constructing and making, such as building a house, arranging a bouquet, or modeling a sculpture. Sometimes creation is followed by *destruction* of plants, animals, and people as well as objects. They are eaten, swallowed or killed. Quite a number of story drawings deal with *death*. Children are no more immune to contemplations of death than any other group.[19]

Other themes included origins, growth, failure, success, freedom, and daily rhythms; the slice-of-life themes of going to school, going on a picnic and returning, or going to the playground. Although children may first depict nothing but the objects they mention in the titles of their output, they soon begin to provide a setting or background for objects, and they produce graphic narratives.

Children's Use of Space. As children's use of symbols broadens and their expression consequently grows in complexity, the task of finding adequate graphic modes to make their meanings clear becomes increasingly difficult. Their strong desire to express themselves with clarity leads them to adopt many curious artistic conventions. The ingenuity exhibited by children in overcoming their lack of technical devices such as linear perspective, and in substituting acceptable and expressive devices of their own is nearly always interesting and, indeed, is sometimes miraculous.

Children are confronted with unavoidable spatial problems in their drawings and other two-dimensional work. At first, objects and symbols produced or placed on paper are not related to each other by the child. There is no up or down, or surface on which people or objects are made to stand. For the child, the sheet of paper (picture space) is a place, and all the objects are together in this place within the edges of the paper. An obvious device utilized by children to make their artistic expression clear is to vary the relative sizes of the symbols used in their work. A symbol having emotional or intellectual importance to the pupils may be made larger than others related to it. "Mother," for example, may be depicted as being larger than a house; or perhaps more frequently, children—who are generally egocentric at this stage—will delineate themselves as towering over their associates. The children will employ this device in connection with all the familiar art materials, but it is especially noticeable in their painting, as illustrated on page 158. When they use paint, they not only give a greater size to the object that appeals most to them, but also may paint it in a favorite color. Color is often chosen for its emotional appeal rather than for its resemblance to a natural object. Soon, of course, the children's observation of the world affects their choice of color—sky becomes blue and grass green. When this happens, at about seven years of age, their paintings tend to lose some of their naiveté.

[19] Wilson and Wilson, p. 15.

"I am skipping." The girl who painted this, at just under the age of seven, has added many details to her symbols. Notice that she makes herself much larger than her playmates.

Even though young children lack the technical ability to express themselves through visual forms, they are extraordinarily inventive in devising relatively complicated modes of composition through which to present their emotional and intellectual reactions to life. Through normal development, however, children become increasingly aware of relationships between the objects that they create. They want to make objects or people "stand up" or stand together, and they seek a place that will serve to support them. The bottom edge of the paper often is chosen to perform this function, and people, houses, and trees are lined up nicely along this initial *baseline*. Before long, other baselines are drawn higher on the paper, usually horizontal to match the bottom edge. Sometimes multiple baselines are drawn and objects are lined up on each of them.

The invention of a baseline on which to place objects is an example of what Arnheim terms "representational concepts," which are "the conception of the form by which the perceived structure of the object can be represented with the properties of a given medium."[20] The baseline is a graphic solution in two dimensions that adequately represents the relationships of objects in the real three-dimensional world, at least for the child at this level of development. It is interesting to note that the baseline, multiple baselines, and virtually all of the other representational concepts found in children's art can also be found in examples of fine adult art in many cultures and times. These representational concepts are used because they work well to convey what is required.

[20] Arnheim, p. 163.

This marvelous drawing includes schematic figures and two definite baselines, plus a sophisticated sun symbol.

At the same stage that children develop baselines, it is not unusual for them to place a strip of color or line at the top of the paper to represent the sky. Between the sky and the ground is air, which is not necessary to represent because it is invisible. Often accompanying the strip of color as sky is a symbol for the sun, which is depicted as a circular shape with radiating lines. Starlike shapes are sometimes added as a further indication of sky. These symbols often persist for many years, and the sky does not appear as a solid mass of color touching the earth until the child has developed greater maturity of expression, probably between the eighth and tenth years.

Another spatial problem that must also be dealt with by young symbol-makers is *overlap*. Because children realize that two objects cannot occupy the same space at the same time, they typically avoid overlapping objects in their drawings. Because paper is flat, unlike the real world, overlapping appears to be inconsistent in drawings. Nevertheless, children often represent houses with people inside or show a baby inside the mother's stomach in apparent *X-ray views*. This convention is a logical one to solve a difficult artistic problem: how to represent the interior of a closed object. It is similar to the theater stage where one side of the set is open to allow the audience to look in.

As children become less egocentric and more interested in how the world functions, the subject matter of their art often becomes more complex. They encounter numerous representational problems such as including many parts of an event or representing a comprehensive view. Children often solve such representational problems by utilizing a *bird's-eye*

Two views of a football game, showing children's treatment of representational concepts. An example of multiple views in a single drawing by an eight-year-old boy and a drawing by a ten-year-old boy utilizing some of the conventions of perspective: converging lines, placement of figures, and diminishing size.

view, a *foldover view,* or *multiple views* in one drawing or painting. For example, in a drawing of a football game, the symbol-making child might draw the field and the yard stripes from a bird's-eye view to depict the space on which the players run. The football players are drawn from a side view, which is much more useful for pictorial purposes than the bird's-eye view and is also easier to represent. Even in drawing a single figure, it is not unusual for children to combine profile and front views to best represent the sitting or moving posture of the person.[21]

In a picture of a hockey game or of people seated around a table, some of the participants may appear to be lying flat or to be standing on their heads. The many children who produce compositions of this type usually do so by moving their picture in a circular fashion as they delineate objects or people. Thus a child may draw a table and place Mother or Father at the head of it. Then, by turning the paper slightly, the child may place Brother in the now upright position. This process continues until all are shown seated at the table. As an alternative to moving the drawing or painting surface, children may walk around the work, drawing as they go. The illustration shows several different ways children will render circle games.

The foldover view is an interesting phenomenon, seen in the drawings and paintings of numerous children. Again, it is a logical solution

---

[21] Judith M. Burton, "Representing Experience from Imagination and Observation," *School Arts,* December 1980.

After they played circle games, first graders were asked to draw their favorite games. Note the treatment of people in a circle. Note also the wide range of expression as each child extracted that part of the experience which had the most meaning. To one child, it was a fashion parade; to another, the game Rabbit Run was meant to be taken literally. Another child, evicted from the games for misbehavior, shows himself sulking on the Jungle Jim, while a fourth child, likewise ostracized, was obviously less disturbed by the situation. The fifth child is interested in the problem of shifting views of people standing on the playground.

developed by inventive children to a difficult representational problem. For example, the child wishes to draw a scene including a street, with sidewalks and buildings on both sides. The child draws the street and sidewalks using a bird's-eye view. The buildings on the one side of the street are drawn up from the sidewalk and the sky is above the buildings. The child then turns the paper around and draws the buildings and sky on the other side of the street up from the sidewalk. The drawing appears to have half of the buildings right-side up and the other half upside down. There is sky at the top and at the bottom of the picture. The logic of this graphic convention can be demonstrated by folding the picture on both sides of the street at the base of the buildings and tipping the buildings up vertically. Now the scene is like a diorama, and a person walking down the street could look left or right and see buildings and sky in proper placement.

Adult artists from various times, places, and cultures have all dealt with these problems associated with spatial representation. Egyptian art is typified by a rigid convention for the human figure with particular representations of the eye, the profile head, hair, and so on. Chinese artists developed conventional ways to represent mountains rising from the mist, bamboo plants, and the human figure. Renaissance artists developed the conventions of linear perspective, which is one way artists deal systematically with the problems of representing the three-dimensional world on a two-dimensional surface. Artists of every era learn the artistic conventions of their culture and use them, reject them, or develop new solutions to problems that in turn become artistic conventions. Artists learn the available conventions and apply them in unique and expressive ways in their own work. This process of learning conventions, applying them, and innovating with them is useful also for children, especially as they approach adolescence and their critical awareness becomes more acute.

The Schema and the Stereotype. Symbol-making children develop ways of drawing objects or figures so that they become graphic equivalents of what they represent. A *schema* is a drawing (or painting, or clay form) developed by a child that has a degree of resemblance to an actual object. The arms of a man, for example, are drawn differently from the branches of a tree. Children use these simple drawings consistently again and again to designate the same objects.[22] To create a schema, "the child not only has to fashion a graphic equivalent of objects in the world, but also has to design each solution so as to differentiate the marks from others that she makes."[23]

[22] Betty Lark-Horovitz, Hilda P. Lewis, and Mark Luca, *Understanding Children's Art for Better Teaching* (Columbus, Ohio: Charles E. Merrill, 1967), p. 7.
[23] Howard Gardner, *Artful Scribbles: The Significance of Children's Drawings* (New York: Basic Books, 1980), p. 67.

Children learn to render the petals of a flower, the rays of the sun, the parts of people and animals in ways that communicate. Children who develop their own schemata naturally understand them and are able to use them in flexible ways. A child who has developed a schema for the figure of a girl, for example, is able to draw girls with different clothing or different hair or different poses. The basic schema for *girl* remains fairly uniform, but the child can accomplish reasonable variations. Sometimes children will alter their schema by leaving parts out or by exaggerating certain parts that are especially significant. Drawings are sometimes left unfinished or some parts are obviously unattended to by the child. These variations should serve to remind adults that children often are more interested in the process of drawing or painting than they are in the result of their efforts as a work of art. The child who draws a picture of his interaction with the neighborhood bully is emotionally more involved with the situation than with the outcome of the drawing as a finished piece. In the child's depiction of the story, it matters little if the fence is not completed—the child knows it is there. The legs that are running and the arm that is throwing are the essential and emotionally significant parts that receive the child's careful attention. Burton reminds us that children's art does not so much make visual statements as make experience visible.[24] The distinction is an important one for understanding children's art.

Children who continue to make art as they progress through the typical symbol-making ages of seven, eight, and nine usually develop a number of schemata that change and gain in sophistication and detail as the children's understanding progresses. Some children focus almost exclusively on the human figure; others draw mostly horses or cars or airplanes. Many develop in several directions and are able to draw many objects. The Wilsons view these graphic specialties as "programs."[25] Because of the time and effort required to develop an advanced schema or program, most children (and adults) are able to draw some objects much better than others. It depends on what each person has developed during the schematic years.

Left to their own devices, children in the primary grades are self-accepting. True primitives, they approach art as though it were their own private discovery, working freely and unself-consciously, despite the profusion of visual influences around them. Allowing children in this stage to use a coloring book opens the door to self-doubt, because they are dramatically confronted with the gap between an adult's image and their own. In attempting to draw a clown at a later time, they may recall a "grown-up" clown they had once colored, and either try unsuccessfully to emulate it or suddenly become dissatisfied with their own rendering.

[24] Judith M. Burton, "Visual Events," *School Arts*, November 1980, p. 63.
[25] Brent Wilson and Marjorie Wilson, "An Iconoclastic View of the Imagery Sources in the Drawings of Young People," *Art Education*, Vol. 30, No. 1 (January 1977).

Artistic *stereotypes* are images that children repeat from another source without real understanding. Because children do not understand the stereotypes, they can only repeat them inflexibly, and often incorrectly or inappropriately. A pervasive example is the looped V shape that represents birds in flight. This was developed by artists to represent birds in the distance where the details of body, tail, head, and feet are not distinguishable. Watercolor artists who paint coastal scenes with seagulls often make this shorthand image with expressive brushlines but usually vary the position of the wings so that the wings do not appear to flap in unison. Artists also often make visual reference to the birds' bodies, and then paint the birds in the foreground in greater detail.

All of these variations of the looped V shape and the concurrent understandings are not available to children who pick up the stereotype for flying birds and apply it inappropriately. Children demonstrate their lack of understanding of the meaning and origin of the stereotype in drawings where the looped V is upside down and the birds are apparently flapping their wings upward instead of downward. Sometimes the children's marks look more like the letter *M*.

Many stereotypes are available to children through television, advertising, and cartoon strips in newspapers and comic books. Others are passed on from child to child. There are two problems with children's use of stereotypes. First, children cannot utilize stereotypes for the central purposes of their artistic development because the stereotypes are not their own schemata and they cannot use them to communicate. Second, reliance on copying stereotypes robs children of the confidence required to develop their own schemata. The slick cartoon images created by adult artists often induce young children to believe that their own drawings do not compare favorably and therefore become discouraged with their own production.

The Wilsons have pointed out that children and adults learn to make graphic images by copying to some degree the graphic images already in their environment.[26] The pervasiveness of adult graphic images (potential stereotypes) in most children's environment suggests that there is no sure way to protect children from these influences if, indeed, protection is warranted. Children will continue to be influenced by Snoopy, smile buttons, Star Wars characters and the like, regardless of what adults do or say. Yet several observations regarding stereotypes and copying are useful for parents and teachers.

1. Graphic images become stereotypes for children only when they are unable to utilize them with flexibility and understanding. A teacher might lead a child away from the use of stereotypes by

[26] Wilson and Wilson, "An Iconoclastic View."

suggesting that the child draw a story using the stereotype as a character. The child might learn enough about the graphic image to apply it flexibly, in which case it is no longer a stereotype; or the child might discover that the stereotype has no useful place in the drawing repertoire and abandon it.

2. When copying tends to stultify or intimidate the individual, it is harmful. In dealing with children who are involved in copying, the teacher can help them identify what they might learn from their efforts and how they might apply this learning in their own original art work.

3. Because it is inevitable that children will be exposed to adult graphic images, many of which may be of low artistic quality, it makes good sense for teachers to expose children to high-quality art works. Slides, reproductions, films, and books of great art are readily available. Just as in literature, music, or mathematics, children should become aware of the best that the world has to offer in art.

Children are much less likely to rely on stereotypes when they are engaged in a regular program of art. Children who develop their own artistic skills are much too interested in their own work to be sidetracked into copying images that are of no expressive value to them.

THE PREADOLESCENT STAGE (AGES 10–13, GRADES 5–8)

The preadolescent stage includes children from approximately the fourth to the seventh grades. Again, it is well to acknowledge the wide variation in rates of maturity among children. This range can be seen quite obviously in sixth and seventh grade classrooms, where girls are usually more physically mature than boys. Preadolescent children's approach to expression in art is different from that of young children in the symbol-making stage. Although preadolescent children are still naturally inquisitive and creative, they have learned to be more cautious. Younger children work in art with abandon; they "try anything once"—often regardless of the consequences. To them, practically every experience in art is a new one, and they enjoy working on unfamiliar ground. Preadolescents, however, are much more socially aware and are extremely sensitive to peer opinion.

The art teacher in the middle grades faces a special problem, for the new social awareness of the fourth and fifth graders tends to make them dissatisfied with their work. Their critical sense has developed far in advance of their ability to draw and paint in ways that are satisfactory to them. As a result, verbal and written communication, which they have learned to control, have supplanted the excitement of the language of art. Furthermore, the potency of the visual symbol leads them to unrealistic expectations. They accept the fact that they cannot read or write or speak on an adult level, but the shock of seeing their immaturity in visual terms is often difficult to accept. One of the teacher's important tasks at this time is to find ways to lead children toward self-acceptance. In extreme cases, it might even be wise to concentrate more on crafts activities than on the more expressive areas of drawing and painting.

The preadolescent's work tends to be relatively complete in statement. Central objects are depicted with increasing reality, so that details of features and clothing appear. Backgrounds are given attention, sometimes to such an extent that they become confused with the main objects in the composition. Light and shade and textural effects are employed not so much for aesthetic ends as to give the work great authenticity or reality. In the same way, color, gradually refined through the use of tints and shades, tends to approximate the actual hues of the objects depicted. Instead of presenting a flat appearance, the drawing and painting of older children often can indicate depth. This effect is achieved by overlapping objects, tone, color, and linear perspective—devices that are taught to the children as their need and readiness becomes apparent.

In later childhood, young people often band together in groups of the same sex. In Western culture, this is the only period in life when the sexes willingly and consciously draw apart, and the division immediately precedes the marked commingling of the sexes during adolescence. Expression in art is affected by activities and interests arising from the group and peculiar to the sex of the child. Certain tendencies in subject preferences are apparent. Some boys gravitate toward machines and speed symbols,

Machines and space flight are interesting to the eleven-year-old boy who made this drawing.

166

acting out masculine roles in their drawings. Some girls become quite interested in drawing animals. Children should be encouraged to avoid sexual stereotyping as well as any other attitude that inhibits variety of expression. There is no reason why both boys and girls cannot draw subjects that have a wide appeal, such as sports events or domestic scenes.

The cultural backgrounds of children account for variations in sex differences from one geographical region to another. A study of East Indian children found that girls drew work tools more frequently than did boys, who preferred spirits and flowers.[27] Differences in choice of subject matter also hold true when American children select topics and titles from vicarious experiences (A Hero's Welcome, Lost in Death Valley, The Last Desperado) or real-life situations (Camping Out, My First Party Dress, Open House for the PTA). No one can deny the catholic taste of the preadolescent.

The age range from 10 to 12 or 13 is most crucial from the standpoint of art education. It is during these years that most children cease to be significantly involved in making art. Indeed, when asked to make a drawing, the majority of adults will refer back to images that they made before reaching the teen years. Drawings of human figures made by adults are very often difficult to distinguish from the figure drawings of preadolescent children. This is because when individuals give up drawing, their development is virtually arrested at that level. Gardner points out that children's critical skills develop later than their capacities to act as artists, art historians, or audience members.[28] With the development of critical skills at about age 11, children become critically aware of the qualities of their own art products. If their own drawings and paintings appear to them more closely related to childhood than to the approaching adolescent years, they become self-conscious and dissatisfied with their art work and tend to produce less or quit altogether. Nine- or ten-year-old children's dissatisfaction with their own best efforts to produce art marks the beginning of a representational stage when children desire to develop technical competencies and expand their repertoire of representational skills.[29]

Dudek also describes qualitative changes in children's mental development around age 9 or 10 and attributes changes in art production to this maturation. "The child becomes interested in testing his greater cognitive ability by attempting to use a more realistic and disciplined approach."[30] Dudek also agrees with Barron that the spontaneity and lack of convention in earlier child art is not necessarily evidence of creativity. Barron states

[27] Cora Dubois, *The People of Alor* (Cambridge, Ma.: Harvard University Press, 1960).
[28] Howard Gardner, *The Arts and Human Development* (New York: Wiley, 1973).
[29] Harris, *Children's Drawings as Measures of Intellectual Maturity.*
[30] Stephanie Z. Dudek, "Teachers Stifle Children's Creativity/A Change Too Easily Made," *Learning,* August–September 1976, p. 102.

that "a certain amount of maturation of the talent, and discipline in its exercise, must precede its full expression. Since this also *takes time*, the complex creative act can be expected to occur only rarely in childhood, or before maturation has taken place."[31]

The solution to the problem of decline in art production prior to the teen years seems relatively clear. The preadolescent years are critical in the artistic development of children. They must make enough progress during this period so that, when they become capable of self-criticism, they will not find their own work too wanting. If children are to continue artistic production during adulthood, they must work with diligence, mastering the technical and expressive conventions of adult art that provide a bridge between the art worlds of the child and the adult.[32] The Wilsons have pointed out in their important article on imagery sources[33] that children do learn from the multitude of graphic images that are part of our environment and that isolation from adult influence is virtually impossible. They suggest that, since children already undergo constant influence, art educators might upgrade the level of influence by providing them with examples of the best imagery that our culture has to offer.

The role of the art teacher also changes during students' preadolescent years. Instruction in art principles and techniques gains in priority as children seek competency. Children want to know how to handle overlap, size, and placement relationships, and convergence of lines for representing space and depth in their drawings and paintings. They are receptive to instruction in shading and proportion in drawing. They are interested in the technical aspects of painting, color mixing, composition, and so on. They are ready to learn about what artists of the past have created and what contemporary artists are doing and why.

These years can be tremendously rich and exciting for children and for their teachers as the world of art unfolds before them. The direction of the child's gaze is toward the teen and adult years, and it is there that the content of art as a subject lies. It is the responsibility of art education to foster the transition from enthusiastic and involved child artists to enthusiastic and involved adults who value art and for whom art is a meaningful and vital part of life.

Why Children Make Art

The virtually universal participation of children in marking, scribbling, and graphic symbol-making strongly suggests that basic reasons exist for

---

[31] Frank Barron, "Creativity in Children," in *Child Art: The Beginnings of Self-Affirmation,* ed. Hilda Lewis (Berkeley: Diablo Press, 1966), p. 17.

[32] Gardner, *The Arts and Human Development,* p. 257.

[33] Wilson and Wilson, "An Iconoclastic View."

these behaviors. Children must gain satisfaction from these activities or they would not engage in them spontaneously. On this topic, however, writers and educators must speculate, because they are unable either to communicate sufficiently well with young children or to recall their own early art experiences. Nevertheless, through lengthy and careful observation of children and through the application of useful psychological theory, it is possible to speculate with some confidence.

For children, art is a means to engage all of their senses for learning and expression. Creating art heightens children's sensitivity to the physical world and fosters a more perceptive appreciation of the environment. Art helps children order their sense impressions and provides a means for them to express imagination and feelings. In his argument for education through art, Read asserts that art is "the only human activity that can establish a universal order in all we do and make, in thought and imagination."[34]

The effects of art activity on children's self-concept and general personality development can be very beneficial. Art can provide a means for children to develop their inherent creative abilities and, in the process, to integrate other personality dimensions, such as the emotional, social, and aesthetic. Children's art is often seen as instrumental in fostering and preserving each individual's identity, uniqueness, self-esteem, and accomplishment.[35]

In addition, some art educators claim that art activity contributes to cognitive development. Nearly fifty years ago Dewey stated:

> To think effectively in terms of relations of qualities is as severe a demand upon thought as to think in terms of symbols, verbal and mathematical. Indeed, since words are easily manipulated in mechanical ways, the production of a work of genuine art probably demands more intelligence than does most of the so-called thinking that goes on among those who pride themselves on being "intellectuals."[36]

Eisner has outlined no fewer than nine things, from symbol-formation and symbolic play to the expressive function of visual forms, that children can learn through the act of painting.[37] Children's early graphic behavior—the marking, scribbling, and manipulation of materials—appears to be intrinsically pleasurable. As they move into the symbol-making phase, these psychomotor and kinesthetic rewards are reinforced

[34] Herbert Read, "Art as a Unifying Principle in Education," in *Child Art: The Beginnings of Self-Affirmation,* ed. Hilda Lewis (Berkeley: Diablo Press, 1966).

[35] Viktor Lowenfeld and W. Lambert Brittain, *Creative and Mental Growth,* 6th ed. (New York: Macmillan, 1975).

[36] John Dewey, *Art as Experience* (New York: G.P. Putnam's Sons, 1938), p. 46.

[37] Eisner, "What Do Children Learn When They Paint?"

by children's newly developed ability to conceive and convey meanings. This power to use the images that they create as symbols for the world allows children to construct their own knowable world and to convey what they know to others. Eisner writes:

> Children learn that the images and symbols they create can be used to transport them into a fantasy world, that they can create an imaginary world through the use of their own images and through them become a part of other situations in which they can play other roles.
>
> For children the taking of new roles through imagination is an important source of learning. It allows them to practice in the context of play what they cannot actually do in the "real world." It affords them opportunities to empathetically participate in the life of another.[38]

As we watch children draw or paint we are often struck by their concentration and involvement in what they are doing. Children often talk as they draw, and it is only through close observation that an adult can gain an understanding of what has been created by a particular child. Through discussion with the child artist, a four-year-old boy, his mother learned that his drawing was a picture of the family. The figure on the right with lots of dark hair is the mother; the short figure is the father; next is the child who drew the picture. The small figure next to the boy is his baby

[38] Eisner, p. 7.

The four-year-old boy who drew this family group was able to identify and describe the figures.

The Development of Children's Art

sister. When asked by his mother where his brother (a sibling rival) was, the child quickly made the scribble on the left and said, "Here he is, he is hiding behind a bush." In this drawing we see several things:

1. The child is developing symbols for the human figure and can make basic differentiations to represent specific individuals.
2. The child is able not only to represent figures, but also to consider family relationships in his drawing.
3. The emotions of the child are important and obvious in his drawing. Mother is most important in his life and is made prominent in the drawing. His own figure is large. The brother with whom he feels competitive is conveniently left out of the picture. Later he is represented only in a hurried scribble.
4. The child has been able to relate several symbols together in the picture space. At this point no environment is indicated.

One of the fascinating and charming aspects of children's art is that it can often serve as a window into the minds and emotions of the children. The series of drawings on page 172 was done spontaneously by a seven-year-old girl as a response to her experience at school. The first drawing shows the girl admiring a classmate who has pretty curls and is neat and prim. The child artist is an active girl, her hair is stringy, and she is disheveled. Her classmates note these characteristics and comment unfavorably. This motivates the girl to ask her mother to give her a permanent wave. She has the permanent and puts ribbons in her neat hair. After a few hours at school, running and playing, her hair is stringy and the ribbons are untied. The pretty classmate is as neat as ever.

This art product reveals several things.

1. The child is very aware of peer social relationships at school, and she is concerned about her appearance.
2. She is able to reconstruct the series of events in her drawings and to identify her feelings.
3. She is able to tell her story with graphic images in a direct and effective way.

The therapeutic value of making these drawings is not possible to determine. The child was motivated to make them, however, and she did sort out the experience through her art.

In similar ways, children deal with many of life's concerns, joys, and trials through their art products. A child is afraid of fire and paints a picture of someone escaping from a burning building. A child is fascinated with football, invents team players, and draws them in action. The favorite

This spontaneous narrative of a personal experience by a seven-year-old girl shows her awareness of social relationships and her ability to tell a story.

team wins. A child hears a fairy tale and draws a picture illustrating the story. A child visits a grandparent and makes a painting of the experience. The list of possible subjects for child art is as endless as the list of life experiences.

The Wilsons emphasize the narrative dimension of children's drawings. Drawings are produced, they believe, to tell a story, to relate an event, or to tell what some object is like.

> We think that visual narratives are told as part of the process of making personal symbolic models of the world—actually not just *the world*, but *worlds*. . . . To understand himself or herself or his or her environment, the child makes drawings that serve as models for how things might be. Thus the drawings provide a means for constructing, testing, and prophesizing what can be. . . . In their fantasy worlds, children are able to create all the characters, all the settings, and all the rules. Thus they are able to experiment at will in an open, stress-free situation; reliving and rehearsing birth, growth, trials, what is right and what is wrong; the consequences of this and that action and what will happen now and what will happen next.[39]

[39] Brent Wilson and Marjorie Wilson, "Children's Story Drawings: Reinventing Worlds," *School Arts*, April 1979, p. 8.

The Development of Children's Art

The narrative function of art is apparent in this sequence from a major effort by a fourteen-year-old boy. He tells of his traditionally unsuccessful high-school football team triumphing over the opposition. This is an example of world-making through art: characters, story, dialog, action, and composition were all developed by the youngster.

These three drawings by a boy at the ages of nine, twelve, and fifteen document his progress in representing action in the human figure. In the absence of appropriate instruction and encouragement, many young people cease to draw by the age of twelve.

The Development of Children's Art

Through their art, children can create worlds and can control actions and outcomes as they investigate in a safe way concepts, relationships, understandings, and models of behavior.

Children can create fantasy, narrative, and "other worlds" through plays, songs, and stories as well as through the visual arts, although drawing seems to be a very significant medium for such accomplishments. Beyond these functions of art in the lives of children, there are several other aspects of learning that are unique to the visual arts. As children create visual representations, they are required to combine the elements of design into structures with meaning and then to judge the adequacy and quality of their own work. Then they must proceed on the basis of their own judgments. This type of mental activity can be quite stimulating and often results in creative behavior, which is also satisfying. The flexibility of art activity, where even the purpose of the process can change on the basis of the individual's judgment, is very different from other areas of learning that rely on the achievement of stated criteria and the memorizing and recitation of correct answers.[40]

As children enter the preadolescent stage, their interest in art moves from using it as an exclusive vehicle for personal expression to creating satisfying visual forms. Children become interested in the visual properties of their works—composition, the elements of design—and in the technical aspects of materials and processes. There are very few activities available to people of any age that allow the personal control from initiation to completion that is typical of art activity. Those children who maintain their interest in art and who receive appropriate instruction to develop artistic competencies experience great satisfaction in the visual qualities of their art. They also enjoy the self-confidence that attends the achievement of competency in any worthwhile field of human endeavor.

Artists and Children's Art

The art of the child, in its spontaneity, directness, and relevance to the life of its creator, is often discussed in relation to the works of mature artists. Examples of similarities are many. Children's treatment of sky areas, for example, has its counterpart in some Oriental paintings. The flat painting of children finds its sophisticated echo in contemporary Hard Edge paintings. Enlargement of important figures in painting and sculpture has been used expressively by many great artists; by Duccio, for example, in his *Maestà*, painted for the cathedral of Siena. The X-ray type of picture so common in the work of young children is found frequently in professional

---

[40] Eisner, "What Do Children Learn When They Paint?"

The *Maestà* altarpiece by Duccio (c. 1255–1319) illustrates the enlargement of the important figures. Compare the use of this convention here with that found in the child's painting on page 158. (Alinari. Museum of the Duomo, Siena.)

work, not only in painting but also in theater stage-sets. As a means of depicting movement, space, and time, Marcel Duchamp, in his well-known *Nude Descending a Staircase*, produced a work of art reminiscent of the space-time compositions developed intuitively by children. Is the art of children, then, to be considered in the same way as the work of mature artists? In what ways are child artists similar to adult artists, and in what ways are they different?

The relationship between the artistic style of the child and that of the adult artist may be an unplanned one, as in the case of primitives such as Grandma Moses, Horace Pippin, and Henri Rousseau, whose works contain distinctively childlike qualities. The fact that primitive painters and children both lack professional training and enjoy an independence from the mainstream of art accounts for such common pictorial traits as crude perspective, hard edges, flat patterning, preoccupation with detail, and arbitrary use of space.

There are also some professional painters who consciously use one characteristic or another of children's art as a determining factor in their own work. The potency of color and boldness of line of the group of

The Development of Children's Art

German artists known as Die Brücke (The Bridge) was in part the result of an awareness of these characteristics in children's painting. Others such as Paul Klee saw mystical "interiors"—values that were quite different from the more painterly qualities prized by Die Brücke. Klee's pursuit of what is seen by the innocent eye, uncorrupted by a technological society, left us a body of work noted for its remarkable range—humorous, delicate, and mystical—drawing its strength from the shapes and symbols of the four- to six-year-old child. If Klee entices us into a delicate world of quiet fantasy, then Jean Dubuffet jars us with raw, brutal forms reminiscent of graffiti left by children on sidewalks and walls. Dubuffet establishes an "anti-art" attitude by utilizing the crude, tactile aspects of children's art, thus reflecting the child's independence from the traditions of aesthetic value and technique.

Children's art is typified by great pleasure and intense involvement in the making. Young children are willing to disregard what others are doing and to pursue their own ideas to conclusion. Children seem to have an intuitive sense of design or composition even before they are able to use symbols fluently. As children make art they explore, take risks, and solve problems of representation and communication. They are often flexible and open to suggestion as visual accidents occur; dribbles of paint, unintended marks, bleeding, and commingling coloring suggest new forms and expressions. All of these characteristics also describe various adult artists.

There are also important differences, however, between the art of children and the art of the professional artist. Dudek reminds us that much of the spontaneity in children's art is due to lack of convention. Small children paint the sky yellow and the tree red because they have not yet developed the conventions of local color, of making objects approximate their appearance, or of controlling the mixing of hues, values, and intensities. The Fauve artists, who were known for their "wild" use of color, disregarded the conventions of local color with which they were quite familiar, and did so for their own expressive purposes. Although Picasso displayed attributes in his work similar to children's artistic production, we see at work "a host of factors that separate him from the child: his perfected technical facility, his ability to render almost instantly the exact image he desires, the capacity to plan ahead for periods of time and to follow through a project over a great period of time."[41] Picasso also had a tremendous knowledge of the works of other artists and how they were made, and he was very much aware of the techniques, norms, and conventions of art and of the expressive consequences in his own work when he chose to violate them. Beyond this technical and expressive dimension of art, there is also the development of the adult artist's personality that is

[41] Gardner, *Artful Scribbles*, p. 268.

unavailable to the child because of a lack of experience. Life's events, crises, responsibilities, hardships, and satisfactions are the stuff out of which art is made, and it is the person with the most developed feeling for life who is most likely to create art that will speak with significance.

Given these differences, we can celebrate the art of children as well as the art of adults. We can be charmed and delighted by the work of children and we can see in their art production the crucial seeds of the greatest artistic achievements. The value of children's art varies according to the point of view of the observer. The educator may view it as one route to the development of personality; the psychologist as a key to understanding behavior; and the artist may see it as the child's most direct confrontation with the inner world of sensation and feeling. But educator, psychologist, and artist all view children's art as a "reflection of the unconscious and as a non-verbal and pre-verbal mode of expression providing a direct access to the unconscious and pre-conscious processes."[42]

[42] Elliot Eisner, *A Comparison of the Developmental Drawing Character of Culturally Advantaged and Culturally Disadvantaged Children,* Project No. 3086 (Washington, D.C.: U.S. Office of Education, September 1967), p. 9.

Activities for the Reader

1. Collect from a kindergarten and a first grade class a series of drawings and paintings that illustrate the three phases of the manipulative stage.
2. Collect some drawings or paintings by a single child to illustrate the development of a symbol such as that for "person," "toy," or "animal."
3. Collect from several children in the first to third grades a series of drawings and paintings that illustrate developments in symbolic expression.
4. Collect from pupils enrolled in the third to sixth grades drawings and paintings that illustrate some of the major developments in the preadolescent stage.
5. Make one collection of drawings and paintings that is representative of artistic development from kindergarten to the end of sixth grade.
6. Collect work in three-dimensional materials, such as clay or paper, from the pupils in situations identical with, and for purposes similar to, those mentioned in the five activities above.
7. Make a collection of children's work to illustrate the normal development in design from kindergarten to the end of sixth grade.

Suggested Readings

Burton, Judith M. A series of articles on children's artistic development in *School Arts,* September, October, November, December 1980, January 1981. This series of five articles with illustrations is an excellent overview of children's artistic development.

Eisner, Elliot. "What Do Children Learn When They Paint?" *Art Education,* Vol. 31, No. 3 (March 1978). An analysis of types of learning that children can experience as they engage in making art products.
Gardner, Howard. *Artful Scribbles: The Significance of*

Children's Drawings. New York: Basic Books, 1980. An insightful analysis of the development of the author's own children in their art-making, and of the significance of child art.

————. *The Arts and Human Development: A Psychological Study of the Artistic Process*. New York: Wiley, 1973. A broad view of children's development in all the arts, with psychological theory as a basis for explanation.

Golomb, Claire. *Young Children's Sculpture and Drawing: A Study in Representational Development*. Cambridge, Ma.: Harvard University Press, 1974. The report of a study comparing children's use of artistic symbols, and the effects of two media on their art products.

Harris, Dale B. *Children's Drawings as Measures of Intellectual Maturity*. New York: Harcourt Brace Jovanovich, 1963. A detailed review of research and theory in children's artistic development precedes a discussion and expansion of the Goodenough Drawing Test.

Lark-Horovitz, Betty, Hilda Present Lewis, and Mark Luca. *Understanding Children's Art for Better Teaching*. Columbus, Ohio: Charles Merrill, 1967. Chapters 1, 3, 4, 5. This book is unique in its record of research studies that relate to major issues.

Lowenfeld, Viktor, and W. Lambert Brittain. *Creative and Mental Growth*, 6th ed. New York: Macmillan, 1975. An update of what still remains a classic work in art education.

MacGregor, Ronald M. *Art Plus*. New York: McGraw-Hill, 1977. Chapter 1, "Perceiving: Making Sense Out of What We See."

Wilson, Brent, and Marjorie Wilson. A series of articles on children's drawings in *School Arts*, April, May, June 1979. The series, with illustrations, provides practical teaching applications of the authors' theories of children's development in drawing.

PART TWO

TEACHING:

THE ART PROGRAM

IN ACTION

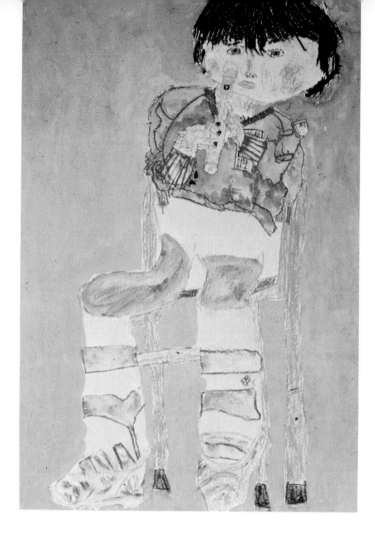

drawing

and painting

Duplicating the outward appearance of a thing as exactly as possible is no longer a job for the artist—if it ever was. The camera can do this well enough if such a record is required. The artist must occupy himself with something far more important than mere "recording"—he must interpret, penetrate, reveal—say something meaningful. He must show the spectator more than "what is there."*

six

Drawing and painting are probably the most pervasive of all art activities engaged in by children. Through these two modes of art production children can very quickly and directly participate in the exploration of media, the creation of symbols, the development of narrative themes, and the solving of visual problems using the elements and principles of design. The emphasis in contemporary art education is on these expressive aspects of art, with support and instruction by the teacher appropriate for the levels of development of the children and suited to their individual needs.

*From Robert C. Niece, *Art: An Approach* (Dubuque, Iowa: Wm. C. Brown Co., 1963), p. 69.

Children produce drawings and paintings that say something about their reactions to experience or that heighten their abilities to observe. Indeed, many art educators are inclined to believe that these activities, often called picture-making, are the most important work in the entire art program. Certainly, when taught effectively, drawing and painting activities are universally enjoyed and provide a very flexible and practical means of expression for the young at all stages of artistic development.

This chapter will describe the tools and materials for drawing and painting and comment on their use at various developmental levels. We will also refer to certain problems related to the teaching of drawing and painting, such as working with color; dealing with space; producing figure, landscape, portrait, and still-life compositions; using mixed media; and, finally, improving pictorial composition.

The Manipulative Stage

The chief purposes in encouraging very young children to draw and paint are, first, to allow them to become familiar with the materials associated with picture-making, and second, to help them develop sufficient skill so that they can produce symbols easily when they reach the symbol stage. As we saw in Chapter 5 on children's artistic development, children draw and paint for several reasons, and these reasons change as children grow and mature. From the manipulation of materials to the creation of symbols to an emerging interest in aesthetic qualities and the elements and principles of design, children make and respond to art in dynamic ways. Very young children require little or no external motivation to engage in art activities, but as they grow older, more aware of their capacities, and more critical of their abilities, children can benefit increasingly from the guidance and support of a knowledgeable and sensitive art teacher. Numerous suggestions are provided in this chapter to help teachers foster artistic growth in their students.

One approach is exemplified in the work of Brent and Marjorie Wilson and their emphasis on narrative drawing, graphic storytelling, and the creation of new and exciting worlds by children.[1] The Wilsons' research has centered on the ways children learn to draw from the graphic models of other children, of adults, and of the media, and on the way children use their drawings to tell stories, stories that motivate them to depict people and action and events.

[1] Brent Wilson and Marjorie Wilson, "Children's Story Drawings: Reinventing Worlds," *School Arts*, April 1979, p. 8.

Children like to tell as well as listen to stories. Narrative art encourages both visual and ideational fluency. One picture becomes a beginning for an entire scenario rather than an end in itself, as one image and event set the stage for succeeding ones.

This five-frame story drawing collected by the Wilsons is an example of the influence of stories and images derived from the entertainment media. In response to a request to tell a story with drawings within the frame format, this sixth grader chose to represent a simple vignette based on a television commercial for a fast-food chain. Quite simply, the story deals with the typical advertising theme of initial deprivation and ultimate acquisition—the character in the story is suffering a "Big Mac attack." He breaks through the wall of the restaurant in his haste to obtain and eventually bite into the desired hamburger sandwich. Television has also taught the young boy the sophisticated devices of the closeup—witness the lusciously drippy, well-packed sandwich in the second frame—and the long shot—in the next frame—as well as the ability to zoom in and out of the action.

The Wilsons have developed several methods for encouraging children to develop graphic skills. These skills are viewed as a graphic vocabulary and grammar, and they assist the child in producing drawings that are satisfying and meaningful. Following are several of the exercises:

1. Ask children to draw as many versions of a single object as possible. Examples might be different types of people, shoes, cars, trees, insects, and so on.

2. Ask children to think of a person, such as a dancer, acrobat, sports player, or superhero, who goes through lots of motions. On a long strip of paper, show the figure going through its action as it moves from side to side across the paper.

3. Ask the children to think about excesses and then to draw people who are too tall, too thin, situations that are too bad, too weird, and so on.

4. Using the concept of metamorphosis, ask children to start with one object, such as a car, and to gradually change it in a series of steps until it looks like something else, perhaps an elephant.

5. Ask children to draw a face, and then to draw the same face with a series of expressions, such as sad, happy, excited, or frightened.[2]

MEDIA AND TECHNIQUES

In selecting media for children who are in the manipulative stage, the teacher must keep in mind the children's working methods and their natural inclination to work quickly and spontaneously. Paints or crayons should be easy to handle and should yield a rich and satisfying sweep of color when applied to a surface. For beginners, soft chalk and charcoal are too dusty and tend to smear and break too easily. These media are more acceptable when the child has progressed well into the symbol stage, in about the second grade.

Young children who are beginning to draw seem to prefer felt-tip pens and wax crayons to other media. A box of crayons contains a wide variety of colors. The crayons should be firm enough not to break but soft enough for the color to adhere to the paper without undue pressure. Felt-tip pens are especially popular because of their vivid colors and ease of handling. They are available in a variety of sizes, colors, and prices and can be very stimulating for all age groups. Even very young children will sometimes draw in great detail with fine-point pens, even though the details are marks and scribbles.

Teachers must be careful when selecting pens for school use. Use of nontoxic pens prevents health hazards. Teachers should avoid using pens with fruit aromas or flavors, particularly with young children who will tend to taste the ink. Crayon-pastels combine the soft, richly colored qualities of pastels (colored chalks) with the dustless quality of crayons. These are usually more expensive than crayons but are well received as art media by all age groups.

[2] For more detail see Brent Wilson and Marjorie Wilson, "Of Graphic Vocabularies and Grammars: Teaching Drawing Skills for Worldmaking," *School Arts*, June 1979.

Drawing and Painting

There is a wide variety of papers appropriate for drawing, and a range of sizes and shapes of paper provides interesting alternatives for young artists. Regular 9-by-12-inch white drawing paper is a standard. Manila paper is inexpensive and has sufficient "tooth" for crayon. Newsprint is also suitable, but although it is cheaper than manila paper, it's texture is too smooth and it tears easily. It is often possible to find discarded papers, such as computer printout or the back of obsolete forms, which cost virtually nothing.

Children in kindergarten should learn to work with paint, an exciting medium that they find attractive. The most suitable paint for the beginner is an opaque medium usually called *tempera*, which may be purchased in several forms, the most usual being liquid or powder. The powdered variety is somewhat less expensive than the liquid but must be mixed with water before it is used. (With beginning pupils, the teacher must mix all the paint.) Powdered tempera has one advantage over liquid tempera: its textural qualities can be varied as desired. The liquid paint tends to go on with a uniform smoothness, whereas the powdered variety can be applied with varying degrees of roughness or smoothness depending on how much water is mixed with it.

The broad, muscular fashion in which young children naturally work is even more noticeable with paint than with crayon. Large sheets of paper (18 by 24 inches) allow for young painters' large strokes and exhuberant movements. The teacher should use a variety of paper and brush sizes so that the children can explore different ways of controlling the paint. Newsprint and manila paper are both suitable, as are the thicker papers such as bogus and kraft. The children can also use newspapers and colored poster paper.

Paintbrushes are usually flat or round, and the coarseness of the

These illustrations by kindergarten and first grade pupils show children's early linear orientation as well as the broad, muscular fashion and fairly large area in which they work.

bristles varies from very stiff to very soft. Cost is always a factor in purchasing art materials for schools, but it is inconsiderate to ask children to express themselves with materials that even an experienced adult could not control. The poorest-quality brushes, although usually the least expensive, might not be the best value. Cheap brushes often have uneven shapes and are difficult to control, thus frustrating the painter. Bristles can fall out in the process of painting and during vigorous cleaning. It is better to invest in decent-quality paintbrushes for better service and less frequent replacement. Purchase a variety of brushes, particularly large bristle brushes (10-inch handle, $\frac{1}{2}$-inch flat bristles) for young children. After use, wash brushes in water and store in jars with the bristles up to avoid permanent creases.

Finger paint is a medium that lends itself readily to manipulation, but it is of decidedly limited artistic value. To start work with this medium, the teacher should place several spoonfuls of finger paint on a well-dampened sheet of glazed paper. After the children spread the paint over the dampened surface of the paper, they can use their fingers, knuckles, and the palms of their hands to create rhythmic patterns. They can quickly erase a pattern by smoothing the paint with the flat of their hands.

Children must exercise some care in finger-painting to keep from spilling the paint on their clothing, on the desks, or on the floor. They should wear aprons or old shirts, and the painting surface (paper) should rest on a protective covering such as oilcloth, cardboard, or absorbent paper. Newspapers make a good covering for the working surface and, because of adhesion resulting from excess paint, have the added advantage of keeping the sheets of finished work flat.

Of all painting methods, finger-painting is the most fun—so much so that children are seldom critical of the results. The most sensuous and muscular of "flat" activities, finger-painting lends itself to total physical involvement far more than tempera painting. It is inappropriate, however, for subjects that require handling of detail. Thus the choice of medium affects how the subject matter is handled: crayon gives linear qualities to children's work, finger paint allows broad sweeps, and tempera enables children to use line, shape, and texture.

Very young children are usually anxious to experiment with media and will use whatever crayons, paint, and paper they find within reach. Their attention span is short, however, so within five minutes they may exhaust their interest in one kind of work and seek a new activity. The more children experiment with art media the longer their attention span becomes, and some children remain involved in art activities for extended periods of time.

When children first use paint, it is a wise practice to offer them only one color. When they have gained some familiarity with the manipulation of the paint, the teacher can give them two colors, then three, then four. By providing children with the primary hues—red, yellow, and blue—plus black and white paints, the teacher can encourage them to discover the basics of color mixing at a very early age. Colors will mix at first by accident (the red and yellow miraculously turning orange can be quite exciting).

The paint should be distributed in small containers such as glass jars, milk cartons, or orange juice cans. Place these containers firmly in a wire basket or a cardboard or wooden box to prevent accidents. Very young children should have one brush for each color because they cannot at first be expected to wash their equipment between changes of color. The attentive teacher can give simple instructions on how to clean brushes in water and how to mix or lighten colors.

From the beginning of the children's experience with paint, the teacher should attempt to enlarge their color vocabulary. This can occur naturally by naming colors as they are used. The use of "coloring drills," often seen in some kindergartens, seems unnatural and should be avoided. Children learn about color most effectively by using it and talking about it.

Because many children come to school with a linear orientation to picture-making, their first experiments in painting during both the manipulative and symbolic stages are likely to be brush drawings. Picture-making in its early stages is generally a matter of enclosing images with lines rather than the more sophisticated work of placing areas of color next to each other. Even if they begin as painters, children will often complete their work by going over it with black lines to lend greater clarity to the shapes. At first the teacher should accept whatever strategies the children happen to use, but should keep an eye on their work habits and handling of materials and should get them to talk about their work during the evaluation period.

When the children are familiar with crayons, paints, and brushes, the teacher may try a few simple teaching methods to encourage them and perhaps to help them improve their technique. Sometimes background music helps children improve the rhythm of their lines or color areas. When certain children in the group make discoveries, such as stipple or dry-brush effects, the teacher might draw the attention of the entire class to these discoveries. The teacher should also, in a general way, praise each child's industry or some other broad aspect of the child's endeavor.

When children reach the phase of named manipulation, that is, the creation of a symbol, the teacher should encourage them to talk about the subject matter of their painting. In so doing, the pupils tend to clarify their ideas and thus progress into further stages of development. The relation between ideas, language, and images is very intense at this age and should be encouraged. Whatever learning takes place at the stage of manipulation, however, depends largely on the children. A pleasant working environment and one in which suitable materials are readily at hand are the main ingredients of a successful program during this stage of expression. The teacher must give much thought to preparing and distributing sup-

Paintings by two six-year-olds, one from the United States, the other from France. Children in the primary grades normally do not fill the pictorial space as completely as they have here. For children at this age, art largely is a graphic—that is, drawing—process. Paintings first emerge as brush drawings, which then may be filled in with areas of color. The teachers of these children have made a conscious attempt to direct attention to certain "painterly" approaches, such as color against color, color and moving line, and forms that cover the complete surface of the paper.

plies and equipment and must work out satisfactory procedures for collecting work and cleaning up after each session.

The Symbol-Making Stage

MEDIA AND TECHNIQUES

In earlier art sessions little or no chalk is used, but in the symbol-making stage, with their newly acquired skills, children will probably be ready to use soft chalk, or "pastels," as they are sometimes called, which may be purchased in sets of ten to twelve colors. "Dustless" chalk, while lacking in color potency, leaves less residue on children's clothing. Charcoal is another medium that might be used. Pressed charcoal in hard sticks is better than the "willow vine" variety, which breaks easily. Chalk and charcoal can be used conveniently on manila and some newsprint papers, which should be large, about 12 by 18 inches. Use spray fixative to seal the chalk or charcoal and avoid smudging. Always be sure to use any spray materials in a well-ventilated space or under an exhaust hood. If prolonged use is required, use a filter mask. The crayon-pastels mentioned earlier are appropriate also for school-age children and require no fixative.

It is possible to use transparent watercolor for painting, but the teacher must realize that it is difficult to control and proceed accordingly. Watercolors require more instruction and more structured supervision for children to use them successfully. Some teachers prefer to wait until children are older before introducing watercolor painting.

In the symbol-making stage, drawings and paintings represent subject matter derived directly from the children's experiences in life. The teacher may thus from time to time assist the children in recalling the important facts and features of the depicted objects. For example, for those children developing symbols for "man" or "woman," the teacher could draw attention to such activities as running, jumping, climbing, brushing teeth, wearing shoes, combing hair, and washing hands. If the children act out these activities, the concept inherent in the symbol is expressed more completely. Judicious questioning by the teacher concerning both the appearance of the symbol in the children's work and its actual appearance as observed by the children in their environment might also be effective. These teaching methods, it should be noted, are not suggested for the purpose of producing "realistic" work, but rather to help the children concentrate on an item of experience so that their statements concerning it may grow more complete.

When the children relate their symbols to an environment, their chief difficulty often arises from an inability to make the symbol sufficiently distinct from the background of a picture. The following dialog between a teacher and a third grade pupil relates to such a problem.

TEACHER: Mark, it looks as if you're about finished. What do you think?
MARK: I don't like it.
TEACHER: What's the matter with it?
MARK: I don't know.
TEACHER: You know, there comes a time when every artist has to stop and look at his work. You notice things you don't see up close. (*Tacks painting on easel.*) Now look at it hard.

TEACHING

Complexity can be a factor even in the earliest stages of symbolic development. Although most of the figures in this drawing are free-floating and minimal in concept, the one at the bottom left is distinctly different in form—indicating that it is a subject of considerably greater importance than the others. Age four.

MARK: You can't see it too clear—
TEACHER: You mean the tent?
MARK: It doesn't show up.
TEACHER: What we need is a way to make the subject—that is, the tent—
stand out. What can you do? I can think of something right off.
MARK: I know—paint stripes on it.
TEACHER: Try it and see what happens. You can paint over it if you don't
like it.

There could have been other solutions, such as using an outline or increasing the size of the tent. The important point of this dialog is that the teacher got Mark to discover his own solution without requiring him to give a single correct answer. The problem of developing contrasts between figure and ground, especially in color, light and shade, and sometimes texture, is an important one that the pupil should be helped to solve at this time.

The Preadolescent Stage

Preadolescent children are ready to develop real competencies in drawing and painting activities. By the time children reach the fourth and fifth grades, they will probably have had considerable experience with art media and will have developed many skills in their use. A brush or crayon should now do what the child wants it to do.

MEDIA AND TECHNIQUES

The teacher should provide a wide variety of brushes, ranging from about size 4 to size 10 of the soft, pointed type made of sable or camel hair. The teacher should also make available the bristle-type brush in long flat, short flat, and round types and in all sizes from $\frac{1}{8}$ inch to 1 inch in width. Since children at this stage will sooner or later use tints and shades of color, it is sometimes a good idea to provide a neutral-toned paper to make the tonalities of paint more effective. Some pupils avoid pure white paper because of its confusing glare. Pupils in the preadolescent stage will require not only the standard opaque and transparent paints but also inks, crayons, pressed charcoal, pastels, and drawing pencils of reasonably good quality. Conté crayon, which is available in both black and sepia, makes an excellent drawing medium and may be used effectively with white chalk on gray paper. Crayon can have a range of some twenty colors. Soft lead pencils should range in weight from about 3B to 8B.

The discussion that follows will focus on several important techniques that preadolescents are expected to develop at this stage—techniques involving facility in use of color, understanding of space, skills in drawing from observation, and ability to mix media. Because the teacher's role is central to the process of developing these techniques, comments on how to teach them are incorporated into this discussion rather than set forth in a separate section.

Developing Facility with Color. In the early preadolescent stage, children are concerned with the relationship of background to foreground. This concern, together with their interest in the effects of light and shade, involves them in problems related to the tonalities of color. By learning more about mixing colors, children increase their choices, thereby using a wider range of colors. They also learn how to lower color intensity by adding small amounts of the complementary color and how to lighten color by adding white.

Once it is decided that pupils will mix colors themselves, the physical arrangements in the classroom for the distribution of pigments must be carefully planned. The "cafeteria" system allows the pupils to select their colors from jars of powdered or liquid tempera. Using a spoon or wooden paddle, they place the desired quantity of each color in a muffin tin. The mixing of paint and water and mixing of colors can be done directly in the tins. Because children sometimes waste paint, the teacher should tell them to take only enough pigment for their painting. They should be cautioned not to mix too large a quantity. By adding colors, such as blue to yellow to make green, or red to white to make pink, they can save paint.

There are a variety of ways to alter the standard hues. Mixing black with a standard tempera color creates a shade, while adding white to a color produces a tint. If watercolor is used, adding black creates a shade, but the white paper showing through the watered-down pigment creates the tint. Light areas must be carefully planned in advance. The ability to mix tints and shades and thus arrive at different values greatly broadens pupils' ability to use color. Preadolescent children can also alter hues without undue difficulty by mixing the standard hue with its complement. Hence, when green is added to red the character of red is altered; the more green added, the greater the change in the red, until finally it turns a brownish gray. Grays achieved this way have a varied character and are different from those achieved by mixing black and white. When used in a composition, these grays give dramatic emphasis to the areas of bright color.

By the time the children have gained some ability in mixing colors, they should have a reasonably broad range of standard hues, including red, yellow, blue, green, violet, orange, magenta, turquoise, and brown. Because the choice of colors is so wide, however, the teacher may find it necessary from time to time to caution pupils against using too broad a palette. Children often attempt to use too many colors; in fact, they sometimes try to use every available color in one painting. They then find it difficult to build a unified composition.

Children in the upper elementary-school grades are capable not only of looking analytically at how color behaves, as in the color wheel (see Chapter 3), but also of using what they learn about color in their paintings. This is not as true of children who have not yet reached the preadolescent stage, since young children tend to work intuitively; the works of first graders often exhibit exciting, "painterly" qualities. But the upper grader, being more cautious and less spontaneous in expression, requires stronger and more specific motivation. Color activities built around problems posed by the teacher enable the student to learn more about the interaction of color as well as to arrive at a more personal, expressive use of color.

Here are some problems and questions for the pupils to consider:

1. Questions about sensitivity to color in the environment:
   How many colors can you see in this room?
   Would everyone who is wearing red please stand together?
   Name the colors you see outside the window. Can you grade them according to brightness or dullness?
2. Problems relating to color investigation:
   First make a painting with just three primary colors—red, yellow, and blue. Mix them any way you like. In a second painting, add black and white to the three colors.
   Compare the brown in the bottle with a brown of your own, made by mixing black and red. Which do you like better?
   Mix your own orange and compare it with the prepared orange in the bottle. Which do you prefer?
3. Problems relating to the nature of pigment:
   What happens when you use color on wet paper?
   What happens when you use color on black paper?
   What happens when you combine painting and collage? Notice how a separation of color and texture appears. How can you bring the painted part and the collage section together?
4. Problems relating to the emotive power of color:
   Mix a group of colors suitable for a painting about a hurricane, a picnic, a carnival.
   Prepare little "families" or related groups of color around specific ideas and see how close you can get to what you are trying to express. For example, for a blazing house, you might group red, black, and orange; for an autumn scene, yellow, red, brown, and orange.

Such problems may be viewed as ends unto themselves or as preliminary stages to more complete picture-making. They lead into the area of art appreciation when the children are asked to relate their class activities

As the child grows older the approach to painting becomes less intuitive. The painting above, by a second grader, exhibits exciting, "painterly" qualities, but the one below, by a fifth grader, seems less spontaneous.

Children should learn to express their feelings by experimenting with the emotive power of color, as in this painting from life by a fifth grader.

to the solutions developed by artists. Thus, in conjunction with exercises in the emotive power of color, the teacher may refer to El Greco's *View of Toledo*, Léger's series *Le Cirque*, and many of Picasso's Blue Period paintings.

Masses and Shapes in Space. The problem of rendering space often frustrates the older child, who will require the help of the teacher. Teaching perspective is similar to teaching sensitivity to color in that in neither case does an *intellectual* approach assure the teacher that personally expressive use will follow. Children can have their attention directed to the fact that distance may be achieved through overlapping, diminution of size, consistency of vertical edges, atmospheric perspective or neutralization of receding color, and convergence of lines. This knowledge, however, has only limited value if the children are not able to see the many ways in which perspective may be used; indeed, effective pictorial expression may occur without recourse to linear perspective. Such painters as Feininger, Picasso, de Chirico, Marin, Dalí, and Braque (as illustrated) should be studied as examples of artists who have distorted, adjusted, and exaggerated the laws of perspective for particular artistic ends.

The teacher's job is not so much to decide that a particular treatment of space is to be used in the children's work as it is to keep the children moving by helping them through any phases of dissatisfaction. Calling the children's attention to perspective as seen in the natural world and the realm of painting can help the students in such cases. It is wise, therefore, to have on hand several examples of the different ways space may be treated. Such examples might show:

1. The Oriental placement of objects, which usually disregards the deep, penetrating space of Western art.
2. The Renaissance use of linear perspective, with its vanishing points and diminishing verticals and horizontals.
3. Cubist dissolution of Renaissance-type space, with its substitution of multiple views, shifting planes, and disregard of "local" (realistic) color.
4. Photographic techniques using aerial views, linear perspective, and unusual points of view in landscape subjects.

Space may also be studied by examining color in abstract paintings in which very few familiar associations come between the viewer and the painting. Children can describe which colors seem to come forward and which recede, which ones "fight" with each other and which are harmonious. Hans Hofmann[3] refers to the tensions of color as a process of "push and pull."

[3] Hans Hofmann was a world-renowned Abstract Expressionist painter during the 1940s and 1950s. He was also recognized as one of the great art teachers of the time.

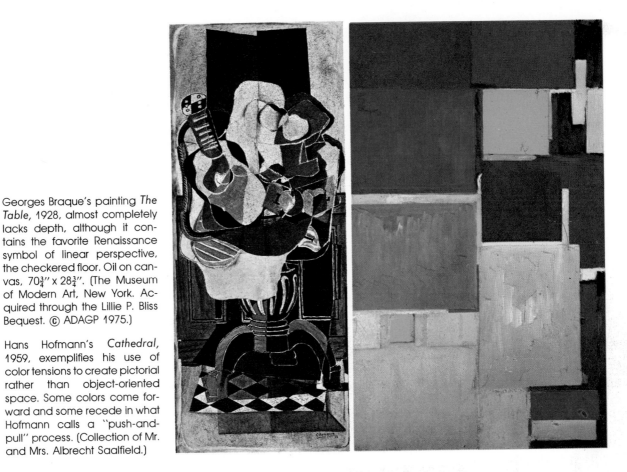

Georges Braque's painting *The Table*, 1928, almost completely lacks depth, although it contains the favorite Renaissance symbol of linear perspective, the checkered floor. Oil on canvas, 70¾″ x 28¾″. (The Museum of Modern Art, New York. Acquired through the Lillie P. Bliss Bequest. © ADAGP 1975.)

Hans Hofmann's *Cathedral*, 1959, exemplifies his use of color tensions to create pictorial rather than object-oriented space. Some colors come forward and some recede in what Hofmann calls a ''push-and-pull'' process. (Collection of Mr. and Mrs. Albrecht Saalfield.)

In teaching perspective, as in teaching color, the teacher should keep in mind that children may produce successful paintings without using linear perspective. If elementary-school children do not exhibit an inclination to adopt linear perspective, they should be encouraged to master such alternate modes of composition as the overlapping of planes and the toning of colors. On the other hand, if pupils do show an interest in this type of perspective, judicious teaching will allow their expression of it to grow in clarity and power. There are good books and sound filmstrips available on teaching perspective.[4]

Developing Skills in Drawing from Observation. Herbert Read makes a distinction between three categories of activity: the activity of *self-expression*, the activity of *observation*, and the activity of *appreciation*.[5]

[4] For example, see ''Perspective Drawing,'' a sound filmstrip in two parts by Educational Dimension Group, Stamford, Ct., 1977.
[5] Herbert Read, *Education Through Art*, rev. ed. (New York: Pantheon, 1958).

In terms of child development, self-expression has greater implications for the lower elementary grades, and observation is more relevant to the capabilities of elementary-school children in the upper graders. Although art educators are still divided as to when drawing from observation should begin, a growing number feel that directed perception satisfies a strong desire among older children to depict subject matter.[6]

One area of misunderstanding that accounts for this division of opinion is the assumption by some educators that any form of directed vision implies a staunch devotion to realism, a violation of the "creative, expressive" self, or both. Any teacher who has ever asked a class of thirty children to draw the same object knows it is erroneous to assume that instruction automatically robs children of individual responses. Unless instruction is of an aggressively inhibiting nature, the child's "self" will be asserted. What is not certain is whether the self will attempt to enrich and expand its vision in specific directions. The teacher is needed to direct this operation.

We need to ask the question: Is "realistic" drawing necessarily "good" or "bad" drawing? The issue of good or bad exists apart from any particular style, for values in drawing, as in painting, reside chiefly in form rather than in the degree of realistic representation. In an attempt to find a place in art for realistic drawing, "the painter may . . . imitate what he sees," says L. A. Reid, "but he imitates what he sees, because what he sees fulfills and satisfies his needs."[7] Good drawing necessarily occurs, then, when the artists select, interpret, and present in a personal, aesthetically coherent composition those items of experience that move them, regardless of whether or not the presentation is realistic. Weak drawing occurs when the forms used are drawn merely to fill gaps in the pictorial surface, without regard for the unity of the composition. In accomplishing the feat of organization, an artist may purposely depart from nature to varying degrees in the interest of design.

There is little merit in encouraging children of any age to draw with photographic accuracy. But a distinction must be made between requiring children to work for realism in drawing and using certain drawing techniques to heighten their visual acuity. Few teachers who use nature as a model or have the class work with contour line really believe that they are forcing their students to conform to photographic realism. In the first place this kind of professional facility is impossible to achieve on the elementary level, and secondly, there would be very little point to such a goal,

---

[6] Pearl Greenberg recommends the use of models, still life, and landscape as early as the second grade (*Children's Experiences in Art* [New York: Reinhold, 1977]), and Helen Merritt devotes a full chapter to the problem in *Guiding Free Expression in Children's Art* (New York: Holt, Rinehart and Winston, 1964). Miriam Lindstrom, in her detailed description of the art program of the De Young Memorial Museum in San Francisco, emphasizes the use of observation as a primary basis for art activity (*Children's Art* [Berkeley: University of California Press, 1957]), as does Adelaide Sproul in *With a Free Hand* (New York: Reinhold, 1968).

[7] L. A. Reid, *A Study in Aesthetics* (New York: Macmillan, 1931), p. 236.

Drawing and Painting

even if it were possible to attain. The argument that working from nature is inhibiting to children is no longer accepted by most art educators. As Roettger and Klante point out:

> Play with line leads logically to a fresh way of looking at nature. Today this is often thought outmoded, because some blinkered minds will not realize that it does not need a great effort of imagination to break nature's spell. Observation and imagination thus merge inextricably, as when children (whether from imagination or memory is immaterial) try to draw objects, flowers, animals or their own reflections in the mirror.[8]

The question a teacher must inevitably ask is, "What can the child learn from drawing activities?" Obviously, there is not enough time for some children who lack the perceptual development required of drawing to master it. Nor is mastery of any one skill a definable goal of an elementary art program. Drawing activities can, however, serve to:

1. Provide pleasurable art activity that allows children to attain a degree of success.
2. Direct children away from stereotypes.
3. Provide children with usable skills that may be employed in other art activities.
4. Offer an opportunity to study works of outstanding professional artists.

[8] Ernst Roettger and Dieter Klante, *Creative Drawing* (New York: Reinhold, 1964), p. 3.

Examples of drawing from observation. Jeep, fourth grade; imaginary bug based on a study of a real object, sixth grade; drawing from model in period costume (the pupil decided to leave the face blank because of difficulty with the features), sixth grade; still life composed of a cluster of music stands, fifth grade.

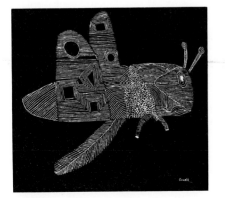

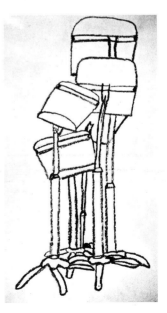

5. Provide a process of observation that can reveal such factors as the structure and texture of objects and the relation of parts to wholes.
6. Develop in children a sensitivity to design and to the structural uses of line.

Sources of Observation. Good drawing depends in no small measure on the producer's experience of the things drawn. Such experience, it should be noted, depends not only on the eye, but on a total reaction of the artist, involving, ideally, all the senses. Often in the fifth and sixth grades, good drawing may be developed through the use of some time-honored subjects that demand a comprehensive reaction to experience. Using sources grounded in experience, the child may produce drawings of the human face and figure, landscapes, and still-life subjects. The teacher should not be bound by the traditions associated with such subject matter. According to what subjects, materials, visual references, and motivating forces the teacher selects, drawing can be an exciting and pleasurable activity, or an academic and inhibiting one. Table 6.1 compares two approaches to teaching drawing activities for a sixth grade class.

TABLE 6.1

Two Approaches to Teaching Drawing

	Subject	Materials	Instructions for Visual Reference	Motivation and Historical Reference
Negative Instruction	*Still life:* A wine bottle, a tennis ball, and a plate on a table at the front of the room.	Hard pencil on newsprint, 8 by 10 inches, flat desk tops used as work surface.	"Draw everything you see—light and dark, lines, and so on."	None.
	Human figure: A girl posed sitting in a chair, which is on the floor.	Ballpoint pens on newsprint, 18 by 24 inches.	"Make the drawing as real as you can; make the folds really stand out."	None.
Positive Instruction	*Still life:* Four still-life centers, each composed of large shapes of interesting objects—pieces of machinery, drapery, and so on.	Dustless chalk on black construction paper, 12 by 18 inches; drawing boards used as work surface.	"Concentrate just on contour. Use a different color chalk for each object and let the lines for the shapes flow through one another."	Contour drawing demonstrated (see dialog, pp. 203–205). Line drawings by Matisse, Picasso, or good commercial illustrations shown.
	Human figure: A boy and a girl, one sitting, one standing, dressed in odd bits of costume and holding musical instruments; placed above eye level.	Black crayon and watercolor wash on 40-pound white paper (size optional).	"Balance light washes of watercolor against line. Lay in the broad directions of the figures in wash, and when it dries, work the lines over the wash."	Demonstration given; wash and line drawings by Rembrandt, Tiepolo, and Daumier shown. Lesson related to a previous lesson.

As far as is practicable, the children should be responsible for arranging their sources of observation. For example, they should have some control in posing the model for life drawing. The teacher, of course, will have to oversee the lighting and the setting of reasonable time limits for poses. Artificial lighting by one or more spotlights can be used, and these lights must be moved until anatomical details are clearly revealed and an interesting pattern of the elements, especially line and light and shade, is visible. Models must not be asked to pose for too long (usually for a preadolescent youngster, ten minutes is a lifetime). However, if the pose is too brief for a complete drawing to be made, the teacher merely needs to remind the model to memorize the position in order to return to it after a rest. The teacher, of course, should also remember the pose in case the pupil forgets it. Chalk marks to indicate the position of the feet often help the model to resume the pose.

In producing life drawings and portraits, older pupils will be assisted by an elementary study both of pertinent relationships among parts of the body and of approximate sizes of parts of the figure. The pupil who is maturing physiologically often shows an interest in the human body by drawing certain anatomical details in a rather pronounced manner. Any emphasis beyond the requirements of aesthetics may be counteracted to some degree by a study of the human body. The teacher should point out

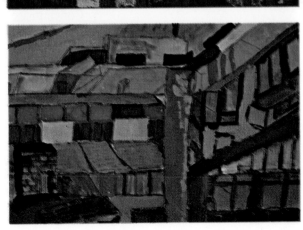

In this neighborhood study by a nine-year-old girl in Hungary, the forms of buildings are the subject. The use of color is more advanced than is the level of drawing, which suggests that graphic skill is an inadequate basis for judging a child's visual sensitivity. Some children reach for color; some can group forms better than others; and some have special capability for drawing.

An eleven-year-old Japanese boy developed this painting from a drawing made by observing a section of his school. It was sketched directly with felt pen; tempera was added where needed. Of course, the teacher provided some preliminary experience in line drawing. Drawing outdoors is an important part of the art program in the schools of Korea, Taiwan, and Japan.

the nature of the mechanically independent body blocks—the head, the torso, and the pelvic girdle.

The human figure lends itself to interpretation. Once the children have closely examined the figure, they might be asked to interpret it in terms of fantasy or qualities of mood—joy, doom, strength, violence. Such subjects can be drawn from observation as well as imagination, for students can be posed displaying these moods.

In still-life work, the pupils should not only arrange their own groups of objects, but they should also be given the opportunity to become thoroughly familiar with each item. By handling the objects they may make note of differences in textures and degrees of hardness and softness. Sole dependence on the eye in art work limits unnecessarily the experience of the creator.

Selection of still-life material is another instance of the need for the teacher to plan a program with the pupils' preferences in mind. The teacher must, of course, ensure the adequacy of still-life arrangements. They must have a challenging variety of objects, in which there are various types of contrasting surfaces, such as the textures found in glass, fur, metal, cloth, and wood. Contrast in the shapes of objects must also be arresting. The other elements—line, space, light and shade, texture, and color—should also be considered for the variety they can bring to a still-life arrangement. As the objects are assembled, however, they should be brought together into a unified composition.

Once the objects of the still life have been selected and arranged, the teacher must establish some visual points of reference with which the pupils can work. These might include getting them to:

1. Search for size relationships among various objects.
2. Concentrate on the edges of objects (contour drawing).
3. Use crayon to indicate shadows.
4. Use one object (an ink bottle, a wine bottle, a hammer) to arrange repeated shapes, overlapping portions of the object to obtain a pleasing flow.
5. Concentrate only on shape by drawing the forms, each on a different color paper, cutting them out, and pasting them on neutral-toned paper in overlapping planes.
6. Relate the objects to the size and shape of the paper. Students will find they can work on rectangular surfaces (12 by 18 inches), on squares, and even on circular shapes; they can draw small objects many times their size and reduce large objects to paper size.

In general, landscapes selected for outdoor painting or for preliminary studies to be finished in the classroom should have a reasonable number of objects in them that can be used as a basis for composition.

Drawing and Painting

Hence a scene with a barn, some animals, a silo, and some farm machinery is preferable to a sky and a wheatfield, or a lake and a distant shore. By having many objects before them, the pupils may select items that they think will make an interesting composition. The wheatfield or the lake may not give them enough material to draw. Children can be sent outside the classroom to bring back sketches of the environment for their classmates to identify. A simple homework assignment is to have the students bring in drawings of their homes that show the surrounding landscape.

The work in these activities need not be of long duration. Some pupils, however, may wish to produce a more finished work and, of course, should be encouraged to do so.

Contour Drawing as a Basis for Observation. Contour-line drawing, which can be applied to landscape, figures, or objects, is considered by many educators to be a sound basis of perception. The contour approach requires the children to focus their visual attention on the edges of a form and to note detail and structure; they are thus encouraged to move away from visual clichés to a fresh regard for subjects they may have lived with but never truly examined. The following teaching session demonstrates how one teacher went about introducing this method of drawing.

TEACHER: . . . I need someone . . . to pose. Michael, how about you? (*Michael is chosen because he is the tallest boy with the tightest pants. He will do very well for the purpose of the lesson. The teacher has him sit above eye level in a chair placed on a table.*) Now listen carefully. First, is there anyone here who is not able to draw a picture of Michael in the air by following the edge of his body with his finger? . . . Then let's try it. (*The teacher closes his right eye and slowly follows the outer edge of the subject in the air. The class follows, feeling fairly certain of success, at least at this stage.*) Very good. That wasn't too bad, was it?

PAUL: But that's not drawing.

TEACHER: Let's wait and see. Now, suppose I had a pane of glass hanging from the ceiling and some white paint. Couldn't you *trace* the lines in Michael's body right on the glass? (*They think about this for a moment.*) After all, it's the next thing to drawing a line in the air, isn't it?

ALICE: We don't have any glass.

TEACHER: True. I wish we did. But if we did you could do it, couldn't you? (*All agree they could.*) O.K.—then if you can follow the lines through the glass, you can *see* them. If I ask you to put them on your paper instead, what will your problem be?

ANDY: How can we look at Michael and at our paper at the same time?

TEACHER: Andy is right. We can't do it, so we just won't look at our paper. . . . May I show you what I mean? (*The class heartily approves of this. The teacher goes to the blackboard.*) Now, I'm not going to look at the blackboard because I'm more interested in training my eye than

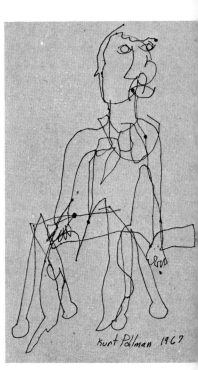

One type of contour drawing is this continuous contour of a figure; fifth grade. Another approach can be made using light and allowing children to work on a large scale. Light casts shadows of shapes on the paper. The lamps can be adjusted to attain the desired shapes, which are overlapped before being painted. When the shapes are the children's own bodies, the artists become their own subjects.

in making a pretty picture. I'm going to concentrate just on following the edge. Do you know what the word *concentrate* means? Who knows?

ALICE: To think very hard about something.

TEACHER: Exactly. So I'm going to think very hard—to concentrate—on the outside edges of Michael. We call this *contour-line drawing*. (*Writes it on blackboard.*) Contours are edges of shapes. You don't see *lines* in nature as a rule. . . . What you see mostly are dark shapes against light shapes, and where they meet you have *lines*. Who can see some in this room? (*Among those mentioned are where walls meet the ceiling, where books touch one another, and where the dark silhouette of the plants meets the light sky.*) Very good, you get the idea. We start with edges—or contours—then. Another example is my arm. (*He puts it up against the blackboard.*) If I ask you to draw my arm from *memory*, you might come up with something that looks like this (*draws several schematic arms—a sausage shape, a stick arm, a segmented form divided into fingers, hand, forearm and upper arm divisions, and so on. The class is visibly amused*). Now, watch this carefully and see what happens when I concentrate on the contour of my arm. (*With his right hand he follows the top contour and the underside of his arm. As he removes his arm from the blackboard the class is delighted to see a line drawing of the teacher's arm remain on the board.*)

VERNON: I used to draw around my fingers that way.

TEACHER: Well, it's kind of hard to trace around every object you'll ever want to draw, and even if you could, would that teach you how to look?

VERNON: But you just did it on the blackboard.

TEACHER: What was I trying to show you?

ALICE: You were trying to show what the *eye* is supposed to do.

TEACHER: Exactly. I showed you what the eye must do *without* a subject to feel. What did the eye show me about my arm? (*The class notes wrinkles, the separation of shirtsleeve and wristwatch and hand.*) I'll bet you didn't realize there were so many dips and squiggles in just one arm, even without shading—that is, without dark and light. Once a contour drawing is finished, the eye fills *in between* the lines. Now, let me try Michael. (*As he draws he describes what is happening.*) Now, I'm starting at the top of his head, working down to his toe, I'm going up over the ear, down to the neck, and on to the collar. Now I move away, along the shoulder, and here the line turns down the arm. (*He continues in this manner until the line reaches the foot of the model and starts the process over again, moving the line down the opposite side of the figure.*)

The discussion points made by the teacher in the dialog were arrived at after careful study of the kinds of problems children face when attempting contour-line drawing. Their confusion arises in part from the necessity to coordinate eye and hand in analytic drawing skills. Because the contour-line drawing focuses on only one aspect of form—that of the edges of the subject—it cannot be expected that the relationship of parts will follow. This problem should be taken up as a second stage in the activity of contour-line drawing.

Developing Methods of Mixing Media. Children can mix media from an early age, so that by the time they reach the higher elementary grades they may achieve some outstandingly successful results by this means. The use of resist techniques, for example, is practical for preadolescents and tends to maintain their interest in their work. Scratchboard techniques may also be handled effectively by older pupils.

The technique of using resists relies on the fact that waxy media will shed liquid color if the color has been sufficiently thinned with water. A reasonably heavy paper or cardboard having a mat, or nonshiny, surface is required. Ordinary wax crayons are suitable and may be used with watercolor, thinned tempera paint, or colored inks. The last are particularly pleasant to use with this technique. In producing a picture, the pupil first makes a drawing with wax crayon and then lays down a wash of color or colors. To provide accents in the work, thicker paint or India ink may be used. The ink may be applied with either a pen or a brush, or with both tools.

In using a scratchboard, the pupil scratches away an overall dark coating to expose selected parts of an under-surface. Scratchboard may be

In this exercise in observation through mixed media, a class was asked to depict the artroom as art object. A twelve-year-old boy drew the room in oil-base crayons and then covered the drawing with India ink. When the work was rinsed with water, the ink settled in the spaces between the colors, thus adding emphasis in line and texture.

Scratchboard and crayon were the media chosen by an eleven-year-old Austrian boy for his portrayal of an automobile junkyard.

either purchased or made by the pupils. If it is to be made, Bristol board is probably the most desirable to use. The surface is prepared by covering the Bristol board, or other glazed cardboard, with a heavy coat of wax crayons in light colors. A coating of tempera paint or India ink sufficiently thick to cover the wax should then be applied and left to dry. Later, the drawing may be made with a variety of tools, including pen points, bobby pins, scissors, and so on. A careful handling of black, white, and textured areas has highly dramatic effects.

The techniques described above are basic and may be expanded in several ways. For example, white wax crayon may be used in the resist painting, with paint providing color. Another resist technique is to "paint" the design with rubber cement and then float tempera or watercolor over the surface. The next day, the cement can be peeled off, revealing broken white areas against the color ground.

Lines in dark ink or tempera work well over collages of colored tissues, and rich effects can be obtained by covering thick tempera paintings with India ink and washing the ink away under a faucet. The danger of mixing media lies in a tendency toward gimmickry, but often the use of combined materials can solve special design problems. We should not consider these techniques as merely child's play. Many reputable artists have used them to produce significant drawings and paintings. Some of Henry Moore's sketches, for example, produced with wax and watercolor in the London air-raid shelters during World War II, are particularly noteworthy.[9]

Other forms of mixed media are as follows:

India ink and watercolor. The child may draw in ink first, then add color or reverse the procedure.

Watercolor washes over crayon drawings. This is a way of increasing an awareness of "negative space" or background areas.

Black tempera or India ink over crayon or colored chalk. Here the black paint settles in the unpainted areas. The student can wash away the paint, controlling the amount left on the surface of the colored areas.[10]

The Development of Pictorial Composition

Some assistance in pictorial composition must occasionally be offered if the children are to realize their goals of expression (see Chapter 3). This

[9] See Henry Moore, *Shelter Sketch Book* (New York: Wittenborn, 1946) and *Sculpture and Drawings*, 3 vols., rev. ed. (New York: Wittenborn, 1957–65).

[10] The most thorough treatment of mixed-media processes is to be found in Frank Wachowiak and Theodore Ramsay, *Emphasis: Art* (Scranton, Pa.: International Textbook, 1965).

means that children should be helped toward an understanding of design and a feeling for it, largely in connection with their general picture-making. As they gain experience with the elements of design, children should be praised for any discoveries they make, and any obvious advances might be discussed informally by the class. There is no reason why some professional work emphasizing certain elements of design should not be brought to the attention of even those pupils who are still in the early symbol stage. The works of Picasso, Matisse, Johns, Wyeth, Frankenthaler, and others may be viewed by children with much pleasure and considerable profit if related to their own acts of expression. The teacher should also use slides and originals of work by the children to demonstrate the possibilities of design on their own level.

As they grow older, children tend to become more concerned with certain elements of design than others. Somewhere between the third and fifth grades, for example, preadolescents begin to incorporate shadow effects in their pictures and to pay some attention to background details. It is then that they require assistance in arriving at suitable tonalities of color.

From time to time some children need help in arriving at a successful composition. In cases of this kind the teacher must resist the impulse to supply formulas for the designs of pictures. It would be a simple matter, for example, to tell children who are having difficulty in creating a center of interest to draw a central object on a large scale. Children instructed to do this would undoubtedly establish a desirable focal point, but in so doing they would be following an ultimately stultifying formula. Instead they should be exposed to or discover for themselves through carefully arranged activities many various means of developing centers of interest. No single method should receive undue prominence.

Questions directed at the children are valuable for yielding visual information that can lead to more satisfactory picture-making. When this technique is used, the teacher should try to establish the connection between *ideas* and *pictorial form*. This can begin when the children are at an early age by playing a *memory game*. Here the teacher simply draws a large rectangle on the chalkboard and asks someone in the class to draw a subject in the center, say a turtle. The teacher then draws a second rectangle next to the first and puts the same subject in it. What then follows is a series of questions about the turtle. The children answer the questions by coming up and adding details to the turtle in the second rectangle. As shapes, ideas, and forms are added, the picture becomes enriched and the space *around* the turtle is filled as a result of the information acquired. When the picture is finished the first one looks quite barren by comparison. The questions surrounding the subject might be posed as follows:

Q. Where does a turtle live?
A. In and around the water.

Q. How will we know it's water?
A. Water has waves and fishes.
Q. How will we know there is land next to the water?
A. There is grass, rocks, and trees.
Q. What does a turtle eat? Wheaties? Canned pineapple? Peanut butter? What does he eat?
A. He eats insects, bugs.
A. He can eat his food from a can, too.
Q. Think hard now: Where are there interesting designs on a turtle?
A. On his shell. . . .

Composition is thus approached through the grouping and arranging of a number of ideas. As each answer provides additional visual information, the picture takes on a life of its own by the relation of memory to drawing. The teacher can play this simple game with third graders, and it can provide a way of thinking about picture-making.

Another important task for the teacher is the development of a vocabulary of design terms. In all other subject areas, attention is paid to the exact meanings of words. This has not always been the case in art education, partly because the vocabulary of art in general has tended at times to be nebulous, and partly because teachers have not always attempted to build for themselves a precise vocabulary of art terms.

Some teachers have been eminently successful in assisting children to use words about design with precise meaning. They have done so, of course, with due regard for the fact that art learning should not be primarily verbal but rather should consist largely of visual and tactile experi-

"My Village," by a nine-year-old girl, Sweden. Much class discussion preceded this chalk drawing of the child's environment, in this case a country road in a rural village. The forms of the landscape—roads, trees, buildings, signs—were all used to generate ideas. Since the perspective is not accurate (the land tips upward to the horizon), more space is available for subject matter.

ences. These teachers have made sure that, if not at first, then eventually the terms are used with understanding and precision. Thus, although the teacher might at first compliment a child on the rhythmic flow of lines in a composition by saying that the quality of line was like the "blowing of the wind," later the teacher would use the word *rhythm*. In this incidental but natural manner the vocabulary of even the youngest child can be developed.

If continual attention has been paid to such informal vocabulary-building, pupils may leave the elementary school with a reasonably adequate command of art terms that will enable them to participate later in a more formal program of composition and art appreciation. It is necessary for pupils to have a working vocabulary in art by the time they reach adolescence. At that period in their development, they are often ready and in fact eager to approach design in a more intellectual manner. Without at least a rudimentary vocabulary, they will have difficulty engaging in the type of art work their stage of development requires.

Memory is a form of stored experience, and it plays a much more important role in the arts than most people realize. Actors must memorize their lines, musicians their notes, and orchestral conductors a complex array of instrumentation. Writers rely on memory of their own personal histories, dancers display choreographic memory, and artists develop a kind of visual encyclopedia of images and forms that they have encountered. Most of us do this casually—on the run, so to speak—but the memory of an artist is trained as conscientiously as a pianist practices the scales. It is important that children become aware of the powers of their own memory, not only to retain forms that they may want to depict later but also to gain the insight that memory can give to their own sense of self. The process of "becoming" is more fulfilling if we retain some sense of continuity with former states of being.

MEMORY AND DRAWING

If asked to work in the abstract, children rely on judgment, both conscious and intuitive. When asked to deal with a subject from their own lives, such as A Visit to the Doctor, they must deal not only with the memory of form but also with its surrounding knowledge. Preschool children are content with graphic symbols, but older children are often frustrated by their inability to capture memory and match it with form as they know it. To be able to recall the shape of a tractor and to describe it is one thing, but to find the right lines and shapes to depict it does not come as easily. Here are some suggestions to help children utilize their memories.

1. Divide the class into pairs, and have the children study their partners closely for two minutes. Everyone then turns around and makes some change or adjustment in clothing, hair, facial expression, and so on. Turning back to each other, the partners are asked to note the changes.

"Building an Apartment House." Here a six-year-old boy has worked from both memory and observation to convey a wide array of ideas associated with the subject. Note how details diminish as the subject extends away from the child's eye level.

2. Before going on a field trip, discuss things to look for; call attention to shapes, patterns, colors; and tell the class before leaving that they will be expected to draw what they have seen. This will sharpen their perceptions.

3. Have each child in the class draw a scene from his or her neighborhood to send to a class in a foreign country. Remind the children that those receiving the collection may not read English and that art, as a universal language, will have to tell the story of life in their country.

4. Prepare a still life of contrasting shapes and have the class draw it from observation, putting in as many details as they can. Take the still life away and ask the children to draw it from memory. Check these drawings against the original. What was not included?

5. Ask the children to draw a picture of their very first memory of school. Again, they are to put in as many details as possible. How early can memory be pushed back? What details remain?

6. Take the class outside to study a tree or a house. Discuss the characteristics that make the object special. Return to the classroom and draw the object from memory.

7. Have the children close their eyes. Describe a scene with which the class is familiar. Be precise with large things such as buildings and streets, and do not worry about details. Ask the children to build up the picture in their minds as it is described and then draw it or paint it.

8. Show a slide of a painting—one with a strong composition that is not too complex. Let the class study it for three minutes, then turn on the lights and ask them to draw it. Do this several times with pictures of increasing complexity of design.

9. Ask the children to pretend they are on the back of a giant bird who will fly them to school. How many street corners, stores, streets, and the like will they see from the air? Have them draw a diagram of the aerial view just as they would walk it.

10. To demonstrate how conscious a process memorization can be, have the children draw the entrance to their house, extending the doorway and its surroundings to both sides of the paper. Then ask the children to either draw the same subject from observation or to study it consciously, with an eye for another memory drawing the following day.

Activities for the Reader

Teachers should be thoroughly familiar with the tools, media, and techniques they will use in the classroom. The following activities are suggested to help them gain this familiarity. Because knowledge of the processes of art, in this instance, is more important than the art produced, teachers should not feel hampered by technical inabilities. Experience with art media is what counts at this stage.

1. Using a large-bristle brush for broad work, paint in tempera an interesting arrangement of color areas on a sheet of dark paper. Try to develop varied textural effects over these areas in the following ways:

    a. *By using dry-brush:* Dip the brush in paint and rub it nearly dry on a piece of scrap paper. Then "dry-brush" an area where the new color will show.

    b. *By stippling:* Holding a nearly dry brush upright so that the bristles strike the paper vertically, stamp it lightly so that a stipple pattern of paint shows.

    c. *By brush drawing:* Select a sable brush and load it with paint. Paint a pattern over a color area with wavy or crisscrossed lines, small circles, or

some other marks to give a rougher-looking texture than is found in surrounding areas.

    d. *By using powdered paint:* Apply liberal amounts of powdered paint mixed with very little water to your composition to obtain some rough areas (add sawdust or sand to liquid tempera if you have no powdered tempera).

    e. *By using a sponge:* Paint the surface of the sponge or dip it into the paint and rub the sponge on your composition.

    f. *By using a brayer:* Roll the brayer in paint and pull it over cut-paper forms. Experiment with the roller by using the edge or by wrapping string around it. Place small pools of color next to each other and pull the brayer over them, changing directions until you have blocks of broken color that lock into each other.

2. Select a small segment of a landscape and make a preliminary sketch with Conté crayon or 5B to 8B pencil on drawing paper. Keep working at your sketch, rearranging the positions of items until you think you have an interesting variety and unity of shapes, spaces, light, and shade. With watercolor or

thin tempera, paint over parts of your drawing to form an interesting color pattern. In another composition, try limiting your dark areas to just black or brown for dark wash tones.

3. Select some objects you think are interesting and use them to make a still-life arrangement. Sketch the arrangement with wax crayons, using light, bright color where you see the highlights at their brightest, and using dark-colored crayons where you see the darkest shadows.

4. Using heavy drawing pencil, try to draw the following subjects in a strictly accurate, photographically correct manner. (Remember that lines below the horizon line rise to this level; lines above fall to this level; all lines meet at the horizon line.)

    a. A sidewalk or passageway as though you were standing in the center.

    b. A cup and saucer on a table below your eye level.

    c. A chimney stack, silo, or gas storage tank, the top of which is above your eye level.

    d. A group of various-sized boxes piled on a table or on the floor. (It is easier to draw if you first paint the boxes one unifying color, such as gray or white.)

5. Sketch a house or a collection of houses or other objects with crayon or heavy pencil, following the rules of linear perspective. In another drawing, rearrange the areas you drew to change the patterns of masses and spaces. Carry the lines through each other, taking liberties with the spaces between the lines. Notice how this freedom gives your picture more variety.

6. Have a friend pose for you. On manila or newsprint measuring at least 12 by 18 inches, make contour drawings in Conté crayon or heavy pencil. Draw quickly, taking no longer than three to five minutes for each sketch. Do not erase mistakes—simply draw new lines. Make many drawings of this type based on standing, sitting, and reclining poses.

    Now begin to draw more carefully, thinking of places where bones are close to the surface and where flesh is thicker. Heavy pressure with the drawing medium will indicate shadows; the reverse will indicate light areas. Think also of the torso, the head, and the pelvic region as moving somewhat independently of each other. Begin to check body proportions.

    Later make drawings with ink and a sable brush. Always work quickly and fearlessly. Try using some of the suggested visual references for drawing listed in the section "Sources of Observation."

7. Place yourself before a mirror for a self-portrait. Study the different flat areas, or planes, of your face. Notice the position of prominent features (especially eyes, which are about halfway between the top of your head and the bottom of your chin). Quickly draw a life-size head in charcoal, crayon, or

Self-portrait, left, by an eight-year-old girl, South Africa. The subject is carefully integrated into the background space. Forms are broken as they flow through and around the figure. This is one of many ways of dealing with the problem of figure-to-ground, positive-negative, and subject-background relationships.

Students drawing portraits of each other will learn that there can be as many different versions of the same subject as there are artists with individual styles. Displaying the children's work illustrates the point vividly.

chalk. When your features have become more familiar to you, try some other media, such as ink or paint. Try a self-portrait that is many times larger than life-size.

8. The formal exercises listed below express nothing and are valueless for children, but they can help you develop technique.

a. Draw about a dozen 2-by-2-inch squares, one below the other. Paint the top square a standard hue; leave the bottom one white. Make a gradation of color areas ranging from the standard hue to white by progressively adding white to the standard hue. The "jumps" between areas should appear even.

b. Repeat a, using some other hues. Use transparent watercolor as well as tempera for some exercises, adding water instead of white paint to the watercolor pigment.

c. Repeat, this time adding the complementary color to the first one chosen. Now the gradations will go from standard to gray rather than to white.

d. Add black progressively to a standard hue to obtain twelve "jumps" from standard to black.

e. Try shading about six 3-inch-square areas with Conté crayon, charcoal, or heavy pencil so that you progress from very light gray to very dark gray.

f. Draw textures in four 3-inch-square areas so that each square appears "rougher" than the next. Crisscrossed lines, wavy lines, circles, dots, and crosses are some devices to use. India ink and a writing pen are useful tools in this exercise.

g. Using the side of a crayon, take a series of "rubbings" from such surfaces as wood, sidewalks, rough walls, and so on. Create a design using the rubbings you have collected.

Suggested Readings

Chaet, Bernard. *An Artist's Notebook*. New York: Holt, Rinehart & Winston, 1979. Discussion of materials and techniques for drawing and painting, beautifully illustrated with reproductions of the works of many great artists.

———. *The Art of Drawing*. New York: Holt, Rinehart & Winston. A course in drawing with projects and exercises for teaching, profusely illustrated with drawings by professional artists and students.

Dobin, Jay. *Perspective: A New System for Designers*. New York: Hill and Wang, 1957. The fundamentals of linear perspective.

Edwards, Betty. *Drawing on the Right Side of the Brain*. Los Angeles: J. P. Tarcher, 1979. This book illustrates a number of time-tested drawing exercises for beginning and intermediate students.

Fein, Sylvia. *Heidi's Horse*. Pleasant Hills, Ca.: Exelrod Press, 1976. A delightful book that documents the horse drawings of a girl named Heidi from her early years through adolescence.

Goldsmith, Lawrence C. *Watercolor Bold and Free*. New York: Watson-Guptill, 1980. Beautifully illustrated in color, this book presents paintings by many watercolorists in a variety of styles. Each painting exemplifies a different painting lesson explained in the text.

McFee, June King, and Degge, Rogena M. *Art, Culture, and Environment*. Belmont, Ca.: Wadsworth, 1977. Part I, "Seeing to Draw and Drawing to See."

Nicolaides, Kimon. *The Natural Way to Draw*. Boston: Houghton Mifflin, 1941. The classic drawing text that presents the author's sound and successful approach to drawing instruction.

Wilson, Brent, and Marjorie Wilson. *Teaching Children to Draw: A Guide for Parents*. Englewood Cliffs: Prentice-Hall, 1982.

Filmstrips

Perspective Drawing, Parts I and II. Sound filmstrips. Stamford, Ct.: Educational Dimensions, 1978. Very useful for teaching perspective, these filmstrips offer explicit instruction and show examples of perspective in the works of professional artists.

working

with paper

Tear it. Fold it. Rip it out and bend it. Slash it. Mend it. Twist it or crumple it. Tape it, glue it. Dissolve it. Score it, scratch it. Emboss it. Toss it away. "It," of course, is paper.*

SEVEN

Paper is one of the most accessible, least expensive, and versatile materials for the making of art. Not only is paper used as a surface on which to draw, paint, print, and make collage, but it is an art medium in its own right. Paper can be cut into intricate patterns, built into sturdy and detailed sculptures; it can be cut, folded, expanded, curled, twisted, torn, rolled, laminated, creped, and scored. The art world is undergoing a resurgence today in the use of paper as a medium of artistic expression. More artists today are hand-making papers as works of art, including prominent contemporary artists such as Frank Stella, Louise Nevelson, Sam Gilliam, and Ellsworth Kelly.[1]

[1] Jules Heller, *Papermaking* (New York: Watson-Guptill, 1978), p. 11.
*From Robert Munaff, "Think Paper," *Craft Horizons*, Vol. 27 (November–December 1967), p. 11.

Technological advances now permit us to think of paper in terms of furniture, clothing, boat hulls, and even geodesic domes. It is estimated that there are more than 14,000 different paper products and that each person in the United States uses nearly 600 pounds of paper per year.[2] It is no wonder that paper interests artists or that it is a basic medium for school art programs.

Because paper has so many uses as a medium of art expression, there are no firm rules about when paper work should be offered in the art program. Sometimes paper work can introduce art activities; sometimes it can supplement expression in paint. Sometimes it can serve as the major activity, since paper can also be used in sculpture or as part of a mixed-media process. The teacher should encourage children to test paper and to get some sense of its special qualities of strength, tension, and resilience. Children should learn that if they tear paper, it offers little resistance; yet if they pull it, another kind of force is involved. The many different types of paper, from heavy cardboard to delicate rice paper, and its numerous forms, such as boxes, cans, cups, and cartons, make paper an ideal medium for experimentation by children. Even very young children can make pictures by tearing or cutting different colored and textured papers. More sophisticated paper projects continue to interest children even into their adolescent years. The fact that mature artists use paper as a medium lends validity and integrity to its use in the school art program. In this chapter we will describe how to use paper and its derivatives in picture-making, modeling, and general construction work, as well as how to use paper as a plastic medium. We will also briefly discuss making paper by hand with inexpensive and accessible tools and materials.

Picture-Making with Paper

Media and Techniques. Every child from kindergarten through sixth grade can profit from picture-making with paper. Papers can be in a variety of colors, textures, weights, shapes, and sizes. Cartons filled with odds and ends of paper, from newsprint to corrugated cardboard to metallic and transparent papers, could be provided so that children can select the type of paper they want. The very fact that they are able to select from many kinds of paper stimulates children working in this medium, whatever their stage of development.

At early ages, children will tear and glue colored papers in very much the same manner as they scribble with crayons or work with paints. The kinesthetic qualities of the activity will sustain their interest, and they will learn about the properties of the medium through exploration. Children in

[2]Thelma Newman, J. Newman, and L. Newman, *Paper as Art and Craft* (New York: Crown, 1973).

the symbol-making stage will use the paper medium to make symbols, which will become increasingly easy to recognize as the children progress in age and experience. As in their drawings, common objects from life, such as people, houses, trees, cars, the sun, and so on, will appear as scraps of paper cut or torn and combined in appropriate shapes. The motivation for this type of activity often results, as with drawing and painting, from the children's natural interest in the medium and from their desire to depict and narrate.

Tools and materials for picture-making with paper may be quite simple. At the most basic level, all that is required is paper and paste or glue. White glue can be squeezed from the plastic bottle onto small scraps of paper or in small jar lids and distributed to each child. Glue can also be thinned with water and applied with inexpensive brushes. Children in the early manipulative stage can create pictures merely by tearing paper. Very soon, however, they will wish to use scissors, and these should be chosen with care. For young children, the scissors should be short and light; for more experienced pupils, they may be heavier and have longer cutting edges.[3] Although their cutting edges should be kept sharp, the scissors should not have pointed tips, since although these may be convenient to use, they are dangerous. It is quite important that left-handed pupils use left-handed scissors and that they also have an appropriate desk or work space. The pupils in the preadolescent stage might also be allowed to use artist's knives as well as scissors. These are artist's precision knives (often commercially known as X-acto knives, but available from several suppliers), which can be used for fine cutting. Remember to place a wooden or cardboard surface under the paper so table tops will not be ruined by the knife blade.

Children who work with paper to make pictures find that the new medium and tools do not present insurmountable difficulties although there are a few mechanical problems not found in painting. Beginners frequently have difficulty holding scissors in a cutting position. The teacher will have to use considerable judgment in determining whether or not the children possess sufficient muscular coordination to use scissors. Until the children are ready to use scissors, the teacher should encourage them to tear paper. At first, the pupils tear robustly and therefore with little control, but with practice they learn to be more exact.

Teaching. Older children, from first grade onward, might benefit from organized instruction by the teacher, who should at the same time recognize and respect each child's need to make personal expressive decisions. The following is an example of a picture-making project with paper as medium.

[3] Some children can use scissors successfully at ages 3 and 4, but many will not develop this skill until age 5.

The teacher begins by showing the children a large reproduction of a landscape painting by Kokoschka and asks the class, "Tell me what you see in this painting." The children respond by pointing to various parts of the picture and naming hills, trees, water, houses, and sky. Another landscape by Renoir (or any other accomplished painter) is shown, and the class is asked to respond again, naming the objects depicted by the artist. Possibly a third landscape might be used in a similar way.

The teacher continues, "These three paintings are different in many ways, but how are they the same?" Individual children respond by pointing out that they all have land, sky, trees. "Do you know what word we use for paintings like these?" asks the teacher. If a child knows and responds with the term *landscape*, the teacher reinforces and discusses the concept. If the children are unable to provide the term, the teacher does so. After discussion and clarification of the concept of landscape, the teacher asks the children to make a landscape of their own using the various papers that are ready for this purpose. The teacher's task then is to assist individuals with their work and to answer any questions.

The teacher may display the results of this activity on a wall so that the children can see the results of their creativity and at the same time be reminded of the concept that has been added to their store of knowledge about art. The teacher can organize similar activities around other fundamental art concepts, such as still life, figure, seascape, or abstraction.

Picture-making with paper will help children expand their ideas about design. As children in the manipulative stage become familiar with this medium, they find it possible to develop many interesting effects peculiar to it. The teacher should encourage children to play not only color against color but also texture against texture, metallic surface against the usual paper surface, and matte finish against glazed finish. Transparent papers might be used to add more variety to the design: overlapping two or more transparent papers with ordinary papers of varying hues produces particularly interesting effects. Children might be encouraged to make use of various textiles, string, and thin wood in their compositions.

Eventually childen, particularly those in the symbol stage, should learn how to build up their paper compositions from a support such as cardboard, thus developing three-dimensional effects. In working on a theme of flowers, for example, children can first glue the paper flowers flat to the support. The teacher can then demonstrate how petals can be curled by running the paper between the thumb and scissors and gluing the center portion of the flower. Three-dimensional effects can be achieved by scoring, say, the center veins of the leaves or petals. Other three-dimensional effects are obtained by bending, folding, twisting, cutting, and stretching. The illustration shows sculptural relief forms. The surfaces of the forms, rising from their support, catch the light in patterns determined by the manner in which the paper is cut, scored, and folded.

Working with Paper

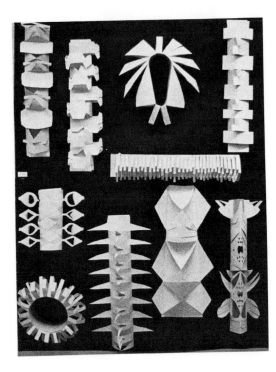

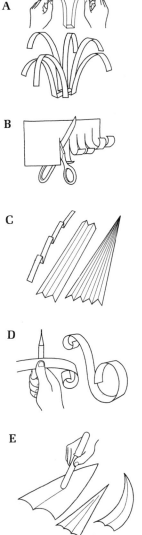

Fifth graders achieved these three-dimensional effects by cutting, scoring, and folding. (Photo by Rick Steadry). At the far right are some ways of developing three-dimensional forms in paper: (**A**) folding and bending, (**B**) frilling, (**C**) pleating, (**D**) stretching, (**E**) scoring, and (**F**) twisting.

Although the teacher will have to demonstrate certain techniques, demonstration as a teaching device should be used with restraint. Demonstration is a necessary and effective practice, but wrongly used it can inhibit the children, especially those in the manipulative and symbol stages.[4] Classes have been observed in which the paper work displayed an unfortunate uniformity resulting directly from an overeffective lesson on how to work with paper. The folds and cuts that the teacher carefully demonstrated were observed by the class to be practical: as a result, the children tended to rely on the teacher's thinking. Since children do have the ability to develop suitable methods on their own, it is not always good to cut short the struggle for mastery of the medium in order to arrive at quick results. Significant development in paper technique often occurs as a result of a child's personal conquest of the medium.

Actually, successful pictures in paper result from many teaching devices other than demonstration. In the initial phases of manipulation, most children will stick the torn or cut paper to a background without much help or suggestion from the teacher. The bright paper and the natural curiosity of children are sufficient motivations to start the production of

[4]See research on this point in "A Comparison of Instructional Methods for Teaching Contour Drawing to Children," in Jean Rush, J. Weckesser, and D. Sabers, *Studies in Art Education*, Vol. 21, No. 2 (1980).

pictures. Praise for being adventurous will encourage further experimentation. As children progress from manipulation to the production of symbols, the teacher's pleased and vocal recognition of well-established centers of interest, rhythms, and balances in the work of some individuals will help the whole class improve on design.

Eventually the characteristics of preadolescent art emerge. The problems of depth, tonality of color, pictorial composition, and more exact representation of objects arise in paper work just as they do in painting. Paper work, however, tends to move the child away from a concern with realism toward a greater awareness of the vivid effects of pattern and shape. Problems will arise from pupils' desire to make more realistic statements. The ranges of paper colors should then be expanded so that the pupils can employ tints and shades for depth and emphasis. The teacher should also see that many different textured papers are readily available. If pupils appear to feel handicapped by having to rely entirely on cutting and tearing, they should be allowed to draw or paint over some areas that require detail.

Sculpture with Paper

The most common form in which paper is used in schools is sheets, but paper also is found in many three-dimensional forms—such as boxes, cartons, and tubes—that are very useful for making sculpture. Paper can also be shaped into three dimensions through the process of papier-mâché.

BOX SCULPTURE

Media and Techniques. Probably the simplest type of sculpture for very young children is that made with paper or cardboard boxes. The only supplies necessary are an assortment of small cardboard containers, masking tape or other sticky paper tape, and possibly white glue. Tempera paint and suitable brushes can also be supplied. The containers should vary in shape and range in size from, say, about 1 inch to 1 foot on each side. If possible, cardboard tubes of different diameters and lengths and perhaps a few empty thread spools should also be provided.

The beginning of this activity is very much like building with blocks. Young children are able to innovate and learn as they stack the boxes and watch them tumble down. Then the children can use masking tape to secure the paper containers and build a permanent structure. For a more stable structure, children can glue the boxes and secure them with tape until the glue dries.

Young children delight in gluing containers together to build shapes at random, and later they like to paint them. As might be expected, they

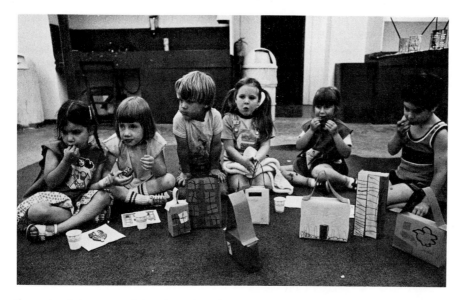

These simple box or container forms have been painted as architectural subjects and will be grouped to create a community. The children are six years old. At this stage, environmental education need not be separated from art-centered activities.

first build without apparent plan or subject matter in mind. Very quickly, however, children begin to name their constructions. "This is a bridge," says five-year-old Peter to his classmates, describing an object that faintly resembles such a structure. "This is my dad's factory," says Arthur, who has placed a chimneylike object on top of a box. "I guess it's a castle," says Mary, describing a gaily painted construction. This parallels the naming stage in drawing that occurs at an earlier age. Soon children begin to make plans before starting their work. One child might decide to make a boat;

Sculpture with boxes and bags turns into costume as these eleven-year-olds turn themselves into robots for a school play. The simple processes of pasting, joining, painting, and collage can be used to create sculpture, stage properties, or costumes.

another, to construct a house, paint it red, and build a garden around it. Thus, when working in sculpture, children tend to progress through the usual stages of manipulation and symbolic expression.

Teaching. For children in the manipulative stage, little teaching is required apart from the usual general encouragement and an attempt to keep the children free of glue and paint. In the symbol stage, the children should have ample opportunity to discuss their symbols with the teacher and with one another. In this way their work will grow in clarity and completeness. The teacher should encourage children in this stage to add significant details in cut paper and in paint.

A study of Haida Indian carvings preceded this unit (three class sessions) on totem poles. The students, eleven- and twelve-year-olds, created their own designs without relying on original sources. The surfaces were modeled in papier-mâché and painted with acrylic so that the works could be displayed outdoors. Heavy cardboard tubes were the base for building the forms. Each child or team of children worked on an individual unit. The sections were regrouped each day in order to maintain an ongoing sense of variety.

Older children, in the preadolescent stage, construct marvelous sculptural forms using paper containers. These sculptures can become quite large—taller than the young artists—and still remain lightweight and easy to move. The teacher can provide motivation by showing pictures or slides of sculpture. Modern, nonobjective, or abstract sculptures interest children and, at the same time, expose them to the real world of art. The sculptural forms of other cultures can be studied; for example, the monumental sculpture of ancient Egypt or the abstract forms of African carvings. The following text describes how to implement a paper-sculpture project based on the totem poles of the Indians of North America.

The teacher might begin by asking students what they know about totem poles; where they are found, how large they are, what they are made of, and what their purposes are. The teacher can supply information that is not forthcoming in the discussion or can assign individuals or groups of students to investigate and report. Pictures of totem poles can be shown, studied, and discussed. When the children have become sufficiently knowledgeable about totem poles to understand a related project, the teacher suggests that they make totem poles out of paper and cardboard containers. Depending on the ages of the group and the level of detail desired by the teacher, the children might begin planning totem poles with some symbolic meaning given to each figure and a definite order for the figures from bottom to top just as real totems have. In such a project, it is often desirable to encourage the children to work in groups of three or four.

The students begin construction by gathering a variety of rectangular, round, and unusually shaped containers and stacking them to create a pole-like form. Flexible cardboard can be cut and shaped into tubes, triangular forms, and so on, according to need. The pieces are taped together as the pole takes shape. At this point the class should decide what holes and notches to cut with a knife or scissors to make facial features, and what shapes to add to make wings, arms, headpieces, fabricated from paper and taped onto the pole.

When the basic pole is completed, surface decorations of cut colored paper can be glued on or tempera paint applied. The entire construction and decoration can follow a traditional Indian theme or can be a contemporary example of the totem concept. The results are often striking and impressive in their size and visual presence. In this type of project, children learn not only about an art medium, design, and technique, but also about the art of another culture.

Children in the upper elementary grades find other freestanding forms of paper sculpture challenging. The supplies required for such sculpture include the usual scissors, knife, construction paper, and cardboard; odds

OTHER FREESTANDING FORMS

and ends of colored paper, tape, and glue; and a vast array of miscellaneous articles such as drinking straws, toothpicks, and pins with colored heads.

The chief problem in developing freestanding forms in paper lies in the necessity to develop a shape that will support the completed object. A tentlike form is perhaps the first such shape children will devise. Later they may fashion a paper tube or cone strong enough to support whatever details they plan to add. In constructing a figure of a clown, for example, the children might make a cylinder of paper for the head, body, and legs. The arms might be cut from flat paper and glued to the sides of the cylinder. A hat could be made in a conical shape from more paper. Details of features and clothing might then be added with either paint or more paper.

Media and Techniques. For preadolescent children, it is practical to use rolled paper to construct objects. Old newspapers may be used together with glue, tape, and sometimes wire. Children who begin this work obviously must possess some ability to make plans in advance of production. Their plans must include an idea of the nature and size of the object to be fashioned. Will it be a person or a bear, a chicken or a giraffe? What will be its general shape? When this is decided, the underlying structure is easily developed. Arms, legs, body, and head may all be produced from rolled newspapers. A chief component, say, the body, should be taped at several places and other components taped to it. Should one part of the creation tend to be flimsy because of extreme length—perhaps the giraffe's neck—it can be reinforced by wire or strips of cardboard or wood.

When the main structure is complete, it is strengthened by carefully wrapping one-inch-wide strips of newspaper, dipped in art paste, around all parts of the object—until it looks like an Egyptian mummy. While it is still wet, the children can add details, such as eyes, ears, tail, and nose made of buttons, scraps of fur, and other odds and ends. When dry, the creation may be painted and covered with shellac or varnish. Paste for this project and for papier-mâché should be one of the nontoxic plastics such as the powdered vinyl Metylan, which is mixed with water, or a polyvinyl acetate such as the various brands of white glue. Wheat paste is not recommended because of possible allergic reactions, the difficulty in storing the wheat paste and water solution, and its attraction for insect and animal pests. The new vinyl wallpaper pastes are generally superior to wheat paste.

Preadolescent children may use heavy construction paper or thin cardboard to fashion miniature buildings. Also required are a ruler, scissors, knife, and strong glue. Although children in kindergarten and perhaps the first grade also construct buildings, these are very simple and symbolic in character. Usually only the facade is produced, which must be glued to a small box in order to stand upright. Preadolescent pupils gener-

Rolled-paper animals made by fifth grade pupils. (Photo by Royal Studio.)

ally wish to develop more realistic four-sided structures. After folding the four sides of a construction-paper house into a hollow square, the children can add a roof—which the child at first may make flat but later will give a peak. Gradually children improve the structures, and in time they learn to plan in advance even the details of cutting and folding. They learn to leave tabs for gluing; details such as windows, doors, and porches may be painted on or cut from other paper and fixed in place. To the basic structure, moreover, children will probably add wings, garages, and so on. Drinking straws, tongue depressors, swab sticks, wire, and string are among the items that children eventually use to enlarge on architectural ideas.

Teaching.   The teacher will often find it necessary to resort to demonstrations of the techniques involved in general freestanding paper sculpture, rolled-paper sculpture, and miniature architectural work in paper. It is important that teachers always try art projects themselves before introducing them to students. This is the best way to anticipate problems and the need for demonstrations. As a project progresses, teachers should observe each pupil and be ready to make suggestions, so that an otherwise impractical improvisation in a paper technique can be successfully altered. For example, a pupil may have forgotten to leave sufficient paper to make tabs for fastening two pieces of paper together. The teacher could suggest sticky tape to replace the tabs. If a horse's head in rolled paper is so heavy that it droops, a thin stick of wood, wired to the neck from body to head, might be suggested as a solution to the problem.

The teacher may also find it necessary, at least with less-experienced pupils, to offer many suggestions on how to finish the articles. After studying a pupil's rolled-paper figure of a clown, the teacher might suggest, for example, that absorbent cotton from the scrap box would make a good beard, or that small buttons glued to the main paper figure would complete the clown's costume.

As the pupils gain experience, the teacher must emphasize the necessity of making reasonably detailed plans in advance. The pupils might make sketches of the basic shape of a figure so that it can be accurately cut out. Even a sketch of a rolled-paper figure in which some indication of proportions and reinforcement points is given is occasionally helpful. In fact, the pupils and teacher together might well go through all stages of using a medium in advance of individual construction.

Architectural construction sometimes requires even more detailed plans in which every tab and fold, together with each component of the planned assembly, is decided on before starting work. Such details, however, need not always be planned in advance. Much of the fun in this, as in other art work, comes from improvisation. Nor should the teacher expect perfection in the children's work. They must be permitted to develop both their thinking and their skills at their own pace. Preadolescents are usually no more ready to construct, say, a well-made model of a house than to produce a professional painting. The same kinds of flaw will be found in other early paper construction. Only time, experience, and effort will allow them to master the difficult feat of constructing in paper. The teacher must accept learners' initial efforts until their skill grows more exact.

MOLDED PAPER AND PAPIER-MÂCHÉ

There are two types of paper work in which the material is sufficiently plastic to be molded and modeled. The first type, molded paper, uses dampened paper; the second uses mashed paper, or as it is more commonly known, papier-mâché. Dampened paper is suitable for children in the advanced symbol stage; papier-mâché can be used by children in all stages.

Media and Techniques. To work in molded paper, old newspapers, art paste, tape, tempera paint, shellac, perhaps some clay, scissors, and a willing pair of hands are all that are necessary.

Model igloos, tunnels, mountains, and the like are easily produced by covering different types of substructures with the sticky strips of newsprint. The substructures can be made with fine wire netting, clay, balls, or slightly dampened newspaper that has been pressed into the desired shape. In producing paper forms over these constructed molds, the first step is to make the substructure as close to the desired shape as possible. Wads of slightly dampened newspaper can be used to produce the mold. Plastic wrap or waxed paper placed over the mold will keep it from sticking to the next layers. The entire assembly should then be covered with strips of newsprint that have been dipped in paste. Each layer of paper should be laid down in the opposite direction from the preceding layer. Crisscrossing the strips adds strength to the construction. By using papers of different colors (like classified ads and comic strips), children can distinguish one layer from another. When the paper has dried into a hard shell, the inner wads of newsprint can be removed. Details can be developed further from paper or various scrap materials. Paint and shellac are added to color the finished product.

Modeled clay, the surface of which has been thoroughly greased or covered with plastic wrap before the strips of paper are set down, can also be used as a base for much of this type of work. Firing clay or oil-based plasticine is particularly recommended if children possess special ability in art, because it lends itself to a greater variety of modeling effects. If plasticine is in short supply, a substructure of scrap wood can be used to support the sculpted surface. Earth clay must be kept under plastic to preserve dampness from one day to the next. When using either, pupils should keep the substructure smooth and free of undercuts so that the paper "skin" will come off easily.

A popular variation of the paper-modeling process is the use of inflated balloons of various sizes and shapes as the foundation. The resulting three-dimensional forms are quite useful for making masks. The round form of dried paper strips can be cut in half with a knife, and eyes and mouth can be cut away if desired. Additional forms can be applied and covered with more paper strips and art paste to make protruding noses, facial features, or decorative embellishments. The possibilities of combining forms are endless. Heads of animals can be made and embellished with yarn, fur pieces, colored paper, and so on.

Papier-Mâché.   Papier-mâché, or mashed paper, has been used as a modeling medium for centuries. Chinese soldiers of antiquity are said to have made their armor with this material. Mashed paper is strong and may be put to many uses in an art class. To prepare this claylike medium, tear newsprint into small pieces. (Do not use magazine paper with a glazed surface, because fibers do not break down as readily into a mash.) Leave the torn paper to soak overnight in water. It is possible to use an electric blender to mash the paper in water, but is not necessary. Instead, mash the paper in a strainer to remove the water, or wring it in a cotton cloth. Four sheets of newspaper shredded will need four tablespoons of white glue (polyvinyl acetate) as a binder. Stir until the pulp has a claylike consistency. If desired, a spoonful of linseed oil can be added for smoothness and a few drops of oil of cloves or wintergreen as a preservative. This mixture can be wrapped in plastic and stored in the refrigerator. The teacher can also purchase commercially prepared mixtures of papier-mâché that require only the addition of water.

Children in the manipulative stage can roll papier-mâché and pum-

Because paper is both versatile and inexpensive, papier-mâché can be used to create large forms. Papier-mâché can be draped or pressed on any surface, from balloons to modeled clay. It can also be squeezed into soft pulp and modeled very much like clay. When dry, it can be lifted off the base and painted.

mel it; in the symbol stage they can produce three-dimensional forms with it—shapes of different fruits, for example. Preadolescent children can learn to control the medium further and model sculptured pieces. After the mashed paper has dried—a process that takes about a week—it can be worked with hand tools. The dried papier-mâché forms can be sandpapered; holes can be bored in it; it can be carved and painted. Acrylic paint is particularly useful both for its brilliant color and its protective qualities. Objects painted with other types of paint should be shellacked if possible.

Teaching. Because a kind of metamorphosis occurs in both modeling and molding between the beginning and end of the process, children may become confused unless they have a clear picture of the entire process before they begin. The teacher, therefore, should prepare a step-by-step display of paper as it changes from flimsy newspaper to the hard, painted shell resulting from the papier-mâché process.

Paper-Making

The ultimate use of paper as an art medium is the actual making of paper by hand from vegetable sources. The paper-making process is a fascinating one, somewhat similar to pottery-making in that it has evolved from primitive sources over many centuries and involves the creation of useful and beautiful objects from the basic resources of the earth. Today, although methods and materials have not changed, contemporary artists are not only making paper for drawing, painting, printmaking, and even photography, but they are molding and casting paper, using paper for sculpture, and making paper from unusual natural materials. This process has received much attention from contemporary artists, causing Jules Heller to comment:

> We are witness to the revolution in paper. This revolution will no longer allow a sensitive individual to examine a figure without equally inspecting the ground on which it sits . . . paper.[5]

Under the guidance of a teacher, children can make papers for similar purposes.

Tools and Techniques. A basic paper-making project requires a blender or mixer; a bucket to hold the pulp; an electric iron (this is optional); a sink or laundry tub; a mold (a wooden frame and screen); deckle (a wooden frame that holds wet pulp on the mold); and paper or felt for blotting. The actual materials from which the paper can be made vary widely, but the most common is probably cotton rag. Beginners should use papers and vegetable materials that will break down easily in the blender to form the pulp. This is a suggested recipe and method:

1. Make two wooden frames the same size out of 1-by-2-inch wood. The size of the frames can vary according to the desired paper size and the size of the tub. Tack or staple a piece of plastic screening (the type used for screen doors) onto one frame. This is the mold, and the other frame, the deckle, fits on top of the mold.
2. Soak about 30 sheets of facial tissue overnight in about 1 liter of water (4 cups). Other papers, such as toilet paper, napkins, newspaper, and paper bags, can also be used.
3. Pour the paper into the blender and blend. The result is called *pulp* or *stock.*
4. Pour the pulp into about 9 liters (10 quarts) of clean water and stir. This is called the *slurry.* Add about 1 tablespoon of instant starch dissolved in 2 cups of water. This is not essential, but helps the paper to take ink well.
5. Place the deckle on the mold, hold tightly with both hands, and dip the mold into the tub of slurry.
6. Hold the mold level in a horizontal position and raise it out of the slurry. Quickly shake the mold and deckle sideways to lock the fibers and form an even sheet.
7. Set the mold and deckle on a sheet of felt or blotting paper (newsprint will do) and remove the deckle. The sheet of paper, very wet and thick, is now resting on the mold.

[5] Heller, *Papermaking.*

8. Place a blotter sheet on top of the wet pulp and turn the mold over, face down, on the table. Sponge or blot excess water away through the screen.
9. Carefully remove the screen: there is the sheet of handmade paper. Place another blotter sheet on the wet paper and iron dry, or leave the pulp on the mold to dry.

Children can experiment with many variations of this basic process. Paper can be made from numerous vegetable sources, such as onion skins, cornhusks, sawdust, straw, carrots, banana peels, and leaves. Almost any natural fiber that contains cellulose will provide the bonding quality necessary for making paper. Numerous paper products, such as egg cartons, cardboard, and newspaper, also can be recycled into handmade paper. Lint from a clothes dryer, thread, and strong, thin natural objects can be incorporated into the paper. The slurry can be colored with dyes, and the molds can be made with raised portions for relief design and texture. The paper-making process is simple and inexpensive, and the possibilities are endless.

Teaching. Paper-making works well both with small groups of children and with an entire class. A few sessions of paper-making will provide the teacher with the experience necessary to decide how the process might best fit into the curriculum. Some teachers help their pupils to make greeting cards from their handmade paper. Using it in conjunction with printmaking (such as vegetable printing or block printing), the children can experience two art media simultaneously. They can make small books or even bookcovers from their handmade paper, or the paper itself can be mounted and displayed as art.[6]

[6] See the beautiful papers in *American Craft,* February–March, 1981.

Group mural in collage of a Bedouin Village by ten- and eleven-year-olds, Israel. The group used whatever materials were at hand: cloth, cardboard, paper, sections of weaving from a previous project. Background areas were set in first, and subjects were then glued in place.

"Stop," second grade. Collage made by cutting and tearing the paper.

Making pictures with paper

1. With a range of colored papers (including some light, dark, and middle grays, and black and white) and rubber cement or paste, make a nonobjective picture on a piece of heavy paper or cardboard no smaller than 18 by 24 inches. You might start by developing a colorful center of interest out of an irregularly shaped area cut from a bright piece of paper. Thin strips of paper in contrasting colors, acting as a contrast to this center, could be used to develop interesting and useful rhythms. Watch the balance of your composition as the background becomes covered up. Stop before the work becomes cluttered.

2. Cut pieces of paper from the colored, the halftone, and the black-and-white pages of a magazine. Make a picture using these pieces, recutting them where necessary. Use the differences in texture of the various scraps to good aesthetic effect. Your theme may be realistic, abstract, or completely nonfigurative.

3. Set up a still life and base a paper picture on the arrangement. Watch tonalities of color and other aspects of general composition.

4. Make a collage using a subject like a portrait of an old man or an old house. Use such materials as absorbent cotton, felt, and printed cottons, as well as paper, in your work. Absorbent cotton might suggest hair or eyebrows, for example; felt or sandpaper, a man's beard; printed cloth, a background. For the house use such textures as sandpaper, painted paper, wallpaper, and so on. Use a little paint for details if you wish. Try to be imaginative, but be restrained in achieving variety in your design.

Other activities

5. Prepare a chart showing paper that has been scored, twisted, frayed, stretched, curled, torn, and so on, until you have included all the ways you can think of for treating paper for picture-making.

6. Make a collection of papers to develop a graduated range of textures from roughest to smoothest.

7. Make a collection of gray papers and show their gradations in tone. Do the same with a range of papers in one hue.

8. Collect some cardboard boxes and wooden spools. Select a relatively large box for the body of some animal. Add smaller boxes or spools for the legs, neck, and finally the head. Add paper, felt, or cloth ears; a string or paper tail; paper, button, or large pin-head eyes. Paint with tempera color, and when dry, cover with one or two coats of varnish, shellac, or acrylic polymer. A brush 1 inch wide is useful for applying the acrylic, varnish, or shellac. After shellacking, wash the brush in methyl alcohol (which is a poison). After using varnish, wash the brush in turpentine or a turpentine substitute. The brush used to apply the acrylic polymer can be washed simply in water.

9. Make freestanding figures of animals or people based on each of the following basic forms: (a) a tent made with one simple fold; (b) a cylinder; (c) a cone that may be cut to shape after twisting and gluing. Heads and legs should be devised by cutting and shaping paper and gluing it in place. Add features and details of clothing by gluing cut-paper pieces to the basic shape.

10. Make an object out of rolled newspaper. Roll the newspaper into a tight cylinder for the body and tie it with string in three or four places. For arms and legs, make thinner cylinders of newspaper tied with string as above. Tie the arms and legs to the body. Next the neck and head should either be modeled separately and attached to the body or be bent under as an extension of the body cylinder. Dip strips of newspaper or paper toweling about 1 inch wide into paste and wrap them around the figure. When the object is dry add details with colored paper, scraps of fur, and so on. Finish with paint and shellac.

11. Make a model building out of cardboard. Sketch your plan beforehand, working out the position of tabs. Draw the plan accurately on cardboard. Cut away excess cardboard and score the cardboard with the back of a pair of scissors where the folds are to be made. Fold and glue. Add details such as drinking straws for veranda posts and cut paper for windows. Prepare a landscape for the model, perhaps using green and gray paper for lawns and paths, twigs with green paper leaves for trees, and paper in bright colors for flower beds.

12. Make a mask over a clay base. On a workboard, model a mold for the mask in clay. Leave the clay to dry overnight; then cover it with cooking oil or small pieces of wax paper. Dip 1-inch strips of newspaper into paste and lay them over the clay mold, pressing them gently to the wax paper (or oil) covering the clay. Crisscross paper strips until they make four or more layers. To help keep track of the layers, alternate layers of the Sunday comics with black-and-white newsprint. When dry, lift the shell away from the mold, trim the edges, cut holes for the mouth and eyes, paint, shellac, and add other features from a "junk" collection, such as curtain rings for earrings, fur for hair, and so on.

13. Practice laying a shell of newspaper strips over a mold made of wads of dampened newspaper. After doing exercise 12, the reader will find the directions offered earlier in the chapter sufficient.

14. Prepare papier-mâché according to the directions on page 227. While it is wet, model some of this plastic medium on a workboard into a nonobjective form. With the rest of the pulp, model a representational form. Be sure to keep these objects solid and chunky rather than spindly; the solid form will more readily stay in one piece as it dries. When the objects are dry, try making one of them smoother by rubbing it lightly with fine sandpaper. Paint both the smooth and the rough object with tempera paint to enhance the designs already created.

15. Using pieces of decorative wrapping paper in a wide variety of patterns, make a collage of a city scene, showing architectural forms; unite the different patterns with paint or create an abstract design.

16. Prepare an attractive and easily understood exhibit for classroom display, showing the papier-mâché process from newsprint to finished object.[7]

[7] See Victoria Betts, *Exploring Papier-Mâché* (Worcester, Ma.: Davis, 1966).

Betts, Victoria. *Exploring Papier-Mâché.* Worcester, Ma.: Davis, 1966. Media and techniques for work with papier-mâché.

Heller, Jules. *Papermaking.* New York: Watson-Guptill, 1978. An articulate text on the topic with excellent illustrations and beautiful color reproductions of paper works by contemporary artists.

Johnson, Pauline. *Creating with Paper.* Seattle: University of Washington Press, 1966. A fine book for projects in paper, well written and illustrated.

Lord, Lois. *Collage and Construction.* Rev. ed. Worcester, Ma.: Davis, 1970. Projects from two-dimensional collage to three-dimensional construction, often utilizing found or inexpensive materials.

Newman, Thelma, J. Newman, and L. Newman. *Paper as Art and Craft.* New York: Crown, 1973. A helpful book on the use of paper as an art form.

Roettger, Ernst. *Creative Paper Design.* New York: Reinhold, 1961. One of a series of excellent design books by this author, it displays an amazing range of possibilities for creating with paper.

sculpture and pottery:
modeling, carving,
and constructing

Essentially sculpture means taking possession of a space, the construction of an object by means of hollows and volumes, fullnesses and voids: their alternations, their contrasts, their constant and reciprocal tension, and in final form, their equilibrium.[*]

EiGHT

Drawing and painting are accomplished primarily on two-dimensional surfaces, usually paper, canvas, or board. Sculpture is fashioned in three dimensions and is classified as free-standing or relief. Free-standing sculpture, or sculpture in the round, is the type that can be viewed from many angles, such as a statue. Relief sculpture is usually viewed from the front, like a painting, and is seen on a wall or other surface that cannot be viewed from behind.

Modeling, carving, and construction are typical processes involved in making sculpture. Modeling involves building up a form from material, such as clay, and then adding and shaping the material. For example,

[*]From Henri Laurens, quoted in Andrew Carnduff Ritchie, *Sculpture of the Twentieth Century* (New York: Museum of Modern Art, 1953), p. 43.

235

when modeling a head in clay, the basic form is modeled and then more clay is added and shaped to develop the nose, hair, ears, and other features. Modeling, then, is usually an additive process. Carving is typically a subtractive process in which the material, such as wood or plaster, is carved or chipped away until the desired sculptural form emerges. Sculpture also involves a process of construction in which the materials are cut or shaped or found, and bound together with appropriate materials. Welded metal, nailed or glued wood, and a limitless array of materials, from sheet plastic and glass to driftwood and junk, can all be used to create sculpture. Selecting materials and experimenting with methods of modeling, carving, and constructing provide much of the excitement in making sculpture.

Today's art requires a rather broad definition of sculpture, one that takes into account the mixed-media approach and the interrelation of art and technology. "Shaped canvases" can be viewed as painted sculpture or as painting that moves into space. In assemblage, artists create unusual contexts for mundane "found objects." The Pop artist Marisol combines whimsical and traditional drawing with carved and geometric forms. Jean Tinguely animates his constructions with intricate mechanical devices; other artists experiment with sound and light as components of the total sculptural experience. Because children respond positively to many of the concepts inherent in sculpture today, problems of both a traditional and a contemporary nature should be considered when planning activities that are built around forming, shaping, and constructing.

In the traditional sense, carving and modeling are activities in which raw materials from the earth and the forest are directly manipulated by the artist. In modeling, artists may approach clay with no tools other than their bare hands, while in carving wood and other media, a tool as primitive as a knife allows artists to pit their skill against the material. If the artist shows respect for it, the primary characteristics of the original material remain in the finished product. Wood remains wood, clay remains clay, and each substance clearly demonstrates its influence on the art form into which it was fashioned.

Children in all stages of development can work successfully in modeling clay and in one or another form of wood sculpture. Only older preadolescents, however, are able to carve wood and plaster of Paris, since the skills involved are beyond the ability of younger children and some of the tools required are too dangerous for them to use. It is important when considering the appropriateness of art activities for various grade levels to make a distinction between *media* and *concepts*. Instead of arbitrarily relegating any one type of material to a particular grade level, the teacher should examine the material in terms of the specific problem to be explored. While it is true that the range of manual control varies with the age of the children, there are some concepts associated with a particular medium that are within the children's capability on every grade level. For

Sculpture and Pottery: Modeling, Carving, and Constructing

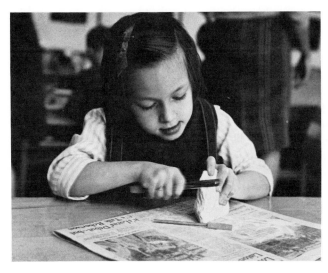

Carving may begin in the primary grades, as evidenced by this second grader's handling of soft soapstone. Tools are simple rasps, files, and cut pipe. (Photo by Education Development Center.)

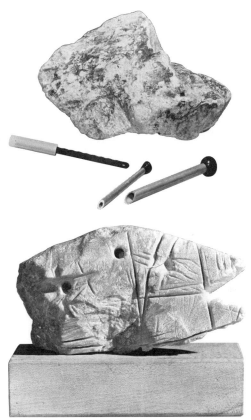

instance, even elementary-school children engaged in making animal figures can be encouraged to "pull out the shapes" and to "piece the figure together so that the parts don't fall off." They can practice maintaining uniform thickness of the side of a pinch pot and can press patterns of found objects into clay tiles. These concepts might be presented to the children with such remarks as:

> "There are many ways of making sculpture. As all artists do, choose the one that is most comfortable for you."
> "Some kinds of modeling (or sculpture) require practice, just like learning a musical instrument or handling a ball. It may be difficult at first, but practice will help you to make something that you will want to keep."
> "Even a flat piece of sculpture (relief) can be made to catch light. Then it will make interesting surface patterns."
> "There is an animal form trapped in this piece of clay. Can you help it come out, so we can see what it is?"

Sculpture and Pottery: Modeling, Carving, and Constructing

Sculpture has a universal appeal, and the problems of creating forms in space and of wedding materials and processes to ideas engages the interest of people of all age groups. Indeed, the ideas discussed in this chapter are as useful to senior-high-school or even college students as they are to elementary-school students. The children who make their first papier-mâché masks and the team of teenagers involved in carving totemic figures out of discarded telephone poles can benefit equally from the practical suggestions found here. In this chapter, we will deal mainly with the basic sculptural materials of clay, wood, and plaster of Paris. Cardboard and found materials also can be used with many of the ideas presented here.

Sculpture in Wood

USING SCRAPS OF WOOD

Children can handle wood in many ways. Odd shapes can be glued into structures just as they are, or they can be adjusted by carving, sawing, and planing. The surface of the wood in turn can be left as is, or it can be painted or stained. Surfaces can also be sanded smooth or "pebbled" with carving tools; edges can be rounded with a file or plane. The options for design in wood, as in painting, are many, the only limitations being the child's manual control and the tools available.

Simple materials such as scrap pieces of wood, glue, tempera or acrylic paints, and colored tapes can be arranged by children to form elegant sculptures. Children explore relationships of mass, space, and balance as they make these sculptural forms.

Media and Techniques. If access to an industrial arts shop in a nearby secondary school is available, the teacher may obtain scraps of wood varying in shape and size. These scraps should be inspected to see that they have no dangerous splinters. In addition to scraps of wood the children might be supplied with tongue depressors, swab sticks, and wooden spools. To fix pieces of wood together, use a particularly strong glue such as white vinyl, which can be purchased at any hardware store. As with all materials used to make art, care should be exercised for the health and safety of students and teachers. Avoid glues that might have toxic fumes, and be wary of fast-sticking glues that can stick fingers or objects together.

Children in the manipulative and symbol stages put together pieces of wood much as they put together the boxes and tubes in box sculpture. They select two pieces of wood, smear both with glue along the edges to be stuck, and then press them firmly together. If hammers and nails are available, children can nail together the pieces of wood to make a strong, permanent bond. The process is continued until several pieces of wood form one solid structure. A swab stick or a tongue depressor can be used to apply the glue. After assembling the pieces, children often like to paint their structures. A complex piece, composed of eight or nine wood scraps varying in size and shape, can be given unity through the addition of a single color or through color patterns that correspond to sharply articulated planes. Whereas older children may use paint and sculpture to solve a problem in design, younger children may color surfaces only for decoration.

The distribution of supplies causes few special problems. Scraps of wood may be placed in cartons from which each child can select a number of pieces. The glue is best distributed by the teacher, who should place a dab of it on paper or cardboard and set it before each child. Paint is handled in the usual manner described for picture-making.

Media and Techniques. Only older preadolescent children, usually in about the fifth and sixth grades, will be able to produce wood sculpture in the traditional manner. Traditional wood sculpture consists of carving bumps and hollows in a suitable piece of wood. Neither very hard woods like oak nor very soft woods like balsa are suitable for children's work. The hard woods, of course, demand more strength than children possess, while the soft woods fail to offer the resistance that children's developing muscles require.

Wherever possible, woods from the local environment should be selected. By using local wood, children explore their immediate environment and capitalize on their own resources. Wood from poplars, pines, birches, and many other trees, when seasoned, has excellent qualities for sculpture.

SCULPTURE IN THE ROUND

One of Picasso's many sculptures from wood scraps, *Musical Instruments*, 1914. His playfulness led Picasso to discover surprising uses for castoff materials. (Owned by the artist's estate. Photo by John Webb, FRPS. © 1974 by SPADEM PARIS.)

Lumber yards often sell suitable scraps of these woods. If the wood is damp, it should be stacked under cover outdoors until it dries. Wind dries the wood, and stacking prevents it from warping.

Some schools might have to depend on scraps of wood from discarded objects, such as old boxes or broken furniture, or from friendly fruit dealers or building contractors. If there is no source of discarded wood, the school can usually purchase sufficient wood for its needs at reasonable cost. A call to the local telephone company might yield free telephone poles, sometimes delivered directly to the schools.

Wood can be worked with a considerable degree of satisfaction with merely a strong, sharp pocketknife. Sets of carving tools may be bought, however, that allow children to produce a wide variety of cuts. These tools are obtainable in a number of shapes, such as straight-edged knives, V-gouges, and U-gouges. All tools should be kept sharp. In addition, some files, rasps, and sandpaper, from coarse to fine grain, may be required.

Wood can be cut on a piece of plywood placed over a school desk, but wood sculpture is best performed on an industrial arts (carpenter's) bench. These benches usually are fitted with vises that allow the student to place both hands on the cutting tools. (Without a vise, the student must hold the wood with one hand and carve with the other. Unless great care is exercised injuries can occur.) In general, the wood should be cut in the direction away from the body. Rough two-by-four strips bolted to the side

Sculpture and Pottery: Modeling, Carving, and Constructing

of the work table will provide a protective surface against which pupils who work without a vise can carve. This permits students to sit while carving.

The method of working with wood recommended here is that of "roughing out" the subject from all sides. The student holds the wood in one hand and presses it against the bench, or places it in the vise, if one is available, while applying the carving tool along the grain. Turning the piece and cutting, the student gets rid of excess wood until the desired shape begins to be formed. Rasps—very coarse files—may be used at the close of the roughing-out process if the vise is used. The sculpting-in-the-round approach allows the student to create a solid, chunky piece of sculpture that is attractive in its "woodiness."

The piece must be finished with some care, so that neither the design nor the inherent quality of the wood is spoiled. For a smooth finish, the student can use a rasp followed by a file and later by sandpaper on the surface. Wood usually requires the application of a preservative; perhaps the most acceptable is wax. A thin coat of solidified wax can be applied with a cloth and then polished vigorously. Successive coats should follow until the wood glows. A thin oil stain might occasionally be employed to enhance the wood, but this preservative should be used with caution. For one thing, it is often difficult to maintain a desired uniformity of tone because of the effect of the grain of the wood. Also, a bright stain may distort the natural appearance of the wood. Too often, a fine white wood can be spoiled by the application of a "mahogany" stain. Other than wax, perhaps the safest and most satisfactory finishes for wood are clear varnish and colorless shellac, both of which may be applied with a brush. Even with these coverings, however, there is a danger of making the wood look like toffee. In short, unless the wood is to be painted, nothing is better than the quality of wood itself.

Teaching. Sculpture in wood affords many opportunities for effective teaching; in particular it calls for discussion and demonstration. Wood is a medium with many excellent qualities that must not be destroyed through clumsy and inappropriate working techniques. The teacher's first task is to discuss with the class the fine qualities of wood—its color; its grain; its various surface qualities enhanced by different finishes, including sanding, waxing, and painting. Studies might be made of the various uses to which wood may be put and of how people have often relied on it to develop civilization.[1] Included in these studies might be examples of faulty as well as successful treatment of wood. It is always useful to show children examples of good quality art done by adult artists and to discuss the works with them. This is especially true if pieces can be found that exemplify and illustrate the goals set by the teacher, such as respecting the

[1] See Lewis Mumford, *Technics and Civilization* (New York: Harcourt Brace Jovanovich, 1963).

This wood sculpture by Louise Nevelson demonstrates the rhythmic possibilities of the medium. *Case with Five Balusters*, 1959. White wood. (Courtesy of Martha Jackson Gallery.) Nevelson's approach contrasts with that of Picasso (p. 240); a comparison of the two works can help make children aware of the handling of pattern, the unifying effect of color, and the difference between machine-tooled and "raw" wood forms.

natural properties of the material and allowing the material to contribute to the total expressiveness of the sculpture. Viewing and discussing art can also assist children to clarify the artistic purposes in their own work. The teacher will also find it necessary to discuss the subject matter suitable for wood sculpture. Making references to sculpture in wood, from medieval German sculptors to moderns such as Louise Nevelson, will teach students that sculpture is a form of expression as personal as painting.[2] In addition

[2] For information about modern sculpture, see Barbara Rose, *American Art Since 1900* (New York: Holt, Rinehart and Winston, 1975).

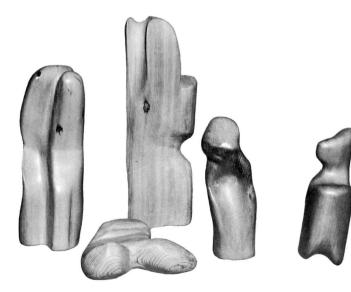

Wood sculpture made by sixth graders. These objects are similar to the "feelies" of the Bauhaus school. They provide a basic lesson in the various stages of wood sculpture—shaping, filing, sanding, staining. (Photo by Royal Studio.)

to suggesting expression based on representational themes, the teacher might encourage students to do some nonobjective work. In this way students can concentrate on troublesome aspects of technique without being concerned with subject matter.

Because most tools for working with wood are dangerous, the teacher should demonstrate the correct ways of handling them and, perhaps, discuss safety in using tools and procedures for giving first aid for a cut. The teacher should give lessons concerning the sharpening and care of tools, emphasizing the pride good artisans have in their tools. A class trip to a sculptor's studio would be very worthwhile. A suitable project at this point might be the making of "feelies," small, highly polished carved objects designed to feel good in the hand.[3] Before working with wood itself, it might be a good idea for children to experiment with clay and soap to find out how material can relate to the hand. Because the "feelie" is hand-sized, the student has no difficulty giving the wood a high finish by sawing, filing, sanding, polishing, and waxing.

The child who works with wood in the round should learn that the chunky appearance of this sculpture is a natural outcome of the technique. The teacher should emphasize the fact that flimsy protuberances of any kind are not in keeping with this type of wood sculpture and tend to affect the design adversely. The child should also be taught that any detail that is cut into the main contours must be developed with some restraint lest the distinctive wood quality of the piece be lost. Such insights into the technique will develop through practice.

As the children work in wood, they should be taught that the bumps, hollows, and textures they have carved must be studied for the patterns of light and shade they produce. By holding a child's sculpture in a reasonably strong light coming from one source, the teacher can demonstrate how to study the highlights and shadows. As in other art forms, it is far more important for children to learn to judge the quality of sculpture from the point of view of design than to judge it for its "realistic" appearance.

A constant challenge in teaching sculpture is to select and employ only those teaching methods that develop students' artistic integrity and taste. The search for excellence of craftsmanship will show clearly in wood sculpture, as will the growing mastery of tools. Any subterfuge in the treatment of wood soon becomes evident. For example, pupils should not be obliged to obliterate the tool marks from the surface of their work if they do not wish to do so. Tool marks may add greatly to the design quality and particularly to the texture of a piece of sculpture.

[3]The Bauhaus included such exercises in its design course. The artists began by rolling the wood over and over again in their hands until a certain shape began to suggest itself. This experimentation often led to the solution of such varied industrial problems as developing handles for gun stocks and designing refrigerator doors.

Sculpture in Plaster of Paris

For most children in the preadolescent stage, a suitable medium for sculpture is plaster of Paris. A child who is capable of using any kind of cutting tool safely can use this material successfully. Plaster of Paris can produce sculpted pieces displaying satisfying qualities either in relief or in the round.

Media and Techniques. The plaster is usually bought in sacks. It should be mixed by sifting handfuls of the plaster into a pail of water until the plaster reaches the water level. The mixture should then be activated by sliding the hand under the plaster and moving the fingers around the bottom of the pail. This attains a creamy consistency without lumps. Waterproof gloves or other protection prevents possible skin reactions to the plaster. If the plaster tends to dry too quickly, the rate of drying may be slowed by adding about a teaspoonful of salt for every two cups of plaster.

After it is mixed with water, the plaster must be poured quickly into a mold to dry and harden. Small cardboard containers make suitable molds. (Children may also create their own molds by taping sections of heavy cardboard together.) The container is selected according to the type of work intended; a shoe box, for example, might have the right length and

Two ways of mounting children's work in plaster of Paris. The group on the left clusters the work of the class on a vertical totem-pole shape; the group on the right is mounted for hanging on a wall. Mysterious visages like these can also be carved from other materials. (From the sculpture garden of the Ashkelon Children's Art Center, Israel.)

Girl Putting on Her Shoe, 1968, one of George Segal's plaster body-castings placed in its own environment. Since it appears to be an exact replica, the teacher may have to justify it as art. Segal's pieces, like all sculpture, are transformations, not replicas—they bring about distinctive changes in their surrounding area. Plaster, wood, plastic, 37″ × 24″ × 48″. (Collection of Mr. and Mrs. William Paley, New York. Courtesy, Sidney Janis Gallery, New York.)

height for a plaque on which a relief sculpture could be carved, and a carton that held a large tube of toothpaste would serve as a mold for plaster to be carved in the round. When the plaster dries, which it does with extraordinary rapidity, it contracts slightly so that the cardboard is easily peeled away.

Plaster may be combined with other materials, thus allowing for a choice in the degree of density. Students can mix, in various proportions, plaster, vermiculite, pearlite, sawdust, dirt, and sand. Samples of these aggregate combinations might be prepared and records kept of the degrees of hardness, kinds of texture, and so on that are obtainable with different proportions. Students might want to add some tempera for color and thus create truly personalized carving media.

The techniques used in cutting plaster are somewhat less difficult for children than those used with wood. Almost any cutting tool may be used on plaster—pocketknives, woodworking tools, or linoleum cutters. Even wornout dentist's tools can be used. No special accommodation is necessary for this work; the cutting can be done on an old drawing board. When cutting is satisfactorily completed, the plaster should be lightly rubbed with fine sandpaper to obtain smooth surfaces where they are desired. A preservative finish is not necessary, and would in fact spoil the attractive appearance of the medium.

Another method of working with plaster is to dip surgical bandages or strips of cloth into plaster and drape them over armatures or other substructures. Rolls of plaster-infused gauze used for medical casts is excellent for this method. The sculptor George Segal has been responsible for a whole new direction in art with his plaster body-castings placed in complete environments.

Sculpture in Plaster of Paris

245

Plaster is one of the most versatile and least expensive of all art media. It does require more preparation and cleanup than many other activities, but it lends itself to working outdoors. Considerable care must be taken to keep the classroom floor clean, preferably with a damp cloth or mop to avoid making dust. If plaster bits are walked on they are ground into powder and, when stirred up by activity, can cause an unhealthy breathing environment. Students leaving an untidy room after working with plaster can be identified by the trail of white footprints. Plaster and wood are in themselves two very good reasons for separate art rooms in all schools.

Teaching. Because this medium is easier to cut than wood, demonstration need occupy relatively little time. Students often require more assistance in preparing the plaster than they do in working with it. The teacher should be sure that the children know what their subject matter and technique will be before they mold their plaster. Low relief requires a flat slab, while sculpture in the round requires a block of plaster. Obviously, once the plaster is molded the children are committed to work that suits the shape of the material. As for carving, the suggestions made earlier about wood-carving are generally applicable to the problems that arise in working with plaster of Paris.

Modeling with Clay

Modeling is another activity in which children in all stages of development may participate. Clay has been a standard modeling medium in the schools for many years because it is inexpensive and easily manipulated.

Media and Techniques. Clay may be purchased or it may be found in the ground in some localities, especially along lakes, bays, or small creeks. Any slippery, soapy earth having a red, blue, or whitish tinge and adhering tenaciously to the hands is probably clay. Working with the earth, however, will soon reveal whether or not it is suitable for modeling.[4] Natural clay must usually be refined before it can be used as a modeling medium. If dry, it should be powdered and put through a sieve to remove lumps, pebbles, and other foreign matter. If wet, it must be rolled and kneaded on a *bat*, a porous slab, and any lumps or foreign substances removed by hand as they come to the surface. A suitable porous bat can be made of plaster of Paris prepared in the manner outlined on page 244. If

[4] See Michael Casson, *The Craft of the Potter* (Woodbury, N.Y.: Barron's Educational Series, 1979).

Sculpture and Pottery: Modeling, Carving, and Constructing

Clay is a popular medium for elementary art because it lends itself to table projects like the modeling these primary grade children are doing.

clay is too wet, it can be dried relatively quickly by placing it on a plaster bat and turning it over every thirty minutes or so. The plaster tends to draw moisture from the clay.

When purchased, dry standard clay (always cheaper than prepared clay) is usually packaged in 50- or 100-pound bags. In preparation for use, water should be poured over about half a pail of clay and mixed in with a spoon. It takes about 5 quarts of warm water to thoroughly soak 25 pounds of dry clay. A tablespoon of vinegar added to the water will neutralize any alkaline content and make it easier on the hands. After the clay has settled overnight, any excess water can be poured off. Clay also comes in a plastic state, usually in 25- to 100-pound bags. It is more expensive than dry clay because of the shipping charge for the added water content, but it is still relatively inexpensive. One pound of clay makes a ball the size of an adult's fist, and this is a good average amount for a child to work with.

The youngest children are not able to prepare the clay for modeling and must depend on the teacher to perform this task. For this reason some teachers have turned to the commercially prepared oil clays (such as plasticine). While substances can be substituted, nothing can entirely replace natural, water-based clay as a modeling medium.

Before modeling can be successfully performed, the refined and dampened clay should be kneaded and rolled on the porous surface until it is almost rubbery. When a coil of it can be twisted and bent so that it neither breaks readily nor adheres unpleasantly to the hands, it is ready for modeling. To assist in working with clay to the necessary condition, an apparatus called a "wedging table" is useful. The wedging table consists merely of two boards about $\frac{1}{2}$ inch thick, on 5-ply wood, fixed at right angles to each other with screws. Brackets strengthen this assembly. The measurements of each board should be at least 18 by 24 inches. A length of fine but strong wire should be attached from the top center of the upright board to the outside center of the lower board. *Wedging* makes the clay uniformly moist and free of air bubbles. A lump of clay is cut by pressing it into the wire. The resulting two pieces are then thrown with force onto the surface of the wedging table or slapped together. If the slapping of clay gets out of hand, the children should be encouraged to *knead* the clay from a standing position. This entails folding the clay back into itself, without trapping any air in the folds, until it has the proper rubbery texture. This process is continued until no tiny bubble holes are to be seen in the cut clay.

A reasonably large quantity of clay for modeling may be prepared in advance and stored for a short time in airtight tins or earthenware containers. Indeed, this storing tends to make it more workable. Small pieces of clay for each pupil may subsequently be cut away by means of a wire. Used clay can often be reclaimed by soaking it in water for about forty-eight hours and then placing it on a plaster bat to dry to a workable consistency.

Before the children work with clay or other modeling materials, the working surfaces should be protected with newspapers, cardboard sheets, clear plastic, or oilcloth. The children will find it convenient to model the clay on a board placed on the protective covering. While working, the children can turn the board to view the sculpture from all sides. Plaster bats provide both a working and a kneading surface.

Modeling in clay and other materials is essentially an activity for the hands, and requires no tools. Sets of tools are available, however, to assist more experienced children in producing details in their pieces. Tools can be made easily from wide tongue depressors broken lengthwise and sanded with sandpaper or shaped with a knife or file. Pointed or round-ended tools can be made from dowels. A damp sponge or cloth is useful to moisten the fingers and partially clean them at the close of the activity. The teacher should not use the sponge to smooth out objects. The surface of the clay is a record of the children's individuality, as is the texture of their crayons or the marks of their brushes and, as such, should be preserved as part of their total response.

The child's stage of development in pictorial work is reflected in the output in clay. The youngest and most inexperienced children are satisfied with a short period of manipulation, after which the clay is left in a shape resembling nothing in particular. Later, the children may give a name to shapes of this kind.[5] Still later, the symbols associated with drawing and

[5]See *Young Children's Sculpture and Drawing: A Study in Representational Development* (Cambridge, Ma.: Harvard University Press, 1974).

Sculpture and Pottery: Modeling, Carving, and Constructing

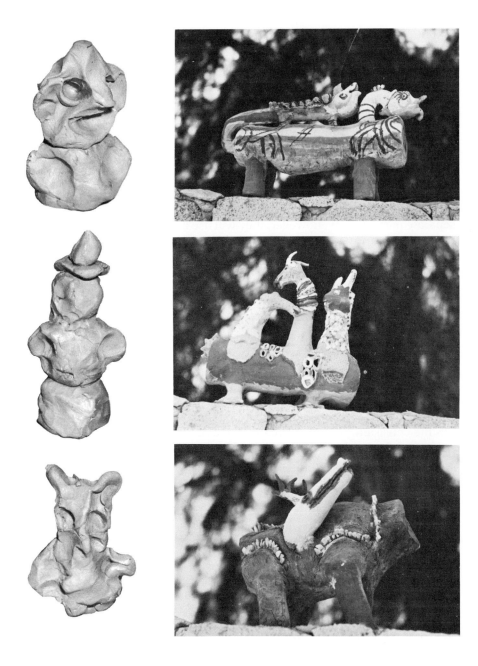

Symbols in clay by first grade pupils, left. The class was encouraged to pull shapes from a central mass of clay. The child who made the middle work could not resist adding the hat as a separate form. These free-standing beasts, right, by upper-elementary grade children were begun with thick slabs of clay. Details were added by raising the surface (with coils) or carving into it. All pieces were fired; some were glazed partially or completely.

Modeling with Clay

249

painting may appear in the clay in three-dimensional form. Finally, preadolescents refine their symbols, aiming at greater detail and realistic proportion. Younger children are less concerned about the permanence of their objects than are older ones, who want to see their pieces fired and carried to completion through the use of glazes.

There is no one technique recommended for modeling. Children begin to model naturally with considerable energy, enthusiasm, and, generally, dexterity. Given a piece of clay weighing from half a pound for kindergarten and first grade pupils to 2 pounds for those in higher grades, children will squeeze, stroke, pinch, and pat it to get a satisfactory result. Whereas younger children may pull out their subject from a central mass of clay, they seldom draw this way, preferring to assemble objects out of separate parts. In clay, however, they will use both methods and should be encouraged to proceed in any manner they find satisfactory.

The finished product in clay must be a solid, compact composition. As they gain confidence in the medium, children attempt to form slender protuberances. These usually fall off, and children quickly learn not to draw out the clay too far from the central mass. They may add little pellets of clay for, say, eyes and buttons, but even these must be kept reasonably flat if they are to adhere to the main body of the clay. It is important to understand that clay shrinks as it dries, so that if a wet piece is adhered to a drier piece, the wet one will shrink more in drying and will break off. Pieces to be joined must be similar in moisture content. The use of watery clay, or *slip*, may help children fix these extra pieces. Slip is prepared by mixing some of the clay used in the modeling with water until the mixture has the consistency of thick cream. The child *scores*, or roughens, the two surfaces to be stuck together with the teeth of a comb, a knitting needle, or a pointed stick, and then paints or dabs on the slip with the fingers before pressing the pieces together.

If worked on too long, clay becomes too dry to manipulate. In order for it to be kept sufficiently moist from one day to the next, it should be wrapped in a damp cloth over which is wrapped a rubber or plastic sheet, and, if possible, the whole should be placed in a covered tin until it is to be worked again. When the work is finished and left on a shelf to dry, it should be dampened from time to time with water applied with a paintbrush. The small protuberances will thus be prevented from cracking or dropping off before the main body of the work has dried.

In some forms of advanced modeling, malleable wires called *armatures* are sometimes fixed to a base and then twisted to form the general outline of the object. These devices are a convenience to the experienced artist because once they have been arranged, the clay can be built up around them to form a more delicate, open type of work. For most elementary-school children, however, the use of armatures is too difficult and should be avoided, except in cases where the child exhibits a marked abil-

Sculpture and Pottery: Modeling, Carving, and Constructing

ity in clay work. The simple, solid mass of unsupported clay is challenging enough for most young children and results in a wide variety of significant output. Occasionally, however, a small pointed stick can be thrust up from the base of the partially completed object to assist, say, in keeping a head erect.

Teaching.   The teacher must be concerned with the preparation of the clay, the physical arrangements for handling it in the classroom, and the subject matter selected by the children.

For the youngest children the teacher must prepare the clay. For the older children, step-by-step instructions and then careful supervision of their preparation of the medium are needed. The clay must be prepared correctly if the work is to be successful. The room and its furnishings must be adequately protected from clay dust and particles. The teacher should ask each child to spread newspaper on the floor under the work area. Desks or tables on which the work is performed should be covered with oilcloth, rubber, or plastic sheeting, or with more paper. Many cleaning cloths dampened with water should be readily at hand, and the pupils should be taught to use them both when the work is in progress and when it is finished. The pupils must also learn to pick up the protective coverings carefully so that clay particles are not left on the desks or floor.

Drawing and modeling can complement each other, yet are rarely used to deal with the same artistic problem. Modeling from observation and memory is closely related to drawing, and children who are sensitive to form in one medium usually do as well in the other. Here, left, the teacher calls attention to the "action" of the figure. A group of completed figures, about to be fired, right, generates an aura of mystery. Sixth grade. (Photos by Rick Steadry.)

Good teachers will see that adequate shelves are provided for storing clay work. Teachers should carefully supervise as each child stores the work and make sure that the products are in no way damaged during the storage process.

Subject matter for modeling in clay is somewhat restricted. Usually it involves one person or thing, or at the most two persons or things resolved into a closely knit composition. Only objects or shapes that are chunky and solid can be successfully rendered. Thus the human figure and certain animals such as owls, squirrels, or pigs, which can be successfully stylized into a solid form, are more suitable subjects than naturally spindly creatures such as giraffes, spiders, and flamingos. Students should discuss and select a subject in keeping with the nature of clay before they begin work.

Working from a posed figure can be a desirable activity for more experienced children. Positioning the human body and interpreting its proportions can be exciting art experiences when carried through in both the flat and in-the-round approaches. The upper grade child can establish a basic standing figure without too much difficulty, but to make the figure sit, crawl, sleep, and perform other such activities often requires a posed model.

Often, before the actual modeling occurs, the teacher will be obliged to demonstrate some of the techniques of handling clay, especially for preadolescent pupils, who generally wish to arrive at an exact representation of the objects they are fashioning. Included among the demonstrations should be the two chief methods of modeling—pulling out from a central mass, and shaping or welding, in which prepared pieces such as arms and legs are scored and treated with slip. The use of some modeling tools to produce details may also require demonstration.

There is no reason why modeling in clay cannot be used to reinforce other learning in art. If fifth and sixth graders sketch the human figure, they can sculpt it as well, working either for heightened observation or for purposes of personal expression. If they are examining texture through collage, children can study texture further by impressing found objects— bark, string, burlap, and the like—into the responsive surface of clay. Plaster casts can be made of such exercises and then combined into attractive wall panels for the school.

LONG-RANGE PLANNING IN CLAY

One teacher who used clay as a major medium planned a complete sequence of activities as follows:

Early Grades
> Make a flat slab of clay with the palms of the hands.
> Roll the clay into a thick coil, a thin coil, a big clay ball, and several small clay balls.

Sculpture and Pottery: Modeling, Carving, and Constructing

Make a bird out of one lump of clay using a particular texture for feathers.

Make a pinch pot out of one small ball of clay.

Middle Grades

Join two pieces of clay together.

Show a film, slides, or books illustrating the clay process and finished clay objects.

Make a mother and child sculpture of one kind of animal.

Make a prehistoric creature, embellishing it with natural textures by imprinting objects such as leaves or fir cones.

Make a clay figure showing a particular emotional state.

Make a clay figure showing physical action.

Make a fantasy clay world or an imaginary environment.

Allow a small group of the most advanced students to be responsible for firing clay objects under the supervision of the teacher.

Upper Grades

Make a large pinch pot.

Make a clay container. Decorate it with a pattern consisting of either an incised texture or added bits of clay.

Make a relief slab puzzle using a drawing or painting as the subject matter.

Make a ceramic slab wall hanging as a group project.

In addition to the activities listed above, the teacher's clay curriculum also included suggestions of a more general pedagogical interest. In order to provide the children with adequate motivation, the teacher showed them photographs of animals and other subjects. To determine the relevant characteristics of the children at a given stage of development, the teacher noted their growing awareness of differences within classes of objects. To emphasize the formal elements of the art form the children were working in, the class discussed the specific properties of clay and glazes.

Stabile Constructions

Stabile constructions are sculptures made of one material, such as wire, straws, or balsa-wood strips, or of combinations of materials, such as string, wood, and cardboard. Although the subject matter may be real—animals, buildings, or people—these *stabiles* are most effective when designed abstractly, with emphasis placed on balance of line against plane, transfer of space into solid areas, relation of parts to wholes, and so on. The mechanically minded pupils may include moving parts in their constructions, and creative individuals may incorporate such materials as ping-pong balls, feathers, and colored cellophane into their work.

Media and Techniques. The wire construction is a practical activity for all children but those in the manipulative stage. Wire lends itself to the creation of a composition that depends largely on a continuous line. When bent into any position the wire should stay there. Copper or aluminum wire, or wires made of alloys of these elements, are suitable. The necessary tools include snips to cut the wire, long-nosed pliers to manipulate it, and a drill to bore holes in a base for the sculpture to stand in. The wire may also be attached to the base by stapling and by bending a nail around the end of the wire.

Teaching. These sculptures are appropriate to our time, since they allow for an open approach to materials and a wide latitude of personal style. The children should therefore be strongly encouraged to approach

Various forms of stabile constructions, using string combined with thin balsa strips, far left, straws, and boxes. Students extend their ideas of design and sculpture by working on a scale related to their own bodies. Problems of structure, balance, and joining must be approached so as to encourage new ways of thinking about three-dimensional form. (Photos by Education Development Center.)

the activity experimentally. The teacher might demonstrate how a length of wire can be bent and then leave the children to make their own discoveries. The first bends may be made with the hands; later the details might be added with pliers. The teacher might suggest, when the desired shape is attained, that either one or both ends of the wire be placed in a base sufficiently heavy to support the sculpture. After further experimentation children may use two separate pieces of wire effectively. By polishing the wire with an appropriate metal cleaner and the wood with wax, students learn to finish the sculpture so that it shines in an attractive fashion.

This craft is a relatively delicate one. It requires no special equipment and makes little mess, except perhaps in the preparation of the wooden bases, and there are no special problems in arranging the classroom for the work involved. The activity allows the teacher to isolate a single idea or material for study; for instance, the manipulation of wire is a logical way to study line in space. Slide reproductions of the works of Calder, Gabo, early Giacometti, Oppenheim, or Snelson[6] will demonstrate to the children that a new kind of space can be controlled and unity and movement can be obtained through constructions as well as paintings.

Making Pottery

Making utilitarian objects out of earth clay and hardening them with fire is one of the oldest and most common craft forms in the world. Beautifully fashioned pots from ancient cultures in China, Greece, South America, and many other parts of the world still exist in museums and private collections. Archeologists learn much about ancient peoples from their artifacts, which in many cases rival or exceed in quality of design and construction the best work that we are able to produce today.

Media and Techniques. The basic pottery hand-forming techniques are the pinch method, the coil method, and the slab method. Each of these methods has varying levels of sophistication and they are often used together by an innovative potter. In the symbol stage, children can make pots by hollowing a solid lump of clay. Preadolescents are capable of what are called the *coil* and *slab* methods. A simple pinch pot is a good project on which to start a child at any age. Children may begin by shaping the clay into a ball and working the thumb of their right hand into the center. They then rotate the ball slowly in the palm of one hand, gently pressing the clay between the thumb and the fingers of the other hand to expand

[6] A good source for pictures of contemporary art are journals such as *Art in America*, and *Art-news*.

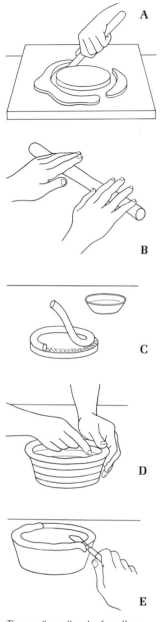

The coil method of pottery-making: (**A**) trimming the base, (**B**) rolling the coil, (**C**) applying the coil, (**D**) smoothing the coil, and (**E**) trimming the lip.

the wall. The wall should be thick and the pot periodically tapped on the table to maintain a flat base. If the walls are thick enough, they may subsequently be decorated by incising lines or pressing hard-edged objects into the surface.

It is useful for children to know and apply a few basic concepts and terms as they make pottery. We have already mentioned that clay shrinks as it dries, so that a bowl, cup, or other object should be made about 25 percent larger than the desired size for the finished piece. Children should be reminded to join pieces of clay that have about the same moisture content and will therefore shrink together about the same amount. Clay that is allowed to dry until it loses most of its elasticity is called *leather hard*. Clay in the leather-hard state is very easy to work with. It is nearly rigid, but not brittle. It is strong and can be carved or scraped easily. As the clay continues to dry it becomes *bone dry*. This is the stage when pieces are extremely brittle and fragile. Bone-dry pieces should not be handled unnecessarily, since this is when most breakage occurs. Pots broken at this stage are very difficult to repair satisfactorily.

When the pottery or clay sculpture pieces are completely dry they will not feel as cool to the touch as pieces that still contain moisture, since the evaporation of water from a clay piece actually cools it. Only bone-dry pieces should be placed (stacked) in the kiln for firing. Pieces that are very thick, that have air bubbles in the clay, or that are not completely dry very often will explode during firing. A slow firing is best to minimize explosions and fractures. Slow cooling helps to avoid breakage caused by uneven contraction between thick and thin parts of a piece of pottery.

Clay that has not been fired is called *greenware*, not because of its color, but because of its immaturity. The firing of greenware is called the *bisque* firing and the fired pieces are labeled *bisqueware*. After firing, the bisqueware is fused and hard and will no longer melt when water is applied. It is ready for glazing or other surface decoration. The firing of glazed bisqueware is called the *glaze* firing.[7]

In producing coil pottery, children will find it convenient to work on a small board or plaster bat. A ball of clay is flattened on the bat until it is about half an inch thick. Then it is trimmed with a knife to the desired size, usually about 3 to 5 inches in diameter. Next, a coil of clay about half an inch in diameter is produced by rolling the clay. The coil is then applied to the edge of the base, which should be scored and dampened with slip so that adhesion is assured. The coil should then be pinched to the base. A second coil is built on the first in the same way. No more than four or five coils should be made in one day, lest the assembly collapse under its own weight. After allowing the clay to dry for a day to become leather hard, the pupil may add another four or five coils. The top coil is covered with

[7]See Hal Riegger, *Electric Kiln Ceramics* (New York: Van Nostrand Reinhold, 1978).

plastic and kept damp so that it will adhere well to the additional coils. This process is repeated until the bowl or pot has reached the desired height and shape.

The position of the coils determines the shape of the bowl. Placing a coil slightly on the outside of the one beneath it will flare the bowl; placing it toward the inside will diminish the bowl in diameter. Although a perfectly uniform bowl is not expected, nor indeed altogether desirable, it is necessary to examine the rising edges from all angles to see that the shape of the object is reasonably symmetrical. A *template*, or contour, cut in cardboard may be applied to the side of the bowl, but this shaping technique is frowned on by some teachers for the good reason that it is mechanical and rather extraneous to the process of coil pottery.

When the outlines of the bowl are formed, pupils should either smooth both the inside and the outside with their fingers or smooth just the inside for support and allow the exterior coil texture to show. Dipping the fingers in slip facilitates the smoothing process. The lip of the bowl should be flattened or tapered and perhaps trimmed with a wire tool or knife. The bowl should then be cut away from the slab with a wire. Its edges may then be gently smoothed with the fingers.

The slab method involves the assembly of a number of flat pieces of clay to form a box. Well-prepared clay is rolled flat, like pastry, with a bottle or rolling pin that rests on wooden guides. The base of the object being made is then cut to size, as are the sides. The bottoms of the sides and edges of the base are scored and dabbed with slip where they are to be joined. A coil of clay, also dabbed with slip, is applied to all sides of the

The slab method of making pottery: (**A**) preparing the clay, (**B**) placing the supporting coil, (**C**) applying the sides, and (**D**) smoothing the sides with sponge and sandpaper.

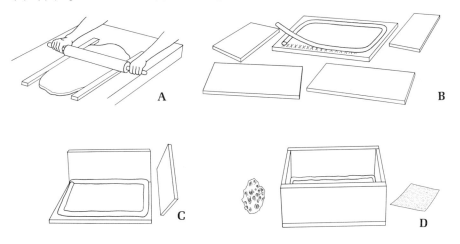

The first problem is to learn to use anything at hand as a source of design; the second is to discover how to maximize the possibilities of neglected objects through a sense of design.

base just inside the edge. A side is put in place and reinforced on the inside by the coil. This process is repeated until all four sides are pressed firmly in place in an upright position. Fine sandpaper or a damp sponge may be used to make the sides smoother once the object is dry.

The box is only one product of slab construction. Slabs have many uses: they can be slotted and joined, and flat and curved sections can be combined. Unbroken surfaces can offset textured sections, and large areas can be created by interlocking slabs, which may, in turn, have smaller sections cut away. Slabs that bisect and interpenetrate one another can result in pleasing nonobjective sculptural forms. Slabs can also be alternated with coils to attain greater variety in constructing containers.

Teaching. Two important demonstrations peculiar to the slab method of construction are necessary. First is the method of rolling clay flat. The teacher should take a ball of well-prepared clay and flatten it to about three-fourths of an inch thick on a piece of plastic or cloth. Two pieces of wood about one-fourth to three-eighths of an inch thick should be placed parallel to each other along two opposite boundaries of the flattened clay. A rolling pin should travel over these pieces of wood until the clay has been rolled to a thickness equal to that of the strips of wood.

The second demonstration involves making slabs without tools. A ball of clay is pressed onto a flexible material such as cloth or several sheets of newspaper. The teacher pounds the clay with the side of the fist, softly, from center to edges. The slab is then turned over. The teacher repeats this process several times until the slab reaches the desired thickness.

Sculpture and Pottery: Modeling, Carving, and Constructing

Media and Techniques. Several techniques may be used to decorate objects made of clay. These include glazing, incising, painting with engobe (colored slip), pressing with various objects, and a technique of incising through engobe known as sgraffito.

The successful glazing of clay requires skill and experience. First, the raw clay must be very carefully wedged to remove air bubbles. Next, after the modeling is done, the object must be dried thoroughly. Then a kiln or oven must be stacked with the pieces for preliminary or bisque firing. When the first firing has been successfully completed, the glazes (of which there are at least five distinct types) must be applied, the kiln stacked in such a way as to prevent the glazes on one object from touching another, and the second process of firing and cooling completed. Although it produces lovely results, glazing is a complicated process, and few people learn to do it merely by reading a book on the subject. To learn how to glaze competently, teachers should enroll in a workshop or course under the guidance of a ceramics expert. Under such conditions, glazing is not too difficult to master in a reasonably short period and the process can be taught to children.

Incising involves scoring the clay with various objects. The clay must be partly dry before incising can be done. Any one of a number of objects, ranging from nails and knitting needles to keys and pieces of comb, can be repeatedly pressed into fairly moist clay to make an interesting pattern.

Engobe, or colored slip, is underglaze pigment. Commercially prepared engobe is available from school-supply houses. The engobe is painted on nearly dry (leather hard) clay with a sable brush. When the

This student is making a pinch pot. The pot and brush contain slip for engobe decoration. Sponges are used to smooth contours of the finished pot; lids and handles have also been dealt with. A well-equipped ceramic workshop can thus provide children with a wide range of experience not normally available.

painted clay is dry, it must be fired as described earlier. A second firing is required if transparent glaze is applied over the bisque-fired engobe.

Sgraffito combines both incising and painting with engobe. Engobe is painted onto the partially dried object. In order to get thorough coverage and avoid streaks, two coats should be applied, the first by brushing consistently in one direction, the second by brushing consistently in another direction. When the engobe coats have almost dried, lines are incised through them—usually with a stick—to the clay before firing the object.

Following the lead of some professional potters, a number of teachers are experimenting with new approaches to surface decoration, which may include polymer acrylics or even tempera paint. In the latter case, when the paint is dry it may be left mat (nonglossy) or covered with a protective coating of shellac. The new polymer paints, unlike tempera, will not come off when the object is handled. Shoe polish gives a pleasing surface tone and may be used in place of paint; it comes in a surprising range of colors. In all cases the clay should be bisque fired before a coating is applied.

Teaching.   Finishing clay objects produced by elementary-school children places the teacher in an educational and artistic dilemma. As Victor D'Amico says in speaking of pottery, glazing is the "crowning experience" of the craft.[8] More than that, glazing is the most acceptable finish for clay. Although clay will take paint, which may in turn be covered with shellac or varnish to give it a shine, such a finish is not suited to clay and tends to make even the best work look cheap and tawdry. On the other hand, children can paint clay easily enough, but most of them cannot successfully fire it without help from the teacher. So much help is required, in fact, that the children must usually surrender their control of this activity to an adult.

Teachers have attempted to solve the dilemma arising from the finishing of clay products in several ways. Some tell the children that it is impossible for them to fire and glaze their work at the present time, but that they might instead try pressing or incising a design into it. The decorated object is then preserved in its natural form. Often teachers glaze for each child one or two products finished in engobe, sgraffito, or another technique that the teacher has demonstrated. Others show the children how to coat the work with shellac and explain that this is merely a makeshift process. Still other teachers, having explained that not all the steps in glazing can be taken by the children themselves, go ahead with glazing but take every opportunity to let the children do whatever lies within their competence. Thus a young child might at first only paint a bowl with

---

[8] Victor D'Amico, *Creative Teaching in Art*, rev. ed. (Scranton, Pa.: International Textbook, 1966), p. 140.

Sculpture and Pottery: Modeling, Carving, and Constructing

engobe but later might help to stack the kiln. None of these alternatives is wholly satisfactory, but perhaps the last provides the children with the most insight into and experience with the craft of pottery.

The Emergence of a New Aesthetic in Sculpture and Ceramics

The art teacher will occasionally be unable to relate sculpture and ceramic activities in an elementary program to the work of professionals. Materials and methods are difficult to duplicate in fields where contemporary artists work with such diverse means as synthetics, electricity, and control of the atmosphere. In general, teachers should be cautioned against concentrating on any extreme approach for the sake of living out their own personal interests. A teacher's indiscriminate pursuit of the avant-garde may have as little meaning to fifth graders as a stubborn reverence for traditional forms.

Sculpture and ceramics, like any art form, should challenge a child within the boundaries of enthusiasm and capability, providing experience in depth and breadth. There is a time to work from observation and a time to work from one's imagination; a time for ideas that move quickly and a time for sequential approaches. Children may carve and model as artists have done for ages or they may combine assembled constructions with light and motion, as is currently practiced. In a broad sense, sculpture in particular may be said to encompass many kinds of volumes and masses

"There are many ways of creating form." A ten-year-old girl applies the finishing touches to a painted sculpture she has assembled from scrap material. (Photo by Troy West.)

261

This group project was performed at an INSEA (International Society for Education through Art) conference held in Rotterdam. A large space, 30 by 30 feet, located at the entrance area, was filled with a variety of materials suitable for creating large-scale structures (poles, wooden blocks, balloons, newspaper, string, muslin, nylon). For five days, different groups of children worked under the direction of five teams of artists. Thirty children, ages six to twelve, were involved for two-hour periods. Each group built on the previous group's structure or began anew. Each day the work was documented with video and black-and-white photography. The photographs were processed that evening and posted the following day, along with statements by the leaders and participants. Equipment for using projections and colored lights was also on hand to create the final effect.

The INSEA conference participants (art teachers and educators) thus had an opportunity to observe a large-scale sculpture in a state of daily change. One group decided to create an intricate labyrinth and, on its completion, invited passersby to join them in crawling through their structure. When asked if they had created a work of sculpture or architecture, the children said, "Both." (Photos copyright Coby van Herk, Rotterdam.)

organized within a spatial context. It can be created with boxes or junk, clay or plaster. During the course of six or seven years in an elementary school, a child should have the pleasure of working with many approaches.

Although a conscientious teacher plans for most of the activities, a portion of the program should be left open for the unexpected. A windfall of unusual materials, a trip to a gallery, a magazine article, or acquaintance with a great artist could capture the interest of both students and teacher in a new activity.

Activities for the Reader

1. Survey the district around your school for materials suitable for sculpture and pottery. Is there any clay, wood, or wire to be had? Test the materials according to the suggestions found earlier in this chapter under the subheadings "Media and Techniques."

2. Seek out an efficient industrial arts teacher who should be only too happy to talk about wood. Ask questions about the types of woods and their various properties, seasoning wood, hand and power tools for woodworking, the care of tools (including sharpening), and finishes for wood. Ask for demonstrations of some of the processes associated with woodworking. Seek advice about brands of tools and types of sharpening stones. Exchange a picture you have made for scraps of wood (sanded ones, if possible).

3. Go to a good furniture store and make a note of the different types of finishes. Speak to an industrial arts teacher in one of your secondary schools if you do not understand how some of the finishes are obtained.

4. Glue scraps of wood together to form a piece of sculpture. Smooth the surfaces of the sculpture with medium and then fine sandpaper. Wax the sculpture and polish it with a soft cloth until it glows. Ordinary solid floor wax is suitable.

5. Experiment with various kinds of woods by cutting them with a heavy pocketknife. (Keep the knife sharp by rubbing it gently over a fine oilstone.) When you find wood that you like to cut, plan, either in your mind's eye or in a pencil sketch first on paper and then on the wood, a nonobjective design that you intend to cut. Start cutting, turning the wood from time to time so that you cut from all angles. Cut away from you and keep your other hand behind the cutting edge. Study the developing design for unity and variety of the elements. If you would like to put some holes in the wood to get three-dimensional effects, you will have to use a large drill or brace-and-bit. When the carving more or less satisfies you, put it gently in a vise and start filing it smooth. Sometimes sculptors protect their work from the jaws of the vise by placing pieces of wood between the sculpture and the jaws. Let the file "bite," by pushing it away from you. Finish with medium and fine sandpaper and, finally, polish with about a dozen coats of wax.

6. Select a flat piece of solid gumwood or pine. Practice using gouging tools by making some V-cuts with two strokes of a knife, making a vertical cut and removing pieces of wood by gouging toward this cut, gouging out a circular depression, and creating many different textural effects by cutting, chipping, and gouging.

7. Cast a plaque about 6 by 9 inches in plaster of Paris. Carve a nonobjective design in the plaque based on overlapping oblongs and squares. In some areas devise textural effects by cutting or gouging.

8. Cast a block of plaster of Paris about 2 by 2 by 8 inches. Plan a representational subject (a torso is excellent) and carve it out of the block.

9. Model a nonobjective shape in clay; model a representational form in clay.

10. Try a life-size self-portrait in clay. Imagine yourself in an unusual role—a king, a slave, a dreamer, or a prophet. Use a soda bottle filled with sand as an armature to control the weight of the clay.

11. Enroll in a clay workshop under the guidance of an expert in ceramics. Learn something about pottery of various kinds—decorating, firing, and glazing.

12. Roll a slab of clay big enough to wrap around an oatmeal box. Press rows of designs into the clay with hard-edged objects such as seed pods, coins, tools, wood ends, and the like. Keep a balance of large and small shapes and deep and shallow marks. Wrap the slab around the oatmeal box and seal the joined edges by pinching them. Remove the oatmeal box. Add a clay base and fire the object. You will have a unique container.

13. Cut a rectangle measuring at least 18 by 20 inches from a half-inch-thick slab of clay. With a nail file, begin cutting out a family of shapes, both curved and angular. Use some linear shapes as links in your design. As you cut out the shapes, place them on a board covered with sand, dirt, or dried clay. (This will keep your forms from sticking.) Make sure that the forms overlap or touch one another. After sprinkling the design with more sand or dried clay, place a second board on top of the pieces and press down hard. (You can even jump up and down on it.) Lift up the board and notice the subtle play of edges and the unifying surface quality attained by the pressure of the board. You can cut the design into sections and begin all over again.

14. Plan a piece of nonobjective wire sculpture in which you use some fine copper wire screen as well as at least two types and sizes of wire—say, heavy copper and fine aluminum wire. Work out the main rhythms with the wire. Then add some screen areas to the composition. The screen pieces may be cut with shears and fixed in place with a clear plastic cement or by weaving the wire through the screen. Work for balance of wire and screen.

Suggested Readings

Andrews, Michael. *Sculpture and Ideas*. Englewood Cliffs: Prentice-Hall, 1966. Good book for use in school projects.

Casson, Michael. *The Craft of the Potter*. Woodbury, N.Y.: Barron's Educational Series, 1979. A relatively inexpensive yet comprehensive book that covers handbuilding, throwing, decorating, glazing, and firing. It is well illustrated.

Nelson, Glenn C. *Ceramics*, 4th ed. New York: Holt, Rinehart and Winston, 1978. A classic text for anyone working in ceramics, this book has a great deal of technical information and includes many excellent color as well as black-and-white illustrations of ceramic pieces from around the world.

Read, Herbert. *A Concise History of Modern Sculpture*. New York: Praeger, 1964. A classic text on sculpture.

Reed, Carol, and Joseph Orze. *Art from Scrap*. Worcester: Davis, 1973. Use of inexpensive and found materials for the making of art, especially sculpture.

Riegger, Hal. *Electric Kiln Ceramics*. New York: Van Nostrand Reinhold, 1978. One of the few books that concentrate on ceramics for electric kilns, the type of kiln found in most schools.

Roettger, Ernst. *Creative Clay Design*. New York: Van Nostrand Reinhold, 1972. Another of Roettger's series of books that apply design principles to various media. This book provides a wealth of ideas for surface decoration in clay.

Stevens, Harold. *Art in the Round*. New York: Reinhold, 1965.

Tyler, Keith. *Pottery Without a Wheel*. London: Dryad, 1955. Emphasis here is on handbuilding, with a number of ingenious techniques that are easily adaptable for classroom use.

Weiss, Harvey. *Clay, Wood and Wire*. New York: William Scott, 1956. Especially good for school use.

Films

Understanding Modern Sculpture, Parts I and II. Sound filmstrips. Stamford, Ct.: Educational Dimensions, 1973. Offers students a discussion of modern sculpture, with a range of contemporary examples.

pRiNTMAKiNG

A fine print may be produced lovingly and patiently, or violently and impetuously—dependent upon the "climate" of the printmaker. From a fleeting idea wrested from the complex of human experience, worked through to the final visual image on paper, the print is employed as a medium in its own right. It is utilized by the printmaker for what it alone can accomplish in serving his particular needs. This precious sheet of paper bears the autographic trace of the printmaker on its surface; in his own "handwriting," then, we read the record of his dreams, his hopes, aspirations, play, loves, and fears.[*]

NiNE

This chapter concentrates largely on the printing process in which an image is transferred from an inked plate to paper. The process may produce multiple prints, like woodcuts and linoleum-block prints, or a single transfer, like monoprints. In contrast to drawing and painting, paper work, and sculpture and pottery, which are largely direct activities, printing is an indirect process; something is done to one substance in order to produce an effect on another substance. Between the child and the finished print, in other words, lies a whole series of moves with intermediary materials that must be completed successfully before the final image itself appears.

It is this emphasis on process that intrigues preadolescents so that they often lose their self-consciousness about the quality of the end prod-

[*] From Jules Heller, *Print Making Today* (New York: Holt, Rinehart and Winston, 1958), p. xiv.

uct. Why worry about accuracy of shape when it is so much fun to gouge the wood, roll on the ink, and transfer the image?

The subject of a print can be a single image, as in pure design, landscape, and figure study, or complex images developed from a number of motifs. However, because printing processes exert especially strong influences on the final product, the treatment of subject matter often requires considerable modification to suit the technique. Children will soon discover that details and shading are more appropriate to drawing than to printmaking and that a successful print makes a strong impact through simplification and contrast.

It is clear, then, that printmaking can be a relatively complicated process for the young. This raises a number of questions about the treatment of subject matter and the influence of technique on design. Printing techniques, however, do lie within the capabilities of all schoolchildren. These include monoprinting and vegetable and "stick" printing, which children at all stages can do successfully. Even the intricacies of linoleum-block printing can be mastered by fourth graders, and sixth graders are perfectly capable of handling woodcuts.

This chapter includes a description of all these types of printing. In addition, stenciling is discussed, since, although this is not strictly a form of printing, it is closely allied to it and makes use of many of the materials required to produce repeated art forms. Experimental printmaking with such unorthodox materials as corrugated cardboard, collographs, collage, and clay is also discussed. The search for new solutions to traditional problems is as much a part of contemporary printmaking as of painting, and every public-school art program should provide for some degree of experimentation in basic art forms.

Rubbings

One way to begin printmaking at any level is by transferring a ready-made surface; that is, by making a rubbing. This is an effective way to draw attention to unusual surfaces that may go unnoticed. A gravestone, a coin, a cracked part of the sidewalk, a manhole cover, or a section of grating, all have a presence that is waiting to be revealed by rubbing the side of a crayon on a sheet of paper placed on the subject. Colors can be changed for different sections of the image, and the paper moved from time to time to create new patterns. Rubbings are not only a way of sensitizing children to the realm of texture, but also a means of attuning them to the "skin" of the environment.

The paper should be any light weight that does not tear easily, and white enough to provide a high rate of contrast. (Ordinary typing paper is

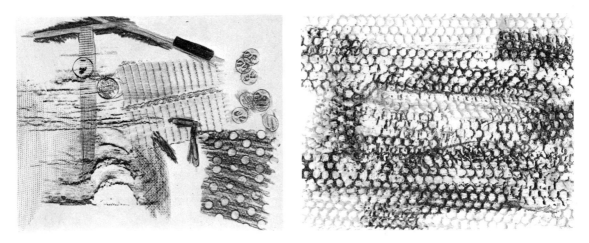

Crayon rubbings of various objects may be used to investigate surface textures. Objects can also be glued to a hard surface and inked to make collage prints. The exploratory stages are usually unplanned, but students can work for some sense of order as they control the overall design of their experiments.

adequate for small objects). When they use crayons, students should be encouraged to blend colors. Large primary-color crayons are fine for this activity, but if the budget will allow, Japanese rice paper and crayon pastels offer the handsomest results. In taking rubbings of raised type—as on manhole covers—students can improvise with the image by rearranging the pattern of form, repeating it, or turning the paper.

Monoprinting

The printing technique most closely allied to drawing and painting, and to which any child may transfer some picture-making ability, is called monoprinting.

Media and Techniques. The supplies required include a sheet of glass with the edges taped so the children cannot cut their hands. Instead of glass, a piece of linoleum may be used, measuring about 6 by 8 inches and preferably glued to a slab of wood. In the lower elementary grades, finger paint or tempera may be used directly on the table, since it is easily cleaned with a damp cloth or sponge. Brayers, brushes, pieces of stiff cardboard, or fingers may all be used, depending on the desired effect. Water-soluble ink and paint in a wide range of colors are available, as are newsprint and other reasonably absorbent paper.

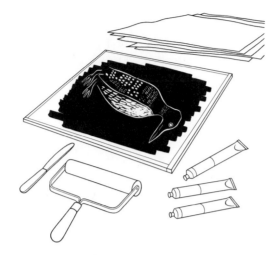

Arrangements for making a monoprint.

To begin the process, the ink is squeezed from the tube onto the
surface of the glass or linoleum and then rolled evenly over the surface.
More than one color may be used if desired. If two colors are used, for
example, they may be dabbed onto the glass and then blended with the
brayer. Another method is to mix the colors lightly with a palette knife
before rolling. Each technique produces its own effect.

A drawing can be produced with almost any implement that can
make a strong mark directly into the ink. The eraser end of a pencil, a
piece of cardboard, and a broad pen point are but a few of the suitable
tools. The drawing, which is made directly in the ink, must be kept bold
because the inked surfaces do not show fine details. Only the ink that is
left on the surface will be recorded in the final printing.

For the printing, a sheet of paper should be placed gently over the
prepared inky surface and pressed to it with the tips of the fingers. A clean
brayer rolled evenly over the paper also produces a good print. The completed print may then be gently peeled away. Sometimes two or three impressions may be taken from one drawing. By using papers with varying
textures an interesting variety of prints can be obtained. Although newsprint is recommended because it is cheap and absorbent, other papers
should be tried also, such as colored tissue, construction and poster papers, and even the coated stock found in magazine advertisements.

In another method of monoprinting, the glass is covered with ink in
the usual manner. The paper is then placed gently over the inked glass.
Next the pupil draws with a pencil on the upper side of the paper, taking
care not to drag the side of the hand on the paper. The resulting print is a
composition of dark lines with some imprint of ink on the background
areas. Since children have a tendency to over-ink the plate, they should try
a test mark on the corner and lift the paper to see if the line is visible.

Printmaking

Drawing in monoprint creates an arresting line quality—soft, rich, and slightly blurred. Because of this, it is particularly appropriate as an adjunct of contour-line drawing in the upper grades.

Another variation of monoprinting is the *paper stop out* method. Paper forms are cut or torn and then placed in a desired pattern on the inked plate. The impression is made by putting fresh paper on the arrangement and rolling it with the brayer. The cut-paper forms beneath serve to "stop out" the ink, and the areas they cover will appear as a negative pattern (that is, as the color of the paper) in the finished print.

Prints may also be produced by arranging objects such as string, a piece of wire screen, burlap, or scraps of rough-textured cardboard on a clean glass. Newsprint is placed over the arrangement and an inked brayer is run over the paper to obtain a print. These techniques may be used as a preliminary for collage prints, which are made by gluing objects to a cardboard base and coating the assembly with shellac. Literally dozens of prints can be rolled off on such a plate. (The shellac keeps soft materials such as yarn and burlap from shedding onto the brayer and paper.) Variations of the same print can be obtained by pulling a second impression that is slightly off register.

Teaching. Four main tasks confront the teacher of monoprinting. The first is to arrange tools and supplies so that printing may be done conveniently; the second is to see that the ink does not get all over the children; the third is to give stimulating demonstrations and continued encouragement; and the fourth is to make certain that there is a cleared area for wet prints to hang or otherwise be stored until dry.

Printing should be done on a long table covered with newspapers or oilcloth. At one end or at several points on the table the teacher should

A fourth grader made this print by arranging string, cut-paper shapes, and cut-paper sculpture of a fish on a clear surface and then inking the paper. One of the goals in this activity is to combine line (string or glue) and shape (cardboard) to achieve a sense of coherence. Dark areas between the raised surfaces can be controlled by gently pressing the surface areas with a fingertip.

arrange the glass, brayers, and inks. Because it would be uneconomical for each pupil to have a separate set of printing tools, the pupils should be given an order in which to work. Those who are not printing should know what other activities are available. As each print is completed the child should place it carefully on the remaining table space. When all the children have finished, the teacher should encourage them to select the prints they consider most interesting. When wet, the prints can be hung with clothespins on an improvised clothesline and then, when dry, pressed between the leaves of a heavy book such as an almanac or a telephone book. When possible, clear a wall on which to mount new prints for drying.

As can be imagined, a large amount of ink comes off on the children's hands. The teacher should make sure that the children either wash their hands often or at least wipe them on a damp cloth. Unless the classroom has a sink, the teacher must provide pails of water, soap, and towels or damp cloths.

The teacher should demonstrate efficiently all methods of monoprinting. Although the techniques are simple enough, it would be wise to practice before the lesson; monoprinting can be very messy unless the teacher has had some previous experience with the work. If the teacher appears clumsy during the demonstration there may be a very inky classroom once the children begin to experiment.

Pupils find monoprinting challenging and stimulating. Once they know how to begin they are eager to discover all the possibilities of this technique. It is a valuable activity not only because it permits spontaneous work but also because it gives children a reasonably accurate idea of the printmaking process in general. Any form of printmaking works well for small groups, especially when they try it for the first time.

Vegetable and Stick Printing

All children can produce work in vegetable printing, and nearly every child in the primary grades can print with sticks.

Media and Techniques. For vegetable printing, children should select pieces of vegetable with a hard consistency such as cabbage, carrot, potato, or celery. The pieces should be large enough for the children to grasp easily and should be cut flat on one side or end. All the children need do is dip the flat side of the vegetable into watercolor, tempera paint, or colored ink and then dab it on a sheet of newsprint. The child in kindergarten at first dabs at random but later controls the pattern and develops a rhythmic order of units. Scraps of sponge may also be used in this type of printing.

The next step is to control the design by cutting into the end of the vegetable. The best vegetable for this purpose is a crisp potato, but carrots are also suitable. The potato should be sliced in half and the design cut into the flat side with a knife. If a design of a different shape is wanted, the printing surface can be trimmed into a square. Tempera may then be painted over the designed end, after which printing on paper may begin.

In addition to vegetables, interesting shapes may be obtained by using a variety of wood scraps. If the wood is soaked in water for an hour

Stick printing in two colors by a fifth grader. Cuts were made in the stick with a knife after careful directions were given. Patterning can provide an interesting entree into tesselation (the combining of single units to create larger figurations), like that found in Islamic tile patterns.

In this mixed-media print, the red and yellow cut-sponge shapes were used to set off the background of colored chalk. Varying background and foreground is a technique that can be applied to realistic subjects, pure design, or abstract compositions. It can be presented as an exercise in planning, or it can evolve spontaneously as the child develops an idea. Fourth grade.

or so, the grain swells and creates circular patterns. The wood scraps may then be dipped in paint and applied to the printing surface. In such cases, the design rests on the arrangement of odd shapes and colors rather than on the broken surface of one piece of wood. The two techniques might be combined.

An easily manipulated material to use instead of vegetables or sticks is the square soap eraser. The surface is soft enough to be cut by a pin, yet the edges can hold up for dozens of impressions. The six available sides also allow for a variety of imprints. When the class is finished with the project, the teacher can glue all the used erasers to a board, run a brayer of paint over the group, make an impression on paper, and thus have an interesting wall piece for the room.

Teaching. Because the techniques involved in vegetable and stick printing are appealing in themselves, the teacher should have no problem motivating the children. The chief task is to encourage every child to explore the numerous possibilities of the process. The children should be encouraged to find and use many kinds of vegetables and other objects suitable for printing. When controlled cutting is used the teacher could suggest that not merely a knife, but forks, fingernail files, and other implements may also be used to cut the ends of vegetables so that different designs may result. The teacher should also suggest that background papers for these types of printing can be specially prepared by laying down thin color with a wide brush. Also, the teacher should note that backgrounds may be prepared with a large vegetable, such as a cabbage sliced in half, over which a potato or a smaller vegetable with the controlled cut may be used for printing in a contrasting color.

Eraser printing should be made equally challenging. The pupils should use several sides of an eraser with different designs on one printing surface. Also, combinations of colors should be tested. Backgrounds might be painted with thin watercolor or patterned with vegetables, sponges, or even crumpled balls of paper that have been dipped in thin paint.

Few, if any, problems will arise over subject matter. Only nonobjective or highly abstract patterns can result from this work, and the techniques lend themselves to repeated patterns rather than to picture-making.

Styrofoam, Linoleum, and Woodcut Printing

A good introduction to the relatively complex method of linoleum and woodcuts is the Styrofoam print. Styrofoam is a soft, inexpensive material that can often be obtained by trimming the sides of food containers. All children need is a pencil to press lines onto the soft surface. The lines will

An eleven-year-old is cutting his design on a large piece of linoleum. Although basic space, shape, and linear decisions should be made in advance, the scale of the print makes it possible to embellish and enrich the surface. (Note the position of the cutting hand in relation to the supporting hand. Safety precautions are vital whenever sharp instruments are involved.)

remain incised and the ink can be rolled over the surface before applying paper for printing. After children make such a print, they understand the process on which more difficult techniques are built.

Media and Techniques. When the linoleum or wood has pieces cut out of it, is inked, and, finally, is pressed to a suitably absorbent surface, a linoleum or woodcut print results. The raised parts of the surface create the pattern. The technique requires sharp tools, some physical strength (particularly in the fingers), and an ability to perform several operations of a relatively delicate nature. Only the more mature students in the upper grades will be capable of this work.

The usual heavy floor linoleum with burlap backing is suitable for cutting. It may be purchased from furniture and hardware stores or from firms that lay floor covering. Linoleum comes in large sizes, but scraps of it can often be obtained at a discount. Small pieces may be cut from a larger piece by scoring the linoleum with a knife and then bending it.[1] The linoleum snaps apart where it is scored, and then only the burlap remains to be cut through with a knife. The pupils will find it convenient but not entirely necessary to glue the linoleum to be carved to any wood scrap that is the exact size of the linoleum. The burlap side of the linoleum should be smeared with a strong carpenter's glue, then pressed against the wood and held firmly in a press until the glue is dry. Linoelum can be bought already affixed to wood blocks, but it is quite expensive.

[1]For beginners, pieces measuring 5 by 6 inches are satisfactory; later, pieces as large as 10 by 12 inches can be used; and for sixth graders, pieces can be even larger.

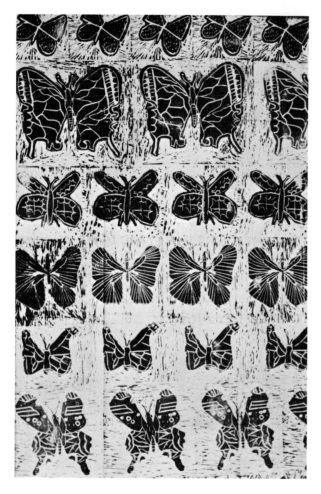

A linoleum-block print by a group of fourth graders. Water-base ink was used on a discarded cotton sheet (which then served as a window curtain). Permanent, washable inks with an oil base may also be used. This is an effective way to utilize an entire class effort for a practical purpose, to establish the relation between fine art (the individual's effort) and applied art (the curtain). Every child's print can be used, since pattern and repetition, by their very nature, will flatter any single unit of the design.

In working on this linoleum cut, a fifth grader had to turn the block to achieve the curve of the elephant's trunk and back. When children stand rather than sit, they have a greater tendency to move the block. Children should be encouraged to be flexible in their positioning and to take greater control of working conditions.

Sets of linoleum cutters and short holders for them are needed. These sets consist of straight knives, V-shaped tools, and U-gouges of varying sizes. The knives and gouges are perhaps the most effective tools, although the V-tool is capable of producing some highly sensitive lines and interesting textural effects. It is especially important to keep the tools sharp, and for this purpose a specially shaped oilstone may be bought.

The same tools are necessary for woodcutting. The best woods to use are maple, pine, and apple.

For receiving the impressions, almost any reasonably absorbent paper is suitable, from inexpensive newsprint to the costly but delightful Japanese rice paper. Generally, paper that is thinner than newsprint tends to stick to the block, and paper heavier than 40-pound bond or construction paper does not have enough resilience to pick up all the details of tool marks. Many textiles, including cottons, linens, and silks, will be found practical for printing if their textures are not rough. For printing on textiles, an oil-based or printer's ink is necessary to obtain a lasting color; otherwise a water-based ink may be used. A few other supplies are also necessary—rubber brayers, a sheet of plate glass to be used as a palette, and, for printing on textiles, a mallet.

In cutting the linoleum, many people use the V-tool to make a preliminary outline of the main areas of the composition. When using this tool, it is often more convenient to move the block against the tool than the reverse. After the outlines have been inscribed the white areas in the design may be cleared away with the gouges. If any textural effects are desired in these areas, the linoleum should be gouged so that some ridges are left. If, however, the worker wishes the areas to print pure white, the linoleum should be gouged out almost to the burlap backing. Various kinds of textured areas may be made by cutting parallel lines, crosshatching lines, or removing "pecks" of linoleum with the V-tool.

Cutting in wood calls for greater manual control and sharper tools. A woodcut generally does not allow for as much detail as a linoleum cut. To make up for these limitations, it offers a grained surface for dark areas. If the stark black-and-white qualities are combined with a surface of a good grain (complete with knots), a more powerful print can be obtained than with linoleum. During cutting the block should be steadied with a vise or cutting board and turned frequently for curved cuts. Naturally, the softer the wood, the easier it is to cut; pine is ideal for this task. Students should learn how to take care of the tools and keep them sharp. However, even the sharpest gouge may require the use of a hammer to move it along the surface, since wood offers much greater resistance than linoleum.

Children generally will find it helpful to take rubbings of their work from time to time to appraise their progress. To do this, they should place a thin sheet of paper over the working surface and, holding it firmly, rub soft pencil or crayon across the paper.

Although no formula can be offered for making a sucessful cut, it may be observed that a composition displaying a balance between lines, white, black, and textured areas will prove to be particularly interesting. Blockprints are distinguished by the distribution of light and dark masses across the surface. Because of the relative difficulty in producing detail, these masses tend to be more prominent than in other forms of the plastic arts. Evidence of tool marks lends great vitality to the surface and gives the print the look and feel of the material. A print from a linoleum cut or woodcut should not be mistaken for a pen-and-ink drawing.

When the children find the cut satisfactory, they are ready to pull an impression of it. Before printing on paper it is wise to dampen all but the softest tissue types of paper with a sponge. After the paper has been dampened, it should be placed between pieces of blotting paper to remove any excess moisture. Then the children coat the brayer by rolling it evenly in water-soluble ink on the glass palette. Next, working in several directions with long sweeps of the brayer, they coat the linoleum or wood evenly with ink. The dampened paper (or dry tissue) should then be placed over the block and in turn covered with a sheet of blotting paper. This covering should be pressed and rubbed gently with the hands until enough contact between the block and the paper has been made to make an impression. In order to pull ink up from the block onto the paper a considerable amount of pressure has to be applied. This is usually done by a press or by prolonged rubbing with the back of a large wooden spoon. The spoon must be used with great care lest the paper tear or crinkle. The print may then be peeled away from the block. To prevent it from wrinkling it should be tacked to a drawing board and allowed to dry before it is removed and perhaps mounted.

For exhibition purposes a mount for the print may be constructed by folding in half a sheet of paper of appropriate size and color and then cutting a "window" in one of the halves through which to display the print. The print may then be fixed in place behind the window by means of rubber cement or tape. If the paper on which the print is taken is translucent, as in the case of certain tissues, an interesting effect may be obtained by fixing colored papers behind it. The "window" approach may also be used without the backing and is as satisfactory with heavy white or black paper as with mat board.

When printing is to be done on textiles, the cloth should be spread over felt or newspapers. The block should be inked in the manner just described for paper, except that, as mentioned previously, an oil-based ink should be used to obtain permanent color. The ink may be thinned with turpentine. Printing can be done with the hands, although much pressure must be exerted. A small wooden mallet is the most effective tool for this job. The block should be tapped smartly, first in the center and then on each corner. Each time the block is used it should be freshly and uniformly inked.

A woodcut print by a sixth grader. Although wood is much more difficult to work with than linoleum, it can often be more satisfying because the quality of the raised surface is usually richer. There is no point in working in wood if the surface is totally flat and ends up looking like linoleum. Wetting the block before printing will raise the surface and provide a more textured, grainier surface. Crayon rubbings will also reveal wood surfaces and should be part of the printing experience.

Teaching. The chief problems in teaching wood- and linoleum-cutting and printing concern the development of skill in cutting and the treatment of subject matter. Organization of the classroom raises problems, of course, but these are similar to the organizational problems that arise with stick printing.

Linoleum- and wood-cutting have often given rise to some unfortunate teaching methods concerning the selection of subject matter. Even teachers who have emphasized the importance of developing original subject matter in the direct processes have allowed pupils to copy designs for their work in linoleum and wood so that they may concentrate on technique. Such a teaching practice, however, proves in the long run to be as ineffective when applied to cutting as it does when applied to other types of art. No matter what the art form being produced, design and technique must develop in close relationship to each other.

The suggestion was made earlier that sculpture in wood might begin with experimental play with the wood. This method is also practical for linoleum and woodcuts. At first, children should work directly with the material. Rather than attempting to follow a drawing, they should explore ways of cutting. After becoming acquainted with the cutting methods, they can follow the teacher's suggestion of making some preliminary sketches with India ink and a brush. By that time they will have insight into the limitations of the medium and will realize to what extent a plan may help them in their work.

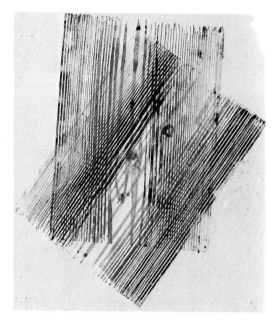

Wood investigations undertaken as a preliminary stage to a woodcut. Portions of the grain are cut away while other sections are retained for their textural effect. This surface was moistened prior to printing, accounting for the clarity of grain. Sixth grade.

In printing, sketches can also be transferred to the plate with carbon paper or by covering the back of the sketch with an even tone from a soft lead pencil. Children should be encouraged to think in terms of print qualities rather than characteristics associated with drawing and painting. Because the children are working in media that do not permit a great amount of detail or halftones, their preliminary sketches and planning should be done in a single tempera or ink tone rather than pencil or crayon.

Linoleum- and wood-cutting lend themselves to picture-making as well as pattern-making, so that the problems arising from the selection and treatment of subject matter are varied. The teacher must, of course, help the children to select suitable subjects from their experience and observations. Beyond that, the work produced is modified both by the children's artistic level and by the technique itself. The children's output in using these media, while related to painting and drawing, is not identical to those processes because of differences in the media and tools. Often a display of the entire process of making a cut is helpful in starting the children to work. After that, further demonstrations of technique may be necessary from time to time. These, however, should be kept to a minimum so that children can develop their own methods of working. Linolcum in particular, unlike some other substances, is a medium that allows many variations of approach to be discovered through experience.

The possibilities for exploration of block-cutting and printing are endless. The various types of cuts, the selection of different papers, the use

A black-and-white linoleum print compared with the same print on a surface prepared with watercolor washes. Sixth grade.

Creating the "ground" is a project in itself. In addition to white and colored papers—from thin tissue to heavy construction paper—children can use collage and photomontage. A fifth grader used magazine advertisements for a printing surface. Backgrounds like these will change the character of the print. It is also possible to press a slab of clay directly into the print, fire the clay, glaze it, and achieve unusual low-relief-sculpture effects.

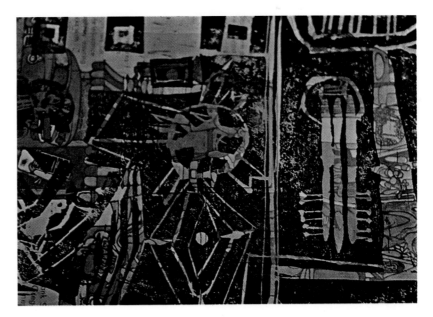

Art history can provide good examples of woodcuts. Note the balance of dark and light areas and the use of tool marks in this portrait by Ernst Kirchner. (© Roman Norbert Ketterer, Lugano, Switzerland.)

of two or more colors on the same block, the placing of units on the textile, and, for sixth grade pupils, even the use of two or more blocks to form a pattern may all be challenging to pupils working in this art form.

The preparation of the print surface is an art project in itself. Consider how the following backgrounds will alter a black-and-white print:

Collage of magazine clippings
A page from a telephone book
Mingling pools of tempera paint on wet paper
Marbleized paper
Handmade paper
Collage of colored tissue paper
Pages from Sunday newspaper comics
Leftover giftwrap and metallic papers

These backgrounds may be used for random effects, or they may be planned with the design of the print in mind.

Some artists whose work in linoleum and wood the children will enjoy are Antonio Frasconi, Pablo Picasso, Leonard Baskin, Sidney Chafetz, Antonio Posada, and several of the German Expressionists. Mexican folk art and medieval and Japanese woodcuts are also rich background sources for appreciation of printmaking.

Printmaking

Another variation of the linoleum method is the *reduction* or *subtractive* print. In this method children can begin by printing "an edition" (a dozen or more impressions) in one color. Another section of the plate is carved or "reduced" away, and a second color is added and printed over the first "reduced" position. When this is repeated a third or fourth time, a very rich surface develops, in addition to the added factor of a multicolored print. The original plate is destroyed in the process, of course, but another print form has been created.

Other Forms of Printmaking

The making of collographs involves cutting shapes out of cardboard, gluing them to another board for backing, inking the entire surface, and printing. The collograph permits the worker to obtain interesting light areas around the edges of the raised surfaces, where the brayer cannot reach. It is best to shellac the plate before inking, since cardboard will weaken with washing.

Corrugated cardboard allows children to work on a large scale, since this material can be obtained in sizes as large as refrigerator cartons. It provides three surface areas to print: (1) the flat exterior surface; (2) the striated pattern of corrugation, which is between the surface "skins"; and (3) the negative areas—sections of the cardboard completely cut away to reveal the paper on which the print is transferred. The illustration shows how these three areas actually print.

Stenciling allows children to print repeated units of design with considerable control. The activity demands a reasonably high degree of skill and an ability to plan in detail before production. For these reasons, it should be performed only by more experienced preadolescents. In stenciling, shapes are cut out of paper; this paper is placed over a surface and then covered with paint. Only where holes (negative areas) have been cut will paint appear on the under-surface, and thus a controlled design is established. The pieces removed by cutting may also be used as "masks" in the stencil process.

Media and Techniques. Strong waterproofed or special stenciling paper as well as oaktag file folders should be used. Such paper may be purchased, or it may be prepared by coating a heavy paper with shellac, varnish, or wax. (If wax is used, the paper should later be smoothed with a hot iron.) Knives are required for cutting the stencil paper, and although a

Fifth graders used cans of spray paint in this stencil mural based on a class study of jungle life. The shapes were cut and pinned into place before spraying. The forms were then moved around for a second and third spraying. (The teacher should always check for proper ventilation for spraying.) If spray paint is not available, stencils can be painted by dipping a toothbrush in tempera paint and brushing it against a stiff wire-mesh surface. Stencil work provides a gradation of tone and clarity of edge that cannot be obtained through conventional painting techniques.

sharp pocketknife or single-edged razor blade will serve, for more detailed work special knives made for the purpose should be bought. Hog-bristle brushes may be used to apply the paint, but inexpensive stencil brushes are obtainable. If stenciling is done on paper, tempera and watercolor are suitable; for stenciling on textiles, ordinary oil colors in tubes may be used. Special stencil paints, however, are available and are very satisfactory to use. Almost any surface, provided it is not too rough, will receive a stenciled pattern. Evenly woven cotton cloth is perhaps the most suitable textile for children to use, and most types of paper for drawing and painting are serviceable.

The paper being cut for the final stencils should be laid over a glass plate or a piece of hard building board. Care must be taken to be exact in cutting, so that a cut stops where it is supposed to stop and joins exactly with another cut. The worker must leave "ties," or narrow bands of paper, to hold parts of the design together. Hence the design must be simple. To perform this relatively delicate cutting, some people find it convenient to push the knife away from themselves in the Japanese manner; others prefer to draw it toward the body.

When paper is being stenciled, it should be pinned to a drawing board. Textile, on the other hand, must be stretched tightly over newsprint or blotting paper and then pinned firmly in place. The paper underneath the textile will absorb any excess paint that might otherwise run and spoil the work.

Paint should be thick enough not to run, yet not so thick as to form an unpleasantly heavy coating on the painted surface. Tempera paint for printing on paper can be placed in a muffin tin. After being dipped into the paint the brush should be scrubbed slightly on scrap paper to rid it of excess paint. Oil paints for textiles should be squeezed from the tube onto a palette, which might be a piece of glass. The amount of paint picked up by the brush can be controlled by gently dabbing the brush on the palette.

Paint should be applied to the holes in the stencil with some care: if the brush is used too vigorously, the stencil may be damaged. For an even spread of color over the entire cut-out area the paint should be applied with a dabbing motion. Stroking from the edge of the stencil into the cut-out area will give a shaded effect.

Teaching. Clean equipment is necessary if smooth work is to result. The brushes in particular should be kept scrupulously clean. While cool water will suffice to wash brushes used with tempera paint, turpentine is the solvent for oil-based colors. Brushes that have been cleaned in turpentine should be washed again with soap and cool water. After the brushes have been washed they should be placed in a container with the bristles up. Students should, of course, be taught to clean their palettes after using them. Should students wish to preserve the stencils from one day to another, they should wash the stencils carefully with water or turpentine, depending on the type of paint used, after which the stencils can be suspended from a line strung in a storage cupboard for the purpose.

A second task for the teacher is to assist the pupils in becoming familiar with the stenciling technique as a means of personal expression. Preliminary practice may be done on ordinary paper or cardboard. Following the teacher's demonstration, and after practice in cutting, children will discover how to leave the "ties," or small bands, to hold parts of the design together. Largely through practice accompanied by the teacher's comments, they will learn that a stencil design must be kept simple and that intricate shapes are generally to be avoided.

Finally, the teacher should encourage experimentation, for which stenciling provides many opportunities. Various colors may be used both separately and blended. A good effect is achieved if the stencil is moved slightly when a second color is used. Furthermore, two or more stencils may be used on the same surface.

Activities for the Reader

1. Produce a monoprint contour-line drawing by using one color and drawing directly in the color after you have applied it to a sheet of glass. Repeat, using two colors lightly blended with the brayer.

2. Produce a monoprint contour-line drawing by drawing on the paper after it has been laid down over the inky glass. Experiment by using several colors of ink at the same time.

3. Produce a nonobjective design in monoprint by laying down an orderly arrangement of string, burlap, and cut cardboard on the inky surface before applying the paper for the impression.

4. Experiment with a number of vegetables, suitably cut, to produce various printed textural effects on paper. Over these effects print an orderly design with a potato or carrot into which you have cut a pattern with a knife.

5. a. Experiment with a potato, scoring it not only with a knife but also with a fork or a spoon. Try printing a sheet of paper with an overall pattern that repeats the unit exactly.

   b. Prepare two soap erasers with different designs ("a" and "b") and print the units as follows:

      a, b, a, b, a
      a, b, a, b, a
      a, b, a, b, a
      a, b, a, b, a, etc.

   c. Now print as follows on black paper:

      a, b, b, a
      b, a, a, b
      a, b, b, a
      b, a, a, b, etc.

   d. Print, turning "a" or "b" upside down.

   e. Print, overlapping "a" and "b."

   f. Print with varying space between the "a"'s and "b"'s:

      a   a   a
        b   b
      a   a   a

   g. Create some different arrangements, perhaps eventually using three and four motifs, or units.

In all cases, the pattern should be repeated exactly.[2]

   h. Combine some of your printed arrangements with interesting backgrounds prepared experimentally.

6. Cut sticks so that they will print a unit and experiment on paper as indicated in 5a–h, above. Combine cut ends with scrap ends of found pieces of wood.

7. Select the arrangement you like best and print it on textile.

8. Experiment with a piece of linoleum, making a nonobjective design to obtain many different types of textures. Take several rubbings of your work as you progress. Finally, print it on paper.

9. Cut a 2-inch square of linoleum and glue it to a block. Cut a nonobjective unit of design in this piece of linoleum. Print the design on paper in repeated patterns in the manner indicated in 5a–h, above.

10. Print the pattern produced according to activity 9, above, on textile rather than paper.

11. From a landscape, still life, life drawing, or some other representational work you have produced, plan a picture to be cut in linoleum. Make an India-ink drawing the exact size you intend your cut to be, say 5 by 8 inches. Cover the linoleum with a thin coat of white tempera paint and then redraw your sketch on the linoleum. Start cutting, taking as many rubbings as you require, and later make some test prints to give you an idea of your progress. When the design is ready, print it in several single colors. Then try printing with two colors simultaneously.

12. Take a plank of wood and make a print of the grain. Use light colors and overlap the grain or turn the wood to create patterns. If the pattern of the grain suggests anything to you, cut away a few sections of the wood to make the movement of the pattern even stronger.

[2]See R. R. Tomlinson, *Picture and Pattern Making by Children* (New York: Viking, 1950).

13. Make a collograph by cutting out cardboard shapes, gluing them to a base, inking the surface, and taking a print. The thicker the cardboard, the greater the play of light around the edges of your shapes in the print.

14. Make a corrugated print at least 18 by 24 inches. Try one print on a surface that is covered with a colored tissue collage.

15. Cut a stencil, using a nonobjective design no smaller than 3 inches square and print it on paper. Experiment on paper as indicated in 5a–h, above.

16. Obtain a styrofoam meat tray from the local supermarket. Using a ballpoint pen or blunt pencil, draw on the tray. Then, using a brayer, ink the drawn area and print the image on paper cut to fit the tray.

17. Decide how you would explain the differences among other graphic techniques such as intaglio, lithography, photography, and silkscreen.

The teacher shares with the student the delight and sense of excitement that only the first print can bring. Changes may have to be made from this point on, but no subsequent printing can offer this sense of surprise when the first print is pulled.

Suggested Readings

Andrews, Michael. *Creative Printmaking.* Englewood Cliffs: Prentice-Hall, 1963.

Romano, Clare, and John Ross. *The Complete Printmaker.* New York: Macmillan, 1972. Updates contemporary print processes, many of which are useable in public schools.

Weiss, Harvey. *Paper, Ink and Roller.* New York: William Scott, 1978.

NEW MEDIA:

COMMUNICATION

AND DESIGN

Adventure and intrigue await the experimenter in design as he improvises with line, form, texture and sometimes with color, for the aesthetic delights he can create. The inherent feature of designing with light is the freedom to improvise, to invent subject matter and to produce an art form in the contemporary idiom.*

TEN

Art teachers customarily associate the word *media* with such accepted materials as paint, clay, and charcoal, and may be unaware of the development of another context—one that refers to the technology of instruction. Instructional media encompass television, films, slides, tapes, and other similar means of communication. The term *media* in this sense implies a rather sophisticated approach to the teaching-learning situation and is associated with advances in learning theory. Vincent Lanier offers a conception of the uses of media that may seem grandiose to the teacher who has not progressed beyond an occasional use of slides or reproductions. He suggests using "prepared units presenting specific content both verbally

*From Robert W. Cooke, *Designing with Light on Paper and Film* (Worcester, Ma.: Davis, 1969), p. 5.

and visually."[1] Instructional media, in Lanier's view, are much more than support material; they can provide the very basis of a curriculum. In Lanier's units, content is broken down into its most manageable segments and sequenced in a logical progression, with a wide range of visual materials suggested for each step.

Media as a Means of Instruction

Indeed, Lanier feels that the entire art program should use media and other forms of popular art (video, comic books, posters, illustrations, films) as its basis, because the world of the growing child is rooted in these forms. He is also more interested in developing a critical understanding of the forms than in using them as a basis for activities. While the authors feel that Lanier's recommendation for a "dialog-" or discussion-based curriculum is unrealistic, Lanier's view must be accepted that new media do provide a legitimate area for concentration and that the development of a critical attitude toward the popular arts has certainly been neglected.

The hardware of media are considerably more than mechanical gadgets for presenting information; they are linked to the very shape and structure of the content being imparted, and thus represent many different ways of learning. Let us consider for a moment the many ways by which instructional media are able to extend students' perceptions of a subject such as painting:

A *film* about a particular artist can show something of the process of change and maturation in an individual.

A *comparison of slides* of works of art can lead to a group discussion of likenesses and differences in style, content, and the like.

Packets of small *reproductions* allow students to investigate at their own pace the visual components of a series of paintings.

A *filmstrip* can provide an inexpensive collection of slides centered on a single idea. For commentary there is usually an accompanying record or lecture notes; students can also work from their own impressions.

A *live television lesson* can bring a professional artist to the class for a single performance.

A *portable video tape machine* can play back a demonstration by a visiting artist for future reference or for classes that could not attend the original performance.

A *tape recording* of an interview with a local artist can be stored for future reference.

[1]Vincent Lanier, "The Language of Education," *Arts and Activities,* Vol. 58, No. 1 (September 1965), p. 37.

It is improbable that any teacher would have access to all of the above modes of instruction, but with time, knowledge, and equipment, teachers can significantly extend their own style of teaching (for both groups and individuals), the pupils' style of learning (through discussion, listening, observing), and the range of subject matter (painting skills, perceptual skills, the creative process).

Let us examine briefly one of the devices mentioned above: television. Here is a perfect example of an instructional tool that has its roots in the life style of the child; yet teaching art through television does not automatically assure a teacher of success. A number of questions regarding its use must be considered:

How relevant is the lesson in relation to what the teacher has planned?

Who can vouch for the quality of the lesson—that is, the validity of its content, the professionalism of the production staff, the choice of the art objects?

Is the level of the dialog suitable for the class scheduled to receive the lesson?

Does the classroom teacher have the materials required for a successful follow-up?

The advantages and the hazards of art instruction are several. The television lesson can rarely be geared to the specific instructional needs of a particular classroom and is therefore not a substitute for regular teaching. It is a basically inflexible medium with regard to timing. In terms of color, moreover, we cannot always trust the quality of color in artworks presented on television. On the other hand, television can support the existing art program by presenting what the average teacher cannot provide: guest artists; closeups of processes such as jewelry-making, pottery-making, and use of tools (although this advantage also has its limitations in that the closeup seems to encourage a "how-to-do-it" approach); access to original works of art from local museums; the opportunity to work with a master teacher who has a great amount of time and a number of production facilities available.

Instructional media require advance planning. A plan may call for a single student to study slides, or it may involve an entire system of instruction in which large segments of the curriculum are related to the equipment deemed most appropriate. The plan may be directed toward exploration of one idea or toward anticipated behavioral changes for the whole class, involving provisions for feedback and evaluation of learning performance. It is unlikely that systems approaches, programed learning, or other instructional packages that require extensive media will reach the average elementary art program. As a rule, these media are expensive to operate, need intensive planning, and imply to most art teachers too great an abrogation of their teaching responsibility.

Art teachers are, however, making increasing use of manageable media, such as those described above for instruction in painting. Yet even on this level, teachers will not accommodate themselves to instruction via media if they have the art teacher's traditional suspicion of mechanical gadgets, or if the school budget will not allow for support materials such as slides, tapes, and rented films.

Media as Art

Media apparently have two roles to play in current education. One has already been discussed—the utilization of communication facilities in instruction. Teachers should also utilize the carriers of information as art forms in themselves; that is, they should place the equipment in the hands of the students for them to make use of its creative potential. In many school situations, such an approach is no longer new. Children are making both live and animated films as well as studying the cinema as an art form. Even first graders are working directly on raw film and projecting images they created. Children in the fourth, fifth, and sixth grades are capable of running tape recorders, handling cameras, and combining several modes of projection in the production of their own "light shows." These activities are described below. First, however, we shall consider how the child's environment today fosters experimentation with the new media.

ENVIRONMENTAL INFLUENCES

Children today are both eager and prepared to engage in media activity. The factors that stand in the way of such activity are the teacher's ignorance of media and unwillingness to recognize them as a valid basis for art instruction. The children, unaware of their teacher's reservations, continue to develop in their own environment. Their visual sense is oriented to motion because of early exposure to television and films. They accept condensed time-space concepts because they view live coverage of news events, and they have never doubted, for instance, that they could breakfast in one part of the world and lunch in another. The camera is probably not a novelty in many families. Many children would rather study structure, perception, and color with a camera than with a box of crayons. The objections of those adults who hold the traditional art activities in high esteem are just academic quibbling to the child with an avid multisensory curiosity.

The art teacher who is truly sensitive to what is happening outside the art room will give serious thought to incorporating media activity into

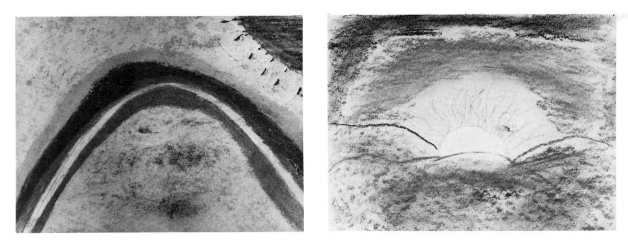

These drawings by fourth graders are an example of the use of media as a means of accelerating perception. The two drawings above were pretest assignments for the topic "Draw anything you like that includes a landscape and clouds." The two below are from the same class a week later. Films of clouds and landscapes followed by discussions were the motivation. While motivation also lies outside the nearest window, films of cloud formations and changing weather conditions showed the children the variety of possible visual effects.

the art program, recognizing the fact that these media are probably the most direct link to the nonschool culture of the child. Society has created the climate for working with media today, just as the numerous art movements of the 1920s liberated contemporary conceptions of painting and helped shape the pattern of many of the art programs of the Progressive education movement. If hesitant art teachers take a fresh look at media, they will have to admit that there is no inherent contradiction in goals or philosophy between creating in either the new or the traditional media. Both kinds of materials provide excitement and challenge in the areas of design, including color, and drawing; both elicit original solutions on the part of the child and call for a high level of creative ingenuity. Newer media have simply added such increasingly relevant ingredients as time, motion, and light to the elements of color, space, mass, line, texture, and shade. Teachers will be shortsighted indeed should they fail to capitalize on the built-in motivations provided by the excitement of matching sound to light or image to movement. They will also deprive themselves of a logical means of combining other arts such as music, dance, and choral reading.

The activities described in this chapter have been tested in elementary schools. They range from simple projects that can be carried out in one learning session to more complex operations requiring several sessions. In most cases, the amount of time spent on the project depends on how deeply the teacher wants to probe the subject.

PROJECTED IMAGES

The creation of designs on slides that can be projected gives the child an opportunity to experiment with light. The materials are not expensive, and the activity can be correlated with music and language arts.

Media and Techniques. The slides should be 2 inches square and made of glass or heavy acetate. These provide the base, or *ground,* for the transparent materials that carry the design. As for these materials, any that permit the passage of light are acceptable—colored cellophane, crystallizing lacquers, theatrical gelatins, colored lacquers, nail polish, and so on. Or the slides may be covered with India ink or tempera paint and sections scratched away to allow passage of light. Applying the color is a simple matter. Nail polish, crystallizing lacquers, and colored lacquers can be painted on with cotton swabs or detail brushes. Colored cellophane and theatrical gelatins can be applied to the slide with white plastic glue that has been thinned out with five parts water to one part glue.

The children should design both sides of the slide; one side might be used for solid color and the other for linear effects with India ink. In such a case the design problem would be to combine the elements of mass and line into a satisfactory whole. Another variant might be to design soft shapes on one side and hard-edged forms on the other. If children want to make a two-slide image, they have not only four sides to plan but also the area between the slides. Here, they may choose to add such "stop outs" as sand, ashes, and thread to create silhouette effects. The edges of the plates should be taped to keep the center of the "sandwich" in place (see illustration). Because of the limited size of the slides, an abstract design is a more appropriate subject than a realistic image. Slides of artworks, landscapes,

New Media: Communication and Design

A *A single slide.*

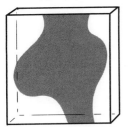

Front side: flowing image (paint, ink, lacquer).

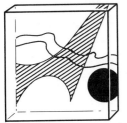

Back side: linear and hard-edged images (ink, cellophane, gelatinate).

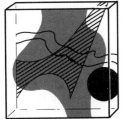

Combined image: hard and soft forms.

B *A two-slide image.*

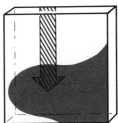

Combined image, slide 1.

Combined image, slide 2.

Center section: string, ashes, and cut gelatin.

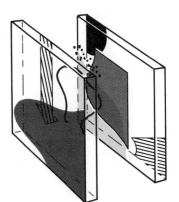

Both slides plus "sandwich" before taping.

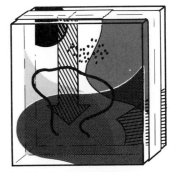

Finished, taped slide showing combined image composed of five patterns.

Various ways of treating glass slides.

buildings, and family groups (provided the owners have decided to discard them) make interesting raw material for photo-collages.

The slides can be projected through a standard school projector. Two projectors allow for overlapping of images. It is safe to say that the more projectors going at once, the larger the image, and the darker the room, the more exciting the possibilities. The projections are often as effective when the images are diffused as when they are sharply in focus. A musical selection that the class enjoys might be used as an accompaniment for the designing of the projections. When the slides are run on two projectors in conjunction with the music the class has a novel program for a school assembly or a PTA meeting.

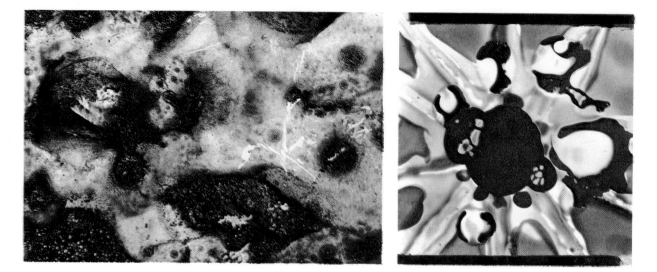

Designing colored slides appeals to children at all grade levels. The age level is not easy to tell in these examples, since experimentation and investigation were more important than obtaining a "finished" product. The drawing, left, by a sixth grader, was made with watercolor, liquid soap, and felt pen; the one at the right, by an eleventh grader, was made with colored lacquer.

Teaching. One way to begin instruction is to let the class manipulate color and light on an overhead projector. If time is limited, the teacher can move about colored cellophane on a sheet of acetate while the class discusses how such movements affect the image. This activity may be followed by some wet mingling of colored lacquers on the acetate. The discussion may then focus on how such activities can be transferred to the smaller confines of a glass slide. The class might list materials that block the passage of light and those that permit light to pass through. If the teacher has any finished slides on hand, the class can look at them and speculate on how the effects were achieved. By this time the class will be more than ready to begin their own slides. The teacher might want to select music for the class to listen to as they work and, later, help organize a light show to project the finished slides.

FILMMAKING WITHOUT A CAMERA

There are several techniques with which to create filmlike effects and moving images without actually using a film camera. The simplest way to acquaint children with the principles of animation is to gather together as many old telephone books as are available and have the students make marks on the margin. By flipping the edge of the book, the images will

New Media: Communication and Design

dance randomly about. Ask the class how to control the motion, and someone will soon suggest a progression. Once a sequential progression is maintained, the flow of images can be controlled. At this point, the class can move on to the next step and draw directly on film.

Media and Techniques. Filmmaking without a camera is accomplished by painting or drawing directly on the actual segments of film. Thus the basic materials for this activity are strips of 16mm film—clear leader or black with an emulsion side—and inks or paint to apply to the film. White leader may also be used; it offers a soft gray background for color. It is also possible to purchase transparent colored leader film.

The most elementary technique is to draw a black line on the clear film. India ink may be used, but it has a tendency to flake off while being used in the projector. The best ink for this technique is Pelikan (K) black, a plastic ink that adheres permanently to the acetate of the film. When black emulsion-type leader film is used, the design consists of white line on a black ground. The white line is produced by scratching through the emulsion with a needlelike tool. Simple etching tools can be made by fixing sewing needles in pencils or sticks. Because it is rather difficult to see the scratched lines, it is advisable to work over a sheet of white paper or on windowpanes. Care should be taken that the lines are not etched too deeply, for the film can be weakened in this way. Another variation of the scratching technique is to punch out a series of holes in varying sizes, thus creating a pattern of flashing lights when the film is projected. Rotating leather punches, which have six or eight sizes of holes, are good to use for this purpose.

Colored lines may be drawn with felt-tip pens. These pens can also be used to make free nonobjective color patterns to serve as background for more controlled black-line exercises. If the student wants to work with color materials of a more plastic nature, two that give excellent results are transparent lacquer and transparent acetate ink. Some fingernail polishes are also transparent and can be used. Transparent lacquer is a thick liquid, so it must be applied to the film with a small brush rather than a pen. Because it has a penetrating odor it should be used only in rooms with proper ventilation. Perhaps the best color medium is acetate ink. It has the brilliant color qualities of transparent lacquer without its offensive fumes, and it can be applied to the film with a pen.

The student should experiment with a variety of pen points or brushes. If the ink resists flowing onto the film, it is possible that the surface is greasy. The film can be cleaned quickly with a rag dampened with alcohol. Sufficient drying time should be allowed before running the film through an editing machine or projector.

The length of the filmstrips need not pose problems as to where to work. The children may work standing up, hanging their strips vertically

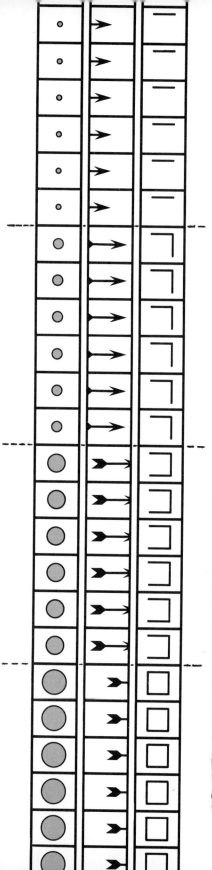

Three basic control activities in painting film segments. All three require the child to maintain a distinct stage of size or motion for six frames. Left: making an object advance toward the viewer; center: making an object travel horizontally; right: metamorphosis of a shape.

on the wall or blackboard; they may tape segments of film to cafeteria-type tables; or they may move the film along their desks. It is recommended that white paper be used as a backing for the section of film being worked on.

Teaching. Before the actual creative work on the film begins the teacher should explain how motion is achieved in filmmaking. The student should understand that twenty-four frames will pass through the projecting lens in one second at "sound" speed.[2] Since twenty-four frames comes to about 7 inches of film, about 2 feet of film per child will allow three seconds of animation.

Because most students have difficulty understanding the frame and time relationship, it is advisable to present them first with some simple activities exploring fundamental paths of motion—horizontal, vertical, and spatial. One basic activity is to have the student develop a series of dots, circles, stars, crosses, or some other objects that advance or recede, as illustrated in the diagram. To advance, the objects should begin very small and gradually increase in size until they take up most of the frame. The objects seem to recede when they gradually diminish in size. At least six frames for each stage of growth should be allowed, for it takes this long for

[2] "Silent" speed slows the film down to sixteen frames per second. But it is recommended that sound speed be used as the basis for designing the film sequence, in case the final result is worthy of having a sound track added.

A third grader draws directly on a piece of film with pen and ink. (Photo by Rick Steadry.)

the eye to accommodate a distinct unit of motion (left column). In order to have a shape travel horizontally from left to right, the student draws the forward part of the object on the left-hand side of the frame for a six-frame segment. Every time the object is advanced toward the right of the frame the position should be held for six frames, until finally only the last portion of the object is visible from the right-hand edge of the frame (center column).[3]

Another activity develops the ability to make a shape grow or change into another shape. This task requires that the student think of the finished product first and then break the design process down into manageable segments that develop logically out of each other. In order to make a line draw itself into a square, for instance, the student might first draw a horizontal line, repeat it for six frames, next draw a connecting vertical line in another six frames, and thus continue until the four sides of the square are completed (right column). This method can be applied to drawing a triangle or even a face.

Ideally, the children should have access to a film-editing machine so that they can view their work immediately. With such a machine, the child can see clearly that each frame is a single discrete image. The flow of one image to the next is controlled in much the same way one controls the movement of "flip books"—by speeding up or retarding the controlling mechanism (see activity 5 at the end of this chapter). By observing how their films work in this machine the students can understand how the movies they see on Saturday afternoons function.

Unless the whole class works in shifts on one large segment of film, it will be necessary to purchase a film splicer to join the segments. There are usually two or three mechanically inclined children in most fifth and sixth grade classes who can be taught to use the splicer. At least five feet of leader should be reserved for splicing at the beginning and at the end of the completed film; this amount is needed to get the film into the projector.

Film animation with a camera is too complex to adequately describe here, but there are several excellent books that explain the process in simple, clear terms.[4] If the teacher has a tripod, an 8- or 16mm movie camera with a stop-action mechanism, and two strong lights, the class can animate anything, from people (*pixillation*), to sand, to pictures. Film animation is valuable because it teaches patience, satisfies the desire to learn purely technical processes, and develops narrative skill. An animated film begins when drawing or painting is completed. It allows a child to move

[3]An excellent film to study in relation to this spatial effect (and others) is Norman McLaron's *Fiddle-dee-dee* (Canadian National Film Board, 1947; distributed by the International Film Bureau).

[4]Yvonne Andersen is a leader in teaching film animation to children, and her book is listed on page 307.

very directly into the world of Walt Disney and Ralph Bakshi. After making their own film, children will never look at professional work in quite the same way.

EXPERIENCES WITH A CAMERA

If a camera is available, whether handmade or on loan from friend or family, it can be used as an instrument for observation and personal commentary. The treatment of one subject in two or more greatly contrasted media (as in sculpture, painting, and photography) is an effective way of attuning children to the possibilities and limitations of art media. Bartow mentions seven tasks for the beginning photographer which are also worth trying in drawing (and writing).

> Make a "living comic strip." Tell a story in a series of pictures using real people.
> Photograph an autobiography. Tell about yourself by taking pictures of your favorite things, your family, where you live, yourself.
> Document your neighborhood. Take pictures of people at work and play, people of different ages, buildings where you and others live, work, spend their time.
> Define a word/feeling with a picture or series of pictures. (Happiness, sadness, cold, hot, hard, soft.)

Anything that can be moved can be animated. These illustrations are two examples. At the left, twelve-year-olds change the shape of a pile of sand so that when it is photographed, one shape will "flow" easily into another. The illustration below shows a basic setup for clay animation. The background is a mural project; the figures are plasticene; and the police wagon is a painted cereal box. Two lights on either side and a 16- or 8mm film camera in the center complete this mini-studio. Working from a storyboard, the animators can enjoy improvising by reshaping the clay and repositioning the objects.

Pretend you're a bug or a giant. Photograph the world through their eyes.

Illustrate a song or a poem or a short story with your own photos.

Film look-alikes. Take a picture of something that looks like an owl but isn't an owl. Does the front of a car look like a smiling face? The branch of a tree like an arm?

Look for patterns. Find repeated designs in the environment, like picket fences, railroad tracks, or bricks.[5]

We mention the storyboard in this chapter, but we could just as easily have discussed it in Chapter 6, "Drawing," or Chapter 11, "Relating Art to the General Curriculum." The storyboard is a transdisciplinary activity that draws in varying degrees on narrative skill, the linking of image to story, and the use of drawing. It can also prepare children to better understand how film-makers, animators, and even writers of commercials think on paper.

A storyboard is a sequence of pictures that tells a story or relates to a given problem. Some students may choose to draw their sequences; others may compile them or paste them up from news or magazine photos. The storyboard can be used to plan an 8mm film or can be an activity in itself.

[5] Ellie Waterston Bartow, *Children are Centers for Understanding Media* (Washington, D.C.: ASCD).

THE STORYBOARD

Making a large-scale storyboard, at right, to plan for the minute transitions required for animation without a camera. Making a storyboard can often clarify the process of image change, and relieve some of the tedium involved in dealing with twenty-four frames per second.

An example of a broad, or generalized, storyboard, which shows key points in the narrative. After this board is completed, the transitional images, which can number into the hundreds, must be supplied. Children can discover new resources of patience within themselves through the animation process.

Specific homework assignments can be made. For example, children in the upper elementary grades are capable of studying a one-minute television commercial by reducing it to a sequence of storyboard frames, thereby recording the timing of shots, distinguishing between tight shots (very close), long shots (at a distance), close-ups, and so on. In making a storyboard, students can apply the basic vocabulary of film and video to extend their own picture-making. Storyboards are the middle ground between the realm of the communications media and the traditional forms of picture-making.

Multimedia: The Light Show

The light show uses media for both their communicative and their creative potential. In addition, the light show allows children to combine many forms of media. For example, consider how a class might treat a holiday or celebration. The class not only has available the traditional performing arts (readings, songs, period music, dramatic scenes), but it also has fresh visual opportunities supplied by the medium of the light show: projection of "fireworks" drawn on clear film, slides of heroes or patriots flashed against a background of moving patterns of stars or flags.[6]

[6] The multimedia treatment of national holidays is an effective way of breaking away from stereotyped school programs that no longer hold any excitement for many of today's students.

In the illustration to the left and the one at the beginning of this chapter, ten-year-olds and their teacher study the interaction between light and painted color. In the chapter-opening illustration, students work with white paint on cardboard; later they will use more colors and project colored light onto them. They can use what they have learned when they design a performance combining the light show with music, movement, mime, and drama. Here, three elements at work together: slides, the "wet" effects of oil and water, and the "hard" patterns of cut paper on overhead projectors.

A "modulator" could be any contrivance that changes the passage of light. Materials used in this example are colored cellophane and strips of cardboard stapled together on a circular structure.

Given a number of multimedia devices to explore for the first time, children will engage in manipulative activities very similar to their first reaction to clay or any other new art material. During this initial stage, the children should be encouraged to experiment freely with the tools of light and motion; they should be allowed to combine fixed and moving images, blend sounds, and work light with color in a random fashion. However, to abandon the challenge of ultimately obtaining some sort of content and meaning in their work would be like cutting off the painting experience after a session or two of dripping and splashing. Ideally, the light show should be planned with some degree of structure around a central idea. If children can be taught to plan a light show with as much care and thought as they bring to the creation of a puppet show or mural, their range of learning can be considerably extended.

There is a very popular but misguided notion that a light show is a "psychedelic" experience. This term lacks validity here, for it implies the use of drugs, from which elementary-school children are still largely exempt. The light show does, however, have the effect of extending the sensory awareness of its participants and as such definitely has a place in today's art program.

No single successful way to prepare a light show can be set forth. Much depends on the equipment to which the class has access. The teacher should first take an inventory of the audio-visual equipment in the school. The following items allow students a wide range of effects to work with:

1. *35mm slide projector:* for use with prepared and original projections.[7]
2. *16mm film projector:* for use with both commercially prepared films and drawings and paintings on clear or black leader film.
3. *Overhead projectors:* may be used to manipulate transparent colored theatrical gels and cellophane, or paper cutouts and grease drawings on acetate, which are placed over the colored transparencies. Interesting effects are obtained by connecting segments of cellophane and pulling them slowly under and over the light. Pieces of colored glass or plastic in a bowl of water, when placed under the light source and stirred, project shifting patterns of color. Similar effects may be had with colored varnish, oil, and water mixed in a bowl or pan; these patterns vary with the ways in which the ingredients are combined. Water prisms, "magic reflectors,"[8] and convex and concave lenses moved in front of the light source project dancing light images.

[7]The various "carousel" models offer flexibility in timing.
[8]Available from Creative Playthings, Princeton, N.J.

4. *Record players:* the tendency today is to use mostly rock music to accompany a light show, but other varieties of music should be investigated—and at decibel levels that are kind to the human eardrum. Of the classical composers, Bach is a favorite. Music poses a problem: the degree to which its style and mood should be accommodated to the visual images. A natural means of achieving consistency of sound and image is to have the children draw or paint to music, take colored slides of the results, and incorporate them as part of the projections.

5. *Tape recorders:* the students can create their own sound effects by collecting the sounds of the street, birds, traffic, playground, and the like on a battery-powered recorder. They can blow into bottles, snap their fingers, or run a block of wood over a series of objects to produce special sounds. Even within the four walls of their classroom there are surfaces such as glass, metal, and wood that yield interesting aural patterns when combined in varying rhythms. The music teacher might be prevailed on to serve as consultant for such investigations in developing awareness of sound.

Before preparing a light show, the teacher should check with the principal or custodian to determine the maximum carrying power of the source of electricity. For best results the room in which the show is projected should be blacked out as completely as possible, and there should be three basic areas of projection. Because a class will rarely have access to more than one large screen, the children should improvise other screens with sheets or large sections of cardboard that have been painted white. When the surfaces of the improvised screens are covered with paper that is rumpled, scored, bent, or curved, the sculptural effects thus derived can add greater variety to the projection. Parachutes and white sheets may be added to the "hard" shapes so that further variety within the images may be obtained. Certain images are even more interesting when taken off the conventional projection screen—the ceiling and the audience itself can be exciting projection surfaces.

Preschool children watch their teacher set up an environmental light show in which they will participate. The older the children, the more materials they can work with in creating environmental effects. (See the environmental sculpture projects in Chapter 8.) Here, light and the surfaces that receive the projections are the elements that can be manipulated. Line (yarn and string) can be an added component, as can plane (cardboard) and volume, both hard and soft, such as balloons, parachutes, mylar, and sheeting. (From "The Space Place," a project of CEMREL Laboratories, St. Louis, Mo.)

The portable Video Tape Retrieval (VTR) unit is gaining popularity in the schools at a rapid rate. However, the VTR has still to gain wide acceptance as part of the art program, and its position at this time is similar to that of the camera a generation ago. If we examine the creative possibilities of the VTR dispassionately, we must admit that it is a truly revolutionary instrument. To children, it means that they can, in a sense, control the very machine that for so many years has dominated their leisure hours. The tables are suddenly turned, and they as viewers are in command, becoming producer, director, or actor. Their new domain is a television studio in miniature, consisting of camera, television monitor, and tape deck for sound and storage of video tape. It is now possible for formerly passive observers to control the camera, create the image, and get immediate feedback on the monitor. Nor do they have to limit their activities to the school; they can extend their control to the playground, the neighborhood—anywhere the VTR can be carried.

The operation of the VTR is far too complex to describe within the limits of this chapter. As with photography, its technical aspects are best learned in a workshop. It is, however, worth noting some of the ways one art teacher with special training went about building a sequence of activities around the VTR. During a summer workshop[9] the children, working in rotating groups, did the following:

> Designed and presented their own commercials. This involved designing the package, writing copy, and delivering the "message," as well as recording the entire experience on tape.
> Designed and assembled several settings for short plays, which were developed from a series of improvisations. Sets were constructed of large sheets of cardboard and included castoff furniture.
> Studied the effects of light and change of scale by examining miniature sets on camera.
> Critiqued commercial programming viewed on the monitor.
> Role-played various social situations derived from their school and home experiences.
> Acted as television art teachers by demonstrating a simple process such as potato printing, stenciling, or collography.
> Took turns as cameraman, director, performer, switcher, designer, and producer. They also learned the basic operation and nomenclature of the equipment.

There were still many activities that the children did not explore. Some techniques planned for the second year were as follows:

[9] This special workshop for fifth and sixth graders was offered by the Newton Creative Arts Summer Program, Newton, Ma.

A number of roles related to video production are in evidence here: actors, camera crew, director, and studio audience. Writer and sound technicians are less evident. During the course of a production, students will change roles.

In what can be the most important phase of the video experience, the teacher critiques the class production on the monitor. The children now can relate performance to criticism.

1. *Projected slides on rear screen:* Slides can be integrated into a tape by recording them with the vidicon camera. Enlarged projections can be scanned by the camera for closer examination.
2. *Projected movies:* Films made by the class can also be incorporated into the same rear-screen-projection technique used for showing slides.
3. *Off-air recording:* Personal reactions can be taped and replayed to provide voice-over content from groups or individuals.
4. *Still images:* By starting the "still" control on the recorder, children can stop visuals and frame them for analysis of any desired special effects.
5. *Infinity:* The camera is aimed at the monitor, so that the monitor shows the monitor, showing the monitor, on *ad infinitum.* With controlled manipulation, interesting wave forms, patterns, and mandalas can be viewed and explored.
6. *TV animation:* By using cardboad figures and inserted tabs, parts of the anatomy, such as mouths, eyes, and hands, can be made to move in interesting ways. Movement can be enhanced by using the figures against both painted and projected slide backgrounds. Puppets and simple objects may also be animated.

The use of television in the art program remains a relatively new and unexplored area. A review of the activities listed above must surely make a curious teacher speculate about the many possibilities offered by the VTR as a means of extending the children's visual awareness. The use of new technology is available; the problem is to get it into the classroom—or to

306

get the students to the machinery. The Apple type of computer is capable of programmed animation, and sixth grades can certainly understand basic principles of computer operation, particularly if taught in the context of a math lesson. Xerography—the use of a photocopying machine—in both black and white and color predicts an array of new images, but these machines are still too costly for most school art programs. Teachers should bear in mind, however, that new technology is always possible if not easily accessible, and that if Leonardo Da Vinci were alive today, he certainly would have used any means at his disposal capable of extending his unique vision.

Activities for the Reader

The chapter itself describes many activities to try with the instruments of light and motion. Included here are some more activities of that type.

1. Run two films simultaneously but eliminate the sound of one and the image of the other. Now try to create connections between the image of the one film and the sound track of the other.
2. Using an overhead projector, improvise a series of shifting color patterns by manipulating colored gels and string. Draw on clear acetate with a grease crayon; note how the scale seems to change when the drawing is projected on the screen.
3. For immediate feedback of projected movement, work directly on those parts of the film that are exposed to view while in the projector. With felt-tip pens or hole punchers, work on a section, advance the film, and work on another part; then watch the results by reversing and advancing the film.
4. Obtain films that have outlived their usefulness and are about to be discarded. Work over the images with marking pens or with watercolor mixed with liquid soap, dyes, and inks. Parts of the image can be scratched away with a razor blade or knife. The work may be done randomly (without regard to content) or with some structure (by relating changes to the content of the film). Old film can be made clear by soaking it overnight in half-strength bleach.
5. Any series of still pictures will give the illusion of motion when viewed in sequence. Create a sequence of "flip cards" by working on one side of a group of index cards. By slightly changing the position of the image from card to card, it is possible to create the illusion of a ball flying off the page, a ship sinking into the sea, a smile appearing on a face, or Dr. Jekyll turning into Mr. Hyde.
6. Experiment with methods of correlating music and media. Select some music and create abstract images on glass slides in any manner suggested by the music. Such elements as line, color, and mass should all reflect the mood of the music. The slides can be grouped according to their relation to the changes in the mood and pace of the music. A roughly synchronized slide production can be made if two projectors are used and the image of one is faded into the image of the other by adjusting the focusing mechanism of the projectors.

Suggested Readings

Andersen, Yvonne. *Make Your Own Animated Movies.* Boston: Little, Brown, 1970.

Cooke, Robert W. *Designing with Light on Paper and Film.* Worcester, Ma.: Davis, 1969.

Doing the Media: A Portfolio of Activities and Resources. New York: Center for Understanding Media, 1973.

Hurwitz, Al. "Redefining the Media of Art." In *Programs of Promise: Art in the Schools.* New York: Harcourt Brace Jovanovich, 1972.

GROUP ACTIVITIES
IN ART

A group of children around a conference table setting up goals, making plans, assuming responsibilities, or evaluating achievements represents an essential prelude to intelligent, responsible citizenship. Children learn from one another through sharing ideas; group action is more effective when several individuals have shared in the planning; individuals find a place in group projects for making contributions in line with special talents; and morale is higher when children work together cooperatively on group projects. This is not meant to imply that there is no place in the modern classroom for individual effort; there should be a time for both individual and group activity.*

ELEVEN

In his book *Democracy as a Way of Life,* Boyd H. Bode says that "teaching democracy in the abstract is on a par with teaching swimming by correspondence."[1] This is why he feels that "the school must undertake to exemplify in its organization and procedures its conception of democratic living."[2] In a democratic community, Bode says, there is provision for all people to share in the common life according to their interests and capacities. A democratic school promotes the doctrine that people are "free and equal" by taking proper account of individual differences and by reliance

[1] Boyd H. Bode, *Democracy as a Way of Life* (New York: Macmillan, 1937), p. 75.
[2] Bode, p. 77.
* From William B. Ragan and C. B. Stendler, *Modern Elementary Curriculum* (New York: Holt, Rinehart and Winston, 1966), p. 192.

on the principle of community living. Such a school neither excuses the individual from a responsibility to the group nor replaces one set of fixed ideas about living with another, equally static, set. The children in a democratic school enjoy a free play of intelligence, and they emerge from this school with their own set of conclusions. The children, asserts Bode, must acquire something "other than a docile acceptance of a point of view."

It is the purpose of this chapter to enlarge on the role that art can play in giving children some understanding of social processes as they operate in the art program. We shall study some artistic activities that are especially suitable for the development of the children's social insight. We will also discuss new concepts of group art that have emerged in recent years, as well as more traditional forms such as puppetry and mural-making.

The Role of the Teacher in Group Activity

While realizing the desirability of including group activities in an art program, the teacher may have certain questions concerning the mechanics of this technique. How does group activity work? How should the activity be chosen? What should be its scope? What is the role of the teacher?

A number of years ago, Kilpatrick outlined the steps in what he called a "purposeful activity." These steps, which have stood the test of time, he called *purposing, planning, executing,* and *judging.*[3] Kilpatrick's steps were to be verified much later in the many descriptions of the creative process that came to light as a result of research into creativity. Creative minds in both the sciences and the arts were found to work in a progression of thought and action similar to Kilpatrick's steps.

Group activities, like those of an individual, must begin with some end in mind. This sense of purpose, Kilpatrick says, supplies the drive necessary to complete the project. Moreover, it is the children who should share a role in the "purposing." The teacher, of course, may make suggestions, but before these suggestions can be effected, the children must accept them wholeheartedly. Both the "planning" and the "executing," which are outcomes of the purposing, must also be controlled by members of the working group. Finally, the children themselves must ask the general and the specific questions concerning the outcome of the activity. Did they do what they planned? What was learned in the doing? What mistakes were made? How could the activity be done better next time? Children, in other words, should also be involved in evaluating the experience.

[3] W. H. Kilpatrick, *Foundations of Method* (New York: Macmillan, 1925), pp. 203ff. See also Frances Pauline Hilliard, *Improving Social Learnings in the Elementary School* (New York: Teachers College, 1954), p. 68, in which the author discusses "the process of cooperative planning and working." Her ideas are clearly an elaboration of those of Kilpatrick.

Group Activities in Art

The functions of the teacher in a group activity in art are parallel to those associated with individual learning.[4] The methods of motivation, the definition of tasks, establishing artistic goals, and selecting media and tools of expression now must be applied to those pupils, whether few or many, who make up the art group.

In the collective life of the school or classroom, occasions requiring group effort in art invariably arise if goals are to be reached. "Let's have a play," the children say, "Let's run a puppet show. . . . Let's make a big picture to go in the hallway. . . . Let's do a light show." Very little suggestion need come from the teacher to set in motion a desirable group project. The children themselves, who are usually quick to realize when working together will get desired results, are often the first to suggest to a teacher that a group activity be considered.

It is in this area that the classroom teacher has an advantage over the art teacher who may see a class for only fifty minutes a week. Children quickly learn that some activities are inappropriate for the typical art schedule and do not even suggest time-consuming group activities. If art teachers are skillful, however, they can sustain interest from one week to the next so that a class is able to paint a wall, build a miniature city, or convert a section of the art room into a spaceship. There will always be some children who want to continue working on such a project after school, and there may even be release time for others to come to the art room as a large project nears completion.

No matter how desirable it may be to encourage children to work cooperatively, the teacher must realize that art is a matter of individual concern and will always remain so. An art form should never be produced by a group unless the size and scope of the work is such that an individual could not possibly master it. Only when a work requires for its successful completion a diversity of skills, a fund of energy, and a span of attention exceeding those of any one child, is the need for group endeavor indicated.

Before encouraging children to proceed with a group project, the teacher must judge not only whether it is sufficiently challenging to occupy the attention of several people, but also whether it may be too large for successful completion by a group. In their enthusiasm for art, children are sometimes willing to plunge into a task that they could never complete. Once fired with the idea of a mural, for example, a group of fifth graders might cheerfully embark on the enormous task of designing murals for all four walls of a school gymnasium. One or even two murals might be made successfully, but production of many more would exhaust the pupils. A group activity in art that comes to a wavering halt because the children have lost interest or lack competence to complete it reflects not only on the

[4] See Arthur D. Hollingshead, *Guidance in Democratic Living* (New York: Appleton-Century-Crofts, 1941), p. 120, for the necessary "personal qualifications" of a successful teacher in a group activity.

The teacher supervises pupils working on a rag tapestry based on the Gilgamesh myth of ancient Babylonia. Although this sort of group craft activity takes considerable preparation, the results are unique in their richness of texture and color; they make an unusual contribution to the school or classroom.

group techniques but also on the teacher's judgment. When failure looms, the teacher must help the pupils alter their plans so that they can achieve success.

Having a greater maturity and insight into group processes, the teacher must fill the role of counselor with tact, sympathy, and skill. As soon as the need for group work in art is apparent, the children must be urged to elect leaders and establish committees necessary for "purposing, planning, executing, and judging" to take place. As stated earlier, the teacher should see that, as far as is practical, the children control these steps. Although teachers have the power of veto, they should be reluctant to use it. If at times the children's decisions seem to be wrong, the teacher should nevertheless allow them to proceed, unless, of course, their chosen course of action would only lead to overwhelmingly disastrous results. It is part of the learning process for people to make mistakes and, profiting from them, subsequently to rectify them.

To one aspect of counseling the teacher must give special attention. Since group procedures depend for success largely on the maximum contribution of each participant, the teacher must see that every child in the group is given a fair opportunity to make a suitable contribution to the project. A good group project should include a wide enough range of tasks to elicit participation from every member of the class.

Often beginners at school, either kindergarten or first grade children, are not mature enough to participate fully in a group enterprise. Nevertheless, a beginning may be made early in their school careers. This takes the form of a quasi-group activity in which children pool work originally completed as a result of individual effort.

Media and Techniques.   The quasi-group activity may be based on any theme that interests young pupils and may make use of any medium and technique that the children are capable of handling. If a kindergarten class happens to be talking about the subject of spring, for example, each child who has reached the symbol stage may select one item of the season to illustrate. The children may draw and paint symbols of lambs, flowers, birds, trees, and other springlike objects. After drawing or painting each item, the children cut away the unused paper around the symbol. Then the drawings and paintings are assembled on a tackboard.

In the primary grades, children like to work simultaneously on four sides of the paper. Later, they will be disturbed by the lack of a baseline and will prefer to work from only one side. If they choose to paint in a nonobjective mode, a common realistic reference point is not as crucial.

313

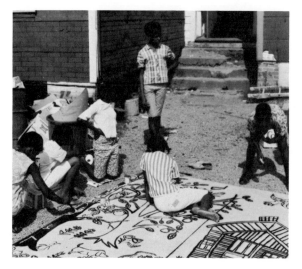

Groups can also function constructively outside the classroom. These youngsters are working on a large drawing of their neighborhood in rural Georgia. The activity, which was preceded by careful instruction in contour-line drawing, requires care and patience on the part of the students. (Photo by Marvin Grossman.)

Many other suitable topics could be treated in a similar fashion. Among them might be the following:

1. Shopping with Mother: Various stores may be drawn and painted, together with people and automobiles. This subject could also be handled as an interior scene showing the articles on display in a supermarket.
2. Our House: Pictures of houses are eventually assembled to form a street.
3. My Friends: The outlines of boys and girls are assembled to form a crowd of children.
4. Spring in the Garden: Gathering associated forms such as bugs, butterflies, and flowers.
5. Above and Below: Including sky shapes (clouds and birds), trees and flowers, and imaginative treatment of what lies below the earth's surface.

Three-dimensional output also lends itself to quasi-group activity. For example, the children can assemble modeling and paper constructions on a table to depict scenes such as "The Farm" with barns, cows, and so forth, and "The Circus" with clowns, elephants, and the like.

One of the simplest and most effective group projects is the "chalk-in," which can be executed on a sidewalk or parking lot. This can be done randomly or with sections marked off in a grid, with each section touching an adjacent one at some point.

Teaching. The teacher begins the group activity in the same way as individual picture-making or three-dimensional work, supplying motivation and teaching as required. Eventually, when the children have produced their work, the teacher, who has reserved a display space in the room, asks each child to bring a piece of work to the board and pin it in place. At first, a rather disorganized arrangement may result. A short discussion with the class, however, will elicit a few suggestions for improving the placement of the individual drawings. Some of the largest and brightest work can be located near the center of the panel, while smaller drawings of the same symbol drawn by several children might be grouped or arranged in a rhythmic line. When the "mural" is made with cut-out shapes, even a first grader can begin to think of subject matter in relation to organization of masses in space. In such cases, it may facilitate matters to do the initial planning on the floor, where shapes may be more easily adjusted than on the wall.

The finished composition will, of course, have a pattern with many small areas of interest reminiscent of some of the output of Grandma Moses and other so-called primitive artists. Teachers should not attempt to improve the layout by adding any of their own work. If they are tempted to provide a fence or road in perspective, or even a horizon line, they should not, first, because the children should learn to depend only on themselves in developing a group activity and, second, because only a muddle could result if adult work (however naive) and children's work were assembled on the same panel. Children should not be used as surrogate artists for the teacher.

The main aim of conducting the quasi-group activity is to lead children to the point at which they can control Kilpatrick's four steps. Therefore, even in this beginning stage, all the teacher's actions must be governed by this aim. The teacher should solicit themes from the children so that "purposing" may develop. Later the children should be urged to decide as a group which items of any class of objects each child should draw. For example, at first all the children might draw lambs for the spring picture, but later the group might decide that certain children should draw chickens, ducklings, and so on. This would lead to better "planning." Then group decisions about, say, media or subject might begin to improve design. Finally, such a simple question as "Could we have made the picture better?" could begin the stage of "judging" even in these early years.

Following practice in quasi-group work the children may exhibit an inclination to band together from the start of a project and work with even a minimum of cooperation. They are then ready for group activities proper. A "group" may be defined as a team ranging from three students to a complete class, depending on the nature of the project. Small groups work very well on dioramas, middle-sized groups can work in the sandbox, and larger groups can take on constructions like model shopping centers and housing communities. Other projects could include decorative maps or a mural that transforms the entire classroom into a medieval environment, complete with mullioned windows and stone walls.

According to most writers on the subject, group development should be fostered at some point in kindergarten and should occupy more and more school time as the child matures. Encouragement of group work becomes much easier for the teacher as the child's age increases. In the third or fourth grade the child becomes especially interested in associating with peer groups. Interests in the "gang" are evident in the children's drawings and paintings. The teacher may capitalize on this interest to promote art activities that lead to a greater social maturity of the young participants. Among the group activities suitable for this purpose and selected for the major part of the discussion here are puppetry and mural-making.

Puppetry

Perhaps some of the most effective group activities lie within the several fields of puppetry. Unfortunately, puppetry has been a casualty in the war between the advocates of a basic education that emphasizes academics and the supporters of an art-centered program that concentrates on activities. Because it is more complex than most art activities, puppetry is often seen as a threat to other priorities in the curriculum. It is therefore neglected in favor of art experiences that require less time and planning and fewer materials. This is to be regretted because, properly conducted, puppetry can carry the children into language arts and history as they go about gathering information, preparing scenarios, and planning and constructing a theater and sets. Work in puppetry is a natural focal point for the various learning styles that educators investigate, and no child should go through elementary school without at least one experience in it.

To produce a successful puppet play the group as a whole must reach decisions, and each member of the group, although maintaining personal identity, must give full cooperation if the enterprise is to succeed. Puppets range in technical complexity from the very simple to the very intricate, so that groups of children at any particular stage of development may select techniques compatible with their capabilities. The two major types of puppets that elementary-school children in one stage or another may select are fist puppets and shadow puppets.

FIST PUPPETS

Media and Techniques. Simple stick puppets—the type operated directly with one hand—may be produced in a variety of ways. The beginner can draw a figure on cardboard and later cut away the excess background. The cut-out figure is then attached to a stick. In place of a cut-out figure, the pupil may use a bag stuffed with paper or absorbent cotton, decorated with paint or cut paper, and tied to the stick.

Group Activities in Art

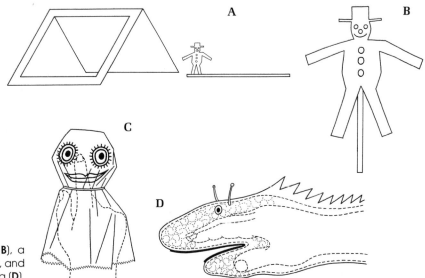

Diagrams of stick puppets (**A** and **B**), a puppet made from a paper bag (**C**), and a puppet made from an old stocking (**D**).

A paper bag may also be used for a puppet that moves its head. A string is tied around the middle of a paper bag, leaving just enough room for inserting the index finger above the middle. A face is painted on the closed upper portion of the bag. To operate the puppet, the hand is thrust into the bag up to the neck and the index finger pushed through the neck to articulate the head.

An old stocking, appropriately decorated with buttons for eyes and pieces of cloth or paper for hair, ears, and other features, also makes an effective puppet when slipped over the hand and arm. Animals such as snakes or dragons may be formed by this means. They become especially fearsome if a mouth is cut into the toe of a sock and cloth is stitched to form a lining to the throat so formed. Both top and bottom jaws should be stuffed with a material like absorbent cotton. The jaws are worked by inserting the fingers in the upper section and the thumb in the lower. The attractiveness of this creation can be enhanced by making a lining of a color contrasting with the sock, or by adding teeth or a tongue made from bright materials.

A fist puppet may be constructed from a wide variety of materials. Some of the modeling media mentioned in earlier chapters, including papier-mâché, are suitable for the construction of heads; plastic wood may also be used. The bodies of the puppets may be made from remnants of most textiles. These more advanced fist puppets should be capable of articulation in both the head and arms. The thumb and little finger are usually employed to create movements in the arms, while the index finger moves a modeled head.

A puppet head modeled over a cardboard fingerstall. The puppet can be manipulated by placing the fingers as shown.

To model a head, children should first cut and glue together a stiff cylinder of cardboard (preferably light Bristol board) large enough in diameter to fit their index finger loosely. The modeling medium, which tends to shrink the cylinder slightly, is then worked directly around the cardboard until the head, including all features, and neck are formed. The neck of the puppet modeled over the lower part of the cylinder, or "fingerstall," should be increased slightly in diameter at its base to hold in place the clothes, which are attached by a drawstring. When the modeling medium is dry, it should be smoothed with sandpaper and then decorated with poster paint. An attractive sparkle can be added to eyes, lips, or teeth by coating them with shellac or, better still, clear nail polish. In character dolls, attention can be drawn to outstanding features by the same means. Most puppets tend to be more appealing if the eyes are considerably enlarged and made conspicuous with a shiny coating. Hair, eyebrows, and beards made from absorbent cotton, yarn, cut paper, or scraps of fur can be pasted or glued in place.

The clothing covers the child's hand and arm and forms the body of the puppet. The outside dimensions of the clothing are determined by the size of the child's hand. The hand should be laid flat on a desk with the thumb and index and little fingers extended. The approximate length of the puppet's arms will be indicated by the distance from the tip of the thumb to the tip of the little finger, and the neckline should come halfway up the index finger. To make clothing, fold a single piece of cloth in two, make a cut in the center of the fold for the neck, and then sew the sides, leaving openings for the fingers. Small mitts may be attached to the openings to cover the fingertips. If children wish their puppets to have interchangeable costumes, a drawstring can be used to tie the clothing to the neck. If they plan on designing only one costume for their puppets, the pupils can glue it into place, as well as tying it for extra security.

Lively puppet costumes can be made with bright textiles; men's old ties are valuable for this purpose. The lining of the ties should first be removed and the material ironed flat before being folded over and sewn to make a garment. Buttons and other decorations may be added, of course, as required.

When children make puppets, they expect to use them in a stage production. In presenting a fist-puppet show, the operators work beneath the set. This means that the stage must be elevated so that the puppeteers can stand or crouch under it while the show goes on. A simple stage can be constructed from a large topless cardboard carton with two sides removed and an opening for the stage cut in its base. The carton is then placed on a table with the opening facing the audience. The puppeteers stand or crouch behind the table and are concealed from the audience by a curtain around the table legs. Teachers can capitalize on the popularity of television's Muppets, but should avoid using commercially manufactured hand puppets, since children may see these as competing with their own efforts.

318

Pupils in about the fifth and sixth grades may wish to construct a more elaborate stage using lumber. A good general plan is a three-panel screen covered with wrapping paper or cloth, with an opening for the stage at the top of the center panel. The frames for the three panels of the screen are formed from 1-by-2-inch lumber, each panel measuring about 3 by 5 feet. Each panel is braced by crossbars of the lumber; the center panel is made so that the crossbars do not interfere with the stage opening, which measures about 2 by 3 feet. The panels are assembled with screws (not nails) so that they can be dismantled easily and are joined by three hinges each. A wire from which to hang the curtain is strung above the stage opening. The three panels are covered with kraft paper or old sheets dyed a dark color. When the screen is set in place for a stage production, the wings of the assembly are held in place by a long piece of the 1-by-2-inch lumber screwed to the top members of the two wings.

The stage settings should be simple. In most cases they may be approached as large paintings, but they should have strong "carrying" power and be rich in a decorative sense. The costumes and backdrops should be designed to provide a visual contrast with each other. Because the stage has no floor, the background is held or fixed in position from below or hung from a frame above. On it may be pinned significant items such as windows and doors. Separate backdrops may be prepared for each scene. Likewise, stage properties—tables, chairs, and the like—must be designed in two dimensions. Spotlights create striking effects and bring out the features of the presentation. Occasionally it may be worthwhile to experiment with projected materials like slides.

The manipulation of fist puppets is not difficult; the pupils can teach themselves the technique merely by practice. They should remember, however, that when more than one puppet is on stage, the puppet that is "speaking" should be in a continual movement, so that the audience may know exactly which puppet is the speaker. The other puppets should be still.

Although shadow puppets are not difficult to make, successful operation of them demands some finesse. In this technique a silk or nylon screen is set up between the operators and the audience. Strong spotlights on the operators' side are then beamed on the screen. The puppets, consisting of cardboard figures[5] attached to a thin control stick, are held close to the screen in the direct path of the light, thus casting a shadow on the screen. Because the puppet appears to the audience only as a shadow silhouette, the figure needs no painting or decorating. The technique of operating is similar to that used with fist puppets, so that the stage for the latter may also be used for shadow puppets.

SHADOW PUPPETS

[5] The Javanese, who are expert at this type of puppetry, use leather.

Children in the earliest phases of the symbol stage can be taught to make shadow puppets. The child simply cuts out a figure drawn on thin cardboard and glues it to a stick. As the children develop their ability to produce symbols and as their skill in using cutting tools improves, they can make much more elaborate puppets. Outlines will become more subtle so that such features as shaggy hair, heavy eyebrows, or turned-up noses can be suggested in the silhouette. By punching holes or cutting inside the puppet, the pupil can depict, say, buttons, eyes, and frilly clothing.

Still more experienced pupils can make shadow puppets with moving parts. To make a dragon, for example, a number of small sections of cardboard are joined with paper fasteners. Two sticks are attached to the assembly. With practice, a child can make the creature wiggle in a highly satisfactory manner. All properties, from tables to houses, must be cut from cardboard, placed on sticks, and also shown in silhouette.[6]

Teaching All Types of Puppetry. As indicated earlier, it is not difficult for a teacher to arouse pupils' interest in puppetry to the point where they desire to produce a play. Most children today are familiar with puppets;

[6]Some of the following should be studied at this time: Marjorie Batchelder, *The Puppet Theater Handbook* (New York: Harper & Row, 1947); Winifred H. Mills and Louise M. Dunn, *Marionettes, Masks and Shadows* (New York: Doubleday, 1927), which contains an excellent section on shadow puppets; Joseph S. Kennard, *Masks and Marionettes* (New York: Macmillan, 1935); F. J. McIsaac, *The Tony Sarg Marionette Book* (New York: Viking, 1930); and Waldo S. Lanchester, *Hand Puppets and String Puppets* (Leicester, Eng.: Dryad, 1948).

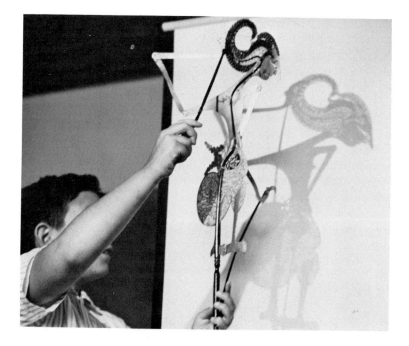

An authentic Javanese puppet, manipulated by a fifth grade boy. Since the construction principle is simple, children can create a Western version of the same puppet; a sheet and two light sources will be needed to create the performance. Javanese puppetry can provide an introduction to Asian art, mythology, religion, and entertainment.

Simple shadow puppets of a human figure and a dragon with moving head and tail.

some puppets have even gained national interest and affection. Short educational films that show puppets in action are available. The screening of such a film in the classroom is often enough to launch a puppetry project. A demonstration by the teacher is another effective way of stimulating interest in puppets.

Cooperative planning of the project is more difficult. Many teachers begin by holding a general discussion of the problems involved. After viewing a film, children are asked to list the various tasks that must be done before a show can be successfully produced. Eventually the main items of work are listed: selecting or writing the play; making the puppets; making the stage scenery and properties (sometimes making a stage, if one is not available); lighting the stage; practicing manipulation and general stagecraft.

Next, committees should be listed to carry out the various tasks. Such committees might include a selecting committee to recommend suitable plays to the general group; a coordinating production committee, or stage committee, to recommend suitable stage properties and backdrops for each scene, the general size of the puppets, and the costumes; and a stage-building committee (if required).

Often the chairmen of the committees are elected with the understanding that they will form a "cabinet" with the duty of overall coordination of the project. Either the members of the cabinet or all the children elect a head chairman, or president, of puppeteers from among the cabinet members, whose duty is to report from time to time to the children about progress and to seek suggestions for improvement.

The teacher's task during these proceedings is to scc that elections take place smoothly. The work intensifies when the "executing" stage is reached. Often demonstrations, short lessons, and informal advice are needed. The teacher must be particularly careful to keep in constant touch with the chairmen, often through the president, to see that they are successful in their efforts. Exactly what a teacher does at this stage, however, would be difficult to define for all cases.[7] Each situation brings its own problems and suggests its own procedures.

Puppetry, like any theatrical activity, culminates in the inevitable presentation of a performance for an audience. The teacher should help the class as a whole to decide who will review the performance—the PTA? the class next door? all the sixth grade classes? and so on. Once the audience has been decided on, publicity must begin; this may involve preparing posters for bulletin boards, a story for the school paper or PTA bulletin, and mimeographed programs, that final testimonial to all who have had a hand in the production.

It is most important that group evaluation or judging take place both as the production proceeds and after the show is finished. With the head chairman presiding, questions should be brought up for discussion. Each chairman's report should be analyzed and suggestions for improvement made. After the performance, the time-honored question must be raised: "How can we improve the show next time?"

[7]For an amplification of this discussion, see Hollingshead, *Guidance in Democratic Living,* especially Chapter 7.

Clair Sterling is the Pied Piper of giant puppetry. Working at outdoor community events, she uses this activity to get children and parents together for both production and performances.

Group Activities in Art

The term *mural* in its strictest sense refers to a painting made directly on a wall. In many schools, however, it has come to denote any large picture, and this is the meaning of the word as used here.

Media and Techniques. What are the technical requirements of this art form? Although the youngest pupils may not understand the significance of all these requirements, the teacher should know about them and, when advisable, teach them. The first technical requirement arises from the architectural quality of a wall. A plain undecorated wall possesses some fundamental architectural characteristics, which it should retain once the mural is in place. The wall is obviously solid and flat rather than undulating. In a mural a wide diversity of depths achieved by linear perspective, or an extreme range of colors, tends to interfere with these basic characteristics of the wall; many people find such interference unpleasant. The design of the mural, therefore, must be kept reasonably flat, if the wall is to maintain its architectural qualities.

A mural should be considered as part of a scheme of interior decoration and should be integrated with it. The color relationships already established in the interior in which the mural is placed should be echoed in the new work. Furthermore, since door and window openings create a design in a room, the mural should be placed so that it does not violate the architectural arrangement of these elements but rather tends to maintain the existing plan or even to improve on it. The architectural limitations of classrooms are so consistently severe that most murals will probably be no larger than 4 by 8 feet—a size convenient for resting on the ledge of the blackboard. Homosote or composition-board backing, which can be purchased at lumberyards or building-supply stores, may be used as a light, portable background for direct painting or as a backing for mural paper.

Despite the technicalities involved in the successful production of a mural, most children find that the activity is generally within their capabilities, and the experience of mural-making is a happy and rewarding one for them. Children in the primary grades will have difficulty in preplanning their work and will probably see mural-making as an activity that allows them to paint large pictures on vertical surfaces. But those who have reached a stage of social maturity that allows them to work with a degree of cooperation and preplanning should find little difficulty in making a mural.

The subject matter for murals may be similar to that used in individual picture-making, or it may derive from a broader frame of reference such as social studies. The most successful murals reflect the children's own experiences and interests. A subject such as "The Western Movement," though not a part of the child's personal background, can still be

These fifth and sixth graders are painting the walls that connect the art and music rooms. The theme is animals making music. The medium is acrylic, and each student was required to submit several suggestions before beginning to paint his or her own subject. The teacher made the final decision on the grouping of the subjects.

worthwhile if due attention is given to motivation by creating the environment of the early settlers with folk music, old prints, posters, and films. Whatever subject is chosen must be sufficiently broad in scope to allow several pupils to elaborate on it. A still-life composition, for example, would not be an appropriate subject for a mural.

The distinction between a painting with a limited focus of attention and a mural with multiple focuses must be made. A subject in which there are many objects of related but differing appearance, such as houses, factory buildings, or crowds of people, would be most suited to group activity. An example of a subject that offers a great variety of shapes is "At the Circus." Members of a third grade class included both circus performers and spectators in the mural. The following are examples of themes that elementary-school pupils have successfully developed:

From the Experience of the Child	*From Other Areas of the Curriculum*
Our School Playground	The Year 2000
A Trip to the Supermarket	The Western Movement
Playing Outside in Winter	Books I Have Liked
Shopping	How People Differ from Animals
The Easter Parade	Our Town
The Seasons Change	Acting My Age in Ancient Greece

Most of the picture-making media can be used in mural production. The paper should be sufficiently heavy and tough to support the weight of the finished product. Kraft paper, the heavy brown wrapping paper that comes in large rolls, is suitable. Many school-supply houses offer a gray mural paper that is pleasant to use. When ordering paper, a 4-foot width is recommended. The most effective coloring medium for young children is tempera paint. This should be applied with the same wide range of the brushes suggested for picture-making. Some especially wide brushes should be available for painting the large areas of the mural. In applying tempera paint excessive thickness should be avoided, since the paint will flake off when the mural is rolled up for storage. Chalk may be used, but it tends to be dusty and to smudge badly when several children are working at one time. Colored cut paper also yields effective results from the first grade on; the cut paper can also be combined with paper collage. Wax crayons are not suitable because they require too much effort to cover large areas, but crayons may be used in some areas as a resist with thin tempera.

The technique of planning and executing the mural varies with the child's social and artistic stage of development. The kindergarten child may begin by working side by side with classmates on the same long strip of paper. Beginners all paint on the same topic suggested by the teacher and use the same medium, but each child actually creates an individual composition without much reference to the work of the others. Not until they reach the third or fourth grade are some children able to plan the mural cooperatively. When they develop this ability they may begin by making sketches lightly in chalk on the area allotted for the mural. Considerable discussion and many alterations may occur before the design satisfies all the participants. By the time they reach the fifth or sixth grade, many pupils are ready to plan a mural on a reduced scale before beginning the work itself. They prepare sketches on paper with dimensions proportionate to those of the mural. These sketches are made in outline and in color. Later, when the mural paper has been laid over a large table or pinned to tackboard, the final sketch is enlarged on the mural surface. Usually this is done freehand, but sometimes teachers suggest that the squaring method of enlargement be used. By this method the sketch and the mural surface are divided into corresponding squares. A pupil redraws in the corresponding area of the mural what is in a specific area of the sketch.[8] Such a procedure, while common practice with professional

[8] This mural-making technique has been developed by Vige Langevin and Jean Lombard, *Peintures et dessins collectifs des enfants* (Paris: Editions du Scarabée, 1950). The members of the class produce small paintings. One painting is selected and divided into squares, which are numbered. Each child in the class is assigned one square to copy on a large scale on another piece of paper. Eventually the large squares are assembled to form a very large picture. Although the children are encouraged to develop details in their copied area, the necessary emphasis on using someone else's idea limits the activity. Considerable work of this kind may be seen in some Paris schools.

This acrylic mural involved a method popular in many European countries. It is a three-stage process: the placement and painting of major areas is followed by two successive stages of enrichment of the large areas with secondary patterns and shapes; occasionally the forms are outlined in color for emphasis and balance. Touches of metallic paint add sparkle and vibrancy.

muralists, may easily inhibit elementary-school children and should be used with caution. Only the most mature children are capable of benefiting from this technique.

After the drawing (or "cartoon," as it is sometimes called) has been satisfactorily transferred to the mural surface, the colors are applied. If tempera paint is to be used, it is usually mixed in advance in a relatively limited number of hues. Tints and shades are also mixed in advance. All colors should be prepared in sufficient quantity to complete all areas in the mural where they are to be used. In this way time and paint are saved, and the unity of the mural created in the sketch is preserved in the larger work. If colored chalk or cut paper is used, of course, the class is not likely to run out of a color. Acrylic paint, which is now comparable in price to tempera, is advisable for murals since it is waterproof, does not flake off if rolled up, and allows sand, paper, and other objects to be embedded in it while the paint is still wet.

When pupils use cut paper, the technique for producing a mural is less formal than when paint or chalk is used. The pupils can push areas of the colored paper around on the mural to find the most satisfying effects. Thus plans may undergo even major revision up to the final moment when the colored paper is stuck to the surface. Colored construction paper is recommended for the main body of the mural because it gives the background areas added interest.

In carrying out the plan of a mural the pupils quickly discover that they must solve other problems of design peculiar to this work. Because the length of a mural in relation to its height is usually much greater than in paintings, the technical problem arises of establishing a satisfactory

326   Group Activities in Art

center of interest. Although only one center of interest may be developed, it must not be so strong that the observer finds it necessary to ignore portions of the work at the extremities of the composition. On the other hand, if a series of centers of interest are placed along the full length of the composition, the observer may consider the result too jumpy and spotty. In general, the composition should be dispersed, the pupils being particularly careful about connecting the rhythms they establish so that no part of the mural is either neglected or unduly emphasized. The balances in a mural made by children, furthermore, have a tendency to get out of hand. Not infrequently children become intrigued with subject matter in one section of the work, with the result that they may give it too much attention and neglect other sections. Profuse detail may overload a favored part, while other areas are overlooked.

One problem of design that rarely occurs in mural-making is lack of variety. Indeed, with many people working on the same surface the problem is usually too much variety. Once they become aware of this difficulty, however, children are usually able to remedy the defect.[9]

Teaching. As with puppetry, it is not difficult to interest children in making murals. Showing a film and slides or going to see a mural in a public building are two fairly practical ways of arousing their interest. Children are also motivated by seeing the murals that other children have made. Perhaps the most effective method is to discuss with the class the needs and benefits of making murals as decorations for specified areas of the school, such as the classroom, the halls, the cafeteria, or the auditorium.

Although in puppetry there is often enough work to be done to permit every member of the class to participate in the endeavor, this is not so in mural-making. The pupils may all discuss the making of murals, including the various media, the most suitable subjects, and the probable locations in which the work might be placed, but eventually the pupils must divide into small groups, probably not to reunite until the final evaluation period. In the elementary school, the small groups may comprise from three to ten pupils each, depending on the size of the mural.

Preadolescents should be able to organize their own mural-making. First, all the pupils in a class interested in mural-making assemble to discuss what the theme should be. After the pupils' suggestions for the main theme have been written on the blackboard, each pupil selects some aspect to work on. Those pupils interested in the same aspect form a team to work on that particular mural. If too many pupils elect one aspect, two teams can be created, each to work separately on the same subject. The teams are finally arranged and each elects its chairman.

[9]See Arne W. Randall, *Murals for Schools* (Worcester, Ma.: Davis, 1956).

Discussion then takes place within each team concerning the size and shape of its particular mural, the medium, and possible techniques. Sketches are then prepared, either cooperatively or individually. The teams can either choose the individual sketch most liked by all or prepare a composite picture, using the best ideas from the several sketches. The cartoon is then drawn, usually with the chairman supervising to see that the chosen sketch is reproduced with reasonable accuracy. Next the color is added. From time to time the chairman may find it necessary to hold a team consultation to appraise the work, so that some of the pitfalls of design in mural-making are avoided. This process goes on until each team's mural is completed. Finally, under a general chairman, all the mural-makers meet to review their work and to discuss the usual topics that arise in the "judging" stage.

During these proceedings the teacher acts as a consultant. If the pupils have previously made individual pictures, the teacher need give few demonstrations. The teacher's tasks consist for the most part in seeing that a working area and suitable materials are available, providing the initial motivation, outlining some of the technical requirements of a mural, and demonstrating the "squaring" method of enlarging, if it is to be used.

A completely different approach allows the children to develop the mural spontaneously. In this approach the children choose only the colors beforehand in order to assure some harmony. The group then gathers around all four sides of the paper that is placed on the floor and begins to paint. If the group is too large to do this comfortably, it is divided into smaller units. The first children paint whatever comes into their minds and succeeding groups try to relate their shapes and colors to those that have preceded them. The entire experience should be as open, and the children as immediately responsive, as possible.

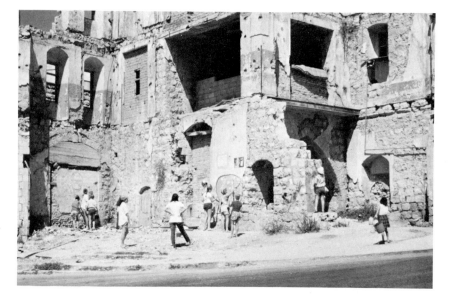

An unusual example of group mural-making: Israeli children are permitted to paint murals on sections of ruined buildings. Since the paint is tempera, the mural is not permanent. This is a community art activity of the Youth Wing of the Israel Museum, Jerusalem.

The teacher should take advantage of the mural-making activity to introduce the children to some great murals in art history. They should be acquainted with the splendor of Michelangelo's Sistine Chapel ceiling, the richness of Chagall's painting in the dome of the Paris Opera House, the massive forms of Diego Rivera, and the dramatic contrasts of José Orozco. Although elementary-school children cannot use oil or do frescoes, they can at least gain familiarity with the terms used in discussing these media. They can also observe how mural materials have changed with advancement of technology: muralists now use such materials as welded metals, fired enamel plates, ceramics, and concrete. David Siqueiros, for example, has used automotive lacquers as well as other industrial materials in his murals. Gyorgy Kepes has produced murals using illuminated glass, and John Mason has used clay. Many muralists today are more likely to be sculptors than painters; children who are exposed to their work may want to make a relief mural rather than a painting in their class activity.

BLOWUPS

"Blowups" are another simple way to begin a mural, and the most manageable way as well, since each child works on his own section in his own space. First, select an interesting image. (Photographs of the facades of older buildings, group portraits, and city views are good subjects.) Then cut the master photo into as many squares as there are students and give each class member his or her own section of the photo to enlarge according to scale (a 1-by-1-inch square equals a 1-by-1-foot square, and so on). They then transfer the small segments to the larger space, heeding whatever problem or technique the class has selected for attention. This is an excellent way to apply a particular skill in color, collage, or pencil. In studying color, children can work in flat tones, blend the tones, or try to match the original color purely as an exercise in color control. When the segments are assembled according to the original, nothing quite goes together; the viewer must accomplish the process of making things "fit"—of perceptual reconstruction—and that makes the viewer a more active participant when studying the final image.

THE ARCHITECTURAL MURAL

One method for making a permanent mural combines mosaic and ceramic sculpture.[10] The method described below allows for a greater range of texture; and since objects are simply embedded or placed in wet cement, large areas can be filled in a very short time. A standard 4-foot-by-6-foot piece of plywood of $\frac{3}{4}$-inch thickness can more than accommodate the work of an entire class. The color added to the cement adds vibrancy and contrast. This is a successful technique for gathering together the efforts of

[10]See Lily Ann Rosenberg, *Children Make Murals and Sculpture* (New York: Reinhold, 1968).

This mural technique involves several stages. First, the children made ceramic inserts and fired and glazed them; they also collected found objects. For the backing, chicken wire was nailed to plywood, and colored cement was poured into sections separated by unfired clay walls. Then the ceramic and other objects were set into place in the wet cement. When the cement hardened, the clay walls were peeled away. The process was repeated, section by section, until the entire surface was covered. Then the whole piece was bolted to the wall. The technique can be applied equally well to one mural or to smaller portions of wood mounted as a group.

several groups of people—children, teachers, parents—to commemorate an event or to dress up a blank wall by adding a note of rich color and texture. The steps are as follows:

1. Have each child prepare a ceramic object based on the main theme or subject. Fire these and glaze them.
2. Nail chickenwire to plywood to hold the cement.
3. Mix ordinary cement and add special cement color or tempera.
4. Trowel on the cement one section at a time, holding it in place with a clay (plasticene) wall surrounding each section. Mix only enough cement for the section to be filled.
5. Lay the ceramic pieces along with shells, small objects, bits of tile, and the like directly into the wet cement.
6. When the cement hardens, remove the clay wall and add a new section. Leave small empty areas to accommodate the bolts that will attach the plywood to the wall.
7. Bolt or screw the final work in place.

Mounting such a heavy mural is sometimes more complicated than making the mural itself. To facilitate mounting, make certain that the school principal approves the project and its location, because he or she may have to ask for assistance from the central office to mount the finished product. When everything is in place, the teacher should plan an installation ceremony, so that the community is aware of the mural. Children will always return to their school to be certain that their contribution is still in place. In so doing, a part of their past will come back to life.

Other Group Activities

A *diorama* re-creates in miniature a three-dimensional subject involving complex spatial relationships. A diorama is usually set into a three-sided container for support and for ease in representing the background. When the diorama is prepared on a flat surface, it is usually referred to as a *panorama*, and when the entire scene is enclosed in a box, except for a viewing aperture, it is a *peep show*. Making panoramas is an excellent extension of mapping exercises, and peep shows lend themselves to experimentation with lighting effects when the walls or ceiling of the container include sections of colored cellophane. The subject matter for these activities is most often derived from social studies and language arts (see Chapter 14).

All three activities call on the ingenuity of students as they search for materials whose qualities approximate those of the objects they are to

DIORAMAS, PANORAMAS, AND PEEP SHOWS

represent and that are in scale with one another (thimbles for tables, bits of dyed sponge for bushes, stippled plasticine for grass, sandpaper for roads). Use of readymade objects such as toy soldiers and model cars is not a recommended practice; the children should learn to create their own symbols, leaving the plastic toys to their model railroads. These activities, which may be performed by groups or individuals, are capable of uniting fantasy and reality: in their creations the children can renew their neighborhoods, plan a city of the future, or speculate about the living patterns of the past. Dioramas test the pupils' ingenuity in finding materials to carry out ideas.

BOOKS

Printmaking activities can lead to the production of books. The class begins the project with individual efforts in making the prints (the contents of the book), but carries the project through as a group in putting the books together. Each child ends up with a copy of the project.

There are two basic methods of book construction. For an *open-fold booklet*, the interior sheets are attached to the folded cover by stapling or by threading heavy yarn through punched holes. The outer cover can be made of cardboard decorated with an overall vegetable- or eraser-print pattern, or it can be covered with cloth or decorative wrapping paper. (Construction paper is not recommended for covers because folded edges will not lie flat unless taped.) The second method involves the *accordion book*. Here, the contents are pasted to both sides of pieces of cardboard. The boards are then connected with yarn and binder tape; like an accordion, the booklet can be folded flat or extended, as the child wishes. When extended, it can be displayed to advantage.

Example of an accordion book.

Group Activities in Art

Group art, like any art, is more than the sum of its parts. The final product comes into being through the efforts of a group of individuals working with visual materials toward some end that ultimately reflects the perceptions of all the participants. All forms of contemporary group art assume that the participant can function both as an individual and as a member of a collectivity; they also assume that the end result of a group activity can be something that by its very nature is beyond the capabilities of any one individual.

Some group activities are spontaneous (chalk-ins, graffiti covering city walls), while others are planned (theater pieces, parades, parties, celebrations). Group activities can be cheap or expensive, and they can cross over, sometimes disconcertingly, into other categories of expression: group drama can become group dance; the delicate art of calligraphy can have a boisterous resurgence in subway graffiti.

The general educator is, as has been mentioned, interested in group activity because it provides one entree into a broader social process and is a vivid means of enlivening the study of geography, history, the language arts, or any other field. The youth of the 1960s, disregarding accepted views of education, embraced the idea of communal art, with its concomitant belief in the shared values of creative social action, and rejected what was felt to be the egocentricity represented by the individual work of art. In many ways they have made possible new attitudes toward group art in the public schools.

Let us examine the major direction from which group art may develop. Random events allow every participant to work independently, yet, through interaction with others, to have a marked impact on the environment. The popular chalk-in, carried on by a group of young people, can make any space take on a new life. Inner-city students who decorate walls around building sites are using the cumulative effect of random design to alter the nature of an entire street. These examples are simultaneously random and planned in that functions, such as the use of a particular color, are clearly defined, and in that no one can completely anticipate what the final result will be.

When making blowups, randomness moves closer to control. In this situation students work strictly on their own but within certain limitations, knowing that a surprise awaits them. For example, a junior-high-school art teacher in the United States wanted to celebrate Washington's birthday in an unusual and memorable way. He cut up a reproduction of Leutze's *Washington Crossing the Delaware* into 1-inch squares. Each student received a square and a large sheet of paper cut to a proportionate size. The class then "blew up," or enlarged to scale, the small segments and transferred them to the large paper. No attempt was made to match colors,

Youngsters create a "Street Dragon" for their neighborhood in Pittsburgh. The structure was assembled from discarded objects under the guidance of Troy West, a local architect. West holds periodic open houses for the children, who must bring interesting junk to be assembled and painted. Some children work in teams, others individually. They are also encouraged to write poetry based on the art work.

since Day-Glo paint was used instead of the standard tempera, watercolor, or chalk. Hence individual students used whatever colors they wanted to without regard for Leutze's painting or the choice of other students. A wall was selected for mounting the project. When the completed pieces were assembled in proper order and fixed in place, a black light was turned on the wall and the effect was overwhelming. The teacher's behavioral goal was reached: "Neither teacher nor students will ever forget Washington's birthday."

The "transformation" activity described by Laliberte is considerably more random than the preceding example in its open-endedness, but it also requires more interaction within the group.

> The instructor or teacher leaves the room for 15 minutes. In his or her absence the students are asked to do something to dramatically alter the physical appearance or change areas of space within the room—i.e., stacking furniture on top of cabinets, everyone standing on top of each other in a corner of the room, all furniture upside down on the floor as if the entire room were now upside down. Variation: cover all the objects in the room with colored paper (or glossy paper, colored cellophane, aluminum foil, newspaper) to create a different mood or atmosphere.[11]

[11]Norman Laliberte, Richey Kehl, et al., *One Hundred Ways to Have Fun with an Alligator and One Hundred Other Involving Art Projects* (Blauvelt, N.Y.: Art Education Inc., 1969), Project 78.

The teacher could refine the activity even more by requiring that only one material such as string, old newspapers, or aluminum foil be used. Or the teacher could use the room for a series of daily changes that involve a sequence of materials.

Another example of a transformation activity that combines both preplanning and spontaneity is the "Woven Playground Sculpture." In this activity a teacher prepared the students by using the jungle gym as a three-dimensional loom. The boundaries between weaving and sculpture disappeared as the entire class used the boxlike structure of the gym to create all manner of volumes and spatial divisions with yarn. When the activity was completed, the class had used a simple craft technique to wholly transform an object for which they held an entirely different set of associations. Once the students sensed their power of transformation, the second stage was begun. This involved a consideration of how they could go about using the entire playground—swings, chinning bars, slides, horizontal ladders—as a dispersed armature for a unified structure. Preplanning required listing the techniques and materials needed. Improvisation occurred when objects such as large paintings and pieces of cardboard sculpture were added as the occasion arose and as a spontaneous response to design requirements occurred. The completed product consisted of units of playground equipment linked together by clotheslines holding planar divisions of sheets and old clothes soaked in plaster of Paris, plus the art work produced for the occasion. Color was added here and there as a final touch.

Group art leaders are intrigued by the promise of more effective communication between individuals and the possibility that numbers of people can produce and share the experience that we normally associate with individual creativity. John Cage sees it as follows:

> Art, instead of being an object made by one person, is a process set in motion by a group of people. Art's socialized. It isn't someone saying something, but people doing things, giving everyone (including those involved) the opportunity to have experiences they would not otherwise have had.[12]

Since group art operates on the levels of both individual and group effort, it is difficult to define. Kultermann,[13] in discussing the roots of the intermedia movement of the late 1960s (itself a form of group art), lists a number of influences on it and then states that it is impossible to explain the developments within the movement as an outgrowth of the history of any one medium. According to Kultermann, "different threads come together in each case," cross traditional boundaries, influence and enrich one another, and ultimately result in a new art form.

[12]John Cage, *Year from Monday: New Lectures and Writings* (Middletown, Ct.: Wesleyan University Press, 1969), p. 151.
[13]Udu Kultermann, *Art and Life* (New York: Praeger, 1971), p. 33.

Kultermann's conclusions could be applied to group art, but with certain differences. The intermedia movement borrows heavily from technology and is synaesthetic in nature (involving total sensory awareness). It draws on the more traditional movements within the arts themselves as sources of form. Group art, as currently practiced, does not rely on traditional artistic forms and owes much of its existence to social forces that function outside the arts. Part of it comes from social and political theory, part of it from consciousness-raising exercises, and part from the heightened sensory perception of the past decade. We might recall the felt need for deeper interpersonal relationships among the youth of the 1960s. Radical changes in the theater, which were formal as well as political in nature, also contributed to the development of group art.

The range of group-art activities is limitless. Dioramas, murals, and puppetry are examples of how the term has been traditionally understood. Light shows and random events are examples of the contemporary understanding of the term. The differences between these understandings of the term reflect the differences that exist in the field of art generally.

Group art is also an act of faith, a gesture toward growth through involvement on a large scale; it requires an ability to minimize the desire for "success," what people *gain* from an activity, in exchange for the values people *bring* to a situation for which nothing in their past may have prepared them. Group art thus comes closer, not to art proper, but to what art ought to be—a model for life. If one can transfer the regenerative power of life to art, then one can ignore the Cassandras who announce the death of art. But if art is not to die, it must redefine itself periodically in order to maintain its vital sense of being. The leader of group art thus redefines art by shifting his attention from the private products to public processes.

The "Woven Playground Sculpture" develops aesthetic awareness in that it produces patterns of color and space. The jungle gym is transformed into a three dimensional loom that becomes a giant square with a linear "skin." The size and scale of the project turns weaving into a type of sculpture, blurring the distinctions between the forms.

1. Study a group activity in a classroom and analyze it according to Kilpatrick's four stages.
2. Describe three quasi-group activities not mentioned in this chapter.
3. Make three fist puppets: a simple stick puppet, a more complicated paper-bag puppet, and, finally, a cloth puppet of an animal whose jaws will move. Improvise dialog around a situation with a fellow student's puppets.
4. Practice manipulating each of your puppets. When skillful, give a short performance for some of your younger friends and see how they react.
5. Study any professional murals in your locality. Make a note of their subject matter in relation to their location, their design, and the media used.
6. Design a small-scale mural suitable for the interior of your local post office, the foyer of a local theater, or the entrance of the local high school. Choose subject matter of local interest.
7. Create a panorama depicting a mythical island or kingdom. Using the top of a card table as a base, turn your panorama into a game in which players race for a buried treasure by throwing dice and drawing directional cards.
8. Select an occasion and plan a party. Think of it as an artwork, unique in conception, compelling in its visual possibilities. Involve the entire class and be sure you have some participatory element. It must not cost more than a small amount per person and should include something to eat and drink.

Suggested Readings

"Art as Celebration," a special issue of *The Structurist*, No. 19–20 (1979–80). Published by the University of Saskatchewan, Saskatoon, Canada.

Hurwitz, Al. *Programs of Promise: Art in the Schools.* New York: Harcourt Brace Jovanovich, 1972. The chapter "Art for Special Planning" describes environmental planning as a basis for learning in a group.

———, and Stanley Madeja. *The Joyous Vision: A Source Book for Elementary Art Appreciation.* Englewood Cliffs: Prentice-Hall, 1977. Chapter 2, "Teaching for Appreciation," describes several group-centered approaches.

Kaprow, Allan. *Assemblages, Environments, and Happenings.* New York: Abrams, 1966.

Pavey, Don. *Art Based Games.* Love Publishing, 1979.

ART ACTIVITIES for children
with special needs

They took away what should have been my eyes,
(But I remembered Milton's Paradise).
They took away what should have been my ears,
(Beethoven came and wiped away my tears).
They took away what should have been my tongue,
(But I had talked with God when I was young).
He would not let them take away my soul—
Possessing that, I still possess the whole.*

TWELVE

Every modern educational system takes pride in the attention it gives to individual pupils. In recent years, many special education programs have been developed for abnormal and atypical children—the blind and partially sighted, the deaf, the retarded, the extremely maladjusted, and the physically handicapped. It is well that this should be so, for classroom teachers who lack training in how to treat these exceptional children will find themselves in difficulty. With many handicapped and retarded children, art activities are used in highly specialized ways for specific and, in an artistic sense, narrow ends. Art is frequently employed, for example, not only as a means of artistic expression in the traditional sense, but as a

*Helen Keller, "On Herself," in *The Faith of Helen Keller*, ed. Jack Belck (Hallmark Editions, 1967).

device by which children reveal their difficulties to a therapist or special teacher. Whatever progress is made by these children occurs as a direct result of highly skilled diagnoses and subsequent clinical treatment.[1]

Recent legislation in the United States has drawn attention to the need for educational programs for the handicapped. Federal Chapter 766 has mandated the "mainstreaming" of children with special needs into integrated situations with "normal" children. That legislation seeks to meet the educational needs of every handicapped student on an individual basis while at the same time integrating (mainstreaming) such students into the normal schoolday's activities, so that each child has as much contact as possible with children who do not share their problems.

The use of all the arts in teaching the handicapped child has also been fostered and developed by the National Committee of Arts for the Handicapped. Through state-run festivals, teacher-training symposiums, and exhibits, the importance of arts programs for children with special needs is gaining public attention. Research by this committee has emphasized the value of arts instruction in special education. Federal and state funding (in Canada, provincial funding) has begun to open professional opportunities within the public sector in the fields of special education and art, integrated arts, dance, and music therapy. While these areas are not entirely new, their entrance into the educational community has been slow. As these approaches become more accepted, however, their balance of visual, manipulative, and kinesthetic expression with verbal expression will undoubtedly produce learning materials to aid the concrete learner— the child whose learning style is visual, manipulative, auditory, and kinesthetic—as well as the verbal learner.

Orville Johnson points out that art provides specific skills for the handicapped child: a means of communication, a way to express feelings and emotions, improved observation and awareness, sensory stimulation, and improved motor skills. The ability of many handicapped children to use oral and written language is limited.

> The deaf child cannot hear spoken words, the cerebral palsied child may have difficulty in speaking, the mentally retarded child is limited in his vocabulary, a child with a specific learning disability may be deficient in visual and auditory decoding and encoding, and for the emotionally disturbed child oral communication may be associated with unpleasant and traumatic experiences. The arts can provide many of these children with a means of communication that is less dependent upon their areas of disabilities and that is not associated with previous frustrating and failure experiences. . . .

[1]See, for example, Emery I. Gondor, *Art and Play Therapy* (New York: Random House, 1954), a booklet written in simple language by a sensitive clinician.

Above, the illustration for the story of Noah's Ark was drawn by the attendant of a boy who was incapacitated in speech and movement. His nurse developed the picture from whatever sounds the boy conveyed. The boy's desire to contribute personally was so strong that a brush was strapped to his wrist so that he could add his own concluding touches in watercolor—an example of the will to create, which cannot be stifled even under the most limiting circumstances. Below, another version of the Noah story, by a twelve-year-old retarded Hungarian child. His conception of God as well as the idea of each person as victim of his own private thunderstorm is strikingly original.

341

A comprehensive arts program has the means of providing activities for the development of needed skills to help physically, learning, and mentally handicapped children become more effective totally. It can help make the total educational program become of maximum value in the physical, motor, cognitive, and effective development of handicapped children. It must be remembered, however, that each of these children is unique, requiring the kinds of experiences he can deal with and from which he will derive maximum benefit. In other words, there is no program for the mentally retarded, for specific learning disabilities, for the deaf, the blind, or the physically handicapped. There is a program for each child at his particular developmental level and in consideration of his disability and previous learnings.[2]

A distinction should be made, however, between the exceptional child who receives special schooling and the slow-learning child who is capable of functioning within the framework of a normal school situation.[3] *Slow learners* are those pupils who make considerably lower than average scores on intelligence tests and who progress in academic subjects at a pace manifestly slower than that displayed by the majority of their fellow students. But if Henry Schaefer-Simmern's experiments are any indication, a sensitive and deeply committed teacher can attain remarkable artistic results with the slow learner. His case study of "Selma" demonstrated that the subject's personality, as well as the visual quality of her work, showed remarkable progress under his supervision.[4]

The slow or retarded learner is but one of the many types of handicapped children that the art or classroom teacher is likely to encounter in the course of a normal teaching situation.

The current tendency, as mandated by Federal Chapter 766, is to move handicapped children out of specialized schools and into the more normal environment of the regular school. As a result, there is an increasing likelihood that all teachers will have to reeducate themselves, at least to some degree, in order to serve the handicapped student more effectively. Teachers will have to reexamine their particular subject area in search of more effective means than were used in the past for dealing with the gifted, the emotionally disturbed, the physically impaired, and the mentally retarded.

[2]G. Orville Johnson, "Art and the Special Education Teacher," *Viewpoints: Dialogue in Art Education,* Vol. 3, No. 1 (1976).

[3]For a detailed analysis of the intellectual characteristics of mentally retarded children, see Karl C. Garrison and D. G. Force, Jr., *The Psychology of Exceptional Children,* 4th ed. (New York: Ronald, 1965). For further information, see Christine P. Ingram, *Education for the Slow-Learning Child,* 3rd ed. (New York: Ronald, 1960); Maida Abrams and Lori Schill, "Art in Special Education," *Art Education, Elementary* (Washington, D.C.: National Art Education Association, 1972).

[4]Henry Schaefer-Simmern, *The Unfolding of Artistic Activity* (Berkeley: University of California Press, 1948).

Art Activities for Children with Special Needs

This chapter will concentrate on the learner who has mental retardation rather than children with other types of handicap, because of the greater likelihood that these learners will be encountered in the average classroom. First the characteristics of the art of slow learners and the subject matter they are likely to select will be considered. Then the teaching methods and art activities especially suitable for these children will be discussed.[5]

The Art of Slow Learners

The causes for retardation should be noted. While some children may indeed be suffering from cerebral or neurological dysfunctions, the deficiency of others may be due to a lack of family (loving, touching, and playing) or to general sensory and environmental deprivation. Both Uhlin[6] and Lindsay[7] therefore view the concrete, sensory nature of art experiences as vital to the development of a sense of self in the child. Art experiences, crafts in particular, can involve the student in learning situations that are tactile, sensory, and stimulating physically as well as mentally. Identifying the causes for retardation are best accomplished through a team approach when the art or classroom teacher has a psychologist, physician, or psychiatrist to consult.

The implementation of what is known as the *core evaluation* by a team including a psychologist, a social worker, a classroom teacher, and various specialists helps to develop the educational plan best suited to the student's learning style. The arts specialists can provide valuable information in developing behaviorial objectives and learning goals for the child with special needs.

The classification of mental ability by I.Q. varies according to different systems. Table 12.1 gives some indication of differences suggested by four major agencies. Any child who functions below 70 I.Q. can be considered a slow learner as dealt with in this chapter.

Slow learners enrolled in a regular classroom begin their artistic career, like normal children, by manipulating art materials rather than by drawing or modeling recognizable objects.[8] They are sometimes slower

[5]Much of the subject matter of this chapter is condensed from the statements made in C. D. and M. R. Gaitskell, *Art Education for Slow Learners* (Toronto: Ryerson Press, and Peoria, Ill.: Bennett, 1953), by special permission.

[6]Donald Uhlin, *Art for Exceptional Children* (Dubuque, Iowa: Wm. C. Brown, 1972), Chapter 3, "The Mentally Deficient Personality in Art."

[7]Zaidee Lindsay, *Art and the Handicapped Child* (New York: Van Nostrand Reinhold, 1972), pp. 18–45.

[8]The study on which this and the following statements are largely based included 514 children enrolled in 55 schools. The I.Q. range was 50 to 89, with a median I.Q. of 70 and a C.A. range of 7 years, 6 months, to 16 years; they produced 3,674 pieces of art for analysis.

TABLE 12.1

Comparative Systems of Classifying Retardation by I.Q.

U.S. President's Panel on Mental Retardation		English System	National Association for Retarded Children and American Association on Mental Deficiency
I.Q.	*Classification*		
50–70	Mild	ESN (Education-ally subnormal)	70–85 mildly retarded
35–49	Moderate	SSN (severely subnormal)	below 70 moderately retarded
20–34	Severe	SSN	
Below 20	Profound	SSN	

than normal children to play with the materials given to them and may not initially explore their possibilities fully. However, with patience and encouragement the repetition of skills will enable the child to feel more comfortable with new media. Even so, the child's symbol formation will reflect its developmental level. Thus a child of chronological age 15 whose developmental age is 4 can be expected to create symbols appropriate only to a four-year-old.

Whereas a normal five-year-old may arrive at the symbol stage within three weeks to six months, the five-year-old slow learner who has an I.Q. of about 70 may not reach this stage for a year or more. In time, however, slow learners arrive at the symbol stage in a manner resembling that of normal children. Once the symbol stage has been reached, several symbols may appear in their output in quick succession.

Because of their greater chronological age, mentally retarded children often possess powers of physical coordination superior to those of normal children of the same mental age. These physical powers, of course, help them to master drawing skills more readily and allow them to repeat a recently developed symbol without much practice. Repetition that requires little thought suits slow learners and gives their work a characteristic rhythmic quality. Their tendency to repeat a discovery interferes with their creation of new symbols and at the same time retards their development of the symbols already discovered. In other words, they are as slow to make progress in the stage of symbols as they are to pass through the period of manipulation. Nevertheless a slow learner, like a normal child, will sometimes surprise a teacher with a burst of progress.

As noted in Chapter 5, regression from the symbol stage to that of manipulation will sometimes occur in the work of all children as a result of such factors as fatigue, ill health, temporary emotional disturbances, periods of intense concentration, interruptions of various kinds, absence from

Art Activities for Children with Special Needs

school, or faulty teaching methods. Reversion of this kind occurs more frequently with mentally retarded children than with normal children.

Gradually, slow learners come to spend more time on their work and thus begin to add details to their symbols. Sometimes they learn to relate their symbols to one another. The progress they make depends largely, or course, on the attention they give to their work. Slow learners' attention span tends to increase with both their chronological age and their mental age. Of 342 mentally retarded children studied for their retention of interest in making a picture, some lost interest in their work within a few minutes, but others worked as long as an hour and a half. The older children tended to work longer than the younger. Moreover, many of the older children were willing to return to the same picture for days on end.

The forms used by slow learners to extend the meaning of their symbols have some peculiar characteristics. The length of limbs in a human symbol may be greatly exaggerated, for example, if children feel such distortion is necessary to tell their story. Although this type of distortion may be seen in the work of normal children, it seems to be more pronounced in that of slow learners. Details added to the symbols may fail to show uniform development. An otherwise crude symbol of a human being might include a most detailed and relatively accurate delineation of facial features or of certain small particulars of clothing that have special significance for the children. Because of their concern only with details that hold their interest and because of their limited powers of concentration, slow learners may omit some items that normal children would probably include in their symbols.

A type of symbol or mark used more frequently by slow learners than by normal children of the same mental or chronological age is an artificial, conventionalized notation like that found in professional cartoons. Lines,

Slow learners sometimes continue in the manipulative stage longer than normal children. This painting by a retarded eight-year-old displays considerable spontaneity and improvisation.

for example, may be employed to show noise emanating from a particular source—a flow of music from a radio or a rush of air from a window. Sometimes feelings of excitement or happiness ascribed to a symbol of a human being are also represented by this type of notation. Slow learners also sometimes employ writing with their symbols in an attempt to clarify their pictorial statement.

A few observations must be made concerning the general composition and aesthetic qualities of the pictorial output of slow learners. These children often use the usual childlike conventions, like X-rays, series, and fold-over pictures, but they adopt these relatively complicated conventions only after much practice in art. Even when retarded children use one of the above conventions, they do not, as a rule, use it throughout their composition, but apply it only to some selected point of emphasis.

Slow learners often fail to achieve unity in their compositions. The rhythms they adopt become monotonous; centers of interest that may appear as they begin work are later destroyed, and almost half the work they produce fails to establish a reasonable balance. Slow learners, however, are usually successful in achieving variety in their use of the elements of design, although this variety is rarely as interesting as that found in the work of normal children. They appear to have most success in their use of color, although they make relatively little use of tints and shades, and rely instead on unmixed colors. In fact, rarely will light and shade in any form be found in their output. Some slow learners use line quite successfully. Occasionally the lines are either vigorous or delicate enough to be very interesting. Textural effects achieved by means of drawing occur extremely infrequently in any of their work.

Sometimes a retarded child may produce work that has some extremely attractive detail. On even rarer occasions, a slow learner may develop a composition both charming and original in either its pattern or its subject matter, or both. Art work is significant, however, largely in relation to the child who produces it. The art activities may be serving primarily therapeutic purposes. The quality of the finished work is not as important as the feeling of well-being and stability that attends the working process.

The teacher's attitude in approaching children with special needs is of utmost importance. Patience and respect for the individual help to develop trust. Accepting the children as they are and guiding them to progress at their own rate will enable children to explore the world with confidence. An awareness of the particular learning style of each child will aid the teacher in developing a program of appropriate activities. As the teacher helps the child to expand and broaden a sensory vocabulary, the child's ability to grasp abstract concepts will deepen. Art activities are based on and nurtured by sensory information, so that the stimulation of the visual, auditory, tactile, and olfactory senses will give the child a sharpened ability with which to approach communication and expression in various media.

Art Activities for Children with Special Needs

As indicated earlier, all children who have the aptitude to do so pass through the normal stages of pictorial expression mentioned in Chapter 5—the manipulation, symbol, and preadolescent stages. The child with a mental age of around three and a chronological age of six will not go beyond manipulating materials; however, the child with the same chronological age and a mental age of four or more may begin to enter the symbol stage. With a mental age of five, the child will even place symbols within their environment.

Once they progress beyond the stage of manipulation, slow learners, like normal children, discover subject matter for expression in their own experiences. Many of the titles they give to their works are little different from those selected by normal children. The titles describe events that occur at home, at school, at play, or in the community. The following are representative:

> We are working in the garden
> Our class went to visit a farm
> I saw a big fire
> I helped my dad wash the car

Titles such as these are usually selected by those slow learners in the late symbol or preadolescent stage of expression with the highest I.Q.'s. The titles are concise and in most of them the children have identified themselves with their environment. The less able the slow learners, the less inclined they are to relate themselves to the world in which they live. In other words, an ability to identify oneself with the environment seems to vary directly with intelligence.

The themes that many slow learners select are often closely connected with little intimate events in life. A normal child might overlook them, or, having touched on them once or twice, would then find other interests. Many slow learners, on the other hand, seem to find constant interest in pictures of this nature. Some representative titles are as follows:

> I sat on our steps
> The birds are in the trees
> I am walking to school

In some of their titles, slow learners seem to place considerable emphasis on authoritarian actions, either their own or those of others. This emphasis may indicate the child's desire to assume command, or conversely to see those in authority as oppressive in a world in which the child finds few opportunities to be a leader. Examples of such an apparently compensatory attitude may be found in the following descriptive titles:

The guard is telling those boys when they can cross the street
The soldiers are keeping us back as the parade goes by
There were two children in our tree; I told them to come down or I
 would fight them

Frequently, the various objects or actions depicted in the work of slow learners have little or no clear and logical connection. Their titles may illustrate their general inability to organize thoughts or to cope with strong emotional experiences. When the child shows deep concern about the subject matter included in this type of expression, the teacher must take the work especially seriously. The following titles are illustrative of this class of expression:

The car went bang and I was eating candy and then I cried
I wish I had a doll and maybe Lucy is coming over to my house and I
 guess she is mad

In some of their titles, slow learners anticipate future consequences of the actions depicted in their illustrations. Here the statements are usually logical and serve to complete a little story begun in the picture itself. These titles sometimes appear to illustrate the child's confusion between present and future action. The following indicate this form of anticipatory statement:

This boy is going to be hit by a car
This is my uncle; he has a big farm and I am going to visit him
Our school is playing ball and we are going to win

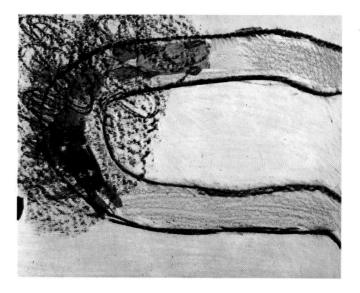

"Accident in My Neighborhood," crayon drawing by a boy, C.A. twelve, I.Q. 80. The impulse to exaggerate form and subject matter to create a more vivid and effective expression extends from professional artists to people with severe learning problems.

Like normal children, mentally retarded children frequently like to depict their reactions to vicarious experience, even though they are more attracted to actual experience. Dramatized versions of familiar stories and events shown on the movie or television screen may excite them to visual expression. However, the teacher should, whenever possible, connect the physical experiences of the children and their drawings. Situations that deal with personal accidents ("falling down," "bumping my head") make effective sources for drawing, as do activities such as rolling or bouncing balls and using playground equipment. If there is any clear agreement among authorities on this topic, it is a belief in the need for motor experiences to develop a sense of space and relationships between objects.

Adolescent slow learners with an I.Q. of at least 70, no matter what their grade level, tend to use some of the subject matter found in the art work of the normal adolescent. Their work often exhibits a growing interest in social events at which both sexes are present. Boys, especially, make pictures about sports and sporting contests, deeds of daring, and many kinds of mechanical objects. Considerable attention is often given to anatomical detail of human beings shown in the pictures.

Methods of Teaching

The fact that mental retardation usually affects the whole personality makes the task of the teacher of slow learners difficult. Often, as the result of external pressures, a mentally retarded child suffers from emotional disturbances. Thus each slow learner, not only because of the mental handicap but also because of unfortunate accompaniments, may exhibit behavior that makes extraordinary demands on the teacher's understanding.

To teach slow learners, a teacher must possess a number of commendable personal qualities and professional abilities. The teacher must above all be patient, for these children progress slowly in their work. The teacher of slow learners must, furthermore, be able to stimulate these children so that they improve mentally, but at the same time not hurry them into work that is beyond their abilities. Finally, the teacher must treat every slow learner as a unique being. The fact that all such pupils suffer from a similar handicap does not mean that they lose identity as individuals. A study of their output in art offers a striking illustration of the fact that the personalities of slow learners differ widely.

Bryant and Schwann were interested in seeing if the design sense of retarded children could be improved, and developed a test to assess sensitivities to five art elements: line, shape, color, value, and texture. Based on these elements, fifteen lessons of half an hour each were provided over a period of time. Their study suggests that children with substandard I.Q.'s (23–80) can learn design concepts through systematic teaching. They discovered that children can

> learn art terminology by direct exposure to concrete objects, which they are able to observe, examine, manipulate, verbalize about, react to, and put together in some artistic way. They can get involved in producing art, which they understand and enjoy. The materials needed in the art lessons do not have to be expensive or elaborate; rather, they can be readily procured from the home, the school supply room, and the local community store.[9]

If in an otherwise normal class the teacher finds one or two particularly slow learners in art who require special attention, this should not create problems. Obviously, the teacher should in no way indicate to other members of the class the deficiencies of their mentally retarded classmates. Since all successful teaching in art rests on a methodology that demands that the teacher treat all pupils as individuals, the fact that the slow learners are afforded certain special attention should in no sense make them unique in the eyes of their fellows. Every child in the class, whether handicapped, normal, or gifted, will require individual treatment. If the teacher is placed in charge of a whole class of slow learners, the

[9]Antusa P. Bryant and Leroy B. Schwann, "Art and Mentally Retarded Children," *Studies in Art Education*, Vol. 12, No. 3 (Spring, 1971), 56.

Music stands around me
While I stand alone .
Birds flutter back and forth
From here to there
Until they're tired ,
Then they go home .

The trees stand sturdy and strong
While the leaves blow along .
The people move here and there ,
The waves toss everywhere .
Music stands around me
While I stand alone .
　　　　　　Perry Hunkins

An example of graphic design that combines printmaking, poetry, and typography. This picture is from a publication of the Dr. Francis Perkins School, Lancaster, Massachusetts.

same educational principles apply. Although every member of the group is a slow learner, no two children will react in an identical manner to art. Here, as elsewhere, every child must be offered an educational program tailored to individual needs and capacities.

Some teachers of mentally retarded children have been tempted to obtain more skillful-looking results by mechanical busywork. Exercises in tracing, copying, and coloring the work of others constitute one such type of work. Activities involving "chance" techniques constitute another type, and activities that are taught step by step tend also to become busywork.

As stated earlier, the educational values of copying, even for normal children, are dubious; such work is, therefore, not recommended. Copying also interferes with the ability of mentally retarded children to participate in a creative art program. Indeed, research has indicated that undesirable as this busywork may be with normal children, it appears to have even more inhibiting effects on less robust minds.[10] A child generally does enjoy a certain sense of security in such activities as copying and tracing; however, the teacher who tries to encourage original thinking later will find it difficult to wean the child away from what can only be described as emotional and visual crutches. The benefits to be achieved from approaching art as a thinking, feeling process should be available to children of all mental ages.

On the other hand, step-by-step teaching practices, while rarely of value to normal pupils because they present no real challenge, may often give the slow learner a valuable and necessary sense of achievement. Frequently this teaching method, if used wisely, may lead slow learners into more creative endeavors.

The approved methods now used with normal children are to a large extent also practical and effective when used with slow learners. The handicapped children, however, require more individual attention than their normal counterparts, and the pace of teaching often has to be slowed. Motivation, classroom arrangements, and appraisal of the effectiveness of the program in progress, nevertheless, require little or no modification in principle when applied to retarded pupils.

Teaching the slow learner does not require as much reorientation on the part of the teacher as one might suppose. It does require teaching in concrete terms, hence the importance of demonstrating craft processes, of simplifying, of slowing down verbal instructions, of having the patience to repeat directions, and above all of breaking down the learning experience into manageable stages. These few suggestions are also recommended for teaching certain types of emotionally and physically handicapped children.

---

[10] Some of the harmful effects of busywork on normal children are outlined in Viktor Lowenfeld, ed., *Workbooks and Art Education*, Research Bulletin of the Eastern Arts Association (Kutztown, Pa.: 1952–53).

USING MUSEUMS

Innovative approaches such as taking handicapped children to art museums have proved valuable in stimulating perceptual awareness and in developing an appreciation of the larger artistic world. A program developed at the Boston Museum of Fine Arts in conjunction with the Newton Public Schools enables the student with special needs to participate in an integrated program with normal learners. Activities include responding to artwork in the museum and then creating artwork in the museum's education department. Cooperative activities that enable normal and special-needs youngsters to share feelings, thoughts, and group projects bring the qualities common to all human beings—as well as mutual respect and greater understanding—to the surface in a healthy and supportive atmosphere. One teacher describes a typical session of this program as follows:

> During one lesson at the museum, each child in the classroom was handed a color card—theirs for the day. After talking about the color cards, the children watched slides of painting—in this instance abstract painting. The colors were bright and bold and the children were interested. The slides remained on the screen as the children were asked to identify the colors and as they successfully did so, they beamed with pleasure and pride. The lesson was skillfully repetitive and afterwards, the children visited a gallery where they saw the paintings they had just seen on the screen.

In the gallery, the children were asked to "look for colors" in the paintings as, with their teachers' help, they began to learn the names of colors they saw in the paintings.[11]

SPECIAL ENVIRONMENTS

A stimulating environment fosters increased interest in learning. The use of color and adaptive equipment encourages the developmentally delayed or handicapped child. Programs such as the Adaptive Environments Center in Boston train educators, therapists, and architects to adapt classrooms to the needs of such children. The increasing awareness of such needs by public-service institutions is making it possible to create environments specifically geared to handicapped children and adults. This is being done not only in public schools but in hospitals, daycare centers, nursery schools, and residential treatment centers.

Suitable Individual Activities

Having discussed the characteristics of slow learners, as well as effective methods of teaching them, we may now consider in detail some art activities especially suitable for them. Stimulating a sensory vocabulary in each

[11] Eleanor Siegel, "Utilizing Art as a Learning Tool," *Newton Graphic*, December 15, 1977.

Art Activities for Children with Special Needs

student is an important step in developing an art program for the handicapped. Children whose cognitive ability is limited to concrete thinking will need more visual, kinesthetic, and manipulative activities to aid them in experiencing the world. As their sensory experience is broadened, their expressive ability and self-confidence in the art-making process will increase.

Most art activities have proved to be sufficiently flexible to be performed by slow learners either in special classes or in regular classrooms. These activities include some types of drawing and painting, some forms of paper and cardboard work, a certain amount of sculpture and pottery, and some types of printing, all of which have been described earlier and hence require only brief mention here. Little additional comment about teaching these activities will be offered, since the reader may refer to other chapters where teaching methods were discussed at length.

Other activities, including certain kinds of weaving, stitchery, and bookcraft, are particularly valuable for slow learners. These activities and methods of teaching them are described in some detail below.

Media and Techniques. In drawing and painting, slow learners may use the standard tools and equipment recommended for other pupils. Hence wax crayons, tempera paint, the usual types of brushes and papers, and so on may be employed. Nearly all slow learners are capable of producing creative paper work. Most of these pupils achieve greatest success when cut paper is used as a medium for two-dimensional pictures. Some pupils, however, may begin to build their pictures into three dimensions. Nearly all these children enjoy box sculpture, and many of them seem capable of doing some freestanding paper sculpture. Many slow learners can use molds to make simple masks, and nearly all of them can work successfully with papier-mâché if it is prepared in advance for them.

BASIC ACTIVITIES

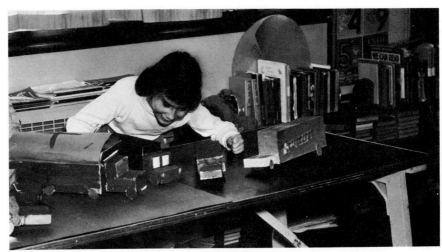

Box sculptures by pupils ranging in C.A. from nine years to twelve years, five months, and in I.Q. from 60 to 75. The challenge of combining and rearranging a variety of shapes to illustrate a particular theme has value for children of all abilities. (Photo by Royal Studio.)

Carving in wood and other substances is not recommended for most slow learners. The tools required in much of this work are too dangerous for them, and the technique is beyond their ability. Simple forms of modeling and pottery, however, are recommended. The direct nature of modeling pleases these pupils, and the repetitive character of most pottery makes this craft highly suitable. Both stick and vegetable printing are also useful techniques, largely because they are repetitive, whereas stencil and linoleum work may be too difficult to master.

Teaching. With all the basic activities mentioned above, the teacher of slow learners must modify classroom techniques to suit the creative abilities of these pupils. A step-by-step approach becomes necessary not only in the work itself but also in the selection of tools and media. If their I.Q. scores fall below 70, preadolescent slow learners usually experience difficulty when confronted by a wide range of color or by the problems of mixing tints, shades, and even secondary hues. The teacher will therefore often find it necessary to supply all colors ready-mixed. Chalk and charcoal also create difficulties for many of these slow learners, as does the mixing of media.

When three-dimensional work such as pottery or box sculpture is being taught to slow learners, the teacher would be wise to analyze the process from start to finish in terms of separate operations. Then, before the pupils begin work, they should be shown a finished object, so they know what to expect at the end of their work. After that, however, demonstrations and general teaching should be performed only one operation at a time. The pupils should select the tools only for the one operation, complete the operation, and then return the tools. This process should then be repeated until all the necessary operations have been mastered.

ACTIVITIES FOR MAKING SENSORY CONNECTIONS

Integrating arts activities within the special-needs classroom enables the teacher to thread specific learning concepts through several areas. Movement and art provide a particularly good way to bridge gross-motor and fine-motor activities. One example would be a movement activity focusing on large movements such as kneading, pressing, pushing, and pulling. The corresponding art activity would use these qualities in the fine-motor manipulation of clay.

Another art and movement combination might be the forming of letters by having the body assume various letter shapes, and by using different body parts to trace letters in the air. A corresponding activity would be to paint or draw the letters on large sheets of mural paper to maximize bodily involvement. Since all children enjoy tactile experience, collage materials including sandpaper, cotton, velvet, and foil could be used to reinforce and ensure sensory integration of the letter concepts.

Art Activities for Children with Special Needs

The length of each operation depends on the class. Pupils with lower I.Q.'s are able to master only very short and simple operations. Perhaps the greatest challenge facing the teacher of slow learners is to judge correctly the length and complexity of a unit of work, so that each pupil is stimulated but not confused. An example of a step-by-step analysis of work is set forth in the section that follows.

To replace some of the activities that slow learners may have difficulty with, certain weaving techniques are useful. Because weaving is an extremely flexible technique and depends largely on a repetition of movement, it is especially suitable for slow learners.

CARD-LOOM WEAVING

Media and Techniques. The process called *card-loom weaving* allows children to produce a number of practical articles such as mats or baskets without too much difficulty. To make a container, for example, the teacher should draw on fairly heavy cardboard a circle having a radius of 3 to 6 inches and inside that circle, a smaller circle having half that radius. Spokes about $\frac{3}{4}$ inch to 1 inch wide should be drawn from the circumference of the smaller circle to the circumference of the larger circle. A space about $\frac{1}{8}$ inch wide should be left between the spokes. It is recommended that an uneven number of spokes be drawn at first. The space between the spokes should be cut out and the spokes should then be bent upward.

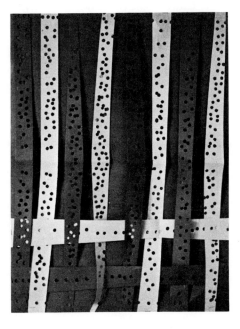

Slow learners are capable of experimenting with paper weaving. A hole punch was used to decorate these strips of colored paper. This activity could be expanded to include a wide range of tactile experiences, with cardboard, yarn, and strips of cloth added to the warp. (Photo by Rick Steadry.)

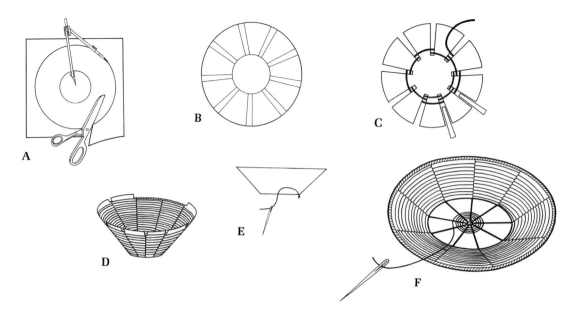

Processes in card-loom weaving: (**A**) drawing and cutting the cardboard base; (**B**) marking the spokes; (**C**) weaving; (**D**) finishing the rim of the basket; (**E**) sewing in strips of material for weaving the base; and (**F**) weaving the base.

Children may now begin weaving, with wool, string, or raffia (a grasslike substance having a long fiber). Starting from the base circle, the weaving material is simply taken over one spoke and under the next until each spoke is entirely covered, except for about $\frac{1}{4}$ inch of cardboard at the outside extremity of the spokes. This may be doubled over from the inside to the outside to form an edge to the container. Any ends of weaving material that are sticking out should be cut off.

To finish the base of the article, children may glue felt to the center, both on the inside and the outside. The base may also be woven. With a large needle, the child takes one strip of weaving material from the inside extremity of each spoke to the center of the base; over-and-under weaving may then be done with the needle. This technique may be used, of course, only in a basket with an uneven number of spokes. The rim of the article may be finished by binding the edge with the same material as was used for weaving. If holes are first pierced through the edge of the spokes before binding begins, the task will be easier. Binding is done by sewing over and over the edge.

To make a mat, children can cut a circle of cardboard of convenient size, and then cut out a small circle from the center of the cardboard. The rim of the cardboard should be notched; then the weaving material is looped repeatedly from the rim to the center of the cardboard. Binding the edge in the manner mentioned above completes the mat.

Many slow learners will eventually be able to try some simple experiments with card-loom weaving. Various colors of weaving material may first be introduced; later, perhaps material with a variety of both texture and color might be used. The shape of the cardboard might be altered; an oval may be used instead of a circle. An even number of spokes may be used, in which case two weaving materials of different colors can be used simultaneously to produce an interesting design. Handles for objects can be made by running a strand of weaving material over and under three long strands of the same material. Such handles may be attached merely by sewing.

Teaching. Suppose the teacher plans to have a class of very slow-learning pupils make woven containers. To arouse interest and to make sure that all members of the class realize what the finished object should look like, the teacher exhibits and talks about three containers. These objects are finished identically at the edges and centers but are made in different colors. The following separate operations and demonstrations are considered to be necessary for this group of children.*

OPERATION A.   *Preparing the cards*

Demonstration   1. Obtain cards, scissors, and compasses
2. Describe inner and outer circles; cut away excess cardboard
3. Draw spokes
4. Cut away cardboard between spokes

OPERATION B.   *Weaving*

Demonstration   1. Select weaving material
2. Begin weaving
3. Weave
4. Finish weaving

OPERATION C.   *Finishing center*

Demonstration   1. Obtain felt and glue jar containing brush
2. Measure center with compasses, transferring measurements to paper; cut out paper as guide for cutting felt, cut felt
3. Glue cut felt to center
4. Return compasses

*This lesson was planned for a class of boys, I.Q. range 50 to 70, C.A. range 11 years to 15 years, 5 months.

OPERATION D.   *Finishing edge*

Demonstration   1. Obtain large needle and binding material
2. Pierce cardboard
3. Sew edge over and over
4. Sew between spokes, through weaving material
5. Finish binding, knotting, and cutting material

OPERATION E.   *Returning all tools*

(no demonstration, but a verbal reminder to be orderly)

OPERATION F.   *Picking up scraps and general tidying up*

(no demonstration, but a verbal request to do a good job)

In another class the teacher might combine some operations, should the intelligence of pupils allow this. Also, more choice in materials and techniques might be permitted.

BOX-LOOM WEAVING

The more advanced preadolescent slow learners—usually those who score over 70 on an I.Q. test—are able to weave successfully on a simple "cradle" or "box" loom. The loom is so simply constructed that the pupils may easily make it themselves. It consists of what looks like two sets of miniature goalposts joined by four dowel rods, which can be made from old broom handles. At one end of the apparatus, slots should be made in the posts for a tension bar.

Media and Techniques.   Three items of equipment are required before weaving can begin. The first of these is what is called a "heddle." This is a frame of metal or wood about the same width as the loom, containing bars pierced by holes. The heddle is the mechanism that allows the cross threads to be put through the warp threads. Since heddles are made with considerable precision, they must be bought rather than made by the pupils. Most school-supply firms sell heddles of various sizes, with differing numbers of bars to the inch. The number of bars determines the texture of the woven cloth. The second item is called a "shuttle." This is a flat piece of wood with notches cut at each end to hold the weaving material, which is wound lengthwise around it. Pupils will find it a simple matter to make shuttles. The third item is known as a "warping frame," a piece of wood with a nail at each end. It is used to measure yarn, and can be made by the pupils.

The first step in the actual weaving process is to mount on the loom the threads running lengthwise (called the warp threads) and at the same time to thread the heddle. To make the warp threads the pupil must first tie

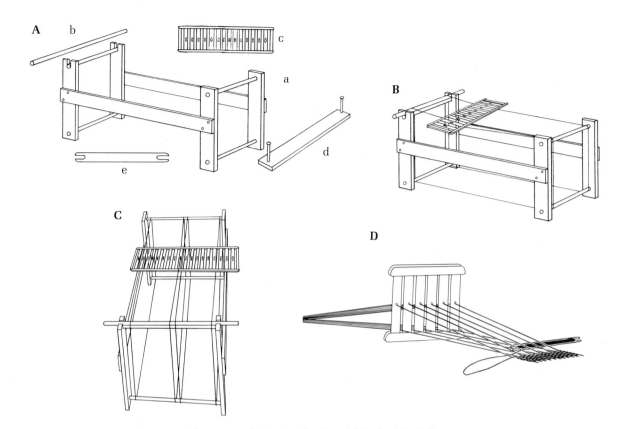

Equipment (**A**) for box-loom weaving: (a) the loom, (b) the tension bar, (c) the heddle, (d) the warping frame, and (e) the shuttle; (**B**) the loom with the tension bar in place and the heddle resting on the supporting threads; (**C**) the first two warp threads in place; and (**D**) the shuttle passing through the warp threads.

the weaving material to one nail on the warping frame and wind several turns around both nails. Then, with a pair of scissors, the threads should be cut where they meet one of the nails, thus providing a number of warp threads of equal and correct length. The mounting of the warp threads and the simultaneous threading of the heddle may now begin. First the tension bar should be placed in the slots at one end of the loom.

Next, two strings should be tied from the ends of the top dowels, so that the pupil may rest the heddle on them. Next, taking one warp thread already prepared on the warping frame, the pupil passes it through the center hole of the heddle and around all the dowel rods and the tension bar of the loom. The ends of this encircling warp thread should be tied together at the top dowel rod opposite the end supporting the tension bar. This process must be repeated with another warp thread, this time passing the thread through the adjoining space on the heddle instead of through the hole. The pupil must continue to thread the loom in this fashion, working on each side of the center of the heddle and passing the warp threads alternately, first through a hole in the heddle and then through a space, until the desired width of the material to be woven is reached. The function of the heddle will now be clear. By either pulling up or depressing the heddle, the pupil will observe that "sheds" are made, through which the shuttle may be thrust with the cross weaver or "weft" thread.

To weave, the pupil should first wind the yarn thread around the shuttle. Then the heddle should be raised and the shuttle passed through the shed on the near side of the heddle. With the heddle, the weft thread should then be pressed to the end of the loom (beaten) toward the pupil. Next, the pupil must press the heddle down and again pass the shuttle through the shed. This process is continued with the sheds being formed by the alternate raising and lowering of the heddle, the shuttle going from side to side, until the desired length of cloth is produced.

A certain degree of skill is necessary, of course, to perform well on a loom. The weft threads must be placed at equal distances from each other. If they are beaten too vigorously with the heddle, the weaving will be bulky. If the weft is not pressed closely enough, the cloth will be flimsy in places. Again, skill is required to keep the edges of the woven material straight and tidy. If the weft thread is pulled too tight, the edge will have a wave; if the weft is not pulled tight enough, the edge will display unsightly little loops. Difficult though the skill of weaving may appear to the beginner, the technique can soon be mastered satisfactorily on the loom described above.

Once pupils have developed an ability to use this loom, they will no doubt become very fond of weaving, and may wish to make articles such as scarves or placemats requiring the full length of the warp thread. In such cases, they must learn to move the weaving around the loom so that they may continue to use the heddle in its normal place. To move the weaving, they need merely to remove the tension bar, and then, using the heddle, to ease the woven material around the dowel rods until only warp threads are visible. After they have replaced the tension bar, they may continue weaving as described previously.

To finish the edges of an article after they have cut it from the loom, the pupils may knot together the warp threads by twos and then trim the strands to form a fringe. To make the edge more secure, they may also sew the last two or three strands of weft to the warp threads.

Experimentation in weaving is within the capabilities of many slow learners. Although 4-ply wool is perhaps the best material with which to learn weaving, various types of both warp and weft material may eventually be used. Interesting patterns may be developed by using materials of different colors and textures.

Art Activities for Children with Special Needs

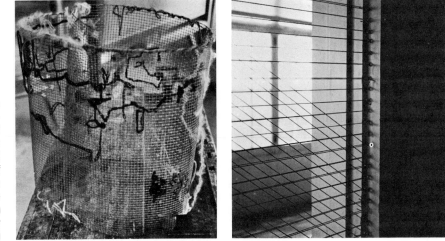

Two of the more unusual forms of weaving to which slow learners will respond. A cylinder of wire mesh permits circular weaving patterns; an unused entryway allows the creation of string and yarn patterns on a grand scale. Screw eyes were placed at 1-inch intervals along the sides and top of the door frame. (Photos by Rick Steadry.)

Teaching. Before slow learners are taught to weave on a loom, the teacher should analyze the operations and list the demonstrations, as was done above for card-weaving.

Loom-weaving creates storage problems, since both the loom and the wool are bulky. These problems may be partially solved by having collapsible looms that can be dismantled when not in use. Another solution to the difficulty, of course, is to have only a few looms that are used by the pupils on a rotation basis.

Good weaving depends on the tension of the strands. We learn to control tension largely through feeling, in the same way that we learn to skate or ride a bicycle. Before attempting to teach, the teacher should practice maintaining an even tension until it is almost automatic. Because each type of loom has its own peculiarities, the teacher should practice on the type of loom that the pupils will use. As each step of setting up the loom is taught, the teacher should inspect the assembly of every pupil. The warp threads should be tapped with the palm of the hand to see that each strand is secure and that tension is right. The tension should be such that tapping the threads causes a vigorous rebound of the hand.

When everything is ready for weaving, the teacher can often help slow learners by standing behind them, lightly holding their hands, and going through the motions of using heddle and shuttle until the pupils can acquire the correct rhythmic motion.[12]

[12]Recommended references for weaving are Harriette J. Brown, *Handweaving: For Pleasure and Profit* (New York: Harper & Row, 1952), and Mary Kirby, *Designing on the Loom* (New York: Viking, 1955).

STITCHERY

Another activity that need not be confined to slow learners but is especially suitable for them because of its repetitious character is stitchery. Stitchery need not mean commercially stamped products depicting old-fashioned ladies or forget-me-nots; it can be as stimulating and original as many other contemporary art forms. In one form or another stitchery is popular with children in all grades. The products of their work can be purely decorative, such as wall hangings, or they can be practical, such as pillow covers, purses, and aprons. The subject matter of the designs may be nonobjective or representational. Appliqué techniques are also possible with stitches. Stitchery is a good activity for a group or for the individual child.

Media and Techniques. To a large extent this activity makes use of scrap materials. Cotton and burlap are very good materials on which to work. If colored burlap is not available, potato or apple sacks will do just as well. Needles may be purchased in almost any department store, as may embroidery cottons in many colors. Yarns in different weights and colors add variety to the work.

Many kinds of stitches are used in this activity, among them the simple running stitch and the more complicated stitches such as the blanket, buttonhole, chain, daisy, outline, and feather stitches.[13] The design, which can be planned in advance or created on the cloth, is outlined with a simple stitch, and areas are given texture with the more complicated stitches. Buttons, beads, and brightly colored felts may be incorporated into the design for accents. As in any design, too many conflicting patterns in the same piece should be avoided; it is advisable to work for a few "balances"—line and mass, pattern and solid, large and small. When the work is completed, it may be mounted in a picture frame for display.

Teaching. The most practical way to teach stitchery is to treat it as a form of picture-making. With the simple materials mentioned above, even mentally retarded children may immediately set to work. There is no need at first to show them a number of complicated stitches, because what is known as the *running stitch* comes quite naturally to them. Mariska Karasz says:

> If you have ever held a needle in your hand you know how to do this stitch without being told. It . . . consists simply of running the needle in and out through the fabric at fairly regular intervals. It is the simplest kind of stitch with which to draw a line or outline a shape. But you will be missing its best use if you don't try it also as a filler.[14]

[13]A good introductory booklet on embroidery is Mildred Ryan, *Needlecraft Handbook* (New York: Arco, 1954). A good general sourcebook is Lili Blumeneau, *Creative Design in Wall Hangings* (New York: Crown, 1967).
[14]Mariska Karasz, "Creative Arts of the Needle," *House Beautiful*, January 1952, p. 85.

In this well-appointed art class-room, slow learners have ample space to explore weaving, stitchery, and knitting. (Photo by Bradford Herzog.)

Thus, children may use the needle directly as a means of expression. After selecting their cotton or burlap background material, they may start working without drawing lines. When they have gained experience in the technique, they might later sketch some ideas in pencil before they begin the actual stitchery. After this they may be taught the more complicated stitches, some of which are rather easy to learn.

Slow learners have little difficulty in acquiring the skills needed for stitchery and are generally very creative in this activity. They can experiment with using threads and backgrounds of varying colors, weights, and textures, or explore the potentialities of a newly discovered stitch.

The pedagogical case for weaving and stitchery has been stated by Schill and Abrams in their discussion of the role of manipulation of media in teaching retarded children. They state:

> Various forms of conceptual thinking can be initiated for these children through art. Color, perception, size and shape discrimination and light and dark, over and under, around and through, and numerous others can be integrated into the total art program. However, the retarded child will not develop them unless they are consciously and overtly taught.[15]

"Conscious" and "overt" teaching, as has been stated, imply simplification, concrete presentation, and above all, repetition.

[15] Abrams and Schill, "Art in Special Education," p. 164.

BOOKCRAFT

Bookcraft has been mentioned as one possibility for group work. But it is also suitable as an individual activity for children of all ages. Most slow learners can learn to make books, which may be used as attractive scrapbooks or notebooks, with decorated covers and end pages. Much of this work appeals to slow learners because the techniques used to decorate the books are simple and yet result in quite spectacular designs.

Media and Techniques. First, the pupil decorates the front and back of the cover paper. This may be done by stick or vegetable printing, finger painting, or some "chance" effects. Some of the techniques depending on chance are as follows.[16]

1. Tempera colors are splashed over paper that has been dampened with water. The colors will run and blend in a pleasing manner.
2. A few drops of thin oil paint of various colors are placed in a shallow pan of water. By gently blowing on the surface of the water, the pupils develop a swirling pattern of color. Paper should then be slipped into the water at one end of the pan, submerged completely, and then raised gently. The oil paint will adhere to the paper to form a unique pattern.
3. A toothbrush loaded with tempera paint is held over a sheet of paper. Using a scraper such as a knife, pupils draw the blade toward themselves over the toothbrush, thereby spraying the paper. Several colors may be used. This technique can be controlled by using a "mask," or covering paper, to block off areas where the spray is not desired.

[16]These techniques are also suitable for producing gift-wrapping papers or for backgrounds for various forms of printing.

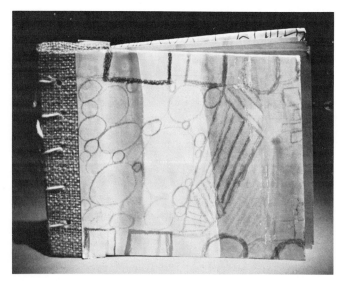

In this open-fold book made by a slow learner, yarn holds the spine in place; heavy cloth remnants and a crayon-and-watercolor resist make the cover decoration. Both the picture and the cloth were pasted to heavy cardboard backing with white glue. The book contains prints made by the pupil's classmates.

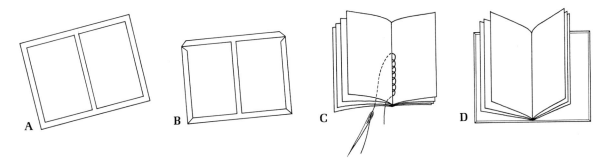

Processes in making a simple booklet: (**A**) placing cardboard on treated cover paper; (**B**) mitering and folding the cover paper; and (**C**) sewing the page inserts. The finished booklet is shown in **D**.

4. Tempera paint in two or more colors is placed thickly on paper. The sheet is folded in half with the painted surface inside. When drawn apart, the paper displays a bisymmetrical pattern.

To make the cover of the book, pupils place the prepared cover paper on the desk, with the reverse side of the cover paper facing them. Next they cut a sheet of stiff cardboard slightly smaller than the cover sheet. They then cut the cardboard into two pieces of equal size and lay the two pieces side by side over the cover paper, leaving a small gap between them to form the spine of the book. The cardboard and cover paper are pasted together; the corners are carefully folded and, if the pupils are capable of doing so, mitered. The pupils then fold the edges of the cover paper over the cardboard.

To prepare the inside of the book, sheets of paper about one-quarter of an inch smaller than the cover are folded to form pages. These are lightly stitched together with a needle and thread along their spine. The front and back pages of this assembly are then pasted and pressed to the covers. To complete the book, the pupil may shellac the cover.

Many other types of bookcraft are possible, of course, but most of them are too exacting to be considered for slow learners.[17]

Teaching. Although the exact steps of making a book must be taught to slow learners, the teacher can employ a creative approach both in the "chance" effects of decorating paper and to some extent in the actual making of the book. The techniques leading to a chance pattern should be demonstrated one at a time, so that the pupils will not become confused

[17]For bookcraft, the following references are recommended: Chris Groneman, *General Bookbinding* (New York: Taplinger, 1958); Lawrence Town, *Bookbinding by Hand* (New York: Pitman, 1952); Douglas Cockerell, *Bookbinding and the Care of Books*, 5th ed. (New York: Pitman, 1953).

by a multiplicity of materials and ways of using them. Maximum and minimum size limits for the book should be established, but the pupils can decide on the exact dimensions they want to use within those limitations.

Suitable Group Activities

Whether in special classes comprising only slow learners, or in classes in which there are only one or two slow learners, the mentally retarded require thoughtful consideration when group activities take place.

Most retarded pupils have difficulty participating in class or group art activities largely because of considerable differences in the mental and chronological ages of individual members of the group, even among pupils in special classes for the retarded. Group activity presents many difficulties for normal people; for the mentally retarded, who have usually suffered from frustrations in life and hence are often emotionally volatile, the group activity must be very carefully chosen and supervised, if it is to succeed.

A highly recommended group activity for slow learners is puppetry. This activity allows children to work both as an individual and as a member of a group. Only the simplest of puppets described in Chapter 11 need be made for a successful group performance. Stick and fist puppets are suitable for most slow learners. The child's own symbols, cut in cardboard and tacked to sticks, or doll-like creatures made from old socks or paper bags and manipulated with the fingers, will serve as suitable characters for a play. A large cardboard carton provides a simple stage. The spoken lines and the action of the play may be derived from a well-liked story or based on some experience in the children's lives.

Because mural-making demands a high level of group cooperation and organization, this activity as handled in conventional situations is not generally recommended for slow learners. The quasi-group activity, how-

Tapestry weaving is a quasi-group activity suitable for slow learners. Each child contributes his or her own square of weaving; then all the pieces are sewn together and attached to a frame. Although this tapestry is designed for random arrangement, children should be encouraged to decide where their own portions will be placed.

This mural (of a monster) by slow learners is the product of a quasi-group activity. Two children drew the outline, and each child in the group filled in a section of the work. (Photo by Rick Steadry.)

ever, in which the general plan is discussed and decided on by a group but in which each child works independently on a section of the display, is more practical for slow learners, as it is for young children. Slow learners may not be able to grasp the design concept of a mural, nor is it important that they do. What they do know is that working on a large scale is a pleasurable experience. Many partly cooperative activities of this type may be carried out in clay or in other modeling or building materials, including empty boxes and odd pieces of wood. A service station, a farm, a village, or a playground are subjects that slow learners might be interested in developing.

When only one or two noticeably slow learners are found in a class of normal children, the difficulties arising from group work are greater, since these pupils must participate and attempt to hold their own with their classmates. The problem of having these pupils purposefully occupied is not too great when the whole class is engaged in a group activity such as puppetry. That activity involves a variety of tasks, such as assembling the stage or hemming curtains, to which slow workers can contribute if given some guidance. In the more difficult activities involving only a few major tasks, such as, say, mural-making, the slow learners' relative lack of ability tends to become conspicuous. Obviously they cannot be asked to do only such menial jobs as washing brushes or cleaning paint tins. They must be given more important jobs, if they are to retain their self-respect.

Some teachers arrange privately with one of the more intelligent and sympathetic class members who have been chosen as leaders, to elect a slow learner to the team. This leader provides the slow learner with some aspect of the drawing and painting, and coaches and supervises the slow learner carefully. The contribution of the slow learner in the mural activity may range from filling in areas of color, outlining areas, creating repeat borders—tasks that can be undertaken with the knowledge that they contribute materially to the activity.

The Value of Art for Children with Special Needs

Slow learners will display difficulty in working on some art projects, especially those that involve a high risk of failure. Nevertheless, wherever possible they must be stimulated by work of a creative nature rather than lulled by copy work. Most art activities are sufficiently flexible to engage their attention profitably.

Many teachers feel that process-oriented activities provide the slow learner with much-needed specific, concrete operations. Schaefer-Simmern's comments on the learning process of the mentally retarded may have some relevance here. He states: "Creating order and organization in the realm of concrete, visual experience is a discipline thoroughly suited to the nature of mentally defective individuals. . . . These patients who are taught embroidery, weaving, rug making and the like, often surprise one with the accurateness of their work." Schaefer-Simmern also cautions against falling into the trap of providing such children with packaged designs, stating that "for the sake of their inner stability and satisfaction, for the sake of their own enjoyment in the realization of their own world, they should be led to create their own cultural pattern."[18]

For this reason the activities involving fabric design and construction have been left to this chapter. It must be remembered, however, that bright children in their own way gain even more from weaving or stitchery than do slow learners. One difference between the two groups is that slow learners have a tendency to enjoy an activity for the *pleasure* of the process, whereas the above-average child uses technical knowledge more readily as a *means to an end*. In addition, the bright child has a greater ability to pursue and develop ideas in art activity. The bright child can, moreover, deal consciously with the problems of design.

Art education may have considerable significance in the general education of most slow learners. There is wide agreement that a child who is adversely affected in one area of personality is likely to be adversely af-

[18] Schaefer-Simmern, *The Unfolding of Artistic Activity*, p. 187.

fected in other areas. It is reasonable to suppose that this process could operate in reverse, and that a slow learner who profits from art activities might undergo desirable changes in personality. Whatever progress in art is made by slow learners depends primarily on the patience and sympathetic understanding of the teacher.

The gains to be derived for slow learners working in art may be summarized by the following seven points:

1. Through art activity, slow learners may create a product that is not necessarily inferior to that of their neighbors. Their efforts need not suffer by comparison.

2. The process of concept-formation through symbolization takes place for slow learners as it does for average and above-average children. Through art, slow learners can present ideas that may otherwise be denied expression because of limited ability in handling language skills.

3. For the trained observer, the drawings of slow learners may provide diagnostic clues to emotional difficulties that sometimes accompany retardation.

4. Art activity can function as therapy, providing a source of satisfaction and stability to children who have a history of failure.

5. Working in art provides vital sensory and motor experiences that involve the total mental and physical capabilities of the workers. The integration of physical and mental operations in turn facilitates the union of thought and feeling. In this respect, art serves the same unifying function for subnormal children that it does for normal ones.

6. Artistic activity provides slow learners with experience in decision-making and problem-solving, which are socially useful skills.

7. The art room can provide a nonthreatening atmosphere in which to begin the mainstreaming process of integrating normal children and children with special needs.

Other Kinds of Handicaps

Although this chapter has concentrated on art and retardation, teachers may be faced with other kinds of handicaps, as children with disabilities are moved from special learning situations into the regular classroom. Teachers cannot become instant authorities on the many problems that may confront them, but Table 12.2 provides a guideline for beginning to deal with problems that may arise. This chart was organized by a group of art teachers who were interested in preparing themselves for those handi-

TABLE 12.2

Suggested Teaching Methods for Special Needs

Identification	Characteristics	Appropriate Approach	Suggested Activities
Mentally Retarded	Slower to learn and to perform. Short attention span, impaired self-image. Limited spatial perception. Difficulty in socialization. Poor body awareness. Learns through concrete approaches.	Overteaching and repetition. Specific instruction in specific skills. Regular follow-up imperative. Simplification of concepts and skills in lessons. Gradual addition of steps in sequential order.	Activities relating to emotions. Direct manipulation of materials: finger paint, fabrics, clay, etc. Body sensory awareness through motion and tactile experiences. Simple puppets (paper bag, paper plate, sock). Unconventional media (shaving cream, vanilla pudding, chocolate syrup) on formica surfaces. Painting on a mirror. Self-adornment (costumes, hats, jewelry, body paint). Thickened tempera paint (with soap flakes). Sand casting, Play Dough, simple weaving, papier-mâché. Tactile boards and boxes. Junk and body printing. Constructions, stuffed shapes.
Visually Impaired (blind or partially sighted)	Limited or no visual field. Uncomfortable in unfamiliar physical setting. Difficulty in perceiving total image. Learns through tactile and auditory experiences. Lack of environmental awareness.	Organize materials so child has same place to work each time. Develop familiarity with environment. Develop tactile sense to the fullest. Develop sense of rhythm, patterns, motion sequencing, body awareness, and sense of space.	Tactile experiences. Matching and sorting textures, texture boards, texture walls, aprons with textures. Feely boxes. Clay. Collages of wide range of textures. Sand casting. Construction and junk sculpture. All tactile media as above. Weaving, macramé. Shape-discrimination games.
Perceptually Handicapped (extreme reading disability)	Lack of form discrimination. Lack of spacial orientation. Hyperactive, especially in periods of frustration. Poor eye-hand coordination. Impaired visual reception. Poor kinesthetic performance. Distractable. Failure syndrome.	Keep visual distraction to a minimum. Repetition. Develop sense of rhythm, pattern, motion.	Body awareness exercises, calisthenics and movement to music. Sequencing activities. Matching colors, sizes, shapes. Letter, number, and shape collages. Use of tactile media to develop eye-hand coordination. Construction. Hammer and nail letters. Pencil drawings. Drama, puppetry. Stuffed letters.
Hearing Impaired (deaf or partially deaf)	Limited language. Difficulty in communication. Lack of conceptual language. Limited environmental awareness. Tends to withdraw. Difficult to motivate. Sensitivity to visual world.	Develop nonverbal communication. Instruct through demonstration and illustration of work. Emphasize visual and tactile experiences. Develop sense of rhythm, pattern, motion, sequencing, body awareness, and space.	Drawing or painting based on bodily movements. Drawing on blackboard. Any activity based on clear, well-trained demonstration by teacher (clay, sculpture, collage, etc.). Color discrimination. Weaving, sewing. Printing, painting.

370

Art Activities for Children with Special Needs

TABLE 12.2 cont.

Identification	Characteristics	Appropriate Approach	Suggested Activities
Orthopedic Problems (cerebral palsy)	Spastic, rigid, jerky, involuntary movement. Impaired eye-hand coordination, impaired speech and general communication. Lack of muscular control.	Extend art time. Secure materials and sufficient space. Teach through actual manipulation, direct tactile experiences before using tools. Build up handles on tools with plasticene or foam rubber. Attach drawing instruments to wrists.	Large felt-tip pens provide emphatic lines and bright colors. Thickened tempera paint. All tactile media as above. Water play. Any activity that uses the hands and body in a physiotherapeutic manner.
Emotionally Disturbed	Short attention span and easily distracted. Failure syndrome. Lacks self-confidence. Hyperactive. Poor self-image. Egocentric.	Create a code of acceptable behavior. Limits are imperative. Provide security through repetition of activities and single tasks. Experiences should be "open." Encourage expression of feelings.	Stuffing precut shapes. Making media such as Play Dough, papier-mâché pulp. Constructions (glued). Body awareness. Costumes and puppets. Painting with thickened paint. All tactile media as above. Water play. Bookmaking.

capped children they might be teaching the following year. The chart, while incomplete, reflects not only their own experience and judgment, but that of others cited in the bibliography. It can also provide readers with a format within which to add their own observations and findings. Therapists urge us to view a handicap not so much as a defect but rather as a difference, and so to discover in it the potential for a specific and unique creativity—one through which other sensory modes may even be heightened.

> As we opened ourselves to their [blind children's] unique ways of being, we learned to value their otherness, to treasure the ways in which they sensitized us. The children expanded our sensory awareness by referring to "clay that smells like candy," "ether markers," or "soft paper." They tuned us in to sounds, like Billy, who took intense pleasure in "a marker that squeaks a whole lot . . . that makes a whole lotta noise." Although one would not have chosen a felt-tip marker as the most appropriate tool for a boy with no vision, Billy taught us not to allow our own preconceptions to interfere with what media we might offer a handicapped child.
>
> Through their sensitive use of their hands, those who could see nothing taught us about a kind of "free-floating tactile attention" in their approach to shape, form, and texture. . . . They seemed to know where to position their wood-scraps, suggesting a "tactile aesthetic" different from a visual one.

The therapist also tells how a child with limited vision experienced a "kind of 'color-shock'" from the intense hues of tempera paint. "And Terry, a deaf-blind child, literally jumped for joy when she accidently dis-

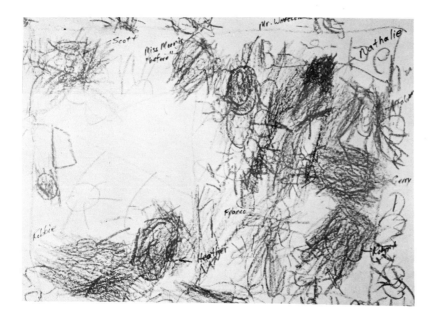

The artwork of children with behavioral problems—another type of handicap—often reflects their moods, as in this drawing by a nine-year-old Canadian girl from a broken home. She drew people she knew; then in a rage obliterated them with scribbles. After such outbursts, however, her drawings took on firmer and more organized patterns.

covered that wet clay pressed on the white paper made a visible mark. . . . The art program . . . opened our eyes to their need and capacity for joy. . . . The intensity of the children's sensory-motor pleasure in the art experience was inescapable."[19]

Trainable mentally retarded children make advances in behavior, speech, and language through arts programs. Through creative drama, deaf children can shed the fear of using words. Music has helped to develop a rhythmical sense in handicapped children, as well as to aid them in relaxing their muscles. Movement activities can help the blind child gain the freedom to explore space.

In a study by Greene and Hasselbrings, a curriculum was "designed so that the students actually were exposed to language concepts within the process of making art objects. Through a concrete method, abstract verbal concepts were learned and integrated into each student's life." A multisensory approach can foster greater understanding of abstract concepts. "A highly visual curriculum which attempts to unify the total learning experience of the hearing impaired child" can often be achieved through arts activities. Using the visual, tactile, and linguistic modes results in a "greater concept attainment."[20]

[19]Judith Rubin, "Growing Through Art with the Multiple Handicapped," *Viewpoints: Dialogue in Art Education* (1976).

[20]J. Craig Greene and T. S. Hasselbrings, "The Acquisition of Language Concepts by Hearing Impaired Children Through Selected Aspects of Experimental Core Art Curriculum," *Studies in Art Education*, Vol. 22, No. 2 (1981).

1. Collect drawings and paintings done by slow learners in various grades and with various I.Q.'s. Compare the work of each group of slow learners with that of a group of normal children who (a) are in corresponding grades and (b) have corresponding chronological ages. List the differences between the work of slow learners and that of normal pupils in each instance.

2. Compare the work habits of the slow learners with those of the normal pupils in the instances described in the activity above.

3. From a collection of work by slow learners, select pieces of art having some pleasing aesthetic qualities. How would the number of pieces selected compare with the number obtained from a collection of equal size comprising the work of normal children in corresponding stages? List some of the chief characteristics of the work chosen from the slow learners' collection.

4. Make a list of titles that slow learners give to their drawings and paintings. Can you give any explanations for the titles?

5. Describe the personal characteristics of a teacher of slow learners whom you know well.

6. In preparing to teach a class of slow-learning boys and girls (I.Q. range 50 to 70, C.A. range 11 to 15), analyze the *operations* and *demonstrations* considered necessary for a successful outcome in each of the following activities: (a) making a design in stitchery; (b) making a small clay bowl by the coil method; (c) making a tempera painting.

7. Build a small box loom as described in this chapter and, using heavy weaving material, wave two placemats.

8. On a piece of burlap or cotton about 12 inches square, create a nonobjective design in stitchery. Using a lightweight cotton and a running stitch, make an interesting line arrangement that has a variety of enclosed areas. Using wools, cottons, and yarns of different weights and colors, create textural effects in some of the outlined areas. If you are satisfied with your work, frame it under glass as you would a drawing.

9. Using materials similar to those suggested in 8, above, make a representational picture in stitchery. Choose subject matter from life, such as a still life or landscape.

10. Observe an art class that has one or two slow learners at work on group activities. Note the techniques used to assist the slow learners. Describe any opportunities missed to help the handicapped children. Suggest practical steps that might have been taken to assist them.

Suggested Readings

Lark-Horovitz, Betty, Hilda Present Lewis, and Mark Luca. *Understanding Children's Art for Better Teaching.* Columbus, Ohio: Charles Merrill, 1967. Chapter 6, "The Exceptional Child," covers children who have disabilities and children who are gifted.

Uhlin, Donald. *Art for Exceptional Children.* Dubuque, Iowa: Wm. C. Brown, 1972. Part II is particularly valuable for definitions, classifications, and suggestions for instruction.

Although art therapy is different from the education of special learners, the following books are instructive for both topics.

Rubin, Judith Aron. *Child Art Therapy.* New York: Van Nostrand Reinhold, 1978.

Ulman, Elinor, and Penny Dachinger, eds. *Art Therapy in Theory and Practice.* New York: Schocken Books, 1975.

ART ACTIVITIES

for gifted children

Any inquiry in art, and especially one concerned with the sources of artistic accomplishment, must necessarily confront the issue of talent—the status of those individuals who, owing to nature, nurture, or some indissoluble blend, possess special gifts.[*]

THIRTEEN

In considering the gifted or talented child we are confronted with something of an educational mystery.[1] Strangely enough for a society that looks to the gifted for its leaders, the gifted child was until recently perhaps the most neglected of all types in the public schools. This neglect cannot be excused on the grounds that gifted children are able to make satisfactory progress without help. On the contrary, there is much evidence that cases of failure, delinquency, laziness, and general maladjustment easily occur among gifted children as a result of educational neglect.[2] Since the Sput-

[1] In most educational writing *gifted* refers to children with a high general intelligence, while *talented* refers to a special capability in one field of endeavor. This differentiation of meaning is by no means universal and has not been adopted here. In this chapter the words are used interchangeably.

[2] An excellent general reference is Paul Witty, ed., *The Gifted Child* (Boston: Heath, 1953).

[*] Howard Gardner, *Artful Scribbles* (New York: Basic Books, 1980), p. 17.

nik crisis in 1957 the lot of the academically talented has improved through the addition of special programs, grouping arrangements, the re-organization of faculty into teams, teaching aids, and paraprofessionals. The child who is gifted in art, however, is to a large extent still not adequately provided for.

A cautionary note must be sounded at this point. Even if artistically talented children are singled out and supported, they may still be discontented. The intensity of the children's preoccupation with art may lead them to view other school obligations in a negative light, and the fact that they are singled out for attention may cause them to withdraw from art activity. De Francesco cautions against "exhibitionism, exploitation, and pressures. Public performances for their own sake . . . contests," while at the same time pointing to existing "inadequacy of the regular instruction, or even of the special instruction."[3]

Art educators have ambivalent attitudes regarding the gifted in art. An examination of art education literature shows that many writers do not even discuss the gifted. There is, undoubtedly, a mystique surrounding artistic talent. Even the students, echoing the attitudes of their parents, may profess to have misgivings about art activity, protesting to the teacher that "I can't draw a straight line" or "I'm no artist." It is important that students, administrators, and the public alike recognize the fact that all children are capable of creative activity, and that the benefits obtained from the study of art should be available to them all. It is desirable, therefore, that not too much fuss be made over the gifted, who constitute a relatively small minority among those studying art. But talent does exist, manifesting itself as early as the kindergarten; when it shows itself, the teacher should be prepared to deal with it constructively.

This chapter deals with three main topics: how to identify gifted children, how best to educate them, and what art experiences they should have. Unsolved problems remain, but research offers at least partial solutions.[4] If we can tackle these problems, talent that otherwise might never be developed may blossom.

Identifying the Gifted Child

It seems to be more difficult to identify the artistically talented child than the academically gifted child. With the latter, investigators can rely to a

[3] Italo de Francesco, *Art Education: Its Means and Ends* (New York: Harper & Row, 1958), p. 404.
[4] Betty Lark-Horovitz, Hilda Present Lewis, and Mark Luca, *Understanding Children's Art for Better Teaching* (Columbus, Ohio: Merrill, 1967), offers the reader forty-two research references in Chapter 6, "The Exceptional Child." See also Robert J. Havighurst, Eugene Stivers, and Robert F. De Haan, *A Survey of the Education of Gifted Children* (Chicago: University of Chicago Press, 1955).

Art Activities for Gifted Children

very large extent on pupils' I.Q. scores.[5] The determination of artistic talent is not so simple. While the results of one study indicate that every child who seems gifted in art also scores above average on I.Q. tests, not every child with a high I.Q. score possesses artistic talent.[6] Some, indeed, with exceptionally high I.Q.'s may appear to be lacking in even normal artistic skills and sensibilities.[7]

One of the greatest difficulties in discovering artistic talent arises from the fact that no reliable measures exist to judge either art production or appreciation. Whatever beliefs we may hold about a particular child's abilities in art are usually based on personal appraisal rather than on data gathered objectively. Most experts hold that subjective appraisals are not so important in reading, spelling, and number work, where fundamental abilities can be measured fairly accurately and, as a consequence, talent can be identified. We might suspect, however, that the expressive and appreciative aspects of even these academic fields are no more amenable to a reliable measurement than they are in art.

Since most teachers depend on subjective means to identify artistically talented youngsters, their estimate of the children's artistic future can be relied on only with reservations. Nevertheless, the pooled opinion of informed people has frequently led to surprisingly accurate judgments concerning artistic talent.[8]

Several authorities have made the study of artistically gifted children a special concern. One of the earliest efforts to characterize the special capacity for art was made by Norman Meier, a psychologist whose interest in the subject led him to design tests to assess the degree and kind of artistic talent among children. Meier claimed that gifted children derive their artistic ability from superior manual skill, energy, aesthetic intelligence, perceptual facility, and creative imagination. His study of gifted and average children led him to conclude that, since youngsters with the greatest artistic aptitude had a greater number of artists in their family

Special programs should encourage gifted children to go beyond the usual classroom experience. This eleven-year-old is working comfortably beside a seventeen-year-old, drawing a larger-than-life-size animal head.

CHARACTERISTICS OF GIFTED CHILDREN

[5] Among psychologists, L. M. Terman applied the term *gifted* to all those with I.Q.'s of 140 or over; L. S. Hollingworth suggested 130; H. H. Goddard, 120.

[6] In the classes sponsored by Ontario Department of Education, the lowest I.Q. among the children gifted in art was 112; the lowest C.A. was 9 years, 3 months.

[7] Adding a further difficulty, some writers maintain that artistic talent appears to have a slower rate of maturation than other talents, particularly musical talent. See Florence L. Goodenough, *Exceptional Children* (New York: Appleton-Century-Crofts, 1956). The author cites Catharine Morris Cox, *The Early Mental Traits of Three Hundred Geniuses,* Vol. 2 (Stanford, Calif.: Stanford University Press, 1926), which discusses thirteen great artists and suggests that their early work did not compare in stature with that of young musicians of similar chronological age. The differences in rate of maturation in the two artistic fields might be questioned, as Goodenough rightly suggests, on the grounds that we do not possess suitable measuring devices for artistic talent.

[8] Pooled judgments have been important in Goodenough and Harris' "Draw-a-Man" test, the Cleveland Studies, and Eisner's *A Comparison of the Developmental Drawing Characteristics of Culturally Advantaged and Culturally Disadvantaged Children.*

histories, the genetic factor played a major role in determining artistic abilities.

Let us compare the conclusions of some other writers as they describe the phenomenon of talent among elementary-school children.

According to Miriam Lindstrom, an art teacher,[9] gifted children:

1. Are extraordinarily perceptive in both objective fact and subjective effect.
2. Are better able to indicate a clear sense of structure in the interrelationships of parts.
3. Show deeper appreciation of significant expressive gesture or attitude.
4. Possess a generous unspoiled readiness to respond to the challenge of new experience.
5. Enjoy a relative freedom from the ordinary frustrations of most children.

According to Howard Conant, an educator, painter, and writer,[10] gifted children:

1. Possess heightened visual acuity and interest in both idea and detail.
2. Are better able to see the underlying artistic structure of realistic subject matter.
3. Are characterized by a level of persistence and interest far beyond their classmates.
4. Demonstrate unusual attention to detail and precocious representational ability, and possess a photographic mind and acute powers of visualization and draftsmanship.

According to Lark-Horovitz, Lewis, and Luca, art educators and psychologists,[11] gifted children:

1. Are usually beyond the norm of their age group in developmental status, technical skill, and aesthetic judgment.
2. Excel in compositional arrangement and enrichment in decorative and aesthetic qualities.
3. Show great ease in working with media.
4. Present a commonplace subject more imaginatively and with a greater variety of detail.
5. Possess a richer storehouse of images.
6. Show greater facility with the "true to life" appearance level.

[9] *Children's Art* (Berkeley: University of California Press, 1957), p. 49.
[10] *Art in Education* (Peoria, Ill.: Bennett, 1963), p. 183.
[11] *Understanding Children's Art for Better Teaching,* Chapter 6, *passim.*

Art Activities for Gifted Children

7. Are both original and fertile in their fantasies, and possess imaginative ability to an extraordinary degree.
8. Can more readily depict movement.
9. Can better handle symmetry.
10. Can use color with subtlety as well as brilliance, and are able to achieve contrast by well-balanced and integrated coloring.
11. Are more eager to explore media for original effects.
12. Display effective interplay between selective visual observations and a strong visual memory; retain impressions of things seen long ago.
13. Have a stronger desire to learn; ask for explanation and instruction.

Any discussion of the differences of art products of average and talented children must include mention of the studies conducted at the Cleveland Museum. In these studies, art products rather than behavior were analyzed; it was concluded that gifted children surpass their classmates in portraying motion, grouping objects (composition), using media, handling line, and in representational skills such as perspective.[12]

Using the points on which there was greatest consensus, we might construct a profile of a gifted child as follows. A gifted child observes acutely and has a vivid memory, is adept at handling problems requiring imagination, and is open to new experiences, yet can delve deeply into a limited area. The child takes art seriously and derives great personal satisfaction from the work. Indeed, the gifted child may sometimes be obsessive or compulsive about art work, often neglecting other areas of study for it.

Thus stated, this composite of the qualities of a gifted child reads very much like a list of acceptable goals for any art program. If this is so, can we not assume that the character and behavior of the gifted child provides us with very definite clues as to the nature of an art program for average students? This is mentioned as more hypothesis than recommendation, yet the idea seems worth pursuing.

As special programs for artistically gifted children have grown in number in both schools and museums, teachers have come to realize that many traits of creative behavior are shared by average or nonartistic as well as gifted children. Attitudes toward art such as self-direction and commitment merit attention and are best noted through observation. The following list of characteristics, both general and artistic, has been divided into categories of behavior relevant to artistic talent.[13]

[12] Thomas Munro, Betty Lark-Horovitz, and E. N. Bernhart, "Children's Art Abilities: Studies at the Cleveland Museum of Art," *Journal of Experimental Education*, Vol. 11, No. 2 (1942), pp. 97–155.
[13] Al Hurwitz, *Talent in Art* (Worcester, Ma.: Davis, 1982).

The rich variety of forms, ideas, and uses of the human figure in this drawing by a sixth grader shows a gifted child's range of interest and conceptualization. It also demonstrates the child's narrative sense, patience, and ability to depict a strong emotional experience. Nothing in the composition is static; everything is in a state of turmoil and change.

GENERAL CHARACTERISTICS

Precocity: Children who are gifted in art usually begin at an early age—in many cases before starting school and often as early as age 3.

Emergence through drawing: Giftedness first evinces itself through drawing, and for the most part will remain in this realm of expression until the child tries other forms of expression or becomes bored with drawing. Drawing dominates not only because it is accessible, but because it fulfills the need for rendering detail.

Art Activities for Gifted Children

Rapidity of development: All children progress through certain stages of visual development. The gifted child may traverse such stages at an accelerated pace, often condensing a year's progress into months or weeks.

Extended concentration: Visually gifted children stay with an artistic problem longer than others, because they both derive greater pleasure from it and see more possibilities in it.

Self-directedness: Gifted children are highly self-motivated and have the drive to work on their own.

This pencil drawing of a fruit stall is an example of acute observation and very personal handling of the medium. The gestural quality of line is advanced for a twelve-year-old; most youngsters of that age seek the security of more clearly defined forms.

Possible inconsistency with creative behavior: The behavior of the artistically gifted is not necessarily consistent with characteristics usually associated with creativity; in many cases the opposite may be true. The success won through long hours of practice is not easily relinquished in favor of journeys into the unknown. Young people's reluctance to make fools of themselves, to appear ridiculous, or to lose face before their peers tends to instill attitudes of extreme caution when confronting new problems.

Another twelve-year-old, an Italian girl, depicts a scene of student protest in her native Milan. Her handling of proportion, detail, and depth is sophisticated for her age group.

The class cartoonist may have more wit, inventiveness, and persistence than the "serious" artist. The ten-year-old boy who made this drawing had been interested in cartoons since the age of six. His drawing shows a keen observation of people, places, and events.

Art as an escape: The gifted child may use art as a retreat from responsibility and spend more than a normal amount of time drawing. This is often accompanied by the kind of fantasizing reflected in the artwork. No talent, however impressive, is beneficial if used as an escape from other realities, and precocity in and of itself should not absolve a child from fulfilling the same responsibilities required of others.

CHARACTERISTICS OF WORK

Verisimilitude, being true to life: Although most children develop the desire to depict people and other subjects from their environment in the upper elementary years, gifted children develop both the skills and the inclination at an earlier age.

Visual fluency: Perhaps the most significant of all, this characteristic is most similar to that of the trained artist. Visually fluent children may have more ideas than they have time to depict. Asked to draw a still life, they will include details missed by others; given a story to illustrate, they present many episodes rather than just one. They draw as spontaneously as most people talk, because through drawing they maintain a dialog with the world.

Complexity and elaboration: In their drawings, most children create "schemas" that are adequate to their needs; the gifted child goes beyond these and elaborates upon them, sometimes as an adjunct of story-telling or fantasizing, and sometimes for the sheer fun of adding details of clothes, body parts, or objects related to the schema. Wholes are related to parts as powers of recollection are tested and transformed into a growing repertoire of images.

Sensitivity to art media: Since one of the characteristics of giftedness is immersion, it is logical to assume that through hours of practice the child will master any media of particular interest. Where most fourth graders are content to use a color straight out of the box or tube, a gifted one may become quickly bored with packaged color and combine several colors to achieve desired effects. A child may be instinctively sensitive to what a particular medium can do, or may consciously try to attain mastery through practice. Older children (ages 10 to 12) are more apt to do this than are younger ones.

Random improvisation: Gifted children often doodle: they improvise with lines, shapes, and patterns, and seem conscious of negative areas or spaces between the lines and absorbed with the effects of lines. They transfer this interest to subjects such as the human face; like cartoonists, they experiment with the influence of minute changes on facial expression, noting the differences that the slightest shift in the direction of a line can make.

Table 13.1 is an attempt to place visual and artistic intelligence in an appropriate context. Using three categories—cognitive, artistic, and creative—it indicates the manifestation of each type in the child's behavior, the tests that identify each, and the artistic career suitable to each type.

Since all three areas reflect forms of intelligence, intelligence can be regarded not as a single characteristic but as a phenomenon that contains multiple ways of dealing with knowledge. Throughout the primary grades, the child is holistic and makes no distinctions between the three categories. Task commitment is an overriding cluster of attributes without which none of the other three kinds of intelligence can reach fruition. It should be noted, moreover, that all three realms may interact as they are influenced by three factors: environment, genetics, and personality. The last two factors, however, are less open to change than the first.

CASE HISTORIES OF GIFTED CHILDREN

Strong indications of the nature of talent may sometimes be found in case histories of artistically gifted people, but it is often difficult to unearth actual evidence of their early work. A child's art is usually lost, and both parents and teachers are generally unable to recall accurately the child's early behavior. For some cases, however, there are reasonably detailed and apparently accurate data.

TABLE 13.1

Defining Artistic Intelligence

Task Commitment: An Overriding Attitudinal Factor

Personal traits such as

Desire to succeed
Goal orientation
Persistence
Extended concentration
Positive self-image
Independent action

General Pool of Artistic Intelligence

Cognitive Characteristics (Convergent Thinking)	Artistic Characteristics (Convergent and Divergent Thinking)	Creative Characteristics (Divergent Thinking)
Verbal facility	Strong feelings	Problem-solving skills
Computational facility	Sensory attunement	Imagination
Abstract reasoning skills	Imaging impulse	Originality
Synthesizing ability	Visual fluency	Risk-taking
	Fluency of ideas	Elaboration
	Perceptual awareness	Flexibility
	Skills related to memory, spatial relationships, etc.	

Examples of Instruments for Identification†

Perceptual Acuity Test	Child's Aesthetic Judgment Test	Barron Threshold Test
Differential Aptitude (verbal, abstract, spatial, mechanical skills)	Hall Mosaic Construction Test	Torrance Tests for Creative Thinking
	Welsh Figure Preference Test	Purdue Creativity Tests
Barron Symbol Equivalents	Tests in Fundamental Abilities of Visual Arts (Lewerenz)	Southern California Tests of Divergent Production
Stanford-Binet Test		
Iowa Tests of Basic Skills (cognitive abilities)		
Otis Lennon Mental Ability		
Rutgers Drawing Test*		
Goodenough-Harris "Draw-a-Man" Test*		

Emergence of talent through drawing; branching into arts areas

Professional Levels

Draws on all modes of intelligence as required

Art director	Craftsperson	Architect
Art critic	Fine artist	Industrial designer
Art historian		Film, video, special effects technician

*Can have implications for artistic assessment.
†A full listing of tests is published by The Psychological Corporation, 757 Third Avenue, New York, N.Y. 10017.

Among these cases are the histories of two girls of the same age from upper-middle-class homes, Susan McF and Mary M.[14] These girls gave promise of talent in art very early in their lives. A study of their production shows that both of them began manipulating media just before they were a year old and that they had passed beyond the stage of manipulation before their second birthdays. Around fifteen months Susan was naming the marks she was producing in crayon. Mary did the same when she was sixteen months old. Around this age Mary began to use some spoken words clearly, but Susan was slower to learn to speak and instead was producing sounds such as "rrrr," which consistently stood for "automobile," and "goong" for "duck." When she depicted such objects in her paintings by the use of symbols, she named them in this vocabulary. When twenty-five months old, Susan produced an attractive montage with sticky tape and colored paper. Around twenty-seven months of age, both girls could delineate many different symbols and give them some relationship in the same composition.

Both children led normal, active lives and during warm weather neglected their art for outdoor games. A study of their work (which their parents carefully dated) reveals, however, that inactivity in art did not seem to interfere with their continuous development. By the time both children were three years old they were overlapping objects in their drawings and paintings, and at four Mary seemed to recognize texture as an expressive element of design. By six, they were skilled in a variety of techniques—toning colors, devising textural effects, and inventing outstanding compositions. Before she was seven, Mary even gave hints of linear perspective in her work. It is important to note that both girls attended elementary schools that apparently provided progressive and highly commendable art programs.

By the time Susan was ten years old and Mary ten years and eight months, their work had lost most of its childlike qualities. Each girl passed through a realistic stage in which objects were rendered rather photographically. Then Susan's work became distinctly mannered in its rhythms, and Mary's output became reminiscent of that of several artists. In quick succession, she went through an Aubrey Beardsley period, followed by one reflecting the influence of Degas and later of Matisse. When they were twelve years old, the girls first met and became friends. They attended the same art classes in high school and produced paintings in a style obviously derived from that of the Impressionists.

[14] Because each girl has highly educated parents who are especially interested in art and are knowledgeable about both child psychology and pedagogy, records of their art were preserved. The parents systematically filed the children's work after writing comments about each piece on its reverse side. Both children eventually enrolled in the Ontario classes for gifted children, at which time the parents disclosed the girls' records. The girls' I.Q.'s are as follows: Mary, 120; Susan, 130.

Art Activities for Gifted Children

Fortunately, their secondary-school art program proved almost as efficient as that of their elementary schooling. After a time their work became noticeably more personal. Eventually both girls attended special classes for children with artistic talent, where they remained for four years. Here they produced some sensitive paintings and sculpture in forms that continued to be recognizably personal. Both girls went on to attend a college of art where, according to their teachers, they gave evidence of outstanding artistic ability.

There seems to be little doubt that Mary and Susan were talented. What characteristics common to both might identify them as such? First, an almost lifelong preoccupation with art. Although their interest in art was at times intermittent, their production of art forms was for the most part uninterrupted. Second, both girls came from cultured homes in which the parents enjoyed artistic interests. Both environment and biological inheritance often contribute to talent. Children of artistic parents have the double advantage of artistic "nature" and artistic "nurture" often denied the children of parents who lack these interests and abilities.

Third, the progress of Mary and Susan throughout the phases of their childlike expression was both richer and more rapid than normal. Although both girls developed a skill in handling tools and materials that was obviously above average, neither allowed her skill to assume paramount importance in her output. Again, at one period the girls apparently became dominated by technique, and the work of other artists whom they admired strongly influenced their output. Fortunately, however, their insight into artistic processes and their personal integrity, intellectual vigor, and vision were sufficient to overcome these powerful influences, which can be very seductive to the gifted young person who seeks a satisfying means of artistic expression.

Another form of case history may be gathered from listening to the earliest memories of adult artists. When asked to reflect on their earliest artistic experiences, artists seem to have remarkable powers of recall. Much of what they describe, however, may on first reading appear to have little to do with conventional views of art. This is evidenced by the following reminiscence by a professor, art historian, and critic.

Let me emphasize at the outset that neither the concepts to which I refer, nor the vocabulary used to express them, were available in the milieu in which I grew up. Ideas like creativity, imagination, originality, and self-expression simply were not elements of the conceptual framework of my family, my friends, or my teachers until I entered high school. For example: I have been told by my parents that at the age of nine or ten months I would play with buttons for long periods of time, grouping them by size, shape, and color, and various combinations of these characteristics, as well as by the patterns and designs that I could form on the tray of my highchair. I could distinguish very subtle differences in color.

An old rabbi visited us and when he saw me playing thusly, he tried to confuse me by mixing buttons that were nearly alike. I got very angry, at which he commented that my activity was a sign of superior intelligence. My family accepted this judgment of "intelligence" rather than any thoughts of artistic ability or aesthetic sensitivity. As I grew up, family and friends interpreted my ability to paint and draw as a "gift" or an inherited trait.

We were a poor immigrant working-class family. My father was a cutter in a garment sweatshop. I had very few toys and preferred to play with household objects and spools of thread that my father brought from the factory.

I do remember that already at age two I was scribbling frantically and constantly on every available surface. I tore open grocery bags to make larger surfaces. At this age I remember being scolded for drawing on the sidewalk, the front stoop, and all over the steel-gray surface of the porch. I liked the light chalk lines on the dark background.

About the time of my third birthday, I became aware of the compulsiveness of what I was doing. My mother bought a new oilcloth to cover the kitchen table for Passover. I noticed that the backing was textured like canvas and I remember that *at that time*, I was conscious of my *compulsion qua compulsion* to draw on it. I knew beforehand that I would be spanked, but I literally could not stop myself. . . .

At about age 5 or 6 I made my own greeting cards, and as I learned to read and write, I combined pictures with words in many different ways. Magazine pictures, fabrics, candy wrappers, and other textures were added to my designs, although of course I had never heard of collage. I made my own comic books and I experimented with three-dimensional ideas such as pop-ups. . . .

"Pennsylvania," drawn from memory by a fifth grader a year after he moved away. He later attended art school and is now a successful furniture designer. Like most artists, he began by drawing far more frequently and intensely than his classmates did. For this drawing, the child's memory fueled his sense of structure and ability to create patterns from nature.

I was acknowledged as the "artist" of the school where, as with my family, the criterion for judging my work as good was my ability to draw and paint realistically. Consequently, this recognition was a kind of exploitation. . . . I spent very little time in the classroom. I was released from classes to paint hall murals, Christmas murals, stage sets, and posters.

There were no art books in the school. When I was about nine years old, I started to copy paintings from art books in the public library and soon commenced to make composite copies of the great masters. At about this time, the librarian refused to let me borrow books on Greek sculpture. "I know why you want them," she said. "You want to look at the dirty pictures." [15]

Burt Silverman, a well-known illustrator, recalls his childhood in art is as follows.

Beginnings

I was born in Brooklyn in 1928. Compared to many kids born during the Depression, I had a comfortable childhood. But by current middle class standards, my cultural life was really rather deprived. No puppet shows, children's theaters, museum tours, or marvelously illustrated children's books. Yet something *was* different for me. I could draw very well. I also had parents who recognized that painting pictures *could* be a valid substitute for the Stradivarius. I'm sure that they were also encouraged by the fact that my talents were clearly recognized by others. Special attention at school—a sense of being better at art than the other kids—made up for the fact that I was a rotten third baseman on the stickball team.

I drew and painted that special world of daydreams and fantasies that is so much a part of a child's life. My pictures were images of faraway places and exotic people—sunset landscapes, sailing ships, and ancient Roman soldiers. (Indeed, these were the characteristic elements of the Romantic paintings of the nineteenth century; years later I discovered Turner and Constable with a sense of immediate recognition.) I was fascinated by illustrations in romantic adventure stories for kids. I lay in wait lustfully for N. C. Wyeth's and Howard Pyle's books in the local library. Beset by boyhood reveries, I drew pictures to give them substance, and I attempted to draw them as realistically as possible.

My efforts were reinforced by the admiration of my peers and adults alike. And so at the age of nine, I got thirty-five cents every Saturday morning for the subway ride (and a malted) to Pratt Institute's children's classes.

I was also given my first art book at this time. It was a history of Northern European Renaissance artists like Van Eyck and Van der Weyden—strange names and forbiddingly austere paintings of people in long cloaks. I began to learn of a whole new world of great art. Other books followed. One in particular, called *Modern American Painting*, was a favorite. It was a

[15] Dr. Phyllis Gold Gluck, Brooklyn College, N.Y. Used by permission.

pictorial survey of American art from the Colonial period up to the late 1930s, with marvelous full-page reproductions of Homer, Whistler, Ryder, and Sargent. I was nine or ten years old when I painted my first oil, a copy of Hopper's *Lighthouse*, from this book. But curiously enough, I had never seen an original painting, nor even the *outside* of a museum or gallery. In those days a kid from Brooklyn went to Manhattan only to see a specialist.

The World's Fair

That was all to change, however, with the arrival of the first New York World's Fair in 1939. For with it came a mammoth exhibition of the world's great masterpieces. The show was dazzling in its scope and quality, covering 400 years of Western art and including all the giants—Caravaggio, Rembrandt, Velásquez, Tintoretto, Veronese, Titian, and on and on. I wandered awestruck through the three vast pavilions. I felt a surge of excitement that was to transform me. I'd had no prior experience to prepare me for the impact of these paintings. The size and color—the *aliveness* of the work—hit me almost like a physical blow. But it was the more naturalistic painters who were especially absorbing. The paintings of Eakins, Homer, and Sargent were breathtaking. I couldn't believe that it was possible for anyone to *really* paint these pictures. Even now, I can recall the feeling: a childlike gasp, almost an unwillingness to look too long, lest it somehow be "used up."

I came away from that show forever stamped a realist. I wasn't aware then of any movements in art history or even of the concept of realism. But the paintings suddenly brought into focus all my aspirations about art. I wanted to paint the world as beautifully—and as accurately—as those great artists did. To this moment, I can say that some of that original feeling still persists—that thirsting for the world made more real through paint.[16]

Silverman, Gluck, and many other artists have certain memories in common—parents who were ignorant of art yet sympathetic to their children's interests; an impulse to copy; and an affinity for realism. Their first experiences with museums were definitely positive, and, as with many writers and actors, their lives as children were particularly rich in fantasy, daydreams, and reveries.

THE EVALUATION OF TALENT

Witty says that "perhaps it is desirable . . . to consider any child gifted whose performance, in a potentially valuable line of human activity, is consistently remarkable."[17] This statement can be accepted in relation to a creative field such as art only if the phrase "consistently remarkable" is interpreted broadly. Because people employed in art are continually exploring new fields, they cannot always be expected to produce work of a

[16] Burt Silverman, *Painting People* (New York: Watson-Guptill, 1977), p. 10.
[17] Paul Witty, "The Gifted Child," *Exceptional Children*, Vol. 19 (April 1953), p. 255.

Art Activities for Gifted Children

consistently high quality. Sometimes their experiments fail and then their efforts, however commendable, will probably result in bad art. The art careers of both Susan and Mary show ups and downs. "Consistently remarkable" must therefore allow for plateaus as well as peaks of productivity.

There is no denying, however, that "gifted is as gifted does." The child whose performance in art more often than not is "remarkable" may be suspected of being gifted. Such a child will almost inevitably possess above-average intelligence, display skill beyond the ordinary, give noticeable evidence of sensitivity in organizing the elements of design, and be capable of producing work bearing the stamp of a distinctive personality.

Because the data used in the evaluation of talent must be subjective to a degree, judgment cannot be made either lightly or hastily.[18] Herbert A. Carroll, in his study of teachers' judgments of children's intelligence,[19] discovered that only 15.7 percent of students suggested by 6,000 teachers were accurately assessed, a fact corroborated by another report issued by the Education Policies Commission.[20] The teacher who suspects a child of possessing unusual artistic talent might be wise to enlist the opinions of others, including artists and art teachers. Opinions of such well-informed people, furthermore, might well be sought over a relatively long period of time. A sudden appearance of talent may later prove to be merely a remarkable but temporary development of skill. Again, what appears to be artistic talent in early years may disappear as the child develops other interests into which energies and abilities are channeled.

When teachers want information on a particular aspect of talent, they can devise certain tasks to reveal particular skills. Characteristics to be studied in the area of art might include observational ability; color sensitivity; ability to fuse drawing and imagination; emotional expressiveness; memory; handling of space; sensitivity to media.[21]

The problem of assessing giftedness continues throughout a child's school career. Those who are most concerned with its identification are the admissions personnel of art schools. While the traditional means of admission rests on the applicant's portfolio (which reflects the child's capabilities in drawing, color, or design), many art schools have for some time used other criteria for admission, such as problem-solving abilities, evidence of creative thinking, and personality traits that are assessed through personal interviews. In other words, an alert student with a flexible and inventive mind may now have an advantage over an applicant whose main talent lies in skillful watercolors.

---

[18] A discussion of objective art tests will be found in Chapter 17.

[19] *Genius in the Making* (New York: Hill & Wang, 1940).

[20] *The Education of Gifted Children*, Bulletin of the National Art Education Association (December 1957).

[21] For specific suggestions see Hurwitz, *Talent in Art.*

The system of identification that is based on both time and the opinion of many specialists seems to function with reasonable efficiency.[22] In the Ontario experiment, pupils who, in the opinion of their classroom teachers and art consultants, had talent were recommended to attend special art classes. Recommendations were based not only on their ability in art, but also on their intelligence rating and success in other areas of school life. After pupils had attended the special classes for eight months, the staff passed judgment on their progress. If, in the unanimous opinion of the staff members, pupils had failed to show outstanding talent, they were usually removed from the classes so that room was made for other, more promising pupils. By these procedures the staff seemed to be able to select only the most gifted children with whom to do research.

In the special art classes offered the children of the Newton schools, the major criterion for admission was commitment to art rather than talent as such. These special classes demonstrated that skill did indeed improve in many instances, once children worked in an environment of a shared enthusiasm. The classes were specifically designed for those whose hunger for art was simply not satisfied by the amount of activity the normal school could allow.

Special Arrangements in Art for Gifted Children

When gifted children have been identified, the problem concerning suitable educational treatment for them arises. An "enriched" program may be offered by the classroom teacher or art consultant whereby the pupil is assigned advanced work, given special materials, and allowed to take time from other obligations to work in art. The danger here is that the classroom teacher might not be equipped to provide special help, or that excusing the child from nonart activities to work in art might arouse adverse reactions from the rest of the class. We also must bear in mind the negative attitude that many teachers take toward children who are particularly nonconformist in their creative behavior.

Another arrangement for helping the gifted is the "special class" in which only talented children are enrolled. Such classes may be offered during school hours, after school, or on Saturday mornings. Educators believe these classes provide the best solution to the problem of meeting

---

[22] For a description of two other systems of selection, see Havighurst and others, *A Survey of the Education of Gifted Children*. Neither the Quincy nor the Portland test described in this publication seems to be wholly acceptable. The Quincy test apparently includes such items as the drawing of "stick men," which can scarcely be described as art activity in any sense. The Portland test appears to rely to some degree either on a laissez-faire technique in which the pupils are given "free choice" of subject matter, or on assigned subjects in which, as far as one can ascertain from the account, the pupils may have little or no real interest. For further discussion about "identifying the child talented in art," see Witty, "The Gifted Child."

the needs of the gifted. Teachers can be engaged who possess capabilities in special artistic fields. Much as a sympathetic teacher of general subjects may help a gifted child in art, a specialist can provide even more assistance. In the special classes the need to provide for individual differences will be even more apparent. According to David Manzella:

> These classes should be taught by producing and exhibiting art educators or by professional artists. They should be real studio experiences with a real aura of art about them—not ersatz . . . fabrications. These would not be general art classes in which a little of this and a little of that was presented, and a ceramist taught painting, and a painter, weaving. My recommendation would be to secure the services of good artists who love to teach and are sympathetic with and have an understanding of children and young people. And I would have these artists teach in whatever medium and in whatever way they found most satisfactory. . . . The nature of the particular medium is not important. A youngster's abilities can be challenged and nurtured by good teaching in all forms of the visual arts.[23]

Whatever special arrangements are made for the child with artistic talent, two considerations of paramount importance to the child's future development must be kept in mind. In the first place, on no account should the child's artistic development be unduly hastened into adult forms of expression. In the elementary school, the talented youngster is still a youngster, and artistic growth must occur with due regard for this fact. "Overstimulation, growing from the drive of eager adults . . . has often killed the child's urge for artistic expression."[24] Even so, in the second place, every talented child must be provided with sufficient challenge to work to capacity. Unless this condition prevails, the gifted pupil may lose interest in the work, and considerable energies and abilities may be dissipated in less worthwhile ways.

Under what circumstances will talent flourish? To begin with, the home should, at best, encourage an interest in art and, at worst, not discourage it. While it may be true in some cases that, no matter what the circumstances, "genius will out," a sympathetic home environment is extremely stimulating. The home that provides suitable art media, a library of art books, and a convenient place to work, together with loving and intelligent parents to admire the work being produced and to encourage further production, will aid substantially in fostering talent. Next, the elementary and secondary schools that the gifted pupil attends should provide a sufficiently stimulating and challenging art program. Finally, somewhere along the line of artistic progress, the gifted pupil should be afforded special opportunities for the cultivation of talent and should have

[23] *Educationists and the Evisceration of the Visual Arts* (Scranton, Pa.: International Textbook, 1963), pp. 91–92.
[24] Viktor Lowenfeld, *Your Child and His Art* (New York: Macmillan, 1954), p. 176.

A ten-year-old girl in the special art classes at the Pioneer Youth Palace in Moscow. Children in these classes are encouraged to work large in clay-modeling and to combine animal and human forms into fantastic figures.

the opportunity to encounter a supportive teacher who is sensitive to any capabilities that set the gifted child apart from other pupils. Some questions teachers and administrators might ask themselves when identifying and planning for gifted children are the following:

> Have I notified the parents that their child has special talents that deserve support?
>
> In dealing with gifted children, am I being overly solicitous—giving more attention than needed?
>
> Am I adding an appreciative or critical dimension to the activities by showing and discussing artworks that are related to studio activities?
>
> Have I investigated any sources of additional help from the community, such as special classes in museums?
>
> Do I have rapport with the children? Do they respect my opinions?
>
> Has their ability in self-appraisal improved?
>
> Do I know how to deal with and interpret the extreme attitudes sometimes displayed by gifted children?

Suitable Art Activities

It is unwise to offer the gifted a curriculum that is oriented primarily toward media. The talented child can be challenged by ideas as well as by materials in special classes. Moreover, there should be opportunities for students to work in one area in depth.[25] A conceptual approach to art

[25] The Saturday morning classes in the Newton Schools of Newton, Mass., offer in-depth approaches to such activities as drawing, painting, and filmmaking. Student interest has been high over the year—95 percent of those attending elected to remain in the area they first chose rather than change at the semester break.

activities begins with an idea and then asks the child to use materials merely as a means of solving a problem. The problem may be stated as follows: "One characteristic of human beings is that they design their environment for pleasure and for aesthetic purposes as well as for function and utility. In creating your own environment, take into consideration purpose, scale, and materials." Stating the problem in this manner opens up a number of choices for the student and encourages decision-making that is different from the kind that results when the child is given such directions as: "On the table you will find cardboard, pins, knives, and rulers. These are the materials to be used in making a scale model of a vacation home."

A series of sculpture lessons might be used as a focal point for the idea of *opposition*—that is, of hard and soft, open and closed forms. The children are encouraged to obtain an understanding of this concept through their own investigation of the materials. This approach obviously offers greater opportunity for growth in problem-solving than is allowed by concentrating only on how to use a particular medium. The gifted children in the special class, then, can be guided away from object-making into the kind of visual thinking that might not occur until a later stage.

The teacher of the special class or the art consultant teaching in an after-school program should take an inventory of art activities offered prior to the special class in order to better plan the new program. Thus a child who is interested in sculpture but has worked only in clay might try a large-scale plaster or wood carving. In printmaking, a child who has worked only in linoleum may try a woodcut, or one who has handled both of these could attempt a multicolor silkscreen or any other problem beyond the capabilities of the other children. These activities extend the range of the child's experience and serve to compensate for the relatively limited exposure to the art in the regular school program.

Gifted children demonstrate a number of peculiarities in their selection of art activities. Their interests in such basic types of art work as cartooning, still life, landscape, portraiture, and sculpture develop early, and they appear to find greater challenge and deeper satisfaction in these than they do in some of the craft fields such as weaving and paper construction. While they may occasionally turn to these for their novelty, they generally return with renewed interest to what might be described as the more classic or traditional art forms, possibly because these art forms afford an opportunity to display the children's special brand of precocity.

Gifted children usually prefer to work at art by themselves rather than participate in group endeavors. Although as a group the gifted are socially inclined, they seem to recognize in art a subject that demands individual deliberation and effort. They are not entirely adverse to participating in puppet shows, mural-making, and other art forms requiring a pooled effort, but most are happiest when they are submerged as individuals in artistic problems.

GENERAL ACTIVITIES

In working on this landscape, a ten-year-old girl showed a strong affinity for oil paint. This was her first painting and was followed by many more in oils, before she moved on to other media.

PAINTING IN OILS

Painting in oils is a good example of a special activity suitable for the gifted. It offers the student an effective means of identifying with "real artists." The oils are rich and sensual in color and are far more versatile than most water-based paints. The slow-drying quality of oil paint makes it suitable for art projects undertaken over a period of time. By the time they reach preadolescence, gifted children should have had an opportunity to work with it. However, not even the most gifted children can use it effectively until they have had experience with many other types of paint.[26]

OTHER MEDIA FOR DRAWING AND PAINTING

Gifted pupils in the preadolescent stage will find several other challenging media that may not be available in the regular art program. Some of the more expensive colored drawing inks, for example, might be used in conjunction with India ink or in some of the mixed-media techniques mentioned in Chapter 6. Work with steel pens and pointed brushes might be explored. Charcoal and conté crayon in black and brown can also be used fairly extensively, either in quick sketching or in more deliberate drawing.

[26] See Ralph Mayer, *The Painter's Craft*, 2nd ed. (New York: Van Nostrand, 1966); Frederic Taubes, *The Technique of Oil Painting* (New York: Dodd, Mead, 1946); Max Doerner, *The Materials of the Artist*, rev. ed., trans. by Eugene Neuhaus (New York: Harcourt Brace Jovanovich, 1949); W. G. Constable, *The Painter's Workshop* (New York: Oxford University Press, 1954). These publications are clearly written and cover the subject in sufficient detail. Before holding classes in oil painting, a teacher should not only be able to paint but also be familiar with at least one of these books.

Some of this line drawing might lead to a consideration of etching and other graphic processes like dry-point, aquatint, and mezzotint.[27]

Some gifted children in the preadolescent stage become proficient in the use of various types of watercolor. In the opinion of many painters, transparent watercolor is one of the most subtle and difficult of media. It must be used with precision and speed, and its "wetness," or watery character, should be reflected in the finished work. Good watercolor paints, brushes, and especially papers are relatively expensive. The pigments in tubes are more convenient to use than those in cake form. When gifted pupils begin to paint seriously in watercolors, they should be provided with materials of a higher quality than is usually found in the school art program. The many acrylic paints on the market offer colors as intense as oils as well as quick drying properties. Gouache is similar in handling to oils and acrylic paints; it dries quickly and, unlike tempera, is both water soluble and, when dry, waterproof. The use of these media may require demonstrations, which specialists are usually more capable of handling than classroom teachers.

It would be a mistake, however, to be preoccupied with adding more kinds of media. Instead, the emphasis should be upon the nature of the art problem (more challenging) and the instruction (more specific, where needed), and upon the creation of additional time, preferably in a peer group. Teachers should require more of gifted children, set higher standards of work, and be more directive when the occasion demands it. Instruction, therefore, differs as much in intensity as in kind.

Teaching the Gifted Child

The young gifted child will, of course, make use of the usual materials and perform the basic activities mentioned in earlier chapters in connection with the general art program for normal children. Since the gifted can be recognized only over a period of time, they must obviously take part in the art program designed for all until their talent is discovered. When it is clear that individuals possess gifts above the ordinary, the teacher, using the teaching principles suggested in Chapter 2, can help the children to progress at their optimum level of accomplishment. This may be done through any art form. In drawing and painting, it means more drawing and painting; in sculpture, more three-dimensional activities. Progress in art occurs when the worker keeps producing art. Mere quantity of production or

[27] See Victor D'Amico, *Creative Teaching in Art*, rev. ed. (Scranton, Pa.: International Textbook, 1966) for a description of these processes. Before exposing gifted children to any of them, a teacher should be skilled in the use of all relevant tools and materials. Furthermore, the teacher should have a well-equipped room in which the children can explore the processes.

repetition of forms previously created is not progress, but production that leads to improved skill, more penetrating insight, and greater mastery of media will help to develop a child's talent.

The principle of teaching in response to the needs of the learner has been emphasized throughout this book. The preceding chapter observed that, in order to profit from art at all, some slow learners need to be subjected to a step-by-step method of instruction. With the gifted the reverse is necessary. Here the teacher is faced with the necessity for what might be described as "under-teaching." Every attempt must be made to challenge the greater abilities of gifted children. Whenever they can learn a fact or a technique for themselves, they should do so. Assistance must in general be withheld until the children have explored their own avenues for solutions to their problems. Gifted pupils who are given this type of educational treatment thrive on it, and so does their art.

Whether in a special classroom or as individuals in a normal classroom, artistically gifted children must be continually challenged with drawing and painting and three-dimensional media of all types, and with examples of fine production in these media. Artistically gifted children are normally motivated to express themselves with drawing and painting media. They should always have access to fine works of art in the media of their choice or, failing the actual works, good reproductions of them. The teacher should suggest certain outstanding works for them to study at art galleries and museums. Talented children can be assumed to be capable of extending their passion for creating works of art to the appreciation or criticism of art. Art works should be discussed—both for their own sake and for the problems they pose as regards the work currently in progress.

The teacher will have to make special efforts with gifted pupils from underprivileged homes to encourage them to see the best art and to read good books on art. Gifted children from well-endowed homes generally have many opportunities to add to their knowledge of art. Underprivileged children enjoy few, if any, such opportunities. Indeed, their gift must often be an especially vital one if it is to survive. In their case, the teacher's duty is to supply the inspiration and sources of knowledge that their home environment has denied them.

It was noted earlier that gifted pupils, evidently sensing the importance of personal expression in art, tend to prefer individual to group activity. However, when gifted learners are found in general classrooms, their classmates often elect them to key positions in the committees established to perform group work. Indeed, they are frequently elected to chairmanships of various enterprises. With their special abilities in art, these children are thus placed in a position to do much of the difficult work, thereby depriving their classmates of tasks that they should do themselves. Gifted children, however, should not be encouraged to dominate the activities of the class. Fortunately, gifted pupils tend to be well adjusted in other ways, and a teacher can appeal to their reason and good judgment

Art Activities for Gifted Children

with better than average results. Hence, when gifted pupils appear to be assuming more than their share of responsibility in group work, a short, forthright, and friendly discussion about the situation usually results in their relinquishing some tasks to their fellow classmates.

In cases where a group of gifted pupils shows a disinclination to perform group work in art, it seems reasonable to suggest that the teacher respect their wishes. After all, the pupils are probably well adjusted socially without group work. Whatever further practice they need in working cooperatively can be assigned in other areas of learning, thus leaving them free to exercise their remarkable individual talents in art—the area best suited for a personal contribution.

Activities for the Reader

1. Study some children considered to be artistically gifted. Make a note of their outstanding personal qualities and work habits, and their attitude toward their contemporaries.
2. Make a collection of drawings and paintings by artistically gifted children. Analyze the work for its subject matter, design, and technique. Compare this collection with one composed of the work of normal children of the same chronological ages as those in the gifted group.
3. Study the home environment of several artistically gifted pupils. How does this environment rate culturally and economically?
4. Set up a still-life arrangement and sketch it on paper in pencil or ink. Then outline the general composition in thin paint on canvas and begin to paint with oils or acrylics. It is wise to keep to a few pigments at first—say, one bright one, like yellow, and umber, black, and white. Paint bold strokes with medium thick paint on the areas having middle light values. Later add highlights in thicker paint, using a palette knife if desired. Paint the shadow areas in thinner paint.
5. Paint a landscape or portrait in oils, but continue to keep the number of colors restricted.
6. Contact some artists and request that they lend you a drawing from their schooldays, if one still exists. Talk to several artists and ask them to recall their earliest associations with art. Recount similar associations of your own.
7. Get a copy of the Advanced Placement course description in studio art. How is giftedness implied in the description of the course requirements?

Suggested Readings

Baker, Catherine. *The Innocent Artists*. Pool, England: Blandford, 1980. A personal record of an art teacher's experiences in Papua New Guinea. Vivid evidence that exceptional visual sensitivity exists as a phenomenon in all cultures.

Carl, Florence. *The Artist in Each of Us*. New York: Pantheon, 1951. Contains a number of valuable case studies of artistic children.

Gardner, Howard. *Artful Scribbles: The Significance of Children's Drawings*. New York: Basic Books, 1980. See "Portraits of an Adolescent Artist" and the account of Nadia (pp. 180–91) for one of the few references to the subject of artistic talent.

Hurwitz, Al. *Talent in Art*. Worcester, Ma.: Davis, 1982.

RELATING ART TO THE GENERAL CURRICULUM

The only value of integrated work is when it enables the art teacher to achieve all he could have achieved previously plus the bonus of breadth of study and the excitement of working in a mutually sympathetic relationship with a colleague from another discipline.*

fOURTEEN

Stimulus for valid artistic expression may derive from any area of a child's life. If a child is genuinely moved by an experience, it makes little difference from an artistic standpoint what the source of stimulation is. Since children live a large part of their lives in school, one might expect that many situations found in play or study at school can promote expression. Such, in fact, is the case. Life at school may, and indeed should, be the source of many and varied significant artistic statements.

*From Maurice Barrett, *Art Education* (London: Heinemann, 1979), p. 125.

The Nature of Correlation:
Art as an Integrative Force

That other subjects should serve as a basis for children's art work is educationally sound in principle. In Chapter 1 we noted that whereas the mechanistic psychologists believed that learning can best occur when school subjects are broken down into their smallest parts, the Gestalt psychologists disputed this assertion and asserted the reverse is true. Wholes, not parts, are primary, they asserted. Learning occurs best not when subjects are dissected, but when they are combined.

Through the practice of correlation, school subjects formerly considered discrete are closely related. Reading, composition, spelling, grammar, and handwriting, for example, have become one area of study known as the "language arts," and history, geography, and civics are called "social studies." As a result of such groupings of subject matter, the pupils are said to gain greater insight into all the areas of learning involved.

Further grouping occurs in the unit (or "area" or "experience") curriculum. Here, the broad areas of learning that result from correlation of subjects are superseded by even broader themes. In place of "language arts," "social studies," and "general science," one may find in some school curriculums such items as "living together in the home," "how people make a living," or "how we are fed, clothed, and sheltered." In working on these themes, children are able to learn many facts related to various subject areas and to develop the necessary skills in such areas as spelling, computing, and penmanship. A large part of the day is spent in doing research on the main theme and the problems associated with it, during which time the pupils may draw, write, read, sing, build, and measure. A part of each day is set aside not only for the evaluation of products and

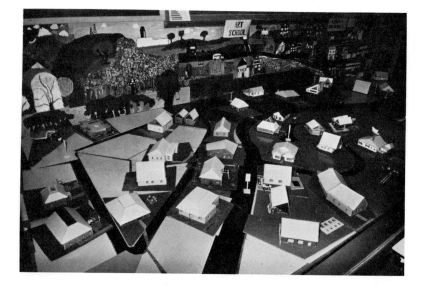

The environment studied through art experiences can range from the classroom to the home, neighborhood, town, and city. Using the city as a core subject, a combined fifth and sixth grade studied everything from legal institutions to the metric system. After learning about the city as a topic in art history, the class prepared posters and other graphics and painted the background mural for the city they "designed." The project, which lasted a full semester, took place at the Hyde School, Newton, Massachusetts.

procedures, but also for the practice of skills that the learners need to improve. In a well-conducted unit, pupils are able to develop skills in a functional manner that rivals in efficiency the methods of developing skills by drills used when subjects are studied independently. Besides helping pupils to learn facts and develop skills, the unit approach provides ample opportunities for them to develop social skills in group activities. The children must cooperate with one another for the successful outcome of their efforts (see Chapter 11).

Schools may someday place art within a broader context of a "related arts" division, so that art, music, dance, and drama can have perhaps the same status that nature study, biology, physics, and chemistry now enjoy under the more general heading of "science." The number of articles, conferences, and grants relating art to other areas of learning indicates a national trend toward new liaisons for art specialists.[1]

CORRELATIONS IN ART

Three main directions seem to be followed by the many new programs now being developed. These are (1) the use of art to develop varieties of sensory awareness, (2) integration within the various arts, and (3) the integration of art with academic subjects. The conscious seeking of relationships between separate disciplines is assumed to be educationally desirable in any discussion of art beyond its customary function. If one examines the "grass roots of art," to borrow Sir Herbert Read's phrase, the distinctive qualities of visual art become less apparent as one compares the formal characteristics of art to those of its neighbors. As an example, design features such as line, rhythm, and pattern have their counterparts in music, drama, and dance. For this reason, design components are often used as the basis for many related art programs. The visual arts all involve perception, emotion, and the creative processes: a love of manipulation (of both forms and materials), a delight in sensations, and considerable pleasure in the contemplation as well as creation of structured experiences.

It is precisely because of these shared characteristics of art that art is so suitable as an adjunct of other activities. Since the major interest in the correlation of art with the general curriculum lies in its integration with academic subjects, this chapter will focus on that area. Before we examine this direction, however, let us look at a few examples of the way art is employed in the first two areas mentioned above.

ART AND SENSORY AWARENESS

In this instance, art is used more to enhance a process that gives children a more vivid awareness of some aspect of themselves than to achieve a product. In many cases, however, a sensory exercise can be a vivid prelim-

[1] An indication of interest in this area was the NAEA-sponsored "mini-conference" on "Art in Interdisciplinary Contexts" (Boston: October 1973). See also Al Hurwitz, "Integrated Arts in the Public Schools," *Issues in Art Education*, Vol. 1, No. 5 (1970–71).

Left: as the "surrogate artist," one student tries to draw "through" another. To achieve success, the two must cooperate closely. Close cooperation is also needed in "blind sculpture," which involves working with an "invisible" partner. (Photos by Roger Graves.)

inary to the creation of a painting or sculpture. Below are listed a number of activities based on the theme "Receiving and Responding Through Art."

1. *Speaking the Pattern:* The class is divided into pairs. The partners sit back to back, each with a set of matching cut-paper shapes. Partner A builds a composition using the design units, while partner B attempts to build the same pattern using only A's verbal directions. When the design is complete, A and B look at their designs and discuss any mismatching. Question: Was mismatching the result of a failure in communication on A's part or in listening on B's part?

2. *Surrogate Artist:* A draws slowly with a finger on B's back. B then attempts to reconstruct with chalk or crayon the image A has developed. Questions: Is A going too fast? Is B attending closely enough to the image produced by A?

3. *Blind Sculpture:* A and B are both blindfolded and not allowed to speak. Thus neither knows the identity of the other. A piece of clay is placed between the partners, and they are asked to create together a piece of sculpture using only the cues communicated through the clay and each other's fingers. Music may be played throughout the experience. Question: Are A and B responding to the changes in the clay produced by each other?

Blind sculpture may also be extended into a visual stage. Children can join the individual sculptures by twos, then extend the connections until all pieces flow together in one rambling work. Questions: Where are the connecting points? Where can you join a shape so that it continues the flow of the forms?

The above exercises are intended to encourage children to pay careful attention to each other and to develop powers of concentration. In all cases the process is indeed the product, with the end result simply emerging as a record of the process.

In a situation in which the different arts interrelate in a broad context, some principle or concept is selected because it is a part of the artistic experience, while at the same time existing separately from a particular art category. Let us take one concept that many artists face at various times in their careers—*improvisation*—and examine its possibilities as a "connector" between several art forms.

As a rule, improvisations do not allow any preplanning. They are spontaneous acts that are created from moment to moment, using some stimulus in the immediate situation as a point of departure. Improvisations always call on the inventiveness of the participants, thus developing such creative attributes as flexibility, fluency, and imagination. Participants in improvisational situations learn to respond to the moment at hand and to trust in their ability to embellish, expand, and develop an idea. Below are several suggested improvisational activities organized by category.

RELATIONSHIPS WITHIN THE ARTS

VISUAL ARTS
1. *Graphic Improvisation:* Pupil A draws a line, B counters with another, and C follows suit. The idea is to work from the previous image, relating new images as intimately as possible to the preceding ones, thus provoking each pupil to respond immediately to the partners' work. Have each pupil use individual colors, or have them all use one color as a means of gaining cohesiveness. The criterion for success is the sense of unity that is attained.
2. *Musical Improvisation:* Select two or three violently contrasting musical pieces (such as Mozart's *Eine kleine Nachtmusik* and Ravel's *Bolero*). While listening to each, pupils can allow their crayons to roam freely over sheets of paper. They should allow themselves to respond completely to the suggestiveness of the music, especially in terms of color and rhythm. When the music has ended, set up a section of the wall on which to hang the pictures for class criticism and discuss differences and similarities in structure, choice of colors, and the like.
3. *Word Images:* The teacher calls out words that have strong emotional overtones, and the pupils improvise drawings suggested by

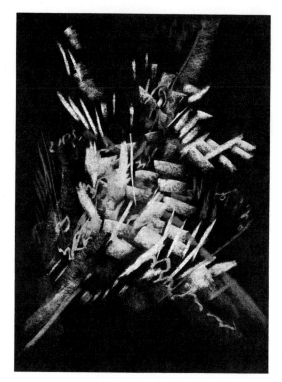

A chalk drawing on black paper by a gifted boy in the sixth grade, based on the "Saber Dance" from Khachaturian's *Gayne Ballet,* Suite No. 1.

the words. As an alternative, pupils can respond with their bodies, reacting either physically or pictorially to onomotopoetic words such as *explosion, piston,* and *eggbeater.*

DRAMA

Situational Improvisations: Select several pupils and ask them to imagine themselves in the following situation. Two people are making camp in a deserted place. At some point, two unknown people appear on the scene. The pupils should decide for themselves what roles or characters they are playing and why they are in this place. All players should agree on where this place is, but neither pair of participants should know in advance the roles the other pair has decided to adopt. What would the members of each pair say? Does a plot or "situation" develop out of the dialog? An infinite number of variations on this scene can be developed.

Another improvisation can be developed by setting the scene at the departure gate of an airport near which a number of people are waiting. At some point the teacher interjects an unexpected occurrence: announcing that the flight is cancelled or that there has been an accident; or instructing another student to play a

Relating Art to the General Curriculum

hijacker, to become violently ill, or to behave in some eccentric manner. The participants should know nothing of the teacher's plan in advance of the scene; they should respond to the incident as they would in a life situation.

After dramatic improvisation has been completed, the class can draw or paint their visualization of the setting. The children should try to be as spontaneous in their art work as in their acting.

MOVEMENT AND MUSIC

Sculpture Machines: The class is divided into four groups. A leader is selected for each group and creates a "living sculpture," designing the team for visual interest as well as for the possibility of movement. Each member of the team should adopt a frozen posture showing movement of the torso, arms, or legs. Working to the music of a Sousa march, for instance, the sculpture should activate itself in time to the musical beat. The basic form of the sculpture (the position of the pupils) remains in place while the separate parts (their bodies) move.

Connections and Sequences. Although the arts lend themselves to many styles of related instruction, teachers must learn to distinguish between forced and natural ways of connecting one experience to another. If the planning for sequences of activities can be shared by two or more arts specialists, the pooling of ideas can lead to rich possibilities for arts experiences. One arts area can provide motivation for another and so on, creating a sequential flow of activities. *Exercises* can free the body and attune it to *movement* to music, which in turn can set the stage for a more *formalized dance experience*. Since there is no dance without *rhythm*, exploration and creation of rhythmic patterns can lead to *creating sound-making instruments*. Rhythm can also be translated visually into *large-scale drawings* based on principles of conducting (imagine holding a brush instead of a baton). Making a spontaneous *graphic* record of a musical experience can then provide the basis for more thoughtful works, developed with care at the student's own pace rather than that of the music.

Experiences in related arts can also be connected through the grouping of activities around some common element. For example, *observation* is a skill that actors use in studying characteristics of various kinds of people (babies and very old people have their own way of walking, for example—hesitant, halting, insecure). Such observation helps in the actor's creation of a character. Artists use their powers of observation as a means of memory development and analysis of form. *Memory* can be developed, as can visual acuity; many kinds of artists store and call upon recollected experience. The actor must learn the lines of *King Lear*, the pianist commits musical scores to memory before a concert, the dancer must recall dozens of minute bodily movements within fixed time frames, and the artist develops a mental storehouse of shapes. *Improvisation* is part of every actor's training; and the painter who develops an image from each preceding stage without any preplanning or the jazz trombonist who picks up cues from what the clarinetist is playing, also is improvising. These are three of the many shared characteristics of the arts that suggest groupings of activities.

Sensory Experiences as Motivation. An arts sensory experience can be used as motivation for another activity. This arrangement differs from the groups of independent or separate exercises previously mentioned, which share a larger unifying idea. In the arts sensory experience, each activity prepares the child for and is subordinate to some culminating activity. In the independent exercises, all activities are seen as equals and ends in themselves, and have in common one core idea. Below are a few examples of both approaches. A sensory activity can also be so close to another art form that it is difficult to separate them; because of this, such activities are referred to as arts sensory experiences.

SENSORY ACTIVITIES AS MOTIVATION FOR ART

1. *Kinetic Body Sculpture.* Stage 1: The class is divided into teams of four, three of whom will be parts of a sculpture machine (see page 407) while the fourth is the "designer." The designer arranges the other three into a single piece, then animates it by setting different body parts in motion. Stage 2. The class draws an imaginary machine based on the kinetic body sculpture just created. Stage 3 (culminating activity). Each student writes a composition describing the function of the machine.
2. *Picture People:* Stage 1. The class is divided into teams of four or five, each with a reproduction of a painting of people, such as Cézanne's *Card Players* (see Chapter 3). The teams have ten minutes to plan an improvisation in which each team member assumes the position of one of the people in the picture. Stage 2. Each child draws a picture involving people in some predicament. When finished, each picture is passed to another child, who is given five minutes to reconstruct the circumstances leading up to the moment illustrated in the picture.

ARTS SENSORY ACTIVITIES BASED ON A THEME: "MYSELF"

1. The children feel their pulse and heartbeat, then beat out the rhythm they feel. They can walk to that rhythm and then draw a line that imitates the rhythm.
2. Each child speaks his or her full name, then claps its rhythm. Then the child draws a line that is like the rhythm, and develops it into a design.

Relating Art to the General Curriculum

3. Children explore their own voices by making the softest sound they can; the highest; the saddest; the funniest; and so on. Then the idea is transferred to imaginative listening. The class is asked to identify the same types of sounds in a marching band, waves hitting the beach, and so on.

4. The children make four or five three-second scribbles on 12-by-16-inch sheets of newsprint. Lay them out in rows and see which are least alike and most alike. Ask the children to think of words that would distinguish the character of one set from another. Then have the class create an abstract design based on one characteristic that all the scribbles share. This activity relates the child's personal rhythm to the visual rhythms in their drawings.

5. Spontaneous-response exercises: The class is divided into pairs. Partner A says a word and B says the first word that pops into mind. Then the teacher claps out a rhythm and the class duplicates it. This is repeated with more complex rhythms. Next, the teacher draws a line on the blackboard and each student adds one line to it. Each successive line must relate to all the previous ones. (This can also be done with two teams.) Finally, the teacher makes a movement and each member of the class responds with a body motion that extends or builds upon the teacher's movement.

ARTS IMPROVISATION EXERCISES

1. A team of players (no more than three) is selected to "perform" for the class. The team decides upon a topic worth discussing such as a morsel of juicy gossip, but instead of speaking English, they use either numbers or letters of the alphabet. The problem here is to allow meanings to surface without relying on the language of the audience.

2. To improvise through mime and movement, have each student prepare a two-minute pantomime based on phrases assigned by the teacher. Examples: avoiding work; caught between television and homework; a failure in the kitchen. It is important that the assignment come as a surprise. If students have too much time to think about it, the improvisational emphasis is lessened.

3. To improvise visually, ask each pupil to draw with appropriate colors, lines, and shapes related to one word selected from a list (*anger, sorrow, joy, nightmare,* and so on).

Some of these improvisations take very little time and are a good way to begin a day or an art period. The preceding sensory and improvisational activities are inspired by the desire to extend the base of art education, a desire that is reflected in new approaches to team teaching. The art teacher of the future may be expected to think and function beyond the

An eleven-year-old girl began improvising by writing her name several times. She then selected the version she felt was most pleasing and used the letter forms as a basis for a watercolor painting.

immediate demands of the art program. There is also evidence that the education of art and classroom teachers is beginning to include art electives drawn from fields outside the visual arts. Additional knowledge of related arts is easier for the prospective art teacher to acquire than is some expert familiarity with academic subjects, yet it is in the academic areas of language arts and social studies that the new art teacher is often asked to contribute special skills. Therefore, the major portion of this chapter discusses the correlation of art with the existing academic curriculum of the schools.

OVERLAPPING GOALS

Many of the claims art teachers make for their subject are parallel to goals in other subject areas. Recently a group of social studies specialists specified the goals for which they teach. Their choices indicate some very obvious analogies to art. Listed below are eight points they felt were vital for any current social studies program. These assumptions may be similar to those made for an art program, but the teacher should be cognizant of the art program's unique features, as the comments in parentheses indicate.[2]

1. Man in relation to the natural environment and the cultural environment is a proper subject for the elementary-school social studies curriculum. (This is also proper subject matter for art activities.)
2. Contrast is a powerful pedagogical tool: look at unfamiliar cultures to understand one's own; look at animal behavior to understand what characteristics man and animals have in common and

[2] The list of goals is taken from "Curriculum Study Group: Social Studies" (Newton, Ma.: Newton Public Schools).

Relating Art to the General Curriculum

what differentiates them. (The art teacher utilizes the contrasts found in works of art to reinforce learnings in criticism and appreciation. Polarities of style and technique are stressed to heighten the child's perceptions of likenesses and differences in artworks.)

3. "Ways of knowing" are important, such as the way of the anthropologist, the archeologist, and others. ("Ways of knowing" in art implies understanding not only the functions of critic, historian, and artist, but also of the kinds of "knowing," perceiving, and experiencing that differentiate the painter from the sculptor, the architect from the potter.)

4. Studies in depth provide a thorough foundation and a point of reference around which later learnings may cluster. (An art program that included in-depth studies would give a great deal of time to a few selected concepts deemed important, such as drawing, color, and painting, rather than skipping to a different activity each week without making any connections among the activities.)

5. Discovering how things are related and discovering how to discover are the ends of learning; the end should not be just mastery of the subject matter. (Discovery is a part of the process in art as well. Sensitive teachers are aware of the importance of the changes that may occur when children are taught for discovery as well as for adult-inspired goals.)

6. The students are participants; they can be self-motivated inquirers rather than just passive receivers. (The taped dialogs transcribed in this book testify to the value of interactions between teacher and pupil in discussions of art activities.)

7. Students should find their own meaning in the material, some of which should be "raw data." (Raw data have always been at the heart of the art program. The raw data the art student should encounter are creative studio experiences and original works of art, be they buildings, paintings, or craft objects.)

8. The gap between current research in curriculum and methodology in social studies should be narrowed. (No one has yet assessed the effects of research on art education in the classroom. The results obtained from doctoral dissertations are rarely read by classroom teachers, and much research is unfortunately too limited in nature to be of use. Art teachers need the kinds of broad curriculum investigation that have taken place in mathematics and physics; these are slow in coming to the humanities. A gap does exist and it must be narrowed if the teacher is to reflect the findings of the researcher.)

The eight points have been included here to emphasize the need for art teachers to define the special nature of art, even when art appears to be close to other subjects in its ultimate objectives.

In any case, the teacher who correlates art with other subjects will have to determine when an activity ceases to be art or when it may even go against the very nature of art. When in doubt, a teacher should ask a few basic questions:

Does the activity allow for freedom of decision in interpretation, design, and choice of subject?

Does the task call for strong personal identification with the subject, or does it rest primarily on someone else's solution?

Can the pupils take the information beyond the source material and add something of their own?

It is instructive to study both some of the developing techniques involved in correlations between art and other subjects, and some of the results of using art activity as part of a larger unit of study.

Problems of Correlation

THE NEED FOR MOTIVATION

The teaching of art has, of course, been affected by both the correlation of subjects and their fusion in the unit curriculum. In certain circumstances art education has benefited from the grouping of areas of learning; in other circumstances, however, it has suffered.

As has been noted, artistic expression is based on a series of delicate circumstances (see Chapter 2). Not the least of these is a definite reaction to an experience on the part of a person prior to expression. The production of art, therefore, does not occur automatically as a result of correlation or a general fusion of school subjects. Only a child who is emotionally and intellectually moved by an experience in another area of learning is in a position to relate artistic expression to other school subjects. Then the fusion of art and other subjects may be said to be strong, and learning, both artistic and academic, is gratifying.

Perhaps the strongest case to be made for correlation is that art, a sensory experience, can provide a tactile basis for learning in general. This is certainly a useful idea for nonart teachers, but where does it leave the art teacher who has a particular agenda for instruction?

Many educators feel that art is often abused in the process of integration—that in serving the rest of the curriculum, the creative drive necessary to art becomes diluted, and means are often confused with ends. Many activities, such as copying maps and model construction, are labeled "art" simply because art media are used. In these instances, the art teacher should say to the colleague in the classroom, "It is your right to have them color in mimeographed maps of the Western movement, but let's not call it

Relating Art to the General Curriculum

art." Activities correlated with social studies, for example, involve art only if the lives of the pioneers and Indians can be linked to some sort of life experience, personal identification, or visual problem-solving of the child. To copy Indian designs in crayon is not art, but to study the design style of the Indian, weaving one's own pattern on a loom that one has assembled, comes much closer to art.

Correlation or integration need not debase an authentic art experience. In two pilot programs, both dealing with language development, the resulting artworks reflected as much original thinking as those produced in the regular art program.[3] In Group A, children of Italian parents worked on mosaics, simulated frescoes, and travel posters. They studied Venice and created a city of islands in clay. In Group B, children of Cambodian, Vietnamese, and Laotian parents made paintings and drawings of their personal histories. In both cases, language developed out of labeling, naming, and using new language in the art activities. Both programs were conducted by art teachers who felt that, far from being an inhibiting factor, the thematic use of Italian and Asian cultures actually stimulated art activity.

Generally, stories and poems may encourage children in the symbol or later stages of expression to make two- and three-dimensional illustrations. The media associated with picture-making or paper work serve best in this type of work, although modeling materials may also be useful. Either the stories and poems the children read and study in class, or in some cases those they write themselves, may be used as the basis for pictorial or three-dimensional expression. Certain teaching precautions must be observed if the correlation is to be successful. In illustrating published stories, the children's experience is vicarious. Only when the literary source has aroused them to the extent that they strongly wish to express something about it is the vicarious experience suitable subject matter for art. If they have failed to respond sufficiently to the work under consideration, they cannot be expected to react artistically to it, and hence no correlative output of this kind should be encouraged.

The same is true of the children's own literary expression. Only when children retain a strong interest in the experience suggested in their written work can they be expected to express a similar reaction in art. Should their interest remain high after written expression, a further expressive act in another medium might lead to further clarification of their reaction. In such a case the teacher may safely encourage a correlated activity.

One very natural way to relate language, art, and imagination is to ask children to write about what they have drawn. If the subject is selected

LANGUAGE ARTS

[3]"English as a Second Language" (Newton, Ma.: Newton Public Schools).

In a study by the author of art inspired by the story of Noah and the Ark, children from various nations produced work reflecting three major influences: cultural, educational, and personal. The children, ages ten to twelve, were told the same story, often through interpreters. Upper left: a Maori boy in New Zealand integrates designs from traditional Maori woodcarving into wave and sky patterns. Strong art program in the school. Lower left: a Bedouin child in the Negev area of Israel uses linear patterns from Arabic calligraphy to create the sea. The delicate broken lines of rain were also typical of his class. Art teacher not present. Right: a child in rural Kenya emphasizes the path to the ark because of the importance, in the child's homeland, of footpaths. The animals were traced, but the humans and ark were done freehand. No art instructor present. Opposite page, upper left: the orderly patterning of rain, waves, and wood distinguishes this rendering of the story by an Australian Aboriginal child. Art teacher present. The watercolors at lower left and lower right are from two matched groups in separate schools in Seoul, South Korea. The two groups (like children in Taiwan, Hong Kong, and Japan, as well), shared a sensitivity to art media, drawing skills, and an ability to activate the human figure. But the tendency among the Korean children to depict the Noah story in human terms is unique. In the left-hand picture, animals dance in celebration at the end of the deluge; in the other picture, Noah and his family are busy at work. Upper right, a gypsy girl in a rural settlement in Hungary, considered gifted by her teacher, placed the dove inside another bird and combined olive branches, Mt. Ararat, and the ark in a forceful, coherent design. From an after-school art program in a special-interest center. Strong art teacher present.

Literature would seem a natural source of subject matter for art. Children can illustrate favorite stories, as a fourth grade girl has done here.

with care (such as "Machines Designed to Perform Unusual Tasks"), then the interplay between idea and image grows dramatically. Children can speak and write about things they may not draw, and vice versa. Combining the two can enhance the development of both linguistic and graphic forms.

Puppetry is another useful means of correlation. A strong interrelationship exists between puppetry and other theater arts on the one hand, and spoken and written English on the other. The subject matter of a puppet or stage play may be derived, first, from a play already written by someone else; second, from one the children prepare after reading a narrative poem or a story; and finally, from one written entirely by the children. All three sources demand the use of English, spoken in a natural, functional setting. The last two require, furthermore, a high degree of ingenuity and creative effort, which is not beyond the capabilities of most groups of elementary-school children. Drama for children is, after all, a form of make-believe that occurs frequently in their free play.

SOCIAL STUDIES

For children, social studies begin in their immediate environment. The geography, history, and civics they first consider are found close to home. Because children are naturally interested in what goes on around them, few problems arise when they base their art on this area of learning. Their paintings, murals, and three-dimensional work may depict such themes as "Our Neighborhood," "Our Waterfront," "Families Who Have Lived Longest in Our District," "What Our Firemen Do," "How We Travel in Our City."

416

In the lower grades, a topic frequently related to social studies is "Our Friends and Neighbors in Other Lands" or "Boys and Girls in Faraway Places." Here the subject takes the children away from the environment they know, and as a result their art work often deteriorates. The chief reason for this deterioration is that the children frequently do not know enough about the remote region to express much about it, with the consequence that the teacher may substitute stereotyped symbols for true information. How often have we seen such ethnic stereotypes in children's work as a tulip, a windmill, and a boy in baggy trousers to represent the Netherlands; a man sleeping under a cactus plant for Mexico; or a mounted policeman in a red coat for Canada. These banal symbols—a species of adult pictogram—give so restricted an idea of a country that they interfere with the child's understanding of the true character of the foreign land. Granted that the Netherlands has tulips, that Mexicans sleep, and that Canada maintains the Royal Canadian Mounted Police, such images do not represent the heart of these lands.

Before children can be expected to give expression in art to a theme based on remote regions, they must gain a wide knowledge of them, and they must be stirred by some aspects of this knowledge. By reading books and looking at moving pictures, by singing songs of the countries, by studying the work of their artists, and so forth, in course of time they may gain a body of knowledge and a sense of the true character of distant places that will allow them to express something worthwhile.

The same principle applies to the output of pupils in the upper elementary grades. Frequently more mature pupils may be inspired by events and conditions remote in time and place. In their natural history, for example, they may be stirred by events in the American Revolution, the Civil War, the winning of the West, or the exploration of the Antarctic, and may be ready to give expression to them. If, for the lack of knowledge, they find

Current events provided the motivation for a fifth grader's portrait of former president Richard Nixon.

Mapmaking can bring together many disciplines. This imitation of an ancient parchment map led to a written composition describing the dramatic events that took place on the island depicted. Science and art thus extended into language arts. When examples of Portuguese cartography of the age of exploration were shown, both social studies and art history came into play.

it necessary to copy the work of others, they are not engaging in art and are probably learning little about history. Their time could be more profitably occupied elsewhere. If, on the contrary, they have equipped themselves with a sufficient background of the period that interests them and are thereby capable of giving a knowledgeable account of it, they are in a position both to gain historical knowledge and to produce art of some consequence.

Mapmaking is not art but science. It is an extraordinary fact that even today a few teachers seem to consider the making of maps, either drawn and painted or molded in flour and salt mixtures, to be a form of artistic effort. If a map is to be of any use at all, it must be scientifically accurate and allow no liberties of form for artistic purposes. No personal statement, therefore, can be permitted to influence the outline being produced. It is possible, however, to make an art experience of mapmaking if the task is divided into two clearly defined phases: the *scientific*, wherein accurate boundaries, coastlines, rivers, and so on, are located, and the *imaginative*, wherein the children add their own pictographs or symbols for trees, ships, physical features, decorative tiles, borders, and legends. Children also enjoy "aging" the paper by crumpling it, shellacking or oiling it, or tearing and, under the teacher's supervision, singeing the edges. Purely imaginative maps can also provide the basis for creative writing in the language arts. Maps can, and often do, evoke fantasies in addition to providing information.

Just as writing and drawing can be combined, so imaginative writing can follow decorative map-making. An incredible journey between the harbor and the buried treasure can be detailed, for example. A composition can be the culmination of a project that began in science and was carried into art, with a sidelong glance at the fascinating world of pictorial maps during the time, say, of Columbus.

Racial Awareness Through Art. To satisfy the desire of racial and ethnic minority groups for improved recognition of their cultural histories, teachers can easily incorporate relevant information into both art-work and appreciation activities. Collage, murals, and mask-making—which most teachers already include in their programs—can make clear references to Afro-American art and crafts. Activities such as jewelry and basket-making, weaving, and dyeing can also refer to cultures other than Western culture. However, this will mean shifting some of the usual historical references. When the class is involved in a problem of collage, the work of Romare Bearden may be of even greater use than that of Picasso or Schwitters. In showing the work of muralists, the Mexican School and the walls of a barrio in Los Angeles may be as exciting as an example by WPA artists—although works of all cultures rather than one single group should be shown. Every urban area also has artists from minority cultures to draw upon as possible visiting artists. Children need models for emulation and for improving their self-image—there is no reason that children cannot admire artists as well as athletes.

Masks provide one example of how ethnic sources can be utilized. Mask-making is a perennially popular art activity. It combines a wide variety of techniques, transformation, imagination, and even a sense of magic. A mask can be practical—used for Halloween—or decorative. Its effects are achieved quickly—as in adding paint and paper to a paper bag—or can be painstaking, such as careful modeling in clay. The mask-maker can add feathers, buttons, beads, hemp, and any number of objects to enhance the mask's visual appeal. Rarely, however, is the mask presented in any cultural context.

Yet the mask can convey information about the wearer: it can identify a scuba diver, a welder, an astronaut, and so on. Masks certainly can also be used in any racial awareness program to identify cultural figures. Many African folktales for example, involve masks, and mask styles differ from one African tribe or culture to another. All masks use local materials, serve different purposes, and possess their own visual styles. Studying these elements helps aacquaint students with an important phase of another culture.[4]

[4] See Eugene J. Grigsby, Jr., *Art and Ethnics: Background for Teaching Youth in A Pluralistic Society* (Dubuque: William C. Brown, 1977).

This mask of papier-mâché reflects a third grader's examination of African sculpture. In addition to its relevance to cultural studies, mask-making as an art activity has perennial interest because it involves transformation, encourages use of the imagination, and utilizes manual processes.

SCIENCE Although artists like Audubon and da Vinci have been able to bring art and science into close proximity, scientific drawings and artistic expressions differ in intent. Like a map, a scientific drawing is an exact statement of fact, allowing no deviation from the natural appearance of an object.

Many years ago, art programs gave considerable importance to the drawing of natural specimens. The pussywillow was a favorite theme, as were daffodils, tulips, and bunches of grapes. These objects were drawn even by the youngest children with strict respect for photographic accuracy. We now know that children should make use of their own symbols to represent objects. For children, a natural object evokes feelings and holds meanings that a scientific statement could scarcely express. To ask children in an art session to draw scientifically serves merely to curb their expression. However, the objects in the science corner of the classroom, such as fossils, shells, and rocks can provide the basis for invention, as well as for the study of form.

> My art classroom could be mistaken for an extension of the Smithsonian Institution's Natural History Museum. Along with children's art expressions on animal themes, there are continuous displays of real and pictured butterflies, seashells, wasps' nests, rocks, and peacock feathers. The children are constantly exposed to color slides, films, posters, photographs, and books about wild animals, tropical fish, beautiful and bizarre insects, various plant forms, and of course—dinosaurs.[5]

Most elementary-school children, of course, are incapable of drawing with scientific accuracy. This does not mean that they should not be exposed to natural objects or that they should not use them for expressive purposes. On the contrary, flowers, birds, seashells, fish, and animals, as stated previously, may be used with excellent effect in art. Any natural object may be employed as the basis of design, provided the children are also given freedom to depart from the scientific form they observe.

The fact that this freedom is allowed does not retard the children's growth in scientific knowledge. In looking at natural objects and experiencing them in other ways, they come close to nature. Later, should they be of a scientific turn of mind, their art experiences with the natural world will provide them with valuable insights that may lead to scientific inquiry.

A correlated art-science project could work as follows for the fifth and sixth grades. The first step would be an *observational phase*, in which students would be asked to draw as carefully as possible an object or specimen such as bones (skeleton segment); fossils embedded in plastic; flowers; or cellular forms viewed through a microscope. The second step,

[5] Frank J. Chetelat, "Art and Science: An Interdisciplinary Approach," *Art Teacher*, Fall 1979, p. 8.

The art room should contain many different kinds of objects to stimulate a child's imagination and interest. Here a pupil has selected a fossil for study from a collection of natural objects; her initial drawing will be expanded into a large painting or print. (Photo by Roger Graves.)

the *design phase*, would involve using the drawing in one of the following ways:

Fill in areas within outlines with flat tones based on a color theory.
Blow up the drawing to ten times the original size and turn it into a Hard Edge-style painting, following directions in A.
Move a piece of tracing paper over the original, allowing shapes to overlap. Fill in with textured pen-and-ink patterns, a color scheme, or a number of shades of one color.
Select a section for a small linoleum print and make a repeat pattern.

In such a sequence the student moves from observation to design judgment, and in making the print comes to understand how artists use natural forms as a basis for applied design. The entire sequence may take up to four or five class sessions, but it allows the student to "live with" one problem for an extended period of time.

The greatest care, of course, must be taken not to supply children with symbols, considered to be artistic, that tend to replace or interfere with a study of natural objects. The cutting of paper snowflakes, for example, could be approved only after a careful study of these forms, and only

Problems of Correlation

if the activity were entirely creative. The drawing of evergreen trees in the well-known bisymmetrical zigzag design results more often from a teacher's demonstration than from a child's observation of a real tree.

MUSIC

Music and art lend themselves to several types of correlation.[6] As an indirect correlation, a background of music is often valuable to children while they are drawing, painting, or working in three dimensions. The music appears to influence the children's visual output in a subtle fashion.

The teacher may arrange direct correlations between music and art for children at any level in the elementary school. Music with a pronounced rhythmic beat and melodic line may be employed as a basis for drawing nonobjective patterns. The following are well-known selections suitable for elementary-school children:

> J. S. Bach, "Brandenburg" Concerto No. 1
>   *The Wise Virgins* (ballet, arr. Walton)
> Beethoven, Overtures: *Lenore*, No. 3
>   *Egmont*
>   *The Consecration of the House*
> Bizet, *L'Arlésienne*, Suites 1 and 2
> Borodin, *Prince Igor:* "Polovetsian Dances"
> Khachaturian, *Gayne Ballet*, Suite No. 1
> Lalo, *Symphonie Espagnole*
> Liszt, *Hungarian Rhapsodies*, Nos. 1–7
>   *Mephisto Waltzes*
> Prokofiev, *Peter and the Wolf*
> Rossini, Overtures: *The Barber of Seville*
>   *William Tell*
>   *Semiramide*
> Von Suppé, Overtures: *Light Cavalry*
>   *Poet and Peasant*

Music depicting a definite mood may also lead to some interesting pictures, especially in the fifth and sixth grades. Before playing the record, the teacher usually discusses the mood of the selection. After hearing the music the class may discuss possible combinations of colors, lines, and other elements of design to express the mood pictorially. Work then begins, preferably in soft chalk or paint, with the music playing in the background. The following are selections expressing certain moods and are suitable for fifth and sixth grade pupils.

[6] The Activities for the Reader at the end of Chapter 3 suggest methods and media suitable for both teachers and pupils.

Relating Art to the General Curriculum

Bax, *Tintagel*
Borodin, *In the Steppes of Central Asia*
Britten, *Peter Grimes*, "Four Sea Interludes"
Copland, *Appalachian Spring*
       El Salon Mexico
Debussy, *Clair de Lune*
     La Mer
Elgar, *Pomp and Circumstance*, Nos. 1–4
Mussorgsky, *Night on Bald Mountain*
Ravel, *Bolero*
Sibelius, *The Swan of Tuonela*
    Finlandia
Wagner, *Die Walküre*, "Ride of the Valkyries"

Music with a literary theme—*program music*, as it is sometimes called—may also assist in developing noteworthy picture-making by pupils in the symbol or later stages of expression. The teacher gives the outline of the story, plays excerpts from the music, and from time to time draws attention to passages depicting specific events in the narrative. Examples of program music suitable mainly for pupils in the fourth or higher grades are as follows:

Beethoven, Symphony No. 6 in F Major, Op. 68 ("Pastoral")
Bernstein, *West Side Story*, Overture
Bizet, *Carmen*, excerpts
Grofé, *Grand Canyon Suite*
Humperdinck, *Hänsel und Gretel*, excerpts
Mussorgsky, *Pictures at an Exhibition*
Prokofiev, *Cinderella*, excerpts
Respighi, *The Pines of Rome*
Rimsky-Korsakov, *Scheherazade*
Saint-Saëns, *Danse Macabre*
Tchaikovsky, *Sleeping Beauty*

Popular music can be used with equal effectiveness. No listing of jazz or rock music is included because taste in these categories changes so quickly. Dixieland, Duke Ellington, and the Beatles, however, can always be used to motivate art work. And record covers can be studied as a popular art form that links the mood and beat of music to visual experience.

As soon as a child is capable of using a measured line, mathematics may begin to enter into some of the child's art work. Activities such as building model houses, making costumes for puppets, or constructing puppet stages lend themselves to this correlation.

MATHEMATICS

Some teachers have attempted to combine the two fields by having the children work during art sessions with mechanical-drawing tools, such as compasses, triangles, and T-squares, to devise geometric designs. If this type of work is largely mechanical and hence not particularly expressive, there is little to recommend it. However, since children do enjoy the clarity and precision that designing with draftsmen's tools provide, in many situations the teacher may establish creative and aesthetic standards to make the design activities worthwhile. These tools might be combined with work in any number of techniques—crayon and pencil drawing, painting, crayon resist, and etching, among others.

UNPLANNED CORRELATIONS

The preceding examples are correlations that some teachers have consciously developed. Many other correlations may occur that are not arranged formally. Children who develop harmony of movement in physical education, a sense of balance through study of numbers, a concept of unity from some aspect of social studies, or a feeling for rhythm from poetry will find these attainments paralleled in their artistic achievements. Many of the general learnings of this nature are present in many areas of the educational program and can serve as the basis for integrating art into other subjects. So subtle are these correlations in learning, however, that the child and indeed the teacher may be unaware of what is taking place. The most the teacher can do for children is to keep all learning on the highest possible creative and aesthetic levels.

HOLIDAYS

Many of the special days for national observance are important civilizing influences. Most children observe such national and folk holidays as Independence Day, Memorial Day, Halloween, Thanksgiving, and Martin

Finnish children combine art and mathematics by using geometric forms as a basis for collage and design. They can also learn that mathematics is involved in weaving, as in the traditional folk-art patterns in the boy's sweater.

A fourth grader's vision of Halloween goes far beyond the symbols usually associated with that holiday. This painting draws upon several interests of children—giants, science fiction, and speculation about the unknown. It is a long way from the witch, the black cat, and the jack-o'-lantern.

Luther King Day, with which symbols such as the flag, the Christmas candle, the pumpkin, the cornucopia, and portraits of famous people are associated. Unfortunately, these symbols are often used in a standardized, uncreative way in art classes. When they are limited to the mere copying of these symbols, children fail to note the special significance of these events in their own lives. Thanksgiving, for example, is an important American holiday that provides an opportunity for families to gather and eat together. Such an occasion is often charged with feeling and deserving of thoughtful contemplation. Above all, from an art standpoint, it is eminently suitable for expressive purposes. To suggest to children that they should copy a symbol like the shopworn cornucopia instead of offering their own impressions of Thanksgiving is to minimize their creativity. If, of course, children hold a particular symbol very dear, they might work with it not as an isolated object but in close association with the environment in which they found it. As a result, they probably will produce an original design in which the symbol is the chief motif. Picture- and mural-making, modeling, and other art activities based on the children's personal reactions to holidays should be encouraged in every grade; they can result in output rich in subject matter and artistic quality.

Of course, no art program should ever fall into the trap of lurching from holiday to holiday. Every public celebration has in it the germ of some personal connection to remove it from the realm of stereotypes. If the teacher must deal with pumpkins for Halloween, bring in a pumpkin, plus some dried cornstalks or gourds, and give a still-life lesson in tempera. Teachers can also confer with the school librarian to find books and stories that lend themselves to illustration.

Art Activities Especially Suitable for Correlation

Two types of work that serve especially useful purposes in both correlative and unit activities are poster-making and three-dimensional picture-making techniques, generally known as dioramas, panoramas, movies, and peep shows.

POSTER-MAKING

From time to time a classroom project or school activity may require some form of advertising by poster. Ways and means can be devised by which the poster is produced in accordance with sound educational and artistic principles.

Media and Techniques. To be effective and useful, a poster must fulfill several well-defined basic requirements. It must be arresting, it must convey its message briefly, it should usually contain only one idea, and it should be easily readable from a distance. The children should be reminded that a poster is designed to attract attention and convey information. In order to do this, it is recommended that they limit colors and emphasize contrast; avoid clutter in layout (composition); and avoid too much "copy" (words).

The lettering required in most poster work demands practice and provides little scope for the imagination. Letter A must be letter A, and very little deviation can be allowed if the letter is to remain readable. Indeed, to produce acceptable letters and layout for a poster requires a technical competence usually beyond the capabilities of an elementary-school child.

The solution to this problem is to build on whatever abilities the children possess. Most school systems include a carefully graded program to teach writing. The youngest children frequently begin writing in what is called *print script*. This is often subsequently developed into a *joined print script*, and after this stage the children begin cursive writing. Competence at each stage is the result of much painstaking teaching. It is wise, therefore, for the children to use in poster work the abilities gained in the writing program. Whatever alphabet they have learned and mastered as part of the writing program seems to be the logical one to use in a poster, because in both types of work they are employing the hard-earned skill of using words to convey ideas.

In poster-making, children who are beginners in writing should first use the usual large pencils and writing paper to which they are accustomed. Later they can use wax crayons and drawing paper. By the fifth and sixth grades pupils are able to use special equipment for poster-making, such as felt-tip pens, or India ink and large lettering nibs having round, oval, and square tips to make the writing bold enough for a poster. Following a little practice in using special pens and inks, the pupils seem to experience no great difficulty in writing in their accustomed style on the larger scale required for the poster.

Whatever drawings and paintings children use in conjunction with their verbal message should likewise be in keeping with their developmental level and general competence. Children in the symbol stage of expression, for example, obviously should use this form in their poster work.

To make the poster more interesting, the teacher can capitalize on previous art experiences in cut-paper collage (for richness of texture) and

This linoleum print (actual size, 8″ × 10″) has many elements that would make it a good poster—readability, simplicity of design, imaginativeness, and humor.

montage (for arresting images of unusual juxtapositions of photos and advertisements). If posters are assembled from separate segments such as decorative letters, pictures, or other elements, the children can rearrange the shapes and spaces until they find a composition they like. Preparatory activities in lettering, aside from the styles mastered in the writing program, may involve creating designs from the child's own name, printmaking using raised letters mounted on cardboard, and collages of letters taken from newspaper headlines and magazines.

Because all posters need to be seen and understood at a distance, it is a good idea for children to test their poster design by pinning letters and pictures in place and studying them from a distance. In most cases, children become accustomed to scaling their work only according to the distance between them and their desk tops, and will not automatically make the proper adjustment for posters. The study of good professional advertisements and travel posters can help them appreciate the appropriate scale.

Teaching. Poster-making can cause problems for an elementary-school teacher because of the demands made on the school by officials of local charitable organizations who wish to advertise the worthy causes they sponsor. While picture-making teachers are contented with work of a technical competence commensurate with the child's developmental level, such is not always the case when posters are being produced for the community. In an attempt to obtain useful posters, the teacher may apply pressure so that the children are forced both to copy the drawings of others and to spend valuable educational time in outlining letters of the alphabet. All this militates against an expressive art program. Overtures from outside sources to have posters made for events unconnected with the school, therefore, should be resisted. Much as the school wishes to

These playful manipulations of letter forms served as the basis for unusual posters. Their effectiveness results from practice in line control (direction, thickness, and spacing), which preceded the actual designs.

support the community at large, the technical difficulties involved in the making of posters for the community forbid the inclusion of this work in the art program in the elementary grades.

A poster for a school activity is quite a different matter. Then, of course, the teacher should encourage the project and offer assistance as required. The size of the poster, its design, the strength of color used, the boldness of the writing, and the like should be discussed. The teacher should also demonstrate the different types of lettering nibs, brushes, and pens available. Time for practice with these tools should be found before the poster is made. As pupils become more experienced in the work, the teacher should encourage them to make rough layouts before beginning work on the final project.

Thus the poster, if treated as an extension of writing and picture-making, serves a limited but necessary purpose in the art program of the elementary school.

These four types of work are especially valuable for correlations between art and literature or history.

Media and Techniques. A *diorama* is a display having a backdrop and wings rather like a miniature stage. It may be made from a carton or box with the lid and one side removed. The objects placed in this setting may be made from cardboard, carving materials, or a variety of other substances. The backdrop can be painted or designed in paper.

A *panorama* is constructed on an open surface and may be seen from any side. The well-known "sand table" is a kind of panorama arrangement. The supporting surface is a tray of convenient size having wooden sides to prevent objects from falling off. All manner of materials and techniques may be used in the making of the panorama. Sand for deserts, glass for rivers, cardboard for houses, papier-mâché for people and animals, and paper for trees are among the items one might suggest.

A *"movie"* is a series of pictures attached to each other to form a ribbon. For displaying the movie, a cardboard carton may be used. An opening for the "screen" should be cut in the bottom of the carton. Two wooden rollers (old broom handles make good rollers) are then thrust vertically through the carton on either side of the screen opening. The ends of the rollers must project well beyond the sides of the carton. Pictures are stuck together in a ribbon, the ends of which are tacked to the rollers. By turning either of the rollers, the pictures are made to move across the opening. The usual drawing and painting materials are used for the pictures.

The *peep show* is actually a variation of the diorama. An old shoebox provides a good basic unit for this technique. In a small end of the box a

DIORAMAS, PANORAMAS, MOVIES, AND PEEP SHOWS

The panorama approach was used in this sand-table group project depicting a primitive community. Fifth grade. Many natural materials were used; a simpler version would be to roll out heavy, half-inch-thick slabs of clay, adding pinch pots as needed for domes and other simple forms. (Photo by Education Development Center.)

hole about the size of a quarter should be cut. Inside, at the other end of the box and at least halfway up the sides, a background must be painted. Figures and trees in front of the background are best made from cardboard. Other properties may be constructed of a variety of materials, from straw to absorbent cotton. Interesting lighting effects can be obtained by covering the top of the box with colored plastics or tissue papers. (When the peep show is not in use, the covering should be protected by placing the box lid in position.) Moving a straight beam of light, such as that from a pencil-type flashlight, over the colored material gives the viewer many pleasant and surprising design effects.

Teaching. These four techniques essentially constitute group work involving from two to perhaps a dozen pupils, in any grade and in at least the symbol stage of pictorial development. The teacher's work is chiefly that of sponsoring group activities according to the principles outlined in Chapter 11. The techniques of constructing, modeling, drawing, and painting mentioned in earlier chapters should be employed in these activities as well.

The teacher's greatest concern should be to ensure that the pupils give maximum attention to developing designs with artistic qualities. Unless the teacher discusses design from time to time, any one of these four types of work could degenerate into busywork. There is no need for this to happen, however, since each type of work can be an art activity in every sense.

Relating Art to the General Curriculum

Teaching an Integrated Program: Two Case Studies

Since integration opens up an even greater realm of possibilities than art itself, there obviously can be no single route to success. In order to see how an integrated approach differs from art-centered planning, let us look at two different teachers in action.

Mr. A is an art teacher who has interests extending into other areas of the curriculum. During his student teaching he worked with classroom teachers on the elementary level and a history teacher in a junior high school. Currently his title is Art Consultant rather than Art Teacher, and he divides his time between scheduled classroom visitations and "open" or consulting periods, when he can teach or plan some future scheduled class with his colleagues. He spends the first week of a semester familiarizing himself with what is being taught in the other subjects and planning ways in which he can contribute through art.

THE ART CONSULTANT

In correlating his plans with those of the other teachers, Mr. A fills in a grid, such as the following one for social studies.

TABLE 14.1

Correlating Art Activities to Social Studies

Grade	Themes	Resource Units	Art Units
K–1	Family, School, and Community	The Community as Laboratory Social Studies Guide Black Studies Kit	
2	Families and Cultures	Houses and Neighborhoods House of the Navajo K–1–2 Black Studies Unit	
3	Interaction with the Physical Environment	Water: Where Does Our Water Come From? Amazon River Basin 3–4 Black Studies	
4	Cultural Geography of the United States	Geography of the United States People of America City and Suburb 3–4 Black Studies Unit	
5–6	Technology and Change Studying the Past American History	Man: A Course of Study The Toolmakers Topics in American History Sampler of Early American History 5–6 Black Studies Unit	

These simulated Egyptian fresco paintings on low, carved relief were done by drawing the faces on slabs of plaster of Paris. The lines were incised with a sharp tool and the faces painted in tempera. Sandpaper was then lightly applied to contribute to the appearance of age. The thinner the paint, the more delicate the colors. This activity was part of a class unit on ancient Egypt.

Mr. A's task is to fill in the last column to indicate where his own goals as an art teacher can mesh with the subject matter described in the column "Themes."

On a typical day, Mr. A's work extends considerably beyond the subject of social studies.

1st period: Mr. A prepares a unit on book design involving an original story written by the sixth graders for the second graders. The stories will be lettered in a calligraphic form, illustrated, and bound into a book, which will have marbleized endpapers and a cover decorated with a small overall pattern cut from erasers. This is an extended project and will run for four sessions after the story has been written.

2nd period: A third and a fifth grade teacher with a planning period meet with Mr. A to discuss simple geometric structures that students could make in relation to a mathematics unit.

3rd period: Mr. A oversees the final phase of a sixth grade mural on the frontier movement. The mural is nearly complete and must be mounted, captioned, and given a decorative border.

4th period: A first grade teacher has requested a set of large cutout letters with a sandpaper surface painted in a variety of colors. She feels the children need more direct, tactile references to letter forms, but she is not capable of making them. Once made, the set of letters will be shared among the primary grade teachers.

Relating Art to the General Curriculum

5th period: Mr. A has reserved this period for mounting a school display of projects representing some use of art from the work of the entire staff. All work will be accompanied by captions explaining the context of the art work.

6th period: In the sixth grade, Mr. A demonstrates the use of tissue collage and discusses how the nature of shapes and color can reflect the mood and meaning of haiku poetry which the class has written. The children make collages to match their poetry. The following week they will add the poetry to the collage, using Mr. A's calligraphic alphabet and studying how to place the letters in a pleasing composition.

While Mr. A is a hypothetical case, the second art educator we will discuss is actually working with children and with art and classroom teachers.

Don Brigham (his real name) is a supervisor of art education for a public school system in Massachusetts. He has made a provocative departure from conventional applications of the notion of "integrated art education." For more than fifteen years, he has been exploring and demonstrating the possibilities of utilizing the perceptive, imaginative, and productive thinking processes of art as a general method of education for all subject areas of the curriculum.

Brigham has been establishing connections between the ways that artists conceptualize and fashion original artworks and the ways that children conceptualize and communicate their understanding of the raw data of such subjects as English, science, mathematics, history, and geography. He assumes, with Kilpatrick and Dewey (see Chapter 1), that creativity is a characteristic of all learning. His program has provided evidence that

THE ART SUPERVISOR

A fifth grade classroom teacher devoted one entire wall of his room to art projects related to the exploration of outer space. Plaster of Paris, clay, papier-mâché, paint, paper, reassembled toys, and junk were some of the materials used over a period of several weeks.

many schoolchildren can imaginatively deal with various school subjects, converting the raw information into intelligible as well as expressive forms that can still retain the characteristics of authentic art expression.

Brigham avoids the conventional correlational approach to integrated art education. *Correlation*, in his opinion, implies a *parallel* arrangement in which one of the parallels is apt to be subordinate to the other. *Integrated* art education means that the essentials of art—its creativity, its active involvement of all the senses, its syncretic or whole-forming nature, and its symbolizing function in relation to the development of human consciousness—can be applied as a *learning process* to any and all school studies.

Rather than projecting art into the English, social studies, or science curriculum simply to illustrate those subjects, Brigham uses art as a cognitive process for student achievement in those areas. Brigham cites as his authorities distinguished writers on learning and art, including Susanne Langer, Rudolf Arnheim, Jean Piaget, and Jerome Bruner, who continually stress the importance of the child's own actions on individual experiences in formulating knowledge. They agree that the artist's way of acting on experience by constructing forms (or "images" or "conceptual models") is an exemplary demonstration of the fundamental process of cognition. Brigham successfully induces children to act as artists on the basic subject matter of their academic subjects and convert it into art forms. Essential to this success, of course, are imaginative, resourceful, innovative teachers who are willing to explore those subjects with specialists and to implement art instruction that stimulates children to creatively deal with those subjects. The following are examples of teaching methods that elicit children's artistic conceptualizations in various subjects.[7]

Language Development. Upper-elementary-grade students can work on sentence- and story-writing by making storyboards (see Chapter 10), using random assortments of pictures cut from magazines and newspapers. Students select pictures to illustrate a story they make up. Then they letter one or more sentences or perhaps a complete paragraph with felt-tip markers underneath the pictorial sequence. Later, the class reads and critiques the stories in relation to the pictures that inspired them.

Students of the same grade level can create original paintings based on expressive language. They draw and paint more or less literal interpretations of contemporary idiomatic expressions such as "That drives me up a wall," "That freaks me out," "Get off my back," or "She's a real cool kid" (the "kid" being a goat).

"Word attack" art lessons can include the production of "syllable

<hr/>

[7]These ideas were all developed by Don Brigham and his staff in the Attleboro, Ma., schools. See also Russell G. Stauffer, *The Language-Experience Approach to the Teaching of Reading* (New York: Harper & Row, 1970), pp. 1–18.

animals" by third grade students. Analyzing the syllabic subdivisions of two- and three-syllable animal names such as *rab-bit, go-ril-la, gi-raffe, and but-ter-fly*, students separate and rearrange the syllables into new names: *go-raffe, rab-ril-la, rab-ter-fly*. They then draw and paint their visual concepts of such "syllable animals." In the process, of course, they practice syllabication skills, which are vital for reading and writing.

Mathematics. Art activities can be used to help children recognize equivalent fractions. To recognize that $\frac{2}{4} = \frac{1}{2}, \frac{3}{4} = \frac{6}{8}$, or $\frac{6}{8} = \frac{12}{16}$, children must have experience with balance and equivalency. Students use balance scales to measure and counterbalance sand, water in containers of different shapes, different quantities of pebbles, and Cuisinaire cubes and rods. Using cork-stamp printing, children discover, for instance, that six red spots printed in a total field of red and green spots was equivalent to twelve half-sized blue spots in a blue-orange field of sixteen spots. Students then experiment with various regular geometric shapes, folding and cutting fractional subdivisions while examining equivalencies. These geometrics, converted into cardboard and metal forms, are incorporated into mobiles. Quarter-size shapes are made to balance an appropriate quantity of eighth-sized shapes, and so on. These equivalency studies and solutions can become increasingly complex in the production of colorful and well-formed mobiles. These experiences have been found to help students understand the mathematical concept of equivalent fractions.

Geography. An integrated art and geography lesson has been named "Body Maps" by the teacher who devised it. Fifth grade students respond to this posted statement: "Many times an artist sees an *analogy*, that is, a similarity between things otherwise unlike, between nature and himself. After making an outline of your body, look for similarities with our list of land, water, and sky features." Among the listed features were continent, city, peninsula, island, crater, gulf, strait, bay, river, moon, meteor, and constellation. Students lie in different configurations on large sheets of paper while other students trace their outlines. Using felt-tip markers, oil, or wax crayons, each student fills in the outline as a complex topographical image, complete with details of transportation networks, modes of transportation, communities and cities, and ingenious, amusing place names. Various body organs are translated into the analogous forms and functions of a landscape or waterway. Each whole "body map" is a work of expressive and imaginative art, and through the activity, each student gains knowledge of geographical features and terms.

Science. In an eighth grade science lesson on the periodic table of chemical elements and their atomic structure, students learn that an atom is composed of a nucleus of protons and neutrons and a "shell" of elec-

A scientist would label these constructions models of molecular forms; an artist would call them sculpture. Both would be correct. Science and mathematics are rich sources of inspiration for the artist; symmetrical and radial forms, as well as the clustering of modules and units, can serve as the basis for drawings, paintings, or three-dimensional structures.

trons, and that the number of protons of any specific element always equals the number of electrons. Using scrap materials, they construct atomic models of various elements. They learn that the periodic table is a tabular arrangement of chemical elements according to their atomic numbers, and that the atomic number of an element is its number of electrons or equivalent number of protons. The science teacher emphasizes that no one has ever seen an atom, and therefore that models of atomic structure are necessarily conceptual; an artistic conceptualization by a student would be scientifically valid, if it represented quantitative facts of atomic composition.

The cooperating art teacher invites the students to conceptualize the atomic structure of elements in terms of stitchery designs or pictorial forms. Later, each student mounts the stitchery on a piece of colored fabric, which in turn is mounted on an 8-by-8-inch wood frame. Each student explores various schematic possibilities for the representation of a selected chemical element. Some students find they could compose the details of the atomic structure into animal or human forms, if not into formal or informal designs. They choose varieties of threads and yarns and carefully stitch their forms. Finally they arrange all the stitcheries in the periodic order, and unite them into an overall tapestry by stringing wires through small holes in the struts of each individual frame.

1. Prepare detailed plans for three lessons involving a correlation between art and each of the following: physical education, reading, arithmetic.

2. Describe from your classroom observations some attempts at correlation between art and other subjects that degenerated into busywork. Explain in each case how you would have altered the lessons to ensure that art was produced.

3. Analyze a unit of work you have seen in a classroom for the art education that was involved in it. Explain how learning about art might have been improved.

4. Study some workbooks, and list any errors made by the authors when they attempt to correlate what they consider to be art with another subject. Suggest art activities to replace those outlined by the authors.

5. List all the symbols related to holy days and holidays that children have been asked to copy in classrooms you have observed. Suggest some art work to replace this copy work.

6. Experiment with a number of lettering nibs.[8] Use your own handwriting but try to eliminate any wiggles and squiggles. Also, in the interest of clar-ity, reduce the length of ascending and descending letters.

7. Cut out twenty-four 2-by-3-inch rectangles and convert them into cut block letters. Cut by families or groups—those that may be folded vertically or horizontally and those that are based on circles.

8. Make a poster for a school event. (A) Select a title for the headline; if a secondary heading is required, keep it to three or four words. (B) Make a rough layout, including letters and illustration, if any. (C) Outline the poster on Bristol board. (D) Paint the picture, if you have included one. (E) Do the lettering. (F) Analyze your work from a distance of ten feet for clarity, brevity, and design quality.

9. With the help of one or two other interested people, experiment with many materials to make a diorama, a panorama, a peep show, and a "movie." In the movie include a title page and captions as well as drawings to tell your story. Relate all four activities to some other classroom work.

10. Study Mr. A's social studies program (p. 431). Then fill in the column on the right in Table 14.1 with art activities that encourage original thinking in art.

[8] For students who wish to become especially proficient in lettering, see Ross F. George, *Speedball Text Book*, 19th ed. (New York: Landau, 1965). The student who wishes to know more about lettering should see Oscar Ogg, *An Alphabet Source Book* (New York: Dover, 1947); this is a purely technical work. Ogg, *The 26 Letters* (New York: Crowell, 1961), is more historical than the previous works just cited.

Suggested Readings

Dimondstein, Geraldine. *Exploring the Arts with Children*. New York: Macmillan, 1974. Part I, "Learning Through the Arts," states, with passion and clarity, the case for relating the arts to other subjects.

Hurwitz, Al. *Programs of Promise: Art in the Schools*. New York: Harcourt Brace Jovanovich, 1972. The chapter entitled "Art and General Learning" deals with ideas of learning theorists as applied to different modes of learning.

Linderman, Marlene. *Art in the Elementary School*. Dubuque: William C. Brown, 1974. Chapter 4, "Interdisciplinary Art Learning."

Report of the NAEA Commission on Art Education. Reston, Va.: National Art Education Association, 1977. Section III, Appendix, "Relating the Arts: Two Views," compares two approaches to art relationships.

displaying
children's art

The final major responsibility of the teacher of art is to display the children's completed art. Since art is appreciated through visual activity and emotional sensitivity, exhibiting it is a necessary part of the cycle of activity involved in any art project. Children have enjoyed the creating of an art project and they also enjoy their completed work. They want to share with others a part of what is so vital to them. Realizing this need and desire for recognition, the teacher should plan to display the work of the children in whatever way best suits the particular art product.*

fifTEEN

From the art program come tangible visual results of the learning experience; the art program in fact constitutes the only part of the school curriculum whose results are truly visible, because they can be exhibited over a prolonged period. As such, art lends itself to display, which serves as the final communicative stage of the creative process.

Several obvious educational benefits may occur as a result of effective display techniques. It is the purpose of this chapter, therefore, to discuss some of the most important aspects of presenting children's work, including the chief reasons for displaying the work, the problem of selecting pieces for display, the techniques and media involved in arranging displays, and the appropriate teaching methods.

*From Blanche Jefferson, *Teaching Art to Children* (Boston: Allyn and Bacon, 1959), p. 154.

439

Why Display Children's Art?

Perhaps the most important reason for displaying art is simply that the results of children's artistic acts are usually worth observing for their aesthetic qualities. Children's art is often so attractive that it should not be hidden in portfolios but brought forth for people to see and enjoy. The production of any art form is not a casual event; it is an offering of heart and mind from one human being to another. Indeed, the whole character of expression in art has been recognized as *"an overture demanding response from others."*[1] Because children offer in their work something of their true selves, their efforts are worthy of respectful attention.

The display of children's art is an effective teaching device. One common method of display is to group the work according to topics or themes. When twenty-five or more pupils in a class present their reactions to one theme, it is highly educative for all to observe those reactions. If art is suitably taught, no two children make identical statements about an experience. After viewing the various statements the children may gain a broader insight into the topic as a whole.

The display of children's art tends to develop in the pupils certain desirable attitudes toward the school. When young children see their artistic efforts on display among those of their fellows, they tend to sense a oneness with the group. Their participation brings out a feeling of belonging, which often increases the fullness of subsequent participation. Perhaps the children have stated something about a pet at home, their mother, father, brother or sister, toys, or playmates. It is comforting to them that these important aspects of their lives have miraculously found a way into their school and, furthermore, that the school is interested in them.

The display of children's art also has, of course, its decorative purposes. The classroom is usually a very barren place when the teacher enters it, preparatory to the opening of school. Likewise the halls of many schools are drab caverns until suitable decorations have been arranged. Much of the art work of children has highly decorative quality that will quickly change the character of a school building. Often bold and colorful, the work lends attractiveness and an intimate feeling to even the most austere surroundings, particularly in older school buildings. But even the most delightful interior architecture of modern schools can be improved by a judicious display of children's production.

More and more, schools are serving as institutions of learning by day and as community centers by night. Parent-teacher groups, night-school classes (in which, among other subjects, art may be studied), and other

[1]The words are those of I. D. Suttie, in *The Origins of Love and Hate*, quoted by Herbert Read in *Education Through Art*, rev. ed. (New York: Pantheon, 1958), p. 167.

Russian teachers and students study an international exhibition of children's work. The arrangement is pleasing—simple and uncluttered. The top row, however, may be beyond the reach of the two boys.

meetings of interest to the members of a community are causing greater numbers of adults to visit the schools than ever before. This is a desirable development, since it provides the school with an opportunity to show the public what is being done with that sacred commodity, the taxpayer's money. Furthermore, it presents the opportunity of arousing or maintaining public interest in education in general and art education in particular. Art displays operate on three different levels: the classroom, the school, and the community. In the classroom or artroom, display is linked closely to instruction and also enhances the environment. In the school and community, however, it should be used to alert viewers to the nature and goals of the art program. Art teachers can no longer afford the luxury of displays that are simply arrangements of attractive objects. No work should be presented without a label conveying such information as the student's name, school, teacher, grade, title, and—most important—the concept, goal, or unit to which the work is related. Thus when viewers are puzzled by what seems to be an exercise without meaning, they can learn its purpose. The art teacher deals with public naiveté regarding art, as do museums or galleries, but those professional centers of art are not linked directly to local tax support.

Selecting Work for Display

Probably the first question in the teacher's mind is how to choose the work for exhibition. The criteria for selection should be both pedagogical and aesthetic. Although children will find interest in the art output of others, they are also interested in their own work and are usually proud of it. This means that every child in a class sooner or later during the school term should have some work on display. Since space is limited in a classroom, pupils cannot expect their work to appear very often, but they will accept this fact if they feel that their chances to have work displayed are equal to those of others. Awareness of this tends to make them more active participants in all displays that appear on the classroom walls.

As children mature, they develop an ability to appraise the standards of both their behavior and their artistic output. Most children in the upper grades can tell with some accuracy whether they "took it easy" or "worked hard." They are also capable of realizing when their output has not resulted in a success commensurate with their effort. An attempt at expression does not always result in success, as every creating person knows. When children realize that their output has not reached an accustomed standard, displaying their work would in all likelihood be an embarrassment to them. Before a particular child's work is displayed, therefore, a teacher would do well to compare it with previous performances. A deviation from the usual standard may be the result of either a decrease in effort or just an uninspired day.

If work for display is chosen with these ideas in mind, the child of exceptional ability will not create the problems of selection that might otherwise occur. It would be discouraging for the members of the class to see a more gifted child's work repeatedly occupying a major portion of the displays to the partial exclusion of the work of others. The gifted child exhibits a range of success in output, just as everyone else does. This being the case, only the most significant items of that child's expression need appear on display.

Sometimes—indeed perhaps frequently—the most finished and apparently competent work of particular children, no matter what their ability, may be rejected in favor of output showing a child's advance in some specific ability in art, such as an improvement in the handling of a medium or an element of design. Sometimes, on the other hand, during what might be described as a burst of growth, children may pass from one expressive stage or mode to another. On such occasions their development may adversely affect their technique. Skills then seem to deteriorate, or rather do not keep pace with thought, so that the work appears inadequate in composition or in the handling of media. Nevertheless, because an advance has been made in other directions, the output should be displayed, provided the children are willing to have it shown.

The teacher will not have to save all the art work of every pupil during the school year to summarize the general progress of each child. While some of the work may be kept in a folder for reference, the teacher will be able, for the most part, to remember each child's earlier performances. The art output of each child becomes unique in the eyes of an alert, interested, and sensitive teacher.

The selection of work for display is, then, a delicate matter. It depends not only on the outward appearance of each piece but also on an intimate knowledge of every child responsible for it. The teacher must be fully aware of each child's potential and judge the work, not from some preconceived standard of attainment, but rather in relation to the pupil's personal abilities.

What part should the children play in the selection of work? This is a difficult question that the teacher will probably have to answer. It is obviously desirable that the children have some control of the selection of work. However, the teacher is probably in the best position to recognize both the aesthetic growth in individuals and the true aesthetic quality in a large proportion of the output. Perhaps a satisfactory compromise can be reached if individuals are occasionally given the opportunity to indicate their preferences for display of their own work, while committees of children are from time to time made responsible for selecting displays from the various pieces chosen by individuals. At other times, however, it may be necessary for the teacher to choose the arrangement of the display. On these occasions the teacher may still work closely with the children by explaining the reasons for the selection.

In general, it is suggested that the farther the display is removed from the classroom, the more selective should be the process of choosing the works to be displayed. When children's art goes to the front hall or to some location in the community, each piece should be selected for its ability to capture and hold the attention of the viewer. In the classroom, however, there may be times when the work of the entire class will be displayed.

Arranging Displays in the Classroom

Media and Techniques for Displaying Two-Dimensional Work. The display areas should not be overcrowded. Each piece should be set apart and mounted in some way. Mounts should be chosen so that their color unifies the display but does not conflict with the colors used in the drawings and paintings themselves. Grays, browns, and sometimes black are usually suitable colors for mounts. White is also recommended, since it flatters the picture and gives a clean look to the exhibit. When the display panels are made of wood, cork, celotex, or homosote, both mount and

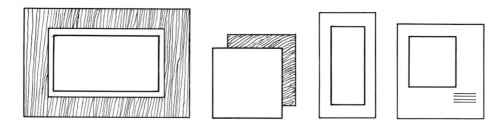

Some methods of mounting two-dimensional works.

picture may most conveniently be fastened to the display area by a gun-type wall stapler or clear-headed pushpins. Thumbtacks should be avoided because they distract the viewer's attention from the work.

Mounts or frames may be devised in a number of ways and with several materials. The simplest, cheapest, and, many think, most attractive method of mounting is to attach a sheet of newsprint, paper, or cardboard to the display board and to fasten on this a drawing or painting having smaller dimensions. A variety of effects may be obtained with this method by altering the proportion of background to picture. Another method of framing a picture is to fix the picture to the board, cut a window the size of the picture in a sheet of paper or cardboard, and then, placing the frame over the picture, attach it to the board. Mounts need not be wide: even a 1-inch border with a 2-inch lower border can be effective, as long as it leaves room for a label.

As mentioned earlier, it is often desirable to exhibit work according to topics or themes. Sometimes a theme depicts a series of events that demand a logical order of display, for example, "Our Trip to the Dairy," which would include the departure from school, the arrival at the plant, the mechanical processes observed, and the return to school. To assist the observer in following the proper sequence of pictures, a series of paper arrows can be used. In addition to providing information, displays can invite the onlooker's participation by asking such questions as "What kinds of shapes do we see in a dairy?" or "How many kinds of workers bring us our milk?"

In some displays no particular topical arrangement is required, but a certain aesthetic order is desired. Those arranging a display will find string convenient in establishing patterns. If various colors and types of string or yarn are strung from one place to another in a panel, some exceptionally interesting rhythms can be achieved throughout the display.

When a display is arranged, a title is usually required. Titles, of course, become part of the general design of a display. A title may be produced in two dimensions with lettering pens and India or colored inks and felt pens.[2] Although they are beyond the ability of most elementary-

[2]See the section on poster-making in Chapter 14.

Displaying Children's Art

school children, three-dimensional titles can be made from cardboard cut-out letters. After it is cut out, each letter is stuck on a long pin that holds it away from the display board. Attractive background papers of contrasting color or texture help to make this type of title particularly arresting. "Primer" typewriters with large type also produce attractive titles.

The simplest and most common arrangement of pictures on a display panel is one that follows the rectangular shape of the board. The pictures are hung so that their edges are parallel to those of the board. More often than not a formal balance is achieved, so that the viewer's attention will be attracted equally around imaginary central axes of the board. The margins established between the picture frames and the outside edges of a display panel that is horizontal should be such that the bottom margin is widest, the top narrowest, and the width of the sides in between. In a vertical panel, the traditional proportions to be observed reverse the proportions of sides and top: the bottom is widest, the top is second in size, and the sides are narrowest. A square panel calls for even margins at top and sides, with a wider margin at the bottom. These classic arrangements are safe, and by using them one may tastefully display any group of pictures.

If display panels are not available, it may prove difficult to exhibit works of art in the school hall because most walls are constructed of tiles. Curls of masking tape on the back of pictures are often used to attach flatwork to such surfaces, but this is far from ideal because of the expense involved and the tendency of pictures to slip. Two permanent solutions are strips of cork bolted to the wall and framed 4-by-8-foot sheets of composition board or any other material that takes staples and pins. Avoid masonite for this reason. Masonite pegboard, however, is excellent because bent metal hooks can be inserted to hang shelves, puppets, and other three-dimensional objects.

Display techniques may be highly informal, as demonstrated by this life-size costume parade taped to the tiled walls of a corridor. (Photo by Rick Steadry.)

The corner of a classroom has been temporarily converted into a gallery. Display units are dispersed to accommodate traffic and facilitate viewing. (Photo by Rick Steadry.)

All exhibitions in a classroom must show an awareness of the display situation and should be considered as designs subject to the discipline of good taste. As each display is added, it must be considered in relation to whatever displays are already on view. In general, it is wise to restrict displays to those areas especially designed for them. A classroom can scarcely appear orderly if drawings and paintings are stuck to blackboards, pinned to chalk-ledges, or plastered on windows. Blackboards, chalk-ledges, and windows are functional parts of the classroom whose efficiency is impaired by displays of art. To interfere with their function through decoration is an act of bad taste.

Here are some other points the teacher might keep in mind when setting up bulletin-board displays and exhibits:

1. A bulletin board has somewhat the same function as a poster. Both must capture attention, provide information, and present a unified design through pleasing relationships of textures, masses, subject matter, and lettering.
2. Pins with clear plastic heads are the best fasteners, metal pins next, and tacks last. Staples may be used if a staple remover is available.
3. Some areas of the background should be uncluttered, to give the eye a rest.
4. The eye level of the viewer should be respected. A good average height is 5 feet, 6 inches.
5. Extreme "artiness," such as complicated diagonal arrangements, should be avoided.
6. Bulletin-board exhibits should seldom be on display for more than two weeks. There is no disgrace in occasionally having a blank display area.

446

7. If possible, a well-lighted area should be used for the display.

8. Usually tops or sides of pictures should be aligned for consistency and order, and vertical and diagonal lettering should be avoided.

9. A supply of materials such as solid-colored burlap and corduroy should be kept on hand. These make excellent background segments to unite a small group of pictures. Any material that detracts from the objects on display should not be used.

10. When "going public," avoid supermarkets and other busy environments.

11. Avoid large groups of objects that are too similar in either size or subject. Twenty drawings or paintings can maintain variety within themselves; the same number of 8-by-10-inch versions of paint blown through straws will convey a depressing similarity.

12. Occasionally, break up displays with a sudden shift of scale. It can be quite exciting to have the usual 12-by-16- or 16-by-24-inch works set off against a life-size painting or mural.

13. Some works are "quieter" (lower-key, smaller-scale, less obtrusive) than others. A group of quiet paintings fare better than a row of loud ones, which tend to cancel out one another's effectiveness. Try alternating works of contrasting character.

14. When appropriate, statements by students or teachers, or Polaroid photographs of a class in action, can add diversity and a documentary effect.

15. Nothing is more barren than a blank wall when the public has become accustomed to a surface filled with art. Leave the walls empty for at least a week before putting up the next show. A neverending exhibit ends up as pure decoration and after a while the public may take it for granted.

Media and Techniques for Displaying Three-Dimensional Work.
Most classrooms are not equipped with display cases for three-dimensional output. It is frequently necessary, therefore, for the class to improvise other means of display. If space is available, a table may be placed directly in front of a display board. The three-dimensional objects may then be set on the table and descriptions of the work, or related two-dimensional work may be pinned to the board. Should it be necessary to link a written description to any particular piece on the table, a colored string may be fixed from the description to the piece of work.

The objects should be arranged according to their bulk and height. Obviously the largest and tallest objects will have to be placed well in the background so that smaller objects will not be hidden. Some groups of objects, particularly modeled or carved forms and pottery, will demand the use of pedestals. The pedestals, which can be made from boxes or blocks of wood, may be painted or covered with textiles. By placing a sheet of glass over one or more of the pedestals, it is possible to arrange a convenient series of shelves of varying heights. Ceiling space can be utilized in many unusual ways, particularly for mobiles and kites. Caution should be used, however, in hanging objects from the ceiling, for certain ceiling surfaces and lighting fixtures must be treated with care. Custodians and principals can give information in this regard.

Display boards themselves may be used to exhibit three-dimensional work. Metal brackets fixed to the boards with screws are able to support glass shelves, which make attractive display space.

In arranging three-dimensional displays, the exhibitors must give the same attention to design that they would in displaying flat work. For example, brilliantly colored pieces or those having outstanding structural or textural qualities must be well placed with respect to the centers of interest, the balance, and the rhythm of the design. To bring unity to the three-dimensional display, it may be necessary to use the same background for the objects.

Some striking results may be obtained by avoiding straight rows of objects, placing them instead at different heights and at various distances from the observer, and by grouping objects within a display, yet maintaining a unity among all such groups. Objects do not arrange themselves; to present them with charm and character, one must give considerable attention to the problems peculiar to three-dimensional display.

Paper fish stuffed with newspaper are hung in an arrangement that simulates a mobile. The strings are tacked to the soft celotex ceiling of the hallway. Many classrooms and other areas have high ceilings; the problem is to decide how to use the overhead space without damaging the ceiling or upsetting custodians or the fire department.

448   Displaying Children's Art

Teaching. Because the displaying of art is an art activity in itself, it is highly desirable for children to take part in it. Even a six-year-old can see how much better a drawing looks when it is mounted and displayed. A simple act such as this can establish the connection between design and order in a young mind. Moreover, display techniques may lead to excellent group endeavors. The kindergarten is not too soon for children to begin this work. Kindergarten children may participate in quasi-group activities in which individuals bring their work to some central area for display.

As in all other art activities the teacher must continually remind the children of the importance of design in display arrangements. Whether children are drawing up plans in advance for a display or working out a display directly on a panel or elsewhere, the teacher must encourage them continually to consider the designs being formed.

The teacher should give every encouragement to the pupils to experiment with new ways of displaying their art. One method is to have members of the class report on any outstanding display techniques observed in store windows or elsewhere. Another method is to have the teacher from time to time arrange a display of children's work in which some new ideas for display are demonstrated. The teacher, however, should exercise caution in arranging the display. The arrangement should never be so active that it draws attention to itself and thus overwhelms the work it is intended to support.

Arranging Displays Outside the Classroom

The problems arising from displays arranged in the halls or elsewhere in a school are little different from those related to classroom exhibits. More people and examples of work are involved, of course, so that organizational problems are intensified.

Media and Techniques. School architects often give attention to display possibilities, so it is not unusual for some elementary schools to have gallery-type walls designed adjacent to the principal's office.

If no gallery space is available, school authorities may be expected to provide suitable panels and even display cases; the cost of these is a relatively minor item in most educational budgets. When the panels and cases are being installed, those responsible for the installations must remember to arrange suitable lighting for each one.

On occasion the school may need additional display facilities. Many extra panels might be required on Parents' Night, for example, when the school wishes to make an exceptional effort to interest the community. The design of panels for extra display facilities has become almost stand-

A large zigzag display in a school gymnasium. Activities that normally take place in the gym must be rescheduled to accommodate the exhibit. Moreover, setting up such an exhibit may involve a good deal of the teacher's time and energy, even though the exhibit itself may be on display for only a short time. (Photo by Jack Engeman Studio.)

ard. The panels consist of sheets of building board, usually measuring from 4 by 4 feet to 4 by 8 feet, to either end of which legs are bolted. The legs are usually in the form of inverted T's, but other ingenious and attractive designs are to be seen. For three-dimensional display a boxlike construction often having shelves takes the place of the panel.

A second type of portable display board has been designed for space-saving and quick assembly. It consists of panels of building board and sturdy legs with slots cut into two adjacent sides. The panels are fitted into the slots to form a zigzag effect which is pleasing and practical. The panels are made secure by lashing the legs together with cord at the top and bottom of the panels.

The illustration shows another portable display unit. The materials needed are 2-by-2-inch wooden rods slightly over 5 feet in length, with holes bored at approximately 30-inch intervals. These rods will receive 1-inch dowels, on which hang metal rings that are attached to the pictures. The placement of the holes on the 2-by-2-inch rods determines how the units may be angled, so that the flow of traffic can be controlled.

The Display as Community Education

The subject matter of art displays for parent and community groups may be different from that of displays for children. Parents and other adults are interested not only in the work as such but also in the pedagogical princi-

Displaying Children's Art

ples supporting the art program. We should remember that for many adults, the present-day program of art in schools is completely different from the so-called art work they were forced to do in their youth. Although ignorance of the contemporary program sometimes leads to disapproval, parents are generally quick to react favorably to present-day trends in art, once they understand those trends. For parents, subjects of exhibitions of children's art might emphasize some of the instructional implications of the art activities. The themes may dramatize the overall structure of the art program or a single aspect of it. The following are a few sample topics that have proved satisfactory for Parents' Night:

> The Art Program: A Grade-Level Approach
> Looking at Nature
> Personal Development Through Art
> Variety in Artistic Expression
> Group Work in Art
> "How I See Myself"
> The Colors of Our Neighborhood
> The Art Program in Our Elementary School

For each exhibition, brief but effective signs should be made to emphasize the points demonstrated by the children's work. Each show, more-

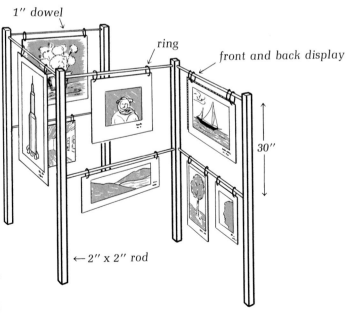

1" dowel

ring

front and back display

30"

← 2" x 2" rod

The units in this display arrangement can be dismantled easily and stored in a small area. Note that both the front and back of the units can be used for display. (Designed by Pat Renick.)

Rarely has there been a more impressive place to set up a display of children's art than in one of the main galleries of the Hermitage Museum, Leningrad. The work comes from special children's art classes in the museum.

over, should have a clearly marked beginning, a logical sequence of ideas throughout the body of the exhibition, and a short summary, either written or pictorial or both, at its close. The exhibit should be more than merely another chore. It is the most dramatic means of communicating the teacher's role in the school to the public, to the administration, and to other teachers.

Activities for the Reader

1. Describe the various criteria used by teachers you have observed to select children's art work for display. Appraise each criterion according to its educational effects on the children concerned.
2. Study and compare the display techniques you have observed in various classrooms.
3. Experiment with mounting and framing a picture on a surface such as a drawing board. Try some of the ways suggested in this chapter and then devise new ways to display the picture.
4. Sketch in pencil or crayon some plans for a display of five pictures. Select the plan you like best and use it in an actual panel display.

5. Repeat 4, this time including at least twelve pictures.
6. Make some plans for the display of three pieces of pottery. Carry out the plan you like best.
7. List some subjects for an art display to be used in the main entrance of a school on Parents' Night. The entrance hall is about 25 feet long and 12 feet wide. After selecting the subject that most appeals to you, indicate in detailed sketches (a) the type and position of the display panels; (b) the number and subject matter of the pictures or three-dimensional objects; (c) the captions to be used; and (d) the route that visitors should follow to view the exhibi-

tion and the means by which they are directed along this route.

8. Pretend you are a new teacher using a spring exhibit to acquaint the community with your art program. You have a dozen 4-by-8-foot panels on which to display the year's work in the gymnasium. What materials would you choose for your panels? How would you organize your display? Present your plan in the form of a real model made of heavy cardboard, using a scale of 1 inch to 1 foot.

9. Assume that you have completed the plans for the installation of an exhibition at your school. Now ask yourself the following questions: Should art work be labeled? Why? If the work should be labeled, what kinds of information should be included? Pupil's name? grade? medium? teacher? school? Should all, part, or none of the foregoing be included? Why?

Suggested Readings

Horn, George. *Bulletin Boards*. New York: Reinhold, 1962. A good source of ideas for school displays of all kinds.

Lindsay, John C. *Art Is . . .* Ontario: General Learning Press, 1975. Chapter 10, "Displaying Student Work."

Wankelman, Willard F., and Philip Wigg. *A Handbook of Arts and Crafts for Elementary and Junior High School*, 4th ed. Dubuque, Iowa: Wm. C. Brown, 1978. Pages 15–21, "Effective Use of Display Areas and Bulletin Boards."

developing

children's appreciation

of art

SiXTEEN

Up to this point we have considered the educational problems arising from the production of art forms. We must now turn to another aspect of art education, that of the pupils' appreciation of the work of others.

The Nature of Art Appreciation

In considering art appreciation we face intangibles. When the pupil has produced a work of art, we have the finished product to study and to

Photos on facing page: left, Amedeo Modigliani, *Woman with Red Hair*, 1917. Oil on canvas, $36\frac{1}{4}''$ x $23\frac{7}{8}''$. (Chester Dale Collection, National Gallery of Art, Washington, D.C.); right, tempera painting by an eleven-year-old boy.

*From Harry S. Broudy, "Contemporary Art and Aesthetic Education," *The School Review*, Vol. 72, No. 3 (Autumn 1964), p. 397. Published by the University of Chicago Press. Copyright 1964 by the University of Chicago.

compare with the output of others. There can be no such tangible evidence of development in the pupils' ability to appreciate art. But we have good reason to believe that not only can children's appreciation of art be heightened, but that progress can be observed and, to some degree, evaluated. The validity of such a claim naturally depends on how *appreciation* is to be defined. If by this word we refer to the final act of criticism—that is, the formation of opinions in the evaluative or judgmental stage—it may indeed be difficult, philosophically as well as practically, to attempt to chart the child's progress. If, however, we refer to stages that precede judgment—that is, describing, analyzing, and interpreting what is revealed in artworks—then it is possible to develop both verbal and nonverbal means of measuring and appraising the gains being made by the student.

Stated simply, art appreciation implies knowing and having information about art works and using such knowledge as a basis for discriminating and interpreting. Knowledge about art refers to information surrounding the work of art (names, dates, places) as well as to facts concerning physical details (subject matter, media, colors) taken from the work itself. Knowledge about art also involves those concepts of design, technique, and style that the teacher feels enable the student to "read" a painting, sculpture, or building with some acuity.

Knowledge about art is rooted in perception. Art appreciation rests on the teacher's skill in developing the perceptual capabilities of the child. The development of perception is usually achieved by focusing attention on aspects of the work of art and is often viewed as a preliminary phase, to be followed by a valuative stage in which the pupils discuss the feelings generated by the work and whether or not they like the piece they are viewing.

Expressive movement can set the stage for art appreciation by encouraging direct physical responses to the structure of artworks. The education department of the Metropolitan Museum of Art in New York has experimented with a variety of multisensory approaches to heighten young people's sense of empathy with art objects—see also page 480. (Photo by Karen Gilborn.)

To accept knowledge as a vital component of art appreciation is not to preclude those highly personal reactions to art that come so naturally to children. Each child is free to react spontaneously to a given artwork. Many critics and aestheticians feel, however, that the children should be made aware of what is involved in the viewing of a work of art.

To what do we react in a work of art and how do we react? Roger Fry offers the argument that in all cases our reactions to works of art are reactions to relationships and not to isolated sensations, objects, persons, or events. He goes on to point out, as an example, that some of the works of the greatest colorists are built up from elements that are of no particular significance when taken separately, but that through interrelationships in their composition gain the utmost significance. His observations concerning our reactions to the relationships of elements extend into the fields of music, poetry, and architecture.[1]

An important distinction can be made between the reaction of "having a good laugh" or "a good cry" at, say, a cinema, and the aesthetic reaction to the screenplay. The former reaction, according to Herbert Read, is one of sentimentality. "Sentimentality," he states, "is a release, but also a loosening, a relaxing of the emotions; art is a release, but also a bracing."[2] Thus, in Read's view, to weep over the trials of the heroine of a play as if we were in the place of the sufferer is not to experience the aesthetic quality of the production. A work of art may lead the mind to delightful fantasies, but such a state is irrelevant if the work of art is the single reference for aesthetic appreciation. John Dewey sums up the matter thus: "Emotion is esthetic when it adheres to an object formed by an expressive act."[3]

An aesthetic response, as distinguished from a sentimental one, seems to involve the total personality. There is probably much truth in the old saw about "a picture judging a person" rather than the reverse. What a person is—emotionally, intellectually, and socially—will determine that person's ability to appreciate art. This ability is not innate, but it seems to be built around innate qualities, so that some people are able to acquire it more quickly than others. Art appreciation, in fact, appears to be the result of prolonged education. "As for appreciation, this can undoubtedly be developed by teaching," says Read, although "the faculty is only likely to develop as one aspect of social adaptation."[4] The problem arises in the elementary school when it wishes to help children learn to appreciate the art of others. The remainder of this chapter will concentrate on some practical ways and means of developing appreciation of art.

[1] Roger Fry, *Transformations* (New York: Doubleday, 1956).
[2] Herbert Read, *The Meaning of Art*, 3rd ed. (New York: Pitman, 1951), p. 39.
[3] John Dewey. *Art as Experience* (New York: Putnam, 1959), p. 76.
[4] Herbert Read, *Education Through Art*, rev. ed. (New York: Pantheon, 1958), p. 209.

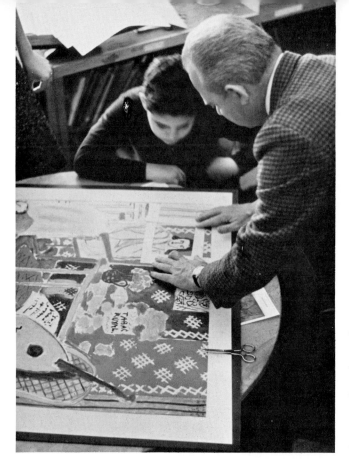

A pupil and his teacher study a reproduction of a Matisse painting to examine the many compositions within the total work and the way the parts relate to the whole. (A pair of two-sided **L** frames allows them to delineate each subcomposition.) Learning to observe, describe, interpret, and understand is integral to the appreciation of art.

PREFERENCE AND JUDGMENT

It is useful to recognize the distinction between preference and judgment in response to works of art. Our preferences are not subject to correction by authority or persuasion. Preference is our personal liking and disliking and is one aspect of our individuality. A sound basis in perception and logic is not required for personal preference. Judgment, however, is subject to argumentation and persuasion. For example, a person might be convinced, on the basis of nutritional evidence and the testimony of great cooks, that asparagus is a fine food, but still dislike asparagus.

When someone makes a statement such as "That is a very strong painting," or "That is a poor example of raku pottery," it is reasonable for someone else to ask, "Why do you say that?" and request some justification for the judgment. If the justification is weak or controversial, a dialog or friendly argument may follow. The person with the soundest evidence and the most convincing justification may persuade the other to alter his or her position.

When someone makes the statement "I like that painting very much," someone else might ask, "Why do you like it?"—but the preference is not subject to the process of justification described above. In fact, it is perfectly reasonable to say, "I know that this drawing is not of high qual-

Developing Children's Appreciation of Art

ity, but I like it nevertheless." Conversely, it is appropriate to remark, "I know that this is an excellent sculpture, but I really don't like it." In most instances, however, we are more apt to like a work of art if we have an understanding of it. Usually we prefer those works that we judge to be of high quality to those that we judge to be of low quality.

Gaining skills for art appreciation—learning to observe, describe, and interpret—will help us to respond more fully to art, but the goal for art appreciation is understanding, not preference. Even the greatest critics maintain their personal likes and dislikes. We find, however, as we learn more about an artist's work, a style of painting, or a process such as print-making, that our preferences normally change and expand; often we come to enjoy more than before. The great barrier to appreciation is lack of familiarity and awareness. We have very little chance of appreciating abstract painting, for example, unless we have been exposed to it and have learned something about it. Through the process of education, we can move from ignorance to understanding and then possibly to enjoyment.

Some Teaching Methods for Developing Appreciation

There are at least four points of view concerning the teaching of art appreciation in the elementary school. The first suggests that there should be no teaching, because children are not sufficiently mature to benefit from it. Instead, the teacher should encourage the pupils to express themselves and then "can only stand over them in a kind of protective awe."[5] The second is that formal lessons should be offered from time to time, particularly with regard to "picture study."

The third view is that appreciation should be taught when such teaching appears to be expedient and when the need for it is clearly apparent. This view implies that the logical juncture for appreciation on the elementary level may well lie in studio activity. Experience with materials may be directly related to the kinds of knowledge needed to extend the pupil's power of appreciation. The fourth viewpoint, already touched on, is that special efforts should be made to make children, even those on the elementary level, so aware of critical processes that they can apply what they have learned when confronted with works of art.

The first point of view seems untenable. The actions of teachers during their daily rounds of duty, their appearance, their care of the classroom, and so on must exert some effect, either good or bad, on the attitudes of children toward art. Furthermore, if expression is to receive any guidance at all, the question of appreciation immediately enters into an art activity. Whether or not teachers believe in teaching for the development of appreciation, they do so teach.

[5]Read, *Education Through Art.*

Few teachers who have ever taught for appreciation and listened to the insights that children bring to viewing would ever take this first position. The freshness, honesty, and directness that characterize the art work of primary pupils, and the imaginative and intuitive capabilities of most children on the elementary level, combine to provide a positive learning climate for their appreciation activities. The increased verbal skill of children in the upper elementary grades can compensate to a large degree for their self-consciousness in certain studio activities, and can often provide academically talented children with an opportunity to excel in another area of art—critical appreciation.

The second point of view had more advocates twenty-five years ago than today. An extraordinary amount of nonsense has been perpetrated in many classrooms through formal lessons in art appreciation, in which irrelevant questions are asked about certain works of art. Sir Joshua Reynolds' *The Age of Innocence,* for example, may be the picture chosen for study. Even when the questions are fairly pertinent to the picture being studied—"Why is the little girl placed where she is in the picture?" or, "What colors has the artist used to make us look at her?"—there is some doubt as to the value of the teaching procedure. But when, as is not infrequently the case, the questions become artistically remote from the work and include sentimental or literary ideas—"Isn't she a pretty little girl? Do you think she is happy? Why isn't she wearing shoes? Will it rain? What will the little girl do then?"—the appreciation of art can never occur. Such questions simply lead the children away from "the sense in which the act of expression has been defined." To offer this type of lesson in picture appreciation, even as a literary exercise, can only intensify an all too prevalent misapprehension as to the nature of art.

Indeed, in recent years any formal teaching of "famous masterpieces" has been held in some suspicion. "Urging people to like things, or preaching about our own likes is not the most effective way to get results."[6] As Dewey says, art can be appreciated only when there is a "hunger and thirst" for it. The formal attempt to motivate children to appreciate famous paintings is rarely as effective as its advocates maintain. But the failure in general of the formal method of teaching appreciation of art in no way obviates the necessity for children to be afforded every possible means of coming into contact with their cultural heritage.

[6]Thomas Munro, "Powers of Art Appreciation and Evaluation," in G. M. Whipple, ed., *Fortieth Yearbook of the National Society for the Study of Education* (Bloomington, Il.: Public School Publishing Co., 1941), p. 340. The extent to which a child's acquaintance with pictures may be at the mercy of a teacher is well illustrated in many of the books on art appreciation that appeared years ago. A typical example is Agnes Hammell, *Advancing in Picture Study* (Toronto: Gage, 1931). Most of the 110 illustrations chosen by this author are of the "realistic" or story-telling, photographic type, by Landseer, Dupré, Breton, Alma-Tadema, Leighton, and others of similar style. Not represented are Michelangelo, Gauguin, El Greco, or Matisse. Rather amazing is the inclusion of some Cézanne apples!

TABLE 16.1

A Comparison of Past and Present Methods of Teaching Art Appreciation

Past	Present
1. Emphasized immediate reactions to a work of art.	1. Defers judgment until the art object has been examined.
2. Instruction was primarily verbal and teacher-centered.	2. Instruction may be based on verbalization, perceptual investigation, studio activity, or combinations of these.
3. Relied primarily on reproductions.	3. Utilizes a wide range of instructional media—slides, books, reproductions, films, and, most important, original works of art, visits to museums and galleries, and visits from local artists.
4. Based primarily on painting, because of its "story-telling" qualities.	4. May encompass the complete range of visual form from "fine arts" (painting, sculpture) to applied arts (industrial design, architecture, and crafts). May also include print media, television, advertising, films, and magazine layouts.
5. Used literary and sentimental associations as a basis for discussion. Concentrated on such elements as beauty and morality to the exclusion of formal qualities.	5. Bases discussion on the formal qualities of the artwork. Recognizes beauty and other sensuously gratifying qualities as only one part of the aesthetic experience, but also recognizes abrasive and shocking images as legitimate expressions of psychological and political motives.
6. Concentrated on the "great monuments" of art.	6. Avoids reverence of the past; shows respect for artistic efforts of all epochs.
7. Drew instructional material from the culture of Western civilization.	7. Allows examples of artworks to encompass whatever cultures are most appropriate to represent a particular artistic point.
8. Spent much time in anecdotal accounts of artist's life.	8. Minimizes the life story of the artist and concentrates instead on the work.

If a stilted, authoritarian, excessively rigorous teaching situation is implied by the word *formal*, then formal instruction is to be avoided; but if it is taken to mean instruction that pertains to the form of a work, then the word becomes less inhibiting when applied to teaching. Table 16.1 may serve as a guide in comparing dated formal teaching methods with a more contemporary point of view.

Many teachers adopt the third viewpoint in devoting much of their time, thought, and energy to a program in which an appreciation of art is taught in close relationship to expression.[7] According to this method a

[7]This method is also advocated for adolescents in a report of the Progressive Education Association, *The Visual Arts in General Education* (New York: Appleton-Century-Crofts, 1940), pp. 72ff.

Pablo Picasso, *Girl Before a Mirror*, 1932. Oil on canvas, 64″ x 51¼″. (Collection, The Museum of Modern Art, New York. Gift of Mrs. Simon Guggenheim. © 1974 by SPADEM PARIS.) Teaching children to recognize important elements in a work of art can enhance their appreciation of the work. A fifth grader's version of the painting illustrates how children also bring their own responses to a work.

teacher seizes every practical opportunity to introduce the subject of appreciation, not only of drawing and painting but also of three-dimensional work such as sculpture and pottery.

This method is based on the belief that one cannot logically divorce expression from appreciation. After working with a medium, we know what to look for in similar work of others. We become conscious of the problems, needs, and goals that have influenced our own expressive acts. It does not matter how limited our present insight into artistic expression may be. As long as we have had some personal problem that has arisen from our own labors, some goal related to the activity, and some need for enlightenment, we are in a position to increase our insight by intelligently appreciating what another has done.

The fourth point of view is a species of formal analysis related to

462

criticism and is really an extension of the third position. This approach requires children to be thoroughly acquainted with the components of artworks and the teacher to be sensitive to children's perceptual and linguistic capabilities. Research offers relatively little information about this kind of teaching, but it represents a mode of instruction that many art educators today feel should be explored, if such goals as aesthetic sensitivity and visual acuity are ever to be realized in behavioral terms.

Teaching the characteristics that provide the structure of a unified work of art is important in this approach to appreciation. Fry has pointed out the dangers inherent in the abuse of this kind of teaching, which he feels can fragment the total aesthetic experience.[8] The teacher who does not abuse recognition and identification of design elements by an undue emphasis will find that children respond most favorably to the challenge of being specific in their discussion of paintings and sculpture.

In commenting on the reciprocity between the creative and critical processes in television art instruction, Manuel Barkan and Laura Chapman state:

> . . . the most sensitive making of art cannot lead to rich comprehension if it is not accompanied by observation of works of art and reflective thought about them. Neither can observation and reflection alone call for the nuances of feeling nor develop the commitment that can result from personal involvement in making works of art. The reciprocal relationship between learning to make art and learning to recognize, attend to, and understand art should guide the planning of art instruction.[9]

It cannot be assumed that children will make a connection between their own painting experience with color and that of an artist such as Monet, unless discussion and activity direct their attention to such a relationship.

This type of art appreciation at the elementary level suggests processes whereby students may engage in both studio and critical activities, gaining relevant information while discussing works of art. It also suggests deferring judgment and interpretation until the art has been examined and discussed. To cite a specific example, let us take a single unit of instruction for sixth graders that would include the above activities.

Stage I: Studio Activity
   A line drawing of a figure and still life. The object is to:
      1. Vary the quality of line.
      2. Take into consideration the spaces between the lines as components of the design.
      3. Relate the lines to the contours, or edges, of the subject.

---

[8] *Transformations.*
[9] *Guidelines for Art Instruction Through Television for Elementary Schools* (Bloomington, Ind.: National Center for School and College Television, 1967), p. 7.

Stage II: Knowledge (Information)

Vocabulary concepts around which the activity is built. These are listed on the blackboard and discussed prior to the activity.

Contour

Mass

Weight (of line)

Positive (line)

Negative (space between lines)

Discussion of artists who reflect these qualities (using slides or reproductions. Some artists for study are:

Pablo Picasso Edgar Degas

Henri Matisse Ronald Searle

Ben Shahn George Grosz

It is possible, of course, to vary the sequence and begin at this stage by using the work of the artists for motivational purposes. Some teachers would question this rearranged sequence on the grounds that it could unduly influence the work of the class.

Stage III: Observation and Perception

The children compare slides or reproductions of works by the above-mentioned artists to observe how their work reflects the concepts already discussed.

Stage IV: Interpretation and Preference

The children are asked to discuss the meaning of what they have seen (interpretation), then voice their opinions (likes and dislikes) of the artworks.

The final stage clearly allows for personal reaction, but the responses have greater critical validity because they are based on preparation through activity and guided discussion. Such an approach to art appreciation compels the children to be aware of the aesthetic constituents of appreciation and draws them away from irrelevant responses that over-emphasize subject matter.

Let us now note the kinds of discussions, activities, and learning instruments that can develop art appreciation, and examine the critical terminology used in the elementary-school classroom. The slide lecture is the most common, but not the most effective, way to teach art appreciation. There are other approaches.

A lesson need not take fifty minutes or an hour. Very effective teaching-learning situations occur in five minutes. Example: "This is a reproduction of a painting by the artist Monet," says the teacher, while displaying a large print. The teacher then asks questions related to recent art experiences, or provides some interesting information about the artist and his work. Each art class could begin with such an introduction to "The Artist of the Week."

Developing Children's Appreciation of Art

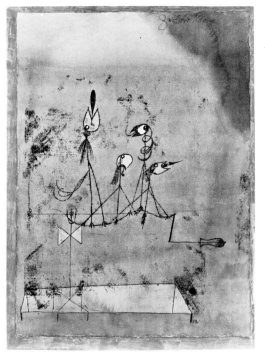

Paul Klee, *The Twittering Machine* (*Zwitscher-Maschine*), 1922. Watercolor, pen, and ink, 16¼" x 12". (Collection, The Museum of Modern Art, New York. Purchase. © 1974 by SPADEM PARIS.) A version by a third grader is on page 454. (The child's work was actually inspired by Gunther Schuller's musical study on Klee's painting.) Klee, who clearly stated his indebtedness to children's art, can be an effective starting point in directing children away from representational art toward the realm of the imaginative and the fantastic.

Teachers can teach art appreciation visually as well as verbally by putting up displays in the classroom. Example: Three color photographs of sculptures are placed on the bulletin board, one the head of an Egyptian woman, one an African woman, and one an Aztec woman. All three are sculpture from ancient times. After the pictures have been on display for a few days, the teacher asks, "What have you learned by looking at these sculptured heads?" Discussion might include concepts of sculpture, the idea of portraiture, apparent differences in style, speculation regarding sources, similarities, differences, and so on. This discussion might even lead to a discussion of what a contemporary American sculptured head would look like.

Teaching for art appreciation can take place in conjunction with studio art projects. When students are working on a visual or technical problem in their own art, they are often receptive to learning from other artists who have confronted similar problems. Example: Children are working on a collage and several are using pictures and fragments of pictures from magazines. Aware of their apparent interest in fantasy, the teacher shows the children pictures of works by artists who specialize in fantasy such as Dalí, Magritte, and Klee.

Children as well as adults can gain appreciation by explicitly trying what artists have tried. Example: The teacher's goal is to help the children understand why the Impressionists are called "painters of light," that is, why and how they captured so much sunlight in their work and why their colors are so light. The teacher takes the students outdoors on a sunny day to do landscape pictures with craypas. The children are encouraged to capture the colors that they see in sunlit areas. When they return to the classroom, they discuss how working outdoors is different from working in the classroom.

Children and Criticism

Criticism, as Feldman succinctly puts it, is "talk about art."[10] Its suggested inclusion in the elementary art program is recognition of the fact that children enjoy talking, arguing, and venturing opinions about art, even if their opinions may be somewhat uninformed. With increasing use of the critical process, however, children can develop a way of organizing their perceptions that provides a more valid basis for judgment.

Verbal skills may also be developed, since critical discussion focuses children's attention on concepts that can be mentioned, pointed to, and used in children's own activities. For instance, the phrase *symmetrical composition* may be meaningless to children until they can point to a medieval icon and say, "This is more symmetrical than the Wyeth."

THE STAGES OF THE CRITICAL PROCESS

The critical process involves certain categories of discourse that pupils may use as broad guidelines for the organization of their comments. Authorities differ in their ordering of "stages" and "taxonomies,"[11] but we are safe in stating that four basic stages of discussion are possible— description, formal analysis, interpretation, and judgment or informed preference. Let us examine these as they might apply to elementary art instruction.

Description. In the descriptive stage the child takes an initial inventory of what is seen. At this first perceptual level, a consensus should be reached that can be referred to in succeeding stages. Description involves noting objects, shapes, colors, and other items with which the children have probably had some prior experience. Children, like adults, will bring to a painting only what they have been prepared to bring. It is the teacher's task to prepare them by broadening their base of experience. Obviously,

[10] Edmund Feldman, *Art: Image and Idea* (Englewood Cliffs, N.J.: Prentice-Hall, 1967), p. 446.
[11] See Feldman, *Art: Image and Idea,* and Stephen Pepper, *Principles of Art Appreciation* (New York: Harcourt Brace Jovanovich, 1949).

Developing Children's Appreciation of Art

children will not compare a Holbein and a Van Gogh in terms of "painterly" textures unless this term has been pointed out to them. Even fourth graders are capable of such distinctions if their attention has been called to changes of appearance and of surface, or if they have been brought to discover it for themselves. A discussion of nonobjective or abstract paintings (those of Kandinsky, for example) will almost of necessity be descriptive.

Although the descriptive level focuses on aspects we generally perceive in ways that are common to most of us, it can lead to some heated discussions—what one person sees as red, another sees as orange; one person may see square shapes, another trapezoidal. In any case, it is an exercise in using precise language.

Formal Analysis. Formal analysis also has a perceptual basis but it takes place at a deeper level. It takes the descriptive stage a step further by requiring the child to analyze the makeup or composition of an art work. The child who can distinguish between symmetry and asymmetry, describe the nature of the material, and be sensitive to the kinds and qualities of color and line can comment about the form of an art work. This is the stage in which the teacher discovers whether the children can use the language of design.

The discourse initiated at both descriptive and formal-analytic stages brings about the intense visual concentration that is necessary if appreciation lessons are to have meaning and substance. Both stages are valuable also for the development of considered opinions about art. They do not allow for premature judgments, requiring instead that the student defer certain decisions until they can be handled with some detachment. At these two stages the teacher is asking, "What do you see?" rather than "What do you *think* about it?" What the child sees will, of course, depend on many factors. Some children will know more than others; that is, they should know more if they have had some experience with light, mass, color, line, and other elements of form.

Children view criticism as a visual-verbal game and will participate with enthusiasm if the discussions are not too lengthy (a half-hour seems to be an outside limit), and if the art works under discussion are selected with care. Works with strong color, interesting subject matter, and clear, indeed obvious, compositional structure seem to elicit the most positive responses.

Interpretation. In the interpretive stage, the child is asked to think about the meaning of the painting. To do this the child is required to establish some connection between the structure that can be discerned in a particular painting and the intent of the artist. For example, if the class has agreed that Orozco in his *Zapatistas* uses sharp contrasts of dark and

José Clemente Orozco, *Zapatistas*, 1931. Oil on canvas, 45″ x 55″. (Collection, The Museum of Modern Art, New York. Given anonymously.) The striking contrasts of light and dark in this work can be a starting point for a discussion of ends in painting.

light and strong directional forces, the next question might be, "To what end?" Would the meaning have been as clear had the artist used Redon's colors? At this vital point the class is getting at an artist's conscious use of compositional elements for a specific end. How does Renoir's sensuous and pleasing color relate to his feelings regarding motherhood and courtship? How do de Kooning's fragmented shapes and strident color tie in with his attitudes regarding certain types of women? Such questions provide material for discussion in the interpretive stage.

Informed Preference. The critical process normally ends with a judgment, that is, a conclusion regarding the success or failure of an artwork and its ranking with other artworks. This stage will not be discussed because it is the province of professional critics and connoisseurs. Judgment, in the mind of a child, is synonymous with preference. Children's opinions regarding the position of Dürer's etchings in the cannon of graphic art would not be terribly meaningful, but the same children's defense of their own acceptance or rejection of an artwork is perfectly possible. The fourth and final stage with which children can become involved, then, is *informed preference*. It is in this stage that the teacher can determine to what degree students can use critical and design vocabulary to articulate their views.

This is the culminating and most demanding stage. Although it invites students to render their opinions regarding the worth of an object, it requires that their opinions be based on what they have learned in the previous stages. Such questions as the following are asked: "Are you moved by this work of art?" "How do you feel about it?" "Would you like to own it or hang it in your room?" "Does it leave you cold?" "Do you dislike it?" "Why?" Most viewers begin at the level of preference: what the process of criticism as set forth here attempts to do is to *defer preference until the matter has been given thought*. In all cases, children should be asked to describe how they arrived at their opinions.

In essence, the four stages are related to four basic questions:

"What do you see?" (description)
"How are things put together?" (formal analysis)
"What is the artist trying to say?" (interpretation)
"What do you think of the work, and why?" (informed preference)

The following segment of an actual teaching session demonstrates what a renowned art historian, Dr. James Ackerman,[12] considered important in discussing painting with sixth graders. Dr. Ackerman began by making the point that the basic task of the session was to *talk* about what was seen as well as to look; and that looking would come naturally to the children, since they lived in a visually oriented society with constant exposure to television, films, and mass-printed media. He then listed on the blackboard four terms he felt were needed to discuss the paintings to be shown:

A HISTORIAN TEACHES

1. *Technique:* the way in which artists use materials.
2. *Form:* the structure and interaction of components of an art work. The class seemed to understand the word *shape* as a component of *form*, and the teacher accepted this.
3. *Meaning:* the intention; the ultimate significance of an artwork. Because the children had some difficulty absorbing this concept, Dr. Ackerman accepted the term *subject* in its place.
4. *Feeling:* the emotive power that is elicited from a work.

Dr. Ackerman used the comparative method to develop the class discussion. On one screen he showed a slide of an Impressionist oil painting of poplars, and on an adjacent screen he projected an Egyptian wall fresco showing trees framing a pool of fish and ducks (see page 470).

DR. A: Who would like to try to describe the painting techniques of these two paintings?
STUDENT: The trees are watercolor. . . .

[12]Dr. James Ackerman is former chairman of the department of fine arts, Harvard University. Because of the length of the tape, excerpts have been interspersed with descriptions of what occurred.

Two paintings discussed in the comparison exercises. Claude Monet, *Poplars*, about 1891. Oil on canvas. (Philadelphia Museum of Art. Gift of Chester Dale. © 1974 by SPADEM PARIS.) Egyptian fresco, XII Dynasty. (The Metropolitan Museum of Art, New York.)

STUDENT: I think they're oil.

DR. A: You're right; that is an oil painting. How about the other. . . ? (*a lot of whispering but no volunteers*) Take a guess.

STUDENT: Watercolor—maybe tempera?

DR. A: Why do you say that?

STUDENT: It's flat and bright, not shaded like oils.

DR. A: Very good—flat is a good word, except that in this case the effect is due to a fresco technique. Anyone know what fresco is? (*silence*) Well, it was used by the Egyptians as a way of making painting part of a wall. They did this by using tempera paint on fresh plaster mixed with water and lime. Now back to your "flatness." If you've ever painted on

Developing Children's Appreciation of Art

plaster you know it gets soaked up and dries quickly. That doesn't allow for much shading or roundness of forms and instead gets the painter to work in clear, flat areas of color. How did this artist make his shapes seem clearer?

STUDENT: He put lines around them.

DR. A: Very good. Would you care to point to one part of the painting to show what you mean? (*Student points to outline of pool.*) Now, let's look at the subject. Can we say that one of these paintings is more true to life than the other? Let's take a vote. How many say the poplar trees are more "true to life"? (*The class votes as a group in favor of this one.*) Why is that?

STUDENT: Well, it doesn't look exactly like a photograph but it almost could be one.

DR. A: Which do you like better? (*The class votes for the Impressionist.*) Let's see how the painter looks at his subject. . . . Anyone care to comment?

STUDENT: Well, it's more like real life in the poplars.

STUDENT: The ducks are real life.

STUDENT: But it's mixed up in the fresco.

DR. A: I think you are trying to say that there are two points of view in the Egyptian's. Who can go to the screen and point to one point of view? (*One student volunteers and points to the bird's eye view of the pool.*) Where are we standing when we look at the pool?

STUDENT: Above—we're above it.

DR. A: How about the ducks?

STUDENT: You're in front of them.

DR. A: Good. Then we might say that in one way the Egyptian artist used his space and subjects with a lot more freedom than the other artists. But what does the Impressionist painting offer us instead of different points of view in the same picture?

STUDENT: You can see more . . . more details . . . more real . . .

DR. A: Would you agree with me that there are many ways of being "true"; that the Egyptian painting shows us the way we know things to be and the Impressionist more the way we are likely to react? . . .

In one research project in art appreciation, Dr. Ackerman's ideas were applied to a method of teaching whereby children were led to discover for themselves a system of criticism.[13] The children were shown four reproductions and were asked to name the differences they could detect among the works. The paintings used were Raphael's *Madonna and Child*, Käthe

THE DISCOVERY METHOD

[13]The material in this as well as the previous section was taken from a research project in art appreciation in the Newton Public Schools, Newton, Ma. The entire project is described in full in Stanley Madeja, ed., *Exemplary Programs in Art Education* (Washington, D.C.: National Art Education Association, May 1969).

Kollwitz's *Killed in Action*, de Kooning's *Marilyn Monroe*, and Kandinsky's *Improvisation*. (The children thus began with an achieved consensus—that the four pictures shown were obviously different in many respects.) As various differences were noted the teacher wrote them on the blackboard, setting them down in columns according to whether they related to materials, subject, meaning, form, or style. When the children's powers of observation were apparently exhausted, the teacher wrote the categorical headings above the columns, pointing out that what the class had really done was create its own critical system. Such an ordering of concepts demonstrated to the children that there were many ways to discuss a work of art. Instead of providing them with answers prior to the discussion, the teacher sought to elicit responses by posing questions that centered on a single conceptual problem—the ways in which artists differ in their work. In order to deal with such a problem, the children had to become engaged in such processes as visual discrimination, ordering, comparison, classification, and generalization.

Paintings used in the discovery exercise: Raphael, *Madonna and Child*, 1508. (Scala: New York, Florence. Alte Pinakothek, Munich.) Käthe Kollwitz, *Killed in Action*, 1921. Lithograph. Willem de Kooning, *Marilyn Monroe*, 1954. (Scala: New York, Florence. Neuberger Museum, State University of New York at Purchase.) Wassily Kandinsky, *Improvisation*, 1912. (The Solomon R. Guggenheim Museum, New York. © ADAGP 1975.)

During the "discovery discussion," the teacher translated the crude vocabulary of the class into a vocabulary for criticism, adding some important characteristics that had been missed. When the task was completed, the comments listed on the board were those shown in Table 16.2.

The discovery discussion laid the groundwork for subsequent lessons. The "materials" column provided the background for a visiting artist to demonstrate the difference between oil and water colors; the "meaning" classification prepared the class for a lesson in comparison of styles, in which they were shown a variety of paintings, each of which took a different stylistic approach to the same theme.

OTHER APPROACHES TO TEACHING CRITICISM

The phase of art appreciation that calls for simple exposure to art is not difficult to manage. A range of techniques is open to the teacher—audiovisual media, field trips to museums, visits by artists, displays of original artworks and reproductions. Teaching for the critical phase of appreciation, however, poses distinct problems. The role of dialog has already been mentioned; although verbalizing about art is central to criticism, nonver-

TABLE 16.2
Results of a Discovery Discussion

Object: To create categories that may serve as a basis for building subsequent sessions in art appreciation

Materials What We Work With	Subject What We Paint	Meaning Why We Paint	Form How a Painting Is Made	Style What Makes Paint- ings Look Different from One Another
"Kollwitz uses crayons; it's more a drawing." (Teacher explains difference between drawing and lithography.) "The Raphael must be oil." "The de Kooning could be tempera or house paint." "The Kandinsky painting is thin, it could be watercolor." (Teacher explains that if oil paint is thinned with enough turpentine, it can have the transparency of watercolor.)	"Kollwitz has a sad mother and hungry children." "Raphael has a happy mother and child." "The de Kooning is called *Marilyn Monroe,* but it takes you a long time to see her." "I can't recognize anything in the Kandinsky like I can in the others." (Teacher defines "non-objective" and "abstract.")	"Kollwitz's mother is worried about how she will feed her children." "Kandinsky's has no meaning; it's just shapes, lines, and colors that go all over the place." "I can't tell you what the Kandinsky and de Kooning are all about." "The Raphael is a religious picture."	"I see a triangle in the Raphael and up-and-down forms painted really sloppy in the de Kooning." (Teacher: "We call this painterly, not sloppy.") "The Raphael is quiet. The Kandinsky is loud." (Teacher: What makes one picture "loud" and another "quiet"?) "Kandinsky makes you look in different 'directions' up, over, and around."	"The Raphael looks so real you could walk into it." "The Kollwitz is real too but in a different way." (Teacher defines "selective realism.") Raphael "smooth" "like a photograph" "done carefully" De Kooning "sloppy" "done really fast" "more wild" "messy" Kandinsky "wild" "like a third grader's picture of space"

Andrew Wyeth, *Christina's World*, 1948. Tempera on gesso panel, 32¼″ x 47¾″. (Collection, The Museum of Modern Art, New York. Purchase.) Many of Wyeth's paintings ask more than they tell. The illustrator may invite us to reconstruct an incident; the fine artist invites us to dig deeper into the human condition.

bal activities must also be considered. Children vary in their inclinations and abilities to speak about art, and class discussions are too often limited to participation by the articulate minority. Moreover, generally there is not enough time for each member of the class to give an opinion; therefore several verbal and nonverbal "testing" instruments are described below that suggest solutions to the problem of how to achieve total class involvement. Each "test" is related to what may reasonably be expected of children in the area of art appreciation, and each of the instruments attempts to reach one of three goals:

1. To enable the children to discuss art works with a knowledge of art terminology and to identify the design, meaning, and media as these function in particular works of art (verbal).
2. To extend the students' range of acceptance of artworks (nonverbal).
3. To sharpen or refine the students' powers of perception of visual elements in artworks (nonverbal).

One way a teacher can involve a full class in working toward the first goal is to have them respond to multiple-choice questions while they progress through a series of slides. The questions should be based on the terminology and concepts the teacher deems valuable. Thus, as the children see their first Wyeth slide, the teacher may want to emphasize the uses of composition and placement of objects:

This painting is called *Christina's World*. You notice that the artist, Andrew Wyeth, has used a high rather than a low horizon line. (*points to line*) Now

474   Developing Children's Appreciation of Art

study it carefully. If you think he did it because the house just happened to be located there, put down A. If you think he did it because it allows for more space between the girl and the house, put down B. If you think he did it because it would look that way if the scene were photographed by a camera, put down C. All right, how many put down A? B? C? How many put down more than one reason? Paul, I notice you didn't raise your hand at all—can't you decide? Mary, you voted for B. How about trying to show Paul why you voted that way? . . .

TABLE 16.3
Sample Questions Utilizing the Terminology of Art

Terminology	Painting	Question
Social Criticism	The Senate (William Gropper)	After a visit to the United States Senate the artist painted his idea of what he saw. In *your* opinion, this artist seemed to feel that: A. The only things senators did were read papers, sit around, or make speeches that no one cared about. B. All senators are not the dedicated public servants we think they are. C. Most senators read papers in order to know what was happening in different parts of the country.
Depth	The Last Supper (Leonardo da Vinci)	In this wall painting, what gives you the feeling of depth? A. The direction of the lines in the construction of the room. B. The strong and bright colors. C. Both A and B.
Paint Quality (Technique)	Lady with a Parasol (Auguste Renoir)	The edges of the objects in this painting are *mostly*: A. Unclear and fuzzy. B. Sharp and exact. C. Both A and B.
Line Quality	Killed in Action (Käthe Kollwitz)	We can describe the line in this print as: A. Delicate and soft. B. Strong and bold. C. Both A and B.
Meaning	Killed in Action (Käthe Kollwitz)	Which statement *best* describes what is going on in this print? A. A mother is resting with her children. B. A mother is expressing misery in front of her children. C. A mother is playing with her children.
Style	Zapatistas (José Orozco)	The style (the artist's own way of painting) of this picture is called: A. Realism (looks lifelike). B. Selective realism (partly real). C. Abstract (simple, unrecognizable shapes).
Composition	Poplars (Claude Monet)	The trees dominate this painting. Monet makes it stand out by: A. Emphasizing the texture of the trees. B. Making the trees large and placing them centrally in the picture. C. Focusing attention on strong vertical shapes.

Because the entire class is involved in the physical process of marking and raising their hands, the number who verbally participate do not appear to be such a minority. The teacher may wish to collect the papers to study the extent of the class's comprehension. It is important in using this device not to stress the rightness or wrongness of the answers. This should be used as a means of opening up discussion of what the teacher feels is worth noting (see Table 16.3).

Another way to involve the whole class in identifying components of design is to give each child a reproduction of the same painting and a sheet of tracing paper. The paper is placed over the reproduction and the class is asked to seek out and define such compositional devices as directional movement and "hidden" structure. This method is particularly effective if first demonstrated on an overhead projector.

The second goal is to extend the children's acceptance of artworks. In order to assess this range of acceptance, the teacher can use a simple preference test based on all the slides and reproductions to be used during the course of the year. This is a simple questionnaire that requires children merely to check off the phrase that best describes their reactions to the

Leonardo da Vinci, *The Last Supper.* (Scala: New York, Florence. Santa Maria de Grazie, Milan.) Auguste Renoir, *Lady with a Parasol.* (Courtesy of The Museum of Fine Arts, Boston. Bequest of John T. Spaulding. © 1974 by SPADEM PARIS.) William Gropper, *The Senate,* 1935. Oil on canvas, 25$\frac{1}{8}$'' x 33$\frac{1}{8}$''. (Collection, The Museum of Modern Art, New York. Gift of A. Conger Goodyear.)

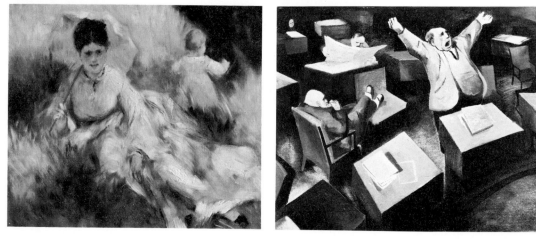

artworks placed before them. Using the children's manner of speaking, the responses to be checked might run as follows:

1. I like this painting and wouldn't mind hanging it in my own room.
2. This painting doesn't affect me one way or the other.
3. I don't like this painting.
4. This painting bothers me; as a matter of fact, I really dislike it.

It may safely be hypothesized that initially most children will gravitate toward the familiar, that is, to realistic treatments of subjects that appeal to them.[14] By consistently exposing children throughout the year to works that range from the representational to the nonobjective, a competent teacher can open their eyes to a wider range of styles. This does not place a premium on any one particular style, but aims at an extension of taste from whatever point the child begins. If the preference test is given at the beginning and at the end of the course, the teacher should be able to determine how the class has progressed—both as a group and as individuals.

The third goal is to refine the children's powers of perception; to achieve this, the children should study paintings that share certain attributes. The preparation of materials might cause the teacher some difficulty, for each participant should have a set of reproductions. The sets may be compiled from inexpensive museum reproductions, which come in manageable sizes (postcards as a rule are too small). Six reproductions seems to be a number that children can handle; more than this tends to confuse them, and there may be occasions when just two or three are appropriate. Whatever the number of pictures, children should examine them and make certain decisions about them. On pages 478 and 479 are a few examples of choices they can make. This comparative study will also lead to increased awareness of the terminology discussed in connection with the first goal. This type of study allows children to proceed at their own rate and find the viewing distance most convenient for them. Spreading the pictures out on the floor or a table is preferable to flipping through them: the pictures are more easily compared when seen simultaneously.

It was stated earlier in this chapter that the problem of appreciation is involved with the acquisition of knowledge; that is, the kinds of information that are relevant both to the student and the artwork being studied. One kind of knowledge that has not been dealt with is that which pertains to the iconographic or symbolic content of paintings. Iconography—the

SYMBOLS, ICONOGRAPHY, AND ASSOCIATIVE MATERIAL

[14] Betty Lark-Horovitz, "On Art Appreciation of Children: Preference of Picture Subjects in General," *Journal of Education*, Vol. 31, No. 2 (1937).

Vincent van Gogh, *Starry Night*, 1889. Oil on canvas, 29" x 36¼". (Collection, The Museum of Modern Art, New York. Acquired through the Lillie P. Bliss Bequest.)

John Marin, *Lower Manhattan (Composing Derived from Top of Woolworth)*, 1922. Watercolor and charcoal with paper cutout attached with thread, 21⅝" x 26⅞". (Collection, The Museum of Modern Art, New York. Acquired through the Lillie P. Bliss Bequest.)

Henri Matisse, *Nuit de Noël*, 1952. Maquette for stained glass window commissioned by *Life* magazine, 1952. Gouache on paper, cut and pasted, 10'7" x 53½". (Collection, The Museum of Modern Art, New York. Gift of Time, Inc. © 1974 by SPADEM PARIS.)

Charles Demuth, *Acrobats*, 1919. Watercolor and pencil, 13" x 7⅞". (Collection, The Museum of Modern Art, New York. Gift of Abby Aldrich Rockefeller.)

André Derain, *London Bridge*, 1906. Oil on canvas, 26″ x 39″. (Collection, The Museum of Modern Art, New York. Gift of Mr. and Mrs. Charles Zadok. © ADAGP 1975.)

Wassily Kandinsky, *Composition 8*, *#260.* 55½″ x 79⅛″. (The Solomon R. Guggenheim Museum, New York City. © ADAGP 1975.)

Stuart Davis, *Owh! In San Pao*, 1951. Oil on canvas, 52¼″ x 41¾″. (Collection of the Whitney Museum of American Art, New York. Photo by Geoffrey Clements.)

Irene Rice Pereira, *White Lines*, 1942. Oil on vellum with marble dust, sand, etc., 25⅞″ x 21⅞″. (Collection, The Museum of Modern Art, New York. Gift of Edgar Kaufmann, Jr.)

A packet of reproductions for teaching. Children can become acquainted with the art terms that are italicized in the activities below by matching certain paintings from a basic collection. The terms progress from simple, usually descriptive to more complex, dealing with qualities in art.

1. Four pictures use the *circle* as an important shape in the composition. (Answer: Van Gogh, Marin, Demuth, Kandinsky)
2. Two are painted in *watercolor*. (Answer: Marin, Demuth)
3. The effectiveness of four paintings rests on the use of colored objects that are *flat* and *hard-edged*. (Answer: Davis, Pereira, Kandinsky, Matisse)
4. Two paintings have a quality of *violence*. (Answer: Van Gogh, Marin)
5. Two of the paintings show obvious uses of *broken color*. (Answer: Van Gogh, Derain)
6. Three paintings use *line* as an important factor. (Answer: Marin, Davis, Kandinsky)

study of symbols—can be of great interest as a teaching tool, since it deals with common objects in totally new contexts and satisfies the child's interest in unusual kinds of information.

The facts that surround an art object and deal with conditions relevant to its execution are what we call *associative*. A secondary teacher who brings up the fact that van Gogh cut off his ear is conveying associative, but not iconographic, information. Unfortunately, most teachers rarely go beyond this level—which belongs in the realm of gossip. While iconography can also be associative, it operates on a higher level.

Since all children love secrets and mysteries, they can be held by the decoding processes that iconographic study involves. As an example, let us study the iconography of a seventeenth-century Dutch painting, Jan Steen's *Tavern Scene*. Like most seventeenth-century paintings, it is filled with symbols,[15] of which some are purely local and bounded by time, while others can be interpreted by alert twelve-year-olds today. If a child's attention is directed to a boy on a balcony who has a skull by his elbow and is blowing bubbles while surveying the carousing below, someone can make a connection between the brevity of life (the soap bubble) and the inevitability of death (the skull). When one explains that an empty parrot cage represents people who have left the Christian faith and who must eventually return if they are to achieve salvation, the meaning of the painting becomes clearer. Other symbols have more specific meanings: the footwarmer (love glowing in embers at the end of life is not the same as the roaring blaze of youthful love), the open oyster, the dancing dog, and so on. All these have special meanings with varying degrees of appropriateness for discussion among different age groups. Symbolization allows an art work to operate on more than one level; helping children understand the importance of symbolic thinking can have implications well beyond the realm of art.

Another reason children are attracted to historical art information is that it is, in a sense, "neutral territory"—it is separate from studio work and does not require, for instance, that the child draw well. Everyone can get involved in learning interesting new facts. Mythology and allegory are forms of storytelling that figure in many artworks, such as those of Jacques-Louis David, as well as historical incident, as in some of the works of John Singleton Copley and the murals of Orozco. Because of such connections, art appreciation can provide a link between art and literature.

EMPATHIC APPROACHES   Another way to approach art appreciation is to get students to identify, or *empathize*, with a work by taking on the characteristics of a work with their bodies—their actual selves. They can do this by assuming the pose of

[15]Two very useful reference books on iconography are Madlyn Millner Kahr, *Dutch Painting* (New York: Harper & Row, 1978) and Gertrude Grace Sill, *Handbook of Symbols in Christian Art* (New York: Collier Books, 1975).

a figure or the expression on the face of a portrait. The teacher can then ask the questions: What is happening inside you? Have you changed in any way? The teacher can show a slide or reproduction of Rodin's *Burghers of Calais*, for example, and have a group of students adopt the same positions as the figures in the sculpture. The teacher can also show slides of interesting compositional structures in nonrepresentational paintings and ask the class to change their body positions to reflect the forces within the work. (Consider for example the active diagonals of a Kandinsky or the angularity of a Mondrian.) These can be warm-up exercises to precede discussions, or they can be motivational phases for activities with art materials.

Teaching Aids for Developing Appreciation

Among the teaching aids required in the program for the development of appreciation of art are prints; pictures of other art forms; films, filmstrips, and slides dealing with a variety of art topics; and some actual works of art in two and three dimensions. No matter what field of art may be engaging the child's attention—pottery, textiles, drawing, painting—the teacher will find it necessary to have available suitable works for reference, comparison, and study.

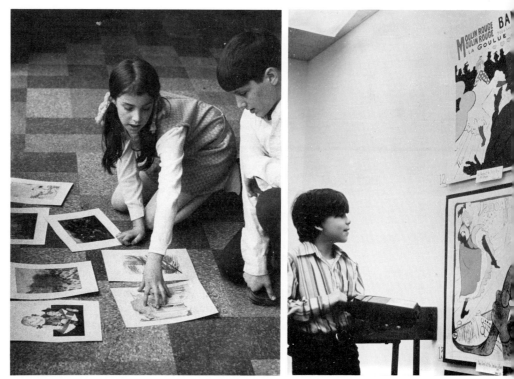

Left: two sixth graders confer over a problem in matching. Teamwork encourages discussion; the teacher becomes arbiter and clarifier. (Photo by Rick Steadry.) Right: a pupil listens to a taped lecture at an exhibition of the posters of Toulouse-Lautrec. The exhibition, the result of a project by a group of parents interested in art history and appreciation, is a good example of the effective use of reproductions when trips to museums are impossible. The parents obtained the materials and also helped the teachers prepare the pupils for the exhibit.

Much of this reference material will represent the contemporary period. Since the children are living in this era, they are probably in a better position to appreciate contemporary than traditional art. Nevertheless, when the children are studying history they should become reasonably familiar with the work of the artists of the period being considered. Artists convey not only factual statements but frequently also emotional reactions to the epoch in which they live, both of which are important in assisting children to acquire insight into life in the past. The same, of course, may be said of artists from other countries. The teacher, therefore, requires a collection of visual aids that illustrate many aspects of art, both contemporary and historical, related to local and other cultures.

The selection of what is to be represented in the visual aids is crucial. The teacher must not only consider the appropriateness of the artwork to the particulars of instruction, but must have some sensitivity to the natural preferences of children. The teacher may avoid frustration at the beginning of the year by noting the following points when selecting visual material:

1. Children generally value subject matter more than elements of form and prefer realistically portrayed content to abstract or non-objective work.
2. As a rule children prefer clearly stated spatial relationships and well-defined form to diffuse or ambiguous rendering.
3. Next to realistically rendered content, color appeals to children most. To this attraction they bring positive emotional associations.
4. Only older students are capable of recognizing design as a harmonious entity composed of interactions of parts; this recognition comes at a relatively sophisticated level of appreciation.
5. Young children prefer simple compositions; older students are able to appreciate some degree of complexity.
6. Young children work best on the descriptive level; beyond that, they have a tendency to ramble.

PICTORIAL REPRODUCTIONS

Today any school can possess a good collection of prints of pictures and pictorial reproductions of other art forms. Never before has so large a selection of these been available. With the refinements of printing processes today, most prints are acceptable, accurate, and, because of large editions, surprisingly inexpensive. Many stationery stores, bookstores, and artists' supply firms act as outlets for both American and imported prints. Books containing excellent reproductions are also available. Finally, popular magazines frequently devote pages in both color and black and white to reproductions of artworks. Although the quality of the printing in these periodicals may not equal that in art books, it is usually good enough for the prints to be kept on file for reference in the classroom.

Developing Children's Appreciation of Art

Reconstruction by Ben Shahn could be among the works studied when pupils are dealing with social themes. (Collection, the Whitney Museum of American Art, New York.)

The file should be constantly added to; every art and classroom teacher should develop the habit of collecting photographs of visual material from museums, magazines, and other sources. Such materials should be mounted on cardboard or stiff paper (discarded oaktag folders are suitable) and stored for future reference. One relatively inexpensive source of reproductions would be two copies of an art-history book, which could be cut up for filing purposes.

One reason to seize every opportunity to add to the classroom collection is that the teacher can never be quite sure what pictures may be required. If some preadolescents are exploring color, for example, works of such painters as El Greco, Rubens, Gauguin, van Gogh, Matisse, and Dufy might be studied. If some are considering social themes, they might look at political posters and reproductions of Daumier's or Ben Shahn's drawings and paintings. If some are concerned with linear perspective, they might compare paintings of the Middle Ages with those of the High Renaissance. If a religious topic holds some pupils' interest, they might see reproductions of works as diverse as the twelfth- to fourteenth-century bronzes of southern India, the figures on the west portal of Chartres Cathedral, and the paintings of Duccio, Rouault, and Stanley Spencer. A high priority should be placed on large-sized reproductions, because of their suitability for class discussion. But small-sized reproductions are adequate for the children to study on their own.

Not only must the collection of reproductions be extensive, but the teacher must be thoroughly familiar with its makeup, so that the right reproductions may be found exactly when they are required. The teacher must also be familiar with each item, so as to be able to emphasize any particular aspect of a composition related to a pupil's interest.

Obviously, nothing could be more desirable than to have on hand a well-stocked library of books in which children can read about art and artists. In the past, most writers of such books gave too little attention to the vocabulary they used—so that few publications of any quality existed that could be mastered by children enrolled in the first six grades. Fortunately, today children's books about art are increasing in quantity and quality; a special listing is offered at the end of this chapter.

FILMS, FILMSTRIPS, AND SLIDES

Each year sees worthwhile additions to a growing library of acceptable art films for the young. These art films are designed to fulfill various purposes. Many of them are intended both to stimulate children to produce art and to assist them in mastering various techniques. Some are produced largely to develop children's insight into art forms. Some films, such as the internationally renowned *Loon's Necklace,* are not produced specifically as art films, but prove highly effective in the classroom in both the production and the appreciation of art.

The teacher who uses films in the art program must understand what constitutes a good film. Before using a film with the class, the teacher obviously must preview it and then decide how effective it may be. What criteria should be used in selecting art films to be shown to young children?

1. The film should be of high technical and artistic quality. Young children see expertly made films in theaters and on television. Similar high-quality work by producers of children's movies should be standard.
2. The film must be suitable to the children's level of understanding and maturity. To show young children the highly competent but rather intellectual production, *An Experience in Cubism,* would probably bore them, but any Norman McLaren film (Canadian Film Board) would delight them with its sparkling sound and movement.
3. The film should be closely related to the children's immediate interests. No matter how excellent a film may be in itself, it tends to be a poor educational device when shown out of context.
4. When a film is of the "how-to-do-it" variety, it must not only stimulate the children but also leave some room for them to use their own initiative. Try to use films that attempt to stimulate produc-

Developing Children's Appreciation of Art

tion, focus attention on design, and give a few basic hints about technique. The content of the films stops there, however, and the child is left with many problems to solve independently.

5. Teachers should feel free to turn down the sound and make their own comments, since they know the language level of their particular class.

Knowing the film intimately, the teacher can use it at the right moment during the art sessions, either as an introduction to a topic, as an aid in teaching a topic, or as a summary for a series of experiences with a topic. Sometimes the teacher may need to comment on the film to the class before it is shown; on other occasions a discussion might take place afterward. Obtaining a film for a specific art class is often difficult. A projector and a screen as well as the film must be scheduled, sometimes three or four weeks in advance. Therefore, as much advance planning as possible must be done so that the film will suit the type of art activity in progress.

The above remarks concerning films also apply to the use of slides and filmstrips. Although these visual aids lack the dynamic qualities of movement and sound, they allow the teacher greater control of presentations. Whereas a film moves at a predetermined speed, the filmstrip frame or slide can be held on the screen for as long as required.

Filmstrips are an excellent value: they take up little space and are usually accompanied by lecture notes (of varying usefulness). They are inflexible, however, in that the images are set in a fixed order. Slides come in a wide range of prices, with the best values to be purchased from the major museums. The cheaper slides should be avoided since their color suffers from being taken from secondary sources of reproductions, usually art books or other slides, rather than from the original works. Subjects such as drawing, architecture, or sculpture, which do not require color fidelity, may be of service even in the inexpensive lines. Slides may be arranged any way the teacher desires and can be used with double or multiple projectors for purposes of comparison.

Poster-sized reproductions of design elements, architecture, and sculpture are most useful, but are unfortunately in very short supply. Of particular merit is the *Reinhold Visual Series*,[16] which treats the elements and principles of art through a variety of visual references.

USING MUSEUMS

Although we may obtain a reasonably accurate idea about many works of art by consulting reproductions of them, nothing can actually replace the work itself. How often we feel we know a work of art through a study of

[16] John Lidstone, Stanley T. Lewis, and Sheldon Brody, eds. (New York: Reinhold, 1968–69).

During a museum visit, a teacher discusses Rembrandt's *Night Watch* with her class. Using museums calls for a teacher skilled in leading group discussion. And children usually need experience with art appreciation before they can spend an extended period of time with a single work. (Photo by Adam Woolfitt.)

reproductions, only to be overwhelmed on first seeing the original! Colors, brushstrokes, textures, and sometimes the scale of the work are never adequately conveyed by a reproduction. It is most desirable, therefore, for children to have the opportunity from time to time to observe original works of art, no matter how familiar they may be with reproductions.

The most obvious sources of originals are art galleries and museums. Schools situated near such institutions would be remiss indeed not to make use of them. Even if a relatively long journey is necessary, the time and effort required may be considered well spent.

Before a class pays a visit to a museum or gallery, the teacher should take the trip alone in order to become acquainted not only with the building and the collections, but also with such mundane but important problems as the location of washrooms for the children, and the special rules and regulations of the institution concerning the general behavior of young visitors. At the same time, the teacher can make arrangements with museum officials concerning the program for the children's visit and the length of time it will take.

Developing Children's Appreciation of Art

Before the pupils set off, they should also have some idea of the reason for their trip. They may be excited about seeing an art show, but without a focus of interest the trip could be largely a waste of time. As a general principle (but subject to many exceptions), it appears wise to organize trips to museums and art galleries only for those pupils who are sufficiently mature to be able to develop a long-range interest in an art problem. In many instances very young children should wait until they can define and retain in their minds a legitimate reason for the visit that is more closely related to art than to entertainment. Some museums and art galleries, however, have lecturers who are talented in talking to children and provide exhibits specially designed for the very young.

Unfortunately, it is not always possible for children to handle the three-dimensional objects on display. The teacher might inquire as to the possibilities of allowing certain less delicate objects to be handled. Children who are allowed to touch many objects learn more about them. There is a growing trend in museums both here and abroad not only to allow children to handle objects, but to encourage them to do so. The Museum of Fine Arts, Boston has established this policy in its programs for children with special needs (see Chapter 12).

On no account should young children be expected to make long reports or detailed drawings of the objects observed during the visit. If reports or scientific drawings are to be made, they should be mere sketches. To ask young children for detailed reports might rob the whole expedition of its good effects. Older children, if time allows, should be encouraged to make studies of specific objects such as costumes and architectural details.

Schools not located sufficiently close to museums and art galleries for visits by pupils will have to depend on other means for bringing original works of art to the children. Many museums and art galleries today maintain extension services by which well-packaged and adequately anno-

A fourth grade class watches as a painter describes his methods of working. Direct contact with professional artists can be an exciting experience for children. The choice of artist and the nature of his or her work are vital factors, since the artist must be able to hold the children's attention for more than a brief period of time.

tated items are shipped to responsible organizations. The teacher should investigate these opportunities; by such means, art can be brought not only to the children but also to the community at large.

Another possible source of original art forms is the area in which the school is situated, where very often creditable local painters and craftsmen can be discovered. The teacher should make an effort to find these local artists and to help them organize shows of their work for the children and others to see.

Finally, it is perfectly reasonable to expect that a school system set aside funds for purchasing original paintings and other works of art as well as reproductions and slides. In time, a school system of any size can possess a permanent exhibition of good pieces in which it can take both interest and pride.

PRACTICAL OBJECTS

The study of utilitarian objects—cups and saucers, coffeepots, knives and forks, telephones, and chairs—can do much to help children to develop an appreciation of art and to elevate their taste.[17]

Although a functional or practical object may not be as profound an artistic expression as, say, a fine painting or a superb piece of sculpture, it may nevertheless have the attributes of true art by virtue of its design (see Chapter 3). Well-conceived practical objects should be brought to the attention of young people as part of the art appreciation program. Every object shown should be chosen for a particular reason.

A teaching difficulty occurs in developing an appreciation of practical objects, because appreciation can only rarely be related to the production of such objects. Although children continually make pictures and produce sculpture that they can compare with professional work, such is not often the case with craft and practical objects. Hence the teacher will sometimes find it necessary to discuss such objects as cups and saucers and television cabinets by themselves rather than in connection with the children's work. The children, however, often find a discussion about such articles interesting, because these are things with which they come in contact in their daily lives. The objects tend to have real meaning even when not associated with the children's expressive acts.

[17]The reader's attention is again directed to the Bauhaus, the school of design founded in 1919 by Walter Gropius at Weimar and later moved to Dessau in Germany. Although painters of note, including Kandinsky, Klee, and Feininger, gathered there, the Bauhaus was an institution dealing primarily with problems related to architecture and industrial design. Here many unique experiments were performed by the students in order to gain experience with materials, tools, and techniques of an industrial nature. As a result, a disciplined and appropriate approach to art forms related to machine production made its appearance. The writings of László Moholy-Nagy and others, describing some of the work at the Bauhaus, have been carefully read by art educators, especially those in high schools and art schools, and have influenced their teaching methods. See for example László Moholy-Nagy, *The New Vision* (New York: Wittenborn, 1964) and Walter Gropius, ed., *Bauhaus 1919–1928* (New York: Museum of Modern Art, 1938), which states that among other reasons the Bauhaus is important "because it courageously accepted the machine as an instrument worthy of the artist."

1. Select three paintings or reproductions—the first by a master, the second by a reputable but not renowned artist, and the third by an amateur—and (a) tell what the paintings all have in common; (b) explain the differences in their significance to you.
2. Describe any occasion on which you gained insight into an artist's work that previously had puzzled you. Can you account for that flash of insight?
3. Describe two paintings that deal with the same subject—one sentimentally and the other artistically.
4. Outline some teaching procedures for helping fifth grade children to appreciate each of the following: (a) a mural by a well-known painter; (b) the design of a frying pan; (c) the design of living-room curtains; (d) a wood sculpture by a well-known artist.
5. Create a visual reduction game by collecting about twenty reproductions and dividing them into subcategories. Directions for such a game might read as follows:

   a. Divide this group of reproductions into two piles, one nonobjective and one realistic.
   b. Now divide the nonobjective pile into two more piles, one emphasizing line and the other solid masses.
   c. Divide the realistic group into two sets, one sentimental in nature and the other aesthetic.
6. Create your own visual game or test instrument that uses perceptual judgment as its basis. The test may involve matching or sorting for a specific visual problem. In selecting your examples, use a broad historical frame of reference.
7. Discuss with your class three problems with art materials that are related to some dominant concern of artists as reflected in a particular work of art.

Suggested Readings

Chapman, Laura. *Approaches to Art Education*. New York: Harcourt Brace Jovanovich, 1978. Chapter 4, "Perceiving and Responding to Visual Forms."

Day, Michael. "Seeing, Knowing, and Doing." *School Arts*, February, March, April 1975. A series of articles that provides examples of instruction for art appreciation.

Eisner, Elliot. *Educating Artistic Vision*. New York: Macmillan, 1972. Suggests that art appreciation be on equal terms with art-making.

Feldman, Edmund B. *Becoming Human Through Art*. Englewood Cliffs: Prentice-Hall, 1970. Chapter 11, "Studying Varieties of Language," and Chapter 12, "Mastering the Techniques of Art Criticism."

——. *Varieties of Visual Experience: Art as Image and Idea, 2nd ed.* Englewood Cliffs: Prentice-Hall, 1972. Part V, "The Problems of Art Criticism."

Hurwitz, Al, and Stanley Madeja. *The Joyous Vision: A Source Book for Elementary Art Appreciation*. Englewood Cliffs: Prentice-Hall, 1977. Chapter 3, "Exemplary Units," cites programs in action.

evaluating

children's progress

in art

A painter had executed a story, for which he had taken so many parts from drawings and other pictures, that there was nothing in it which was not copied: this being shown to Michelangelo, and his opinion requested, he made answer, "It is very well: but at the day of Judgement, when every body shall retake its own limbs, what will this Story do, for then it will have nothing remaining?"—a warning to those who would practice art that they should do something for themselves.*

SEVENTEEN

Evaluation in art education is a process of gaining information about some aspect of the educational enterprise and assigning value to it. Laura Chapman has pointed out that curriculum and teaching can be evaluated as well as learning.[1] Indeed, we regularly make value judgments about many aspects of schooling, ranging from the quality of textbooks to the adequacy of school facilities or the behavior of individual students. Most of the evaluation that goes on is accomplished informally. On entering the classroom, for example, the teacher notices the room temperature, the lighting, and

[1] Laura Chapman, *Approaches to Art Education* (New York: Harcourt Brace Jovanovich, 1978), p. 384.

*From *The Nature of Art* by John Gassner and Sidney Thomas, p. 284. © 1964 by John Gassner and Sidney Thomas. Used by permission of Crown Publishers, Inc.

the arrangement of furniture. The teacher evaluates the situation and makes changes to suit his or her educational purposes. As the students enter the room and the class period progresses, the teacher makes numerous quick assessments of the students, noting who is engaged in activity and who is not, and adjusts teaching strategies accordingly. The teacher speaks quietly with a student, moves on quickly to a restless group, demonstrates a technique, offers words of encouragement, chastises mildly, and so on, as each situation warrants—all the while noticing in what ways students are encountering difficulties in their work and formulating changes in the plans for tomorrow's activity.

The type of evaluation described here is termed *formative* and is used primarily for improving teaching and learning processes and environments. A second type, *summative* evaluation, involves making final judgments after the teaching-learning process is completed. For example, summative evaluation is used to determine grades for students and to assess the effectiveness of teachers at the conclusion of the academic term.[2]

Numerous means for gaining information assist the educator in the evaluation process. Some of these are observation, interview, testing, viewing student work, and reading assigned papers. The results of evaluation are likewise numerous, ranging from the assignment of a grade to the development of new curriculum or a request for a change in school policy.

Evaluation of student learning is the concern of most formal assessment in schools, and since a report of student progress is usually required, this form of evaluation holds a high priority. The basis of appraisal of a pupil's progress in any area of learning can be found in the objectives of that area. If the objectives of a particular subject have been accurately stated, they will reflect not only the specific contributions that the subject has to offer, but also the philosophical purposes and educational practices of the school system. An appraisal of the progress of any pupil involves a judgment of the efficacy of the school system in general and of the teacher's endeavors in particular.

How the Objectives of Art Education Influence Evaluation

Evaluation and instruction are both guided by the educational goals and objectives of those who educate (see Chapter 1). Evaluation must be made compatible with objectives, and the results of evaluation should be re-

[2]Michael Day, "The Use of Formative Evaluation in the Art Classroom," *Art Education*, Vol. 27, No. 2 (1974), p. 5.

ported in ways that are meaningful to those who receive them.[3] Five basic questions can be asked about any system of evaluation:

Who will do the evaluation—teachers, pupils, some outside agency?
What is being evaluated—attitudes, or curriculum content such as skills, knowledge, or processes?
Who will be evaluated—elementary-school children, high-school art majors, retarded children?
What is the range of the evaluation—pupil, class, entire school program?

And finally, perhaps the most difficult:

What is the purpose of the evaluation?

Chapman states that evaluation in an art program can serve to:

inform those interested in the current status of the art program;
persuade people that changes in the art program should or should not be made;
diagnose strengths and weaknesses in planning for change;
predict trends and anticipate problems before they arise;
decide on priorities and select the best direction for change;
guide the step-by-step development of program changes;
confirm that certain values have been achieved through the program.[4]

Evaluation Based on a Taxonomy of Objectives

If the teaching objectives of the art program are given a *taxonomy,* or system of classification, the task of evaluation is made easier. Two such systems are presented below; a study of both is recommended for the teacher who is confounded by the multiplicity of objectives within the art program. Once the objectives of a particular category are clear, the teacher will have a better idea of the type of evaluation required.

The first system utilizes three main categories based on the objectives

[3] Robert Stake, ed., *Evaluating the Arts in Education: A Responsive Approach* (Columbus, Ohio: Charles E. Merrill, 1975).
[4] Laura Chapman, "Evaluating the Total Art Program," Paper presented at the NAEA Study Institute, San Diego, Ca., April 1973, pp. 26–27.

discussed in preceding chapters—artistic expression, art appreciation, and behavior during art activities. The following lists present questions connected with each of these categories that the teacher might find useful in the process of appraisal. These lists are not intended to include all possible questions; rather, they are offered as examples of the type of lists that a teacher might devise.

1. *The quality of pupils' personal artistic expression*[5]

   To what extent have pupils attempted to express their reactions to their own experiences?

   To what extent have they expressed themselves emotionally and intellectually in a form commensurate with their apparent stage of aesthetic development? (See Chapter 5.)

   To what extent does pupils' work show a sensitivity to functional design?

   Does their work indicate that they are aware of the effects of tools and materials on design?

   To what extent does their work show ability to use each element of design—line, shape, space, color, texture?

   Do pupils appear to have developed technical skills in art commensurate with their needs of expression?

   To what extent has their sense of observation improved? To what extent their use of memory? their use of imagination and fantasy? unity and variety?

2. *The quality of pupils' reactions to the work of others*

   Are pupils familiar with and knowledgeable about the works of many artists?

   To what extent do they consult art books?

   What is their apparent attitude toward art as shown in their reactions to films, slides, talks, and visits to institutions?

   Are they able to apply appropriate art vocabulary and concepts in their discussion of art?

   What is their attitude in discussing art by their peers?

3. *The quality of pupils' behavior as exhibited during participation in all types of art activities*

   During art activities, in what respects have pupils demonstrated personal initiative?

   In what respects have they demonstrated through art activities an inner discipline, worthy habits of thinking, commendable attitudes regarding a search for excellence, or other desirable personal qualities?

---

[5] Expression, appreciation, and general behavior cannot in practice be isolated from one another. The division has been made here only for the sake of discussion.

To what extent do they show good judgment in selecting tools and
    media for art work?

Once having selected an artistic goal, to what extent do they strive
    to reach it?

What is their attitude with regard to accepting advice about their
    artistic production?

To what extent have they demonstrated qualities of leadership in
    art activities?

To what extent have they shown themselves willing to cooperate
    generally with the group?

How willing are they to share in the less rewarding tasks, such as
    helping to keep equipment, supplies, and the group's work area
    clean and tidy?

In general, do they seem willing to share ideas about art with oth-
    ers?

Obviously, children cannot be expected to show evidence of positive change in an area that the teacher has not touched on. The teacher, therefore, has as much responsibility as the pupil in the evaluation process.

A second system of classification that is useful in establishing objectives as well as criteria was developed by Benjamin Bloom and his associates.[6] The classifications, or *domains*, that they chose for their taxonomy are the cognitive, the affective, and the psychomotor. The *cognitive domain* includes behaviors and goals having to do with knowledge and the development of intellectual abilities. The *affective* domain embraces objectives dealing with interests, values, attitudes, and appreciations. The *psychomotor* domain involves the manipulative and motor skills. Bloom states:

> It was the view of the group that educational objectives stated in behavioral form have their counterparts in the behavior of individuals. Such behavior can be observed and described and the descriptive statements can be classified. . . . The process of thinking about educational objectives, defining them, and relating them to teaching and testing procedures was regarded as a very important step on the part of teachers.[7]

A brief analysis of an art program using the first two categories of Bloom's taxonomy is offered in Table 17.1 to assist the teacher in planning. The levels into which the categories are subdivided are only suggestions. It is hoped that the teacher will add items appropriate for the grade being taught.

[6] Benjamin Bloom, ed., *Taxonomy of Educational Objectives,* Handbook I: Cognitive Domain (New York: David McKay, 1956); David Krathwohl, Benjamin Bloom, and Bertram Masia, Handbook II: Affective Domain (New York: David McKay, 1964).

[7] Bloom, Handbook I, p. 5.

TABLE 17.1

An Analysis of an Art Program in Terms of Bloom's Taxonomy

Content and Objectives of the Cognitive Domain

Knowledge Level:
    Terminology.
    Art history: facts, names, dates, artistic schools.
    Facts about the education and career possibilities of an artist.
    Facts about processes, tools, and materials.
    Knowledge of criteria for various kinds of art products.

Comprehension Level:
    Recognition of styles and symbols of various periods.
    Ability to understand key ideas in design (unity and variety) and in art history (the hierarchical art of Egypt, the educational and symbolic art of the medieval period, the stylistic breakthroughs of the twentieth century).
    Ability to understand the various roles that the visual arts play and their concomitant satisfactions.
    Ability to direct attention to specific visual references suggested by the teacher.
    Ability to see analogies and to shift frames of reference.
    Ability to summarize.

Application Level:
    Capable of applying visual principles to studio activity: can carry ideas into practice.
    Can function in situations that require assimilation of previous experience, information, and knowledge.

Analysis Level:
    Can identify components of an art work (design).
    Can point to relationships between elements in a particular composition.

Synthesis:
    Ability to unite content, design, materials, and processes into a satisfactory whole.
    Can distinguish between the relevant and irrelevant in solving a particular problem.
    Can point to means-end relationships in discussing the formation of objects or the creation of a painting.

Receiving Level:
    Accepts criticism from teacher.
    Listens to comments of classmates in group evaluation.
    Is open to varying points of views, styles, and philosophies of a wide range of professional artists, sculptors, and architects.

Responding Level:
    Willing to participate in discussion and respond with expressed judgments; capable of an exchange of differing opinions.

Valuing Level:
    Willing to pursue positive, constructive criticism and appreciation of the efforts of classmates and of the works of professional artists.
    Can distinguish between kinds of values; product values, process values, and aesthetic values in a given work.
    Capable of immediate valuing on an emotional level.
    Able to make a judgment about an art problem or an art work within a defined context.
    Capable of relating criteria to judgment and of developing a personal value system in accordance with mutually accepted standards developed in the art program.

Evaluating Children's Progress in Art

Bloom's taxonomy has provided theorists with much of the conceptual framework for the behavioral goals movement, particularly in art education.

Having sorted objectives according to various "levels," the teacher must select activities that will move pupils to the point where they might be evaluated. Obviously, in evaluating the activities some kinds of appraisal will be more appropriate than others. Will the work the children produce provide the point of reference, or will the teacher observe the children in action? Will the tests take a written or a verbal form? The children might be asked to study slides and make judgments, provide information orally or write an essay, or they might keep a notebook, sketchbook, or scrapbook. Whatever the method of appraisal, it is the teacher's responsibility to see that the evaluation is consistent with the objectives and activities of the program.

The National Assessment of Educational Progress, operating under the sponsorship of the Educational Commission of the United States, provided one model for appraisal of achievement in learning. The National Assessment project collected data that helped to describe the knowledge, attitudes, and skills gained by American students from age 9 to approximately age 24. Planners who were involved in the initial phase had to state the goals for their subject area as well as the specific criteria for assessing how well the goals were being met. Brent Wilson, the major consultant to the project, appointed a committee composed of individuals with the highest professional qualifications to take the first step—the development of objectives. Feeling that this committee had produced only a summary of the educational ideas that had appeared during the previous quarter century, Wilson formed a second committee and broadened the conception of art they were to work with. The content of "art" was now to include the environmental arts, popular arts, and the informal art education that children receive at home, while traveling, or through the media, as well as the traditional art forms of painting, sculpture, ceramics, and the like. Wilson's committees jointly produced the following objectives of art education.

1. Perceive and respond to [different] aspects of art.
2. Value art as an important realm of human experience.
3. Produce works of art.
4. Know about art.
5. Make and justify judgments about the aesthetic merit . . . of works of art.[8]

As an example of how these objectives are treated, let us examine an outline of the first one:

[8] National Assessment of Educational Progress, Art Objectives (Ann Arbor, Mi.), p. 6.

I. Perceive and respond to aspects of art

Clarifying Definition: Aspects of art are defined as: sensory qualities of color, line, shape, and texture; compositional elements such as structure, space, . . . balance, movement, placement, closure, contrast, and pattern; expressive qualities such as mood, feeling, and emotion; subject matter, including (1) objects, themes (the general subject of a work, i.e., landscape or battle scene), events, and ideas (general presymbolic meanings) and (2) symbols and expressive content, which is a unique fusion of the foregoing aspects.

A. Recognize and describe the subject matter elements of works of art.

Age 9. Identify themes of specific works of art.
Identify events depicted in specific works of art.
Describe how the themes of two or more specific works of art are similar or different.

B. Go beyond the recognition of subject matter to the perception and description of formal qualities and expressive content (the combined effect of the subject matter and the specific visual form that characterizes a particular work of art).

Age 9. Describe the characteristics of sensory qualities of works of art (that is, tell about colors, shapes, lines, and textures in a painting, building, photograph, etc.).
Describe the expressive character (feelings and moods) of works of art.

These behavioral objectives indicate the need for making reproductions part of the conceptual framework. Indeed, one of the National Assessment's unique contributions has been its imaginative use of visual materials (packaging and sculpture as well as reproductions) as part of the evaluation process.

Evaluation Techniques

STANDARDIZED ART TESTS

Techniques for evaluation range from the most formal test to the most informal conversation with a child. A number of standardized art tests are available, dating back to the 1920s and 1930s and including the Meier-Seashore *Art Judgment Test*, the *McAdory Art Test*, and the *Bryan-Schwamm Test*. Although standardized art tests are interesting and provocative, often they are not very reliable and do not apply to the specific needs of classroom situations.

Since the heyday of standardized testing several decades ago, the trend in testing for art ability has been directed toward specific ends—that is, tests have been designed by teachers or research workers to arrive at limited kinds of information. Tests may be designed for a number of purposes, but in all cases they represent "a judgment of the adequacy of behavior as compared to a set of educational objectives."[9] Any test is a reflection of what a teacher considers important in a student's behavior, studio processes, skills, and knowledge about art. The test may be formal or informal, and it may just as easily precede instruction in the form of a diagnostic device as it may follow the instructional period to measure a student's gain. In any case, the test is but one technique among many to gauge the kind and quality of change in the student.

In addition to the standardized tests devised by experts, there are tests composed by the classroom teacher. Such tests can often be useful, provided the teacher understands their significance. Sometimes the teacher may wish to use a test (usually cognitive) to discover whether or not the pupils have grasped some part of the art program. For example, it may be helpful to present a few questions based on the pupils' knowledge of a specific medium, or of facts surrounding an artist's life, or of techniques in using color.

FORMAL TESTS DEVISED BY THE TEACHER

The following completion-type problem could be used to test knowledge of color mixing:

> Fill in the blanks:
> 1. To obtain a *shade* of red tempera paint, add _____.
> 2. To obtain a *tint* of red watercolor, add _____.
> 3. To turn *blue* into gray, add _____.
> 4. To turn *green* into gray, add _____.

An essay-type answer might be obtained from the following:

> Describe two methods of mixing tempera paint to obtain gray.

Identification and multiple-choice tests are useful for younger children, because they do not require written answers of any kind. For example, one item could be the following:

> Which pigment, when added to red tempera paint, will result in a *shade* of red?
> (a) green
> (b) white
> (c) black

[9] Elliot Eisner and David Ecker, eds., *Readings in Art Education* (Waltham, Ma.: Blaisdell, 1966), p. 384.

Another recognition category might be based on slides and reproductions. After being shown a Rouault and a Rembrandt, a child may be asked the following items:

An art form that had a great influence on Rouault is:
(a) Impressionist paintings
(b) stained-glass windows
(c) sculpture

Which of the following methods did Rembrandt use to achieve his effects?
(a) chiaroscuro
(b) impasto
(c) glazes
(d) all the above

It should be noted that the easiest test items to compose are often technical questions that tend to be trivial compared with the goals of developing personal expressiveness and artistic creativity. The most significant educational objectives are often the most complex and the most difficult to evaluate appropriately.

Elliot Eisner and a group of his doctoral students at Stanford University have pioneered a form of educational evaluation based on the notion of connoisseurship and on the tools of art criticism.[10] This type of evaluation relies on the sensitive and knowledgeable perception of the evaluator, and on the evaluator's ability to express in verbal language the essence of educational encounters. The advantages of this type of evaluation are its direct relation to art criticism and its ability to convey meanings and flavors of situations in ways that the more common statistical evaluations cannot.[11]

INFORMAL METHODS OF EVALUATION

In the world of art, people are continually making unsupported judgments. They might assert, for example, that Seurat's *La Grande Jatte* is a masterpiece; that Leonardo da Vinci is not as good an artist as the public believes; that Bellows is a master of concise statement with a brush. When the opinions of numbers of well-qualified people coincide about a work of art, we are inclined to accept their statements as true. If numbers of such people agree for any considerable period of time that a work is excellent, we begin to call it a masterpiece. By this type of informal critical appraisal, people in our society fill their galleries and select their masterpieces. No great work of art has ever been chosen by any other method.

[10]Elliot Eisner, "On the Uses of Educational Connoisseurship and Educational Criticism for Evaluation of Classroom Life," *Teachers College Record*, Vol. 78, No. 3 (February 1977).
[11]Elliot Eisner, "The Forms and Functions of Educational Connoisseurship and Criticism," *Journal of Aesthetic Education*, Vol. 10, No. 3 and 4 (July–October, 1976).

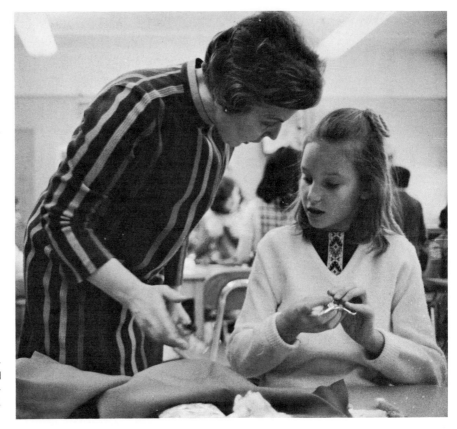

The appraisal of a pupil's progress in art must be derived largely from the teacher's acquaintance with each child. (Photo by Rick Steadry.)

The method has, of course, demonstrable limitations. The history of art is full of painters now considered important, such as Cézanne, who during their lifetimes were either unrecognized or disliked by the critics. Then there are painters like Landseer, who were favored by contemporary critics but who, in the course of time, have lost their esteem in the eyes of reputable judges. With full awareness of the limitations of our method of selecting works of art, however, we retain this method because no better practical means of selection has been devised.

Teachers should first recognize that they are subject to error in their appraisal of the children's patterns of behavior and their ability to produce and appreciate art. Having accepted this fact, they will probably be cautious in jumping to conclusions, painstaking in their efforts to analyze the pupils' progress, and humble in the weight they attach to their opinions. Nevertheless, if they familiarize themselves with art, with the children under their care, and with an acceptable pedagogy in relation to art and children, there is nothing to prevent them from accepting with some confidence the task of appraising the progress that the children make in art education.

The Checklist. A simple method of gathering data about a child's progress in art is to keep a checklist. The most difficult part of this method is to devise a practical list. This teachers must do largely for themselves, because checklists made by others rarely are entirely suitable for them. It is suggested, however, that the list be based on the three general headings mentioned on page 494—namely, expression, appreciation, and behavior. The subheadings might resemble the questions offered under the three general headings. Table 17.2 presents a sample of a short checklist for

TABLE 17.2

Checklist for Art Activities

The Student:	Exceptional	Average	Below Average
1. Was able to use own experiences			
2. Progressed normally through manipulative symbol } stage preadolescent			
3. Work showed personal style			
4. Produced work that showed (a) respect for material (b) respect for function of object			
5. Used tools (a) appropriate to task (b) with dexterity			
6. Showed ability to use (a) line (b) shape (c) color (d) texture (e) space			
7. Work showed unity of design			
8. Work showed variety of design			
9. Work showed development over period of time			
10. Successfully related (a) art work to school experiences (b) other school experiences to artistic expression			
11. Responded positively to new situations in art			

Evaluating Children's Progress in Art

expression. It would have to be altered to suit any specific grade or type of art activity.

The three columns can be designated by any terms teachers deem suitable (I, II, III; excellent, satisfactory, unsatisfactory; exemplary, present, not present). Using three columns allows distinctions to be made between (1) progress that occurs in a particular area because of giftedness (exceptional), (2) the level of work of most children (average), and (3) the difficulties certain individuals experience (below average). Schoolteachers in Japan grade their pupils' pictures on a point system. The North American art teacher is horrified, but the Japanese system indicates that art is considered as having the same importance as other subjects.

The Anecdotal Method.   A second device, known as the *anecdotal* method, is also valuable. With this method the teacher periodically jots down observations about each child, based on the questions in the three categories of criteria. A cumulative record of such specific reactions may become a reliable index of a pupil's progress. It at least furnishes the teacher and the pupil with some concrete evidence of strong and weak points in the pupil's art work and conduct.

As an example, opposite some of the items of the sample checklist previously outlined, the following remarks might be set down for a six-year-old in first grade:

The Student:	*Comments:*
1. Was able to use own experiences	"In general picture-making, yes, but not in correlation with social studies—copied a drawing."
2. Progressed normally through symbol stage	"Normal until absence from school—then regression to manipulation for two days—after that normal—is putting in sky and ground symbols."
3. Work showed personal style	"Nothing special yet."
4. (Not applicable)	
5. Used tools with dexterity	"Using scissors well; can actually 'draw' with them."
6. Showed ability to use line	"A nervous child—and so, nervous line—."

The teacher might also consider using a "Gestalt" anecdotal method—that is, commenting from time to time after periodic examination of portfolios. A checklist might be used as a guide in writing these comments, but need not be referred to item by item. Such records give general, overall impressions of a large body of work. The following are examples of notes about children that a teacher might write for a personal file.

John A (6 years, grade 1)
John uses a variety of personal experiences in his pictures, and he is certainly getting along well lately in trying to develop symbols of houses. It is strange, however, how his work seemed to deteriorate last week. He works hard, though, and participates well in a group.

Robert L (11 years, grade 6)
He has always shown himself to be a sensitive child, and his paintings reflect his feelings. He might concentrate a little more on the use of light and shade and bright color areas. He did not seem to care for working on murals with others, but he participated well in the puppet show. He was obviously moved when he listened to music in preparation for a picture.

Betty McM (10 years, grade 5)
Betty continues to be careless and untidy; her paints are in a mess, her drawings all thumb-marks, her brushes unwashed. As stage manager of our play, nevertheless, she worked well. She seems to be more at home with sculpture than she is in drawing and painting. Her last sculpture in clay was quite vigorous. She likes to explore new materials and last week brought to school some wood for carving.

The data derived from checklists and other notations will greatly assist the teacher in arriving at an appraisal of a pupil's progress, but it is necessary also to keep a file of the child's actual art production for periodic study and comparison with the written notations. Usually lack of space prevents the teacher from keeping any but the flat work.

These methods of evaluation allow the teacher to summarize the child's progress in only the most general of terms. Once made, however, such a summary will prove valuable to the teacher in making progress reports to parents and others interested in the child's welfare. Such methods are difficult for the art teacher to follow, however, since their effectiveness rests on a day-to-day knowledge of the children being evaluated.

Reporting Progress in Art

From time to time every school system reports to parents concerning their children's progress. This is one of the traditional and necessary functions of a school. Every aspect of the program of studies should be mentioned on a report form to parents, if only as a notice to parents that their children have been exposed to the subject. The fact that the art program does not always lend itself to exact measurement does not excuse the teacher from making some sort of report on the pupils who participated in it.

In addition to informing parents of the progress of their offspring, some educators feel that reports have other functions. From the teachers point of view, these are: (1) helping teachers to reach conclusions about their pupils; (2) assisting teachers in making plans for the future; and (3) in general, helping them to appraise the effectiveness of their teaching. From the point of view of the pupils, reports have the purpose of: (1) helping pupils to realize the progress they have made; (2) pointing out where they might improve their work; and (3) indicating what they might do in the future to make further progress. Some educators feel that if children compare their achievements with those of their fellows, reports provide an incentive for them to work harder and more efficiently.

In spite of these opinions, it would seem that in relation to art, the only legitimate function of a report is to let the parents know how their child is progressing in this field. A teacher of art who has waited until report time to reach conclusions about a child's progress can scarcely have acted as an efficient and sympathetic counselor in art. Furthermore, if the pupils must depend on a report card to help them understand their progress, to improve their work, and to give them clues as to future action, communication in the classroom must have reached an extraordinarily low ebb.

Regarding the mechanics of reporting to the parents, several points must be kept in mind. First, the method of reporting must be easily understood by all parents. Any report that makes use of complicated symbols or what is considered by some to be highly professional language (and by others to be an undesirable "pedagese") will not be appreciated by most parents. Second, the report should reflect the objectives and practices of the art program and should attempt to comment on the child, both as an individual and as a member of a group. Third, any good report should, of course, be as accurate and fair as a teacher can make it. Fourth, from the teacher's point of view the system of reporting should not demand a disproportionate amount of clerical work.

In general, since reporting in art is characterized by a number of peculiarities arising from the nature of this area of learning, it might be well for the teacher to discuss these peculiarities frankly with the parents and, in fact, with children who are in a position to understand them. Two of the best means of reporting available to teachers of art are *progress reports* and *narrative reports*. The progress report is based on the use of check marks, symbols, or letters. Often only two marks are used—S for satisfactory and U for unsatisfactory. Sometimes the letter O may be employed to signify outstanding progress. Under the heading "art" on the report form, the subheadings "expression," "appreciation," and "personal and social development" might be listed. The parent would then expect to find either S, U, or O opposite each of these subheadings. This system appears to be theoretically sound for reporting art, in that it is based on each child's individual progress, rather than on progress in comparison with that of other pupils. Children, however, will often make a competition of even these general ratings.

A teacher not thoroughly familiar with every child might, with the parents' consent, wish to make an initial report to them verbally during a short conference. This method tends to be time-consuming, but because of its flexibility it has some obvious advantages over written reports to parents. It demands, of course, that the teacher have some ability to report both good and bad aspects of a child's efforts without arousing the wrath of a parent. No teacher, furthermore, can afford to arrange an interview of this type without first being fully prepared. For the school's permanent records, a teacher must keep on file a complete written report of each pupil, even if this report is available to the parents only on request. Of course, if the child is gifted the teacher should make the parents aware of this, so that the child can gain support that might otherwise be lacking without this knowledge. Many parents are completely unaware of their children's creative abilities.

Activities for the Reader

1. Describe some situations in which the art program reflects the educational outlook of (a) a school principal; (b) a school board; (c) a community.
2. Devise some test items in art as follows:
   a. A true-false type to test third grade pupils' knowledge of handling clay.
   b. A recall or completion type to test fourth grade pupils' knowledge of color mixing.
   c. A multiple-choice type to test sixth grade pupils' knowledge of linear perspective.
   d. A matching items type to test fifth grade pupils' ability to use a mixed-media technique.
   e. A recognition type to test sixth grade pupils' knowledge of art terms.
3. Make checklists for (a) appreciation of sculpture by sixth grade pupils; (b) skills needed by fourth grade pupils while doing puppetry.
4. Over a period of two weeks, study the art output of a group of ten children and write a paragraph of not more than fifty words for each child, summarizing their progress.
5. Describe any results, either good or bad, that you have observed as a result of competitive marking of children's art. How do those who have received a poor grade react?
6. Study the checklist in Table 17.2. Try to rework a portion of it to reflect part or all of Bloom's taxonomy of educational objectives.
7. Imagine yourself to be a parent. How would you want art to change your child? List the outcomes that, in your parental view, would demonstrate the effectiveness of art education. Pick a specific age level.
8. Make a checklist of items that would reflect the attitudinal change of the principal and faculty with respect to the art program.

Ahman, J. Stanley, and Marvin D. Glock. *Evaluating Pupil Growth*, 2nd ed. Boston: Allyn and Bacon, 1963. A general book on evaluation for education.

Bloom, Benjamin, J. Thomas Hastings, and George Madeus, eds. *Handbook of Formative and Summative Evaluation of Student Learning*. New York: McGraw-Hill, 1971. See especially Chapter 17, "Evaluation of Learning in Art Education," by Brent Wilson.

Day, Michael. "The Use of Formative Evaluation in the Art Classroom." *Art Education*, Vol. 27, No. 2 (1974).

Eisner, Elliot. *Educating Artistic Vision*. New York: Macmillan, 1972. Chapter 8, "Children's Growth in Art: Can It Be Evaluated?"

Lansing, Kenneth. *Art, Artists, and Art Education*. Dubuque: Kendall-Hunt, 1976. Chapter 10, "Evaluation and Reporting to Parents."

Stake, Robert, ed. *Evaluating the Arts in Education: A Responsive Approach*. Columbus, Ohio: Charles E. Merrill, 1975. A discussion of problems and issues in evaluation.

Willis, George, ed. *Qualitative Evaluation*. Berkeley: McCutchan, 1978. See especially "A Model for the Art of Teaching and a Critique of Teaching," by W. Dwaine Greer.

Wilson, Brent. "The Other Side of Evaluation of Art Education." In *Curriculum Considerations for Visual Arts Education*. Ed. George Hardiman and Theodore Zernich. Champaign, Il.: Stipes Publishing, 1974.

APPENDIX

FURNISHING A CLASSROOM

FOR ART ACTIVITIES

In order to conduct an art program successfully, the teacher must often plan alterations and additions to the basic classroom that is provided. In this section we will discuss some of the ways in which a general classroom may be modified to accommodate pupils engaged in art work. Some attention will be given also to the planning of an art room, if such a separate room is available. We will deal here only with the physical equipment and functional arrangements for art activities in different types of rooms. The general classroom might not always be adaptable to our suggestions, since certain educational requirements must take precedence over artistic considerations.

Many of the problems that arise from the task of reorganizing a room for art are unique to the particular situation. The size and shape of a room, the number of children in a class, the type of activities in the program, all will modify the arrangements to be made. The making of suitable physical arrangements for art, therefore, presents a challenge that in the long run only the teacher can satisfactorily meet.

Physical Arrangement of the Classroom

A classroom in which art is taught requires physical provisions for the following operations: storing bulk equipment and supplies; preparing current supplies for the class; setting out the supplies for current work. After children learn what to obtain and where to obtain it, and how to move so that they do not get in each other's way (all of which they learn through discussion with the teacher and subsequent practice), they must have suitable places to work. Drawing and painting are quiet activities; cutting and hammering are more robust. Papers for drawing and painting are usually much larger than those for writing, so that surfaces to accommodate them must be larger than most school desks. Certain activities, such as wood sculpture or linoleum-block printing, demand a special surface on which the materials may be cut. Through use this surface will roughen and become unsuitable for drawing and painting and other activities. Two boards, a work board and a drawing board, are necessary. Drying unfinished or completed work, storing unfinished work, and displaying work also require their own spaces. These requirements suggest the following furniture:

1. A storage cupboard with some adjustable shelves, the latter at least 8 inches wide for small items and other shelves at least 18 inches wide for larger items. The outside dimensions of the cupboard will, of course, be determined by the floor and wall space available.
2. Two tables, preferably at least 5 feet long and 30 inches wide, one to be used largely by the teacher in arranging and displaying supplies and the other for children's group work.
3. A sink, or a stand for pails of water. The sink should have two faucets or spigots to hasten the clean-up activity.
4. A drying shelf or battery of shelves near a radiator or other source of heat. The shelf should be about 12 inches wide and as long as space permits.
5. Some display facilities (see Chapter 15).
6. Some chalkboard space—but not so much as to displace needed display areas.

Basic Supplies and Equipment

While each type of art activity, of course, demands particular tools and equipment, and sometimes special room arrangements, the following general list of tools and supplies seems basic to nearly any art program. Miscellaneous supplies and equipment such as scissors, thumbtacks, masking tape, and paper cutter (18-inch minimum) are not listed, since they are part of general equipment for other subjects. Crafts materials are not listed because they vary so much with each teacher.

1. *Brayers:* available in a variety of widths from 3 to 8 inches. Soft rubber rollers are recommended and a set for one class can service the entire school.
2. *Brushes:* for painting: flat, hog-bristle, $\frac{1}{4}$ inch to 1 inch wide. For painting: pointed, sable, large (size 6 or 7) paste brushes.
3. *Chalk:* soft; ten or twelve colors plus black and white; dustless preferred.
4. *Crayons:* wax; soft; ten or twelve colors plus black and white.
5. *Oil crayons:* such as craypas or oil pastels.
6. *Pens:* felt-tip marking pens.
7. *Cutting tools:* sloyd knives, X-acto knives, single-edged razor blades, linoleum carving tools. (One set of linoleum tools can service several upper grades.
8. *Drawing boards:* about 18 by 24 inches; soft plywood at least "BC" grade (that is, clear of knots on at least one side); Masonite, homosote, composition board (optional).
9. *Erasers:* Artgum type.
10. *Inks:* black drawing ink; water-base printing inks in tubes for block printing.
11. *Linoleum:* minimum of 6 square inches per child; also available mounted on plywood blocks, but those are more expensive.
12. *Poster paint:* liquid in pints or powder in pounds (white, black, orange, yellow, blue, green, and red as basic; magenta, purple, and turquoise as luxuries; probably twice the quantity of black, white, and yellow as of other colors chosen).

Tempera or poster paints have been the traditional mainstay of painting activity. Acrylic paint is now priced competitively with tempera and should be considered for its distinguishing properties: it is waterproof, and therefore ideal for interior and exterior wall murals; murals on paper can be rolled up without flaking. It will adhere to any surface—clay, wood, glass, and so on. When it is applied thickly, objects can be embedded into it; when thinned with water, it can serve as a substitute for watercolor. When ap-

510

plied with a soft foam brayer, it can also be used for linoleum printing. Purchase in quarts.

13. *Watercolor paint:* primary colors will do, but secondary colors are recommended if budget permits.

14. *Paint tins:* muffin tins, with at least six depressions; baby-food jars and frozen-juice cans may also be used.

15. *Paper:* roll of kraft (brown wrapping), about 36 inches wide; or "project roll," 36 inches wide.
    Manila: 18 by 24 inches, cream and gray, 40 pound.
    Colored construction: 12 by 18 inches (red, yellow, blue, light green, dark green, black, gray, and perhaps some in-between colors like blue-green and red-orange; about forty colors are available).
    Newsprint, colored tissue: size optional.

16. *Paste and glue:* school paste; in quarts.
    Powdered wheat paste for papier-mâché.
    White glue for wood joining (thinned, it works well as an adhesive for colored tissue).

17. *Pencils:* drawing; black, soft.

18. *Printing plates:* glass trimmed with masking tape.

19. *Firing clay:* 3 pounds per child minimum.

Examples of Classroom Arrangements

To illustrate the manner in which arrangements for art are influenced by the age level of the pupils and by local educational conditions, we will discuss three situations: the primary grade classroom, the modern general classroom, and the art room.

A PRIMARY GRADE CLASSROOM

The problems in arranging the room for the primary grades (K–2) arise largely from the stage of physiological development of the pupils, who use the large muscles in art work and require relatively large tools and bulky media, which create storage problems. The teacher's preparation of art materials for young children is often quite different from that for the upper grades. Older children can usually select art materials for themselves, but the primary teacher must, at least at the beginning of the school term, arrange sets or groupings of materials. These vary greatly in the number of items they contain. For example, for crayon drawing, children need only six crayons and a sheet of manila paper. For painting, they require perhaps an apron or a parent's old shirt, a sheet of newspaper or oilcloth to protect the painting surface, two brushes, a sheet of newsprint, a paint cloth, and some liquid colors.

From a necessarily large and convenient storage space the teacher selects materials and places them on a long table, cafeteria-style. Crayons may be placed on a paper plate and set on the sheet of paper. The painting kit may be assembled in discarded "six-pack" cartons, on a metal or plastic tray, or on a wooden work board. The paint should not be included at this point because children could spill it as they transport the kit to the place where they will be painting. Paint and any other "dangerous" materials should be placed in the work area ahead of time.

The following suggestions may be helpful in storing tools and supplies so that they will be ready for distribution:

1. Brushes and pencils should be placed in glass jars, with bristles and points up. Blocks of wood with holes bored in them, each hole large enough to hold one item, provide another convenient way of arranging this type of tool. This manner of storage also allows the teacher to make a quick visual check for missing brushes.
2. Crayons should be separated according to colors. Each container, which might be a milk carton or a cigar box, should hold only one color.
3. Moistened clay should be rolled into balls and placed in a large earthenware jar or a tin container, either of which should have a tight lid to keep in the moisture.
4. Paper should be cut to size and arranged on a shelf in piles according to size and color.
5. Paper scraps should be separated according to color and saved in small cartons.
6. Paste should be kept in covered glass jars (or, if dry, in the bulk packages). The teacher should place paste on disposable paper plates or simply on pieces of cardboard after it has been mixed for use.

It is fortunate that the furniture in most primary rooms is movable, for the floor provides an excellent work area for art. If the floor is covered with heavy linoleum or linoleum tile, it is necessary to set down only a thin protective covering such as oilcloth, plastic sheets, or wrapping paper before work begins. If the floor is in any way rough, cardboard mats may be put over the areas where the activities are to take place. The type of work being done, whether flat or three-dimensional, often determines the kind of floor or table covering to be set down.

Some teachers like to hang paintings to dry on a clothesline with spring clothespins. Tables are often used for drying three-dimensional projects. The floor, or course, if part of it can be conveniently reserved, is an excellent place for drying all types of work. Not much unfinished work requiring storage is produced in the primary grades, since most projects are completed in one art session.

Because it is desirable, of course, for all children eventually to learn how to procure and replace equipment and supplies for themselves, the room should be so arranged that children can perform the task easily. In the primary grades, as elsewhere in the art program, the cafeteria system is useful. Children must develop the ability to obtain and replace art materials according to a plan that they themselves help to determine. The teacher should discuss with children the necessity of learning these skills. However, in the primary grades the children will usually follow plans willingly and treat the routine as a game. The game can even include a rehearsal or drill of the routine.

A GENERAL CLASSROOM

Many contemporary school plans give considerable thought to suitable accommodation for art activities in general classrooms. A description of the special provisions for art in the general classroom is offered here primarily for those teachers who are provided with a reasonably liberal budget for the modernization of their art facilities.

Because in most classrooms desks are not fixed to the floor, they can be easily arranged to suit the studies in progress. Movable desks are a great convenience for drawing and painting, since they allow a pupil to use a drawing board without interfering with other children. Clusters of desks may be arranged so that large flat areas of working space are available for group activities.

In some contemporary classrooms an entire wall is provided with fixtures that facilitate the teaching of art. These can include a counter covered with linoleum or some other suitably processed material, built from wall to wall. This counter houses probably the most important single convenience for art activities—a large sink supplied with hot and cold water. Below the counter are several storage cupboards equipped with adjustable shelves and swinging doors where all expendable supplies may be stored. A second row of cupboards is suspended about twelve inches above the counter. These cupboards also have adjustable shelves, but the doors are of the sliding variety so that pupils will not bump their heads on them when open. Additional supplies or the pupils' unfinished work may be kept in this storage space. Electrical outlets are frequently provided at convenient intervals along the counter. The whole assemblage, which substantially resembles a work unit in a modern kitchen, occupies relatively little floor space. Sometimes an additional work counter is provided along part of the window wall; more cupboards may be built below this counter.

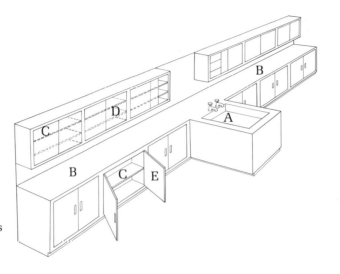

A Sink
B Counter
C Adjustable shelves
D Sliding doors
E Swinging doors

A wall fixture for art activities in a general classroom. (Sketch based on an original design by the Ontario Department of Education.)

Because the teacher in a general classroom requires a relatively large expanse of chalkboard, it is sometimes difficult to find sufficient space to display art. This is often provided, however, on the side wall to the rear of the room, and on two walls above the chalkboards, where a wide strip of tackboard is fastened. But since even these areas are usually insufficient for display purposes, many new schools are being equipped with display boards and cases in the main halls of the building.

THE ART ROOM

In today's educational world, budgets are not always large enough for accommodating a separate art room in a new school, and the wishes of art teachers cannot always be satisfied. If not all the ideas set forth in this section can be adopted, perhaps some of them may be employed as the teachers gradually improve the working conditions in their school.

Design. An art room should be placed near a service entrance on the main floor of a school building, for convenience in delivering supplies and equipment. In junior high schools it is preferable also to have the room situated reasonably close to home economics rooms and industrial arts shops so that pupils may conveniently move from one room to another to use special equipment, such as looms in the home economics room. It is further recommended that the art room be not too far from the auditorium, since puppetry and stagecraft sometimes require ready access to the stage.

The room should be large, with a minimum floor space of about 30 by 60 feet. A spacious floor can provide working centers in which many art

Furnishing a Classroom for Art Activities

activities may be carried out. The floor should be laid in heavy linoleum or rubber tile. Mastic tile may also be used but is rather more tiring to walk on than other types of tile.

Lighting in an art room is of the greatest importance. Fluorescent lighting is recommended and should be arranged so as to cast no pronounced shadows. Preferably the lights should be set flush with the ceiling, with the exception of spotlights for important displays. Unless the room has a daylight screen, blackout curtains for the windows should be provided so that films may be shown. In all matters pertaining to both artificial and natural lighting, architects and lighting engineers should be consulted. Many excellent materials and arrangements are available, including directional glass bricks, opaque louvers, clerestory lighting, and various types of blinds.

The efficient use of space around the walls should also be considered. Along one of the shorter walls, storage rooms jutting into the room might be planned. Two storage areas are desirable—one to house a stock of expendable art materials and the other to store the pupils' unfinished work. Each storage room should be fitted with as many adjustable shelves as convenient. Since the shelves may rise to a considerable height, it would be well to have at least one light stepladder available in either one of the rooms. The outside walls of these storage rooms, facing the classroom, can be faced with tackboard. The long wall area opposite the windows should for the most part be faced with tackboard running from about thirty inches above the floor up to the ceiling. An area of about twenty square feet, however, should be reserved for a chalkboard. Space might be provided for counters and cupboards.

The sink may be located on this long side of the room. Its position should be reasonably central, and it should be accessible from at least three directions (see illustration, p. 514). It may be placed in a separate cabinet so that the pupils can approach it from all directions, or it may be placed at the end of a counter running at right angles from the wall toward the center of the room. However arranged, the sink should be large, deep, acid-resistant, and equipped with hot- and cold-water taps. Clean-out traps should be fitted, and all plumbing leading from them should also be acid-resistant.

Along the entire wall at the end of the room opposite the storage rooms, storage cupboards might alternate with glass-enclosed display cases. These cases should be provided with adjustable glass shelves and illuminated with hidden or indirect lights.

Beneath the windows, a work counter might run almost the full length of the room. Below the counter storage cupboards could be constructed, or the space might be left open to house tools. Jutting out at right angles might be a series of small counters for delicate work. Each small counter, which might be collapsible, should be provided with a stool of convenient height. At the extreme end of this wall an area might be set aside for the teacher's desk and files.

The placement of electrical outlets is a problem for an expert who understands electrical loads, but the teacher must be sure that outlets are placed in correct locations. As well as outlets for ceramic and enameling kilns, and service outlets in general, there should be an outlet for an electric clock. The pupils should always be aware of how much time is available to begin certain phases of their work or to start cleaning up toward the end of the art period.

Furnishings. Certain equipment should be placed in convenient relation to the arrangements around the walls. Such items might include an electric kiln with a firing area of not less than 3000 cubic inches, a pull-out storage bin for clay, a storage box for keeping clay damp, and a spray booth. The clay-working area should be located near the sink. A filing cabinet for storing catalogs, folders containing information about the students, and miscellaneous items useful to the teacher should be placed near the teacher's desk.

Furniture for the art room must be chosen with care. Suitable art desks come in a variety of designs, but a desk with low shelves on which the pupils may place schoolbooks would have optimum utility. Desks with movable tops, by which the slope of the working surface may be regulated, are not proved particularly serviceable because they tend to get out of order. For seating, chairs, stools, and benches all are practical. One or two carpenter's benches as well as desks for drawing and painting should be provided. The benches should be supplied with vises and have storage space beneath them for tools and other equipment.

The colors used to decorate the art room must be carefully planned. Bright colors are generally to be avoided since they "rebound" and confuse a painter. Tints or neutral colors such as pale grays are recommended for the walls and ceiling. The ceiling should be lighter in tone than the walls. The floor should also be neutral, but mottled. Chalkboards come in pale greens or ivory as well as black. Natural or limed wood finishes on cupboards and doors are attractive and serviceable. In general, color in an art room must not interfere with the color work in progress, and it must serve as a background for the displays of the children's work.

Before an elaborate art room of the type described can be set up successfully, much study must be given to the problem and many experts consulted. Not only should plans of the room be drawn but a model also should be made. Particular attention should be given to the grouping of furniture and equipment so as to avoid overcrowding in any one part of the room and to locate in one area everything necessary for any one type

Furnishing a Classroom for Art Activities

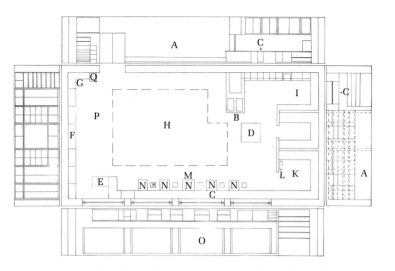

A	Tackboard and screen
B	Sinks
C	Work counters
D	Heavy workbench
E	Teacher's desk
F	Cabinets and display cases
G	Library corner
H	Central space for tables and seats
I	Clay-working area
J	Storage area: expendable art materials
K	Library corner
L	Stepladder
M	Area for 3-dimensional work
N	Solid desks for 3-dimensional work and individual stool for each desk
O	Windows (may not exist if room is air-conditioned): windows should be provided with blackout curtains for showing slides and films
P	Area for easels, posing models, etc.
Q	Filing cabinet

Comprehensive plan for an all-purpose art room. (Based on a design by the Department of Public Instruction, Commonwealth of Pennsylvania.)

of work. Obviously, an art room entails costly construction, and whatever arrangements are made, good or bad, are likely to be in use for a long time. One example to study is the plan shown above.

Creating a Learning Environment. Equipment, facilities, and storage have been considered thus far, but there are also functions other than purely practical ones. The art room can be an environment for learning about art as well as an assembly of hardware. As a learning environment it must contain many stimuli; it must be a place for sensory excitement; it is also the child's link with the world outside the classroom. Here, before painting a favorite animal, a child may have access to slides, paintings, or photographs of animal life. One day the teacher may bring in a live puppy, kitten, or turkey to study. At times the art room may resemble a science laboratory as the teacher attempts to acquaint the children with intricate, hidden forms of nature. The room may contain inexpensive microscopes, aquariums, terrariums, bones, rock formations—anything that can direct the child's attention to visual cues that have bearing on the art experience.

A corner of the room might be reserved for research and supplied with art books, well-illustrated children's books, magazines on a suitable reading level, file material, slides, and filmstrips. Another part of the room might be set aside as a "serendipity corner"—a place for interesting and unusual things to draw. The more provocative these items are, the better.

Each teacher creates a unique collection of objects chosen for their shapes, colors, and associations. This collection provides its own stimulus for any lesson that employs observation.

One way to create a learning environment in the art room is to have the children themselves design portions of the room. Orange crates painted in bright colors and units constructed of wallboard can provide flexibility even beyond purchased components. The teacher who thinks of the child as entering a laboratory of visual delight—a place for looking, feeling, shaping, and forming—will have some idea of what the art room or even a section of the classroom might be. Above all, an art room should have a special character. The moment a child enters should be one of happy anticipation. The art room is a space where creative things happen; it should be the most attractive place in the child's school life.

Suggested Readings

General Equipment Manufacturers. A current brochure with detailed specifications for artrooms is obtainable from this publisher. P.O. Box 836, Crystal Springs, Michigan.

Wachowiak, Frank. *Emphasis: Art*, 3rd ed. New York: Harper & Row, 1977. Appendix F, "Facilities for Art."

film producers and sources for color reproductions

Catalogs are generally available from producers and distributors of films, slides, film strips, and color reproductions.

Film Producers and Distributors

American Handicrafts Company, 6837 W. 159th St., Henley Park, IL 60477.

Brandon Films, 34 MacQuesten Parkway South, Mt. Vernon, NY 10550.

British Information Services, 845 Third Ave., New York, NY 10022.

Churchill Films, 662 North Robertson Blvd., Los Angeles, CA 90069.

Coast Visual Education Company, 5620 Hollywood Blvd., Los Angeles, CA 90028.

Coronet Instructional Media, 65 E. South Water St., Chicago, IL 60601.

Walt Disney Educational Materials Company, 500 South Buena Vista St., Burbank, CA 91521.

Encyclopaedia Britannica Films, 425 North Michigan Ave., Chicago, IL 60611.

Film Classics Exchange, 1914 South Vermont Ave., Los Angeles, CA 90007.

Francis Thompson Productions, 935 Second Ave., New York, NY 10022.

Girl Scouts of America Film Library, 830 Third Ave., New York, NY 10022.

Homer Groening, 1700 S.W. Fourth Ave., Portland, OR 97201.

International Film Bureau, 332 South Michigan Ave., Chicago, IL 60604.

Jeff Dell Film Service, 10 E. 53rd St., New York, NY 10022.

McGraw-Hill, 1221 Ave. of the Americas, New York, NY 10020.

National Film Board of Canada, 111 Wacker Drive, Suite 313, Chicago, IL 60601.

Phoenix Films, 468 Park Ave., New York, NY 10016.

Portafilms, 4180 Dixie Highway, Drayton Plains, MI 48020.

Santa Fe Railway Audio-Visual Services, 80 East Jackson Blvd., Chicago, IL 60604.

University of Southern California, Audio-Visual Services, Dept. of Cinema, 3518 University Ave., Los Angeles, CA 90007.

Wanami Films, Japan.

Weston Woods Studios, Weston, CT 06880.

Yellow Ball Workshop and Newton Mini Films, 62 Tarbell Ave., Lexington, MA 02173.

Slides and Filmstrip Producers and Distributors

American Council on Education, 1 Dupont Circle, Washington, DC 20036.

American Library Color Slide Company, P.O. Box 5810, Grand Central Station, New York, NY 10017.

Carnegie-Mellon University, College of Fine Arts, Schenley Park, Pittsburgh, PA 15213.

Center for Humanities, Two Holland Avenue, White Plains, NY 10603.

Educational Dimensions Corporation, Stamford, CT 06904.

Grolier Educational Corporation, Sherman Turnpike, Danbury, CT.

The Book of Art Filmstrip Library, Herbert Read, ed. Ten filmstrips intended to supplement The Book of Art: A Pictorial Encyclopedia of Painting,

Drawing, and Sculpture. Although the books are beyond the reading level of elementary-school children, the filmstrips can be useful in a basic survey of the history of art.

Life Filmstrips, Time-Life Bldg., Rockefeller Center, New York, NY 10020.

McGraw-Hill, 1221 Ave. of the Americas, New York, NY 10020.

> *Arts of the United States: A Pictorial Survey*, William H. Pierson, Jr., and Mathew Davidson, eds. *The Color Slide Books of the World's Art*

Museum of Modern Art Library, 11 West 53rd St., New York, NY 10019.

National Gallery of Art, Constitution Ave. and 6th St. N.W., Washington, DC 20001.

> *Survey of American Painting*

Phoenix Films, 468 Park Ave., New York, NY 10016.

Philadelphia Museum of Art, Division of Education, 25th St. and Benjamin Franklin Pkwy., Philadelphia, PA 19130.

Dr. Konrad Prothmann, 2378 Soper Ave., Baldwin, NY 11510.

Sandak, Inc., 180 Harvard Ave., Stamford, CT 06902.

> 4000 slides of American art

School of the Art Institute of Chicago, 280 South Columbus Dr., Chicago, IL 60603.

Society for Visual Education, 1345 Diversey Pkwy., Chicago, IL 60614.

University Prints, 21 East St., Winchester, MA 01890.

Color-Reproduction Distributors

Harry N. Abrams, 110 East 59th St., New York, NY 10022.

Art Education, Inc., 28 E. Erie St., Blauvelt, NY 10913.

Art Extension Press, Box 389, Westport, CT 06881.

Associated American Artists, 663 Fifth Ave., New York, NY 10022.

Catalda Fine Arts, 12 W. 27th St., New York, NY 10001.

Metropolitan Museum of Art, Book and Art Shop, Fifth Ave. and 82nd St., New York, NY 10028.

Museum of Modern Art, 11 West 53rd St., New York, NY 10019.

New York Graphic Society, 140 Greenwich Ave., Greenwich, CT 06830.

Oestreicher's Prints, 43 West 46th St., New York, NY 10036.

Penn Prints, 31 W. 46th St., New York, NY 10036.

Dr. Konrad Prothmann, 2378 Soper Ave., Baldwin, NY 11510.

Raymond and Raymond, Inc., 1071 Madison Ave., New York, NY 10028.

Reinhold Publishing Company, 600 Summer St., P.O. Box 1361, Stamford, CT 06904.

> *Reinhold Visual Services*, John Lidstone, Stanley T. Lewis, and Sheldon Brody, eds. A series of eight portfolios, each containing twenty-four prints.

Shorewood Reproductions, Dept. S, 475 10th Ave., New York, NY 10018.

UNESCO Catalogues, Columbia University Press, 562 West 113th St., New York, NY 10025.

University Prints, 21 East St., Winchester, MA 01890.

E. Weyhe, 794 Lexington Ave., New York, NY 10021.

General Information

For a general listing of publications, policy statements, position papers, and so on relating to art education, write to:

National Art Education Association, 1916 Association Dr., Reston, VA 22091.

index

521

526

A 2
B 3
C 4
D 5
E 6
F 7
G 8
H 9
I 0
J 1